The Author

Glenn Shirley, well-known authority on the Old West, has written hundreds of articles for anthologies, journals, and magazines. He is also the author of many books, including *Shotgun for Hire: The Story of "Deacon" Jim Miller, Killer of Pat Garrett*, also published by the University of Oklahoma Press.

UNIVERSITY OF OKLAHOMA PRESS
NORMAN

Crime, Criminals,
and the Federal Peace Officer
in Oklahoma Territory, 1889–1907

University of Oklahoma Press   :   Norman

WEST OF
HELL'S
FRINGE

BY GLENN SHIRLEY

By Glenn Shirley

Toughest of Them All (Albuquerque, 1953)

Six-Gun and Silver Star (Albuquerque, 1955)

Law West of Fort Smith: A History of Frontier Justice in the Indian Territory, 1834-1896 (New York, 1957, 1961; Lincoln, 1968)

Pawnee Bill: A Biography of Gordon W. Lillie (Albuquerque, 1958; Lincoln, 1965)

Buckskin and Spurs: A Gallery of Frontier Rogues and Heroes (New York, 1958)

Outlaw Queen: The Fantastic True Story of Belle Starr (Derby, Conn., 1960)

Heck Thomas, Frontier Marshal (New York & Philadelphia, 1962)

Born to Kill (Derby, Conn., 1963)

Henry Starr, Last of the Real Badmen (New York, 1965)

Buckskin Joe: The Unique and Vivid Memoirs of Edward Jonathan Hoyt, Hunter-Trapper, Scout, Soldier, Showman, Frontiersman, and Friend of the Indians 1840-1918 (Lincoln, 1966)

Shotgun for Hire: The Story of "Deacon" Jim Miller, Killer of Pat Garrett (Norman, 1970)

The Life of Texas Jack: Eight Years a Criminal—41 Years Trusting in God (Quanah, 1973)

Red Yesterdays (Wichita Falls, 1977)

West of Hell's Fringe: Crime, Criminals, and the Federal Peace Officer in Oklahoma Territory, 1889-1907 (Norman, 1978)

Library of Congress Cataloging in Publication Data

Shirley, Glenn.
    West of Hell's Fringe.
    Includes index.
    1. Oklahoma—History.   2. Crime and criminals—Oklahoma—History.   3.   Peace officers—Oklahoma—History.   I.   Title
F699.S47   364.1'5'09766   77-9112
ISBN 0-8061-1444-4

Preface

OKLAHOMA IS KNOWN as the Boomer State and the Sooner State. But for many years the actions of desperate bandit gangs operating across the imaginary border between the Twin Territories, called Hell's Fringe by early U.S. deputy marshals, gave Oklahoma a name synonymous with the word *outlaw*.

Crime in Oklahoma today is at best a shabby, profitless, and seldom spectacular phenomenon, and the reputation is no longer deserved. But from the first opening to white settlement until statehood, outlaw gangs ruled supreme. They robbed banks, trains, stores, post offices, and Indian and homesteader alike. When some member left the stage, another took his place, to bask in notoriety and folklore for a time and then, in turn, be replaced. There were few who did not end their careers in prison or death.

Their names were familiar to everyone in their day: Bill Doolin, the Daltons, Ol Yantis, Black-Faced Charley, Red Buck, Bitter Creek, Charley Pierce, Little Bill, Little Dick, Tulsa Jack, Dynamite Dick, Arkansas Tom, Zip Wyatt, Ike Black, Vic and Jim Casey, Bob and Bill Christian, Al and Frank Jennings, Cattle Annie, and Little Breeches.

Despite the cries of outrage at their actions, most of them were secretly admired for one reason or another. Many people even openly expressed approval when Bill Doolin's Wild Bunch dashed from the town of Ingalls under the withering fire of a dozen marshals waiting for them on almost every side, leaving three federal men dead or dying and the rest amazed that the gang was able to escape temporarily after running such a gauntlet.

The legends of these outlaws even overshadowed the legends of the lawmen who fought them: E. D. Nix, William Grimes, Chris Madsen, Ed Short, John Hixon, John M. Hale, Tom Hueston, Lafe Shadley, Dick Speed, Heck Thomas, Bill Tilghman, William Fossett, Frank Canton, Bud Ledbetter, ad infinitum. These men proved themselves to be as daring as the gangs, bringing them to bay and

v

laying in the raw, wild land the foundation for peace and greatness.

No other set of characters in any section of our country has captivated audiences so extensively. Countless television westerns and motion pictures have told and retold their stories with many variations, their biographies have been published and republished, and scores of western magazines have made newsstand appearances proposing what is to be "true" and "real" and "fact."

Unfortunately, few writers of these scripts, books, and articles have made an effort to dig deeper than original works for information. Errors and legends have been compounded and accepted. Latter-day writers seldom return to primary sources and too often avoid or reject fact for the sake of commercial appeal and not-so-fascinating fiction.

In 1955, I published a book entitled *Six-Gun and Silver Star*, covering much the same theme and material to be found in this volume. *Six Gun* long has been out of print. A continued demand for the work brought many requests that it be reprinted. However, my research during the past twenty years called for so many corrections and additions that it was my decision, in all fairness to the *aficionado* of western history, to present a new work entirely.

Almost every newspaper in the areas where these events occurred and official city, county, and territorial records have been compared and correlated. When available, reminiscences of persons involved have been examined. More important, I have concentrated as much as possible on the water-soaked and dusty records of the U.S. marshal and U.S. district attorney for Oklahoma Territory for the period 1894 to 1920 — about four feet of bound volumes of outgoing correspondence, ten feet of incoming letter-file boxes and a quantity of U.S. Department of Justice registers and reports of the U.S. attorney general — recovered from the old federal building at Guthrie in 1961 and preserved in the Western History Collections, University of Oklahoma Library.

I have allowed quoted items to speak for themselves, not placing undue evaluation or interpretation on them. Considering the several gaps which I have not been able to fill because only meager data exist, this project cannot be definitive. My hope is that it will serve as a middle ground on which historians can meet and compromise their differences.

GLENN SHIRLEY

On the Cimarron
Payne County, Oklahoma

Contents

Illustrations

Unless otherwise credited, all photographs are from the author's collection.

Maps

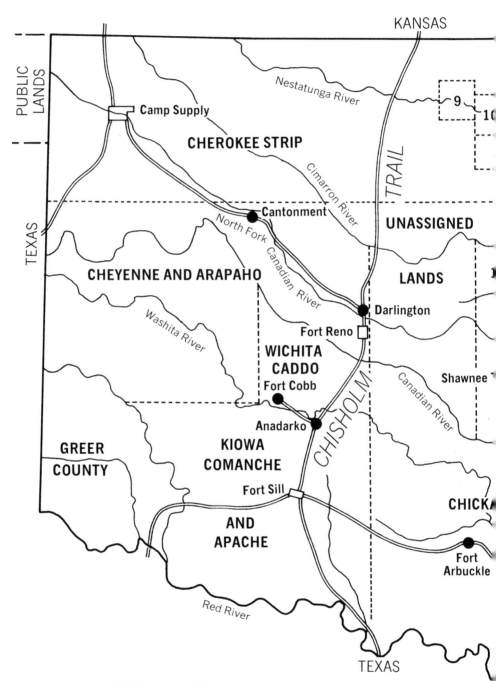

Map 1: Oklahoma in 1875

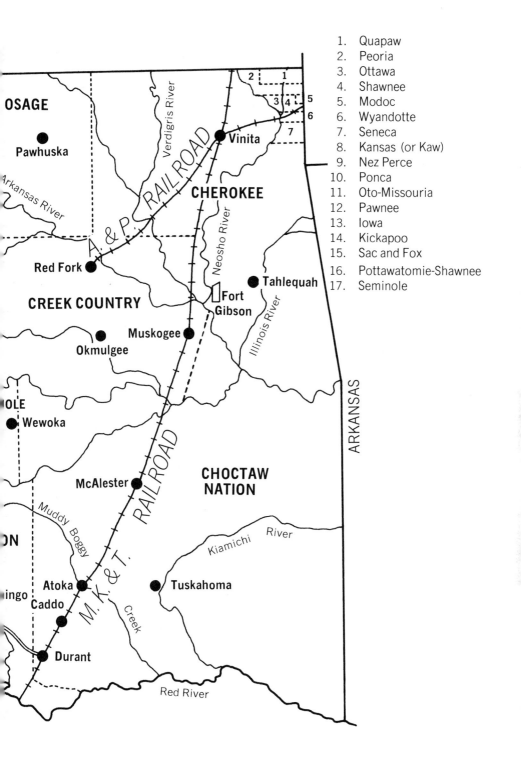

1. Quapaw
2. Peoria
3. Ottawa
4. Shawnee
5. Modoc
6. Wyandotte
7. Seneca
8. Kansas (or Kaw)
9. Nez Perce
10. Ponca
11. Oto-Missouria
12. Pawnee
13. Iowa
14. Kickapoo
15. Sac and Fox
16. Pottawatomie-Shawnee
17. Seminole

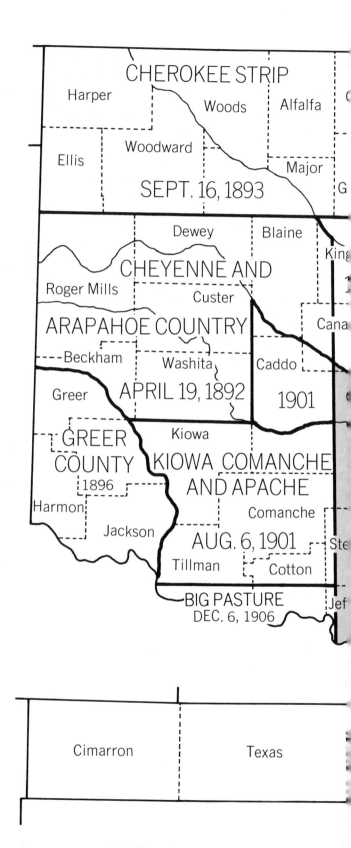

CHEROKEE STRIP

Harper

Woods

Alfalfa

Woodward

Ellis

Major

SEPT. 16, 1893

G

Dewey

Blaine

King

CHEYENNE AND

Roger Mills

Custer

ARAPAHOE COUNTRY

Cana

Beckham

Washita

Caddo

Greer

APRIL 19, 1892

1901

Kiowa

GREER

COUNTY

KIOWA COMANCHE

AND APACHE

1896

Harmon

Comanche

Jackson

AUG. 6, 1901

Ste

Tillman

Cotton

BIG PASTURE

DEC. 6, 1906

Jef

Cimarron

Texas

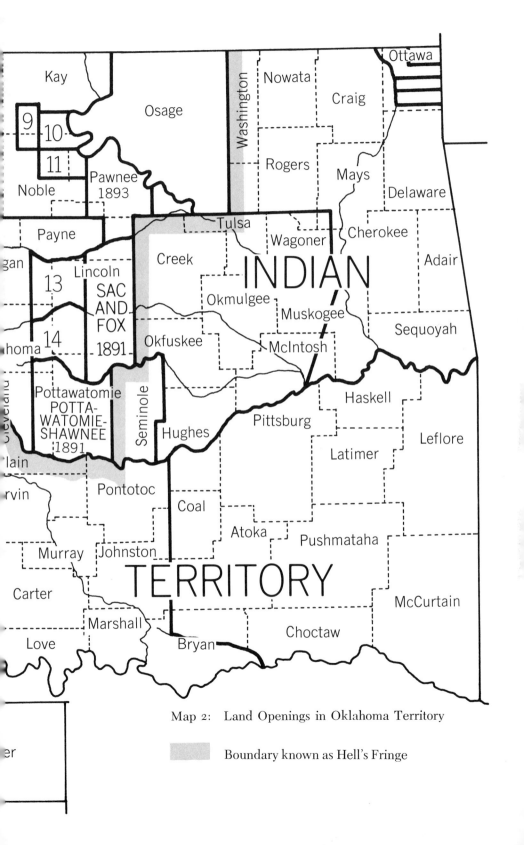

Map 2: Land Openings in Oklahoma Territory

Boundary known as Hell's Fringe

WEST OF HELL'S FRINGE

I Bugles and Carbines

"IT WAS A GREAT DAY to commence the building of an empire," wrote Dr. Delos Walker in 1909. "The sky was as blue as in June. A tonic air, as exhilarating as wine, was fanning down from the north with just force enough to make exertion of man and beast effective and pleasant. Mighty possibilities, sightly lands, fertility equalling the fabled Nile, the garden of the gods, were fenced in by an anxious human wall on that immortal 22nd of April, 1889. No region had been so thoroughly advertised, so favorably advertised. The frequent heroic efforts of the Boomers by the military, at the behest of greed, wakened the world to the belief that a wondrous land was here. The very name Oklahoma was a poem, an inspiration, an invitation irresistible, impossible to ignore or refuse—Oklahoma! A slogan for conquering and conquest! Oh, yes, Oklahoma was advertised. The denizens of all civilization came; came from the hills, from the valleys, from the prairie and forest; came from the caves of the earth, from the isles of the sea and, seemingly, from the clouds of the air. They were here in all tongues, in all colors, in all garbs, with all kinds of profanity and every imaginable odor; were here at high noon."[1]

These settlers were not seeking political freedom. They had much more of that in the states they left than they would find in a territory where governors and judges would be appointed by several presidents and Congress would have veto power over any legislation. It was the consuming land hunger of the American people that had led to the opening of this unassigned district.

The best land in the older states was occupied. Thousands of homesteaders had built sod houses and dugouts on the plains of western Kansas. In Texas, ranchers and farmers had spread across the Staked Plains. This left Old Oklahoma and other unoccupied lands of the Indian country as a broad peninsula between the two states—millions of acres carpeted with buffalo grass and bluestem

3

that could easily be broken to the plow, supporting only sparse herds of cattle and nomadic Indian tribes.

The press painted glowing pictures of the vast area:

In addition to furnishing the farmer a magnificent soil, unsurpassed even by the Illinois bottoms in productiveness, and so favorably situated that it is then and there ready for the plow, being free of rock, swamp, and forest, this superb addition to the public lands of Uncle Sam is blessed with a climate so exquisitely balanced between the long winters of the North and the long summers of the South, that almost all the products of both North and South can be successfully cultivated.

It had long been the topic of conversation around campfires and in the villages and towns of the two states.

Nothing was said of the rights of the Indian or of treaties the white man had made with him. The talk was about the waste of resources under tribal governments. As an example, the land-hungry whites pointed to the fact that in 1883 the Cherokee Nation leased the Cherokee Outlet to a group of feudal cattle barons for five years for $100,000 per year—only a few cents an acre. Each Cherokee would realize perhaps $3 per year while 100,000 white settlers were deprived of rich farms. In 1883, the Cheyennes and Arapahos rented 3,117,880 acres to seven cattlemen for 2¢ an acre.

"Spell that out," cried the *Oklahoma War Chief*, the Boomer newspaper published at Caldwell on the Kansas border. "Three million, one hundred and seventeen thousand, eight hundred and eighty acres! Divide it up into 160-acre farms; just 19,485 farms with 120 acres left over for a soldiers home; on each farm a husband, wife, and three children would be, in round numbers, a thriving, industrious population of 100,000 producers! And their vast domain leased to seven cattle kings!"

Almost directly in the heart of the reserved Indian lands was the unassigned district of 1,888,900 acres. It constituted an uneven quadrangular block bounded on the north by the parallel of thirty-six degrees north latitude, the southern boundary of the Outlet; on the east by the reservations of the Pawnee, Sac and Fox, Iowa, Kickapoo, Pottawatomie, and Shawnee Indian tribes; on the south by the Canadian River, the northern boundary of the Chickasaw Nation; and on the west by the Cheyenne and Arapaho reservations, immediately west of the ninety-eighth meridian. Here the cattlemen had built headquarters ranches, had constructed corrals for branding their animals, had established line camps for use by their cowboys.

"These are not the only public lands thus filched from the people by the cattle kings," the *War Chief* continued. "There are other leases in Oklahoma . . . empires of public lands fenced by these monopolists from Washington territory to the Texas border, hundreds of millions of acres fattening countless herds of stock — at two cents per acre!"

Small wonder, then, in the lean years following the Panic of 1873, when the Civil War inflation bubble burst, that Captain David L. Payne was able to gain increasing support for his demand that Oklahoma be opened to settlement. From 1870 to 1879, thirty-three bills asking creation of Oklahoma Territory from the Indian lands were introduced in Congress. Payne's first Boomers entered the region in 1880 and were thrown out by federal troops again and again until his death in 1884.

A lesser depression in the early 1880's strengthened the demand for opening Oklahoma. William L. Couch, Payne's most active lieutenant, succeeded him as leader of the movement. With the same energy and earnestness for their cause that had characterized Payne, Couch advertized their plans widely, and the railroads with lines in the country, realizing how it would enhance the lines' value if the homeseekers won, added their powerful propaganda and influence. Literally thousands flocked to the Kansas and Texas borders to share this enthusiasm until military authorities found it necessary to call for reinforcements to eject them. The pressure on Congress grew steadily stronger.

The cattlemen were scared. In 1881, they organized at Caldwell an association that wielded tremendous power for good and evil. Besides looking after the cattle business, it took a hand in politics, controlled newspapers, kept sympathetic representatives in Congress, and had much to say even in big New York money centers.

The Five Civilized Tribes opposed the selling of their lands and the opening of the unassigned lands. They were represented in Washington by delegations which included their ablest men and leaders.

Hiram Price, Commissioner of the Bureau of Indian Affairs attempted to discredit the Boomers as a class of people "well armed, mostly with Winchester rifles and carbines, and among them are reported men with full wagon loads of whiskey and cigars intending to open saloons on arriving at their destination. They seem to be, with two or three exceptions, persons without visible means of support, whom the citizens, though deprecating the movement, were glad to get rid of at any cost."

The plea of the Indians and the influence of their allies, the cattlemen, to keep out the settler was doomed. Too many believed what General Nelson A. Miles wrote in his report to the War Department in 1885:

> The object in reserving the Indian Territory as a place where scattered tribes from Texas, Missouri, Kansas and other states and territories could be congregated and removed from before the advancing settlements was humane and judicious and it has accomplished its mission. The Indian Territory is now a block in the pathway of civilization. It is preserved to perpetuate a mongrel race far removed from the influence of civilized people—a refuge of the outlaw and indolent of whites, blacks and Mexicans. The vices introduced by these classes are rapidly destroying the Indians by disease. Without courts of justice or public institutions, without roads, bridges or railways, it is simply a dark blot in the center of the map of the United States. It costs the government hundreds of thousands to peaceably maintain 60,000 to 80,000 Indians there, when the territory is capable of supporting many millions of enlightened people.

The federal government so far realized the ultimate capitulation to settlement that Congress authorized negotiations with the Creeks, Seminoles, and Cherokees to relinquish their claims to all unoccupied lands and appropriated $5,000 to finance such negotiations. The Dawes Act of 1887 cleared the way for the western half of the Indian country—all land except that occupied by the Five Civilized Tribes—to be settled by the white man. In the same year, the Santa Fe was permitted to build a railroad across the territory from Arkansas City to Fort Worth, and on March 2, 1889, news spread that Congress had passed the Indian appropriation bill for the forthcoming fiscal year with a rider opening the unassigned lands under the homestead laws.

President Grover Cleveland was forced to choose between two evils: veto of the bill would wreck Indian administration finances; his signature would mean an end to all hope for an Indian commonwealth. Repudiated by the voters the preceding November and worn out by the stress of a turbulent administration, he "chose to relieve immediate necessity" and signed the bill on his last day in office. Three weeks later, on March 23, his successor, President Benjamin Harrison, issued a proclamation announcing April 22 as the opening day and noon the earliest hour at which one could legally enter the unassigned lands.

Harrison's proclamation expressly declared that "no other portions of lands embraced within Indian territory other than those specifically described and declared to be open for settlement are to be considered open to settlement." It provided further: "Warning is hereby again expressly given that no person entering upon and occupying said lands before the hour of 12 o'clock noon on the 22nd day of April, 1889, *will ever be permitted to enter any of said lands or acquire any rights thereto,*" and the military was ordered to keep them out.

The moment Secretary of State James G. Blaine made the proclamation public, the migration began. For the entire month before the appointed date and hour, Kansas and Texas roads leading toward the Oklahoma District were crowded with every type of conveyance known. The border towns of Caldwell, Arkansas City, Wichita, Hunnewell, and Wellington in Kansas and Denison, Gainesville, and Vernon in Texas were jammed with land seekers and the outcasts and riffraff that went along with them. Before opening day, people were allowed to pass through Indian country and gather on the borders of the unassigned area. The first person on the land was the one to homestead it.

They were lined up by the thousands, mile upon mile, north to south, east to west. The rich and the poor, the refined and the ignorant — all touched elbows in this horde who waited now for the sound of starting bugles and carbines:

> Ten thousand . . . mostly poor people [from western Kansas and Nebraska] . . . gathered along Kingfisher Creek, a mile and a quarter west of Kingfisher. While we were loafing, we had nothing to do except get information and visit. We took an invoice of Democrats and Republicans from the states, and No Man's Land showed up with no party but what they called Presbyterians and sons-of-bitches. We rode up and down, asking the Republicans to get on a certain line or street. Pat [Patrick S.] Nagle unhitched one of his mules and rode bareback up and down the line, asking all Democrats to line up. The Republicans lined up and outnumbered the others about three to one. Then Fatty Smith went up and down the line, asking all the sons-of-bitches to line up, and Dr. Overstreet, riding a fine bay horse, asked the Presbyterians from No Man's Land to line up on his side. There were about three sons-of-bitches and one Presbyterian.[2]

Most of the people were making the run on horseback. There was everything from mules to race horses, some saddled, many bareback. Open buggies, fringed carriages, prairie schooners, light farm wagons, carts, racing sulkies, and even a few five-foot bicycles stood wheel to wheel in that curious assemblage. Hundreds of people had come on foot, trusting to sturdy legs and good lungs to win a piece of land.

7

The Santa Fe had assmbled all the spare equipment it could find. On the northern border, roughly one mile north of present-day Orlando, trains from Arkansas City, eleven in all, were backed as far as the eye could see. Every coach bulged with passengers who jostled in the seats, windows, and aisles. Others rode the platforms and clung desperately to the sides and tops of the cars. The Gulf lines sent six trains from Texas to Purcell, on the South Canadian, "just as jammed."[3] Nanneta Daisey, a noted woman correspondent for the Dallas and Galveston newspapers, had convinced the engineer of the lead train that she was the best reporter covering the run and that he would be doing the entire nation a favor by letting her ride the cowcatcher.[4]

> A score of fords had been selected by which to reach the Oklahoma side of the Canadian, and as the hour drew near, hundreds of homeseekers mounted upon fleet horses formed in line at these different fords . . . like well-trained jockeys seeking for an advantage in the start. All, or many at least, knew the treacherous quicksands of the Canadian, and yet all were eager to be first in plunging into its waters. They saw the signal officer, watch in hand, away on the opposite shore.[5]

Out in front, the soldiers rode back and forth. Two hundred cavalrymen policed the west border near Hennessey, holding back nearly 2,300 vehicles and 7,000 people. Occasionally an impatient rider would cross the line but scamper back with amusing alacrity when challenged by the troops. Every few minutes, scouts could be seen bringing out illegal individuals and small parties who had slipped into the country the night before. On the north, along the southern border of the Outlet, and to the east, on the borders of the Iowa, Kickapoo, and Pottawatomie-Shawnee reservations, the procedure was repeated. Infantry complemented cavalry in stalking strategic points. A few minutes before noon, the bodies of land claimants became so concentrated that it was almost impossible to hold them back. "In all that legion of '89ers, there was not one Joshua who could have forced the sun to stand still, but every devil of them could force their watches ahead and they did. Then, a moment of bated breath, a hush till hearts could be heard to beat."[6]

A call from the bugles, a salvo of shots from the cavalrymen's carbines, and a human flood swept the land. From the Canadian, it was

> a typical Bull Run, a race free for all. None were barred. Neither sex, age or circumstances were imposed as conditions. . . . Cheers and shouts from ten thousand souls, a refrain to the bugle notes, sent their echoes

o'er hill and plain. Fleet racer and plow horse were given free rein and plied with whip and spur. The long railway trains, too, with ear-piercing shrieks from the engine whistles joined in. . . . Ere the stirring notes from the bugle reached the ears of those in the furtherest end of the column, the foremost horsemen . . . with yells that would have done credit to a band of Pawnee warriors, dashed into the fords, followed by hundreds of other equally excited riders. It was a furious dash, and horses and riders were literally drenched with water and covered with sand. Wagons and carriages, as thick as they could be crowded together, followed pell-mell the columns of horsemen through the fords. The opposite bank gained, the immense throng spread out like a great army, covering the entire country for miles, the advance only falling out of the race as they reached a claim that suited them.[7]

At the same moment, the halted masses to the west, east, and north surged forward in a mighty rush to meet them. "A wild shout ascended from forty thousand throats and it was greater by far than the glad cry that echoed across the Red Sea when the children of Israel were delivered from the hosts of Pharoh,"[8] wrote an observer. Pandemonium. A din of confusion. Vehicles broke down and overturned. Horses, freed from their encumbrances, galloped madly with flying harness. As the trains from the north rolled over the prairie, hundreds leaped from the platforms and windows and dashed off in search of quarter-sections. Victorious shouts as they drove identification stakes into the ground, rising above the thunder of hoofs, the clatter of vehicles careening from side to side in wild, uncertain courses, the scream of a man thrown from his mount and trampled to death.

Many never reached claims. Those on horseback and in vehicles paid little attention to those on foot and in a number of instances ran over them. It seemed that people had lost all reason and judgment except to achieve the purpose for which they had long waited and suffered many privations.[9]

By nightfall, the wild flowers in the new spring grass nodding in the morning breeze had been crushed under the feet of hurrying people, the land scarred deeper with horses' hoofs and iron wheels and furrows plowed around new homes. Every desirable claim and town lot had been taken. Guthrie was a city of 15,000, Oklahoma City 5,000, Kingfisher 3,000, and other towns boasting populations of 100 to 1,000 were scattered over the territory. "Their campfires gleam in the darkness," said a news dispatch,[10] "their tents loom athwart the sky like an army in bivouac. Already around the campfires there is talk of mass meetings on the morrow to form local

9

governments . . . and all this was gained in an afternoon. In no country save America, and in no part of that country but the great West, could such a thing be possible. It is a triumph for the Western people such as they may never again have the opportunity of achieving. That they were fully equal to the occasion needs no more proof than the presence of 60,000 persons in this country tonight."

II Hell's Fringe

IT WAS A HAPPY DAY for those lucky enough to secure a piece of
ground. "The possibility of failure or disappointment did not enter
into the consideration of a single individual, but for many, the
anticipations were 'April hopes, the fools of chance.'"[1] Hundreds
went away with empty purses and broken hearts because they had
spent so much time and money trying to get a home and failed.
Many picked claims that were not what they expected and left,
never to return. Others, who found they could not make a crop,
disposed of their claims for little or nothing. "If anything could
exceed the anxiety of boomers and speculators to get into Oklahoma, it is the frantic eagerness of quite a large proportion of them
to get out," said the *St. Louis Globe-Democrat* of April 22. Thousands declared that the country had been "glaringly misrepresented"
and "over praised" and that Payne's Boomers either knew nothing
about the land or had some other object in desiring the opening
of it.

On the other hand, there were those who tried to hold all the
land they could stake, "settling in the names of their sisters, their
cousins and their aunts, or in sheerly fictional names, hoping to
hold them for the arrival of relatives or friends, or to sell their
'possessory rights' after a few days' accretion of value."[2] A. Z.
Clark, who came to Guthrie the first day, found three lots vacant,
and took them all, stated: "It was the accepted ethics of the occasion
for everyone to get all he could and keep all he could get."[3]

An April 23 dispatch reported "an uprising of Indians on the
border on account of boomers who failed to get Oklahoma claims
squatting on Indian land. Troops have been sent to the scene."
That night, one disappointed group which had returned to Arkansas City held a mass meeting in the opera house. The meeting was
well attended and

> the speakers, denouncing the manner in which Oklahoma was settled,
> said if the people could not secure homes in Oklahoma they were going

to have them in the Cherokee strip. About five hundred men pledged to go to the strip and take claims, let the consequences be what they might. The troops in this region, fortunately, are in command of Captain Jack Hayes, an old frontiersman and a cool and discreet officer. There is, nevertheless, going to be great turmoil on the strip unless the government at Washington promptly intervenes.[4]

Most of the misery, however, resulted from finding choice sites occupied by sooners:[5]

There were men who were not disposed to play the game fair . . . and slipped into the forbidden land the night before "by the light of the moon." Those people were called "Moonshiners," and the word "sooner" was not applied for five or six months afterwards. You may imagine the disappointment of a man who had run his horse ten or twelve miles into some beautiful valley and there finding a man on every quarter and sometimes two or three to the quarter. We knew that they were "Moonshiners" but they would all claim that they started from the line at high noon and had just beat us to it. . . . They had come to the country together and had organized a conspiracy to each swear for the other.[6]

The soldiers had made a diligent effort to keep them out. A man named Jackson was so persistent in slipping into the country ahead of schedule that he was arrested several times, but he would be back at the place where he was arrested when the soldiers returned to it. They finally placed a rope around his neck and another around his body beneath his arms, then hoisted him into a tree, tightening the neck rope just enough to make him think he was being hanged. They took a picture of him hanging in the tree before they let him down, and that photograph became his undoing when he appeared at the land office to prove he had not been in the country before the opening.[7]

Several attempts to beat the proclamation were made by organized gangs. One outfit, under the leadership of a smart Bohemian, divided itself into two parties. Half of them crossed the river near Purcell to Mustang Creek, along which lay some of the most fertile country. Each staked two claims: one for himself, the other for a member of the party who had remained at the line to prove those in the forbidden area were with them at Purcell until the opening. The plan worked until special agents from the Interior Department secured evidence which caused the violators to be indicted in federal court at Wichita. Deputy marshals served warrants on twenty-eight of the offenders and took them to Topeka. All except the leader pleaded guilty and were given jail sentences; the leader was tried at Wichita and sentenced to two years in the penitentiary.[8]

Despite the vigilance of the troops, large numbers of people had slipped into the country and concealed themselves in ravines and timber until the opening hour, at which time they popped from their hiding places and occupied the land they had staked.

> The prairie grass was alive with them, crawling out of ditches, dropping from trees, squirming from beneath the freight cars full of raw lumber, hardware, furniture and farm implements that had been allowed entry previous to the opening and stood in long rows on hastily built side-tracks, fifteen or thirty miles inside the border. Before 12:15 a dozen men from the Seminole Land and Town Company . . . were staking out a townsite [Oklahoma City] around the Santa Fe depot and unloading freight cars into wagons. At 12:40 more than forty tents were up, and one settler was busy driving a stake in the center of the Santa Fe tracks and defying the agent and soldier-guards.[9]

The nearest legitimate starting point for them being fifteen miles away, it was obvious that they were sooners.[10]

Fred Wenner, correspondent for the *Kansas City Star* and one of the first newspapermen to arrive on the day of the run, wrote:

> "At dawn a trackless virgin prairie with no human habitation; at sunset a city of tents, homes for a multitude"; "At sunrise a trackless wilderness, at eventide a settled community"; "Rome was not built in a day, Guthrie was"—these and many kindred catch lines had headed our advance stories of the founding of Guthrie. Theoretically and rhetorically they were fine, but historically they failed of realization for, when our train arrived carrying the first legal settlers, the townsite was swarming with sooners who came in on Sunday, the 21st, or early the morning of the 22nd, staked off most of the choice lots, put up their tents, and at one minute after 12, just about the time the law-abiding settlers were starting at the north line, offered two townsite plats for record at the land office!

The homeseekers who made the run from the borders did not give up without a fight. Many rows with sooners were settled with fists, others with six-shooters, and the remainder in the land offices.

> From this situation was developed the long and bitter litigation which filled the federal and territorial courts with an interminable docket of land suits, some of which were contested for nearly twenty years, and in some instances were settled in the supreme court of the United States.[11]

Although *sooner* was generally a term of reproach and is today applied loosely in a significance far from its original meaning,

13

the cause of the "sooner" was one that, in some of its aspects at least, deserved sympathy. . . . They were, as a class, the vanguard of Oklahomans, men who had planned homes in this country long before the great mass of settlers ever considered locating here. Some of them had been in more or less interrupted occupation, though illegally, of land in the Oklahoma country for a year or more, deeming themselves as well justified in living there as the cattlemen whose herds were all around them. After enduring so much for the sake of living in a forbidden land, it was perhaps natural that they regarded with hostility the approach of thousands of newcomers who would have equal chance with themselves in entering this land, and might outrace them at the opening and secure the very homestead around which they had set their stakes and often had improved by the plow and with fences and dug-out homes. The other type of settlers, while anticipating in an equal degree the opening hour, had taken no part in the long campaign for the opening and endured none of the hardships connected with a real "sooner's" experience.[12]

Even arriving on a piece of land first did not always hold it, for some of the land hunters were not easily dissuaded.[13] On April 23, for example, a settler named Goodwin appeared at Fort Reno and made a sworn statement to the post commander that his party of four had been fired upon by twelve Texans who claimed the location by priority of selection, having come there several years earlier with Captain Payne. Goodwin had escaped by hiding in the thick brush along the river; his companions were slain. A detachment of Company C, Thirteenth Infantry, under Lieutenant Buck was quickly dispatched "to recover the bodies and arrest suspicious persons in the vicinity."[14]

The body of another man was found at a crossing on the North Canadian near Council Grove. "He had been dragged some distance . . . on the line between two sections." A man on a gray horse had been seen near the sections. He was arrested, but he proved that he had been miles away on the day of the killing. Officers were unable to determine the victim's identity or the reason for his death, but "the general opinion was that a dispute about the right to the claim was the real cause."[15]

U.S. Deputy Marshal J. C. Varnum rode into Oklahoma City to report that a wealthy Indian half-blood from the Chickasaw Nation had been slain in a quarrel with a man named Nolan. About fourteen miles west of Oklahoma City, he had found another man dead on a claim and his killer sitting on a log nearby, taking the matter "coolly and quietly." The slayer swore that he had been on the property first and that the killing was done in self-defense.[16]

Three miles west of Guthrie, a man who had arrived on the first train staked a quarter-section. When a second claimant refused to leave, he leveled a Winchester and fired three bullets into his body.[17]

Two Boomers who were engaged in a dispute over a town lot attracted the attention of some soldiers. Charley Qinly, one of the contestants, told them not to interfere. One of the troopers disregarded the warning, whereupon Qinly whipped out a pistol and shot him.[18]

North of Guthrie, three "desperate characters" seeking a claim murdered J. C. Chyland of Franklin County, Missouri. A posse of thirty settlers cornered one of the killers in brush near the river; he refused to surrender and was promptly riddled with lead. The posse "made no effort to conceal their action and rely upon the community to sustain them in their efforts to overawe the turbulent and lawless elements of the camp."[19]

Other difficulties were created by professional crooks, who would stand in with some lawyer as crooked as they and file a contest with or without reason. This forced the poor landholder into a lawsuit to defend his claim before the land office, where the person contesting would relinquish his suit for a consideration. The amount depended on the homesteader's purse. A friendly attorney, selected by the contestant, would be recommended to the homesteader and apparently would represent him when, in fact, he was a member of the gang out to skin him.

And there were vicious outlaws who had come for no home, but only to prey on the fat of the land.

"Law? For thirteen months there was no law but what we made ourselves."[20] The rider on the Indian Appropriation Act of March 2, 1889, contained no provision for territorial government. Congress surely

registered amazement on April 23, when they read the headlines . . . which proclaimed that sixty thousand settlers had occupied every available foot of this million and a half acres . . . with no government to restrain their actions and no authority to establish one.[21]

Kansas and Texas, demanding a share of the Indian Territory gravy that for two decades had been going to Arkansas as a result of the ever increasing activity of the federal district and circuit courts at Fort Smith, had caused Congress, in an act approved January 6, 1883, to take all of that region west of the lands of the Five Civilized Tribes from the jurisdiction of these courts and divide it at the Canadian River. Cases from the northern section were shifted to the U.S. Judicial District of Kansas, giving the federal courts at Wichita and Fort Scott exclusive, original jurisdiction. The southern section was annexed to the Northern Judicial District of Texas, the federal court sitting at Graham.[22] The lands of the Five Civilized Tribes remained with the Arkansas courts, but the great bulk of population was in the eastern portion and most of the business still went to Fort Smith.

With the opening of the Oklahoma District imminent, Congress approved on March 1, 1889, an act establishing at Muskogee the first white man's court in Indian Territory. Principally a court of civil jurisdiction and putting into force the laws of the state of Arkansas, it interfered with the criminal jurisdiction of the Fort Smith, Wichita, Fort Scott, and Graham courts to the extent that it was given exclusive, original jurisdiction of all offenses against the laws of the United States not punishable by death or imprisonment at hard labor. By this same act, apparently repealing that part of the 1883 act annexing the southern portion of the western country to the Northern Judicial District of Texas, the Chickasaw Nation and a large portion of the Choctaw Nation north of the Canadian River were annexed to the Eastern Judicial District of Texas, with the court at Paris, and the Paris court was given exclusive, original jurisdiction of all federal law violations not given to the court at Muskogee.[23]

Thus the Oklahoma District became the responsibility of the Muskogee and Wichita courts. Colonel William C. Jones, U.S. marshal for the Judicial District of Kansas, and a number of his men were on hand to assist the cavalry and infantry. On April 10, twelve days before the opening, Attorney General W. H. H. Miller announced that, by direction of President Harrison, the responsibility of keeping the peace in the country rested largely upon the Muskogee marshal, Thomas B. Needles. Needles appointed 300 additional deputies to help hold back the settlers and patrol the interior for sooners and arrived at Guthrie April 16. It was alleged that many of these temporary employees, under guise of their authority; influential parties in the Atchison, Topeka & Santa Fe Railway Company; and other speculators had entered the forbidden area before the official date and had staked off the most valuable property.

John I. Dille, registrar of the Guthrie land office, arriving there by train at dusk on Saturday evening, April 20, found "hundreds of people" already on the townsite "who were or were not officials." According to John A. Pickler and Cornelius MacBride, Interior Department inspectors, two carloads of people arrived at Guthrie on Sunday evening, April 21, "composed of deputy marshals, land officials, railroad employes, railroad stowaways brought here in freight trains, deputy internal revenue collectors, and a host which cannot be classified."[24]

The *Kansas City Journal* of April 24 stated: "In Guthrie all is confusion. . . . the unauthorized and unwarranted settlement of the best portion of this town by government officials and others has complicated the situation." An April 25 dispatch explained: "The present townsite contains 1,923 acres by actual survey and there are six and seven claimants for every lot. The three hundred United States marshals who were there had claims staked before ten o'clock, then threw up their offices. The boomers in the brush saw this and they came from their hiding places and did the same thing. The marshals could do nothing because they had violated the proclamation, and so the brush men and the marshals stand together, while the multitude of home settlers are against them."[25] The *Journal* was more specific:

> Among those who took part in these unlawful proceedings were United States Marshals Jones and Thomas B. Needles, with at least fifty deputies each; United States Attorney Waldron; United States Commissioner Galloway; Register John I. Dille of the land office; Judge Guthrie of Topeka, district judge; Hiram Dillon, master of chancery in the Topeka district; the Commercial bank officers from Newton, and others as prominent. As the *Journal* representative saw the unlawful squatting done, there is no hearsay about it.[26]

One claimant wrote President Harrison that the marshals, U.S. commissioners, and others not only had banded together but had "set themselves up as a board of arbitration" to rob the people. Another gentleman, finding he could not get a lot, filed on the entire townsite.

This caused Secretary of the Interior John W. Noble to declare that any deputy marshal or other government officer who entered the Oklahoma District with a view of locating a claim or town lot "had acquired no rights there," and as for sooners, "not the least shadow of an injustice to settlers would be tolerated for a moment." By telegraph he directed Pickler and MacBride to "pursue a systematic and thorough inquiry into this wrong, preserving evidence

17

with names, circumstances and conclusions, and make a written report."

At the same time, Attorney General Miller called upon Marshals Jones and Needles for an explanation. Pickler and MacBride reported on April 30 that the

> deputy marshals [are] getting rid of their town lots as rapidly as they can. In three days not more than four or five lots will be ostensibly held by them.

Jones said he was responsible for only "27 deputies" and

> while I instructed them not to . . . file on tracts of land in the territory, when they saw themselves surrounded by about 500 to 700 persons at Guthrie and at least one half that number at Oklahoma City waiting for the hour of twelve to come, I do not wonder that some of them, who were serving without pay and only there in the interest of good order, took the fever and attempted to get them a home.

Denying the charges, Marshal Needles wrote Miller on May 17:

> I have not entered any land or lands, town lot or lots in the Oklahoma district and have no interest whatever, directly or indirectly, near or remote of any kind to any land or lots in the territory. . . . I have had an intimation that one of my deputies secured a town lot in Guthrie and one or two have entered a quarter section apiece. I am not positive as to this, but will at once ascertain the facts.

He added in a postscript:

> If the statement made by me and the report of the officers of the Interior Department are not satisfactory . . . I should like a copy of the specifications filed in order that I may furnish testimony in detail to refute them. I should like to meet my accusers face to face before you.

No accusers appeared, and the case against the Guthrie townsite never went to contest.

All in all, it was an instance where men looked with contempt upon the protection Congress had provided and considered the marshals and other federal officials hated tools of an arbitrary government that had so long denied them the right to occupy public domain. Needles said on May 24: "The dissatisfaction with the doings of the government is so great that a conflict is liable to arise almost any moment." But Inspector Pickler concluded in a telegram on the same date: "This people are a reasonable people and I think there is no danger of any conflict. The United States Marshal and deputies can easily keep order."

At the root of the problem lay the fact that the 320 acres set aside for townsites proved entirely inadequate for an estimated 30,000 people who came to Guthrie during the first few days. With two full sections occupied and possessed for townsite purposes, it became necessary to organize separate and distinct town governments. As a result, East Guthrie, West Guthrie, and Capitol Hill sprang into existence around Guthrie proper[27] and the population became a shifting, dust-begrimed throng generally awaiting its turn:

> You waited to file on your land. You waited to get something to eat. A well on Harrison avenue [the principal water supply] was kept going all the time. People waited in line to fill their buckets. There was a public toilet off the main street housed in a tent with an entrance and exit, always a long line in waiting. An enterprising old negro established a private toilet on his lot and charged 10¢ for its use and had a thriving business.[28]

With their patience worn thin and every other man armed with a "belted pistol, often plus a rifle and bowie knife," quick, decisive action was necessary to prevent bloodshed.

Wrote Frank H. Greer, the former city editor of the *Winfield Courier* who established one of Oklahoma's first major newspapers, the *Daily State Capital:*

> Perhaps it was the psychology created by this preparedness that prevented many more brawls than occurred. The second hectic day of Guthrie's existence a general assembly was held on the government square [an acre of land set aside for use of the government on each townsite]. The people gathered around a big farm wagon. Colonel [Charles M.] Constantine [former mayor of Springfield, Ohio] presided. He had a voice that reached to the utmost confines of the vast crowd and his kindly genius kept everybody in good humor. A provisional committee of fifty was elected to select a mayor and other officers to be approved by an assembly meeting a week from that date. Colonel D. B. Dyer, a prominent business man of Kansas City and a gentleman of the highest standing, was selected as mayor with a de facto council and other officers, all being approved by the second assembly meeting. . . . Soon ordinances were passed, a city marshal and policemen appointed, and an occupation tax levied for the expenses of the government. The gamblers were fined, and that was the way we got enough money to run the town.

This amounted to a fair sum, considering that "between the land office and the railroad, flanking each side of Oklahoma Avenue, also on Second and Harrison streets, covering every available foot of ground, were tents and booths where every game of chance from the simple throwing of dice to faro was opening plied night and day."[29]

In one big tent, 90 feet wide and 125 feet long, "every kind of gambling from chuck-a-luck to faro and poker was going every hour of the day and night,"[30] and scores of games, such as blackjack and the shell game, operated on tables outdoors.[31] "If Guthrie proper tolerates gambling houses," said the *Kansas City Times* of July 22, "there is this consolation—they pay in $70 monthly each to the city treasury."

Other places of a sort made contributions:

> The house of ill fame next to the Elephant Dance Hall was being prospered without contributing to the city revenue. [City] Marshal Gebke told the inmates that he wished to see the landlady, the purpose being to arrest and fine her; but the various inmates declined to disclose who the landlady was and, moreover, Frank Scott told the marshal that he would blow a hole through anybody that arrested a person in the house. Being asked his authority, Scott said *he* was the owner of the place and told the marshal to go. Gebke is a man that means business and accordingly did not do as Scott told him. Instead, he gets four men to help him and provides them with Winchesters. Going back to the house the party boldly broke down the door which had been locked and arrested seven of the inmates. Scott was put under guard. A large crowd assembled and excitement ran high. However, Marshal Gebke safely housed his prisoners in jail, and all the girls paid $7.50 fines without further demurrer. Scott, who refused to recognize the court or enter a plea of any kind, was locked up.[32]

The absence of a constituted government to preserve order was not the only oversight of a dilatory Congress. That august body also had failed to visualize the sudden building of cities. The existing statutes, framed to fit normal conditions of development, provided that a townsite plat on public domain must be filled with the registrar of the land office by the corporate authorities of the town, if incorporated; if no incorporated town existed, the plat was to be filed with the judge of the county court in which the townsite was situated.

There being no corporate authorities, no counties, and no county judges, there was no legal authority to lay out streets and alleys, blocks and lots. In Guthrie, everyone had staked lots without regard to streets, locating wherever they could find a vacant spot. The tents were so thick that their ropes crossed, and the passages were mere wagon tracks or footpaths winding between them.

The provisional government was forced to take drastic measures to open streets for traffic. Mayor D. B. Dyer had them laid out by competent surveyors, then issued a proclamation declaring that Oklahoma Avenue would be cleaned on a certain date and that other streets, as designated, would be cleaned daily thereafter until all were open.

At 10 A.M. on the day set, two great logs which had been brought from the woods were fastened together with chains and on each end were put four mules. In front of four of these mules was Jim Masterson [brother of Bat, a well-known gunman of the old Dodge City days] and on the other end before the mules rode Bill Tilghman, who had been city marshal of Dodge City and was famous then as afterwards as a United States deputy marshal. Each was mounted with a rifle on his saddle and two sixes showing on each side. Each made speeches to the people saying that the streets had been fairly surveyed, that no town could be without streets, that they were going right down Oklahoma avenue and were sending men down the street ahead to tell the people to get their tents and luggage out of the way before the mules were ridden over their belongings or they were thrown out.

There were great mutterings. Many men stood with their rifles and revolvers in hand, saying that they had the same right to their lots in the street as others who were lucky enough not to locate in the street and that no one could drive them out without suffering the consequences.

At the appointed time, Tilghman, Masterson, the mules and logs started. In an hour, there was not a tent or piece of luggage in Oklahoma avenue, and for the first time since the occupation of Guthrie you could stand on the hill and look straight down the avenue to the Santa Fe station.[33]

The history made here was reenacted in the provisional organization of other towns as citizens held mass meetings in streets, tents, or saloons and elected officials to lead them through their first wild days and nights. Kingfisher boasted that

Chicago avenue is half a mile long. The town is spreading over the whole section—the liveliest place in America today. Titles are somewhat in dispute. . . . A man named Hoper has a lot here and his sign reads: "Keep off this claim; I have a gun." Almost every man wears a six-shooter and wears it where he can get it very easily, but matters will probably be settled by law.[34]

Cassius M. ("Cash") Cade, prominent pioneer banker and Kingfisher's first provisional mayor, labeled the situation

a hodge-podge mess. The United States land office was called Kingfisher, the stream was called Kingfisher—but the town was called Lisbon. The land office was not even on the 320 acres reserved for town-site purposes but located on the southeast acre of the claim rightfully staked by Bill [William D.] Fossett because he rode the best horse on the west side.

There was only one thing to do—start at the north side and lay off the town in blocks of 300 feet square, making streets and alleys. The Rock Island railroad furnished the surveyor. Many of the settlers were disappointed because they were surveyed into the streets, but it was a square deal and that was all the people asked for. I appointed R. C. Palmer chairman of the board of arbitration for the purpose of deciding the legal owners of the town lots. So just were the decisions made by Palmer and his board and the testimony made a legal record that when appealed to the legally appointed townsite board there were only two reversals.

After provisional government was established, a city election was called. [J. V.] Admire was elected mayor; J. C. Robberts, city attorney; Fatty Smith, city marshal; and myself, city clerk. There were only two offices that drew salaries—Fatty Smith drew $50 a month, and I got $50 a month. We levied an occupation tax by the consent of the people . . . and when we got territorial government the city was turned over to legally elected officers without any debt and, in my opinion, was the best city government that Kingfisher ever had.[35]

Twenty-six miles south of Kingfisher, some two miles south of the North Canadian River and on the very western edge of the Oklahoma District, El Reno struggled for supremacy in its infancy. Unlike Kingfisher and Guthrie, it was "layed out" as a business venture by the Oklahoma Homestead and Town Company, a private corporation organized under the laws of Colorado, which leased one hundred and twenty acres of relinquishments of parts of claims obtained from entrymen. Nearby Fort Reno (established in 1874), Darlington Agency (1870), the Caddo Springs Indian school (later Concho), a substantial bridge across the Canadian (built by Fort Reno troops in February, 1886), and vast cattle-ranching enterprises on the leased lands of the Cheyenne and Arapaho reservations to the west provided the trade area necessary for a fast-growing city.

Challenging El Reno's leadership were Reno City, across the Canadian and three miles north, and Frisco, twelve miles to the east and also on the north side of the river. El Reno won out, and so decisive was its victory that soon there was no trace of Reno City or Frisco. Its period of turmoil, however, did not arrive until 1892, when the town was nearly three years old, with "a county seat war, politics and class struggles in which few of the local factions played the game in perfect fairness."[36]

In 1872, down in the southeast corner, or bootheel, of the Oklahoma District, bordered on three sides by the Pottawatomie and Shawnee reservations and the Chickasaw Nation, a Santa Fe civil engineer named Abner Ernest Norman pitched his tents at a spring of clear water in a beautiful grove near the north bank of the Canadian a short distance west of the area where the projected railroad line was to run. This spot became known as Camp Norman. When the unassigned lands were opened for settlement, James M. Bishop filed on the tract and the spot was renamed Bishop Springs. When the railroad was built in 1886, a boxcar was set on a side-track two miles north of the camp and *Norman Switch* was painted on its side. The name stuck.

On the morning of April 22, 1889, the site was "nothing but three-inch prairie grass, with the Santa Fe station and the engineer's townsite stakes to mark the location of what might become a city." That night, five hundred persons occupied the area, sleeping in makeshift shelters. By the fourth day, several buildings were taking form. The people toiled and built so aggressively that by January 25, 1890, the *Norman Transcript* proudly announced: "The community has two newspapers, four churches, 29 business houses of importance . . . and the Commercial bank has one of the handsomest stone buildings in the territory." Norman continued to thrive and build as the gateway city to the bootheel. Lexington, "the closest settlement of consequence [to the south and across the Canadian from Purcell], boasted more saloons than any other town in existence in proportion to population . . . prohibition across the river, of course, more or less accounting for this fact."[37]

Stillwater, in the northeastern neck of the Oklahoma District between the Cimarron River and the south boundary of the Cherokee Outlet, was not born until almost two months after the opening. Homesteaders had preempted the general area except for an eighty-acre strip of deep, rich, sandy loam just above the confluence of the two branches of Stillwater Creek. Here, Payne's Boomers, numbering more than 200 armed men under the leadership of William L. Couch, had attempted to establish a town during their last invasion of the district in December, 1884.

The eighty acres, overlooked somehow in the land rush, became the nucleus of operations for the Stillwater Townsite Company, organized at Winfield, Kansas. By negotiating agreements with three homesteaders whose farms adjoined the tract, the company increased the townsite to 240 acres. On June 2, 1889, the townsite was surveyed; on June 11, a mass meeting was held, a provisional government was established, and officials were chosen. A drawing of lots followed. The original members of the company were given preference, paying $6.25 each for a choice of one business and two residential lots. Then a "gun wad" drawing was opened to the public at $5 each for three lots. After the drawing, the winners were taken in hand by locating committees appointed by the mayor and escorted to their properties. Thus there were no sooners, no contests, and no disappointed settlers. The proceeds went into the city treasury and were immediately appropriated for the building of streets, bridges, public wells, and other essential municipal needs. Because of the planning and initiative of the townsite company, Stillwater "avoided the consequences of a hit-and-miss arrangement that had prevailed in the other towns founded on the day of the run amidst unavoidable confusion, tension and rivalry."[38]

Trouble reared its head, however. When application was made to enter the townsite in August, 1889, it was learned that Garnett Burks, a member of the townsite company, had surreptitiously filed on the original eighty acres early in June with the intent of forestalling its development. The townspeople protested, and local land officers set a hearing for June 16, 1890. At the hearing, which lasted eight days, the officers held that Burks's entry was made in bad faith and ruled for the settlers. By that time, Stillwater was an enterprising city of 56 business houses and 156 residences.[39]

The civil government of the booming community that was to become the future state's largest city endured somewhat more excitement. In Oklahoma City, the provisional government, installed May 2, did not actively take charge of affairs until May 6, then found itself unable to preserve order without aid of the military. From that date until October 21, Captain D. F. Stiles, Tenth Infantry, the active executive officer and provost marshal for the area, kept a patrol of guards in the town daily as occasion required.[40] An *Oklahoma City Times* reporter, Robe Carl White, recalled:

It was common to see men with ammunition belts strapped around their waists with one or two .45s in their holsters . . . many carrying rifles. Main Street [the principal business section] was the dividing line. The main residential district was located on the highlands extending north. The honky-tonk district, dance halls, cribs, and dives were mostly on the south side. Gambling houses centered on the street fronting the railroad and depot and extended south four or five blocks and

24

was called "Gamblers Row." Every kind of gambling could be found on the "Row". Street fakirs, medicine shows and con-men filled the open space in front. . . .

I entered one of the large places and pushed through the swarming throngs. The first sight that attracted my attention was a large green baize covered table in the center of the room. The table had a two or three inch rail similar to a billiard table and it was pyramided with money — gold, silver and paper money. I never before had seen so much money. I could scarcely turn my eyes away from it and the one man who sat guarding it. This man sat at one side of the table with two .45s in front of him while he calmly and coolly watched the crowd that pushed against the table. I noticed that his hands were never far away from his guns. I did not realize at the time, but I have no doubt now all that money in front of him was just about as safe as it would have been in the Bank of England.

This section of town was crowded night and day . . . it was a feverish atmosphere and excitement ran high. The majority had nothing to do except to hold down their lots; it is no wonder that games of chance attracted great crowds. A dog fight in a street would attract a huge crowd within a few minutes, to say nothing about fights, gun fights . . . arguments of all kinds.[41]

In his book *Thirty Years in Hell,* the first chapter of which is devoted to the beginnings of Oklahoma City, Colonel D. F. Mac-Martin gives the most unusual and colorful description of the camp followers and hangers-on who settled as dregs in the lower levels of the fast-moving community:

History has never recorded an opening of government land whereon there was assembled such a rash and motley colony of gamblers, cutthroats, refugees, demi mondaines, bootleggers and high-hat and low-pressure crooks. . . . The spectacular array included the Kansas Jayhawker, the Arkansas Reuben Glue, shaking with the buck ague; the Missouri puke, the Texas ranger, the Illinois sucker, *et al.* There were nesters, horsethieves, train robbers, hijackers, bank raiders, yeggmen, ragamuffins and vagabonds, brand blotters, broncho busters, sheep herders, cow punchers, spoofers, bull whackers, range riders, minute jacks, wildcatters, fourflushers, *Chevalrie d'industrie,* outlanders, montebanks, confidence men, sand lotters and proletariats, sun-chasers, blown-up suckers, fire-eaters, tenderfeet, land whales, butterfly-chasers, blue-sky promoters, sour-doughs, ticket-of-leavers, fellows with nicked reputations, geezers who had just been liberated from the hulks and had ugly corners of their lives to live down. . . . There was Piute Charley, Cold Deck Mike, Alibi Pete, Alkali Ike, Comanche Hank, False Alarm Andy, Poker Jim, Rattlesnake Jack, Six-shooter Bill and Cactus Sam.

25

There were marksmen who were quick on the draw and who could throw a half dollar in the air and clip it with a bullet from their revolvers three times out of five. . . . Among these prospective settlers were ancient maidens, fainting Berthas, wappened widows, withered amazons. There were scoundrels and camouflage artists—bastard scum of the earth and spawn of the devil who would not scruple to take unfair opportunities of their next door neighbors, glib and slippery creatures, together with a homogeneous smear of other shorthorns . . . offscourings and human birds of passage in every stage of shipwrecked penury. . . . Some of these settlers had left families, creditors and in a paucity of instances even officers of justice, perplexed and lamenting. Some had deserted their wives for the wives of others, for this sanctuary. It is no grotesque assertion to say that some of the best men had the worst antecedents, some of the worst rejoiced in spotless, puritan pedigrees.

The lurid title of MacMartin's book does not refer to Oklahoma City, says Angelo C. Scott,[42] but to "the state of mind and body of the author, induced by unrestrained indulgence in liquor and drugs." Scott describes MacMartin as a brilliant chap, a graduate of Princeton, and a budding lawyer soon to become an attorney for the tenderloin district, who "uses French phrases and Latin quotations with perfect accuracy" and quoted Shakespeare "with scrupulous fidelity" but "so raves in his profusion of epithet and adjective that one is driven to suspect that, like DeQuincey, he wrote under the mighty spell of opium."

However, considering the story of Oklahoma City's early social and political life as presented in the first chapters of Albert McRill's excellent volume *And Satan Came Also*, one can wonder whether MacMartin exaggerated at all. Robe Carl White notes further that

it seemed no time until the town was overrun with "lot jumpers". These men, a reckless and rough class, worked in pairs or groups. They appeared well organized. Apparently they sought out lots or claims held by men known or suspected of being "sooners", then at an opportune time they would come in force and undertake to oust the owner and take possession. All summer long "lot jumpers" were the source of constant trouble.[43]

Some events were amusing, others tragic. A Chicago gambler named George W. Cole took possession of the town's only pump, demanding five cents a drink tribute and enforcing his demands with a pistol. As "dry tongues began sagging," there went to the troops an appeal to run the racketeer out of town. If they didn't, leaders of the angered citizens warned, Cole would be hanged. A sergeant was promptly dispatched and "chased Cole off his perch." The gambler "left the city for more congenial fields of labor."[44]

Two hundred fifty armed men attempted to jump a claim adjoining the city on the north. Ten armed men on the claim opposed them. Troops arrived in time to prevent a pitched battle. Another group of five hundred armed men raided a claim on the west side of the city, staked it in town lots, and named it West Oklahoma. They were run out by a detachment of cavalry. On June 4, the newly appointed city marshal of South Oklahoma was shot and killed by the man he succeeded in office.[45]

A group called the Kickapoos sought to dethrone the city administration, set up an entirely new government, and rewrite the charter. They called an election for July 16, in violation of city ordinances, and pooh-poohed the threat of possible arrest. Four companies of infantry on duty were reinforced by two troops of cavalry. On the sixteenth, more infantry arrived, and all troops, guns loaded, stood ready. The Kickapoos called off the election. They started several riots, but these were "nipped at the roots." Several were wounded and a dozen arrested.[46]

As soon as the community demonstrated that it was able to cope with its rapid development, the troops were withdrawn. But lawlessness continued, and other incidents of the day lent color to the creed of the era: Let the best man live—to hell with weaklings!

The first brick building, situated in the heart of the city, boasted a liquor store on the first floor, police headquarters and police court on the second, and a jail in the basement. At the front door of this building, Sheriff John Fightmaster killed Scarface Joe, an Indian who tried to flee from his cell. Dr. I. W. Folsom, a physician from the Choctaw Nation and the Democratic nominee for mayor, got off to a bad start by trying to kill saloonkeeper Phil Rogers with a Mexican bowie knife. U.S. Deputy Marshal Charles F. Colcord bounced the barrel of his six-shooter off Folsom's head in time to save Rogers' life.[47]

George Shields, known in Texas as Satan Shields, learned that some members of the Wolf gang were in town to "get his friend." They were in the Black and Rogers saloon, a favorite meeting place. Shields quietly went around to a hardware store, bought a hickory ax handle, and returned to the saloon. When he had finished, six bloody and discouraged would-be killers lay on the floor. They were hauled into court and fined one hundred dollars each for "attempting suicide."[48]

Kid Bannister, badman of repute and "obnoxious disturber of

27

the underworld," finally was too slow on the draw and his career was terminated by a gun in the hand of saloon proprietor Tom Cook, who seldom used a pistol. The crowd that witnessed the incident cheered when it was ascertained that Bannister was dead.[49]

When two bad boys named Bud and Ping Fagg went on trial for a misdeed, Police Chief Oscar Lee had to clear the courtroom because it wouldn't hold all the spectators. One man, Bill Mc-Michael, objected and told Lee, "Go to hell!" McMichael landed at the bottom of the courthouse steps. Lee gave him back his gun, fully loaded, and told him not to come back or "I'll have to use force."[50]

Such violence was reduced to a minimum as the towns welded themselves into peace-loving, God-fearing people. But outside the towns, where there was not even provisional government and no laws except those generally applicable to federal territory, outlaw gangs were swiftly organizing.

Despite the work of the federal courts in Kansas and Texas and at Muskogee and Fort Smith, banditry still reigned in Indian Territory. Bank and train robberies occurred more frequently than the change of the moon. Not only was the Indian country thinly populated, but its hills and mountains, streams, dense forests, thickets, and underbrush provided excellent cover from federal and other types of molestation. It was an asylum for fugitives from the States and a breeding ground for local criminal talent.

Robber bands rode over into the Oklahoma District, raided railroads, towns, and settlers, and fled back across the border. All along the line of the Nations, in which intoxicating beverages long had been prohibited, saloons sprang up, and an "inflammatory array of bootleggers" engaged in the illicit traffic of introducing booze to the red men. Whiskey of doubtful varieties flowed freely to those willing to cross into Oklahoma and get it, and "Poor Lo, the Indian whose untutored mind sees God in the clouds and hears him in the wind, was soused with this brand of tailor-made hell-broth to the brink of going on the warpath."[51]

When Congress met in December, 1889, the settlers petitioned for immediate organization of Oklahoma Territory. A memorial drafted at Guthrie by a territorial convention of one hundred delegates proclaimed in part that

> in criminal matters the laws at present in force . . . relate only to crimes against the United States and the primitive forms of violence, such as murder and stock stealing.

There is no provision of law as to child stealing, attempted rape, poisoning, abortion, libel or blackmail, reckless burning of woods or prairies, burglarious entry of houses, trespass, embezzlement, rioting, carrying deadly weapons, disturbing public meetings, seduction, public indecency, profanity, gambling, lotteries, drunkenness, bribery, destroying legal process, official negligence or malfeasance, creating or maintaining a public nuisance, selling unwholesome, diseased, or adulterated provisions or drink, introducing diseased or infected stock into the Territory, swindling, false weights or measures, obtaining money or property under false pretenses, making or using counterfeit labels; nor for many other offenses.

By the exceptional and intelligent employment of United States troops and United States marshals, and by the force of an exceptionally cool and intelligent and honest public opinion, there has been a degree of public order so far preserved in this country that is extremely creditable to the authorities and to the people. But it cannot be hoped that such unusual conditions shall permanently continue.[52]

On May 2, 1890, President Harrison signed the Organic Act, which created six counties and six county seats[53] and extended the territory to include all of the former Indian Territory except the tribal reservations proper of the Five Civilized Tribes, the seven small reservations of the Quapaw Agency northeast of them,[54] and the unoccupied portion of the Cherokee Outlet,[55] but including the Public Land Strip (No Man's Land)[56] and Greer County (which was in dispute between the United States and Texas) in case the title thereto should be adjudged vested in the United States.

The government prescribed was republican in form, consisting of executive, legislative, and judicial branches. The chief executive was to be a governor, appointed for a four-year term by the president of the United States. The legislative assembly was to consist of two houses: a council of thirteen members and a house of representatives with twenty-six members. Section 9 of the act placed the judicial power in a supreme court, district courts, probate courts, and justices of the peace, the supreme court to consist of a chief justice and two associate justices, "any two of whom shall constitute a quorum." They were to hold office four years and until their successors were appointed and qualified, and they were to hold a court term annually at the seat of government of the territory, the supreme and district courts possessing chancery as well as common-law jurisdiction. The section provided further that the territory should be divided into three district-court judicial districts by the supreme court, with one of the three justices holding court in each of the districts at such time and place as might be prescribed by law, as well as serving as a member of the appellate court. A large portion of the general statutes of Nebraska was adopted for temporary use, and Guthrie was designated the seat of territorial government until such time as the legislature and governor might see fit to establish it elsewhere.

Under the provisions of the act, a full complement of officers was provided by President Harrison, who appointed George W. Steele of Indiana as governor. Judge Robert Martin of El Reno was appointed secretary of the territory. It was the secretary's duty to record and preserve all the laws and proceedings of the legislature, transmit copies of same to the president, the secretary of the interior, and both houses of Congress, and execute all the powers and perform all duties of the governor in case of his death, removal, resignation, or necessary absence from the territory. Horace Speed became U.S. district attorney. He had served as assistant to the commissary general in Washington and was a member of the Indianapolis law firm of Harrison, Haines and Miller, of which President Harrison was senior member.[57] Warren S. Lurty of Virginia was named U.S. marshal.

The U.S. marshal was one of the territory's most important officers. Lurty was familiar with political affairs of his state, but when he reached Oklahoma and learned what was expected of him, he seemed to lose his nerve. It has been suggested that other candidates for the appointment described the situation as being much more hazardous than it was and that Lurty went back home before taking the oath of office.[58] Some claim he could not make the necessary bond and therefore did not qualify.[59]

In fact, Lurty executed his official bond, with Joseph W. McNeal and Dennis T. Flynn, prominent Guthrie citizens, as sureties. In June, he became defendant in a Guthrie district court suit for allegedly unlawfully arresting and detaining one A. N. Hally on a charge of assault with intent to do bodily injury to E. M. Bamford, a U.S. commissioner. In July, Lurty was sued on his bond for the alleged unlawful seizure and destruction, by one of his deputies, of liquors and bar fixtures from a Canadian County saloon operated by Barton Smith and William H. Dysart in violation of the revenue laws.[60] Lurty was cleared in both cases, but long after his resignation. On August 22, 1890, he was succeeded by William C. Grimes of Kingfisher.

Grimes was a strong, courageous man, a native of Lexington, Ohio, where he was educated in country schools and grew to manhood. In 1878, he married Mary Cleaver of Harveysburg and moved to Hastings, Nebraska, to begin the printer's trade in the office of the *Harvard Sun*, which he later purchased and moved to Sterling. Within eighteen months he sold the paper and entered the mercantile business. In 1885, he was elected sheriff of Johnson County, becoming the youngest officer in the state. Two years later, he was reelected with one of the largest majorities ever given for that office in Nebraska. After moving to Kingfisher in April, 1889, he engaged in the real estate business and served as chairman of the first anti-provisional government convention petitioning Congress to grant Oklahoma territorial status.[61]

Appointed supreme court justices were Edward B. Green of Mount Carmel, Illinois; John G. Clark of Lancaster, Wisconsin; and Abraham J. Seay of Osage County, Missouri. Green was named chief justice. On May 29, 1890, the court was organized at Guthrie, and the judicial districts of the territory were drawn up. The First Judicial District (embracing Logan and Payne counties, together with the reservations of the Ponca, Tonkawa, Oto-Missouri, Pawnee, Osage, and Kansas tribes; that portion of the Cherokee Outlet lying east of the range line between ranges 3 and 4 West of the Indian Meridian; and all of the lands occupied by the Iowa, Kickapoo, and Sac and Fox Indians lying north of the township line between townships 14 and 15 North of ranges 2, 3, 4, 5, and 6 East of the Indian Meridian) was assigned to Judge Green, with places for holding court at Guthrie and Stillwater. The Second Judicial District (embracing the counties of Canadian, Kingfisher, and Beaver; that part of the Outlet lying west of the range line between ranges 3 and 4 West of the Indian Meridian; and all of the Cheyenne-Arapaho, Wichita, Kiowa, Comanche, and Apache Indian country) was assigned to Judge Seay, with the places for holding court at Beaver, El Reno, and Kingfisher. The Third Judicial District (embracing Oklahoma and Cleveland counties; the lands occupied by the Pottawatomie Indians; and all of the lands occupied by the Iowa, Kickapoo, and Sac and Fox tribes lying south of the township line between townships 14 and 15 North of ranges 1, 2, 3, 4, 5, and 6 East of the Indian Meridian) was assigned to Judge Clark, holding court at Norman and Oklahoma City. Guthrie remained headquarters for the court's appellate function.

Thus only two of President Harrison's appointments were bestowed upon citizens of the new territory, much to the disappointment of its aspiring politicians and people in general, especially since the party platform on which he had been nominated contained a strong declaration in favor of selecting officers of the several territories from the citizens thereof. It is worth noting, also, that four of the five outside appointees immediately left the territory when their official connection with it was terminated.[62]

Governor Steele arrived at Guthrie May 22. He had many duties to perform. County boundaries were defined, county governments established, and the population enumerated so that representation in the first legislature could be apportioned accordingly. The census showed 2,982 inhabitants in No Man's Land and 57,435 persons in the six counties of the Oklahoma district, distributed as follows: Logan, 14,254; Oklahoma, 12,794; Cleveland, 7,011; Canadian, 7,703; Kingfisher, 8,837; Payne, 6,836. Guthrie was the largest city with 5,884 residents; Oklahoma City was second with 5,086. Legislative districts were duly marked off, and the first representatives were elected August 5.[63]

The first legislature assembled at Guthrie on August 27. Even before it convened it became apparent that the chief consideration was whether Guthrie or Oklahoma City should be declared the capital of what every voter assumed soon would become a state. To obtain capital votes, both Oklahoma City and Guthrie promised to locate institutions in cities that would aid in their fight. Edmond got a normal school, Norman a university, and Stillwater the agricultural and mechanical college. As a result, the so-called institutional bloc supported Oklahoma City for the capital. Governor Steele vetoed the bill, however, at Guthrie's urging and after consultation with President Harrison. Guthrie held a memorable celebration.

Oklahoma City then swung its forces to Kingfisher, but the capital was located at Downs (now Cashion), in eastern Kingfisher County, and a capitol was authorized on land homesteaded by the speaker of the house and described as the "greatest prairie dog town in the nation." Downs, too, was eliminated by Governor Steele's veto. The legislature then located the capital at Kingfisher. This decision likewise was disapproved by the chief executive, whereupon the legislature placed the capital at Reno, in Canadian County. This attempt met the same fate as the others.

It was charged that the Republican carpetbagger regime made a trade by which Guthrie would support the party nationally and the Republican Congress would protect Guthrie in its possession of the capital. It is a fact that, in 1892, Congress passed an act forbidding a change in capital location or the erection of any state buildings for such purpose so long as Oklahoma remained a territory.

So much attention was given this turbulent affair that the legislature had only ten days in which to turn out a prodigious amount of work. Revenues for support of government were provided. Congress had approved fifty thousand dollars for temporary support of common schools, and a common school system had to be set up. The settlers did not enter Oklahoma in time to seed their farms. Then the drought of 1890 destroyed their crops, leaving many practically destitute. Congress had appropriated forty-seven thousand dollars for their relief, and a territorial board of three was named to administer the program. A code of laws was adopted. They were good laws, except for their incongruity; they were, in the main, taken from the statute books of various states. For instance, Oklahoma had been range country; farmers had to fight to compel cattlemen to keep their stock fenced, and the act for this purpose was lifted so bodily from the Nebraska statutes that it proved unworkable for years. Finally, the legislature provided for farming out the territory's convicts to the Kansas state penitentiary at Lansing; the insane were sent to Illinois.[64]

Meanwhile, the border between Oklahoma and Indian territories became known as Hell's Fringe. It had become infested with every class of criminal, from the most deadly and ruthless killer to the petty thief.

The most desperate of these outlaws were the Daltons.

Oklahoma's territorial governors.

34

Frank Dale, chief justice of Oklahoma Territory.

Horace Speed, U.S. district attorney for Oklahoma Territory, 1890–94, 1902–1906.

U.S. Marshal William Grimes and part of his headquarters staff at Guthrie, O. T., *circa* 1892. *Standing, left to right:* Heck Thomas, deputy marshal; unidentified jailer; Captain J. S. Prather, deputy marshal; Tillman Lilly, deputy marshal; Warren Cleaver, chief clerk. *Seated, left to right:* Chris Madsen, chief deputy marshal; Miss Florence Hitchcock, stenographer; Marshal Grimes; Mrs. S. M. Burche, stenographer. From the Western History Collections, University of Oklahoma Library.

Federal court officials and others in the jurisdiction of the Fourth Judicial District, Pawnee, 1893. *Standing, left to right:* Charles J. Wrightsman, U.S. commissioner; John Colter, deputy court clerk; John Leahy, attorney; Big Elk, Osage chief; Morris Robacker, deputy marshal and Osage Indian policeman; Bacon Rind, Osage chief; unidentified man. *Seated, left to right:* Roy Hoffman, assistant U.S. district attorney; Will Glenn, court clerk; Judge A. G. C. Bierer; Frank Lake, deputy marshal and Pawnee County sheriff; Charles F. Colcord, deputy marshal in charge of the Fourth District.

Federal officers at Guthrie, O. T., 1895. In front row at right, with left hand on hip, is U.S. District Attorney Caleb R. Brooks. In second row at left is U.S. Marshal E. D. Nix. The others are clerks and deputies.

III   The Desperate Daltons

For more than half a century, outlaws on the Oklahoma frontier have been defended as former cowboys with little or no education, who were forced out of work and driven from the freedom of the range by division of the land into farms and cities, and who could not adjust to trade or agricultural pursuits. They had been bred to the open prairie and the saddle, were accustomed to danger, used the rifle and six-shooter as two of the tools of their occupation; they were a wonderful yet absurd combination of shrewdness, badness, and a sort of Robin Hood chivalry along with their daredeviltry. When the call came to join other outlaws, they went wild, the legend builders tell us, and this explanation has been accepted.[1] It catches the fancy of the reader and delights the collector of western lore. Let's examine some facts.

When the farmer took over this region in the late 1880's and early 1890's, the cattle business was at its peak in Texas, New Mexico, Arizona, and as far north as Wyoming, Montana, and the Dakotas. Moving was not difficult for the average cowboy—he usually owned only a horse, a saddle, and a bedroll. Those with no stomach for such humble work as tilling the soil went with the migrating herds, were paid higher wages and fed better grub than they ever had enjoyed in Oklahoma. Those who stayed and took claims often became rich in land and the fruits of their labor. Some who went into the towns became merchants, bankers, and, later, leading men of the state. They accepted changing conditions and made the best of them. Those who took the bandit trail could have found a niche to fit into had such been their choice.

Which brings us to the second legendary fallacy: that nearly every bandit in the territory had been a cowboy before becoming a lawbreaker.[2] Again, some facts. The robbers, horse and cattle thieves, and daring gunmen who for two decades had infested the Indian Nations remained in the same class after the Oklahoma District was opened to settlement. True, a few disgruntled cowboys, listening to their lurid tales of easy money, joined them, but most were part of the rabble that flocked from Texas, Kansas, Arkansas, and Missouri to this last frontier.

Although a few certainly were men of courage, sentimental glorification of them never impressed the old-timers. Old-timer recollections of Oklahoma badmen are neither admiring nor tolerant.[3] Elmer T. Peterson summed them up in the Golden Anniversary Edition of the *Daily Oklahoman* on April 23, 1939:

> They were lousy loafers . . . who refused to do their share of the back-breaking labor of pioneering, scum of the civilization that came to the far outposts to tame the wilderness. They lived by stealing from those who did the real work, murdering them if they resisted. The real building . . . was done by obscure, leather-faced, toil-bent men and women who never dreamed of notoriety or whiskey-crazed gun-fights, except to uphold the marshals and sheriffs who stood off these criminal camp followers.

Legend has it that Robert Rennick (Bob), Gratton (Grat), and Emmett Dalton, the three brothers who organized the Dalton gang, were among the few who could not change from the wild, free life, that they were infused with the venturesome spirit of the old Southwest and could not be tamed.[4] It also has been stated that, like the Jameses, Youngers, and others who gained similar notoriety before them, they were of a criminal strain that was passed on, unbroken, in a single chain, or dynasty.[5]

Their father, James Lewis[6] Dalton, was a gloomy-looking, dull, morose individual with a gruff disposition whose laziness and love of ease smothered a viciousness which lacked determination to become assertive. He was born in Kentucky in 1824 and served as a fifer under General Zachary Taylor during the Mexican War. At the close of hostilities, he returned to his native state but moved west in 1850, settling near Independence in Jackson County, Missouri. On March 12, 1851, he married sixteen-year-old Adeline Lee Younger, prim but waspish cousin of the Younger boys.[7] A native of Cass County, she had grown to womanhood near Independence, where her parents had moved when she was a child.[8]

Dalton engaged in farming and stock raising. On the side he operated a saloon at Westport Landing (now Kansas City), but he soon disposed of it and built a large house in Cass County on the Little Blue. He put it to good use: he eventually fathered more than a dozen children. Two, a boy and girl, died in infancy. In the fall of 1860, the Daltons moved to Kansas and settled near Lawrence, later moving to Montgomery County four miles west of Coffeyville.

Most of the children grew up on the border of Indian Territory. From here the older brothers scattered. Charles Benjamin (Ben), Henry Coleman, and Littleton (Lit) went to Texas and Montana. They were farmers, quiet and hard working all their lives. William Marion (Bill) went first to Montana, then to California, where he married Jennie Blivins, daughter of a wheat farmer, and settled down in apparent respectability. His letters home indicated some dabbling in politics and that he soon might become a member of the California Legislature, a position, despite claims of early Dalton biographers, he never achieved. In 1881, Grat went to the Pacific coast to live with Bill. In 1882, Lewis Dalton moved the rest of his family into Indian Territory, leasing land south of Vinita near Locust Hill.[9]

This venture, like the previous ones, proved unsuccessful. Dalton's passion for fast horses kept him away from home much of the time following carnivals and county fairs. In this connection, it has been suggested that "imitating their father in becoming expert horsemen may have been the means by which the three sons [Bob, Grat, and Emmett] cultivated the company which resulted in their becoming criminals."[10] Subsequent events show otherwise.

In 1884, while Adeline and the children eked out a living at Locust Hill, Franklin (Frank) Dalton, the eldest son at home, was commissioned U.S. deputy marshal for the federal court at Fort Smith. His income helped support the family, and he was known as a brave and trustworthy officer. A few miles west of Fort Smith on November 27, 1887, he was slain in a gun battle with the Smith-Dixon gang of horse thieves and whiskey peddlers hiding at a wood chopper's camp in the Arkansas River bottoms.[11]

With Frank's death, Lewis Dalton's temper soured. He moved his family back to Montgomery County and worked at odd jobs until early 1890, when he died unexpectedly at the home of a friend near Dearing. He was buried in the Robbins cemetery west of Coffeyville.

Grat Dalton returned from California to take Frank's place as deputy. Twenty-eight years old, tall, blond, with light blue eyes, he was the more venturesome of the brothers. To put it another way, "he had a chip on his shoulder and was prone to take chances."[12] In 1888, he received a bullet wound in the left forearm while attempting to arrest a notorious Indian desperado. In 1889, he was commissioned deputy marshal for the Muskogee court.[13]

Bob Dalton had developed a wanderlust before the family moved to Indian Territory. For more than a year he had been deputy marshal for the federal court of Kansas, transporting prisoners to Wichita for crimes committed in the Osage Nation, and had ridden often in Frank's posses. A smooth-faced youth of twenty-two, blue eyed, blond, six feet tall, he carried himself with a pugnacious air. Fearless to the point of recklessness, a crack marksman with a rifle, and quicker to draw than most gunmen, he was considered "the gunfighter of the brothers."[14] Heck Thomas, a noted law officer of the period, remembered him as "one of the most accurate shots I ever saw . . . fired his rifle mostly from his side or hip, very seldom bringing the gun to his shoulder." Willful, reckless, and impetuous, always wanting to be the leader, he boasted to Thomas that "it would have been different" had he, instead of Frank, gone after the Smith-Dixon outlaws.[15]

Emmett, still a boy, was working on the Bar X Bar Ranch near the Pawnee Agency in the Triangle Country, formed by the confluence of the Arkansas and Cimarron rivers.[16] Owned by cowmen Ed Hewins and Milt Bennett, it consisted of 105,456 acres of leased Indian land and pastured ten thousand head of cattle. Most of these were herds from Texas and Mexico that had been unloaded in nearby Red Fork, the end of the railroad spur on the Frisco line southwest of Tulsa. Here Emmett became the saddle companion of slender, six-foot-two, auburn-haired, drooping-moustached, gander-blue-eyed Bill Doolin and of William St. Power, alias Bill Powers, alias Tom Evans.

Powers, a typical Texas renegade, had drifted into the Oklahoma District with a trail herd from the Pecos. Before the opening, he worked briefly on Oscar D. Halsell's HH Ranch, which lay south of a bend in the Cimarron thirteen miles east of Guthrie in a beautiful ten thousand-acre valley of fine native grassland, post oak, and blackjack timber known as Cowboy Flats. Always ready for a wild scheme or exploit, he enjoyed the frequent beer busts of the X Bar X bunch or riding off with them to some town along the Kansas-Indian Territory border to "paint 'er bright red."

Adjoining the X Bar X south of the Cimarron on the Sac and Fox Reservation and along the western border of the Creek Nation lay the Turkey Track. Here Emmett became acquainted with Charley Pierce, George Newcomb, Charley Bryant, and Richard L. (Dick) Broadwell as they rode line between the two pastures together.[17]

Broadwell traveled under the aliases Texas Jack and John Moore.

Around the cowboys' night fires, he related his tale of woe. He came from a prominent family near Hutchinson, Kansas. In the Oklahoma opening, he had homesteaded a choice quarter-section on Cowboy Flats. A young woman took a quarter-section near by. Dick soon found himself very much in love with her and asked her to marry him. She agreed but did not wish to live on a farm because she had taken the claim only as an investment. She finally persuaded him to sell both claims and go with her to Fort Worth. Dick put the money in her care. At Fort Worth, the girl and money disappeared; in spite of his frantic efforts, he never found a trace of her. He thought about returning to his father's home on Medicine River but decided to make a new start in Indian Territory. He was "not naturally a tough" but "a rather overgrown, awkward, good-natured youth . . . impressionable and greatly attracted by men with visions of adventure and riches easily obtained."[18]

Charley Pierce, a sorry character, was a native of the Blue River country of Missouri who reveled in the tales of old William C. Quantrill's long riders and boasted that someday he would board engines like Cole Younger and Jesse James. He had begun training for this larger career by going on drunken sprees and burglarizing the homes of townspeople. For a time, his family kept him out of the penitentiary by returning the property he stole or paying irate victims its value. Then he got a girl into trouble. This scrape exhausted any sympathies the citizens still felt for his disgraced relatives, and the girl's raft of angry clansmen swore they didn't want him as kinfolk, even by the grace of a shotgun wedding. While they were oiling up their weapons to plant him permanently under the banks of Blue River, Pierce dashed away to the Indian Nations astride a fine running stallion furnished by his brother. Settling in the Pawnee country, he raced horses with the Indians and did rather well as "the race horse man" until he tried his hand at whiskey peddling. After serving a stiff sentence in the federal jail at Fort Smith for introducing, he sought work on the Turkey Track. Scowling, long haired, thick chested, and tobacco chewing, he looked more like an outlaw than any other member of the bandit gangs he would ride with.[19]

Newcomb was best known as Bitter Creek because he was always chanting the lines of a familiar range boast: "I'm a bad man from Bitter Creek, and it's my night to howl!" D. S. McKay, formerly a resident of Fort Scott, Kansas, and U.S. deputy marshal at Guthrie, gave this account of Newcomb's early history to the *Guthrie Daily Leader* on May 5, 1895:

Mr. [James] Newcomb, the father [of George], is a brother-in-law of the late Col. Isaac Stadden, the founder and head of the I. Stadden wholesale grocery company of Fort Scott, one of the largest establishments in the state. Mr. Newcomb was associated with this establishment for some years. . . . In 1878, when George was about twelve years old, a gentleman named Slaughter [Texas cowman C. C. Slaughter, whose Long S Ranch lay at the headwaters of the Colorado River] brought to our city a bunch of Texas ponies to sell. When Slaughter left George went with him, and was afterward known as Slaughter's Kid. After an absence of about a year he returned, only, however, to remain a few months. On hearing of him again, he [had] drifted into the Indian Territory and subsequently was employed by Oscar Halsell to work on his ranch and, I am informed, was considered a valuable man.

Hundreds of people in the city of Fort Scott . . . will now learn with horror that the little pale faced, well mannered boy, George Newcomb, who played around the streets and about his uncle's store, was no other than the daring highwayman, Slaughter Kid. . . . It hardly seems credible that a boy surrounded as he was with influential friends, a kind, honorable and industrious father could so go astray.

Bryant, a rail-thin, sinister-looking, trigger-happy fellow with shining black eyes, came from Wise County, Texas. He fought like a wildcat, was lightning fast with a six-shooter, and had engaged in many brawls in which he claimed to have killed men. In a pistol duel at close quarters, exploding gunpowder had burned his face, making a black splotch over his left cheek; hence his nickname: Black-Faced Charley. He suffered from a ravaging fever for which he had found no cure. It came to him often, leaving him deathly sick and pale, causing him to be doubly reckless and to place little value on his life.[20] "Me," he told Emmett, "I want to get killed—in one hell-firin' minute of smoking action!"[21]

Such statements and rowdiness of the heterogeneous group impressed Emmett and stirred the daring spirit that possessed him. This sextet—Doolin, Broadwell, Powers, Pierce, Newcomb, and Bryant—would play significant roles in the Daltons' future operations.

Emmett returned home when his father died but was soon off again, this time riding with Bob and Grat as a posseman. He loved the excitement but lacked the bravado of his brothers. Perhaps he had inherited too much of the substantial quality and character of his mother. Bob, who had organized an Indian police force for the Osage Nation while serving as a deputy marshal, made Emmett a policeman. They made Pawhuska their headquarters. They nabbed no famous badmen but brought in much criminal small fry and were respected officers until there arose a controversy over their wages.

Bob resigned as head of the Osage police rather than accept a cut in pay, and Emmett refused amounts offered him as policeman. Shortly afterward, Bob was accused of selling protection to whiskey peddlers in the Osage country. Confronted with the evidence, he excused his actions by claiming that the government owed him more than nine hundred dollars in mileage and other fees for services as deputy marshal for the Wichita court. This, he said, he had been "unable to collect because of red tape" and he was "just getting even."[22] Marshal R. L. Walker of Kansas fired him. He was not punished further.

Grat got into trouble about the same time. During his first year of service, he had conducted himself as a model officer and his bravery would have distinguished him except for the peculiar streak of deviltry that seemed to dominate his nature. He was talking to some men in front of a store in Tulsa when a Negro boy walked past on the opposite side of the street, eating an apple. Grat halted him with a drawn revolver and, while the boy trembled and his teeth chattered, compelled him to place the apple on his head so that Grat could "show his companions some fancy shootin'." The boy scarcely could hold the apple. There was a prayer on his lips as Dalton's six-shooter exploded. The bullet struck the apple dead center, knocking pieces in every direction as the boy fled for his life, much to the amusement of the onlookers. When the report reached Fort Smith, U.S. Marshal Jacob Yoes dismissed Grat for conduct unbecoming an officer.[23] His commission with the Muskogee court also was canceled.

Bob, Grat, and Emmett could have turned to farming had they desired, for there was now land in the family. When the Oklahoma District was opened in 1889, sections 16 and 36 of each township were set aside for the support of common schools. These lands were not entrusted to the territory but were administered by the Department of the Interior until statehood. Since no provision had been made for their immediate use, Governor Steele granted permission to settlers who had failed to secure homesteads to move onto the school lands, each reserving one hundred sixty acres. After her husband's death, Adeline Dalton and her teen-aged daughters Eva, Leona, and Nannie made their way to Oklahoma Territory in a covered wagon. The tract Adeline chose was in a school section six miles northeast of Kingfisher. Ben, Henry, and Lit Dalton returned to Oklahoma to live with her.

The quarter-section was all bottom land, with Kingfisher Creek entering the east boundary in a large bend. The Dalton home, a 1½-story affair, was constructed in the bend of the creek, surrounded by ash, elm, and large hackberry trees. The path from the house to the roadway was lined with buckbrush and lilac bushes. When the Cheyenne and Arapaho Reservation was opened in 1892, Adeline secured a homestead on Cooper Creek, ten miles to the west. For the next five years, she would divide her time between the two places.

Ben Dalton, a "slow fellow," batched on the Cooper Creek claim. Nannie later married Charles Clute, who had a claim in the Cheyenne-Arapaho country, and Eva married John W. Whipple, who operated a meat market in Kingfisher and sold farm implements to area settlers from a location on Robberts Avenue. Leona remained single and became the mainstay of the family in later years. Adeline Dalton and this part of her brood were respectable and a credit to the community.

Although Bob, Grat, and Emmett had no stomach for chopping cotton and other farm chores, they could have continued earning fees as *posse comitatus.* Despite cancellation of their commissions, it had always been the custom to allow deputy marshals to choose their posse and guards, and Deputy Marshal Floyd Wilson, one of the most active officers in the Cherokee Nation, had work for them. For instance, near Vinita in February, 1890, Grat assisted in arresting a Missouri Pacific Railroad foreman who was charged with beating an employee almost to death with a shovel; the accused was delivered to the Muskogee court for trial.[24] Near Claremore in April, Bob and Emmett acquitted themselves admirably as members of a Wilson posse which captured Carroll Collier and Bud Maxfield, two dangerous convicts who had escaped from the penitentiary in Arkansas.[25]

The pecuniary compensation was insufficient for the risks they took and a chief cause, the legend builders maintain, for their turn from government service to the robber road. On the contrary, the rules governing deputy marshals gave a guard or posseman by far the best of it.

A deputy received no fixed salary. He depended on fees and mileage: six cents a mile when serving process, seventy-five cents a day for feeding a prisoner, and two dollars for an arrest, even if meant pursuing the suspected or guilty party hundreds of miles, buying information from his own pocket, then having to take his quarry in a bloody fight. The only duty of a posseman was to assist where the nature of the service showed it unsafe for the deputy to act alone. For this a posseman was paid three dollars a day, "based on the time between the date of his employment to the date of his last arrest . . . with additional time as he might require in going from the place of his last arrest to his place of residence."[26]

A guard or posseman averaged at least two dollars per day— considered a fair living wage for the period—and often netted more per month than a deputy. But the work was hard, the hours long, and really big and easy money, such as collecting a reward, was seldom to be had.

The Daltons not only openly criticized the government for their dismissal, they expressed sympathy for many of the men who stole and robbed under conditions then existing in Indian Territory as often more sinned against than sinning. Emmett himself stated: "Our fights were not so much against law, but rather against the law as it was then enforced." Their object, he said, was not so much to rob and terrorize individuals and peaceful communities as "to get the better of the government," against which they imagined they had a grievance.[27] It was that simple.

They made their last trip with Deputy Wilson for the Fort Smith court on June 20, 1890. According to the *Fort Smith Elevator* of May 8, 1891,

> they left here and went to Claremore, where they remained until after the 4th of July, when they visited the Osage country and stole seventeen head of ponies and a pair of mules. This stock they brought to Wagoner, and one or both of the boys [Bob and Emmett] came down here and tried to sell the stock to local buyers in this city, proposing to deliver it at Wagoner or opposite this city in the Cherokee Nation. They failed to make any trade, and started to Kansas, trading the mules to Emmett Vann, in the Cherokee Nation, and disposing of the ponies in Kansas.
>
> They next showed up in the neighborhood of Claremore and boldly rounded up and drove away some twenty-five or thirty horses belonging to Frank Musgrove, Bob Rogers, and other citizens. This stock they sold at Columbus, Kansas, to a horse trader named Scott, referring him to some of the best men in the Territory as to their standing. He gave them a check for seven hundred dollars, which they cashed, endorsing it with their proper names. Scott took the stock to a pasture near Baxter Springs, where the owners afterward found it. In the meantime the boys had gathered up another bunch of horses, and on the very day Rogers

and others were at Baxter Springs for the purpose of recovering the stolen property, the Dalton brothers arrived with them. A posse was hurriedly gotten together for the purpose of capturing them, when they hurriedly saddled fresh horses out of the stolen bunch and lit out with a crowd in hot pursuit. Emmett's horse gave out, and meeting a man driving a team, they took one of his horses, leaving him the jaded steed and Emmett's saddle, bridle and coat, which was tied to the saddle. They were being so closely pressed that they had no time to transfer the saddle from one horse to the other. They made good their escape, however, and their brother Grat was arrested while taking them fresh horses. Grat was lodged in the U. S. jail here, where he remained for several weeks, and Emmett and Bob escaped to California where a brother [Bill] is residing. There being no evidence implicating Grat in the horse stealing business with his brothers, he was released and also went to California.[28]

The activities of the trio after joining brother Bill on the Pacific coast are described in a San Francisco circular dated March 26, 1891:

$3600 REWARD

Supplementing circular letter of W. E. Hickey, Special Officer Southern Pacific Company, dated San Francisco, February 26th, 1891, wherein is offered a reward of $5000 for the arrest and conviction of all parties concerned in the attempted robbery of train No. 17 on the night of February 6th, 1891.

The Grand Jury of Tulare county have indicted Bob and Emmett Dalton as principals in said crime, and William Marion Dalton and Gratton Dalton as accessories; the two latter named being now in jail at Tulare county awaiting trial.

The Southern Pacific Company hereby withdraws said general reward in regard to Bob and Emmett Dalton, and in lieu thereof offers to pay $1,500 each for the arrest of Bob and Emmett Dalton, *upon their delivery to any duly authorized agent or representative of the State of California, or at any jail in any of the States or Territories of the United States.*

In addition to the foregoing the State and Wells Fargo & co., have each a standing reward of $300 for the arrest and conviction of each such offender.

Versions of how California officers and railroad detectives connected Bob, Emmett, Grat, and Bill with the crime vary among Dalton biographers.[29] Generally, it is agreed that the robbery occurred at nine o'clock in the evening near Alila, an isolated village settlement and water stop in the hilly southern section of Tulare County. The express messenger resisted, and in the exchange of gunfire, fireman George W. Radcliff was wounded in the abdomen and died the following day. On March 2, officers learned that Bob and Emmett had left San Luis Obispo on horseback and on March 8 disposed of their mounts at Ludlow, a station on the A & P Railway about one hundred miles east of Mojave, where they purchased tickets on the eastbound train.

Grat and Bill, meanwhile, were making it lively for Tulare County officials. Grat's horse had fallen in his ride from Alila and he had been badly bruised. Since he was relatively unknown west of the Rockies, he boldly rode across the yellow San Joaquin Valley to Bill Dalton's place near Paso Robles. A chain of circumstances enabled detectives to trace him from Alila Canyon to Bill's home, and both the train messenger and the engineer declared under oath that it was his voice they heard that eventful night and that his size and general outlines corresponded exactly with those of the robber left in charge at the engine. This fact saved Grat Dalton from the gallows, for the shots that killed Radcliff were fired by the two bandits who stood at the express car. On the other hand, Bill Dalton furnished an alibi which made Grat an "apparently total stranger" at the holdup. The fact that Bill had sheltered his injured brother "could hardly be counted against him." However, both were jailed at Visalia and indicted as accomplices.

Bob and Emmett reached their mother's home on Kingfisher Creek the end of April, and "word was wired about faster than by any wireless of today" that the Daltons were back in Oklahoma. After staying one night, they headed northeast across the Cimarron for the Triangle Country, where they knew all the hideouts and had friends who would keep them posted.

Shortly after daylight on May 2, they reached a colony of Missourians who had settled on Beaver Creek near Orlando and traversed a pasture where a herd of fine horses was grazing. They had made a long, hard ride and needed fresh mounts, so they took eight or ten head of the best saddle stock and continued east. The irate farmers quickly organized and followed the thieves to a heavily wooded canyon near Twin Mounds in eastern Payne County on the border of Hell's Fringe. Had they known they were dealing with the Daltons and not ordinary rustlers, they might have exercised more caution. As they began dismounting to surround the area, the Daltons opened fire from ambush. The leader of the posse, William T. Starmer, died instantly, and another farmer named Thompson fell badly wounded. The others took to the underbrush and trees, firing in the direction from which the shots had come. The Daltons, well sheltered behind a pile of driftwood, suffered no damage. Another vicious fusillade routed the farmers, and the outlaws escaped with their stolen horses. When Starmer's body was examined, it was found that he had been hit by three bullets so close together that the wounds could be covered with one hand.[30]

Will Smith, the California detective entrusted by the railroad company and Wells Fargo with the task of tracking down the Daltons in Oklahoma, communicated at once with U.S. Marshal William Grimes. As a consequence, Deputy Marshal Ransom Payne was put in charge of the Starmer case with directions to scour the Cimarron country through Payne County and the Iowa, Pawnee, and Sac and Fox reservations to the Creek Nation border and bring in the killers, alive if possible or dead if necessary.

Payne was a tall, strongly built man of forty with clean-cut features and a straggly blond moustache. A native of Iowa educated in Kentucky, he had been on the southwestern frontier about eight years and was a successful real estate agent in Wichita before accepting a commission under Marshal Jones of Kansas to police the Oklahoma District before and after the opening. Since the district's organization into a territory, he had served under Marshal Grimes in the same capacity. He was well known as "a fearless enemy of evil-doers and a shrewd discoverer of apparently lost trails" with "enough deeds of extraordinary bravery to fill a volume."[31] He recruited a posse he could depend on, laid in a supply of provisions, horses, guns, and ammunition sufficient for a full-scale campaign, and hit the trail, accompanied by Detective Smith.

At Muskogee, Marshal Needles of the Northern Judicial District of Indian Territory read the report of Starmer's death. "Nobody in the Territory can shoot like that except Bob Dalton," he commented, and he dispatched Deputy Marshal Heck Thomas and a posse to cover the Cimarron and Arkansas areas in the Creek Nation from the Pawnee and Sac and Fox reservations to Tulsa and Red Fork. The *Fort Smith Elevator* of May 8, 1891, reported that

> the country up there is full of detectives and officers who are endeavoring to secure the big reward. Parties from there state that the Daltons range up in the Turkey Track ranch neighborhood. . . . No one lives in that section, it being 35 to 50 miles from one habitation to another. All manner of rumors reach here as to the movements of the fugitives and those in pursuit of them . . . and it is thought that news of an encounter will be heard of soon.

The officers had little hope of an early encounter, however. It was soon learned that at least two of Emmett's old comrades from

48

the Turkey Track had joined them. Bitter Creek Newcomb and Black-Faced Charley Bryant disappeared from a line camp on the Cimarron the night the Daltons crossed Hell's Fringe.

The *Indian Chieftain* of May 7 viewed the organization of this new gang as gravely serious, explaining that

> few criminals ever turned out in Indian Territory have been more successful in eluding arrest than Bob and Emmett Dalton. Bob Dalton is recognized as one of the best shots with a Winchester rifle in the country. That they will never surrender without a fight is a foregone conclusion.

On that same day, Heck Thomas, posseman Burrell Cox, and Tiger Jack, a noted Yuchi scout and trailer for the Creek Lighthorse (Indian police), discovered the tracks of four riders above Polecat Creek south of the Arkansas in the Creek Nation. One rode a "large-hoofed animal whose hind footprints always cut into the front foot marks."

They followed the riders until late afternoon as the latter split, drifted, reunited, and finally crossed the river into the Pawnee country. Tiger Jack, examining the signs with the patient, canny craft of his race, reported the trail was only three or four hours old. Thomas raised his field glasses and studied the rocky, timbered slopes across the river. It was as close to the Daltons as they had been, and he was anxious to go on, but he said, "We'll have to turn back."

In his book *When the Daltons Rode,*[32] Emmett makes much of the incident, explaining how they "spraddled among the rocks, waiting with ready rifles for the posse to come on." He refers to Cox as a "squint-eyed squaw man, an inveterate cadger," many times the recipient of their benefactions, who even then was riding a saddle and horse that Bob Dalton had given him and was now ready to "mow them down"; claims that the redoubtable Tiger Jack, remembering Bob's "repute as a dead shot," suddenly felt "heap sick" and excused himself with "Maybe so I get to wigwam, 'nother little 'tiger' in family"; and says Will Smith was present, phlegmatic, and sinister as a basilisk, "flanked by the others and baying them on like a bloodhound."

In addition, Emmett says, Smith, sensing the Daltons were near and that he was to be cheated of his quarry as his comrades grew suddenly reluctant, became furious and "blustered" at Thomas, with whom the Daltons often had faced danger on official trails but whose courage now wilted in the face of possible ambush.

49

Exact conversations are quoted, which Bob reportedly was able to read from the lips of the men across the river through his own field glasses![33]

First, Detective Smith was miles away with Ransom Payne's posse. Second, the Daltons, as former deputy marshals, knew better than anyone the hindrance facing Thomas. There was a long-standing regulation that a deputy marshal could not pursue a criminal outside his own district without first obtaining special permission from the marshal of the district into which the culprit had fled. Some deputies became so jealous when their districts were invaded that they resorted to such spiteful tactics as trying to have the enthusiastic officer discharged for overstepping his authority. In some cases, they even helped fugitives escape. By agreement among the district marshals, an interchange of commissions had been provided for a selected few, and this flexible system had made it possible to make some progress against organized banditry in Indian Territory.

Thomas' commission under Marshal Yoes at Fort Smith gave him authority in the unoccupied portion of the Outlet, which was not attached to Oklahoma Territory by the Organic Act but was left under the jurisdiction of the federal court for the Western Judicial District of Arkansas as part of the Cherokee Nation. But the Outlet was the only place he could hunt the Daltons west of Hell's Fringe.

Tiger Jack shrugged blandly. Additional trailing fees could not be paid unless they had been earned legally. It was Cox who argued. Who gave a damn about fees and regulations if the reward was collected? Thomas was adamant. He would not go out of his district without permission. Cox angrily threatened to go on alone, but he "followed with alacrity" when Thomas and Tiger Jack set off for the nearest telegraph station at a lope.

Thomas wired Marshal Needles for authority to pursue the Daltons in the Pawnee country. Needles wired Marshal Grimes. Grimes immediately commissioned Heck Thomas deputy marshal for Oklahoma Territory.

By this time, the Daltons had crossed the Pawnee Reservation. On May 9, they held up the Texas Express at Wharton, a small way station on the Santa Fe railroad sixty miles south of the Kansas border and about thirty miles north of Guthrie in the Outlet.

U.S. Marshal E. D. Nix.

U.S. Marshal E. D. Nix wearing his revolver.

51

U.S. Marshal William D. Fossett.

U.S. Marshal Patrick S. Nagle.

IV   One Hell-Firin' Minute
to Death

IT IS NOT CLEAR how the gang reached its decision to rob the train at Wharton or who suggested it. Bob "burned with wrath" at the price on his own head; Grat was still awaiting trial in California and, from reports received through the grapevine, was almost certain to be convicted. The gang's only purpose, according to Emmett Dalton,[1] was a "blind striking back" in sort of retributive justice against the express company, which they blamed for all the weeks of "dodging and nerve-trying suspense on the borderland between right and wrong." At the same time, he admits that the thought uppermost in their minds was to make a "big haul" and go away to South America, where they had "vaguely contemplated" cattle ranching, but he confuses the issue by saying that Bob and his girl friend, Eugenia Moore, planned to be married and that the loot from the holdup was to pay for their wedding and honeymoon.

Through Eugenia Moore, they had learned that Wells Fargo was sending a large sum of coin and currency from Kansas City to a Guthrie bank on Saturday, May 9. Emmett Dalton would have us believe that Miss Moore, "an amateur telegraphist," obtained the information by listening to casual bits of conversation on the wire at different times. Then, dressed in male attire, she raced to their rendezvous on a horse Bob had given her, Emmett says, informed them of this piece of intelligence, and returned to their friend's house near Guthrie the same night.[2] What wire services she had access to has never been explained.

Harold Preece[3] theorizes it was by "adroitly quizzing" a telegraph officer or local express agent — or by "sleeping with him." He claims Miss Moore was Daisy Bryant, born in Cass County, Missouri, the daughter of poor but respectable parents, who ran away from home and became a harlot and the mistress of Black-Faced Charley. Some say she was Bryant's sister. Other tales, as lurid as anything ever appearing in early yellow-backed journals, purporting to be her "true story" and depicting how she took a shine to Bob Dalton and how Black-Faced Charley stepped aside in Bob's favor, identify her as Flora Quick, alias Flo Mundis, alias Tom King, a female desperado who, dressed as a man, allegedly rode at the head of her own bandit gang. This fiction will be dealt with in a later chapter.

A logical explanation of how the Daltons learned of the Wells Fargo shipment is offered by Frank C. Cooper, whose father, Captain George Cooper, staked a claim April 22, 1889, at Seward, a small station on the Santa Fe southwest of Guthrie. The railroad right-of-way ran through the center of the Cooper claim, and the depot was situated about 200 feet west of the cabin.

Frank's mother, three brothers, and one sister held down the homestead while his father worked as a locomotive engineer on the Santa Fe out of Emporia, Kansas. At three-month intervals, Captain Cooper would take off for a short visit to look after the family and crops. Many riders passed through the area, but the Coopers never thought of them as outlaws. Later, they learned the Daltons had been hiding on the RXL Ranch, about three miles up Cottonwood Creek and twenty-five miles from their mother's home near Kingfisher.

Frank Broadwell, Dick's brother, bought cordwood and ties for the Santa Fe and stayed at the Cooper claim. He was a man of few words, well educated, and had considerable experience as a telegrapher. Albert Davis was the Santa Fe agent at Seward. When Davis went out to eat, he left Broadwell in charge. On several occasions, the Coopers saw the owner of the RXL tie his fine black saddle horse at the depot. Then he and Broadwell would "walk away to the woods and talk a long time." Afterward, the family would hear of a train being robbed. "In looking back and reading between the lines, and just guessing," writes Cooper, "we were led to believe Broadwell may have been the one who tipped the holdup men when large shipments of money were coming through."[4]

One authority believes the Daltons planned their first territorial train robbery at Jim Riley's ranch on the South Canadian River in the Cheyenne-Arapaho country near present-day Taloga.[5] Riley had been a stage driver between Fort Reno and Caldwell, Kansas, before marrying a Cheyenne woman and settling down to raising horses and cattle. Considered well-to-do, he took no part in the gang's operations. However, living as he did, nearly a hundred miles from a railroad or major settlement and where his own safety depended on attending his own business, he reluctantly furnished the outlaws food and shelter and fresh horses.

Emmett Dalton says the plans were made from their camp "some ten miles out" (east of Wharton).[6] This probably is correct, since Deputy Marshal Thomas and his posse tracked them to this location two days after entering the Pawnee Reservation.

Still accompanying them were Emmett's two Turkey Track companions, Black-Faced Charley and Bitter Creek Newcomb. Emmett called them "crack shots and good riders . . . with a recklessness that was second only to that possessed by Bob himself."[7] As the acknowledged leader of the quartet, Bob mapped out each man's duties. The train, southbound,[8] was due in Wharton at 10:30 P.M. It would make only a brief stop for water.

"An Eye Witness"[9] describes Wharton as "not a center of population . . . the whole agglomeration consisting of a small frame station and one or two general stores, with postoffice attachment." Preece[10] states that friction between townspeople and the railroad had caused the Santa Fe to locate its facilities "some distance from Wharton," which he describes as "half a dozen shanty stores that passed for a business section." Actually, Wharton was the depot, with one house back on the hill where the agent lived and the night operator boarded. No town existed in the Outlet until after its opening in 1893, at which time the railway station was included in the southern part of Perry. Half a mile south, the railroad bridge crossed Cow Creek, where loading pens had been constructed for the convenience of cattlemen who leased the surrounding grazing area from the Cherokees.

Bob, Emmett, Bryant, and Newcomb reached the loading pens at ten o'clock. After tying their horses out of sight, Emmett and Bryant took their positions in the darkness on either side of the tracks. Bob and Newcomb moved cautiously toward the depot and waited in the shadows of the water tank.

"Eye Witness"[11] tells us that a few minutes before train time, Bob Dalton, his face covered with a bandanna, entered the station alone, took the agent-operator by surprise, ordered him to put up the signal for the train to stop, and, when this was done, gagged and bound him "solidly in his little office." Harry S. Drago[12] accepts the tale, as does Preece,[13] who adds that the victim was a young citizen whose name has been forgotten and who doubled as station agent and telegraph operator. It didn't happen.

Bob and Newcomb waited quietly in the shadows for the engine's approach. The express was on time. It came with headlight glaring, the engine coughing and choking as it slowed almost to a stop. Then Bob and Newcomb, the lower halves of their faces masked, leaped to the tender, put their guns at the heads of the fireman and en-

55

gineer and commanded them to run the train to the stockyards, where they rejoined Emmett and Bryant. Curious heads popped out of the windows; Emmett and Bryant, appearing from the darkness, fired several shots down the sides of the coaches, and the heads were quickly withdrawn. Up at the depot, the agent, seeing the train stop at the loading pens, remarked to himself, "That's unusual, they must have a hot-box." Hearing the shots down the track, he rushed inside the station and put out the lights.

At this point, according to Emmett Dalton,[14] a tall man "in a big white sombrero and gun belt shining across his waist" stepped onto the smoker platform. Emmett, believing the man was Deputy Marshal Payne returning to Guthrie after delivering some prisoners to Wichita, yelled at him to throw up his hands and come down where he was, which the man did and "remained so during the proceedings." And our anonymous "Eye Witness"[15] quotes Payne as saying that when he heard the shots and concluded it was a holdup by the Daltons, he slipped from the platform and hid in the underbrush close to the track to keep them from pumping his "unworthy — but decidedly precious — frame" full of lead. All this despite the fact that Payne was far from the scene, trying to "strike the Dalton trail" on the Sac and Fox Reservation.

Assured that there would be no interference from the train crew or passengers, Bob and Newcomb marched the engineer and fireman to the express car and ordered the messenger to open up. The messenger refused, and the fireman, says Paul I. Wellman,[16] was forced to tear open the door with his pick. But Emmett Dalton[17] describes how, when Bob rapped on the door, the messenger stuck out his white face, inquiring, "What's up?" In reply, Bob jumped up and inside the car, covering the messenger with his six-shooter before he could make a dash for his own revolver or rifle. According to the *Fort Smith Elevator*,[18]

> when the robbers boarded the tender the messenger was looking out the door of his car and immediately apprended danger. He closed and locked his door and then commenced to hide the money and valuables in his keeping in places of safety. . . . When the robbers appeared at the door, he made a show of resistance, but finally admitted them.

Bob's eyes fell upon two safes: the company's small safe, from which packages were taken at different stops, and a larger, or "through" safe. He backed the messenger into the corner by the small safe and ordered him to open it, which the latter did "with alacrity." Tossing him a gunny sack that he carried on his arm, Bob said, "Throw the stuff in here." The man dumped a handful of packages into the sack. Bob checked the safe and saw that it was empty. "Now, open the big one," he commanded. The messenger hesitated. "They closed it at Kansas City, and wired the combination ahead," he explained. "I can't open it, so help me I can't."

Word had been widely circulated by Wells Fargo that on all trains running through Oklahoma and Indian territories between Missouri and Texas the money vaults were always closed and set at Kansas City or Gainesville and the secret combination wired to the end of the run so that the vault could not be opened en route. Bob knew from his experience as a deputy marshal that it was a lie designed to reach only the ears of outlaws and to give the messengers greater immunity.[19] When the "obdurate messenger again pleaded it as an excuse," Bob became exasperated.

BANG! Bob's six-shooter roared like a cannon in the confines of the express car. The bullet ripped splinters from the floor between the man's feet. At the same instant, from outside, came the rattle of shots. It was Emmett and Bryant firing into the air to "warn back" the restive conductor, who had suddenly put in an appearance on the platform of the rear coach.

It was enough to shake the messenger's determination. He fell to his knees before the vault and in a few seconds had it unlocked. He threw a small sack of silver and a package containing five hundred dollars in currency into the gunny sack.[20] Rummaging through the safe and finding nothing more of value, Bob rejoined Newcomb, Emmett, and Bryant. The engineer and fireman were returned to the cab, and the train was backed to the Wharton station. Then the four men hurried to their horses behind the loading pens. The loot was strapped to Bob's saddle, and they galloped away into the darkness.

In retiring, Emmett takes note,[21] they "cantered within a few yards" of where Deputy Payne lay in the underbrush, gun in hand but afraid to use it for fear that if he winged one of them the others would return and kill him. This is self-contradictory, since Emmett, according to a previous statement, supposedly had the officer in custody during the entire affair.

Another tale is that the departing outlaws saw the young telegraph operator (whom Bob allegedly had bound and gagged in his office) sending a message for help and Black-Faced Charley "shot him dead." This yarn appeared first in Fred E. Sutton's[22] 1927 opus of "true" stories of six-gun fighters of the Wild West as written down by A. B. MacDonald and serialized in *Saturday Evening Post* before they became a book. E. D. Nix[23] not only takes note of the incident, with added detail and color, but reserves it for the Red Rock robbery of June 1, 1892, nearly a year after Bryant was dead. Drago[24] lends it credence, identifying the man who fired the fatal shot as having a powder burn on his left cheek, and Preece[25] even includes a decent burial for the slain telegrapher. The tale apparently originated from a report in the *Oklahoma City Daily Times* of Friday, November 8, 1889, under a Wharton, I.T., November 7 dateline. The account states that

C. M. Smith, night telegraph operator, Wharton, I.T., was murdered by two masked men at about 12:50 Thursday a.m. After the shooting the men rode away and no clue to their identity can be obtained. Smith and a boy, acting as coal heaver, were sitting in the station together, eating lunch, when the two masked men came in and ordered them to throw up their hands. The boy did so, but Smith thinking it a practical joke, made a jocose reply. One of the men fired a Winchester at him, the ball entering his left side, passing clear through his body. He became speechless and died at 1:50 a.m., an hour after being shot. The boy was so frightened he was unable to give any description of the murderers.

As soon as the gang disappeared, the station agent relighted his kerosene lamp and a moment later was chattering a wild message along the wires. "A large force of United States deputy marshals was organized . . . as soon as the news had been received, and pursuit of the robbers was immediately begun."[26] By the time the posse reached Wharton, the robbers were miles away and "nobody knew the direction they took."[27]

The Daltons rode back to their camp east of Wharton, where they tore open the packages Bob carried. Emmett says "about nine thousand dollars . . . was the haul."[28] A report from the Topeka headquarters of the Santa Fe gave the amount as $1,500,[29] while Wells Fargo tallied the loss at $1,745.[30] Emmett maintains the express and railroad officials "minimized it."[31] Apparently, the divvy amounted to a little more than $400 per man. Not until some time later did they learn that the Guthrie bank money had been hidden in the stove, which was not in use at that time of year, and in his hurried search of the car, Bob had overlooked that hiding place.[32]

Wells Fargo detective Fred Dodge of Houston, Texas, was at Pauls Valley, Chickasaw Nation, where he had gone Saturday evening, May 9, after investigating a loss at Berwyn, some thirty miles south. He was asleep in the depot office, waiting to leave on the 4 A.M. train for Oklahoma City, when the telegraph operator awakened him with news of the Wharton robbery. He boarded the northbound train. En route, he met Deputy Marshal George Thornton, who headquartered in Oklahoma City, and acquainted him with the facts he had. Thornton wired ahead to Deputy Sam Bartell, who met them at the station with saddles and supplies sufficient for a hard trail. Since it was Sunday, they had some difficulty arranging for additional possemen and horses, which were to follow on a special train. Dodge, Thornton, and Bartell proceeded to the scene of the robbery. While waiting for the special to arrive, they discovered where the gang had tied their horses and "trailed them about 3 miles on foot."[33]

Meanwhile, Heck Thomas received the news at Pawnee Agency and headed southwest to intercept the gang should they recross the reservation into the Sac and Fox country or the Creek Nation. Shortly after sunup, Thomas, and Burrell Cox, now accompanied by Detective Smith, nearly captured the gang while they were at breakfast. They were "so close in fact," said the *Elevator*, "that the outlaws abandoned camp, leaving their packhorse and camp outfit, which fell into the hands of the officers."[34]

Emmett Dalton[35] acknowledges that it was the only time a posse ever got near them, but he confuses Thomas with Deputy Marshal Payne: "A rancher gave us away . . . told *Payne* the location of our camp. Whether he thought the rancher was trying to put him off the track I do not know but for some reason *Payne* made off in the opposite direction."

Thomas, Cox, and Smith continued west to Wharton and met the special train with fresh horses and additional men from Oklahoma City and Guthrie. Among the new arrivals were Deputy Marshals Ed Short, Frank Kress, Joe P. Jennings, and George Orin Severns. Thornton was put in charge, deputizing all those present who were not officers. During the next forty days, Thornton, Thomas, and their posses and the railroad and express detectives combed the reservations and the Nations — east, north, and south — "apparently impervious to exhaustion and collecting, on the way, with shrewd judgment, a mass of valuable information concerning the Daltons' habits and habitual rendezvous."[36] Other men were added to the posses or took the places of worn-out ones as the search snowballed into the greatest manhunt in territorial history.

The press filled its columns with a hue and cry to capture the outlaws, alive or dead. The rewards for Bob and Emmett offered by the state of California, the Southern Pacific and Wells Fargo interested the natives. Although the outlaws had many friends among both the lawless and law-abiding citizens of Indian Territory, few of these people had any scruples about seeing them exterminated. Dodge[37] tells how some Seminole Indians killed three white men and brought their bodies to the Sac and Fox Agency, believing they were the Daltons. None was a man the marshals were seeking, but they all proved to be "outlaws and whiskey peddlers." An inquest was held June 2, 1891, and six days later, three more whites were slain by the Yuchi Indians. "Another mistake," Dodge says, but they, too, proved to be wanted men who "needed killing." As a result, "all the Indians were called off from trying to apprehend the Dalton Bunch."[38]

Governor Steele, alive to the gravity of this new outbreak of outlawry in the territory, expressed concern but did little to cope with it. The responsibility fell upon the shoulders of U.S. Marshal Grimes.

Grimes, being from Kingfisher, knew the peaceful branch of the Daltons well. "Eye Witness"[39] says he telegraphed Deputy Marshal Payne, "pressing orders not to spare any effort to overtake the assailants of the Texas Fast Express," and suggested a stakeout of the Adeline Dalton, Ben Dalton, and John W. Whipple residences. It is difficult to believe that Grimes could have been so naive. Bob and Emmett, forseeing such a move, gave all three places a wide berth.

It is evident that Payne did carry out such a plan. While nosing about the Kingfisher area, he ran into a man named Fred Carter (identified by "Eye Witness"[40] as "a cattleman from Beaver County" but probably one of the colony of Missourians from Beaver Creek, near Orlando), who reported that as he was riding past Whipple's store he recognized a horse tied to a hitching post "that had been stolen from him, with several others, a couple of months earlier by Bob Dalton's gang."

A cautious inquiry was made, "Eye Witness"[41] continues, with "Fred Carter being recommended in the meantime to keep his own counsel," and "the information collected proved sufficient to establish a *prima facie* case against Whipple, of receiving and keeping stolen goods knowing the same to be stolen." On the same day, two deputy marshals, armed with warrants, "pounced upon Whipple as he was returning to his home . . . riding the very steed Fred Carter claimed as his own." The prisoner was hustled to the Rock Island depot, put on the train, and lodged in jail at Wichita. The arrest had been made with such "lightning rapidity" that Kingfisher citizens were "dumbfounded when they heard of it." Mrs. Whipple, nee Dalton, left to run the store alone, wept bitterly, declared her husband was innocent, received the condolences of friends and neighbors, then set out at once for Kansas "with the necessary money to fight the case to the bitter end."

At this juncture, claims "Eye Witness,"[42] the three Dalton brothers (he includes Grat, who was still in jail in California) were hiding only a short distance from their mother's farm. They sent this unsigned message to the Kingfisher authorities:

> You are making damned fools of yourselves if you think you can tackle any of our people without putting yourselves in a hell of a fix. That Ransom Payne'll have to swing for it, sure, or have so much lead pumped into his damned carcass that his own mother won't know him. Let those that are called as witnesses beware!

Underneath was a rudely drawn skull and crossbones and in big red letters the words WE SHOOT TO KILL!

Not wanting to stampede an already aroused population, Kingfisher authorities kept this "scurrilous epistle" under wraps, increased their patrol of "gambling dens, groggeries and houses of evil-resort where the Daltons counted numberless friends but too ready to help them in any pillaging or burning of houses," and otherwise took precautions to protect the lives and property of citizens. They were soon relieved of their anxiety when the telegraph flashed the news that because of his wife's active interference, the complaint against Whipple had been withdrawn and he had been freed.

The story is mostly fiction. No Dalton threat to the city was ever written. Whipple was not charged with receiving stolen property. Carter swore out a writ of replevin, and when Payne came to seize the horse, Whipple resisted. He was jailed at Wichita for "obstructing an officer" and was discharged without prosecution on May 18, 1891, by order of Marshal Grimes.[43]

The trail had been too hot for the Daltons to go near Kingfisher or their friends on the ranches on the Pawnee and Sac and Fox reservations. It was a couple of months after the Wharton affair before Grimes's office learned that, after two days of hard riding almost due west, the gang had reached the old sod ranch house of Jim Riley in the Cheyenne-Arapaho country. Riley had furnished them fresh horses, but he disclaimed any knowledge of their destination.

Fifteen miles from the ranch house, however, on a high bluff where the cedar brakes slashed away from the river and the surrounding country could be viewed in any direction, the gang had established headquarters. In a red clay bank in the squat-black, gnarled dwarf timber, they had excavated a dugout about eighteen feet square, roofed it with sod and camouflaged it with brush and tree branches, equipped it with bunks and an old stove, and laid in a supply of canned goods, flour, coffee, bacon, and beans. Supplementing this with wild game, they fared well. In a little brush corral near by, they kept their horses, "ready for flight or foray," and there were always twenty or thirty other fine animals available on this remote fringe of Riley's range. Emmett Dalton[44] relates how they even played monte with Riley's cowboys and that "spurs, saddles, boots and other gear, as well as horseflesh" constantly changed hands. They also worked cattle for Riley during this period, and although their "identity was not known to these new and casual acquaintances," Big Jim "was then and always remained one of our most loyal friends."

Drago[45] wonders what they were doing for *thirteen* months after the Wharton robbery, doubts that the loot obtained was sufficient to have sustained them, and finally surmises they were idling their time down in Greer County, where only Texas Rangers searched for wanted men and weren't interested in the Daltons. Preece[46] places them in a hideout far to the southeast "in the black granite crags of the Ouachita Mountains . . . that great Ozark sub-region" on the Arkansas-Indian Territory border. And other interpreters of the Dalton saga suggest such widely divergent points as Bear Creek east of Marlow in the Chickasaw Nation, the Glass Mountains west of Enid, Violet Springs near the crossing on the North Canadian below Shawnee, the Osage, and southwestern Oklahoma's Wichita Mountains, which later gave their brother Bill brief shelter and protection.

Resting at Riley's ranch while the pursuit cooled, they planned their next move. By the end of summer, the gang was riding again. They scouted north and east through the grazing leases along the southern border of the Outlet, carefully avoiding the settlements and farming areas over in Old Oklahoma. Their destination, Bob Dalton had decided, was Wagoner, a hub of activity on the Katy Railroad in the Creek Nation.

The third day out, Bryant was seized by one of his frequent attacks of fever. Bob and Emmett wrapped him in his blanket and left him with some friendly cowboys in a camp near Buffalo Springs, seven miles north of Hennessey, hoping he would rally quickly and rejoin them.

Bryant remained at the cow camp two weeks, and his condition grew worse. Finally, he became so dangerously ill that the cowboys persuaded him to let them take him to Hennessey for medical treatment. A doctor examined the outlaw and ordered him to bed. He was placed in an upstairs room of the Rock Island Hotel with his rifle and six-shooter beside him.

Deputy Marshal Ed Short, who had helped trail the gang after the Wharton robbery, headquartered at Hennessey. Blond, small of stature, quiet in manner, and dudish in dress, he was not a man to inspire fear. He was a bad man in the sense that he was fearless. Like the dime-novel hero, he reveled in deeds of blood and valor, but there was little bravado about him.

Short had filled other positions as a lawman. A native of Indiana, he early adopted the West as his home. He went to Caldwell, Kansas, in 1882 during its violent heyday as a railhead on the Chisholm Trail. He was associated with Colonel Sam Wood in western Kansas as a deputy sheriff and city marshal of Woodsdale during the memorable Stevens County War of 1886–87, in which Colonel Wood and his friends were slain while Woodsdale and Hugoton fought for the dubious distinction of becoming the county seat. In 1889, Short settled at Hennessey, where he became city marshal and a deputy under Grimes.[47]

Short saw Bryant when the cowboys brought him in. While the pain-racked outlaw tossed on his bed, too sick to sleep, yet too groggy to remain fully awake or cautious, the marshal thumbed through warrants and reward posters and read the description of Black-Faced Charley.

The Rock Island Hotel was a two-story wooden structure with outside stairs leading from the corner of the building next to the street to the second-floor hallway. To reach the room Bryant occupied, it was necessary to ascend the stairs. Ben Thorne, a former cattleman, managed the hotel. His sister, Jean Thorne, worked there and took Bryant his medicine and meals.

Short visited with Thorne and his sister but did not mention that their guest was a member of the Dalton gang. On Saturday, August 22, he learned that Bryant had recovered sufficiently to be moved. He asked Miss Thorne to let him accompany her when she took the evening meal to the outlaw's room. She wanted to know why. Short did not answer, and the woman refused.

Waiting until she had gone to the kitchen for Bryant's tray, Short showed the wanted poster to Ben Thorne. Thorne advised him to arrest the outlaw at once and offered to assist in the capture. "No," the marshal said, "I can take him alone." But Thorne insisted. "It's not that I want any part of the reward," he said. "Jean's life will be in danger. I'm going with you." He armed himself with a pistol.

Quickly the men stole up the stairway. They concealed themselves around a corner in the hall and waited until the woman ascended the stairs with Bryant's supper. Her knock and voice were all the assurance Bryant needed. As she opened the door, Short and Thorne leaped past her into the room, revolvers leveled at the outlaw's head. "Hands up!" Short ordered. "You are under arrest!"

Surprise, then fury, swept Bryant's powder-burned face. But it was too late for him to make a move for the rifle or six-shooter lying on the bed. He slowly raised his hands and Short clamped steel handcuffs on his wrists.

The marshal's problem now was how to confine his prisoner safely. There was no jail at Hennessey. The few jails that existed in nearby young towns were too flimsy to hold desperate men. It was 40 miles overland to Guthrie, and this meant almost certain delivery by other members of the gang. If he conveyed Bryant to the territorial capital by rail, he must travel in a roundabout way: north on the Rock Island to Caldwell, east on the Missouri Pacific to Arkansas City, then back through the Outlet on the Santa Fe to Guthrie. Short decided to take his man 150 miles north to Wichita, where federal prisoners were being kept.

The northbound evening train had gone and the next one was not due until 5 P.M. the following day, so the marshal settled down to the task of guarding the outlaw. He sat up all night, never closing his eyes.

Next morning, Sunday, August 23, Short asked the Rock Island agent, S. R. Overton, to guard his captive while he obtained some much needed sleep and rest. Overton, determined to take no chances, had the outlaw's hands cuffed together behind him. Bryant complained that this position caused him a great deal of pain, but the agent insisted on playing it safe. In the afternoon, Bryant asked to be escorted about Hennessey, claiming he needed the exercise because of his long illness. Overton then obliged, walking closely behind him, fully armed.

The outlaw became the center of attraction, and Overton observed several strangers loitering on the streets. Since it was Sunday, when idle persons normally gathered, he paid little attention to them until he and Bryant dropped into J. H. Crider's general store. Three suspicious-looking characters appearing to be cowboys came in, and the agent feared they might be pals of the outlaw bent on his rescue. There was a pile of blankets on the counter, under which

Overton saw one of the strangers slip a revolver. He promptly took possession of the weapon and the men fled.

It was nearly train time when Short appeared, refreshed and ready to relieve Overton of his charge. The agent informed him of the incident in Crider's store, showed him the hidden revolver, and warned Short that an attempt might be made to take his prisoner. "If not here, then when the train stops at Waukomis," he said. Waukomis, a section house on the railroad, was the first stop north in the Outlet.

"The Daltons will go to any extent to rescue a member of their gang; they might even hold up the train in the process," Overton added. "You'd better take some help in case of trouble." He offered to accompany Short. Overton was noted for his bravery and good judgment, and there was nothing forbidding the employment of a trusted guard at government expense. Again, however, Short was sure of his ability to handle one man.

Bryant's hands were still cuffed at his back. When they boarded the train, the outlaw complained so much about the pain that the marshal changed the position of the steel bracelets, placing the outlaw's hands in front of him. Still, he took certain precautions. For the trip, he carried Bryant's Winchester in addition to his own revolver. The outlaw's Colt .45 was thrust under Short's waistband. Instead of sitting in the coaches, where anyone could approach him and his prisoner, he obtained permission from conductor Jim Collins to transport Bryant in the combination mail and baggage car.

During the first lap of the journey, Bryant appeared cheerful. "I'm innocent as a new born babe. The railroad ain't got a damned thing on me, and you know it! Why the first judge hears my case will set me free," he boasted.

As the train drew near Waukomis, Short saw several riders coming across the prairie at a rapid clip. Bryant suddenly became very quiet.

Horsemen approaching a train were not in themselves unusual. Cowboys a long time away from a railroad were, like the Indians, thrilled by the arrival of a locomotive. It was like going to a circus. In fact, Short would not have been concerned except for Overton's warning and the prisoner's sudden silence. He handed the baggage agent the Colt six-shooter from his waistband. Requesting that he keep an eye on Bryant, the marshal, holding the rifle, stepped out onto the platform between the baggage car and smoker to observe the approaching riders.

Inside the car, Black-Faced Charley sat relaxed, staring at the door through which Short had disappeared. The baggage agent, an inexperienced fellow, did not recognize the sinister light building in those shining black eyes. The mail-compartment end of the car was equipped with pigeonholes for sorting letters, and the agent thrust the revolver into one of them and turned to check some mail to be dropped at Waukomis. Black-Faced Charley saw in a flash that the hell-firin' minute he had always talked about was at hand.

In one tigerish leap, Bryant seized the carelessly guarded weapon and forced the agent to the far end of the compartment. At that moment, conductor Collins entered the baggage room. The outlaw ordered him to put up his hands. Keeping both men covered, his black eyes glaring, Bryant noiselessly opened the vestibule door. He saw Short standing on the platform.

Short had finished checking the riders. Satisfied that they were only curious cowhands coming in to pick up their mail, he turned to reenter the car—and looked into the muzzle of the cocked revolver in the manacled hands of the prisoner.

Bryant's first bullet struck Short in the chest below the heart. The marshal, though mortally wounded, threw the rifle to his hip and sent a slug into the outlaw's body. Then commenced the most spectacular gun duel between two men of iron nerve in the history of the West. With Collins standing at one side, holding his hands as high as possible, the passengers in the smoker frantically hiding behind seats, some shrieking, some crying for help—the engine whistle screeching loudly as the train rattled into the station—Ed Short fired the Winchester as fast as he could lever and pull the trigger. Every shot he fired found its mark in Bryant's body.

Black-Faced Charley held on to the gun and continued to fire in mad glee, catching Short with a bullet in the arm; another pierced the wall of the smoker and wounded a Caldwell implement dealer who had taken refuge in the washroom. His other shots went wild as he fell headlong, nearly rolling off the platform. Short caught him by one leg and yelled to Collins, "Help me hold him!" Collins helped the marshal pull Bryant back from the steps. "The damn bastard got me, Jim, but I got him first!" Short gasped, then collapsed, vomiting his lifeblood. When the train stopped at Waukomis, both men lay side by side on the platform, dead.

The bodies were removed from the train at Caldwell, where they were prepared for burial by the Schaeffer Undertaking Parlors. Short's body was shipped home to Osgood, Indiana. Bryant's corpse was claimed by relatives at Decatur, Texas.[48]

This letter from the Santa Fe, received at the marshal's office in Guthrie on September 5, is self-explanatory:

Topeka, Kansas
Sept. 3, 1891

Mr. Grimes
   U.S. Marshal
   Guthrie

Dear Sir:

Your favor of September 1st to Henry Meyer enclosing picture of Charley Bryant, together with identification, is referred to me. I beg leave to advise you that I have today made voucher in favor of Mrs. L. M. Short of Osgood, Ind., for $500, the amount of the reward offered by this company for the arrest and conviction of each and every one engaged in the robbery of our train No. 403 near Wharton, O.T. May 9th.

While the conditions under which the reward was to be paid were for the arrest and conviction, yet the company concluded not to stand on any technical point in the case, having sufficient proof to lead them to believe that Bryant was one of the men engaged in the robbery, and for the further fact that C. E. Short lost his life in his efforts to bring Bryant to justice, the Co. concluded to pay this amount to the mother, Mrs. Short, regardless of any legal rights they may have in the matter.

Yours truly,

G. M. Foulk
General Claim Agent.

The mother of the slain marshal received the reward.

Black-Faced Charley had died as he wished: in one hell-firin' minute of smoking action.[49]

U.S. Marshal Canada H. Thompson.

John L. (Jack) Abernathy, the last U.S. marshal for Oklahoma Territory.

V Leliaetta—
Then Red Rock

"FOR MONTHS," WRITES "EYE WITNESS," in his account of the Daltons,[1] "after this eventful twenty-third of August, 1891, when this bloody drama took place . . . it seemed almost as if the earth had swallowed the whole gang [but] in a cosy [*sic*] little house built by some early settler who had soon tired of the lonesome neighborhood, away in Greer county . . . Daisy Bryant had finally joined her beloved Bob, who had been living there in clover all winter long with his inseparable chum, Emmett."

Colonel Bailey C. Hanes[2] also states that Bob Dalton and his boys "laid low for several months." Then, receiving word on "future prospects," they met at the farm of the Dunn family, who had homesteaded on Council Creek southeast of Ingalls in eastern Payne County. It was here, Hanes believes, that plans were made to rob the southbound Missouri, Kansas & Texas train near Wagoner.

Writes Emmett Dalton: "We were camped at Riley's ranch, two hundred and fifty miles away. . . . Eugenia Moore learned that a large sum of money was to be shipped over the Katy road in September."[3] He has "this girl of unusual tact and wit" at Wagoner, riding up and down the Katy from Parsons, Kansas, to Denison, Texas, constantly on the alert for information which might prove of value to the gang, and tells how the "plucky little woman" saddled the horse Bob had given her and, riding mostly at night through a country infested with Indians and outlaws, finally arrived at Riley's place with the news.

More fiction. Again, Bob knew, from experience as a deputy marshal, that a large amount of money, often more than twenty-five thousand dollars, was consigned the fifteenth of each month to meet the payrolls of the coal companies at Lehigh, Choctaw Nation. By the time he heard of Bryant's demise, he had gathered a "more adequate corps of train boarders" than the mere four used at Wharton. With him now, besides Newcomb and Emmett, rode Bill Doolin, Bill Powers, Dick Broadwell, and Charley Pierce.

They assembled at a point near Wagoner, arriving singly and in pairs to avoid arousing suspicion. On the afternoon of September 15, twenty-three days after Bryant's death, the men ate and smoked over an open fire and heard Bob Dalton's final instructions. They would attack the Katy train, he said, four miles to the north at a little cattle-loading station and water stop called Leliaetta (often misspelled *Lillietta*).

Shortly after dusk, the gang rode down the MK&T tracks toward the water tank and halted in a nearby patch of timber. Emmett stayed with the horses. Powers and Newcomb took positions on one side of the tracks, Pierce and Broadwell on the other. Bob Dalton and Bill Doolin moved cautiously to the tank and waited in the shadows. Bob had selected Doolin to go with him on the engine because "all he knew was fight [and] he had to be kept in restraint, or his quick temper was liable to get all of us into trouble."[4]

The train arrived on time and stopped to take water. Bob and Doolin came out of hiding and took positions close to the engine but still in the shadows. When it was ready to pull out, they boarded the cab with Winchesters and commanded engineer Russell and his fireman to "hold up." Then "the engineer and fireman were taken back to the express car and an entrance effected."[5]

There was some difficulty in persuading the express messenger to open the car. Powers, coming up with Newcomb from their side of the tracks, threatened to use dynamite, but this was a bluff. It was not until Powers fired a couple of hurry-up shots into the door that the messenger decided to take no further risk and opened it. While Doolin kept him covered with a rifle, Bob vaulted inside; soon the messenger appeared, carrying a meal sack so heavy with silver that he was forced to drop it on the platform. Then he was told to get back inside the car and close the door; the engineer and fireman were hustled back to the engine and ordered to get the train under way. Emmett brought up the horses, and the gang thundered away from Leliaetta with the bag of loot swung across Bill Doolin's saddle.

At least four versions of the robbery[6] claim that the four outlaws on outside duty held the entire train at bay with salvos of intimidating gunfire while passengers dived behind seats and other shelter and hid their valuables in case the robbers entered the coaches, but that several of them were foolhardy enough to step outside to see what the shooting was about. Doolin could hear their voices buzzing in angry protest. Realizing that many certainly were carrying firearms and might be "tempted into a counter-offensive" against the gang, he let out a violent curse and shouted, "Watch me scare hell outa them!" Bob allegedly ordered him back, but Doolin ignored the command. Yelling like a drunken cowboy on a Saturday night rampage, he leaped onto his horse and raced the length of the train, firing his six-shooter into the air, and chased everyone back into the coaches.

This didn't happen. The *Vinita Indian Chieftain*[7] reported that

two of the men got inside [the express car], two remained outside, and two guarded the train. The messenger opened the "local" safe and after taking its contents the robbers demanded that he open the "through" safe. This he could not do and finally satisfied them that such was the fact. When anyone came out of the cars they were quietly taken charge of and kept until the work was accomplished.

The *Fort Smith Elevator* of September 18, 1891, added:

The robbers did not molest the passengers and only detained the train a few minutes. So quietly did they do the job that the passengers did not know the train had been robbed until after they had pulled out and were nearly to Wagoner. Reports are conflicting as to the number of robbers, one being that there were only three and another that there were seven.

Further, Emmett Dalton[8] says that when the time "came to reckon up," they had "nine thousand four hundred dollars, or about one thousand eight hundred and eighty pounds, all in silver." That the messenger could have carried this burden from express car to platform or that Doolin rode all night with nearly a ton of loot draped over his saddle is a stretch of imagination. In *When the Daltons Rode*,[9] Emmett increases the amount to "something over nineteen thousand dollars" in greenbacks, "about three thousand in silver," and some nonnegotiable securities. This was divided at three thousand five hundred dollars per man.

Actually, the Lehigh payroll in the through safe was not molested, and the express company's loss was two thousand five hundred dollars in silver,[10] making each outlaw's divvy little more than three hundred dollars—even less than the take at Wharton. Emmett admits that when the loot was counted, their dreams of sudden riches began to evaporate; his share and Bob's combined were hardly enough to start a cattle ranch in the Argentine.[11] Nor did the splitting of spoils occur, as he alleges, in their sunup camp next morning. According to the *Chieftain*,[12] "the agent at Leliaetta went out in the direction the robbers left and run upon them dividing the plunder; also they kept him prisoner until the job was finished."

The gang scattered. Captain Charley LeFlore, chief of the Indian police, told a *Chieftain*[13] reporter that

> twenty miles from the scene of the robbery, about two o'clock the same night, four men were seen riding northwest and leading two horses. The next night a woman who is acquainted with the Dalton boys saw two of them and two others west of Red Fork, riding in the direction of the mouth of the stream of that name. They also had two lead horses and the outfit corresponded with that seen the night of the robbery. The use of bloodhounds [brought from Atoka] the morning after the holdup was rendered impossible because so many persons had been trailing around, but an organized pursuit is being conducted.

"It is the general opinion that the job was done by the Dalton boys, and it is probable that they were 'in it,'" said the *Elevator*.[14] The *Chieftain*[15] was more specific: "Needless to say the Daltons are implicated . . . one of them was seen in that vicinity on Wednesday last week."

Doolin, arriving at the rendezvous on September 9 and unbeknownst to Bob Dalton, had ridden into Wagoner. Cowboying in the Triangle Country, he frequently attended the neighborhood dances along Council Creek and in Ingalls, where he was courting a preacher's daughter, and it was as a gift for her that he entered the studio of a Wagoner photographer and posed for a portrait. A copy of the picture, furnished to the Indian police, became the first link in a chain of circumstances connecting him with the Dalton gang.

While Bob and Emmett drifted back west across the Outlet to Riley's ranch on the Canadian, Broadwell and Powers, who had been seen with them near Red Fork, returned to their respective cow camps on the Cimarron. So did Doolin, Pierce, and Newcomb, taking a separate route but apparently first dropping by Ingalls to deliver Doolin's gift to his sweetheart.

E. Bee Guthrey, an Ann Arbor law school graduate, had come to Ingalls at the opening and started a newspaper, the *Oklahoma Hawk*. He didn't have enough money to buy a press, so he made himself a big roller, filled it with sand, and used it to print his paper. Later, he moved the *Hawk* to Stillwater. A few days after the Leliaetta robbery, he was riding three miles east of Ingalls en route to Pawnee Agency when he met Doolin and his companions. All were armed with "Winchesters and revolvers holstered on well-filled cartridge belts." Shot sacks filled with "something very heavy" hung from the pommel of each man's saddle.

They stopped him and inquired whether he had seen any federal marshals in the area. Guthrey told them he had not and, out of mere curiosity, asked, "What do you boys have in those sacks?"

"None of your damn business!" Doolin snarled.

Guthrey promptly agreed that it wasn't. As he started on, Doolin said, "Say, Bee, you still runnin' that one-hoss newspaper over at Stillwater?"

Guthrey told him that he was, and Doolin asked the price of subscription. Informed that it was a dollar a year, Doolin reached into the sack on his saddle, pulled out a handful of silver dollars, and tossed them in the dust at his horse's feet. He watched as Guthrey dismounted and picked them up. "How many, Bee?" he asked.

"You are paid up for eleven years," Guthrey replied. "Where shall I send the paper?"

"I hadn't thought of that." Doolin paused, then laughed and said, "Send it to Ingalls 'til I'm dead; after that, send it to hell." He set spurs to his mount, and the trio departed.

Later, when Guthrey sold his publishing business to devote full time to his law practice, he told his successor of his meeting with Doolin. By that time, however, both men were at a loss to know how to honor the outlaw's subscription.[16]

Bob and Emmett were still in the Outlet, resting up for the last lap of their long ride to Riley's ranch, when news broke in the territorial press that Grat Dalton had escaped from the county jail at Visalia, California. The facts were brief.

After nearly four weary months of waiting, Grat had gone on trial June 18, 1891, for assault with intent to commit robbery at Alila. For three weeks the prosecution forged a chain of circumstantial evidence while Grat's attorney (the Daltons charged later) "let it be wrapped around his client's neck." On July 7, the jury brought in its verdict: guilty. The judge set sentencing for July 29. Grat's lawyer announced that he would appeal to the California Supreme Court.

The *Visalia Delta* of July 9 ran a full account of the trial's conclusion, and the heated discussion subsided. Those wanting the Daltons' scalps felt it unwise to stir up more public comment until Grat was safely behind prison bars. Bill Dalton's trial for aiding the escape of his fugitive brothers was pending. His was a rather thin case, and authorities were worried by public reaction in his favor. Four Merced County citizens, friends of Bill's father-in-law, had provided the four thousand dollars bond necessary to free him.

On July 29, Grat was brought into court for sentencing. His attorney pleaded for a delay until court reporters could prepare transcripts necessary for the appeal. A postponement until September 21 was granted. Bill Dalton made threats to anyone who would listen that if his brother was sentenced, it would take the entire state militia to get him to San Quentin.

On September 3, two men attempted to rob the Southern Pacific train at Ceres, near Stockton. The messengers resisted, and the robbers shattered the express car door with a bomb. Before they could enter, however, railroad detectives Len Harris and J. Lawson appeared unexpectedly and opened fire. In the exchange of shots, the masked bandits wounded Harris in the head and neck and escaped on horses they had left tied near by. The sheriffs of San Joaquin, Tulare, and Stanislaus counties joined in the manhunt. Wells Fargo and the Southern Pacific offered a joint reward of three thousand dollars for the arrest and conviction of the culprits.

The *Tulare Register*[17] gave a long account of the capture of Bill Dalton and Riley Dean as the cosuspects and said that

> when the news was spread in Visalia Thursday night, Sheriff Kay asked Capt. Byrnes of Company E, N.G.C., to guard the roads leading into town. Within an hour after the request was made every thoroughfare leading out of town was guarded, and they remained guarded during the balance of the night. It was thought the robbery was committed to call out the officials at the county jail. In their absence confederates would overpower Jailor Williams and release Grat Dalton.
>
> It is now known, however, that William Dalton's purpose was to rob a train, furnish bail for his brother and then the two skip the country, but the effort was a dismal failure. . . . There is no question about their being the right men.

But when Dalton and Dean were arraigned before Justice J. J. Townes at Modesto, railroad detectives refused to swear to their original stories, and Bill proved an "ironbound alibi," substantiated by one of the detectives named Devine, that he was a hundred miles from Ceres at the time of the crime. "The truth is," he stated in an interview with the *Fresno Expositor* of September 11, "I am like Paddy Miles' boy—no matter what goes wrong, or what depredation is committed, Bill Dalton is always charged with same." The district attorney moved to dismiss the case. The motion was granted.

The affair influenced popular opinion, however. One of Bill's bondsmen on the Alila charge withdrew, so Bill was promptly rearrested and returned to the Modesto jail. It was enough to make even the Visalia judge want to throw the book at Grat. Meanwhile, Grat began to make arrangements on his own.

At 5:30 on the evening of September 18, jailer Williams locked the prisoners in their individual cells and locked the cellblock. Sometime before eight o'clock, Grat, W. B. Smith (a freight car thief), and John Beck (charged with horse stealing) loosened the nuts on the levers that turned the cell bolts and an accomplice in the cell corridor — allegedly a Negro trusty — pushed back the bolts from the outside. The exit from the cell corridor leading into the empty jail kitchen was unlocked, and the three men excaped through the basement window of the kitchen.

The time of escape was determined by the fact that George Mc-kinley, who lived five miles south of Visalia, had driven into town early to attend a church meeting and tied his team and buggy on one side of the courthouse square. When he returned for them at eight o'clock, they were gone. No one suspected the fugitives from the jail until next morning, when their cells were found empty. By that time, Grat Dalton and his associates had at least a ten-hour lead. Posses were organized, but it was another twelve hours before they knew the direction the fugitives had taken. McKinley's outfit was found hitched to a rack on the Southern Pacific main line at Tulare, ten miles from Visalia, where witnesses said three men had boarded the southbound train.[18]

According to Emmett Dalton,[19] three prisoners accompanied Grat, and the men escaped by severing the jail bars with saw blades smuggled into their cells in the seat of the pants of a "cotton-picking darkey." They then commandeered the team and buggy and drove west four miles to Goshen, where all but Grat caught a freight train. Grat drove to the ranch of a supposed friend named Middleton, and Middleton took the team to Tulare to make pursuers believe all had boarded the train there. Grat hid out in the Sierra foothills above Sanger until Middleton double-crossed him by putting a sheriff's posse on his trail for the reward. In a running gun battle, Grat escaped on a neighboring farmer's plow horse and found refuge with a friendly rancher near Merced until the chase cooled sufficiently for him to slip out of California and back to Oklahoma.

"Eye Witness"[20] claims that Grat had been sentenced to twenty years and that one morning in early April, double-manacled to the wrist of one of two deputy sheriffs, he was put on the train to be taken to the state penitentiary:

> The temperature was very hot . . . the window next to which sat the prisoner had been thrown open. While the train was running at full speed — forty-five miles an hour — between Fresno and Berenda, the deputy sheriff who was tied to the prisoner felt so drowsy that he let his head droop upon his breast, while he sunk in a delightful doze. His companion was having a chat and a smoke with a friend at the further

end of the car. Suddenly Grat Dalton rose from his seat with a jerk that awoke his bewildered neighbor. By a magic that has never been explained to this day, the bracelet around the prisoner's wrist fell upon the seat, while the man himself pitched headforemost and with lightning rapidity through the open window. A great noise of water was heard outside, and the excited passengers, now all shouting and crowding to that side of the train, could just see the form of the escaped prisoner swallowed up by the blue waters of a running stream. . . . The deputy sheriffs started out in hot pursuit [when the train finally stopped], but their search was fruitless. All they found on the river bank . . . was the fresh hoofprints of a couple of horses that had evidently been kept waiting for the prearranged escape of Grat Dalton.

Wellman[21] accepts the "Eye Witness" account, adding that Grat fled back to Oklahoma with his brother Emmett. Drago[22] correctly discounts the story and discusses its preposterous aspects. Burton Rascoe, in his introduction to the 1954 reprint of the account told by "Eye Witness,"[23] is unconvinced that "any of the Daltons" were ever in California and believes their apprenticeship in banditry began with the holdup of the Santa Fe express at Wharton on May 8[9], 1891, contemporary reports and official records to the contrary.

When the gang divided its slender pickings from the Leliaetta robbery, Bob had indicated that he and Emmett "were through." Doolin and the others expressed disbelief, declaring that they were only getting started. But Bob was adamant. "You fellows have your wad," he told Doolin, whereupon he and Emmett rode off, the others staring after them. Not until they were in the Outlet did Bob tell Emmett what he was really thinking. The one grand haul, he had begun to realize, materializes so seldom as to be a devil's miracle; they couldn't hope to play the game forever without being captured or killed. Maybe they would go to South America after all. They had enough of a stake to get them there, and they would be safe.[24]

Now the news of Grat's escape filled them with a new enthusiasm. Grat eventually would make it home, Bob predicted. They would wait for him and see what he wanted to do.[25]

They dropped down from the Outlet to Kingfisher Creek and lay in the brush all day. Since the Wharton holdup, they had "steered clear of the family nest." With news of the Leliaetta robbery and Grat heading back to Oklahoma, the Dalton and Whipple residences would be doubly watched. That night, finding the coast clear, they paid one more visit to their mother. There were warm embraces but "not a word of censure or blame." Only, "Have you boys come home?" Yes, the marshals had been there and were on the watch for Grat as well. A quick supper, then good-bye. More embraces, a mother's tears. "Tell Grat to get in touch with us at Big Jim Riley's." Then they were riding again, waving back to her as she stood in the doorway. It was the last time Adeline Dalton saw Bob alive and the last time she saw Emmett until she came to cheer him as he lay fighting death after the raid at Coffeyville.[26]

Bob and Emmett hid out on the Canadian throughout the fall and winter and into the spring of 1892, working some in the round-ups on Jim Riley's range under their old assumed names. Killings and holdups continued in Oklahoma and Indian territories, and be-cause of their established record, they were accused of having a hand in many of them. But they were waiting for Grat. There was speculation that they had joined him in California as the search in Oklahoma subsided.

Meanwhile, Grat was making his way, horseback and alone, down from the Sierra foothills, over the wild divide of the gaunt Tehachapis, across the Mojave Desert, through Arizona, New Mexico, and the Texas Panhandle. He left California in the drench-ing rains of winter. On the one hundred seventh day of his "record-making flight," he reached his mother's home at Kingfisher. Both horse and rider were "hard as nails," and "a new wolf look" blazed in Grat's eyes.[27]

Bob and Emmett met him toward the end of April. They related their adventures; he told them of his trial and escape, and "the bitterness ... burning within him burst forth." There was no "formal word" that he should join them, Emmett says. "We were Daltons, and Daltons we would remain until the bitter end."[28]

By the end of May, they were riding again with Pierce, Newcomb, Broadwell, Powers, and Bill Doolin. They had word — perhaps again through the brother of Broadwell — that seventy thousand dollars in Indian annuity money was to be expressed on the Santa Fe to the Sac and Fox Agency. Bob decided they should "get the train" at Red Rock.

Red Rock was a stop in the northwest corner of the Oto-Missouri Reservation in the Outlet, twenty-six miles northeast of Wharton and forty miles south of Arkansas City. It consisted of a depot and section house, cattle loading pens, a trader's store, and a few Indian shanties. Never any excitement in Red Rock except when Longhorn herds were being shipped northward. It lay in tranquil slumber the night of June 1, 1892, as the gang concealed their horses in a deep wash near the station and took their positions in the darkness for the arrival of the 10:40 train.

Promptly on time, the small wood-burning engine with half a

dozen coaches labored into the station and eased to a stop. No passengers got on or off. The coaches, with lights dimmed and sleepy heads on the reclining chairs showing through the windows, seemed regular enough. While the engine hissed idly, the agent went to the express car, engaged the messenger in a brief conversation, and returned, whistling softly.

"Come on," said Grat impatiently, "let's take it!"

"No—something's wrong." Bob clamped a restraining hand on his rifle arm. "Look at that smoker." The smoker behind the express car was as dark and sinister as a vault. "It's a deadhead," Bob whispered, "and as dangerous as a rattler."

While the outlaws waited, undecided, the train began to move on. Suddenly, the sleeping passengers came alive, peering intently from the windows as the coaches slipped past. Something expected hadn't come off. Could it be the darkened smoker was filled with armed marshals ready at the first sign of trouble to blast the Dalton gang from their boots?

Powers was doubtful. "We've been buffaloed, that's all."

"Yeah," Doolin growled, watching the red light on the rear of the train vanish in the darkness.

Grat exploded. "We just stood here like a bunch of old women and let all that money get away!"

The rest were inclined to agree, except Bob. Even as they stood arguing, a sudden rumble grew in the north. A second section, which proved to be the regular express, came roaring in so fast that its searching headlight was almost upon them before they leaped back into the shadows. "I thought so," Bob commented, and the others looked a bit sheepish. "She's all lit up. It's the one we want."

As the train squealed to a halt, a blanketed Indian with a woman and two children alighted and moved off toward one of the shanties. The station agent had run to the engine to give engineer D. Carl Mack[29] his orders when Newcomb and Pierce dashed past him and jumped into the cab. Covering Mack and fireman Frank Rogers with revolvers, they marched them back to the express car, which had been surrounded by Bob, Grat, Emmett, Powers, Doolin, and Broadwell.

Realizing what was happening when the first figures emerged from the darkness, messenger Elston C. (Whit) Whittlesey[30] and guard John A. Riehl had blown out the lights in their car and now refused to allow anyone to enter. The bandits opened fire, sending lead whipping through the wooden walls from all quarters, even shooting from under the car through the floor. The firing, however, had no effect, for Whittlesey and Riehl stood their ground. More than sixty shots were exchanged as they drove the robbers back. Finally, Bob seized a coal pick from the engine. Keeping the agent and engineer under watch some distance from the locomotive, he directed the fireman to take the pick and smash through the door of the express car. This placed Rogers between two fires. Realizing it meant death to his companion, Mack begged the men inside to stop shooting.[31]

They allowed Rogers to come up to the car. He chopped a hole in the door large enough to admit a man's body. "Now," snarled Bob Dalton, "crawl in there and unlatch that damned door!" The moment Rogers was inside, Riehl ordered him to go to the opposite end of the car and lie down, then shouted to the bandits that the first man who came through the opening would be killed. Another fusillade ripped the car while the three men hugged the floor. After this siege, Bob yelled, "Lay down your guns and come out and you won't be hurt!" Rogers begged the messenger and guard to give up. After a hurried counsel, they surrendered. Grat and Doolin entered the car and found only a way safe. Whittlesey convinced them that he did not know the combination, so they tore open the door with a sledge hammer and chisel and dumped the contents into a grain sack. Next, they went through the merchandise, taking everything of value they could carry. They also took fifty dollars from Riehl, plus his gold watch. Finally, they gathered up the rifles and revolvers with which the two men had held them at bay. Then the gang walked to their horses and rode southwest into the night. Nobody else on the train offered any resistance.[32]

The first report of the robbery, flashed from the dispatcher's office at Arkansas City to all points in the territories, said the Daltons had escaped with the seventy thousand dollars Sac and Fox annuity. However, the money had gone through on the first train, guarded by an armed posse of marshals and Wells Fargo detectives. In "Beyond the Law,"[33] Emmett sets the gang's take at seven thousand dollars; in *When the Daltons Rode*,[34] the amount is increased to "something short of eleven thousand." "Eye Witness"[35] says, "They hardly got two thousand for their trouble, and swore their choicest curses when thus disappointed," which is more likely correct, for the railroad gave its loss as "only a few hundred dollars." For their courageous efforts in defending the express car and its contents against this "most daring band of outlaws that ever infested the Southwest," Wells Fargo gave Whittlesey and Riehl each a handsome gold watch set with a diamond.[36]

Much hoopla has been written about the manhunt which followed.[37] The *Stillwater Gazette* of June 10, 1892, gives the most comprehensive account:

> On June 4, Sheriff John W. Hixon of Logan county returned from the trail of the Red Rock train robbers. When he left the pursuers . . . they were sixty miles west of Red Rock. There were twenty-five deputies in the party and he said they would press on until the trail ended or the robbers were overtaken. United States Deputy Marshals Payne and [Chris] Madsen were in the Panhandle country at that date with a posse of men watching to prevent their escape. The two posses are now pursuing a northerly course through the strip [Outlet]. A party has started from Caldwell, Kansas, going south, in sufficient numbers and fully armed, to do battle in case they intercept the fleeing road agents. The latest reports state that the robbers were on the trail leading to Fort Supply and their pursuers were following them very close. A posse had started from Fort Supply to intercept them.
>
> It is to be hoped that this band of ruffians may receive a lesson that will deter others from attempting to follow their example.

A fifth posse, under the leadership of Marshal Grimes, hurried west to Riley's ranch on the Canadian. Heck Thomas and Detective Dodge, with separate posses, on a tip that the Daltons had doubled back in an attempt to secure the Indian annuity, combed the Sac and Fox Reservation to the Creek Nation and the Cimarron. And from Purcell at the behest of Dodge, Deputy Marshal John Swain took a carload of men and horses via the Santa Fe to Arkansas City, thence west to the end of track at Englewood, Kansas, to intercept the gang, reportedly fleeing northward.[38]

The *Stillwater Gazette* of June 17 tells how the search ended:

> Deputy Marshals [Frank] Kress and [George] Severns returned yesterday from the pursuit of the train robbers. On the same train were the posse of marshals from Purcell en route home.
>
> All of the pursuing parties have now returned and the chase of the thieves has been entirely abandoned. Marshals Kress and Severns, with eleven others, chased the robbers over two hundred miles before . . . their horses gave out so they saw it would be no use to go further. They chased the thieves into the Cimarron hills in the strip [Outlet], then south into . . . the Cheyenne and Arapaho country and finally back into the Cimarron hills.
>
> The thieves had obtained a relay of fresh horses [at Riley's ranch] and it was then very easy for them to ride away from their pursuers. . . . Four horses which the robbers had abandoned were picked up and brought back by the marshals.

U.S. Deputy Marshal Frank Dalton.

U.S. Deputy Marshal Heck Thomas.

U.S. Deputy Marshal Charles F. Colcord.

81

U.S. Deputy Marshal Ransom Payne

VI   Disaster at Coffeyville

THE TIP RECEIVED by Thomas and Dodge proved to be little less than correct. In the Cimarron Hills, the gang scattered and doubled back, singly and in pairs, not to rob the Sac and Fox Agency, but to reassemble at a new rendezvous in Indian Territory. Riley's ranch had become too popular with the marshals, and Oklahoma Territory was filling up with posses and bounty hunters. In the last week of June, Dodge and Deputy Marshal Sam Bartell pursued a rider eastward through the Deep Fork bottoms on the Sac and Fox Reservation but failed to overtake him. They later learned, from a squaw-man friend of Bartell who had given him food and water for his horse, that the rider was Grat Dalton.[1]

The new Dalton hideout allegedly was a cave in a bluff eleven miles west of what is now downtown Tulsa on the east fork of Shell Creek, which runs through the Charles Page Sand Springs Home lake farm. The mouth of the cave, ten feet in diameter, commanded open terrain between the bluff and timber. The gang concealed their horses in the canyon and secured food from the nearby farmhouse of a friendly Creek half-blood. Bob and Grat had discovered the cave and used it frequently as a camping place while serving as marshals.[2]

Residents of this Creek country area have located it variously as "near a spring south of Sapulpa, between Bristow and Kellyville"[3]; "an old cave one mile east of the little town of Slick, back in the thick brush and rocks about two hundred yards off the Slick and Beggs highway";[4] and "a dugout along the banks of a creek near Broken Arrow, about seven miles southeast of Tulsa."[5] Drago[6] describes it as a limestone cave with an overhanging shelf of rock on the old Berryhill farm just above the confluence of the Cimarron and Arkansas rivers near Mannford, originally a ferry crossing on the Cimarron about twenty-five miles west of Tulsa. Hanes[7] says the gang assembled again on the Dunn farm southeast of Ingalls, where Bob received news about another shipment of money over the Katy.

Neither "Eye Witness"[8] nor Emmett Dalton[9] mentions such a cave; they say the various gang members left their "Western lair" and, by some circuitous route, returned to the Cherokee Nation, where they bivouacked on Pryor Creek a few miles west of Pryor Creek Station, a "petty" stop on the Katy about twenty miles north of Leliaetta. For two days they lay in the brush, waiting: Bob, Grat, Emmett, Powers, Broadwell, Pierce, Newcomb, and Bill Doolin. Their plan was to hold up the Katy express at Pryor Creek Station. They knew that since the Leliaetta robbery Katy officials had ordered every train on the main line guarded by a special force of railroad detectives, marshals, and Indian police "until full information should be received as to the gang's capture or dispersion."

According to the *Vinita Indian Chieftain*,[10] "the Daltons and their associates, numbering in all about eight men," had been camped there "several days" before July 14. That morning, an Indian farmer looking for some stray shoats walked into the clearing, stopped, and gaped in curious surprise at the eight strangers heavily armed with rifles and six-shooters.

"Campin', gents?" he inquired politely.

"Just passin' through," Bob Dalton answered.

Asked if they had seen any stray hogs, the bandit leader shook his head. The farmer thanked him and left, glancing back a couple of times, still puzzled.

"That fellow was a snooper," Grat said, gloomily. All of them realized that he probably would hurry to Pryor Creek Station and tell the agent about the strangers in his timber. In fact, before the day was out, word had been flashed frantically along the line that the Daltons were in the area and Pryor Creek Station was their objective. At Muskogee, the railway and express companies organized for a counter surprise—"an opportunity they had been praying for." Bob Dalton said: "We'll outfox them. They'll be expecting us at Pryor Creek, but we'll be robbing the train at Adair."[11]

Adair, a pleasant little farming community of about 800 persons, lay nine miles north. The Grand River bottoms not far to the east would provide excellent concealment and an escape route. Bob and Grat had marshaled the district many times. They were thoroughly familiar with Adair's streets and had often "tromped along the depot platform" as they boarded the Katy with prisoners bound for Fort Smith. Only twenty-six miles away, near Vinita, was their former home.

The gang reached a wooded draw at the west edge of town at nine o'clock in the evening. Leaving Pierce in charge of the horses, the others "moved [on foot] through the deep pools of shadows cast by scattered elms" to the railway station. Most all the men and boys in Adair came back to town after supper, and business places usually remained open until after train time. For this reason, the bandits approached the depot from the rear. The *Chieftain*[12] said that

> at the muzzles of Winchesters, pointed in the face of night operator Heywood, they ransacked the station office of all its money and valuables. Having accomplished this the robbers, seven in number, stationed themselves at convenient places . . . keeping him [Heywood] in range . . . and coolly awaited the arrival of passenger train No. 2 due at 9:42 o'clock.

The train was on time. As it slowed at the station, Engineer Glen Ewing and his fireman were confronted by two men with revolvers, and no sooner had conductor George W. Scales and his porter stepped down to the platform than both of them faced Winchesters. All were told to "remain quiet or have their brains blown out." Three of the robbers then compelled the fireman to leave the engine with his coal pick and help them gain admittance to the express car. Many published versions of what transpired during the next few minutes are mostly fiction. Here are the events as reported in the *Chieftain*[13] and a Kansas paper, the *Parsons Daily Sun*:[14]

> Simultaneously with the stopping of the train the night operator went to the express car as ordered and called to Messenger George P. Williams, but that party, glancing out the window, saw what was "on" and jumped back. . . . One of the bandits then shouted that he had placed dynamite under the car and would blow it to atoms if the door was not opened. Still Williams persisted in his refusal and the fireman with his coal pick was pressed into service. Telling the messenger who he was and not to shoot he began battering the door, but it was not until one of the bandits fired, by way of emphasis, several shots into the car, which passed uncomfortably near the messenger's head, that he finally gave in. . . . The three bandits sprang inside.
>
> While one covered the terrified messenger with his gun, the other two turned their attention to the safe. Although Williams was threatened with death and stated that he was ignorant of the combination and that if he had it to do over again he could not do so to save his life, he did open it. The robbers made short work of its contents, taking everything they could find, even things that were of no value to them at all.

After relieving the messenger of his watch the robbers bound him and dumped him in a corner. . . .

While the three were in the express car, another robber was seen to back a team and spring wagon [obtained from a nearby hitching rail] up to the door and the contents of the safe and other loot were thrown into the wagon.

Information that the Daltons were rendezvousing in that vicinity had reached the railroad officials and as a consequence the train had been carrying guards between Muskogee and Vinita. There were eight of them . . . among them being J. J. Kinney, special detective of the railroad company, Capt. Charley LeFlore, Alf McCay and Bud Kell of the Indian police, and Sid Johnson, a deputy marshal. Bud Kell, looking from the smoking car window, saw what was happening, gave the alarm and the officers stepped out on the east side—the opposite side from the depot. Such a move had evidently been anticipated and the outlaws were here to meet them. For a few minutes bullets were flying thick and fast, the officers using a coal house standing there as a fort. Why this fight did not last longer is accounted for in several ways, the general belief being that it got altogether too warm for the guards. The robbers however took care to shield themselves with train men, and the fire was to endanger the lives of the latter as much as the former.

In the melee, Kinney received a bullet in the right shoulder and Johnson suffered a slight flesh wound, while Charley LeFlore had the stock of his gun struck with a shot and the slivers driven into his arm. None of the robbers were injured so far as known . . . but they [the officers] made it so hot for the gang that they ran for their horses (brought from the draw by Pierce). The spring wagon loaded, they fired a few more shots, gave some derisive whoops and headed west down main street, one bandit driving the team, the others careening alongside as escorts.

The robbery created intense excitement among the townspeople [many a local man and boy set some kind of record for fast footwork in getting home or under cover], and the train passengers were almost beside themselves. As the raiders were retiring, the most unfortunate occurrence of the evening took place. Dr. W. L. Goff, who has of late been residing at Frederickstown, Mo. but was back at Adair on a visit, and Dr. T. S. Youngblood, engaged in practice at Adair, were on the porch of the Skinner store building, some sixty-five yards from the track [watching the battle]. . . . Three or four of the robbers passed through the street in front of these doctors and as they got opposite fired a volley of eighteen or twenty shots at them. Both were hit in each leg and Dr. Goff fell forward exclaiming "I'm killed." Dr. Youngblood started to run around the building when he was struck by another ball which brought him down. He then made his way as best he could to the depot and told what had happened and the train men went after his companion.

In "Beyond the Law,"[15] Emmett Dalton misspells Goff as *Goss* and claims the physicians were in a drugstore near the depot and were struck by two *stray* bullets in the exchange of gunfire; the incident is ommitted in *When the Daltons Rode.* "Eye Witness"[16] and Preece[17] also say they were struck by "shots that went wild." Hanes[18] accepts but misspells Goff as *Gogg* and Kinney as *Kinnet.* Drago[19] charges that "it was slugs from the high-powered rifles of the cowardly guards that felled the two doctors."

The *Chieftain* and *Sun* reports continue:

> The train, which had been detained forty minutes, now proceeded upon its way, bringing the unfortunate doctors to this place [Vinita]. Drs. Fortner and Bagby had been notified by wire that their services were needed, and as soon as the train arrived they took charge of the sufferers and rendered all possible aid. Dr. Goff's principal wound, which was in the knee, was of a dangerous character, and the only hope for him was to amputate the leg. The operation was carefully performed and the patient recovered from the influence of chloroform, but he had lost too much blood and died next morning at half past five. The body was embalmed and sent home to Fredenckstown on Friday night's train.
>
> On examination of Dr. Youngblood's condition, when daylight came, it was discovered that his right foot was badly shot and it was taken off at the instep. If nothing unforeseen happens he will recover. . . . The officers' wounds were also dressed and all went south on the four o'clock morning train.

The amount of loot obtained in the robbery was not learned, as usual. Emmett Dalton[20] says the spoils approximated seventeen thousand dollars. The *Chieftain* reported: "Express folks say 'very little' as the raid was expected and no shipments of value were made by the night train." In "Beyond the Law,"[21] Emmett acknowledges that when they counted up the money, "we found that the South American trip was far away."

More disturbing to the gang were the repercussions over the senseless shooting of Drs. Goff and Youngblood. Teachers, ministers, and physicians were recognized noncombatants in a rough frontier society that could understand why the Daltons hated express companies and railroads. Now, however, two indispensable citizens had been innocent victims of their wrath against the carriers. Accidental or not, it "dissipated the last ounce of sympathy held for the brothers."[22]

Their bold attack on such an armed force, which they obviously had known to be on the train, spread great alarm throughout the territories and caused "great stirs" in top political circles. From Washington came orders for territorial officials to use every means at their disposal to wipe out these bandits who had become a menace to Oklahoma's march of progress.

On July 15, in a joint telegram, Vice President Purdy of the Katy and Superintendent L. A. Fuller of the Pacific Express Company offered five thousand dollars "for the arrest and conviction of each of the men engaged in this robbery to an amount not exceeding forty thousand dollars." But, as the *Chieftain* pointed out on July 21,

> there will be no pursuit by men of experience in this country. Those who know the Dalton boys know they cannot be captured alive. To kill them does not comply with the terms and will not secure the reward. . . . A call for volunteers to make up a pursuing party met with so few responses the project was abandoned.

Murder warrants were issued for the gang in the U.S. commissioner's court at Fort Smith, Arkansas. At the end of July, U.S. Marshal Yoes wrote the attorney general that

> a large force of my deputies was continually scouring the country, but every attempt at their capture proved a failure. They never remained at any one point more than a few days, so that when located, by the time a force could get there, they were gone again.

First, the gang stopped near Blue Springs in the Grand River Hills. "Gaskell's sawmill hands ran into the bandits with a stack of Winchesters and a blanket spread on the ground covered with six-shooters. The strangers told the sawmill men they had business back the way they came and to go and attend to it. The advice was taken." The robbers remained in the area several days, "buying chickens, eggs, butter, etc. in the neighborhood, and not at all particular as to the prices they paid." Some residents asserted that two camps were maintained—one on either side of the river. On the night of July 21, "eight or nine men, thoroughly armed and well mounted," rode past the house of Willis Woods, three miles east of Big Cabin, toward Vinita. Woods sent word to Big Cabin, and the message was relayed by the first train to reach that city. "It was assumed the robbers were coming here with the intentions of making a raid upon the bank" but "these men have not been seen since."[23]

The gang had turned west. Emmett Dalton[24] tells how they rested at dawn the next day on the banks of the Verdigris River near the old Whiskey Trail, which twisted down over the Kansas line from Coffeyville through Indian Territory to the Tulsa area. Across it, he and Bob and Grat intended taking their further course by way of the Caney River ford south of Bartlesville into the Osage Hills. Internal problems were giving the three brothers deep concern. With a prize of five thousand dollars on each man's head, in addition to the rewards offered already, they "walked now on the brink of gold-lined graves." They felt a need to streamline the organization for the sake of better mobility and safety.

Bob, Grat, and Emmett held a "council of war" in which each member of the gang was appraised in turn. Courage they all had, but tact and shrewdness were just as essential. No objections to Powers and Broadwell; they had followed Bob's orders to the letter. Doolin, however, at both Leliaetta and Adair when the shooting started, had strutted up and down the depot platform, "unruly" and "mentally awkward." He had not the wit to avoid unnecessary danger. Then there was the "dangerous credulity" of Pierce and Newcomb; they were getting too fond of venturing into towns and making friends. Specifically, Bob had commented on their indiscriminate hobnobbing with Oklahoma farmers: the Dunn boys. Such indiscretion, Bob predicted, would someday cost them their lives. Pierce and Newcomb bristled and said, "We ain't no suckin' calves." And finally, the brothers decided, there was not enough divvy when the loot was split eight ways.

So it was that the gang tentatively was pruned down to Bob, Grat, Emmett, Powers, and Broadwell. Doolin, Pierce, and Newcomb were lopped off in such a way that there was no sting in the parting. Bob told them he had nothing in mind but would get in touch with them later. The trio rode off toward Skiatook with a friendly farewell and eventually made their way back to Ingalls and their old haunts along the Cimarron.[25]

Meanwhile, "the wildest rumors concerning the lightning rapidity and secrecy with which Bob Dalton conducted his operations were spreading all over the territory and the bordering Kansas towns, and every act of particularly bold outlawry was placed to his credit." For instance, it was "the general opinion . . . before the first emotions succeeding the Adair holdup died out" that some of the gang "tried their hands at bank robbing at the expense of the little Oklahoma community" of El Reno.[26]

On the morning of July 27, when the streets were crowded with teams and people, two men entered the leading bank of the city. The only person inside was Mrs. S. W. Sawyer, the cashier and wife of the president, who was absent from El Reno on business, and she fainted at the sight of their weapons. The bandits took all the money in the vault and escaped. The raid netted them ten thousand dollars, which was such a loss to the bank that it was forced into liquidation.[27] More than two years passed before federal marshals identified and arrested two men, Smith and Crumm, for the crime at Oklahoma City.[28] As Superintendent C. H. Eppelsheimer of the Pinkerton Detective Agency stated in an interview with a Kansas City reporter,

> many crimes have been laid at the doors of the Daltons that they are not guilty of . . . in this respect they resemble the James boys. In their time every robbery and crime committed in this section was laid to them, while it is an unquestioned fact that they knew nothing of many of the occurrences. So it is with the Daltons.

Within six weeks after the Adair holdup, the ground had become too hot for the gang to circulate. There had been a movement among all railroad and express companies that had suffered from Dalton depredations to finance an outfit that would go after the gang and stay in the field until they were killed, captured, or driven from the territories.

Detective Dodge[29] provides the first insight into the planning of this operation. He arrived in Guthrie on July 28 and spent the day consulting with Marshal Grimes and Chief Deputy Chris Madsen. From here he went to St. Louis to meet with Superintendent G. B. Simpson. Wells, Fargo and Company had succeeded the Pacific Express Company on the St. Louis & San Francisco Railroad, and Simpson had been transferred from Omaha to St. Louis as head of the Missouri Division. After discussing the proposition with the St. Louis people, Dodge proceeded to Kansas City and met with the company's general manager, Amador Andrews. Wells Fargo's president, J. J. Valentine, was in San Francisco; he also represented the Southern Pacific. Contacted by wire, he advised Dodge and Andrews to "go ahead." The next day, they went to Topeka to consult with top officials of the Rock Island and the Atchison, Topeka & Santa Fe. By mid-August, arrangements that were acceptable to everyone had been made. Five railroads (Santa Fe, St. Louis & San Francisco, Katy, Rock Island, and Southern Pacific) and three express companies (United States Express Company, Pacific Express, and Wells Fargo) agreed to share the expenses. New rewards of one thousand dollars were offered for each member of the gang, dead or alive. Dodge was put in charge. His job was to select the posse, coordinate its activities, and authorize payment of rewards and expenses. Andrews was the only person who would be kept advised of his movements.

Dodge wired Heck Thomas to come to Kansas City. Here, Thomas helped him assemble equipment: new rifles, revolvers (all the same caliber so there would be no mixup of ammunition), and saddles, both for riding and for packing. On August 21, they arrived at Arkansas City, where they bought saddle horses, pack horses, raincoats, and other clothing they would need, along with provisions. Heck's old posseman, Burrell Cox, joined them at a friend's house two miles south of town where the animals had been "concentrated." The supplies, firearms, and ammunition had been stored in the Wells Fargo office. They were now loaded into closed wagons at the rear of the office and moved out after dark. Men, horses, and wagons traveled south and east for two days and two nights, camping at Gray Horse, Osage Nation, and on Salt Fork. On August 31, they reached Tulsa, establishing headquarters camp three miles from town.

Cox lived in Tulsa. He was married to a Creek Indian woman and had many friends in the tribe. He and Thomas rounded up half a dozen men they could trust and two more who were not allowed near the outfit at all. Both were squaw men who "rode the country and got any news that was moving" and would send one of their children to report. Another scout was Talbot White, a well-educated Sac and Fox Indian who had worked with Dodge previously. But Cox's wife outdid all of them. She "could go out for a day or two and get more news than the rest could gather in a week."

Making arrangements with Mr. Delaney, the Wells Fargo agent at Guthrie, on where and when to send anything to him, Dodge moved the outfit west into the reservations. They spread the word that anyone caught assisting the outlaws would be sent to Judge Isaac C. Parker's court at Fort Smith. The Daltons got the message and became "afraid to trust anybody."

Many people in the country did what they could to help Dodge and Thomas. One night when the officers moved close to the gang's camp, a cattleman sent a warning to their scouts. When they visited the rancher next day, he told them the outlaws had been there early that morning and that Bob Dalton had remarked, "I was close enough to Thomas and Dodge last night to have cut the buttons off their vests." Dodge was to learn later that this was true, that Grat had "wanted to kill them, but Bob wouldn't let him."

Trailing became more difficult. It rained day and night. They established camp on a high hill where they could observe anyone entering or leaving Ingalls. They used field glasses in daylight and at dark posted lookouts along roadways. None of the outlaws appeared in the settlement.

Then came word that the gang was going to try the train at Wharton again. The posse rode northwest into the Outlet, camped near Wharton, and sent out scouts. Dodge had the agent there do some telegraphing. He asked Delaney at Guthrie to send additional supplies on the morning train. That night, Cox and White came in, reporting that some men had tried to ambush them about six miles out. The posse broke camp at daylight and picked up the trail of three riders. After following it half a mile, they found signs that two more had joined them. They knew the outlaws had discovered their party and that the Wharton robbery was off.

The posse followed the trail east until midafternoon. Then it rained again, a virtual downpour. They lost the trail but cut new sign several miles on and a day later. The gang had beat a course almost due east across the Outlet. To avoid any posse that might be expecting them at the main ford on the Arkansas, they had plunged down the treacherous, precipitous banks of the river and fought their way across the muddy, roaring flood. Their pack animal floundered, lost its footing, and was swept away.[30] Its body was discovered when the waters receded. Heck identified the bald-faced rangy sorrel, which he knew the Daltons had acquired after losing another pack animal and their camping outfit to his posse in the Outlet after the Wharton holdup in 1891.

"My hunch is they're headed back to the Cherokee Nation," he told Dodge. "We'll stick on their trail till we run them to earth." Heck's hunch proved correct. By the end of September, Bob, Grat, Emmett, Powers, and Broadwell gathered in their last bivouac near the Mashed-O Ranch north of Tulsa.

The day-after-day search by the persistent, indefatigable posse had made it strongly apparent that escape by immediate exile from the country was a necessity. Emmett Dalton does not mention Dodge in his writings but refers to Thomas as their "nemesis." Heck tried to "bait" them into various traps; he knew most of the isolated cow camps they visited, and he planted confederates in the guise of cowboys to "take them unprepared." But their friends proved their "reliability" and Heck's traps "yawned unsprung." His continued efforts, however—together with an outraged society and rewards so great as to cause even trusted sympathizers to betray them—moved the outlaws to lay plans for a last big raid from which they could gain a fortune and retire. Nix writes that

Bob Dalton's mad ambition was fired with a desire to commit a robbery so daring and so sensational that the entire nation would be shocked, and that would establish the Dalton gang as more to be feared than the James boys or the Youngers had ever been. Having been reared near Coffeyville, Kansas, the Dalton boys knew the little town, its inhabitants and their habits intimately. Young Bob decided that Coffeyville should be the scene of his *coup de theatre*. . . . They would rob two banks in the same town simultaneously. That would eclipse anything the James or Youngers had ever done. He visualized himself as a romantic hero and he developed a super-ego and an unreasonable confidence . . . that he could lead his impetuous followers to glorious accomplishments greater than America had ever known.[31]

Although Bob's proposal came to the gang as a "startling surprise," the more they discussed it, the more they decided the scheme was feasible. Versions of their final preparations are as varied as Dalton historians. Here are the details from Emmett in "Beyond the Law":

Time after time Bob went over our plans carefully so there should be no mix-up. We chose early morning as the best time to effect the robbery, as the banks would then be opening and there would have been no very large withdrawals. How much we should get we did not attempt to estimate. We knew it would be sufficient for the purpose we had in view. Bob, Grat and I were to have three-fifths of the proceeds. What Broadwell and Powers proposed to do with their share we did not know or care; but neither of them was greatly impressed with our ideas of leaving the country.

Bob decided to leave Doolin, Newcomb and Pierce out of the Coffeyville raid. . . . We were to divide into two parties, Grat, Powers and Broadwell going to the Condon Bank, while Bob and I went to the First National. We were to enter the banks, clean them out, come out together, mount and get away. Then was to come the final separation [from Broadwell and Powers].

Should any posse follow, we intended to aim for the Osage Hills, where we could easily lose it. Our intention then was to make for a certain camping spot in the Cherokee Strip [Outlet]. Here we were to be met by Amos Burton with a good team and wagon, as well as necessary provisions and ammunition. Burton was a typical Texas cowboy . . . and the gamest, most trustworthy negro in that country. He knew nothing about our proposal to hold up the. banks. Arriving at camp, we were to get into the covered wagon with our guns and saddles and lead our horses. Two of us were to sit up on the front seat dressed as farmers, and if asked any questions we were to pretend to be horse-traders.

I subsequently learned that Burton faithfully carried out his part of the program. . . . When we reached him we should have paid him liberally for what he had done, when he would have gone back to his claim, twelve miles east of Guthrie, where he was living with his widowed sister and her children. We planned to go northwest . . . to Seattle, Washington. Here we were to take separate boats, one and two at a time, for South America.

We were now ready for the great adventure.[32]

The gang broke camp on October 2. Emmett's horse had gone lame, so he and Bob circled northeast to W. H. Halsell's Mashed-O headquarters to see whether Bob Thornton, the friendly foreman, could supply a fresh mount. Here they ran into Deputy Marshal Ed Chapman, who was hunting them and had boasted in Tulsa of what he would do if ever he came face to face with the Daltons. In *When the Daltons Rode*,[33] Emmett says Chapman, upon recognizing them, "almost had hysterics," offered to surrender his rifle and six-shooter, and, still hoping to "ingratiate himself," offered his horse when he learned that Emmett's had gone lame. It was a good animal, and when Emmett offered him a hundred dollars and his horse for it, the deputy snapped at the deal, then, "without solicitation," gave Bob all his Winchester cartridges.

Whether or not these are the facts of the transfer, Emmett did obtain Chapman's horse. After eating supper with Thornton, he and Bob departed. The following day, the Daltons reached California Creek, about twenty miles south of the Kansas border.

The Thomas-Dodge posse had located the Daltons' hideout near Tulsa shortly after the gang pulled out for the north. They followed the trail of three men, then five, to the camp on California Creek, which the outlaws left about eight o'clock on the evening of October 3. Then it rained and the posse lost the trail. On October 6, while scouting to find it again, they received word of the Coffeyville disaster.

At three o'clock on the afternoon of October 4, the gang cut a barbed-wire fence and rode across a plowed field five abreast—as tracks of the horses later showed—into the heavy timber of the Onion Creek bottoms on the P. L. Davis farm three miles southwest of Coffeyville. Here they unsaddled, procured corn for their horses from the adjoining field of Mrs. J. F. Savage, ate biscuits and hard-boiled eggs themselves, and lay down to rest until morning.

All awoke early Wednesday, October 5, fed their horses again, and ate a light breakfast. It was sunny and clear, one of those fall days that sharpen the mind and invigorate the body. At 8:45 A.M., they saddled up. Bob's idea was to ride into town at 9:30 because there wouldn't be so many people on the street at that hour and they wouldn't have to hurt anyone.

Mr. and Mrs. R. H. Hollingsworth, who were driving west on Eighth Street, met them just east of the old cheese factory and less than half a mile from the western city limits. Moments later, the gang was met by J. M. and J. L. Seldomridge, who were driving west on the same road. The Hollingsworths and the Seldomridges, according to "Eye Witness,"[34] said there were six men in the party, armed to the teeth and disguised. However, a score of other people along Eighth Street who saw the horsemen pass their residences observed only five. James Brown's young daughter, who was on her way to town horseback, saw the gang emerge single file from the Davis farm, pass under the bridge over the creek, and ride up the opposite bank. She followed them until they reached the road leading directly to Coffeyville and turned east. She counted only five riders. William Gilbert, a farmer living on the same route, saw only five strangers as they passed the spot where he was working. The Hollingsworths and Seldomridges were possibly mistaken, or perhaps it was "Eye Witness," for only in his account, which often is erroneous, does the statement appear.

Accepting the "Eye Witness" version, later writers have conjectured that the sixth rider was Bill Doolin; that his horse suddenly went lame and, bitterly disappointed, he promised Bob Dalton he would rejoin them as soon as he could obtain a big sorrel he had spotted grazing in a pasture a few miles back; that it had been planned to have three men enter each bank but Doolin arrived at the meeting place too late and the gang did not wait for him.

In his book *Oklahoma Outlaws*,[35] Richard S. Graves tells how Doolin topped a hill within sight of the Kansas town and saw a horseman racing toward him. The man reined to a halt in a cloud of dust and, in excitement so great that his words tumbled out incoherently, told the outlaw what had happened in the streets of Coffeyville. There was nothing Doolin could do for his comrades now. His connection with the Daltons was known. Soon the entire country would become aroused and a search spread for him. As soon as his informant had disappeared, he whirled his horse and fled back across the Kansas line. Stopping only to give the animal breathing spells, he "crossed Indian Territory like a flying wraith, flitting by ranch and farm in the night like a ghostly rider saddled

95

upon the wind, reeling off mile after mile until he reached the old rendezvous of the gang, a cow ranch on the Cimarron."

If indeed it occurred, Doolin's escape on his most inexhaustible mount should have gone down as one of the great western rides in history. The tale is repeated by J. A. Newsom,[36] Zoe A. Tilghman in *Outlaw Days*,[37] Sutton,[38] Nix,[39] Wellman,[40] and Drago.[41] I accepted the story in *Six-Gun and Silver Star*[42] but refuted it in *Heck Thomas, Frontier Marshal*.[43] Ramon F. Adams, in his introduction Hanes's *Bill Doolin, Outlaw O. T.*,[44] enumerates the volumes in which the tale appears, including *Six-Gun*, and credits Hanes as being first to explode the legend. Yet Homer Croy doubted the yarn as early as 1958 in *Trigger Marshal*,[45] and Adams obviously had not read *Heck Thomas*, which Hanes used.

Too, what happened in the streets of Coffeyville that eventful day has been rehashed so many times in books, historical periodicals, and "true" western magazines that a volume is needed to separate the wheat from the chaff. That attempt will not be made here. David Stewart Elliott, editor of the *Coffeyville Journal*, was in the plaza area when the battle began, witnessed the entire fight, and was first to reach Emmett Dalton, its lone survivor, after Emmett had been gunned from his horse in the alley. Elliott's account, which appeared in the *Journal* on Friday, October 7, 1892, remains the most reliable report:

> The five men rode boldly and at a swinging trot, raising a cloud of dust which literally enveloped them as they passed down Eighth street. They turned into Maple street and passed along side of the Long-Bell Company's office and entered the alley that runs from Walnut street at Slosson's drug store, to Maple street and thence to the western boundary of the city. There were a number of persons in the alley at the same time and several teams were hitched in the rear of Davis' blacksmith shop. An oil tank of the Consolidated Company, with two horses attached thereto, was standing near McKenna & Adamson's stables, almost in the center of the alley. The party hitched their horses to the fence in the rear of Police Judge Munn's lot, and within a few feet of the temporary residence which he is at present occupying. A stone cutter, who was examining some rock lying near the city jail, observed them riding into the alley and dismounting. They quickly formed into a sort of military line, three in front and two in the rear and walked closely together. The stone cutter walked closely in the rear of the crowd as they passed from their horses through the alley, until they reached the street, when he turned north to his work at the other end of the block. Aleck McKenna was on the pavement in front of his place of business when the men came out of the alley, and when they passed

within five feet of where he was standing. He was close enough to detect the disguises on two of the men, and he recognized one of them as a member of the Dalton family. After passing Mr. McKenna the men quickened their pace and three of them went into C. M. Condon & Co.'s bank at the southwest door, while the two in the rear ran directly across the street to the First National bank, and entered the front door of that institution.

The next thing that greeted Mr. McKenna's eyes was a Winchester in the hands of one of the men, and pointed toward the cashier's counter in the bank. He realized the situation at once, and called out to those in the store, that "the bank was being robbed." The cry was taken up by some others who had been attracted to the men as they entered the bank, and quickly passed from lip to lip all around the square. Persons in the south part of the plaza, the open space between Walnut street and Union street, could plainly see the men as they moved around through the bank. The two men who entered the First National bank were observed by a number of parties, but their presence did not attract any particular attention at first. The scenes that took place in the two banks were wonderfully exciting and must be described in detail in order to be understood. When the three men entered Condon & Co.'s bank, Mr. C. T. Carpenter was alone behind the counter. The first one quickly pointed a Winchester in the direction of Mr. Carpenter's head and sternly commanded him to hand over the cash on hand, and urged him to be quick about it.

He remained near the southwest door whilst the other two men took positions, one on the inside of the southeast door of the bank and the other passed through the hall into a room having a door which leads to the stairway and out upon the street at the north west corner of the building. Mr. C. M. Ball, cashier of the bank, and Mr. T. C. Babb, a bookkeeper of the firm, were in the office. As he entered he covered them with his Winchester and ordered Mr. Ball to bring him the money out of the safe.

The latter undertook to parley with him, and told him that the time lock was on the safe and that he could not get into the money chest. The fellow told him that he would have to get into it, or he would be compelled to kill him. Mr. Ball continued to remonstrate, and in order to appease the unwelcome visitor he went to the vault and dragged out a sack containing about $4,000 in silver. This did not satisfy him, and he inquired how soon the time lock would open. Mr. Ball told him that it was set for 9:45. "That is only three minutes yet, and I will wait," replied the intruder. He amused himself for a minute or two by having Mr. Ball drag the silver around over the floor in order to get it to a point where he could command a view of it. In the meantime Mr. J. D. Levan, an aged gentleman and a customer of the bank unaware that anything unusual was going on, stepped into the bank by the same

97

door that the robbers had entered. Observing the men with guns in their hands, he attempted to retreat, but was grasped by the arm and dragged into the bank and compelled to lie down on the floor. The robber who had Mr. Carpenter in charge gathered up the funds as they were passed over to him and carelessly stuffed them on the inside of his vest. Before the three minutes, which Mr. Ball had claimed for the time lock, had expired, firing began on the outside of the bank and the bullets began to come through the plate glass windows. Messrs. Ball, Carpenter and Babb threw themselves on the floor while the robbers turned their attention to matters on the outside and began firing at the citizens on the plaza. A bullet from the outside struck one of the men and he cried out: "I am shot; my arm is no use to me." About this time all three of the men rushed out at the same door at which they entered and ran across Walnut street, and up the alley from whence they came, and in the direction of the place where their horses were hitched.

At the First National bank nearly the same scene occurred. When the two men entered the bank, Cashier Thomas G. Ayers and W. H. Sheppard, the teller, were in the front room behind the counter and J. H. Brewster was transacting business with the former. They covered all three of these gentlemen with their Winchesters, and addressing Mr. Ayers by name, directed him to hand over all the money in the bank. At the same time one of the men, keeping his Winchester at ready command, ran into the back room and drove Bert S. Ayers, the book-keeper, into the front part of the building, where the vault is located. Cashier Ayers very deliberately handed over the currency and gold on the counter, making as many deliveries as possible, in order to secure delay in hope of help arriving. The bandit then ordered Mr. Ayers to bring out the money that was in the vault. The cashier brought forth a package containing $5,000 and handed that over. About this time the fellow who was behind the counter discovered where the money was located, and proceeded to help himself to the contents of the burglar proof chest, all of which, together with the money taken by the first burglar, were stuffed in a common grain sack and carefully tied up. They then undertook to put the three bankers out at the front door, but a shot from the outside, just as Mr. Ayers reached the pavement, evidently changed their plans, as they hastily closed the door and drove Messrs. Sheppard and Bert Ayers out through the back door of the bank, covering their own persons with those of the teller and book-keeper. When they reached the alley they turned the young men loose. Just at this juncture, Lucius M. Baldwin, a young man of exemplary character and undoubted courage, came out of the rear of Isham Bros.' hardware store and stepped into the alley with a pistol in his hands. One of the robbers ordered him to stop but Mr. Baldwin, as he stated in his dying moments, did not hear the command, and mistaking the parties for men who were guarding the bank, continued to advance toward them. One of the robbers drew up his Winchester and exclaiming: "I have got to get that man," fired. The ball entered Mr. Baldwin's left breast, just below the heart, and he fell dying in the alley. Several persons who were in the alley without arms, seeing the condition of affairs, took refuge in an adjoining building, while the men ran northward in the alley to Eighth street and thence west to Union street near Mahan & Custer's store, the one with the sack keeping in front of the other, the latter carrying his Winchester at ready. As he reached the crossing, near the edge of the pavement in front of the above store, he raised his gun and fired in the direction of the bank, and George W. Cubine, a brave and faithful citizen, who was standing in the door way of Rammel's drug store, with a Winchester in his hands, and his eyes fixed upon the front door of the bank, fell dead from a bullet that entered his back and passed through his heart. Reaching the middle of the street the robber fired another shot, and Charles J. Brown, an old and respected citizen, fell with a bullet through his left breast, within two feet of the prostrate body of George Cubine. Mr. Brown had seized Cubine's Winchester and was looking in the direction of the shot that killed the former, when he became the third victim of the robber's gun. Reaching the elevated pavement of the northeast corner of the brick block in the center of the plaza, the man raised his gun and fired the fourth shot. His victim this time was Thomas G. Ayers, cashier of the First National bank. When the robbers turned him out of the bank, Mr. Ayers ran into the south door of Isham's hardware store and seized a Winchester, took a position in the north door way of that establishment, facing in the direction of the bank. A bullet crashed through his left cheek below the eye and passed out at his neck below the base of the skull, and he fell bleeding and unconscious on the floor. Both robbers then disappeared behind the brick building in the square, and were not seen or recognized by anyone until after they had passed around an entire block of buildings and joined their companions in crime at the conjunction of the alley that runs in the rear of Wells Bros. store, between Slosson's drug store and McKenna & Adamson's store. In the meantime, as many citizens as could do so, had procured arms and secured positions where they could command the point or retreat of the highwaymen.

We desire to state here, in order to contradict some unfounded reports that have been sent out by excited newspaper correspondents to the effect that the citizens were prepared for the attack, that when the robbers were discovered in the square or in the neighborhood. Even Marshal Connelly had lain his pistol aside, and was totally unarmed when the alarm was given. Every gun that was used with the exception of that brought into action by George Cubine, was procured in the hardware store and loaded and brought into play under the pressure of the great exigency that was upon the people.

The firing was rapid and incessant for about three minutes when the cry went up: "They are all down." In an instand the firing ceased.

Several men who had been pressing close after the robbers sprang into the alley and covering them with their guns ordered them to hold up their hands. One hand went up in a feeble manner. Three of the robbers were dead and the fourth helpless. Between the bodies of two of the dead highwaymen, lying upon his face, in the last agonies of death, was Marshal T. Connelly, the bravest of all the brave men who had joined in resisting the terrible raiders in their attempt to rob the banks. Dead and dying horses and smoking Winchesters on the ground added to the horrors of the scene. It took but a few minutes to discover who the desperadoes were. Tearing the disguises from the faces of them, the ghastly features of Gratton Dalton and Bob Dalton, former residents of Coffeyville and well known to many of our citizens, were revealed. The other dead body proved to be that of Tom Evans [Bill Powers], whilst the wounded man was Emmett Dalton, the youngest brother of the two principals of the notorious gang. Great excitement prevailed. Marshal Connelly breathed a few moments, when his brave spirit went out without a struggle. Emmett Dalton was carried to Slosson's drug store and subsequently to Dr. Wells' office. At first he denied his identity, but realizing that he was recognized and likely to die, he admitted that he was Emmett Dalton. It was well known that one of the party had escaped, and a posse was hastily organized and started in pursuit, some on foot and a few on horseback. Those who were mounted had only proceeded a half mile west, on 8th street, [when] they came across the bandit lying beside the road and his horse standing near him. He proved to be the John Moore, or "Texas Jack" of the gang. His proper name was Richard L. Broadwell, and he is connected with one of the best families in Hutchinson, Kansas. He was one of the most experienced and coolest of the gang, and it was he who guarded the southeast door of Condon's bank and fired the shot from inside of that building at the men on Barndollar's awning. It is simply impossible to describe the scenes that followed. Excited men, weeping women and screaming children thronged the square. A few cool-headed citizens kept disorder from ensuing. The dead and dying citizens were removed to their homes or other comfortable locations. The dead raiders were put into the city jail. Guards were thrown out, and the city sat down in sack cloth and ashes, to mourn for the heroic men who had given their lives for the protection of the property of our citizens and the maintenance of law in our midst.

The *Journal* also carried Elliott's "After the Fight: A Careful Review of Wednesday's Events," with added details of how the Daltons died:

The smoke of terrific battle has blown aside, but the excitement . . . has increased until it has gained a fever heat. The trains over the four principal roads leading to the city have brought hundreds of visitors to the scene of the bloody conflict between a desperate and notorious gang of experienced highwaymen and a brave and determined lot of citizens who had the nerve to preserve their rights and protect their property under the most trying circumstances. Telegrams and letters offering assistance and extending condolence to the four stricken and bereaved families have been received, in great numbers from all parts of the country. Those of our citizens who were not in the fight are proud of those who were, and the latter are meekly bearing their laurels and assisting in restoring order and preserving the peace. Less than fifteen minutes passed from the time the Dalton boys entered the bank until four of their party were dead and the remaining one mortally wounded and in the hands of the officers. Bob Dalton, the acknowledged leader of the outfit, disguised by false moustache and goatee, accompanied by his youngest brother, Emmett, entered the First National bank and robbed it, whilst Grat Dalton, disguised by a black moustache and side whiskers, led the raid on Condon and Co.'s bank. Bob and Emmett left the First National by a rear door, passed around two blocks and across two of the principal streets, and joined Grat Dalton and his party at the junction of the two alleys, within two hundred feet of where the latter had left the Condon bank by the same front door at which they had entered. It was at this point, in this now historic alley, that the daring highwaymen met their doom. As Bob and Emmett were going out at the back part of the lot in the rear of the National bank, they were met by the heroic Lucius M. Baldwin with a pistol in his hand. . . . Bob drew his Winchester and shot him through the left breast near the heart. When Bob and Emmett reached the east side of Union street the eye of the former fell on poor George Cubine. . . . Bob fired a ball into the back of this man who had been his acquaintance and friend in former years. . . . As the desperado reached the center of the street he evidently saw Charley Brown, the peaceable and innocent old shoemaker, pick up Cubine's gun, and again brought his Winchester into play and his third victim . . . fell dying almost within reach of the body of the courageous Cubine. Emmett Dalton had run ahead of Bob, in a westerly direction, with the grain sack containing over twenty-one thousand dollars over his shoulder. Bob's bloody and inhuman mission was not yet filled. As he reached the pavement on the west side of the street on which he had been operating, he drew up his gun and sent a ball crashing through the left cheek of Cashier Ayers. . . . Nearly every-body had been attracted to the center of the plaza by firing, hence Bob and Emmett had a clear course until they reached the point in the alley heretofore mentioned. Strange as it may appear, the party . . . Grat Dalton and his pals . . . came together at the intersection of the alleys almost at the same moment. . . . The wait of three minutes for the time lock to go off [at the Condon bank] was the golden opportunity of the gallant citizens on the outside. . . . Mr. Ball's story about the time lock being on was purely fictitious. It was set for eight o'clock and had opened at that hour. The fact that there was over forty thousand dollars in the chest influenced the cool headed cashier to lie to the burglar. The unwelcome visitors at this bank were in plain view of a score or more people on the plaza. Grat Dalton stood guard at the southwest door and John Moore [Broadwell] was at the southeast entrance. The first shot that was fired came from Moore's [Broadwell's] gun. He sent a bullet through the plate glass in the door in the direction of a party on the awning in front of Barndollar's store across the street. The ball passed through the open window in the second story of the clothing department and crashed into some queensware that was stored on the shelves. Just at this moment, Cubine's shot and one from a revolver in the hands of Expressman Cox rang out in front of the National bank. From that until the close of the awful contest, the firing was rapid and incessant. H. H. Isham and L. A. Deitz had stationed themselves behind two cook stoves near the door of the hardware store, where they had a commanding position over Condon's bank and the alley by which the gang had entered. A dozen men with Winchesters and shotguns made a barricade of some wagons that were standing in front of Boswell & Co.'s hardware store, and from this point they poured about eighty shots into the windows of the Condon's bank, through which the forms of the bandits could be plainly seen. Moore returned the fire with another shot through the glass door, when a ball struck him in the left arm. Cashier Ball heard him exclaim: "I'm hit; I can't use my arm."

Grat Dalton was the first to leave the bank, and as he opened the door, he fired two shots in a southwesternly direction, one of which perforated the plate glass in Wilhaf's store, but neither of which hit anyone. As the three men emerged from the bank, they got directly in range of the Winchesters of Isham and Dietz, in the hardware store, and were subjected to a cross-fire from the men at Boswell's and on the south side of the Plaza. . . . The three robbers had to run the gauntlet of three hundred feet with their backs to a dozen Winchesters in the hands of men who knew how to use them. They all kept their feet until within thirty feet of their horses. Bob Dalton was the first to fall. He drew himself up to an old barn, and propping his back against the building, fired four shots in the direction of Isham's store. One of these went high and broke a glass in the large window; another struck a churn on the outside but directly in front of Mr. Isham, and a third went through the bottom of the window frame and lodged in the casing within two inches of where fifty pounds of dynamite were stored. Grat Dalton, very badly wounded, leaned against the west corner of the barn, and was evidently trying to brace up for a final effort just as the brave and dauntless Marshal Connelly, who together with J. J. Kloehr, C. A. Seamen and one or two others had run up Ninth street and through some vacant lots from a southerly direction, emerged into the alley and turned towards where the horses were hitched. Grat Dalton, with apparent great effort, raised his gun to his side and fired a shot into the back of the faithful marshal. The latter fell forward on his face and Grat made another effort to reach his horse, passing right by the prostrate form of his victim. He turned his face toward his pursuers, when John Kloehr's rifle rang out and the oldest of the three Daltons fell on his back with a bullet through his neck.

William Powers, who is known as "Tom Evans," fell about ten feet west of Grat Dalton. He dropped on his face and died where he fell. He was the one with the heavy black moustache. . . . Emmett Dalton, his right arm broken and a ball through both hips, succeeded in reaching his horse and mounting the animal. He had clung to the sack containing the money with wonderful tenacity, and putting it in front of him, he rode back to where Bob was lying and reached down his hand to his dying brother for the purpose of assisting him to get on the horse with him. As he did so a load of shot from Seamen's gun struck him in the back and he fell at the feet of his leader and tutor in crime. John Moore, alias "Texas Jack," had, in the meantime, mounted his horse and started westward. Before he got out of the alley a bullet from Kloehr's rifle and a load of shot from Seamen's gun gave him the wounds from which he fell dead from his horse after riding a half mile over the very road on which he and his pals had entered the town. Emmett Dalton readily responded to the command to hold up his hands by putting up his uninjured hand and making a pathetic appeal for mercy. The scene that presented itself at this juncture was most ghastly. Four men lay dead inside a space thirty feet long and ten feet wide. Three horses were lying near the men, in the agonies of death, and another one went down a few moments later. Five Winchesters were scattered at different points and the hard ground and stones were bespattered with human blood. The citizens left the dead and dying to a few of their number, whilst a well armed party followed the bleeding bandit. His body was found alongside the road . . . placed in a passing farm wagon and brought to the city and laid alongside of his confederates in crime. The dead bandits were photographed and placed in coffins and a guard put around the place.

Thursday afternoon, Powers, Broadwell, and Bob and Grat Dalton were buried at city expense in Coffeyville's Elmwood Cemetery only two cemetery blocks away from the hero's grave occupied by Frank Dalton, who nearly four years before had given his life trying to bring law to Indian Territory.

Friday morning, Broadwell's brother George, a salesman for the Boston Tea Company of Chicago, and E. B. Wilcox, the bandit's brother-in-law, a grocer in Hutchinson, arrived to identify the remains of their "reckless relative." Wilcox told the officials: "We are as greatly shocked by this occurence as you, and entirely ignorant of Dick's being with this gang. We had not heard of him since May. He never was wild or a drinker or gambler, and . . . we always thought him to be straight and law abiding."

The grave containing the coffins of Broadwell and Powers was opened and Broadwell's coffin was removed. The body was then clad in a new suit of clothing, placed in an expensive coffin, and taken to Hutchinson. Powers' body was reinterred. None of his relatives or friends "put in an appearance, nor was anyone ever found who knew anything of his antecedents or history."

Sheriff John Callahan made preparations to remove Emmett Dalton to the jail at Independence but "was compelled to abandon the attempt on account of the manifest disposition of the people to resist anything of the kind. It is safe to say that Dalton would have been taken away from the sheriff and hung" had Callahan removed him from the room where he was confined at the Farmer's Hotel.[46]

On October 22, Elliott's account of the disaster, together with the early life and background of the outlaw brothers and biographical sketches of the living defenders of the town and the fallen brave, was published as a 60-page pamphlet entitled *Last Raid of the Daltons: A Reliable Recital of the Battle With the Bandits.* Affectionately dedicated by the author "to the aged mother, devoted wives and loving children of Lucius M. Baldwin, George B. Cubine, Charles Brown and Charles T. Connelly," it sold out immediately at 25¢ a copy and went into a third printing. Today it is exceedingly rare in any of these editions and is a collector's item.

The little group of citizen heroes won for themselves the everlasting gratitude of law-abiding people everywhere. John J. Kloehr, whose ready aim sent three of the bandits to their deaths, received special recognition. Chicago bankers gave him a magnificent badge. A semicircular plate of gold bears the name "John Joseph Kloehr." Below is a gold ribbon on which is engraved: "The Emergency Arose, The Man Appeared." Suspended from this by three gold links is the badge proper: a gold circle two and one-fourth inches in diameter, with a narrow raised band on the outer edge. Within this is an open scrollwork, another raised band of gold, then a laurel wreath, and a third raised band of gold surrounding an eight-pointed bright gold star set with a diamond. The entire badge is four inches in length. On its back are these words: "Presented by friends in Chicago, who admire nerve and courage when displayed in defense of social order." Today it can be seen in Coffeyville's Dalton Museum.

For Heck Thomas and Detective Dodge, it was the end of the

Dalton trail. They proceeded to Coffeyville to make proof of the deaths for Wells Fargo. Manager Andrews wrote Thomas that

> while it has not been marked by capture, we feel that your work, more than anything, brought about the extermination of this gang . . . and are happy to hand you, from our railway and express pool, a check herewith in the amount of $1,500.

Andrews was hardly correct, however, in saying the gang had been exterminated. Down on the Cimarron, Doolin, Pierce, and Newcomb cursed Bob Dalton but thanked their lucky stars that they had been dropped from the outfit before the disaster. The fate of the Daltons should have caused them to reconsider their program for the future, but they were outlaws, still being hunted throughout Oklahoma and Indian territories. In one short month, they became the nucleus of a more vicious and unholy band led by Bill Doolin.

U. S. Deputy Marshal Chris Madsen.

U.S. Deputy Marshal Bill Tilghman.

106

Bob Dalton robbing the express messenger in the Wharton, I.T., train
robbery on May 9, 1891. From an artist's sketch in Emmett Dalton's "Beyond the Law," *Wide World Magazine*, June, 1918.

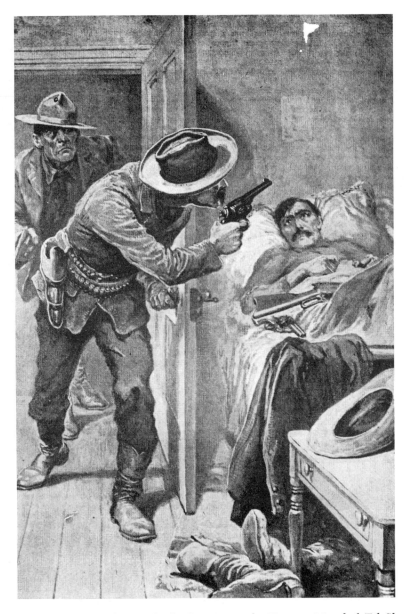

The capture of Black-Faced Charley Bryant by Deputy Marshal Ed Short
and Hennessey hotel manager Ben Thorne. From artist's sketch in Emmett
Dalton's "Beyond the Law," *Wide World Magazine*, July, 1918.

The Condon Bank, one of the two robbed by the Dalton gang at Coffey-ville.

Members of the citizens posse holding up the bodies of Bob and Grat Dalton after the Coffeyville raid.

The Daltons of the Coffeyville raid 1892.

Four members of the Dalton gang killed at Coffeyville. *Left to right:* Bill Powers, Bob Dalton, Grat Dalton, Dick Broadwell.

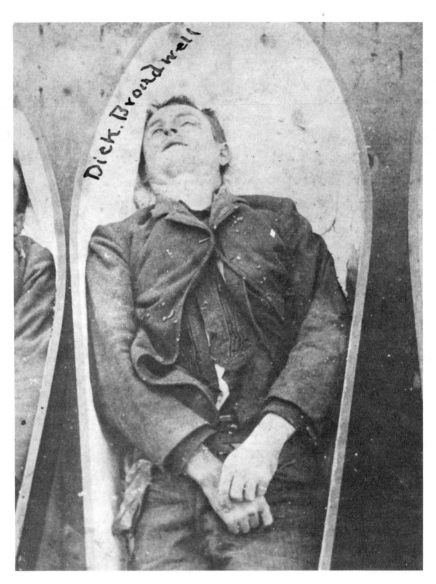

Dick Broadwell in his coffin.

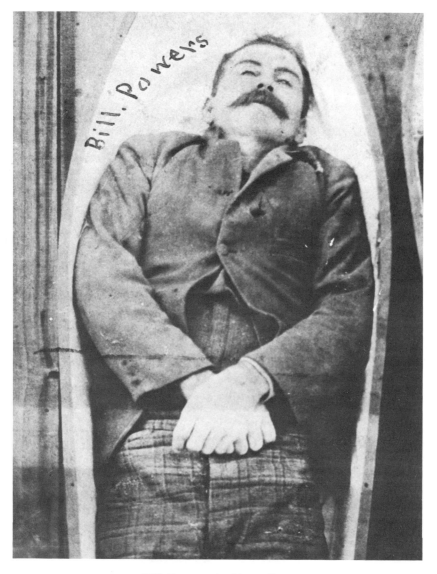

Bill Powers in his coffin.

Portrait of Bill Doolin taken at Wagoner, I. T.

VII Bill Doolin's Wild Bunch

WILLIAM (BILL) DOOLIN WAS BORN in 1858 on a farm in northeastern Johnson County, Arkansas, where his father, 50-year-old Michael (Mack) Doolin, a native Kentuckian, sharecropped until 1860. His mother was Artemina Beller, a woman of 36 whom Mack met and married after moving with his four children—a son, John, and three daughters—from adjoining Newton County following the death of his first wife, Mary, in 1850. In 1860, Mack Doolin bought a forty-acre farm on the Big Piney River in Pilot Rock Township thirty-five miles northeast of the county seat of Clarksville. Here young Bill grew up with his three half-sisters, his half-brother, and another sister, Tennessee, born in 1859. In 1865, Mack died, and Bill helped his mother run the farm for the next several years.

Bill became an expert with a saw and an ax, making fence posts, cutting firewood, and hewing logs for the farm buildings. Fishing was good in the mountain streams. Bill also learned to use his rifle. Game abounded in the surrounding forests, so there was always meat in the family larder.

In 1881, when he was twenty-three, Bill decided to go west, where, he had heard, there were great opportunities for everyone. He signed on as a helper with a freight outfit out of Fort Smith bound for Caldwell, an end-of-track town on the Kansas frontier. There, in 1882, he met Oscar D. Halsell, a Texas cattleman who had just established his new ranch on the Cimarron in Old Oklahoma. Halsell took an immediate liking to the slim, quiet lad who could use a saw and an ax—something his cowboys could not do—and put him to work constructing buildings and corrals on his HH Ranch on lush Cowboy Flats. Oscar's brother, H. H. Halsell, also ran cattle on the flats under his ⊞ brand. Bill worked for him from time to time and soon became a top hand. He could neither read nor write, but Halsell taught him enough about both so that he could keep the ranch books. Halsell often sent him to Caldwell to pick up ranch supplies and considered him completely trustworthy. In the summer

115

of 1883, after the hard winter of 1882–83, when so many cattle were lost, Bill accompanied H. H. Halsell to Texas to pick up a restock herd.

Doolin's activities the next few years are a matter of conjecture. Hanes[1] places him on the payroll of the Open A outfit in the territory, then on the XL Ranch in Wyoming, where he allegedly drifted when "the urge to see the world seized him," and later in Montana, California, Arizona, and New Mexico. He appears, however, to have worked off and on for the Halsell brothers until 1888, when the government issued orders for cattlemen to vacate the land to be opened to homesteaders. The Halsells moved their herds east into the Iowa Reservation and up into the Cherokee Nation of Indian Territory.

Bill drifted down the Cimarron to work on the Bar X Bar, in the Triangle Country. In the fall of 1888, he was employed by T. H. Hill of Arkansas City to work for the Wyeth Cattle Company, which had pastures along Black Bear Creek on the Oto-Missouri Reservation. Bill rode into Arkansas City periodically with the ranch crowd to take the town apart, but he was reportedly the most peaceful man in the outfit.

Tom Waggoner of Texas, who had cattle in both the Outlet and the Oklahoma District, leased the grazing rights to sixty thousand acres from A. W. Hoots, an intermarried Osage, in the Osage Nation. The tribe received three cents an acre for grazing land, paid to the Indian agent at Pawhuska by the Indians or intermarried Osages, who had permission to fence grasslands in the nation. Others with grazing rights covering forty thousand to fifty thousand acres on the west Osage line were Lou Appleby and Green Yeargin. Hoots had no difficulty subleasing to Texas ranchers. In the spring of 1889, Waggoner moved fifteen thousand head of cattle from the Oto Reservation across the Arkansas to his new pasture between Sperry and Hominy, then an Indian trading post on Hominy Creek. His new headquarters was known as the 3-D Ranch and was one of the largest outfits in that country. In his book *The Passing of the 3-D Ranch*,[2] Lon R. Stansbery states that Tom Humphreys was foreman and brought with him from the Oto Reservation Bill Blake (alias Tulsa Jack), Jim Stone, Lee Youngblood, and Bill Doolin— "some of the best cowboys who ever trailed a rein in front of a cow pony."

Doolin was with the 3-D until 1890. After the Oklahoma opening, Oscar Halsell entered the livery business and helped form a whole-sale grocery enterprise in Guthrie. Doolin found employment at

Halsell's livery stable during the winter of 1890–91.[3] In the spring of 1891, he was back with his old cronies on the Bar X Bar. Jim Williams of Guthrie, an old-time cowboy whose father and uncle had a ranch in the Osage at the time,

first met Doolin at a dance that Colonel Harking, in the Kaw country, gave for his daughters when they returned from school at Carlisle. Indian girls and cowboys made up most of the attendance at Oklahoma parties in those days. I was not present when Bill got into his first real trouble, but my uncle and cousin were there and described it like this. . . .

There was some kind of three-day celebration [Fourth of July] going on at Coffeyville, and some of the cowboys decided they would hold a celebration of their own up in the timber about a quarter of a mile. Someone asked my uncle if he didn't want some cold beer, and he said, "Sure," and went along. They had barrels sawed in two and filled with ice and beer bottles. There was a keg or two besides, and everybody could have all he wanted. After drinking their first bottle my uncle and cousin each took a second and stepped into the circle of cowboys that were standing around.

Then a couple of constables appeared [Kansas being a dry state and beer illegal] and asked who owned the beer. Doolin was always the leader and spokesman of his crowd and everybody waited for him to answer. He said, "Why, that beer don't belong to anyone. It's free, gentlemen, help yourselves."

The officers said that if they could not find the owners they would have to take the beer anyway. Bill said, "Don't try to take the beer. . . ." The men started to roll the keg away, a gunfight started, and both constables were badly wounded. Whether Bill fired the shots or not was never proved, but as the leader he was considered responsible. From then on he had to be on the dodge.[4]

Doolin found sanctuary in the familiar reservation cow camps. By September, he was riding with the Daltons in the train robbery at Leliaetta. His long-barreled six-shooter and Winchester rifle, once mere toys in his big fists, had become deadly weapons, and his slow, deliberate nature, which had won him the trust and admiration of many territory cowmen, gave way to the daredevil spirit within him.

He had no wrongs to avenge, no persecutions that drove him into crime. Had he surrendered to Kansas authorities, the assault charges could have been relegated, but hard, rough range work simply had lost its appeal. He had "tasted the fruits of victory in gunfights and known the excitement and glow that came in train robberies . . . a craving for the outlaw life was upon him." In the next several years, he would achieve for himself the longest criminal career of any bandit in Oklahoma, and his gang would figure in more sensational and bloody escapades than any robber band before them.[5]

As he, Newcomb, and Pierce talked it over in their hideout on the Cimarron,[6] they apparently thought how humorous it would be to give Coffeyville citizens another scare before the excitement of the raid had subsided. On October 12, the heroic John J. Kloehr received the following letter from Arkansas City:

Dear Sir:

I take the time to tell you and the city of Coffeyville that all of the gang ain't dead yet by a hell of a sight and don't you forget it. I would have given all I ever made to have been there on the 5th. There are three of the gang left and we shall come to see you . . . we shall have revenge for your killing of Bob and Grat and the rest. . . . You people had no cause to take arms against the gang. The bankers will not help the widows of the men that got killed there and you thought you were playing hell fire when you killed three of us, but your time will soon come when you will go into the grave and pass in your checks. . . . So take warning.

Yours truly,
DALTON GANG.

The startling news swept the town, and irate citizens again armed themselves for the threatened invasion.

In a way, they had been expecting it. Since the Dalton disaster, many persons had been loitering about the city, openly condemning the manner in which the gang had met death. Several sympathizers had been arrested and jailed. Bill Dalton, acquitted in California of participation in the Tulare County holdup, had left his wife and children with Merced County relatives and returned to Oklahoma. Arriving at Coffeyville with his mother, Ben Dalton, and Mrs. John Whipple from Kingfisher, he had announced publicly: "I have never condoned the criminal activities of my brothers. They were wrong in trying to rob the banks, but they were right when they shot the men who were trying to kill them!"

Adeline Dalton, "wrinkled and bowed beyond her years by unspeakable sorrow, and her eyes dim with continuous crying," begged him to keep still. "They can't bluff me," Bill shouted. "I'll say what I please!"

Honest, sturdy Ben tried to ease matters. He told reporters that he

never had much in common with the ones who lie here dead and badly wounded, as I am a farmer and try to be a good citizen. We had not seen

118

the boys for a long time, and I had no idea where they were or what they were doing. . . . I wish you would state that mother and I have no ill feeling against the people of Coffeyville. They simply did their duty. While we naturally deplore the loss of our boys, we also sorrow for the citizens who gave their lives in defense of the town.

But Bill couldn't be muzzled. He threatened to sue the city for damages because the officials in charge of the bodies had allowed unauthorized persons to rifle their pockets of money and valuables which had not been turned over to him or the family—particularly the nine hundred dollars Emmett claimed they had before they went to Coffeyville. The *Journal*[7] declared that

this is . . . the sheerest nonsense, as no one else seems to know anything about it. The chances are that it is only a bluff game, played in order to force those who took articles from the bandits' pockets and are keeping them as relics to return them. . . . He claims that one of the ablest attorneys in the state is backing and instigating the suit on a contingency fee, but refuses to name him. . . . Will's actions and words and his bank account are all interesting straws to watch when considering the question of his being a silent partner in the late firm of "Dalton Brothers, bandits and outlaws," whose business cards should have borne the inscription "train and bank robbery a specialty."

Upon reading the comment, Bill stamped into his hotel, "fuming mad," and announced: "I came near going over just now and shooting me a newspaperman. By God, the next one that braces me *will* be shot!"

Emmett Dalton had passed his first night in constant pain. Amputation of his arm was suggested, but he would not consent. For the next five days, he lay in the hotel, "exposed to the gaze of hundreds . . . his room brightened by bouquets of beautiful flowers sent him by foolish women." By this time he "showed undoubted signs of recovery," and "it was rumored that steps would be taken by his friends to liberate him." Immediately upon receipt of the letter by Kloehr, Emmett was removed to the Independence jail by Sheriff Callahan with no objections from the citizenry. Bill and Ben Dalton, their sister, and their mother accompanied him.

Hardly had the Dalton family departed when Detective Dodge, who had been scouring Oklahoma for Doolin, Pierce, and Newcomb, wired the mayor of Coffeyville that "a large body of desperadoes has passed Wharton station, I.T., presumably en route your city." One of his men, Dodge explained, had picked up information that "forty whites and half-breeds under the command of one of the

119

survivors of the Dalton gang and completely armed" would ride into Coffeyville that night to "wipe out the place." According to Dodge's informant, "no mercy would be given."

There was a new "pandemonium of excitement." Informal meetings were held. Telegrams were sent to Parsons and Kansas City asking that additional rifles and ammunition be shipped at once. By nightfall, every man was ready for the fight. A Katy railroad car filled with armed agents and guards stood at the depot. A huge bonfire was started on the plaza to furnish a reassuring illumination.[8]

Whether Doolin scouted the situation and decided it would be fatal or whether it was part of his strategy to draw full attention and protection to Coffeyville is not known. The attack did not occur. Instead, on the night of October 13, two masked robbers struck the train at Caney, a small station eighteen miles to the west on the Missouri Pacific Railroad:

> Just as the train drew up at Caney at 10:15 o'clock . . . two masked men, heavily armed with Winchesters and revolvers, climbed on the locomotive tender from the front of the combination baggage and express car and covered Engineer Eggleston and his fireman with their rifles. The locomotive men were ordered to pull slowly to the switch, where all was darkness and there was no danger of molestation. This was done.
>
> At the whistling post the outlaws ordered the engineer to stop and made the fireman uncouple the express car from the rest of the train. All this was done so quietly that no one in the coaches was disturbed.
>
> The engineer was then ordered to pull ahead with the express car and obeyed, for the Winchesters held close to his head looked unpleasantly dangerous. When a deep cut, half a mile further on, had been reached, the engine was halted.
>
> Express Messenger J. N. Maxwell, who had witnessed the uncoupling, had in the meantime blown out his lights, barred and barricaded the doors, and made ready for desperate resistance.
>
> The order to open up the car elicited no response and the robbers began firing into the sides of the car with their Winchesters. Maxwell answered the shots with his revolver for a few minutes, but finally received a bullet in his arm, which disabled him and he was fain to surrender.
>
> The robbers ordered him to light his lamps and open the car door and as soon as he had done so they entered the car with the engineer in front of them as a shield. Maxwell was then forced to open his safe and deliver up his watch and personal property. The men then backed off the car and disappeared in the darkness.[9]

"Eye Witness"[10] credits this holdup to the "Dalton survivors." Hanes[11] says four men participated—Doolin, Ol Yantis, Newcomb,

and Bill Dalton—and calls it "Doolin's first adventure on his own"
and "a real success." Actually it was neither because

the regular express money, except what was destined for way stations,
had been transferred at Conway Springs, and the booty was of little
value. Messenger Maxwell, who is now here nursing his wound, which
is not serious, declares that the robbers secured less than $100 . . .
and were probably the same ones who last week held up the station
agent at Sedan.[12]

And Bill Dalton was very much in evidence on the night of the holdup. We shall see why later.

Reaching Coffeyville by courier the next morning, news of the
robbery created another furor. Was the gang approaching the city,
raiding everything in its path? It might ride into town any moment.
Women and children huddled in their homes, frightened at the pros-
pect of another bloody encounter. Attempting to soothe their
anxiety, the mayor told them the size of the attacking party obviously had been greatly magnified, posses already were searching the
area to the west, and a matter of a few hours would result in their
capture. "You people," he added, "have shown your ability to care
for yourselves."

So Coffeyville waited. The attack did not come. And there were
no further sightings of Bill Doolin and his alleged band of "raider-
survivors."

During the third week of October, while officers concentrated
their hunt in southeast Kansas, Doolin and Newcomb, undoubtedly
enjoying their cruel hoax, leisurely made their way up the Cimarron
through the Outlet, entered Kansas near Bluff Creek in Comanche
County, and rode another 100 miles northwest to Garden City. For
some reason, Charlie Pierce remained at the hideout on Cowboy
Flats. Accompanying Doolin and Newcomb on their new campaign
was the first new member of the gang: stocky, black-mustached,
dark-complexioned Oliver (Ol) Yantis (often misspelled *Yountis*).

It is not clear how Yantis met Bill Doolin. Ol farmed cotton on a
homestead occupied by his sister, Mrs. Hugh McGinn, three miles
southeast of Orlando in northeastern Logan County. The homestead being equidistant from Guthrie to the south and Stillwater
twenty miles east, Ol visited both cities often and was well known
to law officers. On nearby Beaver Creek in May, 1891, the Daltons
had stolen the herd of fine horses from the colony of Missourians
and reportedly used the heavy patch of timber on the McGinn claim
as a resting place as they fled west after the Wharton robbery a

few days later. Ol and his sister had brought them grub and kept a wary vigil for marshals until the excitement died and the gang retreated to Riley's ranch on the Canadian. It also was reported that Ol's sister "grew sweet on Bitter Creek" and "lied nobly" to at least one posse that inquired about their guests.[13] Probably, Newcomb, plying Yantis with thrilling tales of his exploits with the Dalton gang, had brought him into Doolin's camp.

The trio reached Garden City on October 21. They left their highly bred mounts with liveryman John Cochran, giving him definite instructions concerning their feed and care, and put up at Mrs. A. C. Bacon's Ohio House. They claimed to be cowboys from the Texas Panhandle and for the next fews days made extended trips out of town by rail and horseback, pretending to look for work. On October 28, they checked out of the Ohio House and rode east. The next day, they stopped at the Jonathan Lee ranch in northern Gray County, where their heavy armament caused no little apprehension. About three o'clock on the afternoon of November 1, "three masked men rode slowly into Spearville," a community of 200 souls on the Santa Fe Railroad seventeen miles east of Dodge City, and halted in front of the Ford County Bank. Obviously, their entry had been planned carefully and "a cold, raw, cloudy day when few people were in town and out on the streets . . . selected."[14]

Doolin and Newcomb dismounted, tossed their reins to Yantis, and quickly entered the front door of the bank.[15] The Spearville report to the press stated simply: "Cashier J. R. Baird, a cripple, was the only employee on duty. . . . Placing a Winchester under his nose," Doolin "compelled him to hand over all the cash on hand," and Newcomb stuffed their "tote bag" with First National Bank of Dodge City and U.S. Treasury notes amounting to $1,697, "in their haste overlooking another large sum in the vault."[16]

The robbery had taken less than three minutes. "What was going on was not discovered by citizens till the men ran out of the bank, mounted their horses, fired several shots in the air and galloped out of town, going south." A party of hunters who had just returned to Spearville "exchanged about fifteen shots with them, but no one was hurt." As many citizens as could procure horses took off in pursuit, but their western ponies were no match for the outlaws' Thoroughbreds. One man, J. M. Leidigh, got close enough to fire at Yantis, who was bringing up the rear, but his shots were ineffective and the trio soon disappeared into the brakes of the Arkansas bottoms. Sheriff Chalkley M. ("Chalk") Beeson was notified and left Dodge with a posse on the Rock Island, going southeast down the river. "Several large posses headed by others started in the same direction."[17]

The robbers were seen at nightfall crossing the Rock Island tracks between Ford and Bucklin. About midnight, they passed east of Ashland, in Clark County, and by daylight reached the Outlet. Here they stopped to rest their horses and divide the loot, then separated to confuse any further pursuit. Doolin and Newcomb agreed to meet later at their Cimarron hideout. Yantis headed for his sister's home near Orlando.

A popular tale told down the years is that the indefatigable Sheriff Beeson struck Yantis' trail and dogged him across the Outlet, finally locating him at Orlando. Proceeding on to Guthrie, Beeson recruited Deputy Marshals Chris Madsen and Thomas J. Hueston (variously spelled *Houston* and *Huston*). Returning to the McGinn farm with a fugitive warrant, they called on Yantis to surrender. The outlaw opened fire on the officers and was slain.[18]

Actually, Beeson quit the chase after the robbers had crossed the Rock Island tracks and headed for Oklahoma. The bank offered a reward, and the sheriff sent the following information on penny post cards to every town and way station where the outlaws might be sighted:

BANK $450
ROBBED.   REWARD.

Ford County Bank, Spearville, Kans., was robbed to-day by three men. One small dark complexioned man 23 years old, small, very dark mustached and dark clothes [Yantis]; one medium sized man, sandy complexioned, short beard, light hat and clothes [Doolin]; one dark man, 25 years old, medium size dark mustache [Newcomb]. Three horses—bay, sorrel and dun, latter with line back, and all of medium size.

Robbers have large number new $5.00 bills issued by First National Bank, Dodge City, Kansas. A reward of $450 is offered.

C. M. BEESON, Sheriff.

Dodge City, Kansas, Nov. 1st, 1892.
N. B.—Keep watch for the $5.00 bills.

On November 15, Beeson received a letter from Hamilton B. (Ham) Hueston of Stillwater. Tom Hueston, Ham's brother, was city marshal and Ham helped him enforce the law in the community. The "small dark complexioned man 23 years old" with the small, very dark moustache, Ham explained, fit the description of Ol Yantis. Ol also "rode a dun pony with dark mane and tail and dark stripe along its back" and was known to "consort with out-laws." Would the sheriff send someone down to make a positive identification?

Beeson was happy to oblige. John Curran of Garden City, who had boarded at the Ohio House at the same time as the robbers, arrived in Stillwater on November 24. The next day, Curran and Ham Hueston rode twenty miles west to the McGinn residence. They claimed to be buying horses. Yantis volunteered the names of a couple of neighbors who had stock they might sell, but he "appeared very uneasy and kept his hand on his pistol all the time they were talking to him." Curran recognized him as one of the trio who had stayed at the Ohio House.

Beeson met Hueston at Stillwater on November 28. Without visiting the McGinn place but convinced that one of the Spearville robbers was hiding there and not having the legal authority to make an arrest, he and Hueston proceeded to Guthrie, where the sheriff made affidavit to the U.S. district attorney, secured a warrant for Yantis, and "was duly commissioned as an officer of said Territory of Oklahoma to execute said warrant . . . then and there placed in his hands."

Returning to Stillwater on November 29, Beeson and Hueston recruited Hueston's brother Tom and George Cox, a constable, to assist in making the capture. The four officers departed that night for Orlando. Arriving at the McGinn farm in a heavy fog before dawn, they concealed their horses and took positions between the house and the barn where Yantis kept his dun pony, hoping the outlaw eventually would show himself. They had no intention of letting him use the house as a fortification.

A half-hour passed. At daybreak, a man emerged from the back door with a feed bag under one arm. He peered through the swirling mist a few moments to see if all was well, then started walking slowly toward the barn. His furtive movements suggested that he was the man they were seeking. When he was within fifty feet of the officers, Ham Hueston whispered to Beeson: "That is Ol Yantis."

Beeson stood up and called to the outlaw to surrender. Instead, Yantis dropped the feed sack, snatched a pistol from a shoulder holster under his left arm, and fired in the direction of the sheriff's voice. The bullet missed Beeson. Ham Hueston triggered his shot-gun, leveled at Yantis, but it was a new weapon selected for the occasion and never tested. It misfired. Yantis heard the snap of the hammer, whirled, and fired at the sound. Again he missed. Then Beeson, Tom Hueston, and Cox opened fire.

"The report was as one gun." Yantis fell backward, badly wounded, and Beeson told the others, "Don't shoot again, he is done for." But Yantis was still in the fight. As he hit the ground, he emptied his pistol, reloaded, and began firing again. Because of the fog, gunsmoke, and half-light, the officers were unable to discern his position. One bullet grazed Cox, who swore he would finish the outlaw, but again Beeson interfered, saying, "He's too badly injured to escape. At that moment, Yantis' sister ran into the yard, crying hysterically, "Run, Ol, run! For God's sake don't kill him!" Beeson demanded that she persuade her brother to surrender. She was "a beautiful young woman and very nervy . . . reluctantly she went over to Yantis, took his gun, and handed it to the sheriff."[19]

The outlaw disarmed, the officers moved forward to survey the results of their work. Yantis was bleeding profusely. One bullet had struck him in the right side and ranged downward, severing his spinal column. Another had struck his heavy leather pocketbook, which contained some of the Spearville bank money. The leather and money had saved him from another severe wound: several of the bills were pierced and torn by the bullet, making a blood-smeared mess.

The officers did what they could to stop the bleeding, loaded Yantis into a wagon, and hauled him to the nearest doctor at Orlando. "The physician's efforts were to no avail." The outlaw died at one o'clock in the afternoon, "game to the last, making no confession or admission . . . cursing the laws and officers of justice." There was "no doubt of his guilt, however, as he wore an overcoat purchased in Garden City just before the crime, and had on his person several silver certificates" later identified by the Spearville bank officials. "Furthermore, his peculiar boots and large sombrero were easily recognized as having been worn at the time of the robbery."[20]

The body was removed to Guthrie, where it was laid out and Lentz Bros., Photographers, called upon to record the dead man in his coffin. The Kansas sheriff needed the photograph as proof of the outlaw's identity in order to collect the reward and show that an innocent man had not been slain. He also obtained a receipt for the bullet-torn money:

> Received of Sheriff C. M. Beeson one pocketbook containing Fifty-five (55.00) dollars taken from one Oliver Yantis when arrested Nov. 30/92. C. M. Madsen, Chief Dep. US. M[arshal].

Mrs. McGinn claimed the body. Its place of burial is unknown. Beeson was paid the reward, which he split, taking three hundred dollars for himself and giving fifty dollars to each member of the posse. The Dodge City press exulted in "the pleasing duty of awarding to our sheriff the homage which we think he has justly earned," but the *Stillwater Gazette* failed to mention Beeson, stating: "Our city marshal T. J. Hueston and Geo. Cox were the officers who did the shooting."

In any case, Tom Hueston took the brunt of a lawsuit filed in Payne County District Court in the spring of 1893 by "S. J. Yantis, Administratrix of the deceased Oliver Yantis," to recover twenty thousand dollars in damages for "killing her husband." It was the first knowledge territorial officials had that Yantis was married. The case was thrown out on a flaw in the petition but was refiled to include Marshal Grimes on grounds that "the acts of the officers complained of were committed in the discharge of their duties as deputy United States Marshals under him." This involved the U.S. attorney, representing Grimes. The case was finally dismissed on a demurrer, filed and sustained, showing the defendants acting under legal warrant and authority and as bona fide *posse comitatus*.[21]

The death of Yantis prompted the *Dodge City Globe* to comment: "The spell is broken . . . it is now only a matter of time when his confederates will be behind bars or meet the fate of their comrade." The editor was right, but this would come only after many hard battles and several years later.

VIII The Crime Fighters Organize

WHILE DOOLIN WAS BUSY launching his Wild Bunch, Bill Dalton was back on the streets of Coffeyville with a complaint about the horse Emmett rode in the raid. Deputy Marshal Chapman, arriving from Indian Territory, had gone to the mayor, identified the animal, and made an affidavit that the gang had caught him unawares and taken the horse from him. The animal was released to Chapman by the Coffeyville authorities.[1] There was enough evidence of Emmett's legal ownership, however, that Bill Dalton was able to obtain re-plevin papers, which he made the mistake of flashing about, leading everyone to believe he had been appointed a U.S. deputy marshal.[2]

The rumor burned the telegraph wires to Washington. Moreover, a particularly hot letter, stating in part that "Bill Dalton, one of the notorious family of that name, is walking through our streets armed with a repeating gun and authority to scour the territory on our border," reached Missouri Senator George G. Vest, a powerful committeeman in Congress. Senator Vest demanded an explanation from Attorney General Miller, [3] and Miller in turn demanded to know on what basis a man like Dalton had been commissioned.

There were immediate denials from the U.S. marshals of Kansas, Texas, Arkansas, and Oklahoma and Indian territories. R. L. Walker of Topeka wrote that

> Wm. Dalton does not now, nor has he ever held a commission as Dep. U.S. Marshal for this District, under me. Bob & Emmett Dalton were deputies under Col. Jones when I came into this office, and I retained them for a few months, but removed them in the fall of 1889.[4]

Thomas B. Needles of Muskogee replied that

> Bill Dalton, nor no other Dalton, has a commission from me. I have always been very careful as to the character of the men whom I have appointed and I do not think that investigation will verify many of the statements made by parties who are not conversant with the facts.[5]

J. J. Dickerson of the Northern District of Texas at Paris wired:

None of the Daltons or any of the gang . . . have had a commission as deputy or posse during my term of office.[6]

Jacob Yoes of Fort Smith was more emphatic:

If William Dalton, bro. of the late notorious robbers of Coffeyville, holds a commission as Deputy U.S. Marshal . . . it is not from this court, as he has not been appointed and never will be![7]

Marshal Grimes submitted the only lengthy report, which clarified the issue to the satisfaction of both Miller and Senator Vest:

I do not think there are any reasons for the newspapers or Senators making any complaint about the selection of deputies, at least in this District. . . . Your honor may understand the peculiar circumstances under which the deputies here are working, and . . . the reasons why sometimes it becomes necessary to employ men who are not the very best class themselves. It takes men of nerve and men who have little concern, so far as comfort and emoluments, to take the trail after such men as those mentioned, and the two dollars a day for endeavoring to arrest far from pays the expenses, but is of course all the law allows. I never appointed one unless he was recommended by the people who knew him, and while I have often made mistakes in appointments I have invariably called in the Commissions as soon as I learned the deputies did not act or conduct themselves in a manner credible to them or to the office.

William Dalton has never had a Commission under this office. . . . While I am not in a position to know what the other marshals may have done, I desire to state that . . . shortly after the killing of the Daltons at Coffeyville, a man appeared at that place and claimed that one of the horses ridden by the Daltons, and which was held by the authorities, had been stolen from him a short time before; that upon his statements to this effect the horse was turned over to him, and he left with it for Indian Territory. One of the deputies under this office [Heck Thomas] had sometime before that . . . learned from reliable parties [Thornton and Halsell] that the horse had been sold by this man to Bob Dalton and that he had paid one hundred dollars for the same. Upon learning of the facts in the case Mr. Thomas informed William Dalton that the horse did really belong to his brother Bob, and it is understood that William Dalton then tried to get lawful possession of the horse, but has so far failed to find the man; it is also understood that the papers which were supposed to be a Commission as a deputy Marshal, or which some people have spoke about as being such, were simply summons issued by some Justice of the Peace for the witnesses in case the horse should be found by William Dalton. . . .

I am personally acquainted with William Dalton, in fact every deputy on the force here knows him, and he came to this office the day after the Coffeyville affair, to inquire about the truth of the killing of his brothers, and requested me to furnish him a certificate that he was not one of the Daltons who had been hunted by the officers . . . this in order that he might go to Coffeyville and see his brothers without being arrested. I notified the Mayor of the town about his going there and informed him that while we had a suspicion that William had had more or less to do with his brothers on the outside, we had no proof against him whatever, and that there were no warrants out for him in this District. While the Daltons have been a bad set of men, William has . . . never been convicted of any of the crimes for which the rest have been tried. He is a bright young man, but considerably given to bragging and no doubt would be willing to take a hand in anything that would give him a reputation like his brothers, but I think he lacks the nerve to do so.[8]

Grimes was correct about Bill Dalton's tendencies but mistaken as to his lack of nerve. Already disgruntled because of his failure to maintain any sort of damage suit against the city of Coffeyville, his disposition worsened when he was unable to locate Chapman or his brother's horse. Then came "the raw deal Emmett got at Independence."

County Attorney J. R. Charlton had charged Emmett with robbery of the First National Bank and two counts of murder in the deaths of George Cubine and Lucius Baldwin. Shortly after his removal to the Montgomery County jail, he was given a preliminary hearing before a justice of the peace and ordered held without bond. On Tuesday, November 1—the day Doolin, Newcomb, and Yantis robbed the Spearville bank—Emmett was arraigned before District Judge J. D. McCue in spite of objections by his two physicians that he was in no condition to stand trial.[9]

Emmett claimed his attorney told him that Judge McCue (then up for reelection with strong opposition) had agreed to *nolle prosequi* the murder charge in the case of Baldwin and the bank robbery if Emmett would plead guilty to murder in the second degree for the killing of Cubine and that the court would give him between fifteen and twenty years. Emmett refused on grounds that he had "actually killed no one." However, after his attorney, friends, and court officials told him the judge would be more willing to help him obtain commutation later, he agreed. He was "heartsick" and "surprised" when he hobbled into court on crutches on March 8, 1893, pleaded guilty to murder in the second degree, and received a life sentence in the state prison at Lansing.[10]

Whether he had been ill advised or erred in trusting the court, considering the magnitude of his crimes, he had not fared badly. But it served as the final excuse for Bill Dalton to throw aside all pretense of respectability and seek out Doolin on the Cimarron.

Doolin resented his presence at first. Already Doolin visualized himself in the light of a romantic hero like Bob Dalton, and he feared that another member of the family might jeopardize his complete control of the Wild Bunch. Bill Dalton, however, seemed to entertain a certain respect for the ability and experience of Doolin and "soon convinced him that they should carry out their plans together."[11]

During the two years of Dalton depredations, embryo Oklahoma had grown rapidly. Under the provisions of the Dawes Act as amended February 28, 1891, each member of an Indian tribe on reservations in the territory could be alloted 80 acres of land, regardless of age or sex, and the surplus lands opened to settlement. In the spring of 1890, negotiations were completed with the Cherokees for relinquishment of the Outlet west of the ninety-sixth meridian. Agreements were made with the Iowas on May 20 and with the Sacs and Foxes on June 12, and both were ratified by Congress on February 13, 1891. Agreements made with the Pottawatomies on June 25 and the Shawnees on June 26, 1890, along with negotiations with the Cheyennes and Arapahos completed in October, were ratified on March 3, 1891. On September 22, the surplus lands of the Iowas, Sacs and Foxes, Pottawatomies and Shawnees, totaling 868,414 acres, were opened by proclamation of President Harrison.[12]

Although these lands were not given away but sold in tracts of 160 acres at $1.25 per acre, this rush for homesteads was a repetition of the run of '89. Nearly every acre was occupied the first day; an estimated twenty thousand persons participated. From this area Logan, Oklahoma, and Cleveland counties were enlarged to the east, Payne County was increased by adding that portion lying south of the Cimarron River, and two new counties, designated A and B, were added to the original seven. In the general election of November, 1892, the residents voted that County A be named Lincoln, with the seat at Chandler; County B chose the name Pottawatomie, and Tecumseh became the seat townsite.[13]

On April 19, 1892, the Cheyenne and Arapaho country was opened by a third run. This area added 3,500,562 acres and six more counties to the territory. The counties were designated C, D, E, F, G, and H and subsequently named Blaine, Dewey, Day (later eliminated to become part of Ellis County), Roger Mills, Custer, and

Washita, respectively. Kingfisher and Canadian counties also were enlarged to the west. As in the 1891 opening, county seat townsites were reserved in advance and homesteads sold under the usual regulations at $1.50 per acre. Anyone who had money could buy acreage by awaiting his turn at the Guthrie or Oklahoma City land offices.[14]

Many, however, refused to waste homestead rights upon this vast area, which they thought too far from a railroad and not desirable for agriculture, and pressed for entry into the Outlet, the only other strip of land negotiated for in 1890. Led to believe that the government meant to open the area at an early date, large camps of men sprang up along its southern border at points where water and fuel were abundant, and along the northern border in Kansas, thousands more waited for homes.

In the older portions of the territory—Old Oklahoma and Beaver County—the $47,000 appropriated by Congress for relief of destitute farmers in 1890 had enabled them to get the hang of the new land. By 1892, they had good crops coming on. Since no farmlands could be taxed, the territorial legislature had to depend on personal property taxes for revenue; a state levy was permitted for roads and bridges and the operation of the universities at Norman, Edmond, and Stillwater. The common school system consisted of four schools to the township and one high school in each township or city over 500 population. Already these districts were making provisions for permanent structures to replace the sod houses and shacks in which classes first had been and were being held. The school population totaled 31,920; the population of the territory had increased to 133,100. The assessed valuation was $11,500,000; there were five national banks with deposits totaling $750,000 and fourteen private banks with $15,000 capital each. There had been much railroad construction. The Rock Island, which had built south from Kansas to El Reno after the '89 opening, was extended into Texas in 1892. The Choctaw Railway Company had built from El Reno to Oklahoma City and was planning extensions both east and west.[15]

Although this new frontier was blessed with honorable men, who were willing to enforce the moral principles for which they stood, and women, whose good influence comprised the very fabric of each community's ideals and ethics, lawlessness thrived because of the unsettled conditions, the constant opening of new lands, and the constant shifting of population. Business between principal towns and outlaying trading posts necessitated overland travel, and it had become almost impossible for money or merchandise to be transported through the territory successfully. Not only trains and banks, but stores, post offices, and the isolated homesteads of settlers were being preyed upon. Responding to the Dalton depredations, big eastern dailies proclaimed Oklahoma "a horrible society" in which it was possible for such gangs to roam at will, without the slightest opposition to discourage their predatory practices, and otherwise painted the territory as a "precarious place to live" at a time when it needed new capital.[16]

The new courts of Oklahoma, although granted jurisdiction to try and to condemn for both federal and territorial violations, were limited in that they might not, under a charge of violation of a law of the United States, try a prisoner for violation of a law of the territory, or vice versa. All offenses committed within any organized county had to be prosecuted in that county, and if they were committed within territory not embraced in any organized county, they had to be prosecuted in the county to which such territory had been attached for judicial purposes. In any case, the courts had the power to transfer for prosecution, by change of venue, any prisoner property-ly charged with an offense, either against territorial or federal law, to a county in any judicial district in the territory.[17]

The marshal's office, with fifty deputies to police thousands of square miles, seemed unable to cope with the situation despite the fact that in three years time it had made nearly fifteen hundred arrests. The demise of the Dalton gang brought a measure of relief to every Oklahoma community, and the killing of Black-Faced Charley Bryant and Oliver Yantis took some of the heat off Marshal Grimes. But rumors of reorganization of the Dalton gang's remnants and the formation of other, smaller outlaw bands aroused new and dire threats against the peace and welfare. The *Stillwater Gazette* of July 8, 1892, charged that

> a tidal wave of criminality is sweeping the country. There is scarcely a county that is not the scene of bloodshed, suicide, rape, robbery or gigantic thefts at the present time. About one murder in fifty is brought to justice. . . . Some of the thieves and highwaymen are apprehended and made to pay the penalty for their crimes. But their punishment . . . does not prevent others from giving loose rein to passion and committing the gravest offenses against the laws of the land.

Disordered political conditions at both the local and territorial levels did more to take the bite out of law enforcement than the constant opening of new lands and the shifting of population. After the long bickering with the first territorial legislature, Governor

Steele grew tired of his job. It also had been his duty, in the face of great rivalry, to appoint the first officers of the new counties into which the territory was divided. The people have never been so hungry, with an average of ten candidates for every one of the ten offices in each county. Little wonder, then, that after his service as an officer in the Regular Army, as a member of Congress, and as a lawyer-citizen of the quiet, orderly town of Marion, Indiana, he resigned as governor, effective October 18, 1891, and returned home to run for senator.[18] His tenure of seventeen months "was long enough to learn that conditions were in such an extricable jumble that the election of United States senators [from Oklahoma] was too remote for the ambitions of an ordinary life time."[19]

True to their office-getting instinct, Kingfisher politicians succeeded in having Abraham J. Seay taken from the supreme court and placed in the executive chair. Seay made his home at Kingfisher, where he was a member of the Episcopal Church, the Masonic fraternities, and the GAR. In Missouri, he had served first as county attorney of Crawford County, then circuit attorney, and two six-year terms as circuit judge of the Ninth Missouri District before resuming private practice, finally entering the banking business at Union and Rolla and becoming president of both institutions. But his heart was in the judiciary, and he so welcomed his Oklahoma appointment that it was February 1, 1892, before he resigned as associate justice to become governor. During the intervening months, Secretary Robert Martin had assumed the territorial responsibilities. On March 8, 1892, President Harrison appointed John H. Burford of Crawfordsville, Indiana, to succeed Seay in the Second Judicial District.

Seay, like Steele, had been a lifelong Republican tormentor of the Democratic party, and territorial Democratic organizations and antiorganizations fought like cats and dogs over the succession and continuing of Steele's appointees in office. When the Cheyenne-Arapaho Reservation was opened in April, Seay also grappled with the county officer problem. An extremely competent man on the bench, he proved equally capable as an administrator. Although he had the reputation of being penurious, he did not mind spending money if he was getting his money's worth. For instance, he vetoed the clerk hire bill of the second legislature, declaring such appropriations too high and plain graft. The clerks all quit, leaving none to enroll bills that had been passed.[20]

On November 8, 1892, Grover Cleveland was elected to his second term as president. He did not allow Governor Seay to remain in office long after his inauguration the following March. Bewildered by claims and counterclaims and complaints of carpetbag rule from territorial leaders, Cleveland agreed on a reliable and trustworthy Democrat, an Oklahoman, for the place and appointed William C. Renfrow, a Norman banker who, shortly after the '89 opening, had suggested that Cleveland County be named in honor of the President.[21]

A nearly clean sweep also was made of lesser Republican appointees. On May 26, Frank Dale, a Guthrie attorney formerly of Wichita, Kansas, was appointed to succeed Judge Green as chief justice, and Henry W. Scott of Oklahoma City, also a former Kansan, replaced Judge Clark in the Third Judicial District. Horace Speed had established himself as a fearless and incorruptible prosecutor; since 1890, he had tried hundreds of cases and had broken up a vicious ring of grafters who by perjury had thwarted the proper administration of the land office. Speed restored public confidence in its function and therefore was not replaced as U.S. district attorney. William Grimes, however, began closing the business of his office and settling the accounts of his deputies. Already attention had centered on Evett Dumas Nix for appointment as U.S. marshal.

Nix was born in rural Kentucky on September 19, 1861. His father, S. S. Nix, had served as lieutenant in the Confederate Army and after the war was for several years a deputy sheriff in Calloway County at Murray. Young Nix finished common school at seventeen, working in a wagon and buggy factory to complete his education. His Grandfather Nix backed him in his first venture, a grocery, hardware, and furniture business at Coldwater, which he sold at a good profit in 1880. Two years later, he joined the staff of J. J. Bondurant and Company, wholesale grocers, at Paducah and in 1889 "caught the Western fever" and came to Oklahoma.

At Guthrie, he entered the general merchandise business with a man named Ed Baldwin. In March, 1890, he purchased Baldwin's interest and began searching for a broader field than the retail business offered. Oscar D. Halsell had opened his livery stable in Guthrie, and he and Nix became close friends. In the fall of 1890, they entered the wholesale grocery business under the firm name of Nix and Halsell Company and soon were supplying most of the small inland towns. For 1891, they had planned a campaign of business expansion to include Indian trading points throughout the territory but, like other Oklahoma businessmen, found themselves facing the hazards of transporting merchandise long distances and returning safely with large amounts of money. They could not afford such risks until the outlaw problem was solved. That same year, the Commercial Bank of Guthrie closed its doors in the territory's first banking failure, and Nix was appointed receiver under bond of $450,000. It was a trying responsibility for a young man of thirty, but he disposed of the ill-fated institution's affairs so satisfactorily that the people, in looking about for someone with executive ability in whom they could place great confidence, suggested him to Cleveland as the man who should conduct the affairs of the marshal's office.[22]

Nix felt considerably flattered, but at the same time flustered, by their proposal. It seemed that

> it would be absolutely impossible for me to consider such a thing. I had my own business to take care of and I hardly wanted to throw the burden of responsibility upon my partner. I refused pointblank. This group of citizens, not to be turned aside, called upon my partner. Halsell came to me and said that he felt we owed as much of our service as we were able to give to the general good of the new country and . . . would do his part by relieving me of a large share of my duties in our wholesale grocery business.
>
> His persuasion caused me to accept . . . the citizens immediately accumulated as fine a collection of endorsements from leading business men of Guthrie and the Territory as any man could hope to have. I then visited Washington, calling on President Cleveland and his Attorney General to discuss territorial conditions and my application.[23]

There were twenty-three applicants for the position: nineteen from Oklahoma, four from outside. Nix's strongest competitor was Heck Thomas, widely known in both territories for his efforts against the Dalton gang. He had moved his family to Guthrie in early 1893. Several leaders of the Democratic Central Committee and county officers throughout the territory endorsed Thomas as "one of the oldest deputies working out of Judge Parker's court at Fort Smith . . . of irreproachable character and whose allegiance to the party is beyond dispute."[24] Judge Parker himself wrote the President that

> I have known Thomas since 1885 . . . and he has done very much service for the Government in breaking up lawless bands of murderers, train and express robbers. I regard him as just the man for the position . . . and would be glad to see him appointed.[25]

Heck prided himself as a "working marshal," but he was not yet a familiar figure in Guthrie, center of all territorial activity. Al-

135

though Thomas was regarded by political "wah-hosses" as "better equipped to meet the emergency that exists" than "this mere boy who had done nothing for democracy," President Cleveland evidently noted his lack of administrative experience. On the other hand, Nix had no experience in law enforcement, but he "held onto the pole and finally knocked the persimmon."[26]

Nix took office July 1, 1893. He bore no enmity for those deputies who had sought the office in Washington and asked Grimes's men to stay on until he could make satisfactory selections for the various positions to be filled.[27]

Richard Olney, Cleveland's new attorney general, had instructed Nix thoroughly concerning the routine of his office and what would be expected of him: find and equip proper quarters for and provide protection for the federal courts; curb the destruction of government timber and the operations of whiskey peddlers on Indian reservations; protect Indian lands from invasion by settlers. Primarily, however, Nix was to solve the outlaw problem and restore unmolested transportation and communication as soon as possible.

In discussing the situation in Washington, Nix had intimated the need of one hundred field deputies—twice the number allowed Grimes. He was advised to use only a force of "reputable" men "adequate" to handle the situation. Nix told the *Guthrie Daily News* on June 6 that

> there will be none but honest men around me . . . who will never compromise the dignity and prestige of the United States government. No man who drinks can have a place on my staff. They will, above all, be courteous, of unimpeachable character and good standing in their communities. . . . The time has gone for swashbucklers who fence themselves round with revolvers and cartridges. A revolver will be for business and not for show. Men will not be dragged from their homes on trumped up charges nor carried hundreds of miles around the country to make fees for speculative deputies . . . and, until found guilty in the courts, considered innocent.

The *Oklahoma State Capital*[28] observed:

> This means that none but Y.M.C.A.'s need apply. It will seem queer to see a lot of dyspeptic cadavers going out to trail the class of criminals who produce the "holdups" in this territory. Think of a gentlemanly moralist running onto a tough out in the jungles and in a plaintive voice, declaring: "My deah suh, we have been sent for you suh, and we would like you to hold up youh hands and be ouh prisoner; if you don't, suh, as much as we dislike to, we will be compelled, suh, to pull ouh guns on you!" And how beautifully "moral suasion" worked the deputy would

have to discover in heaven, for daisies would grow on a premature grave. And think of Mr. Nix searching the ranks of democracy with a microscope to find this brand of Sunday school moralists from which to make sleuth-hound saviours of banks and express trains.

The *News*[29] explained:

It was the spontaneous outburst . . . of a man who knew that the record of his life was clean and that his every act was founded in justice. . . . With a good staff, a picked corps of deputies, we make the prophecy that his conduct the next four years will reflect the highest honor of the man and credit, brilliant and lasting, on the noble territory.

When Nix asked Heck Thomas for an opinion on his policy, Thomas told him frankly: "The strength of your backbone will be shown more by the striking force than the character of the men you choose or the way they wear their weapons." Nix expressed gratitude to Thomas for being outspoken. He admired Heck's lengthy and successful career and appointed him one of the first field deputies.

The initial list included, besides Thomas, John Hixon, Morris Robacker, Frank Hindman, George Orin Severns, and Joe Pentecost at Guthrie; J. M. Jones, John Quimby, Charles F. Colcord, Sam Bartell, and John Hubatka at Oklahoma City; William Banks at Cheyenne; J. H. Gill at Tecumseh; Charles L. Roff at El Reno; Frank Farwell at Anadarko; C. H. Marx at Osage Agency; J. A. Cooper at Kingfisher; James Vandeventer at Orlando; Thomas Tipton and Alonzo Poling at Chandler; C. W. Reynolds at Perkins; William Ivey at Choctaw; S. T. Butner at Crescent City; and George Smith at Norman.

Robacker, Severns, Banks, and Bartell were Grimes men. Hixon had considerable experience as an officer in Kansas before coming to Oklahoma, where he had served as sheriff of Logan County. Although he had waged an energetic campaign in Washington, Nix held him in great respect. Colcord, a Kentuckian, had endured several precarious years on the Texas–Indian Territory–Kansas frontier as a cattle drover and Indian fighter.[30] His term as sheriff of Oklahoma County having expired in January, 1893, he too, was one of Nix's opponents. "He would have made a spendid Marshal," Nix wrote. "He was thoroughly seasoned to the arduous demands our work would make upon him . . . and I was only too glad to have him accept the appointment as deputy in charge at Oklahoma City."[31]

Nix chose John M. Hale as chief deputy. Hale had come to Indian Territory from Virginia several years before as a trader on the Osage and Sac and Fox reservations. For a time, he edited the *Chandler Warrior*, a weekly newspaper which supported the Democratic party. He had many acquaintances and much knowledge of the country and "was soon rated by the Department of Justice as one of the most capable chief deputies in the service."[32] Nix's father, who had joined him some months before, was made chief clerk, with J. K. Goodwin as assistant. W. S. Felts, an accountant in one of the Guthrie banks, was placed in charge of the financial department. These people, together with two stenographers, Mrs. S. M. Burche and Miss Florence Hitchcock, comprised the office force.[33]

Persons committing crimes in the territorial counties often fled into the Nations across Hell's Fringe. Sheriffs and deputies had no authority to cross these borders in pursuit. The Organic Act gave the U.S. marshal concurrent jurisdiction with sheriffs in criminal matters, so Nix compiled a considerable list of eligible local officers and made them federal deputies. Several of them would play important roles in the months ahead: Jim Masterson and Ed Kelley, police chief of Guthrie; J. S. (Steve) Burke, a daring, energetic youth who believed that men would obey the law "if made to see it in the divine light" and later became an evangelist; Dick Speed, city marshal of Perkins; Tom Hueston, now constable at Stillwater; and Lafayette (Lafe) Shadley, a deputy sheriff in Montgomery County, Kansas, at the time of the Dalton raid but now serving as policeman for the Osage Nation at Pawhuska.

Such appointments, at no additional cost to the government except the fees they earned, increased the marshal's force to nearly one hundred men. Calling them together at Guthrie for final instructions, Nix

> looked upon the group as an organization of business men with a very definite obligation to deal fairly and honorably with everyone—citizen or outlaw—who was to come in contact with our department. I considered lack of courtesy and gentlemanly bearing a very serious offense. In my opinion, a man with a smile was more to be feared when it came to a test of real nerve than the would-be man-eater.
>
> In addition to laying down these very iron-clad rules as to personal conduct . . . I urged the men, for their own good to never forget that in many cases they would be going up against some of the wildest characters of the frontier and to always safeguard their own lives . . . to use their guns quickly upon the slightest provocation in their dealings with known bandits . . . to have the drop on the other fellow before they commanded him to hold up his hands, because this order was invariably disregarded by the bad men, provoking a lightning attempt to murder the officer. . . .

I promised to communicate regularly each week with every deputy on my staff, informing them of all our office had learned that might increase the effectiveness of their work. Charged with the seriousness of their responsibilities and with an unfaltering determination to rid Oklahoma of its bandit gangs, my men dispersed to take up the campaign.[34]

Meanwhile, Doolin had added three new members to his own roster—Bill Blake, alias Tulsa Jack; Charles Clifton, alias Dan Clifton, alias Dan Wiley, alias Dynamite Dick; and George (Red Buck) Waightman—bringing the total in his camp to seven. Blake, who worked with Doolin on the Oto Reservation and on the 3-D Ranch in the Osage, had been spending most of his time around the gaming tables in Tulsa, hence his appellation. Clifton had drifted up from the Chickasaw Nation, where he had been stealing horses and cattle and peddling whiskey around Pauls Valley and Ardmore. A heavy-set man, well muscled and of fair intelligence, he had the reputation of being a "shrewd scouter and a dangerous, cunning criminal." He allegedly hollowed the leaden points of his cartridges and filled them with dynamite to give them explosive as well as striking power. Waightman was a Texas horse thief with the reputation of a killer: a surly, vicious fellow, stockily built, with heavy red moustache and deep red hair, which gave him his nickname. He was arrested by Heck Thomas in the fall of 1890 for the theft of some mules in the Cherokee Nation, tried at Muskogee, and sentenced to nine years in federal prison at Detroit. In December, he escaped from a special prison car as it left Lebanon, Missouri, and boarded another train to Texas; there had been no word of his whereabouts until he joined the Wild Bunch.[35]

With Nix in the throes of organizing and assigning his forces, Doolin chose this as the opportune moment to exalt the power of his new band and his own generalship. At 1:20 A.M. on June 11, 1893, five masked members of the gang (Doolin, Dalton, Newcomb, Tulsa Jack, and Dynamite Dick) held up the Santa Fe's Southern California and New Mexico Express No. 3 a half-mile west of Cimarron, Kansas:

The train had hardly got out of sight of this place when the engineer saw a danger signal on the track. A bridge was near and fearing that something was wrong with it, he slowed up. Before the train could come to a stop, two masked men swung themselves onto the locomotive and covered the engineer and fireman with heavy revolvers.

The engineer was forced to take a sledge hammer and go to the express car. Messenger Whittlesey [Elston C., who had suffered a similar experience with the Dalton gang at Red Rock, I.T., a year before] refused to open the door and the engineer was ordered to batter it in, after the outlaws who had been reinforced by three others fired several shots into the car.

When the door had been broken open, it was found that the messenger had received a wound in the left side which disabled him, but will not prove fatal.

Whittlesey was ordered to open the through safe, but could not, and the robbers were forced to content themselves with the contents of the way safe, which were put in a sack.

All this time three of the outlaws stood outside firing at the passenger cars and shouting oaths to intimidate travelers.

No attempt was made to rob the passengers and, as soon as the outlaws had cleaned out the express safe [securing $1,000 in silver consigned to a bank at Trinidad, Colorado], they fired a parting volley, put spurs to their horses and dashed off southward.[36]

Wellman[37] and Drago[38] set the amount taken at thirteen thousand dollars. When it left Kansas City at one o'clock on the afternoon of June 10, the train was made up of a baggage car, a mail car, a chair car, and two Pullman sleepers, one destined for El Paso and the other for San Francisco. At Burrton, Kansas, the train picked up a Wells Fargo car that had been hauled from St. Louis to Burrton over the St. Louis & San Francisco line of the Santa Fe system; it was carrying ten thousand dollars in jewels and currency. However, Wells Fargo officials in Kansas City reported that the through safe had not been molested because "the combination was not known by the express messenger and he could not have opened it if he wanted to."[39]

Not only were the robbers disappointed with the loot they obtained, they fled south with the Gray County sheriff and a posse hot behind them. Within a few miles, the posse reached the spot where the bandits had stopped and divided the money, dropping several of the silver dollars. From there the trail led southeast through the Big Basin section of adjoining Clark County, past Ashland, toward the Deep Hole and Snake Creek tributaries of the Cimarron. The Kansas sheriff wired Sheriff Frank Healy at Beaver and the marshal's office at Guthrie that the gang probably would enter the Outlet above Fort Supply.

Croy[40] says Grimes had relinquished his office and had gone to his farm at Kingfisher, leaving Chief Deputy Madsen in charge at Guthrie, and that Madsen wired the commanding officer at Fort Supply to meet him with a posse of cavalry and Indian scouts at Woodward Station, then "mounted the train" and soon arrived at the scene. On the contrary, Madsen would have been forced to travel nearly three hundred miles. He could go north via the Santa Fe to Arkansas City, west to Anthony, transfer to the St. Louis–Southern line to Kiowa, thence southwest by Santa Fe to Woodward, or he could go overland to Kingfisher, north on the Rock Island to Caldwell, thence to Anthony, and southwest via the same route. Nevertheless, Croy states that Madsen arrived to intercept the robbers shortly after they entered the Outlet and in a running fight that followed was able to "whang Bill Doolin in the foot" with a steel-jacketed bullet from his long-range .30–30 Winchester, that the gang then "rode in separate directions," and that Arkansas Tom took Doolin to the Riley ranch hideout on the Canadian to care for his wound.[41]

Madsen, with Heck Thomas and former Sheriff Hixon of Logan County, did go to Hennessey a few days later to question three men jailed there on suspicion of being the Cimarron bandits, but he "saw at a glance that they were not the men wanted" and ordered them released.[42] Madsen had no contact with the fleeing outlaws and makes no mention of such in his autobiography, "Four Score Years A Fighter."[43]

Doolin *was* wounded. The bullet entered his left heel and tore along the arch to the ball of his foot, shattering the bone. It was a serious and painful wound. But the man who fired the shot was Sheriff Healy.

Upon receiving the wire from the Kansas sheriff, Healy hurried east into the Outlet. He was alone when he sighted four of the outlaws in camp (Tulsa Jack had left the gang after the loot was divided). Since Healy "could hardly tackle four men," he quickly gathered a posse of six "nesters" in the vicinity, "cut in ahead of the robbers" and "rode on them." In the first round of firing, his horse was shot from under him, and his nester posse "quit then and there." Jumping from tree to tree, Healy kept shooting as the outlaws escaped. But the sheriff knew he had wounded their leader, "a tall man, which was Bill Doolin," whom he had met a couple of years earlier. He later found blood on the trail, and he had seen Doolin ride off holding his leg. Healy also wounded one of the robbers' mounts, which died the next day. He removed its shoes and gave them to Wells Fargo Detective Fred Dodge, who had come up from Kingfisher to join the chase. Later, Dodge would use the shoes "to get positive identity" of the Wild Bunch.[44]

After the clash with Healy, the rest of the gang separated to confuse pursuit. Perhaps Doolin thought of Riley's ranch, but the country was being watched by posses from the newly organized counties in the Cheyenne-Arapaho country and his foot was giving him such pain that he was forced to seek relief as soon as possible. He reached the shelter of Wolf Creek and rode southwest.

I am indebted to old-time Oklahoma cowboy Billy McGinty for details of how Arkansas Tom first met Bill Doolin. T. J. McElroy, whose home ranch was thirty miles south of Odessa, Texas, in Crane and Upton counties, had moved a herd of steers from Lipscomb County, above Higgins, into the Outlet to pasture on the Box T range of the Dominion Cattle Company while he arranged for their sale in Kansas City. McGinty was in charge.

> We'd had lots of trouble with them since leaving the Panhandle. This was the year the horn fly came to the country. The fly would set on the horns next to the heads of cattle and worry them, and we had trouble keeping them from bunching while grazing. Our pasture was on the Ivanhoe where it empties into Wolf Creek. The grass was knee high and there was plenty water, but lots of small canyons where a cowboy could lose his life on a dark night—bad country in which to hold mean, nervous steers. The night after Mac left for Kansas City a storm blew up. The whole herd stampeded. Next morning we had bawling cattle all over the hills. We made a circle into the northeast part of the Box T range and threw a roundup together. Then we separated our cattle from Box T stuff with little difficulty. But we were still about 500 short. I wanted to find as many lost steers as possible before Mac got back, so every day we would go through the range, finding a few more and driving them back at night.
>
> While working the Box T, I met another cowboy named Roy Daugherty. The night of the storm his herd of 2800 longhorns from Tom Green County, Texas, had stampeded just south of us near the Fort Elliott–Camp Supply Trail, and his outfit was looking for strays bearing the Long H brand. He was tall and slender, with dark brown eyes and mustache, and soft spoken. He wore the best boots and Stetson, leather chaps and jacket, rode his horses hard, worked hard, and was young and full of devilment. The June sunshine warmed our backs, the Long H cook was a good one, which added to our well being, and we became good friends. He told me he had come from Arkansas and a family of preachers. He had run away from home and a step-mother when he was fourteen to become a cowboy and ended up with this Texas outfit. We worked together about a week and caught 300 cattle belonging to our brands. . . .
>
> One morning he told me a wounded man had come to his camp during the night and was hiding in his tent. The man's foot was so badly swollen Daugherty had to cut his boot off to dress it. Some marshals came through looking for robbers, but none of the boys had seen anybody. I

got a glimpse of Daugherty's guest later, at a distance, and recognized Bill Doolin. I had worked with him on the Bar X Bar in the Triangle country. I didn't know about his trouble then, so said nothing. Doolin was in bad need of medical attention, and Daugherty decided to take him on horseback to Ingalls, the closest place he could obtain a doctor he could trust.

About two months later I saw Daugherty again. McElroy had shipped his herd at Englewood, Kansas, and I had gone to Ingalls, where my family had taken a claim in 1889, to visit my father. The day I arrived, I stepped into a saloon and was surprised to see Daugherty with Doolin and some others. When I called him by name, he took me aside and told me he was now "Arkansas Tom" Jones. Doolin must have paid him well for the trip and filled him up with stories of easy money. We took a ride out to Council Creek and sat down on the bank and I tried to give him some advice. He told me it was none of my business, and that I should never mention the Daugherty name again.[45]

After organizing his new force, Marshal Nix was unable to give serious attention to pursuit of the Wild Bunch. Almost immediately the government thrust upon his office the responsibility of policing the Cherokee Outlet, together with the surplus lands of the Pawnee and Tonkawa reservations, which President Cleveland suddenly had proclaimed would be opened to settlement at high noon on September 16.

No proclamation ever caused more excitement. It made headlines throughout the country. This long-coveted empire, six million acres of rich grasslands stretching sixty miles south from the Kansas border, nearly ten thousand square miles divided into 35,163 claims, was to be broken under the plow.

Washington moved into high gear. Four land offices were established and townsites that were to become boom towns were set aside: Wharton on the Santa Fe, Enid on the Rock Island, and Alva and Woodward on the Southern Kansas Railroad. To prevent sooners and other ineligibles from taking part, nine registration booths were established: five along the Kansas line and four along the southern border in Old Oklahoma. At these booths, settlers were compelled to file their intentions in writing and their qualifications for the right to homestead entry. A certificate issued by the registry clerks and attached to the declaration was then held by the settler as his identification when he appeared at the district land office to file his claim. From August 19, the date of Cleveland's proclamation, the scenes of 1889, 1891, and 1892 were reproduced on a much larger scale. More than one hundred thousand persons registered. From Caldwell to Arkansas City at intermediate points on the Kansas border and at Hennessey, Orlando, and intermediate points on the southern border of the Outlet to northeast of Ingalls, this scrambling, fighting horde gathered to await the zero hour.[46] Nix[47] writes:

> It would be hard for mere words to describe . . . the preliminary planning done in order that the run for claims might be . . . rendered as peaceful and amicable as possible. . . . I appointed one thousand special deputies to assist [the military] in the orderly handling of the tremendous crowds. My men were to patrol the entire boundary between Old Oklahoma and the Cherokee Strip [Outlet]. Immediately upon the opening, we were to take charge of the entire newly-settled area, including all new town-sites.

Naturally, Nix chose Democrats as deputies, but he also realized that partisanship had to be set aside if he were to accomplish his objectives. A case in point was Chris Madsen, whose life had been packed with high adventure.

Madsen was born in Schleswig, Denmark, on February 25, 1851. As a boy, he heard of the Civil War in America, the Archduke Maximilian's audacious acceptance of the throne of the Montezumas, Napoleon's inept namesake in France, and the thundering of the Iron Chancellor in Berlin. When the Franco-Prussian War flared in 1870, young Madsen marched away in the Danish army and was captured by the Germans. He escaped and after several skirmishes made his way back to a detachment whose officers had been killed and led it in a sortie against the Germans to celebrate his successful dash for freedom. After the war, he went to Algiers with the French Foreign Legion, and while riding the sultry Saharan plains of Sudan, heard stories of gold strikes and Indian fights in the United States. At the end of his enlistment, he sailed for America. Landing in New York in 1875, he joined the U.S. Army as a scout and soon was promoted to the rank of quartermaster sergeant with the Old Fightin' Fifth Cavalry. He possessed keen eyesight, an uncanny ability with firearms, and an unruffled temperament, and as his frontier experience ripened, he became one of the chief scouts in Wyoming and the Southwest. He took part in campaigns against the Arapahos and Cheyennes in western Kansas and Indian Territory, fought the powerful Sioux in Nebraska, Dakota, and Montana, and accompanied expeditions against the Nez Percés, Bannocks and Utes. He was a close friend of William F. ("Buffalo Bill") Cody, plumed knight of the Wild West epic, and saw Cody kill Sioux Chief Yellow Hand at Hat Creek with a knife. Hairbreadth escapes from roving bands of warriors were common experiences for Madsen until 1889. When Oklahoma was opened, he took a claim near El Reno, but this gesture toward a quiet life was forgotten when William Grimes appointed him chief deputy marshal.[48]

Madsen and Nix disagreed violently in politics, but the new marshal saw his value and offered him a deputy's commission. Chris accepted. Immediately upon the opening, he would take charge at Enid, Alva, Woodward, and other points west and north. Heck Thomas congratulated Nix for "signing Chris up before his saddle cooled." At the same time, Nix commissioned another of Heck's close friends, Bill Tilghman.

William Matthew Tilghman was born at Fort Dodge, Iowa, on July 4, 1854. When he was three, his parents moved to Atchison, Kansas, where Bill grew up. His father was a freighter, and Bill accompanied him on numerous trips across the plains. At fifteen he had visited most of the forts on the frontier, and at eighteen was a scout for the Army, taking part in the Cheyenne-Arapaho War of 1874 and the campaign against Cheyenne Chief Dull Knife when he and his followers fled the reservation. In 1877, Tilghman settled at Dodge City, where he became the intimate friend of such border peace officers as Wyatt Earp, Charlie Bassett, and Bat Masterson. He remained there fourteen years, serving one term as deputy and one term as undersheriff of Ford County. For three years he was city marshal when Dodge was known as "the toughest cowtown in the West" before coming to Oklahoma in 1889 to play an important role in the early building of Guthrie. In the Sac and Fox opening of 1891, he took a claim near Chandler.[49]

One-hundred eighty pounds of bone and muscle, with kindly blue eyes and a handsome, open countenance that reflected good will and friendliness to all he met, Tilghman became Nix's choice as deputy to take charge at Wharton (destined to become the most important town in the Outlet on the Santa Fe and later renamed Perry). Colcord would assist Tilghman at Perry. Nix personally would supervise the handling of crowds between Hennessey and Orlando.

The marshal departed for Orlando in the last week of August. Tilghman and Colcord were already at Perry, Madsen had gone to Enid, and Chief Deputy Hale was attending a term of district court at Stillwater. Heck Thomas and John Hixon were left in charge at Guthrie to handle any emergencies. Then Nix's office received word that the Doolin gang, enjoying the fruits of the Cimarron robbery, had rendezvoused at Ingalls in Hell's Fringe.

Bill Doolin tips his hat to a photographer. The picture is believed to have been made on the Bar X Bar Ranch on the Cimarron.

The Fitzgerald cabin on Cowboy Flats northeast of Guthrie, often used as a stopping place by the Doolin and Dalton gangs.

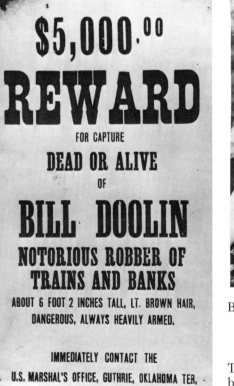

$5,000.⁰⁰

REWARD

FOR CAPTURE

DEAD OR ALIVE

OF

BILL DOOLIN

NOTORIOUS ROBBER OF TRAINS AND BANKS

ABOUT 6 FOOT 2 INCHES TALL, LT. BROWN HAIR, DANGEROUS, ALWAYS HEAVILY ARMED.

IMMEDIATELY CONTACT THE
U.S. MARSHAL'S OFFICE, GUTHRIE, OKLAHOMA TER,

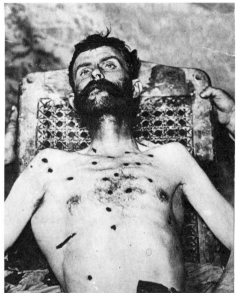

Bill Doolin in death.

Total rewards offered for Bill Doolin by 1894.

147

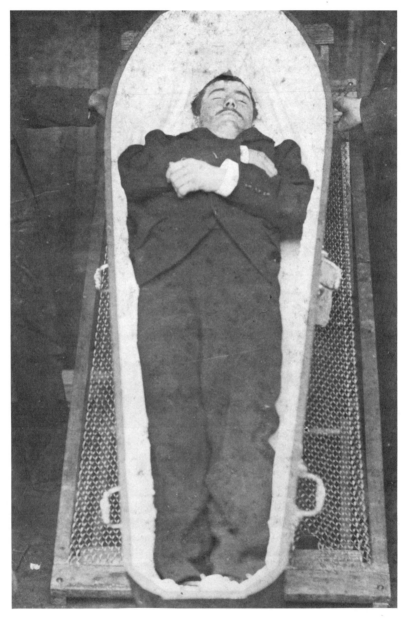

Oliver Yantis in his coffin.

IX The Ingalls Raid

INGALLS LAY THIRTY-FIVE MILES northeast of Guthrie and ten miles east of Stillwater in the eastern edge of Payne County. Far from a railroad and without the advantages of highway connections, there seemed no reason for its birth.

In 1889, Dr. A. G. McMurtry and Robert Beal had leased forty acres from their original quarter-sections to be used as a townsite and named it for John J. Ingalls, a U.S. senator from Kansas who had been instrumental in getting Oklahoma opened to settlement. The east forty was surveyed and platted into nine full and seven fraction blocks, with four streets (Main, Walnut, Ash, and Oak) running north and south, and four avenues (First, Second, Third, and Fourth) running east and west. McMurtry opened a drugstore and undertaking parlor in a small frame building at Oak on Second, and Beal opened a general store on First. A. J. Light put in a blacksmith shop on Ash at First, where the wagon road from the west entered the town limits. A block south, on the northwest corner of Ash and Second, J. W. (Preacher) Perry opened a dry-goods store and, on the southeast corner of the intersection, Jesse D. (Dent) Ramsey, later Perry's son-in-law, constructed another building and put in a stock of hardware and an implement yard.[1]

Falls City,[2] two miles southeast, had a post office that had served the country for miles around since the opening. Even after Ingalls was established, people got their mail at Falls City or Stillwater until Dr. McMurtry obtained a grant for a post office, which he set up in the corner of his drugstore. On January 22, 1890, Robert F. McMurtry was appointed the town's first postmaster.[3] The doctor died about this time; his widow turned the drugstore into a notions shop, and Robert relinquished his position to J. W. Ellsworth, a part-time minister and notary public who had come to Ingalls with his wife and daughter Edith from Iowa via Missouri. Ellsworth soon was succeeded by William Selph, who opened a grocery east

149

of Ramsey's hardware on Second Avenue and built his home a block south of the store on Third.

In 1891, a man named Shassbury, living just west of Ingalls on what later was known as the George Davis place, filed a contest on the west forty of the townsite, claiming abandonment. A town meeting was held and two men were sent to Guthrie to investigate conditions of the contest and report the town's progress to the land commission. They were advised that they possibly could beat the contest but it would be cheaper to compromise with Shassbury. It looked as if Ingalls would be dissolved, and delegations representing six other towns hurried to the territorial capital to present arguments for the community trading point to be placed elsewhere. Another delegation was sent from Ingalls to Guthrie; the commission was satisfied with its report. The representatives from the other places were displeased, and the meeting broke up in a row. Shassbury got the west forty, but Ingalls was there to stay. The survey and plat of the east forty (NW ¼ of the NE ¼ of Section 28, Township 19, Range 4 East of the Indian Meridian) was adopted by the town trustees on September 26, and the town lots were deeded in October, 1892.[4] Afterward, stores from all the places that had cried for the location began moving to Ingalls.

Charley Vaughn's saloon (across Ash Street and down from Light's blacksmith shop), Ketchum's boot and harness store, a cotton gin, a gristmill, a flour mill of fifty barrels daily capacity, another blacksmith shop owned by William Wagner (at Ash and Second across from Perry's dry goods), two restaurants, and Sherman Sanders' barbershop (north of Vaughn's saloon) all did good business. The town's population jumped to 150. Dr. D. R. Pickering, whose office was in his home above Second on the east side of Oak, and Drs. Briggs and D. H. Selph cared for the sick. Dr. W. R. Call, "an expert pharmacist" whose home set west of McMurtry's on Second, "made a specialty of compounding physician's prescriptions and family recipes with accuracy and dispatch." Just south of Light's blacksmith shop on Ash, Henry Pierce and Bill Hostetter built a livery and feed stable. On the southeast corner of Ash and Second (across from Ramsey's hardware), "Old Man" Ransom opened another saloon with a poker table and Neil D. Murray as bartender and built a livery barn on the next lots south.[5] In the center of the intersection stood the town well, with a hand pump and a rough watering trough hewed from a large cottonwood.

The only two-story structure in town was the O. K. Hotel, facing south a half-block east on Second, also owned by Ransom and run by Mary Pierce.[6] West of the hotel, Sadie Comley, nee McCaskey,[7] widow of an old X Bar X cowboy killed in a saloon brawl at Cushing shortly after the Sac and Fox opening, had a small gaming parlor in her home and kept three or four girls around for other diversions.[8] Sadie often dashed about the countryside in a plumed hat and fancy rig behind a team of high-stepping bays and was remembered by old-timers as Belle of the Cimarron.

Ingalls is best described in E. Bee Guthrey's *Oklahoma Hawk* of March 1, 1893, as

> one of the most prosperous and thriving trading points of Payne County. ... The townsite ... well located [on a] slope just enough for drainage which is so essential to good health ... now boasts of twenty-two business houses. ...
>
> It is surrounded by rolling prairie but has plenty of bottom land ... Council Creek only two miles northeast; the Cimarron River only 6 miles southeast; the Little Stillwater about 3½ miles west ... and most of this land will produce from 50 to 75 bushels of corn per acre. ... Among the men holding the fine claims adjacent to Ingalls are the following who are ever ready to exert their best energies toward the upbuilding of the community in general and Ingalls in particular:
>
> J. A. Simmons, John South, Wm. Purcell, James Ashburn, Wm. Wilson, Joseph Simmons, John Irwing, Ernest Chevalier, Wm. Querry, Ed Strange, John Olin, Wm. Stolling, H. Rhode, Frank McDaniel, H. B. Hardy, H. Hammock, W. S. Edmonson, Dr. Samuel Steele, B. Dunn [William B. Dunn, alternately referred to as Bill or Bee to distinguish him from his uncle, Will], Scott Rowden, Clay Windell, B. A. Kelly, Dock Ramsey, Russ Ramsey, Robert VanArsdale, James Duncan and Wm. Thoe.
>
> Ingalls is not what it is as the result of a forced boom. Its natural resources have been its only support and it is a town because there is a demand for one where it is ... in one of the most prosperous agricultural sections of Oklahoma. It will be a city when the balloon towns of the west have exploded.

Nix[9] called it "a sort of pop-off valve for Doolin and his men." While forced to "travel stealthily and avoid the community settlements in the interims between their spectacular hold-ups ... here they could blow the lid off—owned the town, figuratively."

Their frequent camp was an open cave under a large overhang of rocks on Deer Creek near its confluence with the Cimarron in the Creek Nation, and at Bill Dunn's homestead two and one half miles southeast of Ingalls on Council Creek, Doolin, Newcomb, and Pierce often had found sanctuary while riding with the Daltons. Bill Dunn finally constructed a frame house and other good improvements, which it was rumored he financed with money obtained from the outlaws and cattle thievery as a sideline. His original home, however, was a large log cabin on a high slope overlooking the creek; nearby was a plank-covered storm cave, which the gang used as a lodging place. Bill's four brothers—John (the eldest), George, Dal, and Calvin (the youngest)—were "friendly with Doolin and his boys" when the latter came that way but had no connection with the outlaws. An uncle, Will Dunn, took a claim north of Yale in the Pawnee country when the Outlet opened. Bill's thirteen-year-old sister, Rosa, spent most of her time in Ingalls with her mother. Her father was dead, and her mother had married Dr. Call.

Another reason Doolin frequented Ingalls was Edith Ellsworth, whom he had persistently courted the winter of 1891–92 while she was clerking in McMurtry's drugstore. What the town didn't know, and the marshals would not learn until months later, was that the second week in March, 1893, just before her twentieth birthday, Edith had gone north, ostensibly to visit friends, had secretly met the outlaw leader, and had boarded a train to Kingfisher, where, on March 14, she became Mrs. William Doolin.[10] Graves,[11] Newsom,[12] and Zoe A. Tilghman[13] write that

she had no knowledge of Doolin's life before their marriage; he courted her and kept concealed from her all things pertaining to his past or his intentions for the future . . . she likely had reason to believe he was more than a cowboy, a daring rider, an active man of the open . . . but there was about him a dashing and debonair way that attracted her so much she found herself so in love with him that she could not say no when asked to become his wife. . . . After their marriage the girl, without hesitation, accepted her position as the wife of an outlaw.

It waxes romantic and sentimental and is acquiesced in most works on the subject since.

Returning to Ingalls, Edith kept house for Mrs. Selph and helped in Dr. Selph's office, where she was "very efficient in handling the sick." In June, she found employment at the O. K. Hotel, where Mrs. Pierce became her "closest friend." Roy Daugherty took the wounded Doolin there the night of June 17 and Dr. Selph treated his foot, removing Sheriff Healy's bullet and several slivers of bone.

McRill[14] and Hanes[15] tell us that Doolin was treated for his injury by Mrs. Pierce: "She brought out a pan of water and carbolic acid to bathe the foot" and Billy McGinty "came over to wash it." While this was transpiring (on the front porch of the hotel, of all places!), Deputy Marshal Heck Thomas strode by, saw Doolin, and, to prevent the outlaw from drawing on him, "passed on seemingly oblivious of Doolin's presence." Actually, McGinty was still with the McElroy herd in the Outlet. By his own statement he did not see Doolin in Ingalls until nearly two months later, Heck Thomas was checking out the three Cimarron robbery suspects jailed at Hennessey, and the hotel had no front porch.

Scores of stories have been told and have grown with each telling of how the Wild Bunch rode in and out of town until the end of August, boosting a poor frontier economy with stolen money spent in restaurants, barbershops, boot and saddle shops, and on ammunition and whiskey. The outlaws drank and gambled in the saloons, threw beer on customers, and shot empty bottles off the bars with their .45's, yet they are remembered as "likeable fellows," "softspoken," and "friendly." They grubstaked struggling homesteaders, furnished oysters and crackers at picnics and country dances, and even attended church. On one divine occasion in a tent tabernacle near Main Street, when some of the gang became obstreperous, Doolin, carrying his stubby Winchester close to his leg and favoring his left foot (as was his custom after he was wounded), limped grimly down the aisle and muttered from the side of his mouth: "If you bastards don't shut up, I'm goin' to sift lead through some of you." From then on, the service was as demure and orderly as a Puritan Sunday school.

Beginning on June 17, 1893, Dr. Pickering kept a diary of Ingalls events as he saw them, and such tales do not seem so plausible when one examines this early entry:

> In July Wm. Doolan, George Newcomb [alias] bitter Creek, Slaughter Kid, Tom Jones [Arkansas Tom], Danimite, Tulsa Jack, and Bill Dalton began to come here frequently & in a short time they all staid here except Dalton. He was at B. Dunns. . . . They all went hevily armed & constantly on their guard, generly went 2 together. They boarded at the O. K. Hotel [and] staid at B Dunn's when not in town.

It also confirms contemporary reports that

> the majority of the residents were God-fearing, law-abiding people but were so terrorized by the gang that they kept silent. . . . A number of citizens were in full sympathy with the outlaws, shielding them for the sake of getting their trade. . . . Whenever an effort was made to capture the band, they generally had warning and was thus given a chance to escape into the unsettled and uninhabited reservations of the Pawnee and Creek Indians.[16]

Detective Dodge knew the situation from trailing the Daltons.

He took the shoes of the horse killed during the flight of the Cimarron bandits to a friend who lived three miles from Ingalls. The man went into town and returned that night with "a lot of good information." The "Horse-Shoer in Ingalls was a good one" and verified his work. The animal had been one of four brought to him by Doolin, Dalton, Newcomb, and Tulsa Jack "about a week before the Train Robbery."[17]

As a result of Dodge's report, Deputy Marshal Hueston and a posseman named Wilson rode from Stillwater to Ingalls on July 7. They

> rode into the town without thought of danger near. Just as they were dismounting they were covered by guns in the hands of Bill Dalton, Bill Doolin, Newcomb, and a man calling himself Starr [Tulsa Jack], and told not to get off their horses but to move on. [The outlaws] having the drop on them, they had no course but to submit.[18]

Hueston organized a posse and returned to the scene as quickly as possible, but the quarry had fled into the Pawnee country. The *Oklahoma State Capital*[19] commented:

> The same gang were at Ingalls some time ago and had their horses shod at a blacksmith shop. They seem to have some sympathizing friends at that place that need to be looked after.

Allegedly, on the night of June 17, Deputy Sheriff Bob Andrews of Payne County had gone to Ingalls to arrest a small-time thief named Ragged Bill, who had knocked an old man in the head at Stillwater and robbed him of forty dollars. Andrews found him playing poker in Ransom's saloon. Ragged Bill immediately pleaded with the other men at the table not to let the deputy take him back to stand trial. Addressing the tall, drooping-moustached leader as Doolin, he told him that he had come to join his gang.

Andrews, realizing he was at the mercy of the most dangerous band in the territory, explained why he had come for Ragged Bill, and Doolin is credited with saying: "Anybody who would knock an old man in the head for $40 couldn't carry water for our bunch." He told Andrews to handcuff his man, then ordered Bitter Creek to get their horses, and the two outlaws rode out a short distance with the deputy and his prisoner. As they parted, Doolin said, "Andrews, I'm taking your word you won't double cross me. If you do, we'll meet again sometime."

Andrews proceeded to Stillwater with his prisoner and, true to his promise, never mentioned that the gang was making Ingalls its headquarters. Ragged Bill, however, cursed Bill Doolin in jail, and the details of his capture soon were in the hands of the Guthrie marshals.

Contemporary reports mention no such person as Ragged Bill, nor is there reference to a slugging at Stillwater. The Ingalls arrest is an apparent fabrication, especially in light of the reception afforded Hueston and Wilson. The story, first appearing in Stansbery's *The Passing of the 3-D Ranch*[20] and embellished in his later article, "'Cops and Robbers' in Territorial Days,"[21] apparently was based on an interview with Orrington ("Red") Lucas, a retired federal officer then living on his ranch near Wagoner, Oklahoma, who claimed to have witnessed the affair on June 17. This was the night Doolin arrived in Ingalls fresh from the Cimarron robbery with a bullet in his foot, and Lucas was not present until more than a month later, as is attested by this entry in Dr. Pickering's diary:

> The last of this month [July] a man by the name of Dock Roberts and Red Lucas came to town looking up a proposed Rail Road rout. Both parties took in the haunts of the outlaws. They were both jovial fellows & Soon was drinking & playing cards with them. They left & came back in a week & said they were here to locate a booth, a place for intended settlers to register and get certificates to make a race for land or town lots. They staid here until the last week in August then left.

In a 1937 interview,[22] Lucas says he posed as a "fisherman from Black Bear Creek," that he "picked up the ugliest man in the territory called 'Catfish Jack' for a partner" to help with his alibi, and that the two of them sold more than eighteen hundred dollars' worth of yellow catfish to the townspeople while they gained the confidence of the outlaws. Lucas "became such a close friend of Doolin's that when he returned wounded from a raid in Arkansas," Lucas "helped take care of him"; he secretly checked the members of the gang "as to weight, height, scars"; he trained himself to recognize their voices; he even "weighed their guns and checked them as to marks" while he arranged with federal officers for "an opportune time to have them surrounded and taken"; and he gives other erroneous information that renders his account at its best unreliable.

Actually, Lucas had been an officer of the Fort Smith federal court since 1882, operating chiefly in the Creek Nation. In 1889, he obtained a couple of city lots in Guthrie and was commissioned under Marshal Grimes. A native of Ohio, he began his career as a detective in the Muncie, Indiana, police department, where he

155

developed "an uncanny ability to change disguise." There was no mystery that the Wild Bunch was making Ingalls its headquarters, and Nix had ordered Lucas and Captain W. C. ("Doc") Roberts, another federal officer unknown to the outlaws, to "infiltrate the settlement to determine their habits and the best possible way to effect their capture." The two men's operations were essentially as described by Dr. Pickering.

Roberts delivered their final report to Deputy Marshal Hixon at Guthrie on August 30. Hixon conceived the idea of entering Ingalls in two covered wagons. Since the announced opening of the Outlet, homeseekers everywhere were crossing the country bound for the promised land, so they would attract little attention. Heck Thomas thought it a "fool's errand" and refused any part of it. In his long years of man hunting, he had seen too many "large posse" expeditions fail. While trailing the Daltons, he and Detective Dodge had used only three men at the most. Hixon, somewhat irritated, agreed that "one of them ought to stay in Guthrie."

Quietly, Hixon organized his posse. On the night of August 31, a white-topped wagon left Stillwater and another left Guthrie. Each boasted a single driver, but carefully concealed beneath their flapping canvas were arms, ammunition, and thirteen U.S. deputy marshals.[23] Shortly before midnight, the Stillwater wagon, with Tom Hueston in charge, Dick Speed as driver, and manned by Deputies Ham Hueston, Henry Keller, George Cox, M. A. Iauson (given in contemporary reports as *Janson*), and H. A. ("Hi") Thompson, rendezvoused at Red Lucas' camp in a timbered ravine southwest of Ingalls.

According to Hi Thompson,[24] "Lucas reported the Wild Bunch at the O. K. Hotel . . . their horses were in Ransom's livery stable. We expected to surround the hotel at midnight and capture the desperadoes, but the Guthrie wagon was delayed and did not join us till daybreak." In this wagon rode John Hixon, Jim Masterson as driver, and Deputies Doc Roberts, Ike Steel, Steve Burke, and Lafe Shadley.[25] "The delay caused us to revise our plan, and Lucas was sent in to study the situation. He was back at 9 o'clock." Doolin, Dalton, Newcomb, Red Buck Waightman, Dynamite Dick, and Tulsa Jack had gone to Ransom's saloon for their early-morning drinking and to engage in some friendly poker. No sign of Arkansas Tom. He had not been feeling well, and Lucas "thought he had gone out to B. Dunn's."[26]

At that moment, a deputy on picket spotted a "ragged little youngster" hiding in the brush, ears and eyes wide open to everything being discussed. Lucas identified him as one of the local boys who fished in the nearby creek and received generous tips from the outlaws to warn them if any strangers approached. The story goes that he was "captured during the night, but unwisely released in the morning, whereat he ran into Ingalls with the news that 'the law' was coming."[27] Actually, the boy was questioned, then chained to a tree for later disposition.

Hixon, a little shaken now by Heck Thomas' warning, decided the odds of thirteen lawmen against six desperate criminals were not enough. He dispatched a messenger to Chief Deputy Hale at Stillwater. Hale gathered a posse of eleven men and, accompanied by Payne County Sheriff F. M. Burdick and City Marshal O. W. Sollers, started for Ingalls at once.[28]

Meanwhile, Hixon decided to scatter his forces to cut off all avenues of escape.[29] His wagon and party skirted the town, entering from the south on Oak Street. Pickering's diary continues:

> [These marshals] drove up by my house [stopping in a grove of trees to the north] & they all proceeded to unload in a quite maner & take positions. . . . 2 wagons stoped at Lights Black Smith Shop.

Dick Speed, followed by Lucas' "survey outfit," drove his wagon in from the west. At the edge of town, Hueston and the others, heavily armed with ammunition, rifles, and six-shooters, dropped from under the canvas, scattering south to positions behind brush, fences and buildings that lined the west side of Ash Street. Speed and Lucas then turned their vehicles down Ash, stopping just past Light's blacksmith shop at the Pierce and Hostetter feed barn.

The outlaws in Ransom's saloon had seen the wagon from the south disappear in Pickering's grove, but they gave the matter little thought since the grove was a favorite camping spot for travelers. When the other wagon stopped up the street, they recognized Lucas' outfit, and Newcomb left the poker game to investigate. Pickering notes that "Bitter Creek Got his horse & was riding up to a Small building where Said Comley staid & the marshalls thinking he was known to the[ir] move fired on him."

Deputy Speed had climbed down from his wagon with his Winchester and had entered the feed barn, covering its only two occupants. He told them he was a federal officer, that there was going to be a raid, and that if either of them attempted to warn the outlaws, he would be killed. As he stepped back to the open doorway, he saw Bitter Creek walking his horse up the street toward the wagon. At that moment, a boy left Light's blacksmith shop, and

Speed called him to the doorway and inquired the name of "that rider." The incredulous youth (later identified as nineteen-year-old Dell Simmons from Duncan Bend on the Cimarron) exclaimed, "Why, that's Bitter Creek!" and Newcomb saw the lad point his direction.

The outlaw halted his horse and threw up his rifle. Speed whipped his Winchester to his shoulder and fired the opening shot of the famous battle. His bullet knocked the magazine off Bitter Creek's weapon, ricocheted downward, and tore into the outlaw's right leg.[30] Newcomb flinched in pain as he fired, and his shot went wild. Unable to lever for a second shot, he wheeled his horse to escape, and Speed stepped from the doorway to kill him.

Arkansas Tom was on the upper floor of the hotel. The upper story was merely attic-finished, neither ceilinged or plastered. It had a window in the north gable and two windows in the false-fronted gable on the south. Furnished with beds, chairs, and a table, it was used as a sleeping room by the outlaws when they spent the night in town. When Arkansas Tom heard the first shot, he snatched up his Winchester and sprang to the north window. As Speed stepped from the feed barn, he fired at the officer, hitting him in the shoulder. Speed started back to the stable door, then turned and tried to reach the shelter of his wagon. The outlaw fired again, killing him instantly.[31]

This forced the other officers into the fight before they had gained their positions. Hixon's men in Pickering's grove to the east began shooting at Bitter Creek as he rode south out of the town, still clutching his useless rifle. Doolin, Dalton, Tulsa Jack, Dynamite Dick, and Red Buck opened fire from the saloon, covering his escape. The air was thick with flying lead. Young Simmons, who had ducked into Vaughn's saloon, came out the back door and was mortally wounded; he died at six o'clock. Pro-Doolin old-timers swear he was slain by the officers,[32] but he was "in direct range from the north window of the hotel" and "Tom Jones was the only man in a position to have killed him, mistaking him for a marshal."[33] A horse tied in front of Ransom's saloon was "killed intentionally for . . . it was standing broadside of the building and thereby disconcerted the aim of the deputies who managed the front of the place,"[34] and a Cushing man named N. A. Walker, a bar customer when the shooting began, ran into the street and was "shot through the liver by marshals thinking he was one of the outlaws trying to escape."[35] By this time, Bitter Creek had disappeared into the timber, and the first burst of firing ceased.

Hueston and his men moved up behind the buildings on the west side of Ash Street to concentrate their fire on Ransom's saloon, north side and rear. Hixon's men spread from Pickering's grove and advanced through the brush east of the hotel and south across Second Street behind the home of Drs. McMurtry, Selph, and Call, covering both the front of the saloon and the livery stable where the outlaws kept their horses. After several minutes, Hixon shouted to Doolin that the gang was surrounded and had no chance to escape, and Doolin replied with an oath: "Go to hell!"

The marshals opened a withering barrage on the building. Lead ripped into the saloon from the side, front, and rear. Old Man Ransom was hit in the leg, and the fight grew so hot that the outlaws decided to make a run for their horses. Doolin left the saloon first, followed by Dalton and Red Buck, then Dynamite Dick and Tulsa Jack. "Escaping by the side door, the deputies did not know that the building had been deserted until they were fired upon from the livery stable." To detract attention, Murray, "opening the front door [of the saloon] a short distance, put his Winchester to his shoulder in the act of firing. Three of the deputies, seeing him in the position . . . fired at him simultaneously. Two shots struck him in the ribs and one broke his arm . . . his Winchester falling across the threshold."[36]

This surprising, daring move by the outlaws forced Hueston's party to shift positions in order to cover the stable effectively. Hueston himself stepped behind a pile of lumber behind Perry's store where he could command the rear door. "He was facing south, directly west and in easy range of the hotel. He could not have been seen from the gable windows. . . . However, Arkansas Tom punched the shingles off from the inside [making] a hole sufficiently large in the roof, directly in view of the marshal . . . mounted a chair, thus giving him height enough to shoot downward through the hole," and shot the deputy twice in the left side and bowels.[37]

Inside the barn, Doolin and Dynamite Dick saddled the horses while Dalton, Red Buck, and Tulsa Jack pumped a close, accurate fire at Hixon's men from the doorway. Then Doolin and Dynamite Dick mounted and made a wild dash out the rear door to the southwest. Dalton, Red Buck, and Tulsa Jack rode out the front door, heading for a ravine a few hundred yards away in the same direction.

As Dalton galloped into the street, Hixon shot his horse in the jaw. The animal stopped and spun around, becoming almost unmanageable. Pickering writes: "He[Dalton] had a hard time getting him started but finly succeeded. He went probely 75 yards when his horse got his leg broke." Deputy Shadley, firing a long shot from behind Call's residence, hit the horse in the leg. Dalton dropped from the saddle and walked on the opposite side of the animal a short distance, "when Shadley fired again, and Dalton rolled into the grass over an embankment." When the outlaw fell, "Shadley declared he had hit him. He started toward where the other outlaws had reached a wire fence, when Dalton suddenly reappeared from the draw." Realizing that the gang had only one pair of wire cutters and these were in his saddlebags, Dalton ran back to his injured horse. "He fired at Shadley, but missed his mark."[38]

Shadley now was "south and west of Call's house in direct range from the south gable window of the hotel."[39] Disconcerted by other shots coming at him from behind, the deputy ran for some brush between the Ransom home and the William Selph residence. "He encountered a yard fence and in trying to get through it his coat caught throwing him forward. It was while in this position that he received his first wound. The shot was fired from the upper chamber of the hotel. . . . The ball struck him in the right hip, shattering the bone and lodged in his right breast."[40]

Shadley managed to get through the fence and reach the Ransom house, where he tried to obtain assistance. Mrs. Ransom ordered him to leave. McRill[41] states that "a woman was there under the bed screaming for fear so Mrs. Ransom directed him to a cave where several people were." Hanes[42] adds that "the woman was pregnant . . . and nearly frightened to death." Pickering writes:

> He got to Ransom's house & was debating with Mrs. Ransom she ordering him to leave when he got his last shots. He fell there & crawled to Selph's cave.

Hanes[43] thinks that as he staggered around the corner of the house, Dalton saw him and "pumped several shots at him from his Winchester [which] took deadly effect." Pickering disagrees:

> A great many say he [Dalton] shot Shadly . . . in fact Shadly thought so for when I & Dr. Selph was working with him in the cave he said Dalton Shot him 3 times quicker than he could turn around but I think I know better. Shadly was hit [from behind] . . . and all the balls tended downwards. If Dalton had Shot him he would of been Shot in front & balls of ranged up.

When the battle began, Dr. Selph was amputating a finger for a farmer whose hand had been smashed that morning in a threshing-machine accident. Mrs. Selph, deciding to get to a safer place, gathered her children and hurried to William Selph's cave, nearly a block away. By the time Dr. Selph arrived, the cellar was "almost full to suffocation with men, women and children . . . some shouting, some praying, and all terribly excited."[44] Shadley was there. Drs. Selph and Pickering stayed only a few minutes. They dressed the marshal's wounds and gave him some whiskey for a stimulant before leaving to attend the other wounded and dying.

Meanwhile, Dalton had obtained the wire cutters, shot his injured horse in the head, and started back to the fence. "The United States men slowed up some when Shadley was shot. Doolin and the others kept firing at the officers." Deputy Masterson had reached a threatening position behind a blackjack tree about ten inches in diameter. "The tree was soon gashed with bullets that struck above Masterson's head, and twigs and limbs fell everywhere around him. . . . He ran out of ammunition" but, undaunted, "raced back under heavy fire to the covered wagon, filled his pockets with cartridges, and returned to the tree."[45] This gave Dalton a chance to cut the fence and let the gang ride through.

Masterson described what happened next in the *Kansas City Times* of November 15, 1893:

> As they came out of the gully on the jump, Dalton was up behind Tulsa Jack. "Hell," says I, "fellers, they're getting away." Well, we [he, Hixon, Roberts, Steel, and Burke] blazed away at 'em and Dynamite Dick tumbled off his horse. They stopped, lifted him back in the saddle and Doolin rode in behind. I raised my sight to 500 yards, but I couldn't get 'em.

Later, Masterson learned that Dynamite Dick had been hit in the neck; the outlaw had the ball removed, leaving an obvious, identifying scar.[46]

The gang rode southeast to the top of a hill and paused, firing a number of shots along Oak Street. Frank Briggs, Dr. Briggs's teen-aged son, "so intensely interested in the fight that he stood near the officers watching the effects of their broadsides," ran to the intersection in front of the Pickering home for a better view of the departing outlaws and was hit by one of their bullets.[47] Dr. Pickering describes the incident:

> The outlaws crossed the draw south of town & stoped a few minuets shooting up the street my house is on. One of these shots hit Frank Briggs in the shoulder a slight flesh wound. I took him to my cave & dressed his wound then went to Walker & gave him tempery aid [Wal-

ker died on September 16] from there to Murry's & laid his wound
open & removed the shattered bone. Some of the Drs wanted to Ampu-
tate but I fought for his arm 2 inches of raidus was Shot away slight
flesh wounds in the side. About this time I was called aside & told to
go to Hotel that Jones was up there either wounded or killed.

Although the Wild Bunch had fled Ingalls, Hixon and his men
held their positions. It was obvious now that Speed, Hueston, and
Shadley "could not have been hit by the firing from the saloon
or livery stable," and the officers "began tracing the direction from
which the bullets had come. . . . Even as they discovered the hole
in the west roof of the hotel, they were told by a woman that one of
the outlaws was in the two-story building, that she had seen puffs
of smoke rise from the roof and gable windows," and that "this
outlaw did the shooting that proved fatal to the marshals."[48]

The posse surrounded the hotel but "were told by the landlady
[Mrs. Pierce] that none of the outlaws was inside. The woman
who had seen the shooting courageously walked upstairs and found
Jones, returned to the officers and told them the other woman
had lied."[49] Hixon then ordered the occupants out, and all left the
building except Arkansas Tom. "Jones knocked a hole in the east
roof [giving him command of the whole town] and said he knew
he would be taken finally, but in the meantime he would kill at
least seven men, whom he had range on." The officers "began a
continuous firing into the roof and upstairs. . . . it was a miracle
how the outlaw survived, but at eleven o'clock, one hour after the
shot that began the battle was fired, he still pumped lead down at
the besieging party [and] seemed to have an inexhaustible supply
of ammunition."[50]

Chief Deputy Hale arrived from Stillwater. He led his men in
pursuit of the Wild Bunch, and Burdick and Sollers joined the
marshals at the hotel. Again they demanded Arkansas Tom's surrender. "If I come out," the outlaw yelled, "I'll come shootin'!"[51]

Allegedly, at this juncture, Masterson crept to the east side of the
building (while his companions kept Jones busy on the other side),
placed two sticks of dynamite under it, and told Mrs. Pierce that
if she did not bring the outlaw out, he would blow the place "into
the middle of next week." Another popular version is that Masterson "piled kindling wood" against the structure and threatened
to burn it; Mrs. Pierce pleaded that the hotel was her only means
of livelihood and that if he would spare it, she would persuade
the outlaw to lay down his arms. She called out to Arkansas Tom,
went upstairs, and within a few minutes appeared at a window

162

and told the officers that if he was promised protection from mob violence and not put in chains, he would give himself up. The officers "readily accepted the outlaw's proposition." Mrs. Pierce then "threw his rifle and six-shooters out the window and led him, bleeding from bullet wounds, down to the marshals."

The tale appears first in Sutton's *Hands Up!*[52] and gains momentum in Nix's *Oklahombres*,[53] James D. Horan's *Desperate Women*,[54] and Wellman's *A Dynasty of Western Outlaws*,[55] with crocodile tears being shed by Mrs. Pierce when Arkansas Tom says he would not have allowed her place destroyed anyhow. And the legend has become a boon to magazine writers. Here are the facts from Pickering's diary:

> I and Alva Pierce [Mrs. Pierce's son] & boy by name of Wendell boys about 12 years old went over [to the hotel] I went in & called but got no answer & was about to leave when he [Jones] came to top of stairs & says is that you Dock & I told him it was. I asked if he was hurt & he said no. He said for me to come up & I told him if he wasent hurt I would not but he insisted so I went up. He had his coat & vest of[f] also his boots had his Winchester in his hands & revolvers lying on the bed. I said Tom come down & Surender he says I cant do it for I wont get justis he says where is the boys [meaning the outlaws] I told him they had gone. He said he did not think they would leave him it hurt him bad I never seen a man wilt so in my life. He staid in Hotel till after 2 o'clock & then Surendered to a Mr. Mason, a preacher.

Sheriff Burdick took Jones into custody. He asked Sollers whether he could get the prisoner to Stillwater. "I can if I'm not ambushed by his friends on the way," Sollers replied. The outlaw was handcuffed, loaded into a spring wagon guarded by Cox, Thompson, and Iauson, and hauled across open country. Sollers followed immediately in a buggy.[56] The marshal's wagon from Stillwater, driven by Keller and carrying the body of Dick Speed and the wounded Hueston and Shadley, brought up the rear of the grim cortege. Within an hour, Arkansas Tom was in the Payne County jail.

> His arrival . . . together with a report of the fight, caused the most intense excitement, and men in large numbers left immediately for Ingalls; the court room was vacated at once, lawyers, jurors, and witnesses joining in the stampede to the scene of carnage, making it necessary to adjourn court. . . . Several searching parties have spread through the timbered hills and creek bottoms. Another battle may be looked for, and if it comes . . . from the temper of the people . . . it will be a war of extermination.[57]

Hale and his posse had picked up Bitter Creek's trail. At the creek crossing south of Ingalls, they found a bloody pool of water, where he had stopped to bathe his wound, and a spot in a cornfield where he had rested briefly. The trail led south to Falls City, where he had "approached the blacksmith shop of J. D. Vickery [Joseph D. Vickrey] . . . and brandishing a revolver, demanded a bucket of water. He was on horseback and looked very pale. He wanted Vickery to pour the water on his leg, which he did. Vickery asked him how it came the wound wasn't bleeding, and he remarked that he got off at a creek and washed it and succeeded in stopping the blood." Vickrey said the wound was in the fleshy part of Newcomb's thigh and that he (Vickrey) "does not think that any bones were broken. . . [otherwise] he would not have been able to get down from his saddle to wash his leg and get on again."[58]

The *Stillwater Gazette*[59] reported that

Newcomb, alias Bitter Creek, is known to have been shot through the hips, and the last heard of him on Saturday [September 2] was that he was not able to be moved and his death was hourly expected.

Dr. Pickering writes:

The outlaw staid close to town . . . as [he] was not able to travel. Dr. Bland of Cushion [Cushing] tended him I loaned him instruments to work on wound with although I did not know just where he was at. A piece of Magazine [from his rifle] was blown in his leg. It eventually worked out and he got able to again ride.

About four o'clock in the afternoon, Hale's posse reached the Cimarron. They tracked the Wild Bunch along its north bank "for at least two miles" but lost them completely after they crossed the stream into the Sac and Fox country.

Late that evening, Sheriff Burdick and Hixon reached Stillwater with Lon Case, the boy left chained to the tree by the marshals; his brother Al; "two boys belonging to another family of the same name"; and "George Perrin." Steel, Roberts, and Masterson returned to Guthrie with the wounded Murray and Mr. and Mrs. Ransom in custody. Steel led Arkansas Tom's horse, which had been left in the stable, and Roberts carried Bill Dalton's saddle. "The marshals were victorious," observed the *State Capital*,[60] "driving back their opponents, capturing the town and making a number of arrests . . . but it is no easy thing to capture five men, outlawed and having a lot of citizens protecting them." Murray and the Ransoms were charged with harboring, those at Stillwater held as witnesses. Within a few days, all had been released and were back at Ingalls.

When news reached Perkins that Marshal Speed had been "killed outright in the raid," the town was "thrown into a fever of excitement." Many refused to believe the report; others were so incensed that they expressed their willingness to go to Stillwater and lynch Arkansas Tom. By nightfall, rumors of such action were so rife that the outlaw was transferred to the federal jail at Guthrie.[61]

Hundreds of distressed friends and relatives packed the Methodist Episcopal Church at Stillwater on Saturday, September 2, where the funeral of Dick Speed was conducted by AOUW Lodge No. 5, of which he was a valued member. His remains were taken to Perkins, where the last sad rites were performed by lodge members of that city at the cemetery; more than three hundred persons attended. Will G. Hill, editor of the *Perkins Journal,* added this tribute:

Richard Speed was born in Franklin county, Kansas, December 11, 1867, consequently being but 26 years of age at the time of his death. In 1887 he was married in Chautauqua county, where he was constable for four years before his removal to Oklahoma, and in this position he showed himself to be an honest and worthy officer, respected by the law-abiding and feared by the lawbreakers. Of Mr. Speed's career in Perkins I need not speak. Our citizens know . . . of his stainless character as an officer and citizen . . . he had the kindest of dispositions, was a devoted husband and father and a friend of sterling worth, and well deserved his title of "Noble Richard." He leaves a wife and three children.[62]

Tom Hueston died that same afternoon at four o'clock "after thirty hours of excruiating pain." On Sunday, the IOOF and AOUW combined for services conducted in the Methodist Church. "The procession that followed his remains to the cemetery was the largest ever seen in Stillwater, over 1500 people being in line."[63]

Lafe Shadley died Sunday afternoon. On Monday, his remains were placed on the train at Orlando, taken to his home at Independence, Kansas, and laid to rest.[64]

The *Stillwater Gazette* of September 8 lamented:

Dick Speed, Tom Hueston and Lafe Shadley were three as brave and fearless officers as ever operated in support of law and order. They were cut down in the prime of life by assassins, while in defense of our homes and firesides. They are no more, but their memories will live forever. Their labors and deaths will form a page in the history of Oklahoma which will shine all the brighter and read the better when outlawry and organized bands of marauders are completely wiped out of existence.

The *Guthrie Daily Leader* of the same date declared:

> It is a matter of vital necessity that these men [the Doolin gang] shall be caught and made to pay the penalty of their crimes, and it is time that the false glamor surrounding such dastardly deeds be dispelled. . . . Nothing will do this but the killing of the scoundrels as one kills a wild beast.

On September 11, with half of Guthrie's population already departed for the opening of the Outlet, a startling rumor swept the city: the Wild Bunch, rendezvoused "about five miles from Ingalls," nursing their battle wounds, and gathering reinforcements, proposed to raid Guthrie, headquarters of the marshals, to gain revenge for the Ingalls invasion and to liberate Arkansas Tom. "They and their friends threatened to burn down Stillwater a few days ago in order to rescue the outlaw. Finding out that he was here they changed their attention to this place."[65]

A report received by Colonel Dick Reaves of the Guthrie cavalry described "a band of men numbering thirty-five, armed to the teeth, encamped about twenty-two miles northeast of here." Although it was not certain whether "they are the bandits or another party gathered for the opening . . . it behooves the people who remain in Guthrie to be on the lookout."[66]

Two squads totaling forty men were organized under Deputies Hixon and Heck Thomas. It was Thomas' opinion that if the outlaws entered the city, they would "come in separately and concentrate about the jail," and he advised his men to parade the town with Winchesters and arrest all suspicious persons who could give no satisfactory account of themselves. Scores of other armed citizens joined the marshals and promised a repetition of the Coffeyville disaster if the outlaws appeared.[67]

They guarded the city three days and three nights, but nothing happened. A report from Orlando stated the gang had passed that place, headed west. Another report claimed the outlaws were camped on the famous Dalton farm near Kingfisher and the Dalton family was refusing to allow strangers to come near the place. In the federal jail, Arkansas Tom "guffawed loudly" over the scare as an effort by some prankster to confuse the "little army," as he called Nix's force of deputies, and added that Guthrie people "made him weary."[68]

Ingalls, O. T., looking southeast.

The O. K. Hotel in Ingalls at the time of the battle.

The NW.¼ of the NE.¼ of Sec.28, Town. 19, Range 4, East.

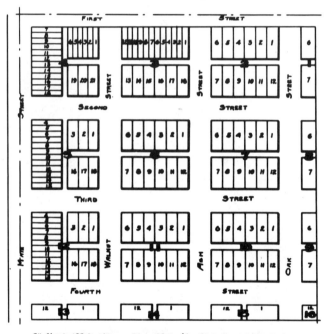

All Streets 100 ft. wide.   Alleys 20 ft. wide. All business lots 25x140 ft. except
Lots 1 to 6 in Blk. 4, which are 23⅓ ft by 140 ft. All residence lots are 90x140 ft.
except the SE.¼ of Block 4, and the East half of Blocks 5 & 12, which are
46²/₃ f. x 140 ft.   Fraction of Block 16 is 70x 70 ft. Lots in all other fractions
70 x 140 ft.

Scale – 150 ft. to the inch.

The above plat and survey is hereby adopted this 26 day of Sept. 1892.

John Foster.
William L. Robinson } Trustees.
Milton ....

Plat of Ingalls, O. T., adopted September 26, 1892.

168

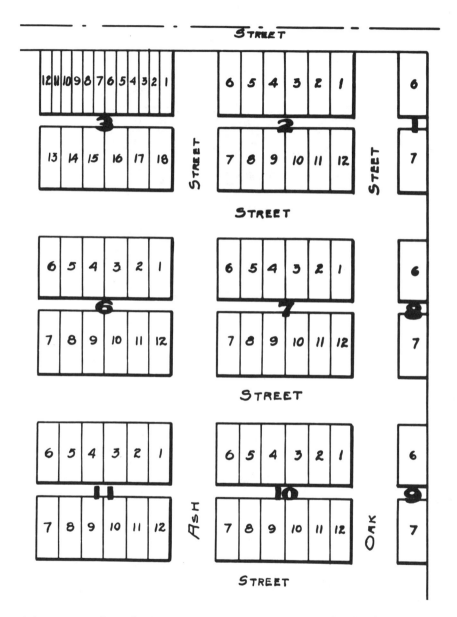

Enlargement of Ingalls plat showing area where the gun battle of September 1, 1893, was fought.

H. F. Pierce's livery stable in Ingalls.

The Ransom-Murray saloon in Ingalls.

X   Cherokee Outlet

DOWN THE YEARS, almost as many versions of the race for homes in the Cherokee Outlet have been given as there were people who participated. The 1893 event is best capsulated from first-hand accounts appearing in the *Oklahoma State Capital* and the *Guthrie Daily Leader* from September 6 through September 16 and several days thereafter.

On the last day at the registration booths in the hundred-foot strip around its borders, with thousands still pouring in, the crush was tremendous. Passenger trains, their seats, aisles, and platforms jammed with homeseekers, rolled into the border cities and were sidetracked; wagon roads teemed with prairie schooners; cavalcades of horsemen in tens, twenties, and fifties rode like an army, until there were "eight persons for every 160 acres, not to mention town lots," and the registration points were unable to accommodate them.

Men and women huddled in lines like swine, the burning sun beating down on their heads. No rain had fallen in weeks. The ground was baked and the tall prairie grass dry as tinder. Soldiers had set fire to huge tracts in forcing the removal of the last grazing herds and to locate sooners, and hot winds sweeping across the plains filled the air with sooty dust which settled on perspiring persons. Water unfit for animals to drink sold at ten cents a cup, and food, poor food that caused much illness, retailed at enormous prices, while "thieves and thugs plied their vocations with zeal for the shekels they could extract from the purse of the honest settler."

The plan of the government to obviate "sooner trouble" by requiring registration proved impracticable. Hundreds of "professional boomers" were on the grounds, holding places in the lines and selling when they had worked to the front at five and twenty-five dollars. Many certificates were bought and sold. Many had "lost their certificates and didn't know what to do. . . . Lots more had

171

been robbed and were wretched because they were a long way from home and penniless."

Women "dirty and tanned to the blackness of a negro were going about looking feeble and wan but still determined to make the race. It was pitiful to see some of them . . . dresses torn and bedraggled, their hair uncombed and disheveled, and looking as if they hadn't partaken of a good square meal for a week. The men also looked particularly hard." Both men and women slept in their places; some died; scores more were carried away, prostrated with the heat, filth, and exhaustion. As time grew precious, the starting lines became "solid walls," and "every heart among them was throbbing with anxiety." Struggling and pushing and cursing, they "presented a very peculiar and sadly interesting spectacle."

By eleven o'clock, the anxiety on their faces was "painful to witness." Men on horseback "chewed tobacco viciously and squirted it out from under their shaggy moustaches as if they didn't care whose eyes they filled or whose garments they spattered. All kinds of vehicles were jammed in together, and all kinds of people were cheek by jowl in this great race for homes and independence."

As the hands on watches approached twelve o'clock, anxiety increased. Men stiffened on the seats of their wagons; men on horseback bent eagerly forward; pedestrians were knocked down and some trampled. Soon all sounds seemed to cease. Then the bugles blew and the signal shots were fired, and the sight was at once sublime and appalling.

"The mobs plunged forward as if some great force had impelled them from behind. The whole mighty lines swayed and pushed and roared then broke asunder as it were, and then began gradually to scatter into fragments of life," while the dust and sand rose up in dense, mighty clouds. "Men knocked each other down as they rushed onward. Horsemen tumbled into the ground. Women shrieked and fell, fainting. . . . Hundreds gave up ere they had gone a mile . . . turned back to the lines from which they started, bleeding, weary of the race, broken hearted. Others continued on only to fall by the wayside. Vehicles of all kinds were smashed and made useless. Men, women and horses were lying all over the prairie. Here and there men were fighting to the death over claims which each maintained he was first to reach. Knives and guns were drawn—it was a terrible and unforgettable scene; no pen can do it justice. . . . Those who got claims earned them dearly. It was a struggle where the game was emphatically every man for himself and devil take the hindmost."

172

As in previous openings, towns sprang up within hours. By nightfall, 12,000 people were encamped on eighty acres at Enid. At Perry, 25,000 found the townsite too small: "thrown, pitched, tumbled into place, the city appeared stretched all over the face of the earth, an inextricable mix-up of horses, mules and equipage . . . a half dozen people seemed to be holding down each lot." As the afternoon waned, there sprang up on the government land around it a North Perry, a West Perry, and Wharton, or South Perry, each the same size. There were 8,000 people at Pond Creek and 1,100 at Alva, with "every business well represented." Woodward, the end of the Santa Fe Division, with roundhouse and repair shop and 350 railroad employees, "had 575 filings," and Pawnee, "32 miles east of Perry on a good wagon road," had "about 1,000, exclusive of the Pawnee Agency population." Other places of promise were Blackwell, Kildare, and Cross (now Ponca City).

Soon the vast prairie was dotted with farms and ranches. Seven new counties were added to Oklahoma Territory, designated K, L, M, N, O, P, and Q and subsequently named Kay, Grant, Woods, Woodward, Garfield, Noble, and Pawnee, with county seats at Newkirk, Medford, Alva, Woodward, Enid, Perry, and Pawnee, respectively.

For thousands who rushed in, full of hope and confidence, there was burning disappointment. Small white flags bearing the words "This claim is taken" were more than a bit of irony. Many were placed so thickly they presaged bitter fights in land office proceedings, and "many murders, which will doubtless forever be shrouded in mystery, occurred."[1] Witness these items from the calendar of violence appearing in the *Guthrie Daily Leader* of September 19 and 20 and the *Oklahoma State Capital* of September 25:

Lewis Rivers, age 20, from Moniteau, Mo. had been left by his folks to watch a team while they went to hunt a claim. Upon returning they found young Rivers in a death struggle, a bullet hole in his side. The body was taken to Orlando and a coroner's jury summoned. . . . The young man had been killed in cold blood.

Near Black Bear Creek to the northwest, the dead body of James Reardon, of Milford, Mass. was found stabbed to death . . . the weapon still sticking in his breast.

Further north the dead body of W. D. Blake, of Gainesville, Texas, was found. He had been shot through the heart.

Madilene Grander of Terre Haute, Ind. was also found on the prairie . . . and a woman, entirely naked, was found Sunday near Woodward. . . . How the poor women met death cannot be told.

173

Another woman who located a claim west of Perry had ridden in alone and picketed her horse while she prepared a shelter for the night. To the windward somebody set a fire in the prairie and the dry grass burned furiously, bearing down upon her. . . . Instead of mounting her horse and riding away, she sought to "fire back," but it was too late, the flames swept over her and she was lost. Her horse escaped.

W. R. Jones, of Moberly, Mo. was found near Newkirk, his body riddled with bullets.

Two miles from Stillwater, in a dense underbrush, the bodies of two boomers and a dead horse were found Sunday evening. Bullets had pierced the hearts of both men.

A negro named Jennings from Dallas, Texas was struck with an ax by A. F. Gilbert, a white man, at Perry, and fatally injured. Gilbert escaped.

James H. Hill, of Kingborn, N.J. was shot and killed at the southwest corner of the Chilocco reservation. . . . He started into the strip before the signal was given and ignored the warning of soldiers to stop.

Fred Hurst and J. L. Tucker, while coming across the strip Saturday four miles north of Black Bear found the body of a man about 50 years of age. A handkerchief around his neck had been used to choke him to death. . . . Papers found on the body show that he is William Klause, of Cedar Vale, Kansas.

Particulars of the tragedy near Waukomis last Friday are to the effect that the killing of William Liddle and his son John was the culmination of a quarrel over a claim located about a quarter of a mile east. . . . It appears that one J. C. Williams was on the land as a contestant and was attacked by the Liddles. Williams was struck with a broad-ax by one of the Liddles, and when he surrendered himself to Special Officer Kent, of the Rock Island detective railway force, claimed that he shot in self-defense. Eber Liddle, another son of William Liddle, was shot by Williams, but not fatally wounded. Williams was taken to the Kingfisher jail. The Liddles were relatives of the notorious Dick Liddle, a member of the Jesse James gang, who escaped the time of the Northfield bank robbery and is now living in New Mexico.

All over the land, men pulled up stakes, and violence against sooners was repeated:[2]

Yesterday three miles from Mulhall the body of a middle-aged man was found with a hatchet buried in his head. . . . No papers were found to identify the corpse, as it was nude and the clothing missing. Near the body was a stake to which was pinned a paper bearing these words, "Death to All Sooners."

Asa Youmans, who formerly lived at Carthage, Mo. came to the strip in a company of Missourians, who were regularly organized and paid by

174

a syndicate of real estate men. When the first runners of the boomers reached Chicaska [near Blackwell], they found fifty men holding down claims with no other baggage than their rifles. This man Youmans was holding two, claiming that his friend and partner had gone on a search for water. The first comers did not attempt to dislodge him but those who came later, to whom the circumstances had been reported, planted their flags, determined to stand by them. Youmans came up to two of them and ordered them off [with] his rifle. One of the men asked him for his certificate. He said he had none and did not propose to get one, that he had support enough to make good his claim, adding: "I am a sooner and I'd like to know what in ---- you are going to do about it."

The two men, covered as they were, went away, but in less than an hour returned with at least two dozen of their friends, captured Youmans and proceeded to make him ready for trial by Judge Lynch. In what was probably a spirit of bravado Youmans said he had killed two settlers and would get away with some more. This so exasperated the men that they placed a lariat about his neck and pulled him up to a tree where they left his body as a warning to others.

The *State Capital*[3] observed:

> There is not a creek bottom claim that was not settled upon illegally and if it is now held by others it is because the sooner was ousted. . . . As sermons were preached before the opening against soonerism, so now a warning can be still given to those who soonered it to not attempt to make permanent settlement. . . .
>
> The sooner will have hell as long as he remains on the land. He will plow and not know whether the other fellow will sow; he will sow and not know whether the other fellow will reap; he will plant trees and not know but the other fellow will eat the fruit.
>
> The hunt after sooners in the strip will be greater than in Oklahoma proper—they will be hunted down like wolves until the last one is found—because the disappointment by active settlers is greater and there is an anger abroad.

Hundreds of dejected boomers "filled the border cities" and drifted about the Outlet, "cursing violently . . . everybody concerned," blaming their failure on the government's planning of this "excruciating game of devilish and ingenious sport," and holding Secretary of the Interior Hoke Smith "responsible for the sick, the wounded and the robbed . . . the graves his registering system dug." One old gentleman who could not restrain himself got up in a meeting at Orlando and gave vent to his feelings in this forcible language: "Damn such an administration, damn such a proclamation, damn such rules and regulations, damn such a set of men that didn't know

175

as much as last year's birdnest." His listeners applauded, and "in all that vast crowd there was not one to lift his voice in defense of the president, secretary or land commissioner."[4] They never considered the damage and injury done to be the result of their own selfishness and greed rather than the method of allocating land.

Townsites had troubles, too. Vice was rampant, and Governor Renfrow ordered that elections be held and town governments organized as quickly as possible. Perry was so tough it became known as Hell's Half Acre, and the chief executive received so many complaints of robberies and homicides occurring in and around its gaming houses that wholesale raids were conducted until "known wheels of fortune, faro layouts, and chuck-a-luck tables were piled in innocuous desuetude on the outside of the principal resorts . . . and the most prominent of these looked like deserted tabernacles."[5]

Enid furnished its quota of sensations. On September 21, the wife and two daughters of Baker Tomlinson, who had settled six miles east, were fatally burned by a prairie fire.[6] All things considered, it

is a poor day in Enid when something does not occur to vary the monotony. A riot and probable lynching was checked in its incipiency [when] a gang of desperadoes . . . rode into town with drawn revolvers. They proceeded to the Cherokee allotments on the east side of the [Rock Island] track and jumped the land. Houses were torn down and women and children terrorized. . . . The citizens turned out and held the outlaws in check until the sheriff and a posse could be summoned, when the entire gang was arrested and taken to the county jail.[7]

John Kelley, who lives alone on the east side of the track, had in his possession a large amount of money belonging to a few friends who were holding down claims outside of town. Yesterday morning an armed band of would-be desperadoes rode up to his shack and ordered him to shell out. He did not comply and they poured the contents of a shotgun into his room, wounding him quite severely. . . . The shooting so alarmed the town that the desperadoes thought it wise to leave and turned their horses west and galloped away at full speed without securing any booty. Feeling runs high at Enid, and people are talking of ropes and telegraph poles.[8]

Most of Enid's troubles resulted from competitive townsites. The Rock Island had established its station at North Enid, a company site in which the railroad was interested, and refused to stop trains at "government" or South Enid, hoping to draw the population to "railroad" Enid. The survey of South Enid was completed September 21 and the lots in both towns are all staked and occupied. Several violent controversies and two or three personal encounters occurred today in the Rock Island Enid, occasioned by disputes over boundary lines and contests.[9]

A similar problem developed in L (Grant) County. The trains stopped at Pond Creek Station north of the Salt Fork, but not at government Pond Creek south of the river. The government changed the name of the south town to Round Pond, but "the people had it changed back to Pond Creek, as the new name loses the town's identity." Mayor H. I. Wasson reported its population to be "fully 4,000 people" and presented "a petition bearing 3,667 names" asking Governor Renfrow to declare Pond Creek a city of the first class. On September 25, a committee went to Topeka to interview the Rock Island about stopping trains south of the river.[10]

The wrangling continued. Railroad officials took no action regarding Pond Creek but agreed to stop trains at South Enid if paid thirty-five hundred dollars. One thousand dollars brought a stop order from the railroad, which reserved the right to refund the money and discontinue service if the balance was not paid. Cash was hard to get. The railroad refused paper securities and precipitated a war with both South Enid and Pond Creek that was to result in much damage to public and private property.[11]

Marshal Nix bent every effort to control such matters until the new city and county governments could take over. He dismissed the temporary deputies employed to police the opening and commissioned regular field deputies at various points in the Outlet. John E. (Jack) Love (who would become sheriff of N county) was in charge at Woodward, Gus Hadwiger and E. W. Snoddy at Alva, W. A. (Pat) Murphy at Pond Creek, and Frank Lake (later sheriff of Pawnee County), at Pawnee.[12] Heck Thomas was sent to assist Bill Tilghman at Perry. On October 21, John M. Brogan defeated his closest opponent by 108 votes to become mayor. He appointed Tilghman city marshal and Heck his assistant, in which capacities they served until February, 1894.[13]

To facilitate the handling of federal matters in the Outlet, the Fifty-third Congress, in an act approved December 21, 1893, added two territorial justices.[14] President Cleveland appointed Guthrie attorney Andrew G. Curtin Bierer, formerly of Garden City, Kansas, and John L. McAtee of Maryland to these positions.[15] The membership of the Supreme Court for Oklahoma Territory thus increased to five, and the judicial districts likewise increased to that number. Judge Dale, who had succeeded Judge Green at Guthrie and Stillwater, became chief justice.

On February 3, 1894, the territory was redistricted, with these judges presiding: First Judicial District, Judge Dale, embracing Payne, Logan, Lincoln, and Q (Pawnee) counties; Second Judicial District, Judge Burford, embracing Canadian, Kingfisher, Blaine, Washita, and O (Garfield) counties; Third Judicial District, Judge Scott, embracing Oklahoma, Cleveland, and Pottawatomie counties; Fourth Judicial District, Judge Bierer, embracing P (Noble), K (Kay), L (Grant), and M (Woods) counties; Fifth Judicial District, Judge McAtee, embracing N (Woodward), Dewey, Custer, Day, Roger Mills, and Beaver counties. All that portion of the Osage Reservation south of the township line between townships 25 and 26 North was attached to Q (Pawnee) County, that portion of the reservation north of the line was attached to K (Kay) County, and the Ponca, Oto and Missouri reservations were attached to P (Noble) County for judicial purposes.[16]

With the Outlet organized into counties and under territorial law, Nix's office had no jurisdiction in the area except in federal offenses, such as cutting timber on government land, breaking the revenue or postal regulations, and selling whiskey to Indians. For such as robbery and murder, his jurisdiction lay only in the Osage, Wichita, Kiowa-Comanche-Apache, and other Indian reservations not ceded for settlement within Oklahoma. Otherwise, these crimes belonged to the sheriffs of the counties in which they were committed, and unless the reward was tempting enough to make a posse for it alone, federal marshals received no pay for going after train and bank bandits. In the general attempt to apprehend and punish these criminals, however, Nix again assured the sheriffs of all possible assistance and continued his policy of deputizing qualified local officers, enabling them to pursue fugitives into the reservations and across county boundaries.[17]

In Grant County, for example, on November 11, 1893, a rancher named Hendrickson went to Deputy Sheriff Paul Jones at Pond Creek and complained that "certain parties were stealing his and his neighbors' cattle and driving them to Kansas . . . stating he knew the cattle thieves to be cowards and easy to arrest." Jones procured warrants and, accompanied by Hendrickson, "drove to the abode of the thieves five miles west." They found the two rustlers in a small cabin. The outlaws opened fire with Winchesters from the cabin door, "shooting Mr. Hendrickson and killing him

178

instantly." Jones returned the fire "until his clothes were riddled with lead and the top of his hat blown off." The men escaped. "A posse . . . followed the outlaws into the sand hills" without capturing them.[18]

Satisfied that the rustlers had been operating across the territorial border, Nix assigned Deputy Marshal Pat Murphy to assist Grant County officers. On October 26, they learned, two carloads of cattle "consigned to the commission firm of C. W. Keys & Co. and netting $1365" had been received at the National Stock Yards in St. Louis. The stock had been shipped from Wichita in the name of Frank Johnson of Caldwell and was accompanied by a man representing himself as Frank Johnson. The cattle were yarded; Johnson received $100 cash, and the balance, subject to his draft, was placed in a bank at Winfield, Kansas. The Oklahoma officers learned that the cattle had been "offered at Wichita, but not sold, it appearing that the commission house there would not guarantee to buyers that they were not stolen." The stockyard authorities at Wichita wired St. Louis to hold the cattle, and on November 20, the officers arrived with John Moffit of Harper, Kansas, who claimed most of the stock, the rest having come from the territory. "Prompt steps were taken to garnishee the money sent to the Winfield bank . . . and Keys & Co. made good to Moffit the $100 paid Johnson." By November 20, Johnson had been identified as Frank Brydson, "living on the claim of Charles Neal near Pond Creek." It was Neal and Brydson whom Deputy Jones and Hendrickson had attempted to arrest on November 11.[19]

On Saturday, November 18, Deputy Marshal William Banks joined Custer County officers in their search for bandits who held up the Hightower store and post office at Arapaho:

It was a cold, raw day. The wind blew straight from the north, accompanied by a drizzle of rain that was almost sleet. The night lowered dark and dreary, and none were astir on the streets. . . . About 8:30 o'clock, Mr. and Mrs. Hightower, Judge VanTrees and daughter, Dora, 'Squire Trigg and Mr. Haney were sitting in the Post office store waiting the coming of mail. Four men quietly stepped in with Winchesters and remarked: "We've got you, boys; throw up your hands."

They then ordered Mr. Hightower to open his safe, from which they took about six hundred dollars of his money and two hundred and fifty dollars that A. G. Boon had deposited with him for safe keeping. They also took his fine watch and a plentiful supply of canned goods and blankets.

The raid over, they ordered the little company to file out to the rear of the store, and two stood guard while two mounted and then the mounted ones guarded while the other two made ready, and on a signal they all disappeared in the darkness.[20]

Banks and his posse started in pursuit Sunday morning and tracked them as far as Dead Woman on the Wichita Reservation, where the trail was lost.

The varied, widening task facing Nix's office is further illustrated by these excerpts from the *State Capital* and the *Oklahoma Daily Press-Gazette* for the four-week period from November 12 through December 10, 1893:

Yesterday was a big day at the federal jail. There were seventeen new prisoners brought in — fourteen full blood Indians from the Seminole, Sac and Fox and Shawnee countries.

R. A. Norvell, who was confined here during the summer months for selling whiskey to the Cheyenne and Arapaho Indians, but who got into the confidence of the turnkeys and was turned out as trusty and ran off the first of September, was brought back yesterday in irons and now occupies a cell in the steel cage. He was captured at Enid.

S. S. Nix committed to jail last night Chas. Vail, alias Chas. F. McDonald, on advice received from New Mexico, where it is claimed the prisoner is wanted for adultery. He was arrested at Oklahoma City.

Hugh Miller, charged with perjury, and James Colbert, charged with murder, were taken to Stillwater this morning for trial.

Deputy Marshal Joe Pentecost arrested Sam Collins, alias Kid Hogan, in the strip this week for horse stealing. The Kid has a record as a horse thief. In bringing his prisoner through Stillwater the local authorities insisted he be tried there. Habeas corpus proceedings were instituted. Joe went before Judge Dale, who had just convened district court, and the judge took immediate action on the case, with the result that the prisoner was bound over in the sum of $800. It was the first case heard by Judge Dale at Stillwater.

Eulallio Horto, a Mexican, confined in the federal jail on the charge of rape brought against him by a Mexican woman in the Cheyenne country, was taken to El Reno yesterday [for trial].

John M. Fuller . . . has been confined in the federal jail for ku-kluxing settlers over in the strip.

John Jones, of African-Creek descent, was brought in yesterday from Tecumseh by Officer Chas. Fults, on the charge of wholesale hog stealing, and lodged in the federal inn.

Thomas Baker . . . is doing fifteen days to balance accounts for introducing and disposing of corn juice in the Osage country.

John Dean, colored, and Jim Green, a white man, were taken to El

180

Reno this morning by Deputy Marshal Madsen for trial. Dean is charged with horse stealing and Green is charged with butchering cattle that were not his own.

Deputy Marshal Heck Thomas passed down yesterday on the noon train . . . and delivered four prisoners from P [Noble] county to the federal jail. All were charged with larceny. We would advise the authorities to box them and ship them to the governor of Kansas [Lansing Prison]. Deputy Marshal Chas. Marx came in yesterday with three prisoners from the Osage country—Chas. Clyne, a white man, and Two Crows and wife, full blood Indians, all charged with handling corn juice.

John Plumer, his father and Jake Mosier were brought in from the Osage last night by Deputy Marshal Robacker. They are all charged with illegally dealing in live pork and were placed in the U.S. jail to await preliminary.

Miffed by the many liquor arrests in the Osage, the *Jordan Valley Journal*[21] at Cleveland criticized

the actions of the majority of the United States deputies [who] seem to have no other business than to go around and work up malicious prosecution against the poor, harmless, dissipating red men . . . and even our most honorable citizens. A great deal of horse stealing is going on in and along the borders of Q [Pawnee] county, and it appears that no effort is being made by the federal officers to stop it. Why do you marshals not go after the Ingalls bandits and the horse thieves of the Osage nation?

The *Guthrie Daily Leader* of November 27 pointed out that

the most common criminals these deputies have to deal with are the lawless characters who persist in introducing and selling ardent spirits in the Indian countries. From one to fifteen men are arrested every day by the deputies, but thanks to Nix's keen-eyed minions this hitherto stereotyped charge is growing rare. The deputies have the whiskey-shovers, as well as other classes of lawbreakers, on the run.

And the editor of the *Pawnee Democrat*[22] barbed his *Journal* counterpart with the observation that

some have been ushered into this world to kick at everything on general principles of adamantic infernality. The U.S. Marshal strives to secure the very best possible deputy service. If he has made bad appointments, he should be credibly informed of such reprobates on his force . . . not indiscriminately complained against . . . then if the recreant deputy is not discharged or his misconduct not properly explained, to censure the Marshal would be within the limits of right.

Meanwhile, the good citizen will aid the officers of the law in all of their just undertakings and will not howl at everything that they may do because of a fancied popularity of such roar.

The *Journal*, however, had made a point. The Ingalls fight had by no means "broken Doolin's power." Four times in one week, the gang had "made public appearances" in settlements along Hell's Fringe, "only to again disappear for a day and reappear at some other point," and had compelled many farmers to feed them and their horses. It was rumored that the band "now consists of a dozen heavily armed men . . . undoubtedly preparing to rob some of the banks in the new Outlet towns or some heavily loaded train on the Santa Fe or Rock Island roads." Nix's office was convinced that "four Doolin cronies had pulled the November robbery at Arapaho," and on December 6, he received "reliable information that the outlaws had left the Stillwater vicinity, their objective points Hoffman, Charles & Conklin's store at Chandler, and the Sac and Fox Agency. People at these places were warned and armed."[23]

No raid occurred. On the evening of January 3, 1894, however, two of the gang entered the store and post office at Clarkson, a Dunker community above Cowboy Flats just across the Payne County line, and "with the help of six-shooters compelled Postmaster Waltman to hold up his hands and keep mum while they looted the place of supplies, tobacco, all money and registered matter, backed out the door, mounted their horses, and after firing a few shots, rode hurriedly toward the Cimarron."[24] A few days later, a drug salesman named Pryer was robbed of his gold watch and sixty dollars at Lost Creek Crossing south of Stillwater by four men led by Tulsa Jack. The following day, a young man who traveled for the Nix and Halsell Company at Guthrie was robbed west of Perkins by the same bandits. Obtaining only some pocket change, they scattered his samples in the roadway and warned that if they ever caught him with so little money again, it would mean his life.

Such outrages stirred the newspaper controversy to fever pitch. The safety of citizens and property could never be achieved until the last member of the Wild Bunch was dead or behind prison bars! On January 16, 1894, Marshal Nix wrote Attorney General Olney:

> By reason of their thorough knowledge of the unsettled portions of the Territory, these men have been able to establish and maintain retreats, and when pursued and pressed by the authorities, flee from one rendezvous to another, making it impracticable to effect a capture.
>
> A very important element which contributes towards the safety of these outlaws . . . is that the inhabitants of the parts of the Territory

infested by them are either on friendly terms with them, or they have been so terrorized and intimidated by threats against their lives and destruction of their property, that they dare not and do not take any step or volunteer the slightest information that would lead to the discovery of their acts, whereabouts, or intentions.

The difficulties attending the organization of a posse of men possessing the necessary qualifications to make a successful raid on the outlaws have been and now are the want of funds to equip and conduct such a campaign and also the want of an adequate pecuniary inducement to tempt them . . . to expose themselves to almost sure death under the unerring aim of the bandits. . . . I earnestly recommend that the U.S. Marshal of Oklahoma be authorized to organize such a posse not to exceed fifteen men . . . that their expenses be limited to Three ($3.00) Dollars per diem for each man . . . and as extra expense the cost of preparation in the way of ammunition, hiring of horses, etc. I would also suggest that the killing of horses owned or hired by the men be considered such an expense as they would be reimbursed for, because of the entire probability that such losses will occur and the men are poorly able to stand such a loss.

While it is far preferable to adopt the proposition as stated, I will make the recommendation, if the Department deems it advisable to offer a reward in lieu of paying the expenses, that a reward of Five Hundred ($500) Dollars be offered for the capture, dead or alive, of . . . Bill Dalton; Bill Doolin; George Newcomb, alias 'Bitter Creek', alias "Slaughter Kid"; "Tulsa Jack"; and "Dynamite Dick."

I . . . desire to impress upon you the importance of early action, as the people of the Territory are appealing to me daily for relief from the terrible suspense hanging over them by reason of the depredations committed by this band of vicious and desperate characters.[25]

Before the attorney general could act on the request, the Wild Bunch struck again.

The new, fast-growing Strip town of Pawnee basked on a rolling prairie and woodland in a horseshoe bend of Black Bear Creek. Across the creek east lay the old Pawnee Indian school and reservation. Every three months, the Indians received annuity payments approximating one hundred thousand dollars, nearly all of which was spent with the more than one hundred merchants of the town. There was also a large trade from the Osage Indians, whose reservation lay only twelve miles distant. One of the leading financial institutions in the Outlet, the Farmers and Citizens Bank, was housed in an elegant, two-story stone building. C. L. Berry, formerly paying teller at the National Bank of Guthrie, was cashier.

At 3:30 P.M. on January 23, the town was startled by the discharge of two volleys from firearms. At the same moment, three horses went tearing down the hill northwest toward Black Bear Creek. Two of the horses bore one rider. On the third, in addition to the man in the saddle, rode cashier Berry.

Only minutes before, Berry had been cashing a check for Dolph Carrion when Bill Doolin entered the bank with revolver drawn and demanded, "Hands up!" He was followed instantly by another armed man, later identified as Tulsa Jack, who stood guard on the customer while Doolin stepped behind the counter, thrust the muzzle of his six-shooter against Berry's head, and ordered him to open the vault. The time lock on the vault was set for four o'clock, when daily balances were made, but Berry turned the dial. When it did not open, Doolin snarled: "Fail on that again, and I'll blow your brains out!" Berry made a second attempt, explaining that the vault could not be opened for half an hour. Finally, Doolin "put his ear to the safe, and hearing the timepiece running, seemed satisfied." Taking $262 that had been left on the counter for ordinary business, he "marched Berry out the door and around the corner of Stewart's hotel," where Bitter Creek Newcomb waited with the horses. Doolin took Berry up behind him to prevent citizens opening fire on them, and the bandits dashed down the street, firing two volleys into Bolton's Meat Market, where Dolph Carrion had fled to give the alarm. Outside town, Doolin ordered Berry to "pile off," which the cashier did "with alacrity." Tulsa Jack, who had lost his hat in the wild ride, took the banker's good beaver cap to replace it and "bade him adieu." A quickly organized posse met Berry walking back to town. At Black Bear Creek, they found signs where the trio had been joined by "four other riders" who "were either in the bank or the near vicinity and will get their pro rata of the $262." The posse lost the trail of the robbers at Gray Horse Ford.[26]

Although the Pawnee raid was the responsibility of local authorities, the *Stillwater Eagle-Gazette*,[27] smarting from the Ingalls fight and the recent Payne County robberies, labeled it "another chapter in the criminal history of this desperate gang of outlaws" and demanded: "Where, oh where, is Marshal Nix and his brave (?) deputies? They seem to be on hand when there is some inoffensive Indian to run in for selling his red brother a drink of whiskey, but conspicuous for their absence when they are needed." Other newspapers declared that Nix "should either get a move on, or surrender the United States to the bandits." The *State Capital*[28] alleged that the Wild Bunch never had been far away but had been seen "off

184

and on for two weeks at a farm eight or ten miles northeast of Guthrie."

These reports, reaching Washington, brought a biting inquiry from Major Frank Strong, general agent of the Department of Justice. Nix, who was confined to his home with a serious attack of influenza, directed Chief Deputy Hale to write Strong on January 31 that

> a few days prior to the Pawnee robbery, I had information that these outlaws intended to raid some of the towns in Oklahoma. My information was not explicit enough to enable me to guard any particular town. I notified the towns most exposed to these outlaws of the contemplated raid, but in this case it did no good.
>
> My deputies are ready at a moment's notice to take the field if Washington informs me that the Department has decided it would give a reward for each of the men I have mentioned, or in lieu thereof pay the expenses of a posse to hunt down the desperadoes. If impossible to have both a reward and expenses, I would respectfully suggest it would be better to pay the expenses. . . . This gang is well organized and each is a man of undoubted courage. This they have proved in actual fight. They know every bridle path in the country and are splendidly mounted and armed, and their protectors and friends are numerous. Any posse that may go after them will do so with the full knowledge that some of them will never return alive should they succeed in trailing the gang down.[29]

There was no response from Major Strong, so Nix wired Attorney General Olney on February 15, asking: "Will authority be granted me to pay expenses of posse as asked for in my letter of Janu. 16."[30] By telegram on February 17, Olney requested the "time, force and amount of money required to exterminate the outlaws," and Nix promptly replied that

> it will require some little time. . . . I will need fifteen men to accomplish the work, expenses not to exceed $3.00 per day for each man, and pay for all horses that may be killed in the fight.
>
> At the above estimate, the total cost will not exceed $1350, with strong probability that one-half that amount will suffice.
>
> If my request is granted, answer by wire.[31]

On February 26, Nix was authorized expenses necessary to "kill, capture or drive" the Wild Bunch out of the country. Any rewards for members of the gang were to come from sources other than the government.

By this time, two more formidable characters had joined the

gang: William F. Raidler, alias Little Bill (to distinguish him from Doolin), and Richard West, alias Little Dick.

Raidler was twenty-eight years old, of good Pennsylvania Dutch ancestry, and well-educated. The cattle ranges early fascinated him, and he had worked several years for Oscar Halsell, first in Texas and later in Oklahoma, where he became a close friend of Doolin.

West was as ignorant of his origin as anybody. "I was just dropped on the prairie somewhere," he once said. "Ma died soon after, and pa broke his life-long rule about sleepin' under a roof. He got caught, and I ain't seen him since." West first appeared as a spindle-legged, sallow-faced waif who washed dishes in greasy-spoon restaurants until he was picked up on the streets of Decatur, Texas, in 1881 by the foreman of the Three Circle Ranch and taken to Clay County to wrangle horses. The following spring, Halsell employed him to bring his remuda north when he established his ranch in Oklahoma. West was then sixteen years old, "wild as a cat and full of cussedness." He would eat his meals away from others, and, summer or winter, he always slept outside. As he grew older and put meat on his bones, his animal qualities disappeared somewhat. He continued to eat and sleep in the open, however, and the wild look never left his eyes. He worked for Halsell until the opening in 1889, then drifted into the Osage, where he worked at odd jobs and discovered a cave which Doolin often had used as a stopping place while riding with the Daltons. West's habit of sleeping in the open while others sought cozy beds and warm houses would make him a valuable lookout for the Wild Bunch. With this in mind, Doolin had invited him to transfer his gear to their hideout on the Cimarron.

On Saturday morning, March 10, a dispatch from Fort Leavenworth appeared in the *Kansas City Times*, which had wide circulation in Oklahoma Territory, describing the intended movements of the army paymaster, the amount of money going to certain posts, and the means of transportation by which it would reach these points. An estimated $10,000 was to be sent by Wells Fargo to Woodward to pay the troops at Fort Supply. How the information got into the hands of the *Times* correspondent is not known, since such matters usually were kept secret.

About one o'clock Tuesday morning, March 13, two men entered the railroad hotel at Woodward and went upstairs to the room of station agent George W. Rourke. They awakened him with six-shooters and told him to dress quietly, then marched him downstairs and over to the depot. En route, they encountered a boy named Sam Peters, who was loitering near the station. Peters was "ordered to throw up his hands and join the procession." Inside the depot, "the railroad safe was opened and robbed of all the currency and checks it contained, which were put in a sack brought for that purpose." The robbers then turned their attention to the small route safe. "Rourke was made to carry the sack and the Peters boy carried the safe about a quarter of a mile east of the depot where it was broken open. It contained nothing to reward the robbers for their trouble. They then marched Rourke and Peters over to the stockyards where their horses were hitched" and mounted. The leader ordered Rourke to hang the money sack on the pommel of his saddle; the other robber "handed the boy $1.50 in silver for his services." The two men rode off in a southwesterly direction. "Neither was masked . . . they were on red bay horses."[32]

Superintendent D. H. Rhoads of the Santa Fe wired Marshal Nix a description of the robbers shortly after daylight. Nix wired Deputy Marshal Jack Love to "start in pursuit of the bold bandits and capture them dead or alive." Love, already apprized of the holdup, "organized a strong posse and took the trail at once." Colonel Dangerfield Parker, commanding Fort Supply, detailed Lieutenant Kirby Walker and twenty cavalrymen for the hunt. Amos Chapman, veteran scout of the Canadian, also was notified, and he organized a company of Cheyennes to "cut the flight of the outlaws toward the bad lands along the river."[33]

Nix and Chief Deputy Hale hurried to Woodward to conduct a full investigation. "Undoubtedly eight men were concerned," for there were indications that six other riders had joined the pair a short distance from the stockyards. Excitement ran high and business was suspended as the news was flashed to other western towns and settlements. A courier from Ochiltree, Texas, brought word that a band of riders answering the description of the bandits had been seen in the vicinity, traveling west. Love and his posse headed that direction, obtained fresh horses at Mose Zeigler's ranch on South Wolf Creek, and continued in hot pursuit. By this time, the outlaws had crossed the Texas border and had vanished in the canyons and gulches near Lipscomb.[34]

On March 14, Major Smith, the army paymaster, arrived at Woodward. He was

non-communicative, and refused to say anything about the money except that . . . the express company was responsible and would be held good for it. . . . He served official notice by wire upon the War Depart-

187

ment that the money had been stolen, and will wait for instructions before proceeding. . . . His chief clerk, however, stated the exact sum [in the packages that were taken] was $6,540.[35]

It was the "unanimous opinion of the Marshal's office," and Woodward authorities "are certain," that "the two who robbed the depot were Bill Dalton and Bill Doolin."[36]

XI Arkansas Tom Gets His—

THE WHEREABOUTS OF THE WILD BUNCH for several weeks after the Woodward holdup is conjecture. There is evidence that the gang, returning from Texas through the Indian reservations south of the settled portions of the territory, crossed the Canadian at the northeast corner of the Wichita-Caddo Reservation in a beeline northeast to their old haunts around Ingalls and in the Pawnee country.

On March 28, Thomas C. Sebring, a farmer living near Edmond, arrived in Guthrie and reported that the outlaws had camped on his place the night before. As he was driving in a bunch of stray cows about half-past eight, a band of horsemen, "dust begrimed and looking rather dilapidated," rode up and asked "whether he had any victuals in his house." He and his wife scraped together enough food to satisfy their "keen appetites," and when the meal was finished, one of the men asked for the bill. "An amount agreed upon was promptly paid"; then the band retired to a small grove near by, built a fire, and began making preparations to spend the night. Later, when Sebring complained about their horses barking his trees, the man replied: "Damn the trees! We'll pay for them." The nettled farmer asked sharply, "Who are you fellows?" and the man said, "Since you're so damned curious, my name is Bill Dalton." This upset Sebring. He tried to suppress his excitement by asking, "Ain't you fellows afraid of being nabbed?" "Naw—we ain't much," replied a gruff, older man, who was warming his hands at the fire. "But say, do you get the papers? Has the government offered that big reward for us yet?" Sebring shook his head, and the man chuckled. "I guess they're waitin' for us to come in." Afterward, the outlaws refused to be disturbed. When Sebring tried to make more conversation, the man at the fire told him: "That's the graveyard, pard; we're tired and need rest. Do any queer business and you'll croak." Sebring averred that he "slept soundly during the night, looked out his window next morning and found the grove deserted."[1]

The day Sebring made his report, a group of riders, "pretty certain" to be part of the Wild Bunch, "armed to the teeth with Winchesters and six-shooters," raided the claim of a man named Hubatka east of Stillwater and escaped toward the Cimarron.[2] On March 30, the *Stillwater Eagle-Gazette* reported that

> a gentleman in today from Ingalls . . . says that the people there live in a constant state of terror from this gang . . . which are making their headquarters at certain places in the town whose owners sympathize with them. Several persons have been held up, and several horses have been stolen in the vicinity.

Nix[3] credited these activities to other scattered bands of ruffians that infested the area:

> My officers had been able to keep hot on the trail and Doolin and Dalton were worried. It seemed no longer possible to conduct their escapades with the wild abandon that had characterized their earlier depredations.

At Ingalls, Dr. Pickering wrote in his diary:

> Danimite, Tulsa [Jack], Pierce & others . . . staid around the Dunns. Danimite ordered a big gun sent from Tulsa the Marshalls got onto it & watched for him thinking he would come in at night to get it but he rode in at 2 P M got his gun & was getting out of town before they knew it They started after him & had a running fight from there to Turky Track ranch they killed 2 horses from under him they thought they had him surrounded in the timber there & sent for more help but when they got it & searched thorough he was gone. Pierce and Tulsa still staid here. . . . Doolin disappeared and no one knew where, also Edith Ellsworth They probely went off together. . . . Dalton drifted away from the crowd.

Dalton was believed to be hiding in the Chickasaw Nation. A few days after the Woodward holdup, his wife and two children, whom he brought from California after the Coffeyville disaster, disappeared from the family home at Kingfisher. Officers traced them to Ardmore, where "the trail vanished completely."

W. H. (Bill) Carr was one of the oldest deputy marshals in Oklahoma. He had served under Marshal Jones and Marshal Walker at Wichita, and after the 1889 opening, he worked in the Indian Nations for the federal courts at Fort Smith, Arkansas, and Paris, Texas. After the Pottawatomie-Shawnee opening, he "settled down as a storekeeper" at Sacred Heart, a residential community of the Sacred Heart Catholic Mission north of the Canadian and near the Seminole border. He still carried his federal commissions, and the last week of March, 1894, Nix wired him that Dalton "might be in his area."

About 8 P.M., Sunday, April 1, "Bill Dalton and one of the gang called Slaughter Kid [Newcomb]" entered the store to buy corn for their horses. Carr was waiting on a seventeen-year-old boy named Lee Hardwick. Glancing up, he "recognized Dalton and the Kid, as he had seen them often." Pistol in hand, he "walked from behind the counter and told Dalton and the Kid to consider themselves under arrest, he having a warrant for Dalton. Kid cried, 'I guess not,' and whipped a revolver from his overcoat pocket." Both men fired simultaneously. "Carr hit the desperado in the left shoulder, receiving in return a wound in his arm above the wrist. This made him drop his pistol. He stooped to get it with his left hand and Kid fired again, the ball passing under him, slivering the floor." Young Hardwick grabbed a shotgun; Dalton whirled and fired at him, but missed him. "Carr raised from the floor and received a ball that struck him two inches above the navel and came out to the right of his backbone." But the old marshal managed to stay on his feet, "firing three more times with his left hand" as the outlaws fled through the door into the darkness.[4] Deputy Marshal W. E. Hocker investigated the shooting. He wired Nix from Purcell on April 3 that

> when I left [Sacred Heart] today about noon, Carr was doing as well as could be expected. He was too sore to think of moving him to town. . . . The men [Dalton and Newcomb] were last seen in the Seminole country. They stopped at an Indian woman's and dressed the wound in the shoulder of Slaughter [Kid].

While Newcomb nursed his second wound received at the hand of a U.S. deputy marshal and dodged posses with Dalton in the Seminole Nation, the rest of the Wild Bunch rendezvoused with Doolin in northwestern Arkansas. A few hours' ride to the north lay Southwest City, a town of about one thousand souls in the heart of a thriving farming and mining section in the extreme southwest corner of Missouri. Its western limit was the Cherokee Nation border. Doolin himself had cased the town's bank and found it "easy and fit to be picked." At three o'clock on the afternoon of May 10, seven outlaws (Doolin, Pierce, Tulsa Jack, Dynamite Dick, Red Buck, Bill Raidler, and Little Dick West) swooped down on the community from the south in one of the most daring raids of their career.[5]

"They did the job in a very business-like manner. Two of them were stationed on the outside and three entered the bank with a sack and two others guarded the horses. . . . The robbers were about ten minutes going through the bank, afterward mounted their horses and started for the Nation at full speed." Those few minutes were time enough for the hill people to arm themselves with such weapons as they could lay hands on, and the gang was forced to fight its way out of the city, firing at anyone on the sidewalks who seemed to offer resistance. A bullet broke the leg of Mart Pembree, a shoemaker. Deputy U.S. Marshal Simpson F. Melton attempted to stop them and was shot in the thigh. J. C. Seaborn, former state auditor and one of Missouri's foremost citizens, and his brother Oscar ran from a hardware store as the robbers swept past. One of the outlaws (West) sent a bullet in the direction of the two men. It passed through Oscar's body without serious effect and lodged in the groin of J. C., who was directly behind him. "As the gang was leaving the outskirts, someone fired several shots at them, killing a horse and wounding a robber, but it is not known how badly he was hurt. He immediately secured another horse from a farmer who was passing and followed his pals. . . . A posse was made up and started in pursuit," but lost them in the Cherokee Nation near Grand River. The robbery netted the gang "between $3,000 and $4,000."[6] J. C. Seaborn died a few days later, and the governor of Missouri posted a reward of $500 for each member of the Wild Bunch, dead or alive.

The outlaws made their way back through the Nations to their old haunts on the Cimarron. On May 17, 1894, Arkansas Tom Jones, the companion they had abandoned in the fight at Ingalls, went on trial at Stillwater before Judge Frank Dale for murder in the first degree in the killing of Deputy Marshal Tom Hueston.

A grand jury in November, 1893, also had indicted Jones for the death of Speed and Shadley. However, Payne County Attorney Sterling Price King, a former judge who believed that "miscreants who fell into his clutches should be prosecuted without fear or favor in such a manner that the law will be fully vindicated," chose the Hueston case, in which he had compiled the strongest evidence, for prosecution. Jones was arraigned at Stillwater on November 26 but was taken back to Guthrie in early February, 1894, because of raids by the Wild Bunch and rumors that "new plans had been laid to release him." On May 14, he was returned to the Stillwater jail.[7]

Before the trial began, Judge Dale received a handful of letters, purported to have been written by members of the Doolin gang, saying his life was in danger. "The whole town is in terror . . . the friends of these outlaws are feared as much as the outlaws themselves." Sheriff Burdick provided a bodyguard for Dale to and from court and at the hotel where he was staying, and a guard was provided at the home of King. The first day of the hearing, more threats poured in—the gang was "expected to attack the court and rescue Tom." Dale was not a nervous man, but he thought the situation "sufficiently critical" to order Marshal Nix "to immediately send a strong posse of deputy marshals." The message was delivered to Nix's residence at Midnight, May 17. By morning, Deputies Hixon, Thomas, Forrest Halsell, Jim Masterson, and Tillman Lilly had arrived in Stillwater.[8]

The trial progressed. "No one was allowed to enter the courtroom without first being searched for concealed weapons . . . as further precaution, guards are distributed about the town at key intervals," and such a "veritable walking arsenal is stationed about the court house that any attempt by the outlaws to rescue the prisoner will surely cost them their lives."[9] Arkansas Tom did not take the witness stand to deny the charge. His lawyer contended that it was physically impossible for him to have killed Hueston from the hole "punched in the hotel roof with the gun" and that he was "an innocent bystander in the fight." Prosecutor King asked that the jury be allowed to visit the scene and judge for themselves the veracity of his contention. The request was granted. The jury made "a first hand survey of the location" and "after deliberating the cause all night [Saturday, May 19] found a verdict for manslaughter in the first degree." On May 21, Judge Dale sentenced Jones to fifty years in the penitentiary at Lansing.[10]

Jones "received the sentence with that composed demeanor and stolid indifference" which had characterized him since his arrest. His motion for a new trial was overruled, and his attorney gave notice of appeal to the Territorial Supreme Court. Judge Dale set his appeal bond at ten thousand dollars, and Jones was whisked back to the Guthrie jail by Sheriff Burdick and the deputy marshals. He was kept in a steel cage just opposite the jail entrance with

John Bray and Lock Langley, each sentenced to eighteen months for horse stealing; George Howell, charged with murder, and C. D. Watkins, with impersonating a United States marshal. At 4 o'clock yesterday afternoon [June 7], Watkins asked Jailer Magill for the privilege of a bath. The bath room is downstairs and he had to be taken out into the corridor. On his return, when Magill unlocked the lever that opened the cage door, Watkins instead of walking in stepped behind Magill and attempted to take hold of him. Magill covered him with his revolver and the fellow threw up his hands. At the same time Arkansas Tom and the other prisoners rushed out of the cage. Arkansas Tom reached for Magill but Magill switched his gun on him. Seeing that the jig was up all five prisoners went back to the cell. All this happened quicker than it takes to tell it. The fact that five men . . . though within a few feet of the open door and in sight of liberty . . . were cowed into submission by the courage of one officer is sufficient commentary. . . . Arkansas Tom has made several attempts to break jail before, and freely acknowledges that this was a deliberate plan to escape.[11]

His time for obtaining bond having expired, Jones again was removed to Stillwater, where commitment papers were issued. Then he was taken to Orlando and put on the train to Lansing. When it was reviewed by the Territorial Supreme Court, the judgment of the Payne County District Court was affirmed.[12] The *Stillwater Eagle-Gazette*[13] commented: "Crime is easy but retribution is hard."

The Ingalls killings had so aroused the ire of Chief Justice Dale that after the trial he called Marshal Nix into his chambers and gave him "a most unusual order," perhaps the only one of its kind ever issued by an Oklahoma judge. "Marshal, this is serious," he said. "I have reached the conclusion that the only good outlaw is a dead one. I hope you will instruct your deputies in the future to bring them in dead."[14]

Since Washington had not found it possible to pay both a reward and the expenses of his man hunters, Nix deposited two thousand dollars of his own money in a posse fund to ensure success of the operation. This, together with rewards offered by express companies, banks, and other corporations, made Doolin alone worth five thousand dollars. Heck Thomas, Bill Tilghman, and Chris Madsen were chosen to lead the campaign. Through their efforts in the desperate months ahead, they became known as Oklahoma's Three Guardsmen.

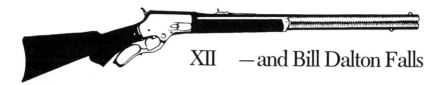

XII — and Bill Dalton Falls

BILL DALTON AND BITTER CREEK NEWCOMB separated after the Sacred
Heart fight. Bitter Creek drifted back to his old haunts on the
Cimarron, and Dalton rode to his hideout on the Houston Wallace
farm near Elk, twenty-five miles northwest of Ardmore. With many
rewards offered for Doolin, dead or alive, Dalton must have considered him too risky to ride with, traveling in large groups in the
territory too dangerous, or perhaps he finally had come to resent
the fact that since its inception the Doolin-Dalton enterprise had
been almost entirely dominated by this "mentally awkward Arkan-
sawyer" his brothers had dumped before the Coffeyville disaster.
Whatever his reason, he and Doolin parted company after the
Woodward robbery. Dalton, however, had no idea of quitting the
business that had brought the family and his own wife and children
shame and disgrace. Already he had planned a spectacular foray of
his own in faraway Gregg County, Texas, near the Louisiana border. Perhaps Bitter Creek's wound at Sacred Heart had prevented
the little outlaw from accompanying him.

Dalton's new companions were Houston Wallace's brother, Jim
Wallace, an inept country loafer using the alias George Bennett,
who in early 1894 married the daughter of a respectable Gregg
County farmer but deserted her, returning to the Chickasaw Nation, and Big Asa and Jim Knight, a pair of outlaw brothers working
for the Brown and Flewellen logging camp near Longview. Dalton
and Jim Wallace joined the Knights in mid-April. While Doolin and
the others were dodging Indian Territory posses in their flight from
the Southwest City raid, Dalton was fishing in the Sabine River,
studying the lay of the Texas town and the habits of its citizens.

At 3 P.M. on May 23, the four men rode into an alley behind the
First National Bank. Wallace and Jim Knight guarded the horses;
Dalton and Big Asa went inside. Dalton wore a long gray duster

195

with a Winchester concealed in its folds. He handed a note to Cashier Tom Clemmons:

Home, May 23

The First National Bank, Longview
This will introduce to you Charles Speckelmeyer, who wants some money and is going to have it. B and F.

It was thought later the signature represented "Bill and Friend." The note was written in pencil "in a fairly good hand" on the back of a poster, and Clemmons, thinking it "an importunate subscription to some charity entertainment," started to donate, but Dalton pointed his Winchester and told him to "hold up." Then Big Asa Knight "rushed into the side wire door and grabbed the cash. The other bank officials were ordered to hold up their hands. The robbers hurriedly emptied the vaults, securing $2,000 in ten-dollar bills numbered 9, and nine $20 bills numbered 20, and a quantity of unsigned bank notes." Meanwhile, the guards in the alley had been spotted. City Marshal Muckley and Deputy Will Stevens opened fire on them. The guards returned the fire and

> would yell at everyone who came in sight and shoot at them instantly. . . . This made the robbers in the bank nervous, and they hurried the officials out and told them to run to the horses. This was done to keep the citizens from shooting, but as the bullets flew thick and fast, the bank men ran around the corner . . . all escaped unhurt. George Buckingham, who was shooting at the robbers, was killed. City Marshal Muckley received a Winchester ball in the bowels. The ball glanced off some silver dollars he had in his pocket, which may save his life. J. W. McQueen, a saloonkeeper, ran out in the alley and was shot in the body and it is thought mortally wounded [he recovered]. Charles S. Leonard, who was walking through the court house yard, was shot in the left hand. Deputy Stevens was not hurt, though he stood in short range and killed one of the robbers. The others, seeing their comrade dead, remarked: "Poor George." He was identified as George Bennett . . . who was well known here. He was dressed like a cowboy, with high heeled boots and spurs, a belt full of cartridges and two double action revolvers. His horse, which was captured, had 300 rounds of ammunition strapped to the saddle. . . . In the thick of the fighting, the robbers mounted their horses and dashed away, furiously, firing as they sped. In a few minutes a score or more of mounted and armed men hotly pursued them.[1]

The posse lost the trail in the pine forests to the north.

At Longview, the bank offered a five hundred dollar reward and citizens added two hundred dollars for the capture of the bandits, dead or alive. The sweatband in the dead robber's hat bore the label of W. O. Duston's Big Cash Store in Ardmore. Sheriff John C. Howard wired Deputy Marshal Seldon T. Lindsey, who worked the Chickasaw and Choctaw nations for the Eastern Judicial District of Texas at Paris, stating that he believed the bandits were from Indian Territory and probably would cross Red River somewhere near Clarksville.

Lindsey and a posseman named Castleman went to Doaksville, across the river from Clarksville in the Choctaw Nation. They learned that the outlaws had passed there "about eight hours before . . . armed with Winchesters, their horses nearly played out," and were last seen going northwest. Lindsey and Castleman trailed them toward Kosoma. On May 29, the deputies found their horses in a cane brake on the Kiamichi River northwest of Antlers, "so exhausted from having been ridden so far and so long that one of the animals had to be shot." The same night, "three men fitting the bandits' descriptions stole fresh horses near Stringtown and headed west across the Muddy Boggy below Coalgate" into the Chickasaw Nation.[2]

Nothing more was learned of the robbers until June 4. Two men appeared at Duncan, thirty-five miles west of Elk, and bought a pair of mules and a wagon with $10 bills that "looked new, but had been wet and creased." When a telegram was sent to Longview, listing the numbers, they were identified as some of the unsigned notes taken in the holdup. The Texas bank refused to redeem them, and U.S. Marshal J. Shelby Williams at Paris wired Deputy Lindsey to be on the lookout for the team and vehicle.[3]

On the afternoon of June 7, Lindsey saw Houston Wallace, "accompanied by two women with sunbonnets pulled close to their faces," drive the wagon into Ardmore. The deputy decided to gather as much evidence as he could before flushing his quarry, so he began to shadow them. "The party proceeded to lay in a large stock of provisions and ammunition and purchased two cots, two pillows and a mattress at a furniture store—$200 worth in all, which Wallace paid in new National bank currency." Having read of the Longview robbery and knowing that the farmer was "proverbially broke," the store owner, Mike Gorman, "carried the bills to Judge [J. C.] Gibbons, U.S. commissioner, who got in touch with the Texas bank and found that the money belonged to them."[4]

Meanwhile, Lindsey had followed the trio to the express office, where Wallace, "presenting an order signed 'Hines', was given a large package. . . . His refusal to sign the receipt book precipitated matters. He was arrested on suspicion and the boxes broken into and found to contain nine quarts of whiskey. The entire party was arrested by Deputy Marshal Lindsey, Wallace for introducing in the Indian country, and the women for being accessories." Then began a questioning in which the farmer admitted the liquor was for "other people" staying at his place; the women, identifying themselves only as Mrs. Smith and Mrs. Pruitt, "refused to talk or verify where they lived," but from their "incautious remarks," Lindsey concluded that Mrs. Smith, "a pretty blond about twenty-seven years old," was the wife of "Hines" and that the Wallace home was the hideout of the Longview bandits. "The farmer was locked up, the women were placed under guard, and a posse at once organized for a raid on the freebooters' rendezvous."[5]

The posse, consisting of Deputies Lindsey, Ed Roberts, D. E. Booker, S. Leatherman, W. H. Glover, Wm. B. Freeman, Caleb Lawson ("Loss") Hart, and two local officers named Denton and Reynolds, reached the Wallace place at 7 A.M. on June 8.[6] The two-room shack faced south; there was a small barn about one hundred yards east of it and a fenced cornfield and feedlot to the southwest. A wooded draw ran north beyond the corn patch into a deep ravine, which paralleled the back of the house. While the others took up positions in the field and feedlot, Hart circled the barn to the rim of the ravine, and Lindsey started up the draw to cover the rear of the shack from the west.

At that moment, a man with "black curly hair, mustache and goatee, clad in a woolen shirt, black pants with yellow suspenders, and top boots," apparently anxious about the women and Wallace, who had failed to return during the night, came out on the porch and looked around. Seeing Lindsey creeping up the draw, he leaped back inside, grabbed a revolver, and jumped from a window on the north, running for the ravine. Hart, who was less than forty yards away, called for him to halt. "Quickening his pace, the man half turned to locate the voice and raised his revolver to fire. This move was the last voluntary act of his life. A .44 ball, hot from the deputy's Winchester, tore into his body at the waistband near the right rear suspender button, and with two convulsive leaps he fell." Hart raced to his side and seized his weapon. "Who are you? Where you from?" the deputy asked. The man glared up at him. Then he smiled, as if experiencing deep satisfaction at not having been recognized, and "expired without a word."[7]

The other officers rushed the house. Inside they found a group of frightened children: six boys and girls. A search of the premises turned up a large handmade calfskin suitcase containing "women shoes and clothes and a lot of silk cloth in bolts." Carefully rolled inside the bolts were "numerous crisp bills and a Longview bank sack," and " $275 was found concealed on the dead man." But the officers did not know "the importance of their game," and "their surprise was great when, in questioning the children, two of them, a small girl and a boy, admitted their name was Dalton."[8]

The officers obtained a hack and a wagon and put the body in the wagon. With some of the posse on horseback, some in the hack, and others guarding the corpse, the cortege started for Ardmore. A short distance from town, they met another wagon occupied by the women, who, because no charges had been preferred, had been released through the efforts of a local attorney. To the blonde woman, Deputy Lindsey said: "Mrs. Dalton, we have your dead husband and in your suitcase and on his person we found considerable money." She glanced in the hack which had come up, and seeing no body, replied: "I am not Mrs. Dalton, and you have not got Bill." The wagon then approached, and when the woman saw the corpse, she "broke down completely and in a hysterical voice admitted her identity and that the dead man was Bill Dalton."

Back in Ardmore, she told the officers how he had left their home in Merced County, California, to come to the Oklahoma country. They had

> kept up a regular correspondence, and though he requested me to address him under various names, I had no thought that he was living other than an honest life. When I came East to his mother's home near Kingfisher, he did not meet me on my arrival, and I was very much surprised. It was only when he came home on the following night during a terrible storm heavily armed that a suspicion that all was not right crossed my mind. When I asked him why he wore his pistols, he laughingly replied: "Oh, it is just for style." He left in the morning at daylight without saying where he was going and after that time I only saw him at long intervals, mostly at night at the home of some of his friends. Soon his name became prominent in the papers, always connecting him with some act of desperation, and gradually I, too, became cautious of his movements.
>
> We came to the Wallace place six weeks ago, where he had engaged board for myself and children, and he left immediately, saying he was going to Texas, and paid Mr. Wallace $40 for our board. I heard nothing more of him until May 30.[9]

She sent two telegrams, signing them Jennie Dalton. The first was to her father in San Francisco: "My husband, Bill Dalton, lies here dead. . . . I want his remains sent home." The other was addressed to Mrs. A. L. Dalton at Kingfisher: "Bill Dalton is here dead. Come at once if you wish to see him."[10]

Adeline Dalton had "scarcely recovered from a severe spell of sickness," and the news "prostrated her." Ben Dalton came to see the body. His lip quivered and his eyes filled with tears as he said, "Yes, this is Bill."[11] Like many others, he had expected to find his brother's death a mistake. Telegrams had been sent to interested railroads, banks, and express agencies, and every train brought eager residents from throughout the territories, "while the roads leading into Ardmore were lined with hundreds who came to view the remains," among them "numerous reputable citizens who knew there had been no mistake in the killing of the celebrated bandit chieftain."[12] Wrote *Daily Oklahoman* correspondent Clarence B. Douglas:

> Stretched out on a pine board in the rooms of Undertaker Appolis, on Caddo street . . . Bill Dalton, terror of the Southwest, the mention of whose name made bank cashiers from Kansas City to the Rio Grande shudder . . . lies stiff and cold . . . a .44 Winchester hole at the pants band on the right side of the spinal column . . . and that small piece of lead has rid the country of the worst outlaw who ever stole a horse or shot a man.[13]

From Texas came Sheriff Howard, accompanied by Tom Clemmons and a farmer who had fished with the outlaws while they were camped near Longview the day preceding the robbery. Clemmons "pronounced Dalton the man who presented the note of introduction and who led the raid," and the farmer "identified the boots he wore by a peculiar patch on the instep."[14]

At the Ardmore jail, J. T. Harris of Duncan identified Houston Wallace as one of the men who had passed the unsigned bank notes for the mules and wagon, which Wallace denied, declaring the men were "Tom Littleton" and "Charles White, alias Jones," who had returned with Dalton on May 30. Wallace was "bound over by Commissioner Gibbons, charged with receiving stolen property."[15] Wallace identified a picture of the robber killed at Longview as his brother Jim.[16] Mrs. Dalton told officers: "Prudy Pruitt, the woman with whom I came to Ardmore, was an utter stranger to me, and represented herself as the wife of White, alias Jones."[17] Littleton and White finally were identified as the Knight brothers. More than a year later, in a battle with a posse on Bear Creek in Menard County, Texas, Big Asa was slain, Jim wounded and captured; Jim was returned to Longview, convicted of bank robbery, and given a life sentence.[18]

The Bill Dalton identification farce continued. His body, which had been embalmed and placed in an airtight metallic casket obtained in Fort Worth, remained on public display. At Guthrie, Marshal Nix received several telegrams that "gave no credence to the report of the bandit's demise." Bill Doolin, allegedly in an interview near Ingalls, asserted that he had been head of the Wild Bunch "for the past year" and that "Bill Dalton was merely withdrawn temporarily, has left Oklahoma for a more congenial clime, and is now living a quiet and peaceful life." In a note to a Perry newspaper, Bitter Creek Newcomb declared that "the whole thing is a ruse to get the $1,700 reward hanging over Bill Dalton's head."[19]

Nix sent Deputy Halsell to Ardmore "to make sure," with instructions that the dead bandit be turned over to the Guthrie office "for official identification in order that the rewards can be paid." Halsell wired him that night: "This is Bill Dalton. Will reach Guthrie with body at 3:20 Sunday afternoon." Nix[20] states: "The body was brought to Guthrie, his mother and older brother claiming it." Again his ghost writer erred; witness this account from the *Guthrie Daily Leader*:[21]

> The telegram from Deputy Marshal Halsell published Sunday morning in the LEADER was the means of causing nearly 2,000 people to congregate at the Santa Fe depot. When the north bound passenger train arrived, people clambered over the cars in an attempt to gain a glance at the outlaw stiff, but all were doomed to disappointment. Bill was not there. At the last moment the Ardmore officers decided not to bring the body to Guthrie, owing to the fact that the embalming was imperfect and the body was in a badly decomposed state.

On June 13, Jennie Dalton returned from the Wallace farm with her personal effects and her two children. The body was put on the midnight train, and Mrs. Dalton and the children accompanied it to its last resting place in Merced County, California.

The *Dallas News* inquired: "Why doesn't some candidate raise thunder with these United States marshals for slaying all of our Daltons?" And the *Fort Worth Gazette* noted: "With Bill Dalton out of the way, Oklahoma and Indian Territory are fully qualified for admission as a state." The *Oklahoma Daily Press-Gazette*[22] replied with this scorching editorial:

The public can scarcely realize the encouragement that has been lent to all forms of outlawry in this and the Indian Territory by the senseless and vicious fulminations of a class of newspapers and news correspondents in regard to the acts and performances of the notorious and infamous Bill Dalton. Columns of space have been used to weave about the personality of this brutal cut-throat the attractive halo of romance and his praises have been sounded as a brave and fearless knight of the road while the officials that have from time to time tried to effect his capture have been sneered at as vile cowards. . . . There is no limit to this mawkish and sentimental drool and people at a distance easily get the idea that our newspapers and people are champions of this class of law breakers. . . . The time for sentiment in dealing with these curses of society has passed and a vigorous prosecution and swift punishment should be meted out to each and every member of the various gangs as fast as they are caught. Notoriety and infamy do not constitute fame even in Oklahoma.

XIII   Robbery at Pond Creek; the Caseys Go Wild

ALTHOUGH MARSHAL NIX ORDERED an all-out search for the Wild Bunch, other problems prevented his staff from concentrating on their apprehension. There had been a new outbreak of outlawry in the Outlet. Although these desperadoes had no connection with the Doolin gang, Doolin's influence was felt in most of the new bands that were organized. "Many wild tales had been told in the territory about the enormous sums bandits were getting away with . . . Bill Doolin was rated as a very rich man."[1]

In March, 1894, federal authorities concerned themselves with the identification of three men who killed Edward H. Townsend, postmaster and general-merchandise storekeeper at Todd, Blaine County, in an attempted robbery of his place the night of the twenty-eighth. Townsend had moved with his wife and seven children from Cloud County, Kansas, to the Cheyenne country soon after the 1892 opening and had started a store on his son's claim, securing the post office in the summer of 1893. According to the first dispatch from Hennessey, dated March 29,[2] the three holdup men were

unknown to him, but they were seen by the family and were unmasked.

One of the three came to Townsend and asked for some supper. Supper was set out in the rear of the postoffice and store building where the family lived. It was prepared by the wife and was very appetizing, but the guest partook of the eatables sparingly and soon said he must go. As Mr. Townsend led the way to the door and began to take down the iron fastening he asked, "Where is your home?"

"Oh! Nowhere, anywhere."

Things began to grow suspicious, the more so since the door was being pushed in from the outside. The merchant then threw his weight against the door to close it. The robber within drew a revolver and pointing it at the merchant fired and disabled the left wrist, but with the iron bar in the right hand the merchant knocked him down only to have his other wrist disabled.

With tremendous oaths the door was forced open and the murderers cried, "Now, God damn you, we have got you," and two shots did the work. One entered the breast and one the head just above the mouth to the left of the nose. He was placed on the bed by his wife and children and within a few minutes was dead. The lamp and stove were knocked over and the room filled with smoke, while the murderers took to their horses. . . .

Mr. Townsend was 48 years of age and . . . well known to every Mason in Oklahoma, having served two terms as territorial lecturer of the Grand Lodge of that body. The citizens of Blaine county are up in arms and declare that if the parties are found justice will be meted out to them in genuine western style.

Townsend was buried Sunday, April 1, at Hennessey. Prominent Masons from every accessible point in the territory participated. A three hundred dollar reward was offered, and Deputy Marshal Thomas Taylor of Hennessey was "specially appointed" to head the search for the killers. Six weeks later, after "a very good piece of detective work" and "over 1000 miles of travel," Taylor arrested 26-year-old Henry M. Shoemaker, a cowboy, who suddenly had left his claim in the Cheyenne country near Oneida for the home of a brother-in-law in Logan County near Cowboy Flats. Blaine County having no place for the safekeeping of prisoners, Shoemaker was lodged in jail, under heavy guard, at Kingfisher, where he was "identified by Mrs. Townsend in a most positive manner" as the "inside robber," and five of the Townsend children swore he was one of the men they had seen shoot down their father.[3]

Shoemaker was indicted by a Blaine County grand jury in September but won a change of venue to Kingfisher County, where he was tried before Judge McAtee, convicted, and his punishment assessed by the jury: imprisonment at hard labor for life. Judge McAtee, overruling motions for a new trial and stay of judgment pending appeal, pronounced sentence and ordered him taken to Lansing. However, Chief Justice Dale promptly issued a stay of execution, giving the prisoner twelve days to secure an eight thousand dollar appeal bond, to be approved by the Territorial Supreme Court. When he returned to Kingfisher the following morning to finish a jury case, McAtee was "very incensed." Declaring Dale's action "a gross insult" to his court and "an outrage his district would resent," McAtee ordered Shoemaker removed to the Kansas prison at once, and a deputy sheriff departed with the prisoner that night.[4]

The prosecution had relied on the testimony of the Townsend family and Deputy Marshal Taylor, but the defendant pleaded an alibi in which more than twenty-five witnesses testified that Shoemaker not only had been seen at Cowboy Flats the day before the

204

killing but had stayed that night at the home of his brother-in-law. The jury, however, believed Mrs. Townsend and her children.[5]

The crux of the issue which caused two federal judges to "lock their judicious horns together" was Judge McAtee's instruction that "the burden is upon the defendant to make out his defense of an alibi, and upon all evidence . . . both that given by the defendant and by the Territory . . . the primary question is . . . is the defendant guilty beyond a reasonable doubt?" Shoemaker's attorneys assigned many errors for reversal but relied on this one jury instruction for consideration of the Territorial Supreme Court. Chief Justice Dale wrote: "The general provision of our statute places the burden of proof upon the Territory, and we have no provision which changes or limits this general provision with reference to proving an *alibi*." Citing many precedents and quoting Greenleaf on evidence, "In criminal cases . . . the burden of proof never shifts upon the defendant but is upon the government throughout," Dale added: "He [the defendant] may desire to meet . . . the testimony of the prosecution . . . in the only way that many a person who is the victim of an honest mistake or a wilful fabrication could meet the seemingly strong proof against him, and that is by evidence tending to show that he was not the person who did the shooting, because he was at some other place than the scene of the shooting when the shooting was done . . . and he certainly, to our minds, no more undertakes the burden of proof in a cause presenting his defense in this way than he would by any other form or name of proof which could be offered under the plea of not guilty." The other justices concurred (Judge McAtee not sitting because he had presided in the case), and the case was remanded for a new trial.[6] Shoemaker's second trial resulted in a hung jury, and finally he was released.

Another suspect in the Townsend murder was Zip Wyatt, a former resident of Cowboy Flats, who had been dodging posses under two aliases: Wild Charlie and Dick Yeager. He had been identified erroneously as one of Doolin's men in the Cimarron, Kansas, robbery.[7] Doubtless he was innocent of many crimes charged to him and guilty of many with which he was never connected.[8] Actually, he was leader of the Wyatt-Black gang, noted for country-store and post-office holdups and the theft of horses and cattle in the Cheyenne country and western reaches of the Outlet since January, 1893.

Zip was born Nathaniel Ellsworth Wyatt in Indiana in 1864, the second of eight children of John T. and Rachel Jane Wyatt, who moved to Oklahoma in 1889, settling on Antelope Creek on Cowboy

Flats. There was a wild strain in the family. Zip's older brother, an expert gambler and notorious in the West as Six-Shooter Jack, was slain in a saloon brawl at Texline, Texas, in 1891. His father, often referred to as Old Six-Shooter Bill, was well known in Guthrie as "a frequent inmate of the city jail . . . for being drunk and disorderly," and Zip was "but a second edition of the elder Wyatt, with trimmings." As a youth, Zip cared nothing for school or religion and had no inclination for a sedate life on an Oklahoma claim. "He became an expert horseman and could shoot like a professional and his delight was to throw his long legs over a forty-pound saddle, fill up on coffin varnish and course wildly out of town, whooping and yelling and firing his Colts 45 at trees and fences."[9]

On June 3, 1891, Zip shot up the town of Mulhall and escaped in a running gunfight during which two citizens were wounded. A warrant was placed in the hands of John Hixon, then sheriff of Logan County. Wyatt fled into the Outlet, then to Kansas. At Greensburg on July 4, he stole several pieces of riding equipment from a livery stable. Deputy Sheriff Andrew W. Balfour trailed him some ten miles north to Pryor's Grove, where a plug-horse race was in progress. When Balfour attempted an arrest, Zip whipped a revolver from his shirt bosom and shot the officer in the abdomen. The ball passed into the spinal column and broke Balfour's back. He died within a few minutes. With a one thousand dollar reward on his head, Wyatt fled to his native Indiana, where he was captured several months later by Terre Haute police at the home of his aunt near Cory. He was returned to Guthrie for trial by right of first warrant. While habeas corpus proceedings were being argued on a requisition from the governor of Kansas to try him there for murder, Wyatt escaped jail. He was recaptured but escaped again by crawling through a sewer pipe in an unfinished section of the prison during a Salvation Army service at the jail on December 31, 1892. Since that time, he and his outlaw pals had "kept the new country in a state of apprehension and terror."[10]

Zip's gang consisted of Isaac (Ike) Black, "an outlaw of so little account as to be hardly worth the trouble of arresting except for mileage";[11] Black's wife, Belle; and Jenny Freeman, wife of Matt Freeman, a former Wyatt partner who operated a horse ranch in the Outlet near Cleo Springs. The Freemans provided Wyatt refuge before his flight to Indiana and after his jailbreak in 1892, but Matt found his wife "so lacking in discretion" that he and Zip "became estranged on her account."[12] The women aided the gang by carrying messages and supplies to their various camps in the cedar-covered canyons and rattlesnake-infested caves of the Gypsum (or Gyp) Hills.

The Gyp Hills, a combination of mesas, buttes, and cap-rock formations rising three hundred feet or more from the plain across the southern part of old Woods County and northern Blaine County, were and are popularly known as the Glass Mountains because the sharply etched selenite deposits on the steep red slopes sparkle in the sun. Unfit for homesteading, the hills were government property and rarely visited except by "cedar haulers" and outlaws. A dozen posses had pursued the gang into this wild, semi-arid section without success.

Cedar haulers enhanced the difficulty. These were settlers who patently needed posts to fence their claims on the treeless plains but who more often decided to raise a little cash during the drought and general hard times in the first years by driving into the Gyp Hills, cutting a load of cedar logs, and selling them at Enid or Alva for eight or ten dollars. Deputy marshals were accused of enforcing the law against cutting timber on government land for the fees they drew on a mileage and arrest basis. Prisoners were taken thirty-five miles to Alva or more than sixty miles to Guthrie. In most cases, because of the law's unpopularity, they would be turned loose and their loads confiscated, but this was after the marshals' vouchers had been approved. The settlers neither appreciated the leniency nor this method of piecing out officers' incomes. So if the lawmen wanted to catch the Wyatt-Black gang in the Gyp Hills, well, that was *their* problem.

The women in the gang were "neither good-looking nor attractive." Belle Black was "heavy set, with stringy dark hair and blue eyes"; Jenny Freeman was "rather tall, skinny build, very light complexion, with hair shingled close." Both frequently traveled in male attire, and it was believed the Wyatt-Black outfit were the "four men" who had robbed the Hightower store and post office at Arapaho in November, 1893.[13] Historical writers down the years also have credited the gang with the Rock Island train robbery at Pond Creek on April 9, 1894, yet every piece of dependable evidence shows that neither Wyatt nor Black participated.

Plans for the Pond Creek holdup appear to have evolved in the brains of Felix Young, a notorious horse and cattle thief, and Nate Sylva, familiar on the streets of almost every town in the territory as a horse trader and jockey, who had served time in a Texas prison and long had been suspected of disposing of stolen stock for the Daltons. The pair decided to emulate Doolin. They recruited four

207

other characters, one being Bill Rhodes, alias Pitts, allegedly an old member of the James gang, who had taken a claim adjoining Coleman Dalton east of North Enid when the Outlet was opened.[14]

The southbound Rock Island passenger and express, carrying a large consignment of Chickasaw money for Fort Sill, left Wichita the evening of April 9 and entered the Outlet about ten o'clock. At Pond Creek station, where it stopped for water, two men slipped on board. One hid himself on the baggage car, the other behind the tender of the locomotive. Pond Creek, on the south bank of the Salt Fork (where the train did not stop), was "run through swiftly" on schedule. About a mile below town, engineer Whitmeyer "noticed a light [small bonfire] on the track and began to slow up," when the man on the baggage car "flashed a pistol in the face of the fireman" and the man behind the tender "presented a revolver to the head of the engineer, and commanded him fiercely to 'stop 'er, you —— ——, or we'll shoot!'" Whitmeyer "ducked apprehensively," and just in time, for the robber's six-shooter "illumined the darkness with a roar." The bullet "slivered the cab window and glanced from the boiler to the roof of the cab." Whitmeyer brought the train to a standstill at a crossing on a section line, where Rhodes and his masked cronies were stationed in a brake near the tracks.[15]

In the style of the Daltons and Doolins, the bandits leaped from the brush, yelling and firing a fusillade alongside the coaches to discourage the passengers while the engineer and fireman were marched back to the express car and messenger John Crosswight was ordered to "open up, or we'll blow it to smithereens!" The car was not opened. Inside with Crosswight was express guard Jake Harmon, a former Wichita policeman, whose run extended to Fort Worth. Harmon was armed with a double-barreled Winchester shotgun loaded with buckshot. He related that

> I heard one of the men outside say: "Get up there!" and another voice [Whitmeyer's] said: "I'm afraid to get up there; there is a guard and he will shoot me"; then the first voice said: "Don't give a damn for the guard; I want the door opened." Someone [Whitmeyer] called out:
> "Don't shoot! It's the engineer and fireman and they have got us in front of them."
> A voice shouted three or four times for us to open the door—under threats of blowing it in. We didn't say anything, but sat perfectly still. It was probably a half minute after the voices had died away when a bomb of some description [a stick of dynamite thrust under the iron plate of the door] went off, shattering the lamps and throwing express all over the car [the concussion knocked Crosswight down, stunning him

for a few moments]. The robbers called out again, saying if we did not open the door they would throw two bombs right in on top of us. The messenger spoke two or three times and said: "Let's open the door." Finally he called out [to the bandits]: "Hold on! I'll open it."

In the meantime I made my way out through the rear of the car . . . went through the chair car . . . stepped off the smoking car [in the darkness], and saw the engineer and fireman climbing into the door of the express car. The robbers were cursing and ordering them to get in or they would kill them. There were three men standing east of the door. One of them held a revolver in his hand pointed in the car. I took aim and fired. The smoke was so dense that I could not see the men after the first shot. . . . [Later, Harmon walked back to the front of the train.] About twenty-five feet from the express car a dead man [Rhodes] was lying on his back with his elbow resting on the ground and a revolver clutched in his right hand pointing straight up in the air.[16]

The warm reception astonished the other bandits, and they fled to their horses. Breaking into the express car had consumed more than twenty minutes, and the passengers were in a state of "great commotion and fright." The brakeman had gone back to flag an oncoming freight. He backed it to Pond Creek and got a posse that arrived at the scene just as Rhodes fell, and it "began an attack at which the outlaws ran in confusion." The sheriff from Pond Creek captured one of the bandits "riding furiously along the road and leading the horse belonging to the dead man." The dead bandit, the captured horses, and the prisoner were put aboard the freight and taken to Pond Creek. The passenger train then proceeded on its way after having been delayed an hour and a half.[17]

The spot chosen for the holdup was singularly unfitted for an enterprise of the kind. Level prairie extended in every direction except north, where river bluffs and scattered timber of the Salt Fork "outlined itself faintly against the sky." Nothing but thick darkness enabled the rest of the gang to escape.[18]

Deputy Marshal Madsen, who hastened to the scene from El Reno, called it "the work of amateurs." The two captured animals were "good horseflesh," lending color to the belief that the bandits were "members of some old organized gang like the Daltons," but the "bungling way in which the fiasco was managed" did not resemble their "polished handicraft." The prisoner was "close mouthed and claimed to be a bum trying to beat a ride," despite the fact he was a "walking arsenal" when arrested. He gave his name as Morgan, then Williams, and finally Will Wade and said he lived on a quarter-section adjoining Rhodes and Coleman Dalton.[19]

A Rock Island detective and Enid officers went to the Rhodes and Wade claims and found two shanties, both deserted.[20] Coleman Dalton, observing the dead Rhodes and Will Wade in jail at Round Pond, denied he knew either man and labeled newspaper accounts of possible Dalton involvement "totally false and misleading."[21]

In a telegram to Marshal Nix on April 10, D. H. Rawson of the Rock Island at Topeka described how agent Overton at Hennessey had caused the arrest of two additional suspects,

> John T. O'Conners, from Trinidad, Colo., and Frank Lacy, from Pond Creek, and they are facing jail. They rode into Hennessey about 10 o'clock today on jaded horses. Their description tallies exactly with that given by parties who saw them at Pond Creek yesterday and . . . they confess being near the place of the holdup and heard shots fired. O'Connor had cartridges on his person, but neither had any weapons. They were trying to trade their jaded horses for fresh ones when taken in. . . . Have asked authorities at Hennessey to hold them at all hazards until information can be filed against them.

On April 12, O'Conners and Lacy were taken to Wichita "to avoid lynching."[22] The ringleaders of the gang, they told Deputy Marshal Pat Murphy, were Felix Young and Nate Sylva.

In the few months since his appointment by Nix, Murphy had achieved fame as "the kid deputy." The press had made much of the fact that he was "small in stature, smooth shaven, looks to be 18 years old, but in reality is over 23." Pat was "strong and active for his size, quiet, cool in time of danger, and one of the best pistol shots in this part of the moral vineyard. . . . If all other marshals were as brave and determined as the kid deputy, Nix would have a crowd he could send after the Doolins . . . and bring them back either captives or feet foremost."[23]

Murphy obtained warrants for Sylva and Young. On May 12, he traced them to El Reno. It was an exciting day. Federal court was in session, attended by Deputies Madsen, Eichoff, and Captain J. S. Prather. The streets were crowded with people "trading and selling horses at public auction." Murphy saw Sylva in the forenoon near the Kerfoot Hotel, but "thought best not to attempt his arrest until Young was located." He notified Madsen, and the street "miraculously filled with marshals." Murphy and Eichoff took Sylva into custody. He offered no resistance.[24]

Madsen spotted Young a block away, standing by his horse in front of a saloon, "talking to two gamblers, Big Hand Donaldson and Slim Jim Hathaway." The deputy walked up to within forty yards of Young "when Young discovered who he was, sprang to his horse and dashed away." Madsen "ordered him to halt, but he did not, and Madsen shot at him some five or six times. One shot hit the horse just above the hock . . . the horse only run a few yards and fell. Young then jumped off and started to run but by this time several parties had come up, among them Captain Prather, who was well mounted. Young ran down to a negro cabin nearby and started in but was soon overtaken [by Prather] and compelled to surrender."[25]

Both prisoners were taken to the federal jail at Guthrie. On May 17, they were removed to Pond Creek for their preliminary hearing. A writ of habeas corpus brought before Judge Bierer at Perry failed, and they were held for action of the Grant County grand jury. Sylva was indicted. Young was released for lack of evidence, but was immediately rearrested on a federal warrant relative to "ten or twelve head of horses officers had found in his possession." On Sunday night, June 3, Will Wade, Sylva, and Young escaped from the Pond Creek jail and fled into the Cherokee Nation.[26]

Available official records provide no dispositions for O'Conners and Lacy, arrested at Hennessey. Nix[27] appears to identify O'Conners as "Jim Fuller," Wade as "Big Jim Bourland," and Rhodes as "Bob Hughes," and states erroneously that "Hughes was killed by Bill Fossett." Bourland fled to Texas, where he had "escaped from the penitentiary at Huntsville . . . was recognized and captured and returned to Oklahoma for trial." He was

pardoned after serving part of his term [in federal prison] and returned to Oklahoma, settling at Anadarko, where he became a respected citizen . . . later appointed a special detective . . . and became a nemesis to lawbreakers. Madsen took up the pursuit of Silva [sic] . . . and discovered he was working in the mines in Colorado. The deputy went to look for him . . . found he had left for Wheatland, California . . . followed him there and arrested him. The man was convicted and sentenced to the federal penitentiary. Young disappeared completely and was never found."

In "Four Score Years a Fighter,"[28] Madsen says "Young was killed in Indian Territory," Bourland was shot and killed in a saloon brawl at Anadarko in 1906, and "Fossett got a bead on Bob Hughes [Rhodes] and dropped him" during the train holdup. He says that it was "Fuller" whom he captured in California, but "his case never came to trial," and that Sylva was apprehended years later in Bates

County, Missouri for "stealing harness" but escaped jail at Butler and was never again arrested.

Authorities apparently were seeking more members of the Rock Island gang than already had been killed or jailed. Witnesses to the holdup had counted at least eight bandits.

On May 21, two riders, "about twenty-two years of age, roughly dressed in cowboy garb, dirty and unshaven, with Winchesters strapped to their saddles," rode into El Reno. The attention they gave the lay of the town, particularly the jail and building where federal court was still in session, aroused the suspicion of Canadian County Sheriff Jackson, who detailed a deputy to "discover their mission." The men rode to Keller's secondhand store on Rock Island Avenue and dismounted. Inside, they examined a stock of six-shooters, finally trading for a .44 double-action Remington revolver. To Keller's question, they replied they were from Chickasha en route to Enid. After riding a short distance north of town, however, they turned east toward Yukon, fifteen miles away, "leisurely following the line of the Choctaw railroad." Between El Reno and Yukon, they met the train from Oklahoma City and "made signals to someone on the coaches." When the train reached El Reno, the party was identified as the wife of Nate Sylva, who thought her husband had been transferred from Guthrie to the El Reno jail rather than Pond Creek. Believing the men were members of the gang not accounted for and that arrangements were under way to "secure Sylva from the clutches of the law," Sheriff Jackson wired Deputy Sam Farris at Yukon to "be on the lookout for them and cause their arrest for investigation."[29]

The pair reached Yukon about three o'clock in the afternoon and stopped for a drink of water. They purchased some small items at a grocery store and were returning to their horses when Deputy Farris stepped from a drugstore next door, approached them, and said: "I have a telegram requesting the arrest of you men. Come in here, and I will read it to you." They started back to the store with him, "when suddenly one of them seized his six-shooter and fired, mortally wounding Farris in the left groin, the ball passing through his body. Farris at once drew his pistol and returned the fire, striking the man in the foot." The man hobbled around the corner of an implement building, "his companion running down the street for their horses, snapping his own pistol in all directions." The deputy "stood his ground until he emptied his weapon" without further effect, "then walked into the drug store and fell to the floor from loss of blood." As the second desperado dashed down the street, Joe Farris, brother of the wounded deputy, ran out, seized him around the waist, and held him in a savage struggle until several other citizens came up to help overpower and disarm him. "While securing the prisoner, the other gunman, who had reloaded [his revolver], reappeared and began shooting upon the crowd." On the sidewalk, a citizen named Ben Wilson snatched a Winchester from the saddle of a horse tied at the rail and opened fire on him, and the gunman "paid his respects" by "emptying his revolver at close range." He missed Wilson, but one bullet "ricocheted from the corrugated seat of a mowing machine nearby, striking an old man named Snyder in the forehead." The gunman, "seeing the citizens were beginning to use the arms taken from his pal," then "made a break for his horse and rode off in the country to the west," closely pursued by a large posse.[30]

"An exciting chase was kept up across the prairie, the pursued and pursuers being not more than half a mile apart at any time." Fourteen miles southwest, the fugitive's mount "became much fagged." One posseman, riding a strong horse, circled ahead, and the fugitive opened fire on him with his Winchester. The pursuers "had only six-shooters and the gunman thus had the advantage . . . two other members closed in on his rear and it looked as if he must be taken, when he ran into the timber on the bottoms of the South Canadian." None of the posse "would venture to follow, darkness having come on, and all returned to Yukon, the chase practically abandoned."[31]

Joe Farris' prisoner refused to give his identity. Sam Farris died at 8 P.M., and many feared for the life of Snyder. Yukon citizens expressed great indignation, and as a precaution against lynching, the prisoner was removed to the guardhouse at Fort Reno. Deputy Marshal Madsen immediately recognized him as James Casey, who three years earlier was living with his parents and brothers in southeast Canadian County.

The Caseys had settled on Mustang Creek near El Reno. Two bachelor brothers living on claims adjoining the Casey farm had been murdered, and "the Caseys were suspected of committing the crime to get hold of the farms of their neighbors." Madsen had developed sufficient evidence to have Old Man Casey and his eldest son indicted. In their trial at El Reno, both were acquitted, whereupon the family moved west, settling near Arapaho.[32] Madsen was confident that the escaped fugitive was Vic Casey, the younger brother of James.

Next morning, May 22, Madsen, accompanied by Deputy Eichoff,

Captain Prather, and an Indian agent named Black Coyote, and Sheriff Jackson, accompanied by Deputies Clay, Hancock, and Williams, left for the South Canadian. They found the killer's trail in the river bottoms and never lost it throughout their 105-mile trek to the Casey home northwest of Arapaho, where Vic Casey was "easily captured, making no resistance."[33]

The brothers denied any connection with the Sylva-Young gang of train robbers. An El Reno grand jury indicted them for the murder of Sam Farris, and they were arraigned before Judge Burford. Vic Casey's foot wound, which had become inflamed during his flight, took a turn for the worse. Blood poisoning set in, and he died while awaiting trial. In June, 1894, James Casey, on a change of venue, was transferred to the Oklahoma County jail to await trial before Judge Scott of the Third Judicial District.

U.S. Deputy Marshal Thomas J. Hueston was slain in the Ingalls battle.

U.S. Deputy Marshal Lafayette (Lafe) Shadley was slain in the Ingalls battle.

Roy Daugherty, alias Arkansas Tom Jones.

LINDSEY

U.S. Deputy Marshal Seldon T. Lindsey.

Bill Dalton in death.

XIV   War on the Rock Island

By JUNE, 1894, the Rock Island's disagreement with the people over stopping trains at the government townsites of Pond Creek and South Enid had erupted into civil war, obstructing the mails and interstate commerce.

In March, 1887, Congress had granted the Rock Island a charter right to cross Indian Territory. During the preceding summer, a junction had been completed at Herington, Kansas, and from this point a new line was run southwest through Wichita and Caldwell to the Salt Fork in the Outlet. It went into operation in April, 1889, just before the Oklahoma opening. Building was resumed in July, 1889, the line following closely the old Chisholm Trail, to Hennessey, crossing the Canadian River below Fort Reno, and running almost due south through Minco and Duncan in the Chickasaw Nation to reach Terral, on the Red River, in September, 1892.[1] Construction was rapidly continued to Fort Worth, and the Rock Island became the main connection between that city and Kansas City, Missouri. It is not clear who dreamed up the idea of developing townsites around the Rock Island depots at Pond Creek Station and North Enid, with the railroad in complete control, but the skulduggery backfired in a sizzling climax that old-timers still remember as Oklahoma's Great Railroad War.[2]

The ruse allegedly was planned by railroad men and a group of Cherokee Indians. The agreement made with the Cherokee Commission in December, 1891, for sale of the Outlet lands to the federal government included authorization for Chief White Feather and sixty-nine other tribal leaders to select the first allotments, not to exceed eighty acres each. The government had planned county seats for L and O counties at Pond Creek and Enid, respectively, but kept the plans secret. The railroad men and Indians learned of the plans, however, and made some of their own. The Indians were to select lands adjoining the depots, then sell to the Rock Island for whatever the railroad was willing to pay for a

217

chance to speculate in townsites. Secretary of the Interior Hoke Smith learned of the deal, and on the eve of the opening sprang his own surprise. He announced that no county seat should be located within three miles of an Indian allotment. Thus Pond Creek and Enid would be located on the railroad as planned—but three miles south of each Rock Island depot.[3]

Sam P. Ridings,[4] early-day Medford attorney and one of the legal advisers of the Rock Island Townsite Company, says the railroad was not interested in allotments and property other than their depots and rights-of-way at the old townsites and "had no connection whatever with the Townsite Company operating at the station of Old Pond Creek"; this company "was incorporated prior to the opening" and the name selected "simply because its holdings were on the line of the Rock Island Railway. The incorporators were citizens of Wichita, Caldwell, and other towns along the railway in Kansas and Oklahoma."

Actually, the Rock Island's problems began September 16, 1893, when it provided two 42-car trains, one south of Caldwell and one north of Hennessey, to haul thousands of homeseekers into the Outlet. Many who boarded the coaches at Hennessey were seeking lots at the land office and county-seat site in O County, while others from Caldwell sought lots in the county seat of L County. Instead of stopping at land-office Enid, the train from the south sped on to depot Enid three miles north, forcing hundreds to jump from the coaches in the mad scramble for claims. Luckily, no one was killed, but several persons were injured. The Caldwell train, much to the chagrin of the contingent from the north, stopped three miles short of the county-seat site of Pond Creek.[5]

When these government sites mushroomed into thriving municipalities, the economic necessity of having depots became increasingly apparent. The civic leaders in Enid and Pond Creek met and decided to ask the railroad either to move its depots or stop trains at the government towns. Whether the charges against the Rock Island were true or false, when the appointed committees went to Herington, Kansas, and talked to Rock Island officials, they were refused.[6] The railroad's side of the argument, according to Ridings,[7] was that the Rock Island had

selected right-of-way to accommodate their conditions at the points where the stations were built. In order to comply with the requests of the new towns, the Railway Company was not only called upon to erect new improvements at the new locations only a few miles away from their regularly established depots, but these new locations lacked the facilities for operating a depot and improvements connected therewith. It also not only rendered the old location practically useless, but if they retained the same it added the extra expense of operating another station and the stopping of trains at intervals only a few miles apart.

On the contrary, the railroad promoted its own sites, selling Indian allotments to settlers with the understanding that it would not recognize the county-seat towns and would force them to move to the stations.[8] The people in the north towns took sides with the Rock Island; those in the south towns sided with the government. These were the grounds for the bitter controversy as all parties concerned prepared to "fight it out."

All four towns petitioned for post offices—two under the name *Enid* and two under the name *Pond Creek*. North Enid was given a post office and held a "jollification" in spite of the fact that its people were obliged to mail their letters from and have their mail sent to a town the name of which they did not own.[9] There was consolation, however, in the fact that south town had to transport all passengers, building materials, and other freight from the depot to the townsite. When south-town citizens went after passengers, their rigs were overturned and harness was cut; it was dangerous even to pick up freight left at the north town until the merchants furnished every wagon with an armed guard. A regular stage was sent to meet the passenger trains, and the driver carried a Winchester.[10]

Finally, the government ordered the railroad to leave mail at both Enid and Pond Creek. The Rock Island erected mail cranes at the town sites and changed the mailbags without even slowing down, often ripping the pouches apart and scattering their contents along the right-of-way.[11] J. L. Isenberg, editor of the *Enid Wave*, called the crane at south town "The Snubbing Post," and stirred the wrath of north-town citizens by referring to North Enid as "The Tank." Wrote Isenberg: "A broad smile perambulates over the faces of the Enid passengers on the Rock Island as they approach this point. The train porter always yells out, 'The next station is Enid; the first stop is at the tank.' The announcement is as true as Holy Writ, the first and only stop is at the Tank; the infernal trains don't stop at Enid, nor do they slow up unless someone expectorates on the track." In another issue of the *Wave*, Isenberg served notice to the world: "There is but one ENID. The post office address of this city is simply Enid. The post office in the addition is called

219

North Enid, but this is positively not South Enid. You uneducated scapegoats, can't you understand that?"[12]

Meanwhile, the settlers at Pond Creek took desperate measures to stop the trains. A house was loaded on wheels and conveniently stalled across the rails. A man ran up the track some distance to flag the southbound freight. The engineer pulled the throttle wide open, blew a shrill blast, and hit the piece of real estate broadside. Boards and splinters flew "helter-skelter," and the train "roared on through town as though it had struck no more formidable obstruction than a tumbleweed."[13] The citizens then moved a heavy freight wagon onto the track. Another faithful engineer was on duty, and the vehicle "soared skyward and separated in small bits." The *Pond Creek Voice* reported: "The wagon tongue stuck in the Milky Way and the kingbolt hit the man in the moon."[14]

As soon as the train had passed, sledge hammers were procured from a blacksmith shop and spikes began to fly from the angle irons. Nearly two hundred men, by sheer strength, then lifted the unjointed track on its edge for nine hundred fifty feet in plain view of the engineer. Again a man ran down the track to flag a northbound freight with several carloads of Texas cattle. But this flagging business had become old hat. Seeing the ties and rails sticking up some distance ahead and recalling that a house and wagon had been placed on the track before, engineer Jim Sullivan told his fireman, "This time they're trying a windmill." He pulled the throttle wide open and thundered on toward town. The engine struck the tilted section and "plowed into the dirt." It did not overturn, but the cars "piled up promiscuously." More than one hundred steers were crippled or killed. The rest escaped from the burst cars and fled bellowing through the streets and over the countryside.[15] This was the first train to stop in Pond Creek, and it brought official interference from Washington.

At Guthrie on April 25, 1894, Horace Speed announced his retirement as U.S. district attorney of Oklahoma Territory because of the serious illness of his wife and his decision to enter private practice; Mrs. Speed died a month later. "For four years," said the *Oklahoma State Capital*,[16] "he has coped with vice and crime of every description, and by his energetic and vigorous prosecution of criminals has done more than any other man in the territory to give them to understand they must respect the law. He goes out with clean hands and the respect of every law-abiding and decent citizen, irrespective of party." On May 14, he was succeeded by his assistant, Caleb R. Brooks, an eminently qualified lawyer who "has had the opportunity to know Speed's careful methods and marked legal ability" and "will no doubt fill the office to the satisfaction of the government and the people."[17] Brooks in turn appointed T. F. McMechan as his assistant. McMechan was a lawyer of "wide experience in the criminal line" in Illinois and Kansas before coming to Oklahoma in 1889, after which he had served as prosecuting attorney of Oklahoma County.[18]

So it was that in response to a telegram from Attorney General Olney, Brooks and McMechan prepared warrants for eighty Pond Creek citizens and ordered Marshal Nix to Pond Creek at once.

Through his deputy, Pat Murphy, Nix had "tried to adjust the matter," and Grant County Attorney C. C. Daniels, although in sympathy with the position of the people, had joined Murphy in an attempt to "convince them of the futility of destructive tactics." Their efforts "were of no avail." Nix, being closer to the situation than the government at Washington,

> realized the fact that diplomacy and not a show of force would be necessary. I was convinced that if I gave information to the newspapers and set out with a trainload of men to enforce my authority, I would probably precipitate a bloody fight. I went into consultation with Justice Frank Dale . . . and my chief deputy, John M. Hale, and we agreed that it would be better for me to take three or four trusted men and go to make an appeal to the better instincts of the citizens of Pond Creek. I gave out no news concerning the trip, but proceeded to the town as quietly as possible. . . . Deputy Pat Murphy met us, telling us that the townspeople were prepared for battle. It seems that the railroad had intercepted the Attorney General's telegram and had informed the Pond Creek people that I was coming to place them under martial law. Murphy's life had been threatened . . . the people were thoroughly convinced that the government was taking an unfair attitude toward them and discriminating in favor of the railroad company.
>
> After a brief conference I decided to go up town alone and, upon reaching the principal street, I found a hundred citizens lined up with Winchesters and shotguns in hand, awaiting what they thought would be an attack by a large group of deputy marshals. As I walked toward them . . . I recognized S. L. Bradley, the county clerk and recorder, whom I had known quite well. Notwithstanding that he was a county official, he stood with his fellow citizens ready to fight. . . .
>
> I motioned to Bradley and he . . . came forward to meet me. County Attorney Daniels joined us in our discussion of the situation. These gentlemen took the position that the government should force the railroads to stop at the townsite that had been set aside for settlement by its citizens. I agreed . . . but explained that they were going at the matter in the wrong way, thereby forcing the government to take action

to protect interstate commerce and the United States mails. I showed them the telegram received from the Attorney General and explained that unless some amicable understanding could be reached . . . there would probably be useless bloodshed. I also explained that I had not attempted to embarrass the Pond Creek people by giving out publicity regarding the situation but that I had come to them in a quiet, respectful way, hoping to be able to adjust conditions without being forced to the martial law order that the government had given.

Bradley turned and made a short talk to the men who were lined up for the battle, after which I was asked to talk to them. County Attorney Daniels followed my remarks, urging that the people follow my suggestion and give the government time to adjust their differences with the railroad. The crowd, much to their own credit, fell into the spirit of the agreement very graciously.

I then told the citizens that I had warrants for eighty of their people. . . . I [again] told them I had no desire to embarrass anyone and that if they would have their citizens appear before me as their names were called, I would check the warrants and allow each one to go on his own recognizance to appear before the United States Commissioner at Kingfisher. They agreed to this and I immediately sent a runner for my deputies to join me and take charge of the work.[19]

A potential riot had been averted. The damaged track was relaid by four o'clock the next morning, thanks to all-night work by a Kansas railroad crew guarded by the deputy marshals. Then all the persons named in federal warrants were loaded on the train to Kingfisher.[20] As they sped through Enid, Editor Mahr of the *Pond Creek Voice* tossed from his car a note addressed to the *Wave* editor: "Isenberg, your turn next. This is my first railroad pass. Justice be-gosh. The United States Constitution is gone."[21]

William Edward Hayes[22] says "a deputy U.S. marshal with 50 men came down from Kansas" and took sixty of the Pond Creek leaders—including City Marshal Charles Curran—to Kingfisher, where the sheriff refused to put them in jail because they had been arrested without warrants. The prisoners were held under guard at a hotel while proper warrants were obtained. Meanwhile, the telegraph wires were kept hot between Kingfisher and Herington, Kansas, and railroad attorneys finally agreed to return the prisoners to Grant County to be tried before a Pond Creek magistrate.

C. E. Lemon[23] states it was Judge A. M. Mackey, of Pond Creek, who pleaded their

right to trial in the county in which the act was committed, which claim was sustained and they all returned on the next train . . . and gave bond to await the action of grand jury. The grand jury was unable to dig up any evidence to link any of the men with the act, and they were freed.

According to U.S. District Attorney Brooks, who submitted his report to Attorney General Olney on June 18,

the citizens of Round Pond [Pond Creek], L County, tore up the track of the Rock Island Railroad for about one hundred yards . . . the freight train was wrecked without loss of human life fortunately but great destruction of property to the Railroad. Two mail and passenger trains came along hours later and were delayed . . . on account of the track being torn up as stated above. . . . I directed the Marshals to go there and protect and prevent the further delay of the mails, which they did, and last week I went there to have preliminary hearing before the U. S. Commissioner of some of the parties under charge of obstructing and delaying the mails, and had a number bound over to the next term of District Court.[24]

Brooks explained that the prisoners were released because

the depredations are committed secretly and the people of the towns will give no aid in apprehending the parties and the local authorities will not lend assistance, claiming all the time to deplore the condition of affairs and asserting their willingness to assist in suppressing the trouble but are always ignorant of the identity of the guilty parties; and the prosecutions must under the Organic Act be had in the County, and the officers and citizens all being in sympathy with the guilty parties it is impossible to secure proof or to get the law enforced. . . . If I could arrest the guilty parties and have their cases heard outside these Counties I could soon break up this work.[25]

The Rock Island employed guards to patrol its track through and near Pond Creek. One night, two citizens concealed themselves in the grass along the right-of-way. As a guard approached, one of the men whispered to the other, "Watch me snuff that lantern." His rifle cracked, the lantern globe exploded into bits, and the frightened guard "fled in the darkness toward Kansas."[26] A small shack with *Depot* painted on it in large letters and bearing a sign reading "All Trains Stop Here" was set within a few feet of the track. At train time, a man sat inside, wearing an agent's cap and posing as a "sure-enough employee of the road."[27] Although harassment continued, Pond Creek was careful not to damage any more railroad property.

Meanwhile, matters had reached a critical stage in Garfield County. Soon after the *Wave* appeared on the streets the night of June 6 with the startling news of the train wreck at Pond Creek, the people of Enid, in great numbers, began to congregate at the E street crossing. The mutterings of discontent were long and loud. . . . It was finally resolved that the railroad track be torn up just south of the city limits, and the crowd was soon hurrying to the pont designated. A few conservative citizens [managed to halt them] with some well chosen remarks that it would ultimate in great injury to the city. Deputy Sheriff Miller appeared on the scene and announced that he would arrest any man who would attempt to disturb the railroad track. . . . While the crowd was occupied listening to the speeches, the railroad bridge was bathed with coal oil and a bundle of baled hay saturated and set against the timbers and fired. Fortunately an officer saw the fire before it gained much headway and put it out.[28]

Trains kept whistling through the south town. Red lanterns, dynamite caps on the tracks, and even bullets failed to stop them. Enid passed an ordinance making it a violation for a train to pass through the city without stopping. However, it proved impossible to arrest a railroad conductor within the city limits while he was on a train that was traveling at fifty miles an hour.

A freight came roaring in from the north. By some act of Providence, the coupling pin connecting the caboose came out and the caboose ran a short distance to a stop. Three city policemen rushed to the scene to place the train crew under arrest. The conductor, brakeman, and several other railroad men resisted their efforts with clubs and revolvers. The engineer backed to the detached caboose, a coupling was quickly made, he opened the throttle, and the train went "tearing off," carrying the policemen. It didn't stop until it had reached Hennessey, where the unfortunate officers, overpowered, bruised, and beaten, were thrown off and the train proceeded on its way. Enraged Enid charged that the Rock Island, in resisting its officers, "are no better than anarchists" and announced a determination to halt such lawless practice if it had to deputize every man in the city.

Petitions demanding legislation to compel the railroad to recognize county-seat towns were sent to Congress in the closing months of 1893. In January, 1894, Mayor John C. Moore and Councilman W. R. Gregg of Enid and Mayor Wasson and Judge Mackey of Pond Creek went to Washington as delegates to work for passage of House Bill 3606, requiring that "all railroad companies operating railroads through the Territories of the United States over a right of way obtained under grant or act of Congress . . . shall establish and maintain passenger stations and freight depots at all town sites established in said Territories on the line of said railroads by authority of the Interior Department." The House of Representatives passed the bill almost unanimously, but it met fiery opposition in the Senate, composed largely of railroad lawyers. Senator James K. Berry of Arkansas championed the cause, while Senator Joseph C. S. Blackburn of Kentucky and his forces insisted on an amendment requiring L and O counties to vote first on where their county seats were to be permanently located. The House disagreed in view of the fact there were enough county-seat troubles already, and the bill went to conference. A Senate committee visited the Outlet towns and reported that they showed every promise of becoming real cities and were in dire need of depot facilities. No further action was taken.[29]

Enid and Pond Creek brought a mandamus action to compel the railroad to put in depots and sidetracks in their corporate limits. On June 18, the Territorial Supreme Court convened at Guthrie, with Justices Dale and Bierer on the bench to hear the case. Rock Island attorneys demanded a full bench before answering the writ or making an argument. The hearing was delayed pending the appearance of Judge Scott, who was holding court in Pottawatomie County.[30] With Scott on the bench, the railroad did not file an answer until June 21, then asked that the case be quashed. The motion was overruled, and the railroad refused to argue the case until the arrival of Judge McAtee.[31] When the court met again July 9, the Rock Island asked for a continuance, claiming it could not get witnesses in time for the session, and asked for a jury. The court agreed to continue the case until its next sitting in August.[32]

Enid's Populist newspaper *Coming Events* concluded on July 12 that "it is evident there is no justice to be found in our courts." And the *Wave*[33] charged that it was

> nothing more than a dodge to gain time. The machinery of justice has slipped a cog . . . and when August comes . . . a half dozen cogs will slip and the court will conclude it is too hot to try the case anyhow. Where is that half carload of giant powder shipped to Enid a few weeks ago?

This was a prelude to the depredations that now occurred in quick succession. A group of daring men assembled, pledged to eclipse anything done by their Pond Creek brethren.

> At dawn [Friday, July 13] a Rock Island freight from the south came thundering onto a bridge built across a dry creek about one mile south of the city and as the engine glided over the structure, the engineer felt the bridge giving under its weight and threw the throttle wide open. The engine and three cars passed over safely but the balance of the train proceeded to pile up along the high grade and under the bridge

225

in a conglomerated but scattered heap. Twelve cars in all [two oil tanks, six cars loaded with wheat, three with lumber, and one with empty beer kegs] were derailed, some of them being smashed into kindling wood, while others were fearfully warped out of shape for business. The caboose tipped over just at the south approach of the bridge. One car load of lumber was smashed into splinters and fine new wheat was knee deep all about the wreck.

The cause was quite visible. Five posts of the center truss had been cut obliquely . . . with a crosscut saw that was quite sharp . . . so that the weight of anything crossing the structure would crush it down. Two outside posts of the adjoining trusses north and south were sawed to swing the bridge with its burden to the west and that is the way she swung and tumbled. . . .

The conductor and one brakeman who were in the overturned caboose were terribly bruised. Two tramps were stealing a ride in one car load of lumber. The car seemed to have simply turned sidewise and dropped into the deepest part of the gully. Their moans were heard and they were soon rescued. One of them was but slightly injured, while it is thought the other will die, having been taken out unconscious.

News of the wreck reached this city, thousands of people flocked to the scene, and the hack drivers did a land office business.[34]

Vice President M. A. Low, general counselor for the Rock Island, wired Governor Renfrow from Topeka, again asking protection "for this company and its property against these outlaws, and if the local authorities cannot afford this protection it seems to me that the president ought to send troops." Governor Renfrow being absent from the territory, Secretary Thomas J. Lowe hurriedly consulted with the Supreme Court, Marshal Nix, and U.S. District Attorney Brooks.[35] That night, Secretary Lowe wired Washington, asking that federal troops be sent to Enid and Pond Creek, and Nix requested from Attorney General Olney "authority to employ a sufficient number of deputies to protect property, enforce the law, and preserve the peace."[36] Brooks advised Olney that the expense of keeping deputy marshals on the ground continuously would be enormous, but unless they were there, or some other federal power was there, the depredations would continue. Olney instructed Brooks "to take immediate steps to prevent such outrages . . . procuring such warrants and orders from court as may be proper and directing the Marshal to execute same by such number of deputies or posse as necessary."[37]

By 6 P.M. on Saturday, July 14, the sawed trestle had been repaired, and one train after another, all freights, came rolling into

South Enid. One carried a troop of cavalrymen and their horses bound for Pond Creek. On Sunday afternoon, sixty additional troops assigned to duty in O County arrived at the E Street crossing. And on Monday, July 16, the angry, impatient citizens of both towns accelerated their protest activities:

> Two more bridges were blown up this morning on the Rock Island, one near Enid and one near Pond Creek. The explosions were terrific and the bridges are total wrecks. They are thirty miles apart, so that no freight or express can be transferred. . . . The enraged citizens are determined that traffic shall be stopped until the trouble is settled.[38]

Two morning trains exchanged passengers at the wrecked bridges. Two trainloads of cattle were sidetracked at Kremlin, and the telegraph lines to Pond Creek were spliced with broom wire to keep messages from going through.[39] South Enid citizens ordered the soldiers to leave town within 24 hours; one soldier was fired upon. Large crowds assembled, loudly proclaiming they would dynamite any train passing through the city without stopping. Pond Creek's mayor wired Secretary Lowe that city authorities there proposed putting into effect its ordinance requiring trains to stop at the principal street of the town and flag the crossings; they requested assistance from the territory in enforcing the regulation should they fail.[40]

There was no reply from the acting governor, so at 1 A.M. on July 17, as the special train from Enid carrying the military approached the South Pond Creek limits, two dynamite bombs exploded. One charge went off immediately under the train, doing no damage; the other blew out a cattle guard and shattered a rail. The wreckers were "decidedly bold, for the night, with a full moon, was almost as clear as day . . . and [they] touched off their shots in full view of the train when so close it could not be stopped."[41]

Deputy Marshal Madsen, who was on the train with his posse, wired Brooks the details, adding that

> while not caring to meddle with Territorial affairs, I must say it will be necessary to at once suspend sheriffs and other officers [of L and O counties] and put in their place men who will attend to their duty fearlessly, and if there is any way by which it can be done lawfully, every house should be searched at once for dynamite.[42]

Brooks wrote Olney:

> The situation is growing worse. . . . The Marshal is preparing to send an additional force of deputies there today. Citizens in the two towns

227

who are inclined to give information are threatened and intimidated and the soldiers are not sufficient in number to deter the mobs. . . . I have requested the Territorial authorities to remove the sheriff and other Territorial officers there and send others in their stead who will aid in suppressing the trouble.[43]

Sheriff R. H. Hager, County Attorney Daniels, and County Commissioner W. B. Cox were called to Guthrie on July 17 to answer for their failure to protect railroad property in L County; they declared they would not resign.[44] Brooks suggested that Secretary of Interior Hoke Smith direct the governor to suspend or remove the sheriff and deputies at Pond Creek; Secretary Smith replied that the exclusive jurisdiction to remove a sheriff from his office lay with the district court for the territory.[45]

Acting Governor Lowe, in a wire to President Ransom R. Cable of the Rock Island in Chicago, proposed to offer a five hundred dollar reward for the arrest and conviction of any person engaged in the destruction of bridges, trestles, cattle guards, crossings, buildings, cars, or other railway property on condition that the Rock Island comply with the ordinances of the cities and construct depots commensurate with their requirements. Cable was adamant; such an agreement, he replied, could be of no profit to anyone so long as the prevailing violence exercised against railroad property continued.[46] He appealed to the attorney general and the secretary of war:

On thirteenth inst. the Acting Governor, United States Attorney Brooks, and United States Marshal Nix of Oklahoma, after consulting with the Supreme Court, requested Secretary of War to send federal troops to Enid and Pond Creek in that Territory. The Marshal assured us that with this he would give us full protection [but] that condition continues and has grown worse, constituting that domestic violence which . . . justifies the interposition of the federal government. I have been in communication with the Sec. of War . . . who today informs me that troops cannot be used except to enforce orders of federal court, after the marshal advises that he cannot execute them unaided. It is difficult to find a judge of the court to whom to submit application for injunction. In the meantime we are being damaged in the actual destruction of property, and the carriage of the mails and interstate commerce seriously interrupted, and actually no adequate power to prevent it. . . . The situation is perilous and urgent. If we cannot have protection, we must abandon operation of line south of Kansas.[47]

Brooks recommended to Olney that, if proper, he

direct the judge of the district, McAtee [at Enid] to hear preliminary trials under warrants for obstructing mails. If I can get him to hear these cases outside of the counties of L and O, say in Kingfisher County, I believe I can check the trouble, but no use to issue warrants to be heard by commissioner in the counties where depredations are occurring.[48]

Olney wired Chief Justice Dale, and Dale replied that he had "directed McAtee to go to Kingfisher and remain until Brooks is through with work in his district."[49] Brooks advised Olney on July 19 that

I have suits prepared. Will go to Kingfisher at noon. Will consult Judge Dale before I leave. Please direct Judge McAtee to remain at Kingfisher and hear cases.[50]

On the same day, Nix telegraphed the attorney general that although he had some of his best deputies along the line with soldiers and railroad guards, the force was insufficient. It was "impossible to find out men connected with these mobs," Nix said, and officers of the counties still refused to cooperate.[51]

Finally, forty-eight men of Company H, Thirteenth Infantry, under Captain William Aurman and Lieutenant Abraham P. Buffington were dispatched from Fort Supply. En route, Lieutenant Buffington and eighteen men were detached to guard the bridges and rails south of Pond Creek; the remainder of the company camped near Enid to guard bridges and rails and handle other matters in that vicinity.

By July 23, the Enid situation was under control. The Fort Supply soldiers were ordered to cooperate with the staff of the commander of the Department of the Missouri, and General Nelson A. Miles telegraphed the adjutant general at Chicago:

Left Enid 4:30 p. m. with all available forces including ten deputy marshals. Arrived at Round Pond [Pond Creek] 5:35. A strong and aggressive display of our forces was made and people notified that any offensive act would be considered as hostile with the result that we met no opposition. Nineteen of the most prominent men of the town were arrested.

That evening, Marshal Nix wired Attorney General Olney from Guthrie:

I have returned from Enid and Round Pond. Am pleased to say the situation is much improved. Attorney Brooks procured order of injunction in L and O counties. Same have been served and are now getting out warrants for preliminary hearing before Judge McAtee in Kingfisher County. Have my best deputies on the ground and am having no trouble in serving papers.[52]

And Brooks wrote to Olney:

Now that the Judges agree with me that the parties can and should be taken out of their county . . . I feel that we are in a fair way to check the trouble. Judge McAtee is holding preliminary hearings and putting the screws to the offenders and it is having a good effect for the time. The culprits are all depending on preventing indictments by having the grand and petit juries in their counties fixed at the next regular fall term of the District Court, and claim that we cannot procure a jury in L or O county who will indict or convict them. I confess that it will be hard to get a jury in either county that will not be favorable to the defendants, but we will try to get over that trouble when we reach it.[53]

Nix added this encouraging note on July 24:

I have been successful in getting the names of about fifty of the men connected with the gang who has committed these depredations at Pond Creek, also have secured the names of a number of parties connected with the mob at Enid, and will doubtless be able to get the names of most all the parties connected with this outlawry by the time the preliminary hearing of the parties now arrested is closed.[54]

The marshal's viewpoint remained sympathetic to the problems of the townspeople in that

some of the best citizens have been connected with this work . . . they are desperate over the situation and claim they settled on the townsites in good faith and that the Government having selected the townsites, given them a name, post office, &c., should now help them to secure railroad facilities. . . .

My opinion is, until there is some influence brought to bear upon the railroad company to put depots at these towns, there will be trouble along this line for a long time.[55]

There was conjecture in spite of the order to conduct the preliminary trials at Kingfisher, Judge McAtee would decide he could not sit as a court there and would refer the cases back to L and O counties to be heard before a justice of the peace. Brooks telegraphed Olney on July 24 that "if he does this, we are utterly without power to enforce the law . . . we will be unable to stop the depredations against the R. R. Please wire him to hear them as first proposed."[56]

Olney declined to interfere. Judge McAtee resumed hearing the Pond Creek and Enid cases the morning of July 25, the question

230

of jurisdiction "still hanging." Brooks asked for an adjournment until one o'clock "to enable him to look up further authorities." This was granted over the protest of Judge Mackey for the defense. At one o'clock, court reconvened. McAtee ruled that although he possessed, as one of the supreme judges of the territory, "a common law right to sit as an examining magistrate," he had "no jurisdiction except [that which] he exercised in the county where the offense alleged is committed." He concluded: "The demurrer to the jurisdiction will be sustained. These cases will be heard in L County and O County beginning tomorrow morning at Pond Creek." The decision "brought a play of satisfaction over the face of the audience" and was accepted by the defendants with "an outbreak of applause," which the judge immediately suppressed, saying he disliked demonstrations in the courtroom either for or against his rulings.[57]

Brooks continued his efforts to obtain convictions and wired Olney from Pond Creek on July 26:

> Twenty-eight offenders were held under bond today to answer before grand jury for obstructing trains. Go to Enid tonight.[58]

On July 27, from Enid:

> Preliminary hearing had here today. Twelve parties held to appear before grand jury under charge of conspiracy to destroy Rock Island property. Will report from Guthrie.[59]

On July 28, Judge McAtee telegraphed the attorney general from Kingfisher:

> Held preliminary hearing in L County Thursday. All defendants in cases for violation Interstate Commerce Act and destruction of railroad property. Forty in number waved examination and gave bond for appearance. Same proceedings in O County yesterday. Ten defendants. Quiet restored and good feeling prevails here. Will be no further violence at present if arrangements are arrived at for depot at those towns.[60]

Returning from Washington, Governor Renfrow, visited Enid and Pond Creek immediately. He talked to the leading citizens calmly and earnestly and assured them they had many friends in public positions who would do everything in their power to secure depots for their cities.[61] With the pledge of these people to prevent further hostilities, he left for Chicago to present his appeal in person to the Rock Island.[62]

Cable listened to Governor Renfrow. He faced a great loss of business on the line through the Outlet. Already people were refusing to take passage or ship freight; the great Texas cattle business was shifting to the Santa Fe. Cable dictated a telegram to general counselor Low at Topeka, advising him to withdraw immediately all opposition to the railroad bill before Congress. Turning to Governor Renfrow, he said: "Tell these people the Rock Island will respect and obey any law the government may enact, but it will never surrender to a mob."

Judge McAtee had set July 28 for hearing the government-site towns' petition for an injunction to compel the Rock Island to slow its trains in obedience to city ordinances. Attorneys W. F. Evans of Topeka and John I. Dille of El Reno represented the railroad. Before the case was called, there arrived a telegram from the mayor of Pond Creek asking that no further action be taken because it would violate the truce agreed upon by the citizens and the company.[63]

On August 1, 1894, by a vote of twenty-four to twenty, the Senate receded from its county-seat amendment to House Bill 3606. The bill passed in its original form and became law on August 8, and the bitter controversy ended.

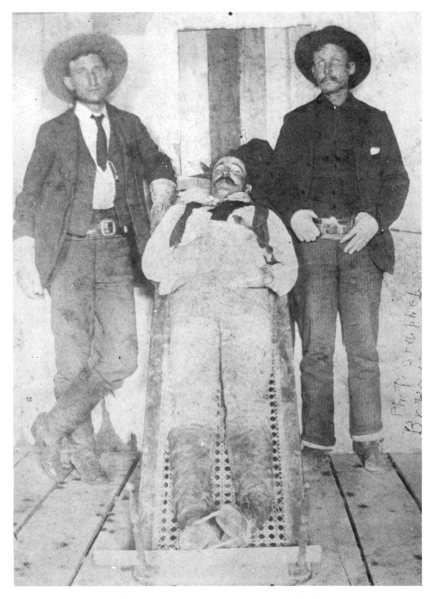

Tulsa Jack Blake, flanked on left by Deputy Marshal William Banks and on right by Captain J. S. Prather.

Tulsa Jack Blake in death.

The federal jail at Guthrie.

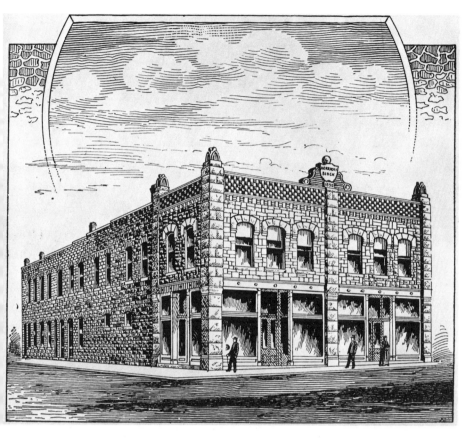

The Herriott Building at Division and Harrison avenues in Guthrie housed the federal court and the U.S. marshal's office.

Pawnee County Deputy Sheriff Frank Canton *(left)* and Pawnee County Sheriff Frank Lake *(right)*, both U.S. deputy marshals, on the trail of the Doolin gang. The officer in the center is Undersheriff T. A. Henry.

Charley Pierce was a member of the Doolin gang.

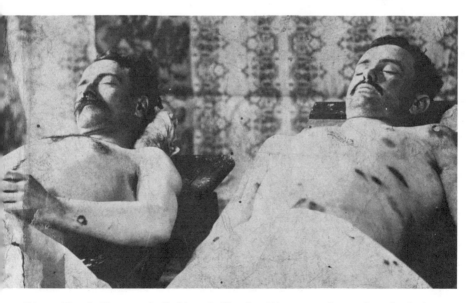

Bitter Creek Newcomb *(left)* and Charley Pierce at the undertaker's in Guthrie.

The Bill Dunn ranch house on Council Creek east of Ingalls, where Bitter Creek Newcomb and Charley Pierce were killed.

Flora Quick Mundis, alias Tom King.

XV   Horse Thieves and Counterfeiters

ALTHOUGH PREOCCUPIED WITH THE POND CREEK train robbery, the Casey brothers' fiasco, and the Rock Island railroad war, Nix's office conducted a hard field campaign against all types of federal offenders in 1894. On February 5,

J. B. Jones, deputy marshal of Tecumseh, came in with a batch of boarders for the federal jail. They were Billie Harris, Pen-ne-she Jee and Jesse Carter, all well known Sac and Fox Indians, and their crime is selling whiskey to their red brothers.

Deputy Marshal Poling transferred James Combest from the federal jail to Chandler today to answer the charge of selling whiskey to the Kickapoos.[1]

Deputy Marshal Robacker and posse . . . that had a fight with a gang of outlaws in the Osage Nation [April 2] returned to Guthrie last night with Sam Johnson, alias Sam Weaver, and William Thomas, whom they lodged in the federal jail. John Baker, another bad man, was released on bond.

Robacker says the battle occurred in a grove 40 miles southeast of Pawhuska . . . was a fierce one and lasted several minutes. Deputy Callahan, who killed bandit Tom Crooks during the fight, was given a hearing at Pawhuska and acquitted. Crooks was buried at Pawhuska. The outlaw band comprised six wild, fierce men who had been terrorizing that section for months. The outlaws would capture inoffensive Indians and string them up to trees in order to capture their guns and other effects. They practiced many other forms of outlawry. Robacker is a good one and is to be commended for annihilating a bad bunch. The remaining two bandits have left the territory.[2]

Deputy Harris, of Norman, and James E. Head, a horse thief and desperate character, came to their deaths at the hands of each other Wednesday evening [May 9], six miles east of Lexington, near the Pot county line. Harris was in search of Head, and stopped at Lexington the night before, and received an intimation that his man was in the vicinity. Mounting his horse, he started for the Pot country, and nearing the line, he encountered Head in the depths of the wood. . . . The details of that desperate fight will probably never be recorded [but] the traces are plainly discernible, and attest to the fierceness of the conflict. The searching party found them exactly as they had fallen, with weapons clasped in their hands . . . both shot in two places, and both stone dead.[3]

Deputy Marshal Banks and posse came in last night [June 5] from the Cheyenne country with James Thurman and Arnold Meines, charged with horse stealing. . . . Dave Patterson was brought over from Pawnee to do a ten days' job at the federal inn for giving an Indian a drink of firewater. . . . Deputy Charles Lowry came down from Ponca with a batch of federal sinners.[4]

Eight deputy marshals [deputy and posse] trailed Bud Smith [a notorious Texas bandit] into Watonga yesterday afternoon [June 19] and attempted to arrest him. When the officers ordered him to throw down his weapons he fired at close range, leaped on his horse and started through the town, firing indiscriminately. One of the deputies rested his Winchester on the saddle and fired at long range at the fleeing bandit, hitting him in the back and killing him instantly. He was taken to the courthouse and an inquest was held by the coroner. There was about $1,500 in rewards on the dead bandit's head.[5]

Monday [July 30] Lon Poling, deputy marshal, killed Bill Baker at Chandler. The trouble was an arrest for cattle stealing. Both men drew their guns.[6]

Deputy Marshal Sam Large shot and killed T. V. Powell Monday morning [August 13] shortly after sunrise . . . ten miles southeast of Cleveland. Deputy Marshals Large and Joe Eads and a posse were after Powell and a man named Mike Guffey. They had warrants for them for horse stealing. They ran across the house of Powell and surrounded it. Powell came out and went to a corral. He was called to halt five times, but he would not, but ran to where his gun was. One of the possemen called to Large to look out for the man's gun. As Powell was getting his hands on his Winchester, Large let him have it and he fell in his tracks. He did not die until yesterday morning. Powell is an old time outlaw. He has been scouting this country for the last four years. The neighbors all feared him, and were afraid to make a complaint. Mike Guffey was captured and brought to this city.[7]

Henry Sparks, a twelve-year-old white boy was brought over this morning from the Kiowa reservation and lodged in the federal jail on the charge of assault to kill Deputy Marshal Choeks. The facts as can be gotten are that the boy had trouble with his parents and left home. The marshal run across him and arrested him. . . . The boy had a sixshooter concealed on his person, the marshal not thinking [it necessary] to search him. The boy watched his chance and when he caught the marshal's back turned deliberately drew his gun and shot the marshal in the head, the ball coming out his right eye. Not being content with that he fired three more shots at him as he lay on the ground. At the time they left for here with the boy the marshal was still alive with little hope of recovery.[8]

Lewis Courtright was taken to Fort Smith yesterday by Deputy Marshal S. S. Nix to answer two charges—one for impersonating a deputy United States marshal and one for highway robbery. For the past year he has been systematically arresting people in the Creek and Seminole country. Bringing them on this side of the line [Hell's Fringe], he would take their personal effects and then turn the victims free. In most cases the victims were poor, ignorant parties or Indians.[9]

Emanual Mills was released from the federal jail today after being incarcerated for some time on the charge of rape. Mills has been making his home in the Kickapoo country for the past three years, when he wasn't in jail. He has been arrested altogether about seven times [for] rape and once [for] highway robbery, and has never had to stand trial yet. It looks very much like someone has been job[b]ing him.[10]

In a drunken fight at Wintan, Deputy Marshal Snoddy and Frank Brown were fatally shot, and James Brown, J. R. Knight and Charles Kitchen severely wounded. The men, it seems, had a grudge against Marshal Snoddy. While intoxicated they met him alone and threatened him. A terrible battle with Winchesters followed. . . . As yet James Brown, Knight and Kitchens have not been taken into custody.[11]

Two Caddo Indians named Caddo Jake and Charley Adams were arraigned before Judge Burford at El Reno yesterday, charged with stealing horses from a white man named Taggett. They pleaded not guilty and were committed to the Guthrie jail to be tried at the next term of court. The Indians' account of the matter . . . was that the Arapahoes came down to visit the Caddoes and danced with them, and the usual Indian custom on such occasions is to load the visitors with presents. The Caddo Indians were poor and had nothing to give the Arapahoes . . . and it would never do to violate the time-honored customs of the noble red man. So the Caddoes went out and stole some horses from the white men in that vicinity and gave them to the Arapahoes, who returned to their tepees on the North Canadian well pleased with the result of their visit to their friends. The Caddoes will be obliged to settle with Uncle Sam for the horses.[12]

There were many arrests for other crimes ranging from sending obscene matter through the mails to conspiracy and perjury. Cattle and horse thievery, however, was the most common complaint.

Settlers living near Watonga decided to put an end to a gang that had been systematically stealing their livestock and driving it into the Texas Panhandle. On April 20, they "ran down Dock Bishop and Frank Latham and made them surrender after exchanging twenty shots, one of which broke Latham's arm." The prisoners were then lynched for "equine abduction."[13] The *Oklahoma Daily Press-Gazette*[14] noted that

> for the first time in the history of Oklahoma, a vigilance committee has been formed and taken summary action on two disreputables. This is to be deeply regretted. But the fault is not to be placed with the settlers. In their five years of settlement the people have proved themselves to be law-abiding and capable of civilized life. But lately there has been a perfect devastation of crime. . . .
>
> The first feeling is to blame the authorities, but they have not been derelict nor cowardly. Their attempts to capture the outlaw have failed . . . because Oklahoma is surrounded by a wild country. The Indian Territory is the cause of all Oklahoma's troubles. It is a refuge for all the outlaws of the west. It is the lair of the robber and murderer, who rushes out and preys upon the settler and then retreats to covert. Settle the Indian Territory and the epidemic will cease. The wolf's den should be wiped out.

The Mutual Protection Association of Oklahoma was chartered by Secretary Lowe "for the purpose of suppressing lawlessness, to cause the speedy arrest and punishment of criminals, to assist the civic authorities in ridding Oklahoma and the Indian nations of the criminal element now menacing our people and retarding progress." Originating in Blaine County, it was "authorized to organize subordinate lodges throughout the territory."[15] And the grand lodge of the Anti–Horse Thief Association of Oklahoma Territory, in session at Armory Hall, Oklahoma City, pledged intentions to make the horse thief hard to catch "if we have to plant more trees to hang him."

In May, 1894, deputies working the Tecumseh district broke up the "most remarkable nest of horse thieves ever known." Twenty-seven head of fine mules and ponies were recovered, seventeen prominent residents and citizens of that community and the Seminole Nation were arrested, and sufficient evidence was unearthed for a federal grand jury to return thirty indictments. The organization extended into Arkansas and Arizona, and all along the route the thieves had caves and other places in which to seclude themselves and stock from pursuers.[16] Of eleven persons finally charged, seven pleaded guilty, one, released on bond, left the territory and was never seen again, and three escaped and were never apprehended.

The most elusive horse thief operating in Oklahoma during this period was a female desperado who dressed in male attire and traveled under a curious appellation: Tom King. The territorial press described her as "medium height, rather prepossessing, and badly tanned. She has the appearance of a well-proportioned boy of 19, and passes herself as part Cherokee."[17] An enthusiastic correspondent for the *Wichita Daily Eagle*[18] observed that

> if she was a man she would be a fine type of the cavalier. She is an elegant rider, very daring. She has a fine suit of hair as black as a raven's wing and eyes like sloes that would tempt a knight of St. John. Notwithstanding her outdoor life she still retains her fine olive complexion, her figure is faultless, and if she had been less wild, better educated and raised in New York or Boston, she would be classed as a positive beauty.

According to contemporary reports,[19] she was born Flora Quick in 1875, the youngest daughter of Daniel Quick, a wealthy farmer and stockman who lived on Big Creek ten miles south of Holden in Johnson County, Missouri. Daniel Quick was "honorable in his dealings, but rough and uncouth in his everyday life." He had married twice and "had an issue of fifteen children, six dying in infancy, the nine surviving being six boys and three girls." Flora was his favorite, "full of nerve and energy, and assisted him in herding cattle and other ranch duties." At age 14, she was sent to Holden College to learn to play the organ and practice the other arts of fine young ladies. But confinement was too much for her. Within a few weeks she returned home to "resume her outdoor mode of living." Her father died a year later, leaving an estate of two thousand four hundred acres of land and thirteen thousand dollars in personal property to be divided among the children. The administrator, Flora's half-brother, sent her to school at Sedalia, "where she remained only one term." She met Ora Mundis, "a dissolute character whose principal object was to get her estate," and, despite the protestations of her sisters and brothers, married him. Flora and Mundis lived in Holden about three weeks, and "it was nothing unusual to see them together night after night in the saloons drinking." From Holden they went to the Indian Nations in a covered wagon, ostensibly on a hunting expedition. They were gone almost a year. When they returned to Holden, "both carried a small armory on their persons" and warned former acquaintances that they were "bad, bad people not to be trifled with." The city marshal promptly relieved them of their weapons. Finally, Flora sold her share of the family estate and they departed for the Oklahoma country, reaching Guthrie in late November, 1892, "where they have since led a checkered life." Novelists have romanticized Flora Quick Mundis as an outlaw queen and leader of a robber gang that terrorized Oklahoma and Indian territories. She was neither, and her delineation by some historians as Bob Dalton's mistress and spy for his bandit legion in all their depredations from 1890 until their demise at Coffeyville in October, 1892, is without logic or documentation.

Flora and Mundis took up residence in the Cottonwood Creek bottoms of West Guthrie and "flitted about the gambling halls nightly"—until Flora's money ran out. Then Mundis galloped off alone. Later, when asked by a *Leader*[20] reporter, "What has become of the man who was with you down below?" Flora replied, "I don't know; we didn't get along well—fought every day. 'Spect he's among better company." She never saw Mundis again.

Flora was not one to be lonely. She became acquainted with Jessie Whitewings, the fleshy, flaxen-haired former mistress of an Indian gambler. Flora was an apt student and in no time had a place of her own on the corner of Fourth Street and Grant Avenue, where she "traded" for horses and money.

She became a familiar figure on the streets, dressed in stunning costumes, and always rode a good animal. Although natural pigmentation and a life in the wind and sun accounted for her coloring, she readily passed for a Cherokee half-blood. No scandal was attached to her name until she swore out a warrant for one Doc Jordan, charging him with assault with intent to rape. Doc didn't stay around long enough to deny the charge; deeming discretion the better part of valor, he hied himself out of the territory and the case was dropped.[21]

After that, no man in his right senses would patronize her place. So Flora stashed her stunning costumes, donned cowboy garb, and instead of trading for horses, began stealing them. There is no record of the extent of her lifting, rebranding, driving, and selling of stock, but during the spring of 1893, she allegedly took horses from field and pasture, off the streets of towns, anywhere, disposing of them across Hell's Fringe. Her known operations were confined to Logan, Canadian, and Oklahoma counties. In June, she was arrested by Deputy Marshals Madsen and Heck Thomas and jailed at Oklahoma City.

Here she met Ernest ("Killer") Lewis, a member of the old Starr gang of Indian Territory, wanted for murder in the state of Washington and the Chickasaw Nation and being held for participation in an 1892 Santa Fe passenger train robbery at Wharton.[22] Although behind bars, Lewis convinced Tom King that there were more opportunities in train robbing than in her line of endeavor. At three o'clock on the morning of June 27, Tom "displayed her charms" to a none-too-bright turnkey, locked him in her cell, and fled with Killer Lewis.[23] In the wild chase that followed, the pair stole two horses at Edmond and escaped into the Outlet.

While officers continued the search, Tom and Lewis camped near a bridge where the Santa Fe crossed Black Bear Creek between Red Rock and Wharton and made plans to rob the train. For this job, they enlisted the help of a half-wit and former acquaintance of Tom named Manvel.

Manvel boarded No. 408 at 3:30 P.M. on June 29, a Winchester wrapped in his coat, and hid himself in a closet of the smoking car. As the train started north, conductor Al Glazier passed through the car. Manvel leaped from the closet and covered him with the rifle. He ordered the conductor to throw up his hands, which the latter did. His next order was "Pull the bell cord." Again the conductor obeyed. When the train stopped, the desperado ordered his man out on the ground, then commanded: "Go to the engine and call down the engineer and fireman." Glazier started, the desperado at his heels. At that instant, Glazier "saw his opportunity." He grabbed the rifle from the would-be robber's hands and "hit him over the head a blow that brought him to the ground." After capturing him, the conductor discovered on his person "two revolvers and four sticks of dynamite with fuse already attached."[24]

There being no officers along the road in the Outlet, Glazier wired the marshal's office at Guthrie: "What shall I do with him? I think I had better take him to Wichita." Here the prisoner stated that "two companions with horses were waiting where he intended to hold up the train."[25]

Chris Madsen and a posse hurried to Black Bear Creek on a special train. As Madsen wrote later,

> we could not do anything except look around. We found a waterhole not far from the road where two people, a man and a woman, had been camped for a while. From the size of their tracks we guessed that it had been Lewis and Tom King, and I learned afterwards that we had guessed correct. . . . Heck Thomas went to Wichita and returned the prisoner to Oklahoma. Manvel was committed to the lunatic asylum at Bloomington, Illinois. We next heard of Lewis in Colorado, where he killed another man and was sent to prison. After serving eight years, he went to Bartlesville, got into a gun fight with the local constable, and both of them died together.[26]

Tom parted company with Lewis after the abortive attempt at

245

train robbery and went back to stealing horses. On July 12, she was sighted in Guthrie. Officers

went on the lookout, but she was too smooth to catch. Last night [July 15] she was reported seen down in the bottoms and the officers made a thorough search. Not finding her, they gave it up and in coming up town Deputy Robacker walked up Second street. As he passed Baxter and Cammack's livery stable, he noticed what appeared to be a cowpuncher perhaps 18 years old sitting in front talking with some men. His suspicions were aroused and stepping up he put his hand on "its" shoulder and felt a quiver of apprehension, which proved he had the one wanted, and made the arrest.[27]

Tom was returned to Oklahoma City. On August 8, she again escaped jail by "tricking and confusing the turnkey." This time, the jailer's name was J. N. Wise. He traced her to a point near Yukon, where he engaged the services of Canadian County Deputy Sheriff J. M. Ogle. Wise and Ogle "kept strict watch in the vicinity" and captured Tom two days later as she came out of a cornfield to get a drink from a farmer's well.[28]

Back in Oklahoma City, "Landlord Wise placed her in a steel cage and pledged to look after her with vigilant care." So Tom decided to employ an attorney. Lawyer D. C. Lewis obtained an order to release her on bail, but another horse theft charge was pending in Canadian County. Madsen and Heck Thomas escorted her, with several other prisoners, by wagon from Oklahoma City to El Reno. En route, Tom asked Madsen: "What's the name of the jailer where you're taking me?"

"Why do you want to know?" Chris asked.

"Every jailer in Oklahoma has his price. If I know who this one is, I'll know his."

On the night of December 8, there swept through the territory the startling report that

TOM KING, THE ROMANTIC HORSE THIEF, BREAKS EL RENO JAIL IN HER THIRD ESCAPE; SHE IS BOUND TO MAKE A RECORD!

It seems there is no jail that can hold her. Even the Oklahoma City jail, which is considered the strongest in the territory, yielded before her magic art. . . . She is very cunning and clever. The vigilant officers usually get her, but getting her does not seem to be of much effect in curing the mania with which she is afflicted. She finds the same delight in horse stealing as other women would in reading novels or playing croquet. It is her ambition to be the most famous horse thief of her generation, and already she has taken more of them than any man in the history of the Southwest.

Canadian County officers have reached a point that no mercy shall be shown her on account of sex. Messengers have been sent post haste to Yukon for bloodhounds there, and they will be put on her trail at once. . . . The chase will be watched with interest. It is very unnatural to see a woman pursued by hounds. It recalls slavery days and brings to mind the sad story of Eliza Harris so beautifully told in Mrs. Stowe's "Uncle Tom's Cabin."[29]

In the excitement of her escape, no one seemed to take time to inquire how it had been accomplished. On December 10, a party who "stood on the ground floor of El Reno affairs" reported that Tom King had fled from the Canadian County jail "on the wings of love." It was

an elopement, and not an escape—with a deputy sheriff. Tom left jail Friday night in the guise of a well dressed lady, and she walked through the open door unmolested. Not many yards from the jail she leaped out of her dresses and petticoats and appeared in her usual suit of men's clothes; hopped on a fleet steed and rode towards the horizon with the speed of the wind.

Somebody finally asked where Deputy Sheriff So-and-so was, and no answer was made. All his haunts were searched, but he could not be found. Wise men shook their heads and said nothing. The sheriff was reticent and made no charges, but it soon leaked out that Deputy So-and-so was then riding over the swelling prairie by the side of the famous outlaw.

Yesterday a grand jury investigated the matter, and while they are silent, there is no doubt they found that the deputy sheriff in question aided Tom King and then eloped with her. His two fine horses were missing . . . and this is what first led to the suspicion that he was implicated. . . . The romance will probably end, however, when the Yukon bloodhounds catch up with them [for] it is said they are pursuing them with all the enthusiastic ferocity of that breed of canines.[30]

It is not clear where Tom and the deputy parted company, but she managed to elude her canine pursuers—except one. Tom rode ahead of the baying brute most of the night, across the South Canadian and the Wichita country to a point near the Kiowa-Comanche-Apache Reservation line, where, next day, the bloodhound was discovered with "his toes turned up." Attached to one ear with a hairpin was a card which read:

Turn luse sum more of your dogs of war. I have still twenty rounds in my belt. If the sheriff of 'L' reno will follow me, I will give him a dose of the saim medisine. TOM KING.

The *Guthrie Daily Leader* of December 17 reported that

the hound was shot under the neck between the forelegs and the bullet passed out between the shoulder blades. This indicates that she shot the dog from her saddle while he was making a lunge at her. . . . He evidently had caught her trousers leg; for beside where he lay a piece of Scotch tweed of irregular form and about the size of the sole of a man's shoe was found, which is said to be a piece of the suit of men's clothes which Miss King was allowed to wear while in jail. Another evidence that the hound was close to her when fired upon is the fact that the hair on the dog's breast was powder-burned.

The animal was discovered by two Comanche Indians who took him into their camp after the day's hunt, to the "great delight of their squaws and papooses." A scout from Anadarko happened to be at the camp, and the card was given to him for interpretation. He had been advised of Tom's flight and explained it "to the astonishment of the Indian maidens." He bought the dog for fifty cents, strung him to his saddle, and took him to El Reno, where "the brute victim of Tom King's unerring aim was placed on exhibition, so to speak, as a warning to her pursuers."[31] The dog, of the highest breed of bloodhound, belonged to a Bohemian, who

> is so enraged that he has tendered the services of himself and two fellow countrymen, fully equipped, to the sheriff of Canadian county to avenge the loss of the animal . . . and the sheriff, as highly enraged as his Bohemian friend on account of Tom's threat, is determined to recapture her if it costs him the entire income of his office.[32]

Tom had recrossed the South Canadian into Oklahoma County, for on December 22, the *Oklahoma Daily Press-Gazette* reported that the El Reno deputy sheriff "alleged to have been captivated by her seductive charms" arrived in town to recover his pony from an unsuspecting local citizen who had obtained it "by virtue of a bill of sale executed by the noted female horsethief."

There was no further trace of Tom in the months that followed. Rumor had it she had organized her own gang and was one of five bandits who held up the post trader's store at Cantonment in Blaine County on March 5, 1894, compelling the proprietor to unlock the safe and hand over nearly one hundred dollars.[33] The identity of the gang was never established.

Many persons believed she was hiding in the Indian Nations and that she was connected with the gang of horse thieves broken up by deputies at Tecumseh in May. This was discounted by attorney Lewis, who had received a letter from his client the last of April. It bore a railroad postmark. The contents did not disclose her whereabouts, but "notified him that she was on her way to South America."[34]

There was an effort to trace Tom through her old friend and tutor Jessie Whitewings. The latter had left Guthrie with the opening of the Outlet. For several months, she frequented the saloons and gambling dens in Perry, then disappeared completely.

On August 7, Sheriff H. S. McCleary of Fredonia, Kansas, wired Nix's office that he had Mrs. Mundis, alias Tom King, in custody. She was "accompanied by another female in male attire, named Ettie McGee, alias Ed Bullock." Ed Bullock proved to be Jessie Whitewings. When arrested, the two women were in camp near Fredonia with a well-provisioned wagon and five stolen horses. In the wagon was a heavy trunk filled with fine jewelry and laces.[35]

The Canadian County sheriff lost no time in returning Tom King to the territory, but he "was not exactly satisfied with himself that he did." The El Reno Democrat[36] explained:

> There is something very ominous in the atmosphere of the jail here . . .
> a death-like quietude and a tip-toe carefulness about the place not common of men used to handling hardened criminals. The officials appear awkward and confused, and the turnkey is beside himself. The famous woman, who has caused so much trouble in the past, is going to cause much more in the immediate future. The jailers have arranged it so that a physician is near at hand . . . although they believe the event will take place without accident.

Tom had seduced one man too many. Who and where were not known. With a baby due and several trials staring her in the face, no judge could be found who would sentence her to a minute's service anywhere. She was released on bail.

Tom left Oklahoma for good. No one ever knew what became of her or the child. One authority[37] says she was killed outside Wichita, Kansas, after an attempted bank holdup in 1893 and lies buried in the family plot of her native Cass (?) County, Missouri.

On April 2, 1896, attorney Lewis received another letter. It, too, bore a railroad postmark and did not disclose her whereabouts:

> I am on a train moving west. I am having a good time. Look after my case at El Reno carefully, for I may be back about Christmas.
>
> TOM KING.[38]

Tom never returned for trial, and Lewis had no further word from her.

Years later, Heck Thomas described to a reporter what was supposed to have been Tom King's end: A young man was killed in a holdup in a border town near Tombstone, Arizona. Upon burial, he proved to be a woman whose body scars and Bertillon measurements, taken in Guthrie, Oklahoma City, and El Reno jails, tallied with Tom King's.[39]

By midsummer, 1894, the government's chief concern had become bands of counterfeiters operating in Oklahoma Territory. Banks and merchants were receiving spurious silver coins, and several thousand light-weight gold coins also had been placed in circulation. The latter had been "impaired by a new and ingenious method of removing the milled or corrugated rim of the coin, decreasing its value by five per cent, with new milling put on the coin and in all appearances made perfect." The Treasury Department sent out warning notices, and Nix's office shouldered the task of attempting to discover the source.[40]

The mystery began unraveling on July 15 when

> Deputy J. J. Graham and posse came up from Pottawatomie County with James Crum and Mrs. Cora Smith. They are charged with passing spurious coin of silver denominations.[41]

On July 20, Deputies J. W. Gill and J. C. Renfrow

> came up from Tecumseh with William Smith, W. T. Gage and Mrs. Anna Crum, all charged with making and passing counterfeit coin. The officers claim positive evidence against them . . . having several dollars of the money already passed, capturing considerable at the time of the arrest, together with the moulds.[42]

And on August 9,

> four more members of the gang . . . working the country west of Oklahoma City were arrested by Deputy Marshals S. S. Nix and Ike Renfro and are now in jail at that place. They are Mrs. Walker and her two sons [J. W. Walker and Joseph Cowden], and John Crilley. The latter seems to be the leader, the others simply circulators. . . . [Assistant] District Attorney McMechan thinks it is the most important capture made.[43]

Crilley, who was about seventy years old, owned a place in Pottawatomie County southeast of Tecumseh where officers found a large quantity of money; bulk metal for making same; a box fitted with dies and plates for dimes, quarters, half-dollars, and dollars; and a set of burglar tools.[44]

The "small operators," tried at Guthrie, were given short prison terms by Judge Dale. Crum, first to plead guilty to a charge of uttering and passing, "played an important part in the conviction of

other members of the gang and got off with a thirty day sentence."
William Smith, who received two years in the penitentiary at Brooklyn, New York, complained in a letter to the *State Capital* that
"Crum is the most guilty man of the outfit." Smith listed people
and places to bear out his allegations and expressed hope that "justice will soon overtake him as there are parties on his trail."[45] Crum
was released from the federal jail on December 16, but "before he
got one breath of fresh air was rearrested and turned over to the
sheriff of Cowley County, Kansas, where he and Gage are wanted
on a charge of stealing a span of mules. The mules were traced to
the Chickasaw Nation where they disposed of them. There were
also papers here from Paris, Texas court, charging him with introducing and selling stolen stock in that district."[46]

Crilley won a change of venue to Oklahoma County. Nix[47] calls
him

the prince of counterfeiters. His specialties were single and double
'Eagles'—ten and twenty dollar gold coins of United States money. He
denied the charge in detail, averring that he maintained his laboratory
for experimental and scientific purposes . . . [however] a number of
eagles had been passed in Tecumseh, and those who had received them
from Crilley identified both the counterfeiter and the coin. Judge Scott
sentenced him to five years in the Kings County Penitentiary at Brooklyn, New York.

The marshals had succeeded in disposing of one gang, but "another source of counterfeit money continued to pour its stream of
coins into circulation."[48] Finally, a spurious coin distributor with
headquarters in Stillwater was arrested at Perry while he was intoxicated, and he unwittingly revealed the location of an underground cave a few miles east of Perkins. The *Daily Oklahoman* of
December 12, 1894, describes how the ring was broken:

After locating the underground mint, the deputies organized and armed
themselves to the teeth. At 2 o'clock yesterday morning the officers
descended into the cavern and after traversing a subterranean passage
for 100 yards, quickly burst in a door and found twenty-five men at
work. The counterfeiters . . . trapped so adroitly and taken by surprise
. . . failed to show fight and scattered like rats through hidden exits. All
escaped except Guy Harper, L. Crawford, Joseph Tillery, Jess Lockett
and Sam Lockett . . . but it develops that they were the leaders and
spurious money makers, and the others were only "shovers" their work
being to float spurious coin. With the prisoners the officers gathered in
three buckets full of counterfeit dollars and two tubs full of dimes, quar-

ters and nickels, besides a splendid and costly assortment of moulds and other queer paraphernalia.

The underground cavern was elaborately furnished, containing folding beds, works of art, divans, fine Brussels carpet and a safe. The men had been operating in the cave nearly eight months, and much of the spurious coin was boxed and expressed to pals in Indiana and Missouri. All of those captured are educated and well-dressed, and two are on the "chappy" order. Tillery was at one time an employee in the Philadelphia mint.

XVI Robbery Sanctioned by Law

ALTHOUGH NIX'S DEPUTIES WERE LAUDED for their successful campaigns against horse thieves and counterfeiters, their continual arresting of homesteaders for cutting timber on government lands and Indian preserves rankled like a festering sore and became a public issue.

On August 8, 1894, U.S. District Attorney Brooks notified Judge McAtee at Kingfisher that

> it is very important that you have a U. S. commissioner at Alva at once. Parties are being arrested in M [Woods] County and brought by the Marshals, with a raft of witnesses, all the way to Guthrie for hearing before the U. S. commissioner here. The expense will break the Government.[1]

At the same time, Brooks directed U.S. Commissioner Charles J. Wrightsman at Pawnee to "use every effort to break up the combination of timber cutters" operating in Q County and that portion of the Osage Reservation attached to the Fifth Judicial District under his jurisdiction, explaining that

> under the Statute all parties interested in cutting timber on Government lands are guilty. Where one procures another to cut he is as guilty as the party cutting and should be punished, and where I thought the parties guilty I would hold them over, ignoring any trumped up testimony. They are not entitled to a regular, thorough hearing before a U. S. commissioner . . . nor is he required to suffer his time taken up by arguments and motions by attorneys for defendants . . . he is only required to hear the witnesses for the United States and a statement from the defendant, if he desires to make one, and if he has probable cause to believe the defendant committed the offense charged, or some other offense, it is his duty to bind them over to the district court. Witnesses should always be sworn to their attendance before commissioners, and the witness is only entitled to mileage from the point where he is summoned, not always from his residence. This is a point that commissioners should be very careful about, there have been great

253

impositions on the Government by false statements of witnesses claiming mileage.[2]

Brooks similarly instructed U.S. Commissioner F. M. Beale at Newkirk:

It is necessary that the commissioners watch these witnesses allowances with great care, and with all their care and caution the witnesses will gorge the government.[3]

And he clarified the government's position to U.S. Commissioner J. M. Morgan at Arapaho:

Referring to your letter of the 9th inst. I have to say that warrants should not be issued for parties cutting dead timber for firewood or posts, or any other purpose where it is used for their family . . . and they should be permitted to cut green timber necessary for improvement of their claim-houses, stables and outbuildings. A settler has the right to cut timber for the purpose of clearing his claim to cultivate, where he has not sufficient tillable land. But they are not permitted to cut standing timber dead or green to sell or speculate on. . . . The object of the law is not to oppress settlers who in good faith cut a little timber for their own use, but to prevent settlers or anyone else from destroying the timber of the Government and selling the same. It is necessary to leave the matter largely to the discretion of the commissioners. Where you know a man is abusing this right he should be arrested.[4]

When U.S. Commissioner T. L. O'Bryan at Woodward asked what disposition should be made of five hundred cedar posts taken from persons who cut them on government land, the district attorney replied that

the deputy should confiscate and mark the posts with the letters "U. S." and put them where they will be safe [until] we can bring action to have same sold.[5]

Concerning a complaint from Captain A. E. Woodson, acting Indian agent at Darlington, that timber was being taken from the Cheyenne and Arapaho reservations, Brooks wrote:

I have called attention of U. S. Marshals at El Reno to this matter, and instructed them to arrest all parties interested in this traffic and confiscate the timber. . . . I understand that the parties claim that the Indians sell the timber to them, but this they have no right to do and it will not protect the parties.[6]

Marshal Nix entered the controversy when Lewis H. Hornbeck, publisher of the *Minco Minstrel*, wrote Governor Renfrow demanding "relief from the outrage of deputy marshals arresting our people for the alleged crime of hauling a few faggots of dead wood out of the Wichita reservation. . . . The idea of the deputies no doubt was to enrich themselves with fees, and they had no hesitancy in tearing these men away from their homes and compelling them to walk across the country and plead before a court."[7] Renfrow handed the letter to Nix, and on November 23 the marshal responded:

> If this is the case, it is in defiance with the orders of this office. . . . United States commissioners have positive instructions from the U. S. attorney to discharge all parties brought before them charged with using dead timber that is only fit for firewood. In such case the deputies are not allowed fees for their work . . . furthermore are not authorized to make an arrest for timber cutting of any kind unless defendant is caught in the act or warrant has been approved by the United States attorney or his assistants.
>
> Now, I would like for you to write me fully regarding the complaint made in your letter, giving the name of the defendants, deputies making such arrests, dispositions that were made of the cases. I assure you that it is my desire to have the deputies do their duty and that they shall do nothing more.[8]

Hornbeck provided no information, and Nix issued new instructions to his deputies. Hereafter, they must procure warrants for timber cutters from the commissioner in the district where the offense was committed. After serving a warrant, they must in every instance take the prisoner before that commissioner for examination, "unless the place where the arrest is made is a considerable distance further than to some other commissioner."

Public criticism continued, however. Oklahoma City's *Times-Journal* repeatedly sympathized with the woodcutters, and called the arrest of homesteaders and ranchers in the western counties "a burning disgrace." The *Kingfisher Free Press*[9] noted that very few such arrests had been made during the summer. Winter was coming on and the settlers would need wood to keep their little ones safe from the gnawing cold, but "the deputies, who are always on another scent when a Yeager or a Black is to be captured, are already cleaning their guns, buckling on their arsenals, and making other preparation to capture the unwary who thrusts an ax blade into a government limb." A special dispatch from Seger, Washita County, reported in February that with its Italian climate suddenly superseded by a howling blizzard, the grass covered by snow which fell to the depth of six inches on the level, and range cattle suffering, "we had the pleasure of a visit from two different gangs of deputy marshals. They were here for the purpose of arresting wood haulers, the snow making it possible for them to be easily tracked. . . . Three of Cloud Chief's most prominent citizens were arrested in the Kiowa country, and as they were informed in regard to the law, they were not taken to [the nearest commissioners at] El Reno or Anadarko, but were brought before the U. S. commissioner at this place."[10]

When it was learned that a deputy had passed through King-fisher en route to Guthrie with five timber cutters from Blaine County, the *Times-Journal*[11] editorialized:

Good timber does not exist in Blaine county on unclaimed land. The government land in Blaine county is either open prairie or scrub oak — blackjack. None of such timber is fit for any purpose except firewood, and the land is worth more with the timber off than as it was when the country was thrown open to settlement. . . . The traffic in Indian liqour sellers is to some extent excusable, for the Indian is not averse to spending a portion of his time in jail, but this timber cutting is such a flimsy pretext for man-hunting that it must bring the blush of shame to the cheek of even a deputy marshal.

The *Pottawatomie County Democrat* asked on February 2:

Why are our citizens arrested and taken to Guthrie when we have a United States commissioner at Tecumseh? Such work is an outrage. . . . The marshals making these arrests do not live in our county, and this is another feature of injustice, as we have marshals here who know the condition of affairs and are capable of attending to these matters. The arrests made are men who have leased land of the Indians, with the privilege of cutting timber necessary to improve the land. The contracts were made in good faith and the Indians are satisfied. It is time these raids on our people were stopped. Robbery is a crime, *even though sanctioned by law.*

Not until September, 1895, did Judge McAtee of the Fifth Judicial District, where most violations occurred, bring an end to such expeditions. In *United States* v. *Joseph Gautier*, against whom complaint was filed and sworn to before a commissioner in Logan County for an offense committed in Grant County, McAtee, taking his cue from Section 10 of the Organic Act, Statutes of 1893, page 44, ruled that "a writ issued by a commissioner of one county for an offense committed in another county cannot be legally served; that no commissioner, other than one in the county where the offense was committed, can hold an examination." He instructed Marshal Nix: "You are hereby notified not to serve any writ from a commissioner's court that does not meet with the requirements of this decision. You are further instructed not to serve capiases issued on information by the U. S. district attorney in cases where the defendant was first arrested on a commissioner's warrant, unless said warrant was issued by a commissioner of the Fifth judicial district and in the county where the offense was committed." Furthermore, the judge declared, any defendants in custody with cases then pending under these circumstances should be discharged. Nix promptly complied, directing his deputies to return all such federal processes to the clerk of the district court, endorsed "unserved, by order of the United States Marshal," and the practice of taking timber-law offenders to a distant commissioner for trial ceased.[12]

Even though the settlers were technically guilty, this work of the deputy marshals, federal commissioners, and prosecutors built a prejudice among old-timers that has not entirely died in this century.

There also were complaints from reservation Indians. On January 11, 1895, venerable old Chief Keokuk and some of the leading men of the Sac and Fox tribe arrived in Washington and presented Attorney General Olney and the Interior Department with "a series of charges of scandalous conduct on the part of United States officials in Oklahoma." Deputy marshals, they said, were "in the habit" of coming into their country, "arresting our people by the wagon load, taking them to Guthrie to get mileage, and charging them as guilty of introducing intoxicants into the tribe, when in many cases the charges are untrue." The deputies had developed a new method. "They took an Indian before the commissioner, said his name was Buffalo Horn, and got $25 fees on him. Buffalo Horn was then taken downstairs, and in a little while another deputy took him before the commissioner as Bitter Creek. Seven times the Indian was taken before the commissioner while in custody, each time under a different name, and $175 collected." The Buffalo Horn trick had been worked "four or five times" with other Indians. Chief Keokuk admitted that he had "some bad Indians" but claimed that the deputies, "instead of discriminating . . . take some of our best members who are guiltless . . . to make fees on them."[13]

Olney was aware of the problem. Brooks had informed him in December that

the question of arresting and punishing Indians on the different Reservations in this Territory, on charge of selling and introducing spirituous liquors into the Reservations, has given my office considerable annoyance. . . . Indian names are difficult to understand, many are known by more than one name, and have been arrested more than once, under different names, for the same offense. I have issued several orders to the Commissioners and the Marshal's office, endeavoring to prevent this wholesale arrest of Indians, and have checked it to some extent. . . . I feel sure [that if] Indian Agents would act in the matter, the trouble could be avoided. The Agents in some instances have hesitated to act, on the ground that it is not their duty. Now if their Department would request or direct the Agents to aid us . . . a great deal of trouble and unnecessary and unjust arrests of the Indians could be avoided.[14]

Brooks's suggestion, Keokuk's allegations, and subsequent orders to Indian agents from the secretary of the interior, had their effect. On March 14, 1895, Brooks advised Olney:

The Secretary and Indian Agents I think should be satisfied with what we have done in the matter; there are comparatively no arrests of Indians being made since these rules were issued requiring warrants to be approved by the Agents, and I feel assured there will be none except where the Indian is clearly guilty.[15]

XVII   The Price of Justice

ANOTHER BIG BONE OF CONTENTION in 1894 was the cost of maintaining law and order. On November 1, Olney inquired of Brooks what were the special causes for the increase of expenses in the federal courts, and Brooks wrote McMechan at Oklahoma City to

> watch the expense of Marshals, witnesses and commissioner and hold them down, otherwise this office will be held responsible for all of it. You should not permit the Marshals to have processes from the courts that are not absolutely necessary, and witnesses should not be brought to court until you need them, nor kept a day longer than is necessary to get through with and discharge them.[1]

In response to press inquiries, the auditor of the treasury in Washington, Thomas Holcomb, made public an account of what the Justice Department had spent during the fiscal year ending June 30 to fight banditry in Oklahoma and Indian territories, the Western Judicial District of Arkansas, and the Eastern Judicial District of Texas. Holcomb pointed up the fact that spending in these districts had been "much greater during the half of the fiscal year just expired than for the corresponding half of the last fiscal year."

The report showed expenditures in the marshal's office for Oklahoma to be $171,155; for Indian Territory, $198,502; Western Arkansas, $210,552; and Eastern Texas, $198,618—a total of $778,829.

The U.S. commissioners in Oklahoma had "pinched out in fees" $13,067; in Indian Territory, $23,638; Western Arkansas, $8,745; and Eastern Texas, $2,389—a total of $47,841.

The clerks of the federal courts in Oklahoma, through fees accounted for to the government, showed they had received $9,908; in Indian Territory, $1,360; Western Arkansas, $7,874; Eastern Texas, $13,930—a total of $33,071.

U.S. attorneys for the same districts "came in as follows": Oklahoma, $7,333; Indian Territory, $9,241; Western Arkansas, $6,207; Eastern Texas, $7,673—a total of $30,457.

"This is a grand total of $890,198," said the *Oklahoma Daily Times-Journal*,[2] observing that

> ninety per cent of the money used by the department in the Western District of Arkansas and Eastern District of Texas is on business that comes to them from the Oklahoma and Indian territories. This makes another showing to the effect that over $600,000 is expended on department of justice business originating in Oklahoma and the Indian country, and the officials spending the most money in this direction have been meeting with little success. . . . The deputy marshals will loot the treasury if not checked.

Attorney General Olney proposed to "fire this information at Congress, insist that something be done to simplify matters in that country . . . and relieve the United States from this burden."[3]

In answering Olney's inquiry of November 1, Brooks explained that

> the opening of the Strip [Outlet] to settlement brought in several thousand settlers, among whom were criminals from all over the world. K, P and Q counties, in the Strip, are contiguous to the Kaw, Otoe, Ponca and Osage Indian Reservations, offering a large field for the operation of criminals in introducing and selling whiskey to Indians, and horse and cattle stealing. The question of the priority of settlement and the settlement of contests have increased, or at any rate opened a new field for perjury in the U. S. Land Offices, and conspiracy to prevent settlement. The scarcity of timber in the Strip counties causes considerable violation of the Statutes by parties in removing timber from the Government sections, and in M and N counties professional wood and post cutters from Southern Kansas are continuously violating the law.
>
> The addition of two new Judges in the Territory, adding two more courts, hear and determine more business; the additional grand and petit juries; the renting of additional courtrooms and offices; the new Judges adding more U. S. commissioners in the new counties; all have naturally increased the expense to the Government.[4]

In Brooks's opinion, holding court in the territory's twenty-two counties twice a year, with grand and petit juries summoned and empaneled at each term (making forty-four panels of grand jurors and forty-four panels of petit jurors, with enormous expenses entailed by each) was preposterous. Moreover, federal offenders in the counties were taken to the federal jail at Guthrie and at each term of court had to be returned, many of them to remote parts of the territory, to answer charges, then conveyed to Guthrie again after indictment or trial, "often to await trial because the court did not have time to hear all the U. S. and Territorial business on docket for the term." Brooks suggested that federal courts convene at only one place in each of the five judicial districts, explaining:

If the home of the Judge (who is required to live in his district) was designated as the place for all U. S. business for that district, we would then have only ten U. S. grand juries and ten petit juries a year. . . . These five courts would be at points along the railroad, three of them within thirty-five miles of Guthrie and the fourth not over sixty miles from Guthrie, and yet each of them convenient to the outlying counties and the Indian country attached.

The U. S. business in this Territory is virtually done in the counties that have the Indian country attached for judicial purposes, and the other counties where the U. S. courts are held create simply an unnecessary expense, with but little or no results. . . . Take the counties in the second district, Blaine, D, Day, Roger Mills, G, Washita and Canadian (the last being the home of the Judge), the Judge was out in the outlying counties for six weeks holding court this fall; in each county he empaneled a U. S. grand and petit jury, and there was not on an average of three U. S. cases in the county, yet [it] was necessary to empanel juries, summon witnesses, and try the cases; and the assistant attorney who attended these courts was necessarily compelled to remain at these courts for the entire six weeks, as it was too far to return home and go back to the next court, and the business he did on the trip did not net the Government or my office enough to pay half his traveling expenses. . . .

The people in these outlying counties, of course, would object seriously if the U. S. did not have a grand and petit jury each term of court in their county, as it would interfere with business to the extent of the U. S. money that is paid to jurors and witnesses, and for the rent of the courtroom and offices; but under the present system it is just a donation by the U. S. without any benefit whatever. A very short amendment to the present law, by Congress, fixing one point in each of the five judicial districts in the Territory for the U. S. business to be heard, will save the Government from twenty-five to fifty thousand dollars each year. In addition, it will separate the Federal from the Territorial business, and make it more satisfactory to the courts and litigants.[5]

The judges of the territory, with whom Brooks discussed the matter, not only approved his suggestion, but in an open letter on December 31, Judge Burford took exception to inferences by the press that every man who carried a marshal's commission was a thief or a rascal:

The people of this territory owe much more to the deputy marshals for the protection of life and property and the enforcement of law and order than the world gives credit for. It may be true, and no doubt is, that some of the deputies are prompted by a desire to make fees, and thus increase their emoluments, but my observation is that this is the exception and not the rule. Several instances have come under my personal observation where the deputies have, at their own expense, performed services that should have been performed by the sheriffs or their deputies, and the marshals are often condemned by the press and public for not apprehending persons who have committed no offense against the laws of the United States, and whose arrest should be made by the county officers. I know of no instance in which a deputy marshal has refused to perform his duty, and but few instances where they have been over vigilant and made arrests of innocent parties without cause. . . .

If there is a criticism that I would offer upon the management of the marshal's office, it is that there are too many deputies. A half dozen competent and willing officers, working in harmony and under a competent chief, are worth more than a hundred deadheads, who wear guns and carry commissions for display, and to make a show of authority. I would cut off all useless branches, and let the efficient force have the benefit of all there is in the work. I would not commission sheriffs, city marshals or any of their deputies unless for special reasons. They have enough work of their own to do, to enforce the laws of the territory, if they will properly attend to it.[6]

The *Kansas City Journal*[7] commented on Nix's being the youngest U.S. marshal in the nation,

a great favorite down in his territory, who handles matters with much style. His force of deputies . . . now reduced to seventy-five . . . are busy all the time doing the business connected with the five federal courts. Salaries and labor run over $50,000 each quarter. He now has claims for $125,000 pending before the department at Washington for the two quarters past.

Nix called attention to the fact that "four of my deputies have been killed in battles with bandits and a score of them have been wounded," and stressed that there was "great risk in the positions." He went to Washington to ask Auditor of the Treasury Holcomb why his claims had not been "moved along" and "discovered a tendency to hold up matters under the plea of being careful, while the real reason for delay was the desire to keep the money in the treasury as long as possible."[8]

Neither Congress nor Olney acted to change conditions. The inquiries from Washington ceased, and the territorial press, apparently reluctant to disturb the goose with the golden eggs, insisted that the only solution to the criminal problem was statehood for Oklahoma and the Indian country.

Throughout his administrative difficulties and his determined field campaign against whiskey peddlers, counterfeiters, livestock, and timber thieves, Nix's primary concern continued to be the Wild Bunch.

It was rumored that the Doolin gang had leased a large pasture in the Wichita Reservation, where for months they had been herding stolen horses and cattle by the score. The Indian agent sent a young Caddo policeman, In-ki-nish, to discover their hiding place; he was captured by the outlaws, tied to a tree, and his body riddled with bullets. A posse gave pursuit, but the gang "repulsed the detachment," killed In-ki-nish's father, and escaped to the Wichita Mountains.[9] Riding from their new lair on November 24, 1894, the gang killed Hemphill County Sheriff Tom McGee at Canadian, Texas, in an attempt to rob the Panhandle Express:[10]

> A package purporting to contain $25,000 was expressed from Kansas City to George Isaacs, a wealthy Chickasaw cattleman at Canadian, arriving at that point Saturday evening. When the train pulled into Canadian station a gang of bandits held up the express car, opening a general fusillade on the train. Sheriff McGee . . . was standing by and took a hand in the protection of the express company, and was literally shot to pieces. Several others were wounded, among them some of the robbers, who were carried away by their pals. The robbers were frightened off without securing anything, and were chased into the Wichita mountains and the Butte lands of the Wichita country . . . and a large force of officers are out from these points looking for the bandits. Isaacs, who shipped the money, was arrested on suspicion of complicity and taken to Texas. The scheme is supposed to be shipment of money that was to be stolen, and the express company made to disgorge and the proceeds to be divided.[11]

"It was a great scheme," said the *Oklahoma State Capital*,[12] "which Geo. Isaacs and other prominent cattlemen of the Chickasaw nation fixed up to bamboozle the express company out of thousands of dollars," but it

> miscarried and left Isaacs and his associates in the soup. The express package purporting to contain $25,000 . . . was opened and found to contain blank paper the size of bills, with a couple of hundred dollars in money on top. . . . Isaacs is in jail, McGee is dead, and the robbers are in the Wichita mountains trying to secret themselves from the officers.

There was some evidence that Red Buck had been involved in the holdup. However, it was "Jim Harbold, Jake McKinzie and two others charged with being implicated" who were captured by Deputy Marshals Eichoff, Prather, Banks, and Madsen and returned to Canadian for trial.[13] George Isaacs obtained a change of venue to Hardeman County; he was tried at Quanah in November, 1895, for the murder of Sheriff McGee and sentenced to Huntsville Prison for life.[14]

On Christmas Eve, 1894, a report describing "the Muskogee Scare" swept the territory. Sunday night, December 23, Tulsa Jack, who had rescued the late Bill Dalton during the battle with deputy marshals in 1893, "rode into Ingalls with six men . . . declaring that Dalton had been betrayed by Saloonkeeper Nicholas and proceeded to demolish his place. It is said that Nicholas gave certain officers the information as to Dalton's whereabouts which led to his death."[15] The outlaws then rode into the Creek Nation. At noon the next day, they were "discovered four miles west of Muskogee in an advanced state of intoxication . . . extremely bold in their defiance of the deputies and sent several messages of a very sarcastic tenor, inviting them out to drink and be sociable. United States Attorney [C. L.] Jackson also came in for a lion's share of the bantering." Muskogee became "an uproar of excitement . . . a raid on the town was momentarily expected." The citizens "armed themselves . . . promising a repetition of the Coffeyville affair if any demonstration was made by the Doolin gang." Marshal J. J. McAlester at McAlester received word of the situation. He gathered all available deputies and departed for the scene on a special train furnished by the Katy Railroad. McAlester's group joined forces with Muskogee officers and citizens, and it was decided to "surround and attack the outlaws before they recovered from their debauch." Meanwhile, the gang had vanished. But night passenger trains were heavily guarded "for fear they had abandoned the Muskogee project for the less dangerous work of train robbing."[16]

A startling dispatch from Hennessey on January 20 claimed that Zip Wyatt had joined forces with Doolin. The authorities

received notice last night that the Doolin gang was in camp near here and a special train was sent by the Rock Island at midnight, while a posse rode to the scene. At 3 o'clock this morning the officers surrounded the camp and found Doolin and five of his confederates. At daylight the shooting began.

Deputy Sheriff Abel Washburn shot and killed Tulsa Jack and Zip Wyatt with a Winchester rifle. Alexander Robinson, a posseman, shot and killed Bill Doolin. . . . Sam Green, an all around desperado, met his fate at Deputy Sheriff Al Burchett's hands.

A desperate running fight is in progress with the other two members of the band, who are entirely surrounded with no hope of escape.[17]

The *Oklahoma State Capital* of January 22 declared emphatically "the report is absolutely without foundation" because no such battle had occurred.

In fact, Nix's office had been unable to obtain reliable information on the Wild Bunch's activity since Arkansas Tom's conviction at Stillwater in May and Bill Dalton's death near Ardmore in June, 1894. The *Ardmore State Herald*[18] offered this explanation:

When looked into there can be little question it is Romance, as Romance, that died several centuries ago. The life of the outlaws of Indian Territory is certainly romantic. Their life is made up of daring. Their courage is always with them and their rifles as well. They are kind to the benighted traveler, and it is not a fiction that when robbing a train they refuse to take from a woman.

It is said that Bill Doolin, at present the reigning highwayman, is friendly to the people in one neighborhood, bestowing all sorts of presents upon the children. It is his boast that he never killed a man.

This is as fully romantic a figure as Robin Hood ever cut.

Frank M. Canton, a former Texas peace officer and a sheriff and stock detective in Wyoming at the beginning of the Johnson County Rustlers War, moved to Oklahoma in the spring of 1894 to accept the position of undersheriff with Frank Lake, a former Texas acquaintance who was now sheriff of Pawnee County. Lake and Canton carried deputy marshal's commissions under Nix and U.S. Marshal George Crump of the Western Judicial District of Arkansas. In his autobiography, *Frontier Trails*,[19] Canton tells of Doolin's many friends among the settlers south of Pawnee, along the Cimarron, and on the Pawnee County line; how the bandit leader had furnished many of them money to buy groceries during the first years of their hard existence; how his kindness had not been forgotten; and how, despite the heavy price on his head, they would get up at midnight and ride to warn him of lawmen seen in the vicinity.

Two of the gang's most dedicated spies were fifteen-year-old Annie McDoulet (alias McDougal, alias McDermot, alias Cattle Annie) who hailed from Skiatook on the Osage border north of Tulsa, and her sixteen-year-old friend Jennie Stevens, who wore men's pants and was called Little Breeches. Together they stole

265

horses and peddled whiskey in the Osage and in Pawnee County. Graves,[20] Newsom,[21] and Zoe A. Tilghman, *Outlaw Days*,[22] recount how a posse met Cattle Annie on the trail in eastern Payne County. Questioned about the "passing of strange men," the girl gave "evasive and unsatisfactory" answers. At the time, her identity was not known. Annie sent a message to the gang's hiding place, and the outlaws "vanished from the district."

Another story rehashed down the years is that Bill Tilghman and Neal Brown (an old friend from Tilghman's Dodge City days), accompanied by former U.S. Army Scout Charley Bearclaw as guide, left Guthrie in January, 1895, in a covered wagon with two saddle horses tied behind, a camping outfit, and supplies to last a month, their mission being "to arrest a ranch owner . . . related to the ranchmen [Dunn brothers] who harbored the bandits." The ranch owner was "under a charge of having stolen thirty-five head of cattle," but it was Tilghman's intention to secure from him "some definite information that would lead to successfully surprising and capturing the outlaws."[23] Here is the original "Tilghman in the Bandits' Dugout" from Graves's *Oklahoma Outlaws*:[24]

The officers came in sight of the Rock Fort [Dunn] ranch on a cold day when a biting wind was blowing. Snow lay a foot deep on the ground and the sky was overcast. At 3 o'clock in the afternoon it was almost as dark as at twilight and a worse storm was threatening.

Tilghman saw that smoke was curling above the chimney of the dugout occupied by the ranchmen as they stopped in front of the door. Nobody was to be seen outside . . . no horses were in sight . . . and except for the smoke there was no indication that the place was occupied. Tilghman alighted and leaving his Winchester in the wagon, walked down the steps and pushed open the door.

At one end of the room a fire of blackjack logs roared cheerfully in the wide fireplace. On both sides of the big room were tiers of bunks, enough of them to bed comfortably fifteen or twenty persons, but they were hung with curtains and there was no way of knowing whether they were occupied or empty. Nobody was in sight except one of the ranchers, who sat hunched in a chair before the huge fireplace with a Winchester across his knee. He was surly and uncivil, and when Tilghman made some inquiries about another ranchman, the replies were given in a way calculated to impart as little information as possible. The marshal made a mental picture of the room as he looked it over.

"I just happened to be passing along this way with my fighting dog and thought maybe I could get Bill [Dunn] to match a fight," Tilghman said, speaking carelessly. "He told me awhile back that he thought his dog could whip mine," he added.

Tilghman was cold from riding in the wind and walking to the fireplace, turned his back to it. As he did so the sight that met his eyes caused every muscle in his body to stiffen. From every bunk the muzzle of a gun had been shoved out, just a little way, but Tilghman knew that behind those bristling weapons were ready hands and gleaming eyes that held a bead on his body. There was no sound except the wind outside as it swept over the bleak scene, heaping the drifting snow deeper and deeper against the side of the lonely dugout.

But there was not the quiver of an eyelash to indicate to those behind the curtains that the marshal knew they were there, or that he expected to be shot to death the next instant. He talked on to the surly ranchman by the fireplace without the slightest shaking of his voice.

"I guess I better be going on," he said, after a time, still speaking carelessly. "Which way does a fellow get out of here?" he asked, moving toward the door, and the ranchman replied: "The same damned way he gets in."

Tilghman walked with a steady stride between the two rows of Winchesters straight to the door, which he opened calmly, and started out slowly, without having shown a tremor. Then he went to where the Indian guide sat in the wagon.

"Drive ahead, but not too fast," he said to his companion. "The dugout is full of outlaws."

. . . It was several months before even Tilghman himself realized the great danger in which he had unwittingly placed himself. It was after he had arrested the ranchman charged with cattle stealing that he learned of what had taken place in the dugout that stormy night when he stumbled into it alone.

All the members of the Doolin gang were hidden in the Rock Fort . . . Bill Doolin, Red Buck, Dynamite Dick, Charley Pierce, Tulsa Jack and Little Bill. . . . One of the outlaws was determined to kill Tilghman and the reason he did not shoot while the marshal stood by the fireplace has never been known.

It was Red Buck who wanted to kill the marshal, and as Tilghman was leaving the place the desperado . . . would have shot him in the back had not . . . Doolin and the ranchman held him.

"Bill Tilghman is too good a man to be shot in the back," Doolin said, as Red Buck struggled toward the door. . . . The ranchman said there should be no killing in or about the dugout.

"If you shoot Tilghman there'll be a hundred men here before morning," he told the enraged bandit. "This place would be dynamited until the last man was dead."

Red Buck cared nothing about death, however, and would have followed Tilghman after the wagon had driven away had not the others restrained him by force.

"You're a lot of cowards," he shouted. "I'll tell you what will happen to us—Tilghman will be back here before sunrise with a big posse and we'll be trapped like rats. Now what are you going to do about it?"

The ranchman advised the bandits to leave at once, fearing an attack later in the night. The outlaws were worn and fatigued . . . they needed the rest and comfort they had found in the dugout, but they knew it would be unsafe to stay. So out into the night they went, into a blinding snowstorm. They saddled their horses and rode away to seek shelter elsewhere, Red Buck still snarling in a towering rage.

Historians have accepted the tale,[25] and scores of magazine writers have turned a quick dollar in retelling it. One has ridiculously suggested that this lawman, who had lived honestly, bravely, and well, and this king of outlaws, whose honor, despite his treacherous, swashbuckling career, was as rigid as the Ten Commandments, respected each other so much that perhaps Tilghman had been put on as Marshal in the Sky, with Bill Doolin as his deputy!

No contemporary report or official record supports the incident; no Rock Fort existed. The plank-covered storm cave at Bill Dunn's homestead on Council Creek was neither rock walled, equipped with a fireplace and tiers of bunks, nor large enough to have accommodated fifteen to twenty men, even in underwear and packed like sardines. The tale was born in Graves's 1915 pamphlet, which sold with *The Passing of the Oklahoma Outlaws*, an historical photodrama then being presented throughout the Southwest by Bill Tilghman.

There was some basis for the yarn Tilghman narrated from the road-show stage. After the Ingalls fight in 1893, Bill, Heck Thomas, and Chris Madsen spearheaded a search for the Doolin gang's hideouts in Payne County and the Creek Nation, assisted by federal deputies from Fort Smith. In the spring of 1894, they surrounded the cave at Bill Dunn's ranch and ordered the occupants to surrender. When they refused, the posse blew off the roof with dynamite. Five men appeared, their hands in the air, all wanted on various charges, but none was the important quarry the marshals sought.[26] In a 1937 letter to Mrs. Matie Thomas of Tulsa,[27] Chris Madsen provided this explanation:

. . . You know that Mrs. Tilghman is employed on the "Writers' Project" whatever that is [a Works Project Administration program in Oklahoma, 1936–38], assembling material for an Oklahoma History, the same as Grant Foreman is. I have given them some points as well as the other writers.

Recently I have received a letter from Mrs. Tilghman to tell her of the exact location where Bill visited the Outlaws in their den, and Bill Doolin saved his life.

I do not know what you think about that affair, which is reported in the pamphlet published in connection with the moving picture. . . .

You probably remember that in April and May, 1894, Heck, Bill and I with a posse were hunting the outlaws, and one cold morning jumped their hiding place at the Dunn ranch. Heck came up from the rear of the dug-out and Bill and I were a short distance from the front door to welcome them when the outlaws would come out. It turned out that when Heck threw a stick of Dynamite on the roof of the dug-out and the inhabitants did come out with their hands in the air, they were not the ones we had expected to find there. There were a second class lot of Horsethieves, so we did not make a dry haul. . . . After disarming the prisoners we made them go back in the dugout and make their own breakfast in which Heck and the Posse participated.

Bill Dunn's dwelling house was only a few steps from the Dug-out and Mrs. Dunn who appeared to be a nice woman made breakfast for Bill and me. When we left there Bill and I rode down the valley and met Dunn, who had a bottle of whiskey, which he offered us, but as neither of us were drinking men we thanked him. . . . He invited us to come back to the house and have breakfast, but we told him his wife had already served us, and he told us that if ever we came there again just to come to the house and stay as long as we liked.

But now Mrs. Tilghman comes with a story that Bill and Neal Brown were driving down through the bottom a cold snowy day in January 1895, about a year after we had visited the place. Bill saw smoke curling up over the dugout *occupied by the ranchmen* as they stopped in front of the door. . . .

Then follows the story how he went into the dugout and found the outlaws all behind curtains hung in front of their beds, — he says there was room for fifteen men.

Well, Bill being a diplomat approached one of the men sitting at the fire place, and asked for some person he knew would not be there, and finally after a few words with the man backed out, while Red Buck was trying to kill him and Bill Doolin kept him from doing it.

He then went to his wagon and drove away from there, but not too fast.

Now, Bill Dunn's house as I mentioned above was right alongside the Dugout, and Bill knew it. He also knew that the dugout, if occupied at all would be housing some outlaws. He did not go into where Mrs. Dunn would have given him shelter in the storm and warned him to keep out of the dugout, but just stepped in there, and even when he saw the guns pointing out from the beds, he deliberately walked down to the fire place instead of backing out while the backing was good.

Now Mrs. Tilghman wants me to give her a description of the location of the dugout and what it was like so she can write it into the history of Oklahoma.

While I [am] willing to go a long way for an old friend and co-worker, I can not see my way to serve Mrs. Tilghman in this case, but would like to hear from you in regard to what Heck may have told you in regard to this matter. . . .

I like Bill Tilghman like I like Heck. Both were good and reliable fellows to travel with, but Bill, when he got in the moving picture business had to make a record whether it was just right or not.

I never knew two better men to work with than Bill and Heck. You could depend on them under all circumstances, but Bill was a little inclined to be romantic. . . .

Bill, besides being a good officer, was also a good politician and not a bad booster for Bill,—which is all right. Like the man said when he was tried for killing his wife: "If I can not kill my own wife, whose wife can I kill?" If you do not occasionally toot your own horn whose horn do you expect to be tooted for you?

Allegedly, Tilghman returned to Dunn's ranch a few days after the raid, talked to him about his good farm and stock and fine family growing up, and convinced him that if he stuck with the outlaws, he would get the short end of the stick. Dunn agreed to assist the officers in wiping out the Wild Bunch if a cattle-stealing charge against him and his brothers was dismissed. Tilghman then rode back to Guthrie and not only convinced a dismayed marshal and U.S. district attorney that they "couldn't prove the charge anyhow," but persuaded Nix to issue Dunn a deputy's commission.[28]

Justice Department records do not reveal that any Dunn was ever deputized. That Nix made a deal with the brothers is true, but it occurred nearly a year later, under different circumstances, and for more logical reasons. On March 3, 1895, "Deputy Will M. Nix, a brother of the Marshal of the Territory, and Heck Thomas, Bill Tilghman and John Hixon" again raided the Dunn cave, again "dynamite was used to blow the outlaws out, but when the Marshals thought they had Bill [Doolin], he slipped out of the cave under cover of darkness." The gang fled northeast across the Arkansas River into the Cherokee Nation and "had a fight" next day with some Indian police, "but the only damage done was the killing of Tulsa Jack's horse. A pal carried the outlaw off on his mount."[29] Canton[30] says that by the spring of 1895 there were "twenty-five or thirty" sympathizers scattered over Payne and Pawnee counties, who worked under cover and acted as fences for the Wild Bunch in disposing of stolen cattle and horses, and that the "most prominent and dangerous of this class were the Dunn boys."

Bill Dunn was the leader. He and G. C. Bolton, a butcher, owned the meat market in Pawnee, where they disposed of the stolen beef. Canton and Sheriff Lake obtained enough evidence to have Bolton indicted and warrants issued for the Dunns. The Dunns gave bond but became "very nervous and restless" and sent word to Lake and Canton that if the charges against them were dismissed, they would furnish information that would lead to Bill Doolin's capture and break up the gang entirely. At a conference in Pawnee, Canton and Lake agreed not to prosecute them further and to use their influence to "get Nix to promise the same." The Dunns were to sever all connections with the Wild Bunch, obey the laws of the territory, and get word to Pawnee authorities the moment Doolin or any member of the gang again entered the country. In the event that any or all of the outlaws were captured, all reward money collected would be turned over to the Dunns after the officers' actual expenses were deducted. At Guthrie, Marshal Nix agreed to the terms. After pledging absolute secrecy (no other officer on his force would be advised of the plans) and promising to report to Canton and Lake periodically, the brothers were allowed to return to their homes.[31]

XVIII   Lucky Lay of the Last Looters

NOTHING HAPPENED FOR A WEEK. Then Canton and Sheriff Lake received word that the Doolin gang had held up the Rock Island train at Dover, nine miles north of Kingfisher.

When the southbound No. 1 passenger and express pulled into Dover at 11:45 P.M. on April 3, two men silently boarded the tender. As the train left the station, they covered engineer Gallagher and his fireman with Winchesters and ordered a stop two hundred yards past the water tank. Gallagher, a little excited, "ran a quarter mile farther and narrowly escaped losing his life . . . the sudden application of air brakes causing one robber to pull the trigger of his gun . . . the ball missed the engineer, passing through the cab window behind him."

Conductor James Mack came forward to investigate; the outlaws relieved him of $11 and ordered him into the cab. Then the train was backed to the point designated, where the bandits were joined by three companions. The passengers, peering from the windows into the moonlight, were "terrified at the sight of five heavily armed men . . . several shots, and the gruff order of one rifleman to 'get your damned heads back inside or we'll blow 'em off!'"

The bandits marched the train crew back to the express car and demanded that messenger J. W. Jones open the door. Jones "declined to obey" and "a fusillade perforated the car from both sides and the bottom, breaking Jones' left wrist and wounding him in the leg." Able to handle his Winchester with his good hand, the "brave messenger still refused." It was not until the robbers threatened to kill the train crew and conductor Mack pleaded with him to "save their lives" that he finally admitted the bandits and surrendered.

The robbers pilfered mailbags and the way safe without finding any money, then ordered Jones to unlock the through safe, reported to contain fifty thousand dollars to pay U.S. troops in Texas. Jones finally convinced them that the large, burglar-proof safe had been locked in Kansas City and could be opened only by the express agent at Fort Worth, so they ordered the engineer and fireman to drill into the vault. The men worked "nearly an hour" but "succeeded in boring less than half an inch." Disgusted, the bandits abandoned the project.

While Newcomb and Pierce continued to patrol the train and Raidler kept an eye on its crew, Tulsa Jack and Red Buck visited the coaches, inviting the passengers to contribute. The porter went ahead with a sack; Tulsa Jack did the "searching" and Red Buck the "bulldozing," the latter walking backward to guard against an attack from the rear.

Former Marshal Grimes was in the chair car. Tulsa Jack (whom he took to be Zip Wyatt) recognized Grimes with the remark: "Ah, there, partner, we meet again. Guess I've got *you* this time. Out with your dough."

The robbers had been so long at the express car that the passengers had time to hide many of their valuables. Grimes had slid his expensive gold watch under the stove. He tossed $1.40 into the bag, stating it was all he had, and Tulsa Jack warned: "You'd better be supplied next time."

Joe Kaufman gave up a Mexican dollar, a Cream Rye check and a ten-cent plug of Piper Heidsick.

Across the aisle, Pete Brough of the grocery firm of Brough & Robinson shelled out $1.05, his watch, a corkscrew, six pieces of string, a barlow knife, two lead pencils, and his laundry bill. The robbers overlooked a $500 roll he had thrust under the seat cushion.

They shook down Lew Fossett. "You are playing on a dead card here," said Lew.

One man, just out of the penitentiary, told his tale of woe. The robbers compelled him to dump his last shekel into the sack, then gave him back a half-dollar "to get his breakfast."

They were "very gallant" to the female passengers, refusing to search their stockings and "other conceivable hiding places," and returned five dollars to one old lady who inadvertently had contributed to the pot. Tulsa Jack tipped his hat, saying: "We are not here to rob or molest women. We came to rob the express company, but have failed and need a little expense money. We will confine ourselves to males in levying this tax."

Bion Cole of the Western Newspaper Union, who provided the press with a graphic account of the affair, contributed nine dollars and a gold ring.

Two farmers from Iowa were the principal losers, each handing over eighty dollars.

A German "yoost from the Faderland thought it was smart a pretty good joke to be . . . a little bit to sleep and maybe somebody fool a little." He didn't fool anybody. Red Buck tapped him on the head with his revolver. When he opened his eyes and stared into the muzzle of the Colt .45, he "yelled like a Comanche and dumped his wealth into the bag."

Altogether, the bandits took $437.50, a half-dozen gold watches, several silver ones, and diamond studs and other jewelry valued at $1,000. Before leaving the train, Tulsa Jack paused again before former Marshal Grimes. "Give my compliments to Chris Madsen," he jested.

The engineer was ordered back into his cab and instructed to wait for the report of a gun from the southeast. Then the gang mounted and rode off into the night. Within a few minutes the report came, and Gallagher pulled out for Kingfisher, where messenger Jones was taken off the train and given medical attention.

The facts were telegraphed to Chris Madsen at El Reno. At 3 A.M., a special engine pulled north with twelve deputy marshals and their horses in a boxcar hooked to the tender. At the same time, a description of the robbers, with an offer from the Chicago, Rock Island & Pacific Railway Company at Topeka of one thousand dollars reward for the arrest and conviction of each, was dispatched to all points in the territory.[1]

Madsen's party struck their trail at daybreak. The gang had gone west four miles and turned north fifteen miles to the southern boundary of the Outlet, then proceeded northwest to Hoil Creek near Ames in Major County. Here they had stopped at a farmhouse for breakfast, then headed west into the sandhills toward the Cimarron. The posse reached the farmhouse at noon. The robbers had made no effort to cover their tracks, remarking that they wanted the marshals to follow them; they planned to bushwhack them.[2]

Madsen split his party into two groups. With five deputies, he circled south and west, hoping to intercept the gang along the river. The second squad, consisting of Deputy Banks, Captain Prather, J. H. Clary, John Phelps, M. S. Hutchison, and W. E. (Billie) Moore, pushed ahead.

At two o'clock in the afternoon,[3] Banks and his men topped a knoll on the edge of a sand basin and saw the outlaws' horses with one man guarding them and the rest of the gang asleep in a small blackjack grove. The guard saw the officers at the same moment and gave the alarm. Without ceremony, Billie Moore yelled, "Throw

274

up your hands, you sons-of-bitches!" The robbers, leaping to their feet, answered with a volley of lead. Then began a fight which

> is without parallel in the annals of Oklahoma. Both sides were equal in numbers as one of the pursuing party had charge of the horses. The robbers scattered among the blackjacks, the deputies following their example, and there a sanguinary battle took place which lasted three-quarters of an hour and in which fully 200 shots were exchanged. The robbers had the advantage, each having a 45-90 Winchester and two re-volvers, the deputies all having lighter guns. About the middle of the fight one of the robbers was killed, a Winchester ball entering his right side, going through his heart and coming out under his left arm. Two others were wounded, one horse was killed and two wounded, one of which was captured. The robbers took advantage of a hollow which was not covered by the deputies and mounted in a running fire.[4]

Later reports[5] boasted that

> none of our boys weakened a little bit or showed the white feather while the bullets whistled. . . . Billie Moore laid flat on the ground and pumped hot shot at the robbers while the Winchester balls were kicking up sand all around him, and of course Clary had to stop and roll a cigarette.

The outlaws, four of them on three horses, raced away,

> leaving the dead man lying where he fell. None of the deputies were injured. After getting themselves together, and considering the fagged condition of their horses, the posse decided to return with the dead man until they met the other party of deputies. They hired a farmer to bring the body and met Madsen's party, who had at once pressed forward to the scene of the fight intending to take the trail from there. They were accompanied by four of the first party [Clay, Phelps, Hutchison, and Moore], Prather and Banks continuing on with the body, arriving at Hennessey about 10 p.m.
>
> Hundreds of Hennessey citizens viewed the dead robber. He wore a pair of light striped pants, light colored flannel shirt, a flowered black silk vest, white cowboy hat and square-toed shop made boots. He has the three front upper teeth filled with gold and a plain gold ring on the little finger and a seal ring on the second finger of his left hand. He is a man about 33 years old, 5 ft. 7 inches in height and weighs 160 pounds, has light colored moustache which has been dyed black, is rather sharp featured and withal a very attractive looking person. . . . Ex-Marshal Grimes and several passengers on the train say he is the man who robbed them, but no one is positive of his identity.[6]

The body was photographed on an undertaker's board with Banks and Prather standing on each side, then the two deputies took it to

El Reno. Here it was viewed in Perry's undertaking parlor by five hundred people.

Still unidentified, the body in its coffin was removed to Oklahoma City and displayed in the hall of the courthouse. Another five hundred people filed past before H. R. Whirtzell of Sterling, Kansas, positively identified the desperado as William Blake, who had worked on the railroad in Rice County several months in 1891, then worked on his ranch near by for a time before coming to the Outlet and finally joining Doolin's train robbers. "In fact," Whirtzell added, "some of his clothes are still at my place."[7] The *Times-Journal*[8] noted that

> there are rewards offered for Tulsa Jack by the Rock Island, Santa Fe, Wells Fargo Express Co., state of Kansas and by several individuals to the amount of $3,000. Deputy Banks, who was in command of the attacking party . . . is a man of coolness and nerve, talks very little. Although his fellow deputies will not say who killed Tulsa Jack, it is certain Marshal Banks did his whole duty in the thick of battle. The rewards will be divided among the six who were in the fight.

The outlaw's remains were returned to El Reno for burial.

Meanwhile, Madsen and his posse continued in pursuit of the gang. A few miles from the battle scene, they found another dead horse. The back of the animal was spattered with blood, and there was "much speculation" as to how badly its rider was wounded.[9] Months later the marshals would learn that one of Raidler's fingers was shattered by a rifle ball during the fight; it was bleeding profusely, so he took out his pocket knife, cut it off, and threw it away.[10] At sundown, the posse reached the farm of an aged preacher named Godfrey, whom the gang had murdered after "going into his barnyard and taking his team . . . the old minister expostulated, whereupon they shot him."[11]

From here the gang rode west. During the night, four men on four horses crossed the Cimarron between the settlements of Elizabeth and Vilas in southeastern Major County about seven miles northeast of Okeene. The marshals passed through Vilas the next morning "two hours after the bandits had left on fresh horses obtained from a nearby stock farm." By this time, they had been joined by Zip Wyatt and Ike Black.[12]

It was thought then and for some time afterward that Wyatt and Black had been with the gang in the fight on the Cimarron. The most dependable evidence, however, denies they had any part in the Rock Island holdup, and their presence with the Dover robbers at Vilas was a coincidence.[13] This was Wyatt-Black country, where tracking was almost impossible. Madsen and his posse returned to El Reno on April 5, having lost the trail in the foothills of the Glass Mountains.[14] Here the outlaws went their separate ways. They were never again united as a gang. Only Bitter Creek and Pierce remained together.

At Pawnee, Canton and Sheriff Lake gathered a mess outfit and a good supply of ammunition and rode to a camp near the Dunn settlement in Payne County. The gang, the Dunns told them, had scattered. Doolin had not been seen since escaping from Bill Dunn's cave on March 3. His wife was living with her parents at the store and post office of Lawson on the Pawnee-Payne county line, and he was seriously considering giving himself up to Marshal Nix in return for "a promise of some clemency." But Bitter Creek and Pierce were "likely to drop in any time." Bitter Creek had left several hundred dollars in Bill Dunn's care and would "come in to get his money if for no other reason." The brothers again assured the officers they would keep their end of the bargain.[15]

Several days passed, with no sign of the outlaws. One evening, Canton and Lake rode over to George McElroy's ranch, about eight miles northeast of Bill Dunn's place, to get some grain for their horses. They notified Dunn that they expected to spend the night there. Next morning, they discovered their horses gone from the corral and "had a long tramp" before finding them. They met one of the Dunn boys, who told them Pierce and Bitter Creek had spent the night at Bill's ranch but had left that morning for the Cherokee Nation. He had hunted for the officers to report but had been unable to contact them.[16]

Canton and Lake doubted the story and suspected that the Dunns knew how their horses had broken out of the corral. Deciding to have nothing more to do with the brothers, they returned to Pawnee to make plans for continuing the hunt on their own. On May 2, they received a telegram to come to Guthrie at once, that the Dunns had just brought in the bodies of two of the Doolin gang.[17]

The *Guthrie Daily Leader* of May 3 published the first account of the affair under the alliterative title "Lucky Lay of the Last Looters":

Shortly after two o'clock yesterday afternoon a covered wagon drawn by two half-famished horses pulled up on the east side of the water tower on Capitol Hill. Two men, armed with Winchesters and furtive glances, dismounted . . . one sped towards Marshal Nix's office. A few minutes later Spengel's undertaking barouche was speeding towards the hill, where two dead bodies were taken from the wagon, placed in the dead cart and hauled to the undertaking rooms. Not long after, the city was filled with all sorts of rumors regarding dead outlaws, and curious crowds gathered at Spengel's became so great that it was found necessary to throw open the doors and . . . allow the public mind to be satisfied. For three hours a stream of people passed through the rooms viewing the bodies. They were fully identified as George Newcomb and Charley Pierce by all the deputies and man killers in the capital, and a camera shot was taken of the dead outlaws stretched out on the embalming boards.

Both Newcomb and Pierce were fairly well dressed and aside from the myriad of bullet punctures the clothes were in good condition. Both men wore blue overalls, calico shirts and string ties . . . high-heeled boots, with broncho spurs [and] around their loins were cartridge belts, half-filled. In Pierce's pockets were found a dirk and a common knife, a few coins, a rabbit's foot and twenty-six Winchester cartridges. Newcomb's pockets also contained a knife, cards, a small hand-mirror, smoking tobacco, sixteen books of cigarette paper and two dozen 45 Colt's and Winchester shells. Near the bodies were deposited the saddles and blankets of the dead men which upon being opened were found well supplied with cartridges, tobacco and other articles necessary for a bandit excursion. In the pockets of Newcomb's saddle were found a Wells Fargo money bag and three pocket knives. On the pile lay two black slouch hats, the one worn by Newcomb being mutilated and covered with blood. Two Winchesters, one shattered at the stock, and two 45 Colt's revolvers made up the collection. Pierce's body, upon being stripped, was found to be literally riddled with bullets, almost any one of which would prove fatal. All the shots had entered the front of the body and ranged backward, the bullets covering a space from the sole of his feet to the top of his head. Newcomb's body showed but five bullet wounds, four of these being in the head and neck; one shot, however, had torn away a part of the forehead, exposing the brain. Another shot had struck the little finger of his right hand as he was pulling a trigger. . . .

The two deputies who brought them in repaired to a private room where to Marshal Nix and THE LEADER man they gave the details of the taking of the territory's terrors. . . .

Two days after the Dover robbery, a tall rawboned man, perhaps 40 years of age, wearing side whiskers and a determined visage, called on Marshal Nix at his office and asked for a commission as a deputy United States marshal. He carried four good recommendations in his pockets, and asked for "just one trial" at the train robbers. Marshal Nix commissioned the Texan temporarily, and next day Samuel Shaffer, for such is the Texan's name, and two other deputy marshals, well known all over the territory but whose names THE LEADER is obliged to suppress for obvious reasons, left this city with three possemen. Several other deputies and possemen chased the fleeing bandits into the fast-nesses of the Glass mountains, but finally returned to El Reno, leaving Shaffer and companions in full hunt. . . . Newcomb and Pierce remained hidden for two days when they emerged from their concealment and traveled towards Payne county where Bill Doolin is now supposed to be in hiding.

Forty-two miles, a little north of east of this city in Payne county, stands a weather-beaten house, owned and occupied by a family named Dunn. For over a year past deputy marshals have suspected that the Dunn family, or at least two brothers of the family, have not only shelved tips to outlaws but have been in league with them. This is now known to be the truth. It is asserted on good authority that Doolin has frequent-ly supped at the Dunn domicile, while lesser lights in outlawry loafed there.

The Dunn homestead, then, was the destination of Newcomb and Pierce. They arrived there last Thursday night [April 25], but imme-diately departed. Twelve hours later Shaffer and his men were en-camped near the Dunn place and in eye-shot of the house. The bandits were not followed. Intuition told the deputies the bandits would return, and they did — reaching the Dunn farm at 10 o'clock Wednesday night [May 1]. The moon was shining, and the figures of Newcomb and Pierce were easily discerned. An hour after the outlaws had entered the house Bacchanalian orgies were in progress. The bold nocturnal riders were "out" or rather "in" for a time, with little thought of impending danger.

At 2 o'clock yesterday morning Shaffer and his men surrounded the Dunn house. The men were stationed at regular intervals of 100 yards, and at a given signal each man fired, alternately, one shot, as an alarm. Immediately a wild commotion ensued within the house, and two lights quickly flickered out. As the lights were extinguished a match was struck in the front room and simultaneously the door opened and Charley Pierce appeared with a Winchester in his hand. As his form loomed up a female voice was heard to cry: "Don't go, Charley!"

Pierce could not see his antagonists, but his figure with the lighted match in the room afforded a bulls eye target for the officers, and in three seconds his breast was transformed into a lead mine. He fell directly back into the room; the leaden hail continued bullets being planted in his arms, legs and even the soles of his feet.

In the meantime Newcomb was endeavoring to climb out of a win-dow, unwisely shooting as he climbed. Three bullets were dexterously driven into his head, one tearing away a portion of his skull and brains. He fell back into the room with the stock of his Winchester shattered.

Both Dunn boys were in the house, but neither fired a shot, although one was wounded by a random bullet. Subsequently both the brothers disappeared. At the time of the killing there were in the house the two desperadoes, the two Dunn boys and a young woman named Sallie

Niles. The latter had cried to Pierce when he stepped to his death. Nothing is known of her, but deputies surmise that she was Pierce's sweetheart. The woman was ordered out of the house and after making sure all was right, the officers entered, secured the bodies and loaded them into a wagon. Shaffer and another deputy at once brought the corpses to town.

The *Leader* concluded:

To Nix belongs the credit for putting out of the way these desperadoes. He spent his own money and personally directed the movement of deputies. . . . Marshal Nix had the bodies embalmed and wired ex-Marshal Grimes and the Rock Island train men who identified them as the parties who made the holdup. The United States Attorney General was also wired regarding the disposition of the dead bandits.

The *State Capital*[18] disagreed on the time and how Pierce and Newcomb were shot:

The outlaws rode to the Dunn house about 8 o'clock. It being moonlight they were easily seen, and Pierce was killed outright . . . with at least thirty buckshot in him, mostly in the right shoulder and side, though he had fully six shots in his stomach and as many in one foot. Bitter Creek made a fight, and two Winchester balls felled him off his horse. One bullet struck him in the forehead and tore out a lot of brains at the back, the other hit his hand as he was pulling the trigger. The horses of the outlaws were also killed.

"Shaffer and deputy" did not stay around to explain discrepancies but immediately returned to Payne County, and Nix declined to discuss the affair, "as the marshals who did the work are still after other gang members" believed to be in the vicinity.[19]

Then word leaked out that Sam Shaffer and his deputy were none other than John and Dal Dunn, whom Canton and Lake recognized upon their arrival at Guthrie. Canton also observed that the buckshot in the soles of Pierce's feet indicated he had been shot with his boots off while lying down and that his body was badly swollen, while Bitter Creek's "looked . . . as though he had not been dead very long." At the marshal's office, Dal Dunn confided to Chief Deputy Hale that he, John, and Bill Dunn were waiting for Newcomb and Pierce at the ranch and had killed them as they dismounted in the yard. They then hitched up a team, put the outlaws and their guns and paraphernalia in the wagon, and covered them with a tarpaulin. Bill remained at the ranch to obliterate all trace of blood in the yard, and Dal and John started cross-country with the bodies to claim the reward. Between Stillwater and Guthrie, they noticed the tarpaulin moving. Lifting the canvas, they discovered that Bitter Creek was still alive and was trying to load a revolver in his hand. Bitter Creek begged them to spare his life. As they were passing a farmhouse and did not care to raise an alarm, Dal knocked him senseless with his six-shooter. After they had gone a safe distance, he shot the outlaw through the head.[20]

Canton neither shared in the rewards nor received his man-hunting expenses. Disgusted with the affair, he gave his story to the *Pawnee Times-Democrat*, and the newspaper declared that "Canton, not Nix, directed the movement of the men who had ended the careers of two principal members of the Doolin gang" and "the Guthrie "Leader's" version of the killing . . . is incorrect." The paper offered no explanation for the buckshot in the soles of Pierce's feet, but allowed that the principal portion of the rewards "should be divided between Canton and his assistants. . . . Canton is a shrewd, fearless officer and Mr. Nix made a wise choice when he selected him to perform the detective work in this matter."[21]

Sam Shaffer remained an enigma, and another legend in the history of Oklahoma outlawry grew.[22] Whoever may have fired the deadly blasts and where, the bandits had died as they had lived: ingloriously and ignominiously.

Nix received authorization from Attorney General Olney to bury the pair in Guthrie's Summit View Cemetery at government expense.[23] Pierce was buried in the Boot Hill section, pauper's grave No. 65, on May 4. But James Newcomb and his wife, Bitter Creek's parents now living in Oklahoma, arrived in time to "identify their erring son" and "take charge of his remains," which they buried on their farm at "Nine Mile Flats" on the north bank of the Canadian west of Norman.[24] A few days later, the father publicly thanked Marshal Nix for his "kind treatment of me and my dead boy," whom "I am pleased to say . . . was an honest and industrious young man until led astray by evil associates. I believe that he was foully murdered by a traitor in the gang and not killed as represented by the press."[25]

The efforts of the marshals to assume responsibility for the killings, together with the belief that Pierce and Bitter Creek had been cowardly assassinated by men they trusted, caused bitter feeling against the Dunns in Payne County. Friends of the two outlaws "openly swore revenge," and the Dunns "barricaded their place, secured a supply of arms and ammunition and made their ranch a veritable arsenal" several days before "their strict vigilance relaxed" and they felt "free of molestation."[26]

Nix himself stalled the attempts of Canton and others to have the Dunns arrested for aiding and abetting outlaws, and Tilghman and Thomas made every effort to protect the family. On May 9, when Canton revived the old charge of cattle stealing against Bill Dunn at Pawnee, Dunn waived examination, gave bond for his appearance at the next term of district court, and returned to Ingalls.[27] Tilghman and Thomas, still heading the outlaw hunt on the east side of the territory, wanted the brothers free as long as possible. Their cooperation, the deputies felt, was necessary for a quick apprehension of the remaining members of the Wild Bunch and the most wanted quarry of all: Bill Doolin.

Before new plans could be formulated, however, the government thrust upon Marshal Nix's office the responsibility of policing another land opening. On May 18, President Cleveland suddenly proclaimed that the Kickapoo Reservation, directly east of Oklahoma County and comprising most of western Lincoln County, would be settled by the last great run for homesteads on May 23, 1895.

XIX Bad Christians

THE AGREEMENT WITH THE KICKAPOOS under which they were to take allotments and cede their surplus lands to the government had been accepted and ratified by Congress on March 3, 1893, but some factions of the tribe had opposed the move so bitterly that the schedules were not approved by the Interior Department until September 12, 1894.[1] Two hundred eighty-three allotments of 80 acres each, or 22,640 acres, were reserved for use of about three hundred Indians, and Governor Renfrow selected 87,668 acres as school indemnity lands, leaving less than half the 206,080-acre reservation for homestead settlement. For filing entries, the district was effectively divided between the Oklahoma City and Guthrie land offices. It was advertised simply as a magnificent park

> bounded on the north by the Deep Fork and on the southeast by the North Canadian River, the eastern bank of which is a succession of rich bottom lands, with soil as black and rich as Illinois prairie loam. The central and eastern portions are high prairie land, interspersed with timber . . . particularly pecan, wild plumb, hickory, elm, red oak, post oak, burr oak, white oak and walnut. Among the woods are beautiful circular glades in which the tall, sweet blue stem grasses wave in the wind . . . where Indian ponies and cattle have browsed until they fairly roll in fat. . . . In one place in the southern central part there are a number of springs within 100 feet of each other, giving forth enough water to supply a city of 50,000 people.[2]

By mid-May, an estimated fifteen thousand persons were camped around its borders, "posed to devour this tenderloin of Oklahoma where not over 550 could be satisfied." The President's proclamation caused such excitement that the slaying of Tulsa Jack, Charley Pierce, and Bitter Creek Newcomb was all but forgotten. The section declaring all men sooners who had entered the country since March 3, 1893, was considered ridiculous. Almost every man in the territory had at one time or another crossed the reservation to attend to business in Shawnee to the south or Chandler on the north.

Although some "first liners" read it and dropped out, most "stood their ground with a do or die look on their faces." No cavalry or infantry was present to restrain them from crossing the lines before the appointed hour, "the Interior Department relying upon the zeal of the individual settlers to secure claims as a check against sooners."[3]

At sharp 12 o'clock noon the signal guns . . . set in motion this vast crowd of homesteaders, boomers, speculators, townsite founders and pleasure seekers on one of these periodical free for all races for which this territory has become noted. The scene was but a repetition, on a smaller scale, of the Cherokee strip opening . . . horses, mules, bicycles, wagons, buggies and other vehicles dashed across the lines and disappeared in a whirlwind of dust. Hundreds of women started and exhibited the same amount of enthusiasm as the men.

Two townsite companies are conspicuous and have capital behind them. One from Chandler has for an objective a place half way between Chandler and Tecumseh and is backed by prominent men from Chandler and Guthrie. The embryo town is to be called "Kickapoo City." The other is on the Choctaw [railroad], midway between Shawnee and Choctaw City, and is to be called "Olney." It is intended as a rival to Shawnee and is backed by Oklahoma City and Tecumseh capital.[4] The two companies combined and located a townsite four or five miles above Dale, called McLoud. Several thousand people rushed over . . . to the railroad on the opposite side of the river. A large number pushed on to near the center of the reservation [and the proposed Kickapoo City], on the prospective route of the C.O.G. road, but here they found sooners claiming the land for homesteads and gobbling all the best lots.[5]

Telegrams received at Oklahoma City from all points show that the entire reservation swarmed with sooners, there being from five to ten illegal settlers to every quarter . . . the woods are full of them. Honest settlers are left, as usual. Much dissatisfaction was expressed at the vast amount of land allotted or reserved for school purposes, and the threat was freely made to occupy the entire country . . . and defy the government.

The U.S. Marshal swore in a large number of deputies, and without any fuss or ado, managed to keep the peace of Oklahoma. . . . Reports of sanguinary conflicts between deputy marshals and whiskey peddlers come from Shawnee, but no killed or wounded have arrived, so we presume that beer, not blood, was spilled.[6]

Persons returning from the Kickapoo borders reported twenty men to every claim. At the Oklahoma City land office, there were two people in line for every claim, a mixed crowd of men and women, and general confusion prevailed. In the first few minutes at the Guthrie land office, eight homestead entries and one soldier's declaratory were made and fifteen applications rejected on "informali-

284

ties and disqualifications." An effort to break the line ended in a free-for-all, but land-office officials soon had matters under control.[7] The *State Capital* of May 24 provided this aftermath:

> Now that the dust and smoke of the opening has blown away, evidences of fraud and soonerism pile up mountain high. Everyone who took part in the race is loud in condemnation of the methods of the administration and angry are the curses hurled at the authorities for the utter lack of provisions to protect honest settlers. . . .
>
> Shawnee and Choctaw City, on the Cherokee, Oklahoma & Gulf road, were principal points for outfitting and were full of gamblers, thugs and thieves. Games were run wide open and many of the prospective settlers were robbed. At Shawnee an infuriated mob threatened to hang "Butterfly Kid" and "Kechi," two noted characters, and had a rope around their necks when stopped by deputies. They had robbed several of the settlers by means of a shell game. There were thirty-six saloons in Shawnee, each with a gambling attachment. Three card monte and shell game men plied their trade on barrels and boxes in front of the saloons unmolested.
>
> It was a harvest for thugs, bums and horse thieves who congregated, and innumerable contests that arise between the entrymen and actual settlers means a rich harvest for lawyers . . . the only class who will make anything out of it. Hoke Smith, with his magnificent penchant for blundering, has eclipsed his former efforts in this line.

The penalty for soonerism was quickly inflicted, however. Of 227 applications offered at Oklahoma City on May 25, only 27 were accepted. The others were rejected because applicants had entered the reservation since March 3, 1893.[8]

At Tecumseh, Judge Scott was extremely busy deciding Indian lease cases and railroad right-of-way matters, and grinding out justice to robbers, whiskey peddlers, and other law violators. Notwithstanding a fake report that one band of culprits had "blown out the north end of the court house," the building remained intact, "as the giant powder used only lifted up the steps over the fence, rods away from it."[9]

In June, the portion of the Kickapoo country lying within Lincoln County was assigned to Judge Dale as the Territorial Supreme Court redistricted Oklahoma and changed judicial boundaries as follows:

> First district, Judge Dale presiding—Logan, Lincoln, Payne and Woodward counties.
> Second district, Judge Burford presiding—Canadian, Blaine, Dewey, Day, Roger Mills, Custer and Washita counties.

Third district, Judge Scott presiding—Oklahoma, Pottawatomie and Woods counties.

Fourth district, Judge Bierer presiding—Noble, Kay, Pawnee and Beaver counties.

Fifth district, Judge McAtee presiding—Grant, Garfield, Kingfisher.[10]

This sudden shift of population and organization of new city and county governments provided the climate for the rise of new bands of brigands:

> At Ingram [one mile northwest of present Wellston], three masked men rode up to the post office, but while they were dismounting the postmaster and several settlers opened fire and drove them off. The men then rode to the house of John Webb [on Deep Fork], and calling him to the door ordered him to bring out his money under penalty of death. He said: "All right, I'll get it," stepped inside, seized a gun and fired through the window, knocking one of the bandits off his horse. They riddled the house with bullets, picked up the wounded man and left without any booty.[11]

The trio was believed to be part of a gang of small-time thieves and whiskey peddlers led by two brothers named Bob (Robert) and Bill (William, Jr.) Christian.

Bob and Bill, the sons of William, Sr., and Sallie Christian, were born near Fort Griffin, Texas, in 1868 and 1871, respectively. Old Man Christian, a Kentuckian, was one of the early settlers in the area after the Civil War, finally taking a homestead in Baylor County in the Round Timbers neighborhood, where his sons spent their boyhoods watching thousands of Longhorns cross the Salt Fork of the Brazos on the San Antonio Trail en route to northern markets. About 1883, the Christians moved farther west into the Texas Panhandle, but nothing of their sojourn here is known. Shortly after the 1891 Pottawatomie-Shawnee opening in Oklahoma, the family appeared in Pottawatomie County, taking residence on an Indian allotment on Little River south of Tecumseh.[12]

Bill Deister, who ranched with his father in Cooke County, Texas, in the '70s and later on the line between Archer and Clay counties, knew the Christians well. In the spring of 1895, when Deister was sixteen, he and his father came to Indian Territory looking for cheap rangeland. The Christians then were living in southeastern Pottawatomie County near Sacred Heart Mission on the Canadian. Deister recalled driving their herd over the river at Young's Crossing, about three miles south of the mission, and "the first man we saw was Old Man Christian. He was getting off his horse, pulling his Winchester—he always carried a rifle . . . his sons carried six-shooters, even when boys. He put the rifle over in his left hand and walked up and shook hands with Pa and patted me on the back, he was [so] glad to see us." The Deisters rented an old Indian log house a half-mile from Sacred Heart, used it for storage, set up their tents, and built a corral. Later, the Christians moved into a one-roomed house farther southeast near Violet Springs. Deister described William, Sr., as "a large man, dark complected . . . didn't everybody know he had been one of old Quantrill's raiders." His wife was a slender blonde. Both "dipped snuff with old-time toothbrushes made of twigs from blackgum trees, and they'd sit and dip for hours . . . never talked a great deal. Pa liked the old man, and mother liked the old lady," but they had little praise for their wastrel sons, who were "on the scout all time."[13]

The *Oklahoma State Capital*[14] described the Christians as

> nervy and reckless men. Bill is said to be the bravest and the one who does the head work. Bob delights in athletic sports, and is never so happy as when showing off his prowess in jumping, boxing and breaking a fractious horse. One of his feats is to take a running leap over . . . a 16-hand animal without touching a hair. As marksmen both are very proficient, and their home is in the saddle.

Here the admiration ended. Too many people were familiar with their larceny and whiskey-selling exploits. Deister remembered how the family would run out of groceries but next morning there would be ham, bacon, and flour for the table. The boys "had been robbing." Their thefts went uninvestigated. "The country was full of outlaws. An officer could not ride in there and take somebody out unless he knew what he was doing . . . he would likely be found dead by the roadside."[15] The Christians had many sympathizers among this heterogeneous populace that had little respect for laws— territorial, tribal, or federal.

Unlike other sections of Oklahoma, where homesteaders found railroads and telegraph lines crossing a country devoid of inhabitants, the Pottawatomie area was untraversed by either, and its Indians, like the Seminoles and Creeks to the east and Chickasaws and Choctaws to the south, lived on farms, possessed cattle and horses, and derived considerable income from leasing land to the whites. The struggle to adjust differences with Indian landowners and establish communication and transportation facilities left Pottawatomie County settlers torn with internal dissension and at cross-purposes with territorial authorities. This and the fact that the country was bordered on two sides by the Indian Nations made it an easy rendezvous for law violators. Many outlaws in both ter-

ritories found the saloon towns that sprang up along these boundaries convenient hangouts for cattle- and horse-stealing operations.

Two definite trails were used to move stolen livestock out of the
country. Both entered the area almost due west of Tecumseh. One
branched off north past old Shawneetown, leaving the county near
Keokuk Falls. The other branched south, leaving the county near
Violet Springs. It was one of the large gangs working these trails
that Marshal Nix's deputies and James H. Gill, Pottawatomie's first
elected sheriff, broke up in May, 1894.

W. B. (Billy) Trousdale, namesake of the town in the southwestern
section of the county established on part of his original homestead
after the railroad came through several years later, succeeded Gill
as sheriff in the 1894 fall elections. By this time, there were sixty-
two saloons and two licensed distilleries in Pottawatomie. Although
each town had its quota of liquor merchants, the saloons that thrived
on the "jug" trade from Indian Territory and contributed to the
county's bloody chapter of thefts, highway robbery, and murder
were at Keokuk Falls, Violet Springs, Young's Crossing, and The
Corner, the latter situated in the extreme southeastern tip of the
county in a jungle of cottonwoods and plum thickets on a river-
bottom parcel of land known as a fraction (less than a quarter-
section), created by the meandering South Canadian.

A quantity of merchandise disappeared from a large mercantile
establishment, owned and controlled by Governor John F. Brown
of the Seminole Nation, where Bill and Bob Christian had been
employed briefly during the spring of 1895, and a warrant charging
grand larceny was issued for Bob Christian. It was delivered to
Sheriff Trousdale of Pottawatomie County and handed to Deputy
Sheriff Will Turner for service. On Saturday morning, April 27,
Turner came upon the Christians and two incipient pals, Buttermilk
John Mackey and Foster Holbrook, in a small grove near Violet
Springs. The deputy informed Bob that he held a warrant for his
arrest. Bob replied, "Damn you, you'd better keep it," and reached
for his gun. Turner beat him to the draw and ordered, "Hands up!"
The outlaw "paid no attention," and the deputy "fired square at his
breast at less than a yard distance." It was thought Christian was
wearing a steel breastplate, "as the shot . . . knocked him down and
appeared to stun him for a moment." Then all four outlaws opened
fire on the deputy, killing him instantly.[16]

Sheriff Trousdale and a posse took Mackey and Holbrook into
custody the next day. Bob and Bill Christian escaped to their Little
River haunts. Three weeks later, for some reason preferring not to

be captured by Pottawatomie County authorities, the two desperadoes surrendered to deputy marshals W. H. Carr and Hank Watts. They were lodged in the Tecumseh jail with Mackey and Holbrook on May 22.[17]

All four men were tried before Judge Scott. Bob Christian took credit for killing Turner but pleaded self-defense. Mackey drew two years for second-degree manslaughter; Holbrook was acquitted. The Christians were convicted of manslaughter in the first degree and each was sentenced to ten years in the territorial prison at Lansing, but they appealed to the Territorial Supreme Court. Tecumseh citizens declared them "a bad lot" who "should get their dues" and that "Oklahoma should raise hemp and start rope factories . . . or we will soon have a worse name than Indian Territory." On June 10, Bob and Bill Christian were transferred to the Oklahoma County jail for safekeeping and an opportunity to perfect an appeal bond.[18]

The Oklahoma County jail, a two-story wooden structure with steel cages on the first floor, was situated at the juncture of an alley running north from Grand Avenue and an alley connecting Broadway and Robinson. The Christians shared a cellblock with James Casey, still awaiting trial for the murder of Deputy Farris at Yukon. Immediately, the trio made plans to escape. Obe Cox, awaiting trial for horse theft, agreed to join them. They were aided by gang sympathizers John Reeves, John Fessenden, and Tullis Welch, a local tough named Louie Miller, the Christians' father, and an "attractive, innocent looking" girl about twenty years old who posed as their sister but actually was Jessie Findlay (spelled *Finlay* and *Finley* in contemporary reports), Bob Christian's sweetheart. Jessie's home was at Paoli, southeast of Purcell in the Chickasaw Nation. Between Monday, June 24, and Thursday, June 27, this sextet smuggled into the jail at least three loaded revolvers while visiting the prisoners and bringing them delicacies and tobacco. Two of these weapons were "blue-steel, black-handled forty-five Colts"; the other was a "white-handled forty-five" decorated with an eagle's head, which Bob Christian had used to kill Turner and which had been placed in the custody of Deputy Marshals Carr and Watts.[19]

There was a stove in the rear of the cellblock. The prisoners unjointed the pipe above the damper, packed it with a piece of blanket to hold the guns on top of the damper, and replaced the pipe. On Sunday afternoon, June 30, while they were allowed the freedom of the corridor, the trio unjointed the pipe, and each armed himself with a six-shooter. At 6:30 jailer J. H. Garver entered the

289

corridor to lock the prisoners in their cells. Mrs. Garver, who had just called at the jail office, stood in the doorway, and Garver instructed her to close the door after him. As he stepped into the corridor,

the two Christians and Casey sprang upon him and hurled him against the iron grating. Then followed a fearful struggle with the jailer engaged by the two Christians, Casey making his escape, pulling the outer door open and passing Mrs. Garver, who in the excitement had forgotten to fasten it. . . . She, however, recovered presence of mind and closed the door and turned the fastenings after Casey passed. She had hardly completed this task, when Casey returned . . . placed his revolver against her head and ordered the jail door opened at once. She complied and the Christians, who had succeeded in overpowering the jailer, passed out.

[At this juncture, Obe Cox lost his nerve and refused to join in the dash to the street.]

On leaving the jail all three prisoners started south in the alley. Chief of Police Milt Jones' horse was tied in the alley about 75 feet from the jail door. One of the Christians [Bill] mounted it and started away on the run. He turned down Broadway and then west in the alley between California and Reno. From the city he struck southwest. . . .

Meanwhile, his two companions were playing a leading part in an awful tragedy. They ran out onto Grand avenue and turned [east] toward Broadway. Almost in the center of Grand they ran up to a buggy in which was Mr. [Gus] White, a carpenter, and Mrs. [Ella] Hurt. [Bob] Christian jumped up into the buggy in front of the couple, and Casey jumped in behind. Christian struck the horse, but it was John Roller's two-year-old high bred colt that had been driven only two or three times. The sudden action frightened the colt and instead of plunging forward it stopped still.

Chief Jones was standing in Broadway a few feet north of the crossing. Officers Jackson and Stafford also were near the corner. The men were recognized and Chief Jones started toward the buggy with his revolver in his hand, but he did not fire. At the same instant Christian jumped from the buggy and fired at Chief Jones. It is believed that Christian's bullet was the one that struck Jones in the breast. His hands dropped and became rigid and he called to a bystander to take his gun. He then turned and walked toward police headquarters, and when opposite the stairway he sank to the sidewalk, W. S. Burnes and Chas. Parker catching him as he sank to the ground. He lived about five minutes.

The assault upon Chief Jones by the escaping prisoners drew the fire of the other officers and one or two citizens. Casey was shot in the head above the ear and also through the neck, death resulting almost instantly. . . . Mr. White received two flesh wounds in the abdomen and leg. Two or three other bullets went through his clothing. Mrs. Hurt was not injured.

After firing at Chief Jones, Christian started down Grand avenue on the run. A dozen shots were fired at him and at least one took effect, for blood was seen streaming from his face. Crossing the Santa Fe, he encountered Frank Berg [a blacksmith] in his road wagon. Christian stuck a gun in his face and ordered him to jump. He obeyed the order and Christian jumped in and lashed the horse into a run, going east to the east side of the military reservation, then south to the bridge [on the North Canadian], across the bridge and east to the Pete Branthouse place where the wagon was abandoned and Christian took to the woods, a posse headed by Deputy Jim DeFord [Sheriff DeFord's son] being about 600 feet behind. Reinforcements were sent for and the timber surrounded, but it soon grew dark and the search was carried on with difficulty.[20]

The *Oklahoma State Capital*[21] added these pertinent details:

Mrs. Hurt's screams vied with the report of the firearms and [as Christian fled down Grand Avenue] she tumbled from the buggy and ran up to the Compton house, where she . . . recovered her composure in part. Dr. Ryan dressed White's wounds and he was taken home. The body of Casey was left in the buggy on the street for an hour or more, viewed by hundreds. It was a ghastly object, the face being covered with blood, which had coagulated and dried. . . . A 45-calibre revolver was taken from Casey's dead hand by Deputy Moors. After being viewed by the coroner's jury the body was removed to Harvey & Reed's undertaking rooms, where it will be prepared for burial.

The *Times-Journal*[22] lamented Chief Jones's passing:

He was only 32 . . . has lived in Oklahoma since the opening and has acted in the capacity of peace officer almost continually since. His modesty, manliness and fine sense of honor endeared him to all his intimate acquaintances and gained for him the respect of the entire community.

Business houses closed Monday morning while thousands attended the funeral. City officials, firemen, and police were in the procession headed by the Hrabe Band, playing a funeral dirge, with AOUW lodge members as pallbearers and escorts. On the coffin rested two floral emblems: the AOUW insigne and the badge of the chief of police.

That afternoon, Old Man Casey claimed his son's body. He had been in El Reno on Saturday getting the bond for his son approved by the county attorney and waiting to see Judge Scott on Monday.

Asked why his son had attempted to escape, he replied: "I think the Christians persuaded him that Judge Scott would not approve the bond." James Casey was buried beside his brother Victor at the home of a sister twelve miles southwest of Oklahoma City.

The posses which pursued the Christians returned without capturing them. DeFord's men found a crimson trail where Bob Christian had entered the North Canadian but no sign that he had left the river, and it was believed, because of his weakened condition from loss of blood and the high stage of the water, which was a boiling torrent from recent rains, that he had drowned. Deputy DeFord soon learned, however, that he had floated downstream several miles on a log and reached his home in the Pottawatomie country two days later. "The party furnishing the information says he is badly wounded, the ball entering the fore part and coming out the back of the neck . . . and does not see how he can recover."[23] Deister[24] recalled that

> he was shot through the neck, and my wife's sister bandaged him up. . . . He went to the home of a neighbor who handled all the Christians' stolen goods and was the go-between for the outlaws. It was close to a week before Bob got able to ride, and left.

After leaving Oklahoma City, Bill Christian continued southwest several miles, then turned east, eluding his pursuers on Little River. On July 5, Chief Jones's horse was recovered at a farm eight miles northwest of Norman, where the fugitive had exchanged it for a fresh mount. By July 8, the Christians were together again,

> holed up in an old dugout twelve miles northeast of Pauls Valley and gathering about them men as desperate as themselves to wreak vengeance on their enemies. The band will rival the Dalton gang in its palmiest days and promises to become a terror . . . it is thought they will either attempt to hold up one of the night trains on the Santa Fe or make a raid on some of the several small towns in the vicinity.[25]

Sheriff C. H. DeFord took the train to Pauls Valley, where a posse was organizing "to go after the outlaws at once." He reached Paoli Wednesday forenoon, July 10, where he learned that Bob Christian had "taken away the woman [Jessie Findlay] who took the arms into the jail." During the night, the gang had stolen six horses near Paoli, and "it is known that they now have four followers who are among the worst of the Indian Territory desperados—John Fessenden, John Reeves, Doc Williams and Ben Brown, a powerful negro and a notorious thief and bad man." They also were accompanied by

Emma Johnson, sweetheart of Bill Christian, "Emma having joined them Tuesday night at her father's, eight miles from Paoli." From this point, the gang "took an easterly direction bound for the Seminole country."[26]

On the evening of July 12, Deputy Marshal Bud Logue and Deputies W. C. Wade and W. H. Springfield of Pottawatomie County raided Brown's hut east of Violet Springs in the Seminole Nation and arrested Doc Williams and Jessie Findlay. Because of an "authenticated rumor that Christian sympathizers would undertake to ambush the officers and recover the girl," they hurriedly placed the prisoners on horseback and struck west fifty miles cross-country to Purcell. Logue wired Sheriff DeFord, who met the officers at daybreak. Logue took Williams to the federal jail at Ardmore on a charge of harboring fugitives in Indian Territory, and the sheriff returned to Oklahoma City with Jessie.[27]

Jessie bore her incarceration without pining, confident that those she had aided to escape would not forget her in "durance vile." Realizing that she could be charged with complicity in the murder of Chief Jones, she decided to do what the Christians had attempted to prevent by hiding her: make a full confession.

From the time the brothers had been placed in the Oklahoma County jail, Jessie told County Attorney J. L. Brown and Sheriff DeFord, she had been allowed to visit them, talking alone with Bob for hours at a time. She had never been questioned or searched by jailer Garver. In fact, the jailer had even allowed her and Bob certain intimacies. On her last visit three days before the escape, she had brought Bob a Colt six-shooter given her by Tullis Welch, carrying it in the bosom of her dress. She identified the gun taken from James Casey's hand and stated that the other revolvers had been smuggled into the jail on June 24 by Reeves, Fessenden, Louie Miller, and Old Man Christian. One belonged to Miller; the other, Bob Christian's white-handled Colt, had been furnished Reeves and Fessenden by Deputy Marshal Carr!

Jailer Garver maintained that he had exercised every precaution while the Christians and Casey were in his custody. Obe Cox, however, supported Jessie Findlay and told how the various persons had come and gone almost at will. Cox saw the gun Jessie brought Bob Christian and the guns delivered by Miller, Reeves, Old Man Christian, and Fessenden. "Watts was there at the time . . . Garver made him take off his gun but allowed him to keep his cartridge belt. While he was in the jail, Bob Christian removed a number of cartridges. We were all locked up in the cage except Bob and Bill . . . and they went around behind the cage with Reeves . . . the jailer stepped out, and Miller put the guns through the door." The most damaging information came from Sheriff Trousdale. On June 27, he learned of a meeting between Bill Carr, Reeves, and Fessenden at a home southeast of Tecumseh where Carr "fitted them out with Bob Christian's pistol." Believing the brothers to be armed and ready to break jail, he promptly wired the information to Jailer Garver. Garver admitted that he received the telegram on June 29 but "believed it to be a fake, and said nothing about it."[28]

County Attorney Brown laid the evidence before an Oklahoma County grand jury, and Sheriff DeFord, "startled by the worst piece of skullduggery ever perpetrated in the territory," proposed to pay from his own pocket the expenses of a large number of extra deputies until all persons implicated were brought to justice.

Tullis Welch was arrested July 15 at his father's home east of Oklahoma City. At his preliminary hearing, Jessie Findlay testified that it was his gun that she delivered to Bob Christian. Welch was bound over to the grand jury without bail on the charge of murder.[29]

On July 18, Sheriff Trousdale arrested Hank Watts at Tecumseh, and Deputy Jim DeFord "went over and got him." Watts denied that he was one of the "king bees" in the conspiracy and pointed out it was he who had induced the Christians to surrender. He did not deny that he had allowed Bob Christian to remove cartridges from his belt while visiting the jail with Old Man Christian, Miller, Reeves, and Fessenden.[30]

Thursday morning, July 19, Deputy Sheriff B. F. Owens and posse left Oklahoma City for Pottawatomie County to assist in the hunt for Carr and Old Man Christian. On Sunday night, "the old man was captured in the brush, he running onto Deputy Marshal Rufe Cannon by accident. . . . Cannon had been hunting the Christians for several days, and was within half a mile of Deputy Owens and posse when he came upon Carr and put him under arrest also."[31]

Carr swore he could prove his innocence and said he had informed Sheriff Trousdale that the Christians had revolvers and cartridges in the jail. He also stated that the Christians had "turned on him . . . and now threatened to burn his store at Violet Springs and kill him on sight."[32] The *Oklahoma State Capital*[33] thought it

quite probable Carr was gaining favor with the Christians with a view of pulling them himself and obtaining the rewards out for their capture . . . he has done as daring deeds in the past. Few of our frontier marshals have lived to rid the country of so many desperate characters as Bill. Whether guilty or not, law-loving people admire the courage of this man's past career.

The *Guthrie Daily Leader*[34] believed that

unjust abuse is being heaped on the deputy marshals on account of the escape of the Christian outlaws. . . . Sheriff DeFord and his wormy underlings are stirring up hard feelings against the deputies in order to throw the blame off themselves. It was through the negligence of the jailer that the outlaws escaped. DeFord's men are now making hippodrome plays to catch them, much to the amusement of the people who are on to their game.

DeFord took the criticism in stride, and County Attorney Brown charged Carr with complicity by introducing into the jail weapons used to murder Chief Jones. Carr's friends, many of them residents of Oklahoma City, rallied to his support. When he was placed under five thousand dollars bond by Probate Judge Harper, "they gave it at once." Carr offered "full cooperation" in hunting down Jones's killers, but DeFord warned his deputies that "he was a traitor and would throw them off if they trusted him." Proof of Carr's guilt or innocence hinged on the capture of Louie Miller, who had vanished from his local haunts, or of Reeves and Fessenden, now riding with the Christians.

With large posses combing the Pottawatomie and Seminole areas, the gang fled to the Choctaw Nation, boasting to make a stake and leave the country. On July 26, they were sighted on the Katy Railroad south of Eufaula. Believing they intended to rob the mail and express train at the South Canadian crossing, Marshal McAlester of the Central District sent a squad of deputies north to "give them a warm reception."[35]

The gang dashed back into the Creek Nation. At 7 P.M. on July 28, they rode up to the door of the Wewoka Trading Company. Leaving one man to guard the horses, Bob and Bill Christian entered,

ordering the clerks, seven or eight in number, to hold up their hands, which they did. They tried to make one of the clerks open the safe, but he informed them that the only man able to work the combination had just gone to supper, and after some parley the clerk's statement was accepted and the robbers contented themselves with $35 cash, two Winchesters, three cartridge belts and scabbards amounting to about $300 value. The clerks and bystanders were marched across Wewoka Creek bridge, and the only horse near was put in condition [hamstrung] to prevent pursuit, and the robbers then rode east, shooting back as they went.[36]

On August 5, they recrossed the Canadian, robbed another store near Calvin, and escaped into the Shawnee Hills. While Marshal McAlester reorganized his forces and telegraphed the Northern District at Muskogee for additional deputies, the gang crossed the Choctaw Coal Railroad near Hartshorne and headed toward the San Bois Mountains.[37]

At sundown on August 9, Deputy Sheriff Springfield and Deputy Marshal F. C. Stockton, who had been trailing the gang since the Wewoka robbery, discovered their camp five miles south of Wilburton. At the order of "Hands up!" the

> four bandits began firing at the deputies, who returned the fire, which lasted about thirty minutes, when the robbers mounted their horses and fled, taking one wounded and leaving one dead. During the fight the marshals lost their horses, and having no means to carry the dead robber, had to leave him and walk to town for assistance. . . . Springfield wired Marshal McAlester to send more men and horses at once.[38]

A special train was sent to the scene, and a posse took the trail of the bandits, who were heading back west. Springfield sent this telegram to Sheriff DeFord at Oklahoma City on August 10:

> Had a fight with Christian gang yesterday. Killed John Fessenden. Do you want his body? Wire Marshal McAlester at South McAlester, I.T.

A few days later, Deputy Marshals Sam Minor and Ed Gardner tracked the remaining bandits to a farmhouse near Hartshorne, where they learned the gang had obtained supplies and fresh horses and had left for the Chickasaw Nation. The farmer and his four sons were "put under arrest for harboring the fugitives. Also taken into custody was Irene Champion [Emma Johnson?], the sweetheart of Bill Christian." All were jailed at South McAlester.[39]

On the evening of August 21, Deputy Marshal Hocker and a Purcell posse surprised John Reeves at the Johnson home near Paoli and took him without a fight. Reeves talked volubly. He had "left the Christians and . . . was at Johnson's to get information respecting the movement of the officers." The Christians were "very much worn, the pursuit of the marshals having been so vigorous that they had had no rest," and were "hiding in one of two big ravines that headed up in a pasture near an old cabin" eight miles west of Purcell. Reeves was to bring food to the cabin, "a gun would be fired, and thereupon they were to come out of hiding and meet him."[40]

Hocker wired Sheriff DeFord. The latter boarded the midnight train to Paoli, picked up the prisoner, and returned him to Oklahoma City. At 1:30 A.M., Deputy Jim DeFord left for Purcell with a posse to join Marshal Hocker, hoping to bag the Christians at daylight.

The pasture was mostly open country with heavy underbrush along the two ravines. The officers surrounded the cabin area and waited all day and night. On Friday morning, August 23, they decided

further watching was useless, and . . . Posseman Martin fired off his Winchester. In a few seconds the two Christians came out of the brush close to Deputy Ben Goode and Hocker, who were twenty or thirty yards apart. Hocker began to shoot at Bob Christian, and while thus engaged Bill Christian got behind Hocker and shot him through the body, the ball entering just below the shoulder blade and passing out under the opposite arm.

During the firing Bill Christian's horse was killed and Hocker is sure he wounded Bob Christian. The Christians immediately sprang to Hocker's horse and both mounted it, Tom Noel [a posseman] having killed Bill Christian's horse and Bob's having gotten away. The two desperadoes rode as fast as the horse could go toward Walnut creek. The belief is strengthened that Bob Christian is wounded by Bill's having to help Bob onto the horse, and when they came to a wire fence Bill got out of the saddle to let down the wire. Under ordinary conditions the one behind would have dismounted.

The tragedy was witnessed by officers on the opposite side of the canyon, a long detour being necessary in order to cross. They were thus unable to lend assistance, although in plain view.

Deputy Jim DeFord secured a fine horse from Bob Christian, Milt Jones' saddle and Bill Christian's rifle.

The officers were in close pursuit at nightfall, and unless the Christians are supplied with fresh horses they are almost certain to be caught.[41]

The Christians, however, escaped again. They

got away from the officers during Monday night [August 26] and have gone in a westerly direction. . . . Deputy Marshal Hocker rested very well last night and the doctors have hopes of his recovery, although his wounds are very serious. The Christians took Hocker's pistol, Winchester and belt full of cartridges. Most of the large posses which went from Ardmore and Davis also have returned home.[42]

At Oklahoma City, John Reeves admitted that Deputy Marshal Carr "knew all about" the contemplated jailbreak but "wasn't certain how Fessenden came in possession of Bob Christian's white-handled Colt's." A new warrant was issued for Carr. Deputy Marshal George Smith had anticipated this maneuver and arrested Carr on a federal warrant for a minor offense "to keep him out of the hands of Sheriff DeFord." As soon as the sheriff heard of the trick, he went to the marshal's office at Guthrie and obtained an order from Chief Deputy Hale for Smith to turn Carr over to DeFord or his deputies. The order and warrant were handed to Deputy Sheriff Owens.

Owens started after Smith's posse at once but failed to overtake it until two days later, when "he slipped up on their camp." Owens covered Carr with his Winchester and told him he was under arrest. Deputy Marshal Fred Jones (Chief Jones's brother) drew his Winchester on Owens. Owens again demanded Carr and showed his warrant and order from the U.S. marshal. Smith informed him that Carr had been turned to the custody of Deputy Marshal C. C. Hutchinson. The latter refused to release his prisoner on grounds that the order was directed to Smith. Hutchinson had seven men and Owens three, so the marshals kept Carr.

On September 1, Hutchinson brought the much wanted deputy to Oklahoma City. Friends again furnished bond in the sum of five thousand dollars, which was approved by Judge Scott. But County Attorney Brown, who knew nothing of the proceedings until Carr had been discharged,

> went to the judge and explained the territory's side of the case . . . the bond was revoked and an order issued for the re-arrest of Carr. He was taken before Justice of the Peace Keys, where he waived examination and was bound over to the grand jury. He was then taken before the district court on a writ of habeas corpus. At the close of the investigation, the court granted Carr bail in the sum of $10,000.[43]

The grand jury indicted Carr, and his trial was set for November 5. He surrendered his federal commission, disposed of his Violet Springs property, and took up temporary residence in Lexington. On the morning of November 4, he boarded a freight at Noble with "$800 or $900 in his pocket," saying he was going to Oklahoma City. "Just as the freight started he jumped off, saying he believed he would wait for the next train," and disappeared. On November 6, the warrant was returned into court with the endorsement "he cannot be found." Judge Scott forfeited Carr's bond and ordered the county attorney to begin suit against his bondsmen to recover the amount.[44]

The grand jury that indicted Carr also indicted John Reeves, Old

Man Christian, and Tullis Welch, but Welch and Old Man Christian were never brought to trial. Reeves obtained a change of venue to Canadian County, where he was convicted as coconspirator in Jones's murder and sentenced to the territorial prison at Lansing for life. He appealed to the Territorial Supreme Court, but the judgment of the district court was affirmed.[45]

No charges were filed against Jessie Findlay. In September, 1896, after fourteen months as an inmate of the county jail, she was released on two thousand dollars bond "in consideration that she be ready at all times to testify in behalf of the territory to any facts in her possession."[46]

It was on her testimony principally that jailer Garver was indicted and tried during the November, 1895, term of Oklahoma County District Court under Section 2010, Statutes of Oklahoma, 1893, for "carelessly permitting the prisoners to escape." Hank Watts and Obe Cox also were damning witnesses. "The verdict of guilty . . . was no surprise to those who had made an unbiased investigation of the escape of the Christians, but to those who saw in the escape an opportunity to malign officers who were endeavoring to do their duty, it was as a clap of thunder out of a clear sky."[47] Garver was sentenced to ten years. He appealed to the Supreme Court, which affirmed the judgment of the district court.[48] He was pardoned two years later and died in 1911.

Louie Miller remained the only coconspirator not dealt with. At three o'clock on the morning of September 30, he was surprised by Deputy Sheriff Owens and posse at Old Man Christian's home near Violet Springs and killed while resisting arrest.

Nothing more was heard of Bill Carr. A couple of years later, it was rumored that he was "making a record by his fearless bravery and unerring aim . . . as captain in the insurgent army of Cuba,"[49] and it was generally assumed that he died on the field of battle. At the turn of the century, an old Lexington acquaintance claimed he saw Carr in the Creek Nation, alive and well, the former deputy marshal having just returned from riding four years "with the Christian boys in southwestern Texas."[50] Neither report was ever verified.

Bob and Bill Christian's Oklahoma trail ended with their escape from the Hocker and DeFord posses west of Purcell.[51] On September 13, 1895, after ten days of scouring the southwestern Indian reservations, deputy marshals returned to Oklahoma City with "definite information" that the brothers were hiding on Red River, somewhere in Greer County or in Texas.[52] Deister[53] recalled that, shortly after the killing of Louie Miller, he was

> at Old Man Christian's on a Sunday . . . the Christian boys were around the border of southern Arizona and the family was waiting for a letter from them about where to go . . . whether to stop in Arizona or over in New Mexico. Next time I went over to their place nobody was there. Nobody knew when they left . . . I never heard from them after that.

Edward Wilson, an old Arizona cowboy, in his curious little memoir entitled *An Unwritten History: A Record From the Exciting Days of Early Arizona*,[54] tells how he came down from the Apache Reservation to Sulphur Springs Valley in the fall of 1895 to work at the Mud Springs ranch for the Erie Cattle Company, a large outfit running more than twenty thousand head. Tom White, the foreman, put him to work breaking some big Colorado horses, and while he was engaged in this venture, he met "a wonderful rider" called 202 (he weighed that many pounds), but better known as Black Jack because of his unusually dark complexion. Wilson and Jack became good friends and later took a contract to break mules for Jim McNair of the Erie Cattle Company, which McNair intended to ship to La-Junta, Colorado. During their association, Jack often remarked how much more profitable it would be to "get up an outfit and go train robbing." He said his real name was Frank Williams—taken from a letter he had received from his mother, then living on the Brazos river in Texas. His brother ("half-brother," Jack alleged), named Tom Anderson, also worked for the Erie. Wilson often made trips with them to Bisbee and "always had a very lively time." He became acquainted with three other men who agreed to join in their plans and tried to get Wilson to join also. Their names were Bob Hayes, Jesse Williams, and Code Young.

Bob Hayes was an alias for Sam Hassells of Iowa, who began his criminal career as a horse thief in Gonzales County, Texas, where he broke jail and fled to New Mexico, cowboying for a time in Chavez County under the alias of John West and changing his name to Hayes upon arriving in Arizona. Jesse Williams was an alias for George Musgrave, a native Texan who had spent most of his twenty-two years in Chavez County; he had left Roswell to avoid trial on a charge of rustling cattle from the Circle Diamond outfit and worked on various ranches in southwestern New Mexico as Jeff Davis, Jesse Miller, and Jesse Johnson before drifting into Arizona's Cochise County. Musgrave's boon companion in the Roswell area had been Code Young, also a native Texan, whose real name was Bob Harris; he was about twenty-four years old and had accompanied Musgrave to southwestern New Mexico for the same reason, using the alias Cole Estes. Later developments revealed that Frank (or Black Jack) Williams and Tom Anderson were Bill and Bob Christian.[55]

By July, 1896, the new gang had been organized. They called themselves the High Fives, after a card game then in vogue. In the months that followed, they robbed stores, post offices, banks, and trains and outdistanced and outmaneuvered posses from Arizona and New Mexico to Sonora and Chihuahua.[56] If they lost a member, they added another. Finally, in April, 1897, Bill Christian was killed by officers in an ambush on Cole Creek near Clifton, Arizona. Bob continued to operate the gang only a short time after his brother's death. On November 25, he was arrested during a Thanksgiving brawl in Fronteras, thirty-five miles below the border in Chihuahua. On December 9, before extradition could be arranged with Mexican authorities, he escaped from the Fronteras jail and rode into the "deepest obscurity." He was never heard from again. It spelled dissolution of the High Fives and ended Oklahoma's hunt for the bold, bad Christians.

Oklahoma City Police
Chief Milt Jones.

Bill (Black Jack) Christian.

Deputies Steve Birchfield and Pink Peters view saddles and guns captured from Black Jack Christian's gang. From the Western History Collections, University of Oklahoma Library.

The possemen who chased Black Jack Christian out of the country and killed some of his gang: 1, Steve Birchfield; 2, Baylor Shannon; 3, Charles Ballard; 4, J. L. Dow; 5, Fred Higgins; 6, C. S. Fly. Western History Collections, University of Oklahoma Library.

XX Doolin Gang Sweethearts

WHILE MARSHAL NIX CONCENTRATED his Oklahoma City forces on attempts to apprehend the Christians, his deputies at Pawnee and
Perry were putting an end to the message-carrying activities of the
two young female spies for the Wild Bunch: Annie McDoulet (Cattle
Annie) and Jennie Stevens (Little Breeches).

Their backgrounds have been dealt with only briefly.[1] Both girls
were "daughters of respectable farmers" who became acquainted
with members of the Doolin gang at a country dance. Annie "fell in
love with one of the bandits [and] probably on account of the love
women are said to have for fighting men [they] imbibed much of the
outlaw spirit" and thereafter "followed, sheltered them when they
could, and acted as assistants and supply carriers." Nix[2] agrees that

> their people were uneducated but considered respectable. I remember
> that the father of one of the girls attributed her wild ideas to the en-
> vironment of some of the hilarious dances that were held in the Indian
> country and to the influence of outlaws who attended these functions.

In an anonymous *Guthrie Daily Leader*[3] entitled "Outlaw Girls
Sassed the Judge," we are told again that

> both came of good, respectable ranch homes . . . but that did not mean
> outlaws and horse thieves could not and did not visit their homes and
> eat and rest between forays. It was a common and accepted thing to
> offer hospitality to any stranger who happened to hitch his horse in front
> of the house. And if the stranger happened to drop a hint that the law
> was after him—well, what could a rancher do? So, the girls grew up,
> having known several of the desperados that the U.S. deputy marshals
> hunted so assiduously. They had eaten with them, shaken out oats and
> fodder for their horses and gazed on their weather-beaten faces while
> they listened to the long and exciting tales of brushes with the law.
>   It was natural, therefore, that the girls should fall in love with des-
> perados. Cattle Annie, young, buxom and high-spirited, fell in love with
> a member of the Doolin gang she met at a little crossroads settlement
> south of Pawnee, at a dance. Introduced to the bandit by a boy friend
> who whispered that the new acquaintance was a member of the notori-

305

ous Doolin gang, Cattle Annie "fell" for him immediately. Little Breeches also was introduced, and became wildly excited at the stories of the wealth and fame that would be theirs if they should turn to banditry.

Several months afterwards, the girls decided to begin their career of outlawry. Not only did they dare to wear men's pants in the sanctimonious but scarlet nineties, but rode horses as men rode them, astride, and with heavy forty-fives swinging at their hips.[4]

According to contemporary accounts,[5] Annie was the daughter of J. C. McDoulet, a preacher-lawyer from Fall River, Kansas, who was "in poor circumstances" when he moved to Skiatook, Indian Territory. Large for her age, she had been allowed to work as a domestic in a neighbor's house, where she met the Doolin outlaws. She "fell in love with Buck Waightman," in whose company she "started out on a career of romance and bullet diet."

Jennie Stevens, "raised on a farm" at Sinnett in southeastern Pawnee County near the Doolin gang's old hideout on the Cimarron,

> made the outlaws' acquaintance while sewing up the bullet holes in their clothes after they would come in from a raid and hear them related their experience, every word of which she drank in as a bootblack does a five-cent detective story. She could stand it no longer, but slipping quietly to the garrett she secured a suit of the hired man's clothes and made ready to go with the boys . . . but on their first night out her horse got away and returned home riderless, and she was taken to a neighbor's and left by the gang only to return home in a couple of days disappointed and heartbroken. . . . To make matters worse, her father gave her a sound thrashing. This, together with the taunts of her friends, was more than the girl could stand, so she skipped again, this time going to New-kirk, where she met a man named [Benjamin F.] Midkiff [corrupted in later writings to *Metcalf*].[6]

Midkiff and Jennie were married on March 5, 1895, and set up housekeeping in a hotel at Perry. In a short time, he learned that she was allowing men to "visit her room" during his absence. This caused the "worst trouble" and he moved her to Osage City, in Pawnee County east of Skedee, but she "acted no better" there. Finally, Midkiff returned her to her father's home, and "almost the next day she started her dishonorable rides up and down the Arkansas River, keeping the lowest company." Midkiff "found her in Cleveland . . . staying in a store with two young men." They again started home, but "fell out and quit on the road."[7]

In the Osage, Jennie met a "rounder" named Wilson, who "thought he had struck a bonanza." Wilson conceived the idea of a partnership: he would bring whiskey into the country and Jennie would peddle it. "She worked as a domestic through the day and at night would don male attire and sail forth, returning toward morning with trouser pockets bulged and all the Indians guessing who the *kin-shin-ka* [boy] was; only by accident was her real identity found out and her capture effected" by Deputy Marshal Canton.[8]

She was arraigned before U.S. Commissioner Wrightsman at Pawnee, bound over for trial in the Fourth Judicial District, and ordered transferred to the federal jail at Guthrie. Deputies Frank Canton, Bush, and Gant Owens reached Guthrie with Jennie and several other federal prisoners on July 5. She had been arrested in male attire and

> still wore the garb when placed in jail here. She naively remarked on the street as she squirted a stream of tobacco juice at a crack in the sidewalk that she liked men's clothes better than those of her own sex, especially for her business. Her general make-up is that of a gadding girl seeking notoriety, her very actions and talk reminds one of the female horse thief, Tom King.[9]

Jennie's stay at the federal inn was brief. She gave bond and rejoined Annie McDoulet in the Pawnee country. With Pierce, Newcomb, and Tulsa Jack dead following the Dover robbery and their "sweethearts" in the gang scattered, the girls returned to their old trade of selling whiskey to the Indians and stealing horses. They became very troublesome, and

> it was evident that they were keeping in fairly close touch with the movements of the officers. . . . Wherever they were seen, they were heavily armed with pistols and Winchesters, and it was reported that they were pretty accurate shots.[10]

On Sunday evening, August 18, the notorious Jennie was

> arrested by Sheriff Lake near Pawnee and taken to that city. There she was taken to a restaurant to eat supper. A guard was placed at the door. When Jennie finished her meal she darted through the back door of the restaurant and quickly tearing off her dress, seized a horse and, mounting it, rode off. Several officers went in pursuit, but darkness came on and she escaped . . . on the horse [stolen] from a deputy marshal [Canton] who had arrested her for selling whiskey to Indians.[11]

On Monday night, August 19, Deputy Marshals Steve Burke, Canton, M. Zuckerman, and Owens

> ran onto the two notorious female outlaws, Mrs. Jennie Midkiff and Miss Annie McDoulet, near Pawnee. . . . The women showed fight and several shots were fired before they gave up. Both were in men's clothing when captured. . . . The girls say that if they had known only four officers were surrounding them . . . they would have fought their way out.[12]

During the first week of September, Cattle Annie and Little Breeches were tried at Pawnee in Fourth Judicial District Court before Judge Andrew G. Curtain Bierer. The anonymous article in the Guthrie *Leader* of April 16, 1939, describes how they taunted the officers as "soft" and "shouted" at the judge and attorneys, and latter-day historians agree that they freely expressed themselves and gloried in their connection with the Doolin gang to the last. On the contrary,

> Annie refused to talk to anyone except . . . to say she was given "good raising," but is now past redemption, and intends to resume her outlaw life when possible. The Midkiff girl sits in jail and sulks . . . afraid to look into a mirror for fear of cracking it.[13]

Annie, being under age, was committed to reform school at South Framingham, Massachusetts. Jennie was convicted of horse stealing and sentenced to two years in the Massachusetts Reformatory prison at Sherborn. Chief Deputy Hale and Guard Ed Kinnan lodged Annie in South Framingham on September 13. Jennie was returned to Guthrie on the old charge of unlawfully dealing in ardent spirits in the Indian country, but because of her "desire to reform" the case was dismissed, and she was recommitted to Sherborn, where Marshal Nix and Deputy Colcord delivered her on November 12.[14]

Within a few months, Annie was released to work as a domestic in Boston, then went into settlement work in New York, where she died of consumption two years later in Bellevue Hospital. Jennie was released in mid-October, 1896, and returned to Oklahoma. She got off the train at Perry

> and was driven to the Pacific hotel. In her healthful appearance, graceful bearing and pleasing countenance no one recognized the once female outlaw . . . known among the various bands of outlaws with whom she formerly associated as "Little Breeches" . . . sentenced by Judge Bierer, in the district court at Pawnee, to two years in the reformatory, where she remained one year, her father and relatives having secured a commutation of her sentence. . . . A gentleman who lives in Perry to whom she spoke freely of her former life and expressed deep regret for her waywardness, says she further stated she was completely reformed. . . . She has returned to her father's home, near Sinnett, in Pawnee county, where she intends to begin a new life.[15]

What finally happened to Jennie remains a mystery, lightened only by a report, many years later, that she "soon lost her identity as an ex-outlaw woman, was living in Tulsa and had reared a fine family." The old-timer who "knew Little Breeches" and provided the information refused to reveal her name.[16]

XXI Zip Wyatt Breaks Corn;
Raidler's Last Stroll

SINCE LOSING THE TRAIL of the Dover train robbers, Chris Madsen had kept several posses in the field searching for Zip Wyatt and Ike Black and their female cohorts, who had helped the fugitives to escape. There was no letup in the quartet's activities. By the summer of 1895, they had "become a terror" to the very settlers who, only a year before, had considered their capture a problem for the marshals.

Most of the time, the two women traveled with a team and wagon, Wyatt and Black following a short distance behind on horseback. They would set up camp near some country store and post office they intended to rob. The women would go to the store and purchase canned goods and other supplies, note any shotguns or rifles that might be setting behind counters, then report to Black and Wyatt, who would ride in at nightfall, hold up the proprietor, loot the place, and dash off the opposite direction, taking a circuitous route to rejoin the women. They would be in a new rendezvous, miles away, the next morning. Occasionally, they would steal a good team. When they had collected a dozen or so horses at one of their canyon strongholds in the Glass Mountains, they would leave the women in camp, run the animals into Kansas, and sell them. Another ruse was

> to offer to pay the poor farmers for their meals with large bills that they knew the farmers couldn't change. The outlaws then would ask the farmers how nearly they could come to changing the bills, and the farmers would tell them just how much they had. . . . The outlaws would take the money from the farmers, keep their greenbacks and ride away.[1]

On the night of June 3, the gang raided the store and post office at Fairview. Several men who were present

> attempted to drive them off, but were themselves badly worsted. The outlaws took everything of value and three of the best horses in the neighborhood and made their escape.[2]

309

Deputy Marshals Gus Hadwinger and J. K. Runnels, riding with
Sheriff Clay McGrath and Deputy Marion Hildreth of Woods County, picked up the trail. On June 4, they surprised Wyatt and Black
in a cave near the Woods County line. The officers

bombarded their fort, which successfully stood the rain of Winchester
and Colts bullets. The fight was kept up one whole day, and the out-
come was the marshals killed one horse . . . captured another, two saddles, bridles and the entire camp outfit . . . shot Wyatt through the left
arm and Ike Black in the left side [right heel]. The outlaws escaped in a
canyon where it is impossible to get to them [and] are still in the gyp
hills where they have friends all through that part of the country. [The
saddle taken from the dead horse belonging to Wyatt] showed nine bullet holes where numerous marshals have come within inches of their
man. [On the evening of June 5] the two women, Belle Black and Jennie
Freeman, who quit her husband last fall and eloped with Wyatt and has
been with her outlaw lover ever since, attempted to make their escape
from a dugout near the cave where the outlaws were quartered. But
they were immediately stopped by the officers and when searched had
in their possession money and valuables . . . taken from the [Fairview]
postoffice.[3]

The women were arraigned at Alva before the U.S. Commis-
sioner, who "bound them over," and Deputy Marshal Runnels and
Sheriff McGrath delivered them to the federal jail at Guthrie on
June 7. When searched at the jail,

the Black woman had the photos of the dead bandit, Tulsa Jack, and
Deputy Marshals Prather and William Banks, concealed on her person.
The photos had been taken in a group [after the Dover robbery] . . .
but the women had cut them all separate and had evidently murdered
the brave deputies in their hearts, as the eyes of Prather had been
rubbed out with a pen and the picture of Banks was punctured in different places.[4]

The hunt for Wyatt and Black quickened as posses totaling more
than two hundred armed men were organized in every direction.
The settlers had "made up their minds" that as long as these "ruf-
fianly, brutal, coldblooded highwaymen" were at large, there was
no security for life or property. Their capture or annihilation had
become a matter of absolute necessity.[5]

Although their safety and freedom depended on it, Wyatt and
Black had no intention of leaving the country, as is indicated in this
colorful piece of territorial journalism:

Love not only laughs at locksmiths, but is the motive power that steels
the heart and strengthens the arm to deeds of daring and almost impos-

sible achievements. Zip Wyatt, known as the bold Colonel Yeager . . . has thrown all his judgment and caution to the winds and sworn a mighty oath that neither bolt nor bar nor prison door shall longer stand between him and his lady fair, who was captured a short time since by unromantic deputy marshals and now languishes in the Guthrie jail.

Word reached this city Monday [July 22] of the wild bandit's mad resolve, and preparations were made to receive him in a manner worthy of so great a malefactor. Twelve deputy marshals, each a walking arsenal . . . were stationed around the prison Monday night, with instructions to prevent the bold Yeager from breaking into jail at all hazards.

No Yeager appeared to storm the castle, but the authorities realize that "eternal vigilance is the price of peace," and have not relaxed their watchfulness. Yeager is desperate. He is like a tiger deprived of his mate, and no attempt is too daring or foolhardy for him that would once more restore his incarcerated companion to his savage breast.[6]

A communication smuggled out by the women outlined a course of action to their gallants. Wyatt and Black were to cut two telephone wires on the outside of the jail to prevent the sounding of an alarm, come to the door, call the turnkey, give their names as deputy marshals, and say they had a prisoner. When the turnkey opened the door, they were to "hold him up and take his keys." The delivery then could be made without fear of detection. The outlaws reached the outskirts of Guthrie July 23 but found the jail heavily guarded and "went away." The marshals "did not learn of their presence in time to catch them."[7]

They fled back toward the Glass Mountains. At dusk on July 26, they stopped at the Oxley post office in eastern Blaine County. A. B. Laswell, postmaster and proprietor of the store, was watering his stock when they covered him with Winchesters. Laswell recognized Wyatt and Black from their descriptions and called them by name, "which they acknowledged to be." They searched the house and store, taking food, tobacco, and thirty-five dollars in cash. Examining the post-office books, they "found that Mrs. McAuntly and Mr. Adams had picked up registered letters that day, rode to their houses, but failed to get anything at either place."[8]

A courier hurried to Okeene, twelve miles north, to give the alarm. At daybreak, a posse of farmers from Homestead found the outlaws asleep six miles northwest of Oxley at the head of Salt Creek, their horses tied to their saddles. R. C. Rhyne, a well-known resident of Cooper and member of the posse, told the *Kingfisher Free Press*[9] that

one of our party crawled up to within a few feet of them and seeing they had their guns in their hands crawled back and informed us. We

311

surrounded them, waked them up, and demanded their surrender. The answer was a volley of bullets, one of which passed through the left shoulder of a man named Richardson. Their horses got scared and ran off about 100 yards from camp, dragging the saddles with them. Yeager and Black then dropped back a short distance and went up the creek, leaving a sack of postoffice plunder and all their effects behind except what they had on, carrying their shoes in their hands. Black was shot in the forehead, but . . . it was only a scalp wound, and did not amount to much. They had to walk over terribly rough country Saturday [July 27], and Black was barefooted and bleeding. They came out of the hills Saturday evening five miles west of Okeene, compelled some farmer to give up his horse and cart, and went out through our pickets that night, Yeager playing a French harp, without being halted. Sunday morning they were near the Glass Mountains with 100 men in hot pursuit. The horse they had to the cart was 26 years old and nearly fagged out at daylight. I had broken down two horses and could not get another. But I feel sure they had them surrounded, as the pursuing parties had Henry Roman Nose, a Cheyenne Indian and experienced trailer, who could tree them in a little while.

Deputy Sheriff Hildreth and a five-man posse left Alva for the Glass Mountains on July 27, and deputy marshals left El Reno the next morning to be in on the final roundup, which they thought could not long be delayed.[10]

Robert Callison, former Union soldier and constable of Forrest Township, and Jack Ward, an old Rebel soldier and a splendid shot, were attending an Anti–Horse Thief Association meeting at Lacey, thirteen miles west of Hennessey, on Saturday evening when word came that Wyatt and Black had stolen a horse and cart and were still going north. Callison promptly organized a party of nine and

started in pursuit. We rode all night . . . being ahead of all others the next morning . . . struck the trail two miles east of the mountains where Yeager and Black had breakfast with a Bohemian who did not know them. We followed them about five miles further in a northwesterly direction where they holed up in a canyon. This canyon is deep and rugged and full of heavy timber. We surrounded the canyon about 10 o'clock . . . John Suit went into the canyon and Jack Ward was guarding the upper end. Yeager and Black opened fire on Ward, and also on the men holding the horses. Frank Pope was shot through the right leg below the knee. The fight lasted about 25 minutes, the outlaws firing faster than we did. It was a running fight. Yeager and Black passed out of the canyon near Ward, and fired at him. . . . Ward fired deliberately at Yeager three times. He was evidently wearing a shield [some kind of steel-link corselet] over his body. Ward feels sure that he struck him once squarely in the breast and once in the back. He fell both times. Four of our horses broke loose and ran down the Cimarron river. Yeager and Black caught two of them, and escaped. About that time a posse from Alva [Hildreth and his men] came up, and continued the pursuit. We left the battlefield at 4 p.m.[11]

Wyatt and Black headed southeast in a zigzagging course across Cottonwood, Elm, and Gypsum creeks. Hildreth and posse followed them as long as their tracks could be seen by moonlight. On Thursday, August 1, the posse took a late dinner at a farmhouse where the outlaws had taken a late breakfast and learned that their mounts were "almost fagged out." The outlaws were "bending a straight course" toward the foothills northeast of Cantonment, where, supposedly, they would attempt to obtain fresh horses. Late in the afternoon, the fugitives suddenly left the hills and struck the bottom lands close to a timbered section, called Cottonwood Grove, six miles northeast of Cantonment. There a farmer saw the two men, Wyatt riding in back and driving Black's exhausted animal along in front of him with a whip.

At six o'clock, they stopped at the shack of a widow and her son, named Jones, about four miles east of Cantonment. Introducing themselves as officers, they asked for horses but were told none was available. A field of high corn surrounded the house to the north and east, offering concealment. The outlaws decided to water and rest their mounts, and ordered supper. The officers rode up and saw their horses hitched near the house. When Wyatt and Black came out,

> they were ordered to throw up their hands, but of course they reached for their guns . . . the posse opened fire and shot Black through the head, then Wyatt ran into the corn while the posse sent Winchester balls after him as rapidly as possible. One ball struck Wyatt in the breast near the left nipple, cutting a deep gash in his side. Despite the wound, he made his way north through the corn, thence east into the sand hills, and escaped. . . .
>
> Black was left lying until a Justice of Peace arrived and held an inquest. His right heel showed where he had been shot in the skirmish with deputy marshals [June 4]. . . . He also had a sore scalp wound above the left temple [received in the battle on Salt Creek]. Nothing was found on his person . . . except a picture of a woman [Belle Black], and $1.50 in silver. He was taken to Alva and photographed and buried at county expense.[12]

Nearly every able-bodied man south of the Cimarron joined in the hunt for Wyatt. Marshal Nix reinforced sheriffs, constables, and city marshals in Kingfisher, Blaine, and the four counties west with federal deputies. Young Indian horsemen and Indian police in the Cheyenne country joined the chase, and Texas Panhandle authorities were alerted in the event Wyatt broke through the lines in that direction.

Wyatt's tracks led through the sand hills to a doctor's house a mile away. The outlaw told the doctor: "I'm an officer. I've just had a fight with Dick Yeager. Fix me up." The doctor bandaged Zip's wounds and gave him a horse. Seven miles northeast, he sent the horse back. Unable to ride because of the pain in his side and chest, Zip went on afoot. Near Homestead, he met a boy with a cart. The outlaw leaped into the seat beside the lad, frightening him half to death, and forced him to drive at top speed twenty-five miles northeast across the Cimarron River before letting him go. Zip continued on in the cart.

Where he hid out that night and why he chose daylight for travel is not known. He knew the entire country to the west had been aroused and apparently decided his only chance lay in reaching Indian Territory. At four o'clock Saturday afternoon, August 3, he was seen crossing the Rock Island Railroad at Waukomis, five miles south of Enid, traveling east.

A wire report to Garfield County Sheriff Elzie Thralls put Deputies A. J. Poak and S. T. Woods on the move, "as well as many volunteers owing to big rewards offered for the capture of the noted criminal." The horse attached to Wyatt's cart showed signs of exhaustion. Fourteen miles east of the railroad, when he struck Skeleton Creek Valley, he deserted the horse and vehicle and ran into a cornfield, closely pursued by the officers and citizens. He was tracked south through the cornfield and then the trail was lost.

At sundown, Wyatt reached the claim of John Daily, who lived alone on Skeleton Creek. Daily was returning to his shack from feeding his ponies when he saw the outlaw, Winchester in hand, approaching up the creekbank. "Old man," Wyatt said, "I want a horse for two or three days to do a little business." Daily noted the bloodstained shirt, the three-week growth of beard, and the tired, worn expression on his face. "I have no horse to hire—who are you?" he asked. "I'm Dick Yeager." Wyatt brandished his Winchester. "Where are your horses?" Daily showed him the ponies. Wyatt complained that they were "a poor lot," but he picked one and ordered Daily to mount another and accompany him.

A mile farther, the outlaw spotted a big roan draft horse in Will Blakely's pasture and compelled Daily to catch it. Leaving Daily's

314

pony by the pasture, he mounted Blakely's roan, and the two men continued riding southeast. After dark, they came to the claim of John Pierce. No one was at home. Wyatt dismounted again, cut himself several feet of well rope, and they rode on. A few miles farther, the outlaw called a halt, improvised a rope bridle, and, removing Daily's bridle from the Blakely roan, placed the rope bridle over its head and told Daily he was free. "Don't give me away too soon," he warned the farmer. "I think I have given them the dodge, but if you see the sons of bitches, tell them that while they are getting me I will get them."

It was now late in the night, but Daily galloped south to spread the alarm. At the home of Horton L. Miles, he found a group of men who had just adjourned an Anti–Horse Thief Association meeting. He told them Wyatt was in the vicinity, and hasty plans were made for his capture. Billy Fox and Ben Vanderwork returned with Daily to the point where the bandit had released the farmer, and waited to take the trail at daybreak. The others dispersed and aroused the community. The posse that was mustered consisted mostly of men from the Sheridan neighborhood.

They followed the trail three miles southeast of Sheridan. At ten o'clock, they were joined by the Enid posse, which had traveled down Skeleton Creek during the night. Wyatt apparently had been striking for the Taylor ranch, where he expected to find a fresh mount, but had missed his mark, going one mile east where the road crossed Skeleton Creek into Logan County. Here the pursuers found Blakely's roan grazing in a bend of the stream and the outlaw's footprints disappearing into a cornfield on the Alvin G. Ross farm five miles southwest of Marshall.

The posses divided their forces to surround their quarry. Enid deputies Poak and Wood, plus Tom Smith, a Sheridan man, were delegated to track the outlaw through the cornfield. The three "ambushed" their horses and moved cautiously into the corn, which rose above their heads. The tracks led north, then east, then south. The men suddenly realized that there was no one with the horses. Fearing that Wyatt might "slip the vigilance" of all and steal one of their mounts, Deputy Woods turned back to guard them.

At that moment, Deputy Poak discovered the bandit sprawled on his stomach at the edge of a sand patch where the corn had failed to grow, feet toward him, a Winchester on his right and a revolver on his left. Poak signaled Smith to come up on the left and a little behind him. Both men brought their cocked rifles to their shoulders. Then Poak called in a loud voice: "Throw up your hands!" Wyatt jerked up his head and grabbed for his guns. Poak and Smith fired simultaneously. Both bullets struck the outlaw in the body within an inch of each other, one shattering his pelvis, the other tearing into his abdomen. He raised one hand. Poak ordered him to throw up the other, but Wyatt could not and implored them not to shoot again.

As they walked up and disarmed him, he inquired: "Who are you?"

"We are deputy sheriffs."

"Thank God for that," he said. "The marshals would kill me." As an afterthought, he remarked: "I must have dropped from my feet asleep."

In the broiling August sun that Sunday morning, Poak, Smith, and Wood cared for their prisoner the best they could. It was an hour before they secured a wagon to remove him from the cornfield to a small church at Sheridan. Sunday services were just over. The Sunday-school blackboard was removed from the wall and laid on the tops of some benches; the wounded outlaw placed thereon and given first aid by Drs. C. R. Jones and Frank Love.

Meanwhile, the "grand army in pursuit" gathered. Sheriff Thralls and his posse were first to arrive and took the prisoner to Hennessey, where the deputy marshals from Kingfisher and Guthrie found them. There arose a controversy over who should have jurisdiction and claim the rewards. The prisoner was now in Kingfisher County, where most of the men in the Sheridan posse lived. They claimed him on grounds that they had been first in tracking him to the cornfield and surrounding him. The capture was made in Logan County, and all the participating officers were from Garfield County. The Sheridan men were "ready to maintain their stand," but the Enid men "would not be shaken." The marshals threatened to wire Judge McAtee for orders to release the prisoner to federal authorities. It was finally agreed that he should be taken to Enid and that Daily and the Sheridan men should share in any rewards paid Sheriff Thralls's deputies.[13]

Wyatt was incarcerated in the Enid jail on the evening of August 4 under heavy guard and was charged with felonies committed in Garfield County. Local jurisdictions continued to quarrel over the right to try him, but doctors said he had no chance to live. Internally, he had been virtually "torn to pieces."

One of his first visitors was Deputy Marshal Ed Kelley, who came to make the official identification for the federal government. Kelley knew Zip well, having arrested him several times while police

316

chief of Guthrie. Wyatt recognized Kelley the moment the officer entered his cell, extending his hand from the cot where he lay.

"How are you, Ed?"

"All right, Zip; how are you?"

"Guess they've got me this time," said Wyatt.

"Those farmers kept you pretty busy breaking corn the past two weeks, didn't they?" asked Kelley.

"You bet; but I kept them just as busy as they did me," responded Zip.

Hundreds of other persons came to see the notorious outlaw, and Wyatt enjoyed the attention. He ate from hampers of fried chicken and fruit piled on his cot by admirers and "embarrassed the predictions" of physicians by growing stronger and livelier each day. He would alternately pet the jail pup or suck a lemon while he confessed every crime committed in the Outlet since the opening, estimating he had killed eleven men. He joshed local attorneys about importing a famous criminal lawyer from the East to defend him because they were "not worth the powder to blow them to hell." But in his stifling cell, "fetid with gangrenous smells and hung with wet blankets to reduce the temperature," the doctors kept him under the influence of morphine and waited. The *Oklahoma State Capital*[14] declared that

> Zip's sun is setting. He is ticketed to that bourne where the spirits of the Jameses, the Youngers, the Daltons and other nineteenth century imitations of Claud Duval have been conveyed by the boatman, Charon, and where, no doubt, after the qualms of sea sickness occasioned by the turbulent waters of the river Styx have subsided, they are most probably now mounted upon centaurs and pursuing the chariot of the great red dragon, and as a divertisement . . . probably sticking fire brands into the tender portions of Dives' anatomy to compel him to divulge the hiding place of his treasures.

On August 12, Zip's mind "seemed to leave him." For two days and nights, he "imagined himself on the road again . . . he would speak to his faithful partners, give orders and commands to an imaginary express messenger or storekeeper and occasionally swear and yell as if participating in some hand to hand encounter with a deputy marshal." On August 18, the *Enid Wave* reported: "He eats little, takes only liquids . . . has no control of his bowels." His pulse quickened, signs of blood poisoning appeared around his abdominal wounds, and on August 28: "His pain at times is almost unbearable. . . . He still lives, a bunch of suffering humanity. . . . He is reduced to a mere skeleton and bed sores are beginning their work." On the evening of September 6, he suffered a "septic chill or putrescent decomposition of the body" and lost consciousness. At six minutes past midnight, "death relieved the sufferer."[15]

The outlaw's relatives did not claim his body. At eleven o'clock Sunday morning, September 8, a small cortege left the jail. It consisted of a spring wagon, the driver, the gravedigger (who sat on the cheap pine coffin), and the jail dog, which followed them to the pauper's field south of the city. Wyatt was buried without ceremony. The county bore the small expense.[16]

Belle Black and Jennie Freeman were taken before a grand jury at Alva the last week in October. The jury found no evidence of a criminal nature against them "other than their presence with the two outlaws," and they were discharged. Both "returned to their friends in the south part of Woods county, and it is hoped that their sad experience will teach them a lesson they will not forget."[17]

While Wyatt and Black were being pursued in the west, Deputies Bill Tilghman and Heck Thomas, still cooperating with Bill Dunn and his brothers on the east side of the territory, learned that Little Bill Raidler, who was to have joined Pierce and Newcomb at the Dunn ranch in Payne County after the Dover robbery, had gone instead to an old gang hideout in the Lower Caney River country of the Cherokee Nation.

In the last week of July, Thomas and two Osage scouts, Howling Wolf and Spotted Dog Eater, "surrounded Raidler in a house near Tallahah [Talala], and after several shots being exchanged he escaped . . . minus several inches of skin from his chin," grazed by a ball from Heck's Winchester. The fugitive's trail led northwest up the Caney near the confluence of Little Caney Creek north of Bartlesville. Thomas enlisted the aid of Deputy Marshals W. C. Smith and Cyrus Longbone of the Bartlesville District, a posseman named Jim Lee, and three other men, but the trail was lost. Tilghman received word of the Talala fight and joined the search. The party split. Thomas and his scouts proceeded upriver, and the posse continued to search the immediate vicinity. Tilghman, Smith, and Longbone made a still hunt to the west. Toward the end of August, they learned that "the outlaw had got a friendly Indian to haul him over into the Osage country." It was rumored that Tilghman paid two hundred fifty dollars for the information. Raidler took refuge on Mission Creek, hiding in the timbered hills in daytime and eating and sleeping at night on the Sam Moore ranch about twenty-five miles northeast of Pawhuska. Tilghman, Smith, and Longbone "went after him," reaching the Moore place in late afternoon on September 6.[18]

318

They found Little Bill absent, but Moore admitted he was "liable to be there any time." He usually walked up the lane past the cattle corral after sundown. Smith and Longbone posted themselves where the outlaw would enter the house. Tilghman, armed with a double-barreled shotgun, hid in an unchinked log hen house near the corral and waited. At dusk, Raidler came walking confidently up the path on his way to supper. When he reached the point where he was completely surrounded, Tilghman stepped from the hen house behind him and ordered him to surrender, but "he had no notion of doing such thing, and drawing a pistol began running and shooting" and "only ceased" when a blast from Tilghman's shotgun knocked him off his feet.[19]

He was still alive when the officers bent over him but was bleeding badly from six buckshot wounds: "one in each side, one through the neck, two in the back of head, and one in the right wrist" which had struck him below the elbow, plowed down his arm, and knocked the revolver and out of his hand. "The neck wound is the most dangerous . . . he said he preferred death to captivity" and told Tilghman he "would have made a fight if the marshal's party had been a hundred strong."[20]

Moore's Indian wife brought a bucket of water and clean rags and did what she could to stanch the flow of blood. The nearest railroad was at Elgin, Kansas, eighteen miles north. The officers borrowed Moore's team and wagon, put some hay and quilts in back, and laid the outlaw on them. Smith drove, Longbone followed with their horses, and Tilghman rode beside the prisoner, bathing his face with water from a jug and checking the bleeding of his wounds, until they reached Elgin and a doctor.

Two days later, Raidler was put aboard the train on a stretcher, transferred to the Santa Fe at Arkansas City, and taken to Guthrie, where he "lies near onto death . . . in a room over the Arlington, attended by Dr. Smith, the government physician." When the doctor gave him only twenty-four hours to live, the outlaw responded, "I will live to attend your funeral," and later that night, "although suffering, he talked like a sailor and entertained 200 people with stories of his exploits."[21]

In the federal jail, Raidler slowly recovered from his wounds. On April 3, 1896, a year from the day of the Dover holdup, he went on trial at Kingfisher on a charge of "attempting to rob the United States mails"—the only grounds on which the government could handle the case, train robbery being a territorial offense. District Attorney Brooks and Assistant Attorney McMechan conducted the prosecution; Joe Wisby of Guthrie and Virgil Hobbs of Kingfisher made up the defense. "It was only by the hardest kind of a legal fight that a conviction was secured." Twenty-three witnesses identified Raidler as one of the five men who looted the express and mail car. A demurrer was argued on the ground that the testimony was not sufficient to convict, but Judge McAtee overruled. No witnesses for the defense were examined, and after arguments were made, the jury retired, coming in with a guilty verdict on the morning of April 9. Raidler was sentenced to ten years in the penitentiary at Columbus, Ohio.[22]

Raidler appealed to the Territorial Supreme Court, and Judge McAtee gave him until April 17 to furnish five thousand dollars' bond. His application for bail was subsequently examined and disapproved. He then petitioned the Supreme Court for a writ of habeas corpus and a writ of certiorari commanding the clerk and judge of the district court "to certify their action" and requesting that the Supreme Court "examine and approve the bond." The petition was denied, and, the time in which to post bail having expired, Judge McAtee ordered him delivered to the penitentiary. He was taken to Columbus by Deputy Marshal Colcord on June 25.[23]

In prison, Raidler developed locomotor ataxia as the result of his wounds. Paroled in 1903 because of his illness, he returned to Oklahoma, but never to ride the bandit trail again. He remained a cripple. For a time he engaged in a tobacco and cigar business at Woodward and finally operated a variety store at Yale, where he died a few years later.

Bill Tilghman received the one-thousand-dollar reward offered by the Rock Island Railroad as soon as the company was notified of the outlaw's conviction.[24] Because Raidler was never indicted or convicted for his part in the Southwest City bank robbery and the slaying of former Missouri State Auditor J. C. Seaborn, the five-hundred-dollar reward posted by the governor of Missouri was not paid.

Tilghman, however, had long since turned his efforts to the apprehension of the remaining members of the Doolin gang. Little Dick West was rumored to be in New Mexico, Dynamite Dick Clifton somewhere in the Chickasaw Nation or Texas, and Red Buck Waightman hiding in the Cheyenne country. There had been no reliable word on Doolin since Tilghman, Thomas, Will Nix, and Hixon raided the Dunn dugout on March 3, at which time the gang had escaped, under cover of darkness, into the Cherokee Nation.

XXII Bill Tilghman Misses a Bath

IN MAY, A FEW DAYS AFTER Newcomb and Pierce were slain at the Dunn ranch, Doolin allegedly called on an old acquaintance, a storekeeper, in Pawnee County and had

> quite a talk with him. His object now is to get away into some new land and lead the right kind of a life. He has only remained in the territory because he would not desert his pals. But now they are gone [Dalton, Tulsa Jack, Bitter Creek, and Pierce]. The merchant asked Bill why he didn't leave . . . that unless he did it would be only a short time until the officers got him too. His reply was that he intended to go. The merchant asked him for a keepsake, and he pulled a large roll of bills from his pocket [taken in a bank robbery and unsigned by the bank cashier], selected a $10 bill, took a pair of scissors and clipped it in two. He gave the merchant one half of the bill and kept the other half himself and soon afterward took his departure.[1]

On July 12, the *Tulsa New Era* reported that the outlaw leader had been seen

> not far from here one evening this week, indeed he spent the night close by, and is reported to have said that he was tired of being hounded all the time and was seriously considering surrendering . . . but said if he should do so he would do it in such a way that no one should get any of the rewards offered for him.

And on December 26, the *Perry Democrat* claimed Doolin had spent Christmas night in that city and

> in an interview, said, "I'm tired of being hunted by these marshals. If I could give up and know I'd get a light sentence, I'd do it tomorrow. I want to get rid of this business. . . . I've done some meanness but some other fellows have done much of which I am charged."

An enthusiastic press picked up the story,[2] and the *Edmond Sun-Democrat*[3] added that Doolin, "after an unsuccessful attempt to compromise with the territorial authorities, is being pursued by armed deputies." The *Oklahoma State Capital*[4] declared the Perry dispatch

> a fake and proves to be born of the festering corpuscal [*sic*] of sumptuous egotism of a deputy marshal named Steve Burke. Burke wants to get his name before the public, and the antics he is playing to do so has given a gestative movement to the bowels of the whole of Marshal Nix's force—they have virtually laughed themselves to death and weakened their intestinal ducts and yet the great marshal at Perry has not taken a tumble to himself.

Actually, three times during the six months from July to December, 1895, Doolin had communicated with Marshal Nix through attorneys, offering to surrender if promised immunity to the extent of being allowed to plead guilty to some charge of robbery and receive a short penitentiary sentence, but his offer was rejected. Nix told Doolin's attorneys: "He has laid low some of my best men . . . I have spent more than $2,000 of my own money, in addition to thousands more expended by the government, in the effort to apprehend him . . . and I propose to make him pay the penalty." Each time, efforts to locate the hiding outlaw were redoubled.[5]

In July, Doolin had joined Little Dick West in New Mexico, where Little Dick had found employment on the ranges of the Socorro County Panhandle, a 45 x 50-mile strip jutting southward between Lincoln and Sierra counties to the Dona Ana and Otero county lines. The panhandle encompassed the San Andres Mountains, a whirlpool of terrain where a man could enjoy solitude unmolested.

In the San Andres east of Engle lay the Eugene Manlove Rhodes ranch, where horse raising and, later, the production of western short stories and novels became serious ventures. "For years," Rhodes once wrote, "I was the only settler in a country larger than the state of Delaware." Unfortunately, his ranch was conveniently located for hideout and lookout points from which badmen could easily depart Outlaws' Paradise, as it was known from the Gulf to Canada because its bootheel southern end touched so many county boundaries where sheriffs' writs stopped short and flight could be extended into Texas or Mexico. If Rhodes knew of the outlaws' presence, he put them to work to earn their keep. To expose them would have been sheer suicide.

Consequently, his ranch became a sanctuary for such luminaries as Tom ("Black Jack") Ketchum of the old Wyoming Wild Bunch. Bill and Bob Christian headquartered in the San Andres during several of their robberies in 1896; the Apache Kid camped in the horse pasture on his journeys between the Black Range and the Mescalero Reservation. The Dalton gang had made the place a way station on their trips between California and Indian Territory in 1891–92, and Doolin found it an ideal refuge while his attorneys attempted to negotiate with Oklahoma territorial authorities.

In the life story of her husband, *The Hired Man on Horseback*,[6] May Davison Rhodes says that Doolin used the ranch as an asylum. And Rhodes himself, commenting on the authenticity of his novel *The Trusty Knaves*, wrote in a 1931 letter to Ferris Greenslet, editor-in-chief of Houghton Mifflin Company:

> This yarn is not the imaginings of a gin-excited mind. Only a few of the events took place as recorded and in the sequence recorded, but these were flesh and blood people whose minds acted just that way—during the brief span of years when they were on their own, without families to disgrace or to be considered. Only three of those people are alive today—Jack Farr [then 84], Lithpin Tham—and myself. . . . I was the boy [Johnny Pardee] the bronc bucked on—and Bill Doolin [Bill Hawkins] shot that luckless horse, as recorded, to keep him from killing me. If you read the story you may remember—along at the last— "Taps"? When Bill Doolin told me goodby—some forty years ago—he rode straight to his death. He was going to quit and settle down in the San Andres.[7]

It was rumored in Oklahoma that Doolin had

> become smitten with Miss Belle Bailey, a Purcell school teacher, who was on a train which he and his gang held up two years ago . . . he made secret visits to Purcell under an assumed name . . . and six months later Miss Bailey left her school and has not been heard of since. . . . It is believed that Miss Bailey is with him as his wife and is working for his reformation.[8]

Like the *Perry Democrat*'s December dispatch, the story was a hoax. Nix's office knew that Doolin had married Edith Ellsworth and that they had a child, a boy, now nearly two years old. Doolin's wife and son and a painful rheumatic condition that had developed in his left leg as a result of the bullet wound he received in his foot during the chase after the Cimarron train robbery were factors that moved him to abandon his wild life as an outlaw. His father-in-law, J. W. Ellsworth, had been appointed postmaster at Lawson, where he moved his family in the winter of 1893–94.[9] Edith Doolin lived with her parents but frequently traveled to Ingalls to see her friend Mary Pierce. Mrs. Pierce was suspected of being the contact between Edith and her husband.

During the summer of 1895, Edith remained at Lawson. By September, Doolin had made his way back from New Mexico across the Texas Panhandle and No Man's Land into southern Kansas, looking for a safe place where his family could join him. Possibly he heard of the capture of Little Bill Raidler and decided against entering Oklahoma Territory. About the same time, although under surveillance, Edith Doolin loaded her personal possessions and child into a covered wagon and vanished.

Tilghman learned of her disappearance when he returned to Guthrie with Raidler. "Fully backed and liberally supplied with funds" by Marshal Nix, he "inaugurated a systematic and thorough quest," checking out reports first in Texas, then Indian Territory, then at a remote point in the Osage, where a woman and child had camped briefly near the Kansas border. In mid-December, he learned that Mrs. Doolin had become ill from her weary journey through the Osage Nation and that "relatives he had followed so long" had been to Burden, Kansas, to "visit and care for her." Burden was a quiet community in east-central Cowley County on the edge of the Flint Hills ranching district, where the Doolins were unknown, and Tilghman "went there at once."[10]

The family was living in a tent pitched near a fine spring on the Uncle Johnnie Wilson farm a mile and a half west of Burden. Unable to go on because of a "sudden flare-up of the husband's rheumatism," they had been there

> fully three months. . . . Doolin would drive into Burden every two weeks for provisions with a dilapidated old wagon hitched to a team managed with rope lines, dressed in ragged clothes and looking the typical played out Oklahoma boomer he pretended to be. He gave the name of Thomas Wilson and affected such poverty that . . . about Christmas season a number of charitable ladies of Burden went about soliciting and raised a purse of money and a goodly supply of provisions for "that poor sufferin' family out there in the tent" and presented them to the astonished Mrs. Doolin.[11]

This unexpected attention apparently disturbed the crafty outlaw. He seemed to sense danger in the air, for one night he packed up and left—"team, wagon and all." Mrs. Doolin and the baby were still at the spring when Tilghman reached Burden. Tilghman

> watched and waited, but Bill did not show. Night and day he kept his vigil, made every train and received much assistance from A. C. Harding, agent of the Santa Fe at that place . . . but all in vain. [On January 6] Mrs. Doolin and the child boarded the train and went to Perry . . .

going from there to the home of her father at Lawson, Pawnee County. The departure of the woman satisfied Tilghman that Doolin would not return to Burden so he started out to try and trace him. After a number of days of fruitless search Tilghman again got a clue and at once followed it up with vigor.[12]

The doctor who attended Edith Doolin during her illness also treated the outlaw for his rheumatism. They had discussed the healing powers of the bath resorts in Arkansas, and Doolin had mentioned he might go there for the cure. Tilghman also learned that when

> Doolin left Burden he had gone east, so I started a search through most of the towns along the southern Kansas border east of the Santa Fe. Finally, on Sunday [January 12], in a town in extreme eastern Kansas, I learned that Doolin had been there and had gone to Eureka Springs. I at once came to Guthrie for instructions, and on Tuesday evening [January 14] at 5 o'clock, left for Arkansas, determined to bring back my man if he was there.[13]

There is no mention of the perennial preacher's disguise. Tilghman didn't need one. What followed was the quickest capture of one of the frontier's most notorious outlaws by a single officer in western history. In less than twenty-four hours, Nix received the following telegram:

> Eureka Springs, Ark., Jan. 15, '96
>
> U.S. Marshal Nix
> Guthrie, Ok.
>   I have him. We be there tomorrow.
>
>   TILGHMAN.

What happened at Eureka Springs in that twenty-four hours has been rehashed by writers for three-quarters of a century. Most versions are happy hybrids of fact and folklore, and some are highly embroidered accounts bordering on the incredible. Mixing fiction and fact is more entertaining, but it is doubtful the story has ever been better or more accurately told than by its participants:

> TILGHMAN: I arrived there [Eureka Springs] at 10:40 Wednesday morning, and, walking up town, one of the first men I met was Bill Doolin. He did not see me at that time and I soon learned that he was stopping at the Davy hotel under the name of Tom Wilson, the same name he had passed under at Burden.
>   I then went to a carpenter and ordered a box made in which I could carry a loaded shotgun, deciding that I would disguise and, carrying the box under my arm, walk about until I met him, the box being arranged

so that with a slight movement of the hand it would drop, leaving the gun in my hand ready for action.

While the carpenter was making the box I determined to take a bath in the mineral waters from the spring and went to a bath house nearby. When I opened the door to step into the gentlemen's waiting room of the bath house who should I see but Bill Doolin sitting on a lounge in the further corner of the room reading a paper. He looked up sharply as I entered and it seemed to me for a second that he recognized me but I walked briskly through the room and into the bath at once.

Once inside the door I turned so I could watch him but his view of me was shut off by the stove. I noticed that for several moments he watched the door through which I had passed, closely, but finally relaxed his vigilance and returned to reading his paper. Now was my chance. With my gun in my hand I slipped quietly into the room up to the stove then jumping around the stove to the position immediately in front of Doolin and told him to throw up his hands and surrender. He got up saying "What do you mean, I have done nothing," but I grabbed his right wrist with my left hand as he raised it to get his gun and with the revolver in my right hand leveled at his head ordered him to throw up his left hand. He put it up part way and then made a pass toward his gun but I told him I would shoot if he made another move.

When I first called on Doolin to surrender the room was full of men, but you should have seen them fall over each other to get out and in half a minute we were alone. I called to the proprietor to come in and help me as I was an officer. He came tremblingly to the door and was finally persuaded to come over where we were. After two or three attempts he managed to get Doolin's vest open and take his revolver out from under his arm and then he wanted to hand the revolver to me notwithstanding the fact that I had my own gun in my right hand. I told him to get out with it and he got, running into the street and holding the gun at arm's length.

When Bill's vest was opened he made a final effort to get loose, and even after his gun was gone protested that he had done nothing. I then said:

"Now, look at me; don't you know me?"

He looked me in the eye and said: "Yes, I know you are Tilghman; where are your other men?"

"Oh, they are all right," I said, and then I told him he knew where he was wanted and it would be best for both of us to get out of that country at once. He agreed with me, said he didn't want to be known in that damned lynching country, and would go along all right.

I then put the nippers on him, got his gun and started for his hotel. On the way he said that if I would take the irons off he would go along all right and that his word was as good as his life and he would not make a move. I told him I would take his word, and took them off, telling him that if he made a single move at any time, I would drop him dead in his tracks. We went to the hotel, got his effects, went to the bank and got $100 he had deposited and left on the first train, not a soul there knowing who either of us were. We came through all right and Doolin was perfectly quiet and docile, nobody knowing who we were until we got into Oklahoma.

DOOLIN [told, unhesitatingly, the same story and laughed heartily when describing the fright of the bathhouse proprietor who was called upon to disarm him]: Why, the damned cuss was so scared he could not unbutton my vest and I had to help him, and then he wanted to hand the gun to Tilghman right on by me, when Bill more than had his hands full.

I was in Eureka Springs to take the baths for rheumatism, which had bothered me much lately, and I was getting some better, though quite lame yet. . . .

I knew Tilghman, and yet, when he walked into the bath house and went right on by me, I could not place him. I was not looking for him over there and, besides, never thought of one man coming after me alone. I was looking for a crowd with guns . . . expected them to shoot me down on sight . . . sooner or later.

I watched the door he passed through for a moment, then went on reading, and the next instant he was on me. I looked in his eye, saw he meant business, and went along. He is a brave man and a true man, or he would have shot me down instead of risking holding me. He has treated me the very best, and I am grateful for it.[14]

News of the capture brought hundreds of people pouring into Guthrie from throughout the territory. At noon on January 16, two thousand were gathered at the Santa Fe depot, and half as many more congregated at the federal jail to see the outlaw come in. When the train arrived at 12:25, there was a great scrambling, pushing, and jamming to catch a glimpse of the bandit leader. When he was escorted from the coach by Deputies Tilghman and Ed Kelley, who had gone north to meet Tilghman and his prisoner at Lawrie, "the people were astonished to see in place of a booted, spurred and bearded desperado a tall, slender man, with a smile on his face, dressed in a suit of well-worn ready-made clothes, and walking with a cane."[15] Marshal Nix, Chief Deputy Hale, and Heck Thomas were waiting with a cab. Doolin was put inside with Tilghman, Nix, Hale, and Kelley. Thomas rode on the outside with the driver.[16] At the marshal's office, Doolin was

greeted by a large number of deputies and leading citizens and ladies, the latter remarking as they shook hands that they were very happy to meet him, and of course courtesy demanded that he made the same remark. Later the press of people became so great that the doors were opened and several thousand allowed to pass through in a steady stream

327

for over an hour. At 2 o'clock, in company with Deputy Tilghman, Marshal Nix and a few other deputies, the noted prisoner took dinner at the Hotel Royal and a half-hour later was escorted to the federal jail and heard the great door of the steel cell clang musically behind him.[17]

Tilghman was the hero of the hour. He bore his honors modestly as hundreds of friends offered their congratulations and hoped that he would collect every cent of the rewards for the outlaw's arrest and conviction. Marshal Nix rejoiced over the capture as "the climax of a continuously successful campaign against outlawry inaugurated at . . . his advent into office."[18]

In his cell that evening, Doolin entertained reporters with tales of his hard life on the range and in camp as a cowboy. "If I had been in all the raids and battles charged me," he said, "it would make a very interesting story, but as I was not in them, I have nothing to tell. I am glad that I will now have a chance to prove myself innocent. . . . I am not married and have not been in Oklahoma nor 150 miles of the territory in two years."[19]

As soon as Edith Doolin received word that her husband was in the federal jail, she hitched a horse to an open cart and, accompanied only by her two-year-old son, started the long, cold drive to Guthrie. She reached Perkins on Monday evening, January 20, and signed her name as "Mrs. Tom Wilson, Lawson, Okla." on the register at the Hicks Hotel. A *Perkins Journal* reporter learned that she was Doolin's wife and was ushered into the dining room and introduced by Hicks. The results of his interview appeared in the January 24 issue of the *Journal*:

> Mrs. Doolin is 25, good looking, above the average in height, dark penetrating eyes and dark complexion. . . . She was modestly attired in a dark dress, with a neat light bodice. She looked somewhat careworn, but was very pleasant and expressed her entire satisfaction that Bill was captured alive.
>
> It was in the winter of '91 she became acquainted with Bill Doolin while she was clerking in McMurtry's drug store in Ingalls. After a year of courtship they were married, and have now a bright, cheerful little boy with golden tresses.
>
> She saw Bill last . . . in Kansas. He was at Eureka Springs for rheumatism; had no wounds on his person, except a scar in the foot cut by a wire fence; is a sufferer from heart trouble and on several occasions when he believed he was dying told her he had never killed or wounded anyone . . . wanted to give himself up long ago . . . had been trying to lead a Christian life; was in the Ingalls raid, but did no shooting. . . . She assigned his bad record to the company he got into.

At times in speaking Mrs. Doolin would caress her boy, who was laughing and rollicking about, little thinking that his papa's name was on everybody's tongue just now.

The reporter bade her good night and withdrew from the hotel, saying to himself "This is indeed a queer world."

Mrs. Doolin left Tuesday morning and arrived in Guthrie at 5 that afternoon. The Guthrie papers say the meeting between man and wife was very affecting.

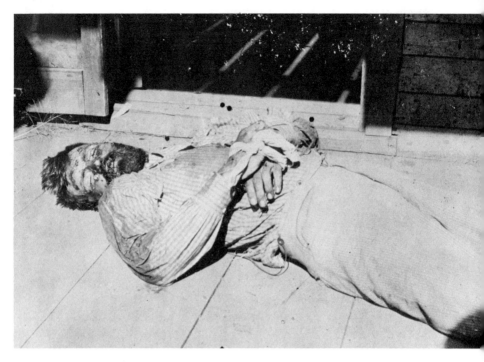

Isaac (Ike) Black in death.

Cattle Annie *(left)* and Little Breeches.

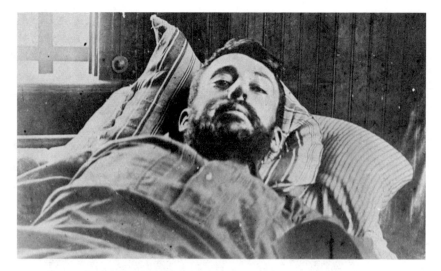

Nathaniel Ellsworth (Zip) Wyatt, alias Dick Yeager, in the Enid jail.

Little Bill Raidler.

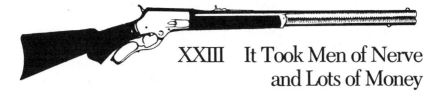

XXIII It Took Men of Nerve and Lots of Money

WHILE MARSHAL NIX TOOK PLEASURE in the fact that his purpose in office was all but accomplished and most citizens were confident and lauded his efforts, many prominent individuals and groups saw it only as publicity clouding the real issue. Republicans dominated the political scene in Oklahoma Territory. There had been one-party domination of the governor's office until the appointment of Renfrow. Both territorial delegates to Congress, David A. Harvey (1890–93) and Dennis T. Flynn, were Republicans. The party also held a substantial majority in both houses of the first, second, and third legislative assemblies. Its leaders expressed dissatisfaction with many of President Cleveland's federal officers and their appointees at the outset, and the federal-court expenses reflected in the report for fiscal year 1894 seemed proof enough that the government's money was being squandered under the guise of law and order.

U.S. District Attorney Brooks's explanation of the special reasons for the increased spending and his recommendations to Attorney General Olney for revamping the judicial system in the territory resulted in some belt tightening, but Olney failed to pursue the matter. The attorney general had become involved in breaking the railroad strike of 1894 by obtaining an injunction in the U.S. Circuit Court of Illinois forbidding the strikers to interfere with interstate commerce and the U.S. mails. The injunction was enforced by federal troops, was sustained by the U.S. Supreme Court, and became the first "government by injunction" in the case of a strike. In 1895, Olney became secretary of state, in which position he had charge of negotiations with England in regard to the bondary dispute with Venezuela and drafted a remarkable official note sustaining the right of the United States to interfere and giving a broad interpretation to the Monroe Doctrine. Judson Harmon, judge of the Superior Court of Cincinnati, became President Cleveland's new attorney general.

Meanwhile, the price of justice for fiscal year 1895 had doubled. Complainants charged that one-fifth of the entire amount appropriated by Congress for court expenses in the Justice Department was being absorbed by the courts and marshals of Oklahoma and Indian territories. The *Oklahoma Daily Times-Journal* espoused the Republican cause: "The devices of the deputy marshals, clerks of courts, and self-sufficient judges to deplete the national treasury and run up expenses against the counties of this territory, will bear the closest scrutiny . . . surely the time has come to call a halt in the career of extravagant and unfaithful officials with which we are afflicted, and it is the duty of all good citizens to aid by all the means of their power in exposing the rottenness which exists." In Washington, Attorney General Harmon told a *Times-Journal* correspondent: "I am investigating the subject . . . due to the paucity of evidence brought to me, I could not impugn the actions of any official [but] have completed arrangements for inspectors to get at the facts so that I may be able to relieve the government of such a heavy outlay of funds annually."[1]

At the same time, Harmon wrote Nix concerning expenses incurred in the wholesale employment of men to do deputy work and asked the marshal to furnish the name and post-office address of each sheriff, deputy sheriff, and city marshal carrying a federal commission. This ignited a controversy, but after conferring with Justice Department inspectors, Nix concluded it would be possible to attend to the business of his office with fewer regular deputies and clerical personnel. In November, 1895, he suggested to Delegate Flynn that he was disgusted with the matter and would resign if he could do so without appearing to evade an investigation. Flynn assured him that "the entire official depravity and corruption of the present administration in Oklahoma would be looked into, and resignations would not arrest the lightning."[2]

On December 13, a grand jury adjourned without indicting

> the awful conspirators against the perpetuity of the American government . . . whom were discovered and arrested in a tangled web of misrule some weeks ago down in the Pott country. . . . The grand jury was too obtuse to recognize the gravity of the situation, the blood-scenting capacity of the sleuth who unearthed the plot, or the valiance of deputy marshals who descended into the heart of the enemy's country to obey the mandate of the stern and unyielding U.S. commissioner.
>
> The United States will, to be sure, pay the heroes mileage and per diem for all the miles traveled and all the days consecrated to the holy

work, and perhaps will pay for more miles than were actually traveled, and more days than were actually consecrated, for the marshals' capacity to swear and Uncle Sam's willingness to pay are not circumscribed.[3]

The *Times-Journal* attacked Judge Scott, suggesting that if Attorney General Harmon

> looked into his record he would reach a conclusion which we hope will rid this judicial district of the incubus that now rests upon it. . . .
>
> It appears that one Crosswaite, an ex-department clerk at Washington, and now a claim agent, is employed by Marshal Nix, and by the clerks and others that are leaching the finances of the department of justice, to manipulate their accounts, so as to make sure that they will pass the scrutiny of the treasury officials. This man Crosswaite is a leading member of the Washington bar and a friend of Judge Scott . . . just what he is paid by the Oklahoma court ring to act as a go-between their official returns and the federal treasury, does not of course appear, but it is understood to be a good round sum in the shape of an annual salary.[4]

On December 19, Delegate Flynn introduced in Congress a resolution that the speaker of the House select a committee of three to investigate the "official conduct, acts and doings of all federal officers and their deputies appointed in the territory of Oklahoma since March 4, 1893." The committee "shall have the power to sit during the session or recess of congress . . . either in the city of Washington or in the territory of Oklahoma, as may best suit and serve their purpose; have the power to send for persons or papers, administer oaths and employ a stenographer, if necessary," and "such expense as may result from the said investigation shall be paid out of the contingent fund of the house." Flynn's "imposed upon" constituents hailed his action but realized the resolution might be months taking its turn with the committees before Congress passed it.[5] The *Times-Journal*[6] pointed out that

> another year of uninterrupted prosperity for the thieves that hold the department of justice offices in Oklahoma would bankrupt the nation and send two-thirds of the reputable citizens to the poor house. . . .
>
> It is doubtless well enough to investigate Marshal Nix, but the marshal could do nothing without accomplices, and those accomplices must be the judges and U.S. attorneys . . . who issue the warrants and endorse them. Are they not the head and front of the conspiracy to rob the government?
>
> The department is aware of the size of the salaries of the three U.S. commissioners who now rule . . . the Pottawatomie country.

335

The *Times-Journal* commented in a later issue[7] that other newspapers which for a year had made

> slight and flippant remarks about our persistent work in exposing the gang . . . now assert they knew all the while that the administration was oppressing poor settlers. . . .
> Cleveland's desire for a business administration has been complied with:
> Nix has done $800,000 worth of business per annum, while Grimes did only one-eighth of that amount. The republican U.S. commissioners did not make a living out of their office, while the democratic commissioners have made about $9,000 per year. M. L. Turner, territorial treasurer [co-owner of the Capitol National Bank] and the Napoleon of shady finance in Oklahoma . . . has been very successful in business. Gov. Renfrow has done very well in a business sense. A few weeks will demonstrate the fact that business has been good all along the line since Cleveland's appointees took possession. A number of experts are now at work on the showing to be made.

The government inspectors zeroed in on the marshal's office. On January 17, while Guthrie was still celebrating Bill Doolin's incarceration in the federal jail, it was announced that an unfavorable report on Nix had gone to the nation's capital. Its full contents were never made public, but a Washington dispatch on January 23 stated that the attorney general

> took up the report today, and after he had gone through it, he applied a match to a fresh cigar and remarked that there was enough on Nix to hang him. He [Harmon] was very warm over the facts set forth, which explained official extravagances . . . the policy of the office in making wholesale arrests; getting long hauls on prisoners by evading near at hand commissioners, by way of getting fees, and the plan of buying up government paper, holding up funds and forcing the sale of the paper.[8]

It also was alleged that Nix had

> compelled deputies and witnesses to discount court and service certificates at a Guthrie bank at 10 per cent when [he] had money on hand to pay them . . . Nix held $150,000 worth of court certificates and Turner holds $40,000 that has been purchased.[9]

When inspectors arrived in Guthrie to investigate the marshal and the judiciary,

> Turner was asked to permit his bank accounts to be examined; that he refused to do; the inspectors telegraphed for a bank inspector, who was promptly sent on to assist; and the result was the laying before the department of justice all the information as to Nix's bank transactions.[10]

Harmon announced his determination to get rid of Nix as soon as possible and said he would "direct his successor to oust every employee in the office unless very sure he had in no wise shared the money fleeced out of the government." The wires to Washington were "thawed out" by messages from Nix's friends on the matter. They asked for time and insinuated that "Assistant Special Agent Tichenor tried to force a consideration out of Nix by way of insuring a favorable report," but "Agent Sheibley explained that Tichenor, as a detective aiding him, played this role by way of catching the marshal."[11]

Nix did not explain that in every case coming to his attention in which a deputy or posseman had sworn to long accounts when, in fact, he had never been within miles of the place shown on the papers or in which men had been jailed on trumped-up charges, the officer had been summarily discharged. Nor did he remind the attorney general that deputies and witnesses had been forced to discount court and service certificates because the Treasury had seen fit to keep available funds in Washington as long as possible. The Guthrie *Leader*[12] however, was explicit:

> A marshal, under the law, can only obtain $500 per month in advance for "fees and expenses." How far would that sum go in defraying the expenses of your five judicial districts in each of which there is as much business as in almost any state in the union? There is no other way for the marshal to obtain money, under the law, except upon settlement of his accounts, by the accounting officers at the treasury.
>
> In justice to Mr. Nix . . . it should be known that the accounting officers of the treasury have not yet paid his accounts for the period ending December 31, 1894, on which there are several thousand dollars yet due, as shown by the books of the treasury, and that balance and whatevery may be due him on his accounts for the six months ended June 30, 1895, which have not yet been settled, can not be paid to him, because the appropriation for "fees and expenses" for the fiscal year ended June 30, 1895, was long since exhausted and he must wait the action of congress appropriating funds to meet such deficiencies.

U.S. District Attorney Brooks wrote Harmon that if it was not against the rules of the department,

> I will be obliged if you will give me a copy of the Inspector's report . . . or that part setting forth the objectionable part of his [Nix's] official conduct. . . .
>
> Enclosed I hand you a copy of a letter written to Attorney General Olney on the 5th of December, 1894, calling his attention to suspicions then in my mind, and asking that an Inspector be sent here to look into . . . the U.S. Commissioners' offices as well as the U.S. Marshal's office.

An Inspector, Mr. Newton, was some months afterward sent . . . he went through the Marshal's office, at any rate represented that he did, and made such a favorable report to the Department . . . and complimented the office so highly that I grew ashamed of my suspicions.

I am not prompted by curiosity to ask for this [information], but that I may be advised and be more able in the future to know what is going on in the Marshal's office.[13]

No reply was forthcoming. Brooks was called to Washington to confer with the attorney general on the matter, but it was some weeks later. On January 24, Nix was summarily relieved of his duties, and he returned to the wholesale business in Guthrie. The *Leader*[14] commented on his capability of earning a good income outside official life and ventured to wager that

he is thankful to be rid of the heavy burden and the atmosphere of contention surrounding it. . . . When he came into office, and until he could organize his forces, the territory was overrun with desperados. Murder, robberies of trains, banks, stores, of farmers at their homes and travelers on the highways were of daily occurrence. The opening of the strip [Outlet] precipitated hundreds of reckless adventurers into our midst and these Ishmaelites banded together in squads too strong to be dealt with by an ordinary quota of posses and deputies. Then the people were denouncing the inertness of the marshals and the absence of a half-dozen at every point where outrages occurred. Mr. Nix left office with no organized band of marauders in the field, but plenty of these erstwhile bandits in their graves or in the penitentiary. It took men of nerve and lots of money to produce this change, and it was worth all it cost to bring it about. . . . He did well and served the people well.

While friends argued Nix's dismissal by wire, a score of applicants for the position, many of them men who sought it when Nix was appointed, made themselves known.[15] Harmon concluded that he could not get a man from Oklahoma who would "conform to his purpose to give its official system a thorough purging" and announced plans to "send" a man to the territory, "probably from Cincinnati."[16] President Cleveland, annoyed by the manner in which his appointments in Oklahoma had been treated, declared he had "about made up his mind to appoint none but outsiders hereafter" and observed that "the senate committee seemed very much imbued with the same idea held by the administration."[17]

This caused a "merry war" in all political circles—Democratic, Populist, and Republican. The attorney general and the President "finally relented" and nominated Patrick S. Nagle, a "home-man" and young lawyer from Kingfisher.

At 35, Nagle already occupied a prominent place in territorial affairs as "a clean and honorable democrat." His brother-in-law had been a member of the first and president pro tempore of the second territorial senates. But local Democrats were

> all in a sweat. Their conflicting interests make them strain their utmost to prevent his confirmation by the senate—the Nix forces are fighting him to save their hides, and the aspirants for Nix's place because they were not given the fat plum that Nix lost.[18]

Populist leaders fought to block Senate action because of some "very ugly and discreditable remarks" made by Nagle about their party; in fact, enough objections were sent to the Senate to delay his confirmation for weeks.[19] On February 18, the Senate committee confirmed Nagle's nomination by a unanimous vote.

The new marshal arrived in Guthrie aboard the 11:20 A.M. Choctaw train from Kingfisher on February 27. He held "quite a levee" at the Royal that evening and shook several hundred hands, after which he held a consultation with several prominent Democrats and announced that some of Nix's old force would remain in office. For instance, Charles F. Colcord was left in charge of the Perry District, Frank Canton at Pawnee, William Banks and Captain Prather in the Cheyenne country, and Tilghman and Heck Thomas on the east side of the territory. During the next few days, Nagle appointed M. J. Kane of Kingfisher chief deputy, retaining Hale as chief clerk; replaced court bailiffs with men of his own choice despite the preferences of the judges; and "chopped down" the field force to thirty-five, with a managing deputy in each judicial district responsible for the good conduct of affairs therein and not to employ more than four men to assist him.[20] With the exception of officer clerks and deputies, the following constituted his entire staff:

> Morris Robacker, Pawhuska; H. Callahan and T. H. Mitchell, Indian reservations; F. B. Farwell, Anadarko; William Tilghman, Chandler; H. A. "Heck" Thomas, Guthrie; E. F. "Frank" Cochran, Oklahoma City; W. J. Brockman, Stillwater; W. H. Warren, Chandler; J. D. Furber, Sac and Fox Agency; Eugene Hall, Woodward; John B. Jones, Tecumseh; George Smith, Norman; Daniel Ryan, Oklahoma City; Charles F. Colcord, Perry; Frank M. Canton, Pawnee; John Smith, Hennessey; J. A. Cooper, Kingfisher; John R. Wisby, Pawnee; William Banks, J. S. Prather, L. Eichoff and Dan W. Peery, El Reno; S. H. Tittle, Greer County; P. I. Brown, Ponca City; R. G. Brown, Newkirk; George H. Mouser, George G. Stormer and I. A. "Ike" Steel, Perry; Sam Large and John Quimby, Shawnee; Clarence R. Young, Pawnee; J. S. Markham, Woodward; John J. McCartney, Alva; John Ventioner, Taloga.

Chris Madsen took a youth east to the federal reform school in Washington. While in the capital, he dropped in for a visit with Attorney General Harmon, who asked Chris if he would like to go to Kansas City as office deputy under the well-known Confederate general Joseph O. ("Jo") Shelby, then U.S. marshal of the Western Judicial District of Missouri. An inspector had just examined Shelby's books and recommended that he obtain a man who understood government red tape. Madsen's wife, a frail woman, had long borne the fear and anxiety of his long days and nights in the saddle while caring for their two small children, and Chris welcomed the opportunity to spend more time with his family. He returned to Oklahoma, wound up his affairs, and moved to Kansas City.

Citizens generally seemed satisfied with Nagle's actions. It was his desire not to create business for the office of U.S. marshal but to conduct it with the greatest degree of efficiency that industry and caution could give. Homesteaders no longer would be carried one hundred miles to answer to a U.S. commissioner for cutting a blackjack tree on their own claims.

The *Times-Journal*[21] remained unconvinced. Nagle no doubt would endeavor to conduct the affairs of his office honestly, but he

> is surrounded by the same villainous gang that brought Nix to grief. . . . How can Marshal Nagle stop the awful abuses without assistance? The U.S. commissioners and U.S. attorneys are more guilty than Nix, for they had it in their power to stop the abuse that they fostered and built up. One word from any district judge would have stopped it in his district . . . what can they say—that the matter was never brought before them in their official capacity? The commissioners are creatures of the court, and held their offices at the will of the judge. The appointing power is held responsible for the acts of its agents. In this case the principal should be held to a strict accounting.

The *Leader*[22] replied:

> Do you readers know that Oklahoma contains a greater number of "all around kickers" to the square mile than any territory that has ever knocked at the doors of congress for admission to the union? There is not one federal officer holder in your territory whose name and character has not been assaulted, not only before the department under which he is employed, but before the committees of the United States senate and house of representatives. . . . Under the circumstances . . . can Oklahoma blame the house committee on territories and the heads of the several executive departments at Washington for turning a deaf ear on any claim for recognition or favor from your territory?
>
> The assault on the character and judicial acts of your federal judges

is most remarkable and is a serious reflection against the name of your fair country, because they have not been and cannot be substantiated.

The *Times-Journal*[23] countered:

> What a despicable threat! The *Leader* is desperate. For three years the paper has divided the ill gotten spoils of corrupt federal officials. Every fresh complaint on the part of the people against the scandalous conduct of officers brought a burst of humor . . . but there is no mirth in the *Leader* office now. The *Leader* has gone so far as to take up such vulgar things as commerce and territorial prosperity.

And on March 23, the *Times-Journal* announced that

> Inspector Sheibley, of the department of justice, left Washington for the west last night. . . . He has with him a bundle of charges against Judges Scott and Dale and various United States commissioners. It was through Mr. Sheibley's work that Marshal Nix was ousted, and it is the same line of business that he is planning a return engagement.

Little came of the additional investigation except the reshuffling of U.S. commissioners, the curtailment of district clerk fees and emoluments, and orders from the attorney general that "hereafter all prisoners convicted and sentenced in the U.S. courts of the Territory to a penitentiary shall be confined in the U.S. Penitentiary at Fort Leavenworth."

The district judges weathered the storm. Judge Burford, whose term expired in May, was succeeded in the Second District by John C. Tarsney, a Kansas City attorney and former congressman from Missouri. Judge Scott resigned toward the end of Cleveland's administration to form a law partnership in New York City. He was succeeded in the Third District by Guthrie attorney J. R. Keaton. In March, Nix settled his accounts with the government. "Uncle Sam found himself indebted to the ex-Marshal about $34,000, warrants for which will be issued."[24]

Meanwhile, there had been no cessation of criminal activity. The territorial political hassle and perpetual nagging at operations of the marshal's office encouraged it. In the Cheyenne country, Red Buck Waightman, using the aliases Buck Gant and White Horse Doolin (because of the "mettlesome gray horse" he rode), had organized a new band of outlaws. On September 1, 1895, in the company of one Charlie Smith, he murdered Gus Holland and stole his cattle from the head of Cheyenne Creek in D (Dewey) County. Local officers took their trail, and the county commissioners offered a $150 reward.[25] A week later, the pair was seen in the vicinity of

Woodward, accompanied by two Texas fugitives, Joe Beckham and Elmer ("Kid") Lewis.

Lewis hailed from Neosho, Missouri, and had worked as a cowboy on Burke Burnett's T Fork Ranch near Wichita Falls before turning to thievery and robbery. Beckham had been sheriff of Motley County, Texas, until he "got as short as possible in his accounts," walked out of his office in Matador with full saddlebags hanging over his shoulder (they contained what was left of the county's money), and set out for old Greer County across Red River. The ownership of this section was in dispute between Texas and Oklahoma Territory before the U.S. Supreme Court. It was a thinly populated area, and its vast pastures north of the river were leased by the Waggoner brothers, prominent ranchers on China and Beaver creeks in Wichita and Wilbarger counties between Wichita Falls and Vernon. Texas Ranger Bob McClure captured Beckham at Horse Creek west of present Frederick, Oklahoma, but lost his prisoner through a writ of habeas corpus because he had overstepped his authority and state jurisdiction. The absconding Beckham finally surrendered to Texas authorities and won a change of venue to Baylor County. However, when his case came up for trial and his old rival, named Cook (a Motley citizen with ambitions for Beckham's office and now his successor by election), came over to testify, Beckham met the train and promptly shot Cook dead as he stepped onto the Seymour station platform.[26]

Beckham mounted a fast horse and cantered back across Red River with Kid Lewis. The pair sought shelter at Altus, near Beckham's sister. The sister had been insulted by a store proprietor there, and Beckham and Lewis, according to the story, "destroyed the general store, beating senseless the man alleged to have been responsible for the insults." The next morning, an Indian trader named Old Nels was robbed and killed east of Altus, near Headrick, as the fugitives fled north ahead of an angry posse into Oklahoma Territory. Somewhere in the Cheyenne country, they joined Smith and Waightman.

At 3:15 on the afternoon of September 12, four masked men held up the westbound Santa Fe passenger train at a deep cut two and a half miles out of Curtis, fourteen miles east of Woodward. Section foreman Miller was

> forced by the robbers to draw spikes, pile ties across the track and flag the train. The train was in charge of Conductor Garfield, Engineer Bob Buswell and Fireman Tom Parks. The robbers were concealed till the train stopped. Two of them ordered the engineer and fireman to get

342

off the engine and go up the track. Several shots were fired through the express car, one barely missing Messenger Kleaver, who retreated to the baggage car and remained there during the hold-up.

Conductor Garfield and Brakeman Ireland stepped off to see what was the matter and were told to get back, which they did without delay. The robbers entered the mail car, through mistake doubtless, as the mail car was not disturbed. They then proceeded to go through the express car, from which they took nothing but a revolver and some shells from the messenger's shotgun. The robbers asked the engineer if he could identify the messenger. He said he did not know who came down today. The robbers left without getting the safe open, leaving orders not to move the train until signaled by them. The passengers were not robbed. Pocket books were secreted in every imaginable place. . . .

A special train carrying Deputy Sheriff Ben Wolforth, Deputy Marshal Eugene Hall and three other officers from here [Woodward] reached the scene one and a half hours after the robbery. The officers immediately struck the trail which leads southeast toward Black Jack.[27]

That night, Hall wired the marshal's office at Guthrie. The robbers were "on fleet horses" and had escaped "towards the Glass Mountains."[28]

The Waightman gang never was officially charged with the Curtis train robbery, and the mysterious Charlie Smith dropped from the picture. But Red Buck, Lewis, and Beckham were positively identified as the trio who, a month later, in October, looted the Charles E. Noyes general store at Arapaho.[29] Noyes, who had gained considerable capital from two previous ventures in Siloam Springs, Arkansas, and the bustling mining town of Bonners Ferry, Idaho, had brought his family to the enterprising young city of Arapaho in 1894 and had erected a solid, prosperous-looking structure between the town's two thriving saloons. The apparent affluence the shelves of the establishment represented attracted the Waightman outlaws.

Noyes and his wife, Alice, were closing up one evening when Red Buck and associates entered with guns drawn. Red Buck thrust the muzzle of his six-shooter under Noyes's chin and demanded to know where he kept his money. Noyes explained that his cash had been sent to an El Reno bank by mail hack that morning, so Red Buck relieved him of a fine gold watch. Afterward, the gang "loaded up" with long black overcoats, boots, food, and ammunition. As they were about to depart, Red Buck grabbed Mrs. Noyes and demanded the diamond ring she wore. "Take your hands off me!" Mrs. Noyes screamed. "The only way you'll get that ring is by cutting it off my finger!"

Red Buck laid his gun on the counter and began struggling with the woman. Mrs. Noyes reached for the weapon. Red Buck wrenched it from her grasp. Jamming the six-shooter against her chest, he seized her by the throat with his left hand and said: "I'll kill you, Alice."

Mrs. Noyes screamed back: "You wouldn't have the nerve to kill a woman."

Red Buck glared at her for a moment, then whirled and left the store. But in that moment, Mrs. Noyes got a close look at his unusually bright auburn hair and moustache and the outlaw's eyes, which she never forgot. She told officers: "They were mean and cold—coyote eyes."

Again the gang escaped. About 7 P.M. on December 4, the trio rode into Taloga, thirty miles north of Arapaho on the South Canadian, held up the Shultz & Alderice store and fifteen occupants of the place, and galloped away with a quantity of clothing and one hundred dollars and a dozen irate citizens in pursuit.[30]

By now, officers knew the "full identity of their quarry," and posses swarmed throughout sparsely settled Custer and Dewey counties, reminiscent of the vast man hunt conducted a few months earlier for Zip Wyatt and Ike Black. The gang decided to quit Oklahoma and headed south. Two weeks later, they were sighted on West Cache Creek near the Wichita Mountains. By December 24, they had reentered Texas, reaching the Waggoner range on Beaver Creek in Wilbarger County.

That night, Sergeant W. J. L. Sullivan of B Company, Texas Rangers, and Wilbarger County Sheriff Dick Sanders were on Beaver Creek twenty miles below Vernon, hunting for a train robber. Not finding their man, they ate dinner and spent most of Christmas Day with a farm family in the vicinity before returning to Vernon. There Sullivan found waiting for him a telegram from Taylor Holt, the bookkeeper at Waggoner's store, saying that four men had come to the place and "beat one of the clerks nearly to death," presumably for refusing to reveal where the store's money was kept.

In his exceedingly scarce biography, *Twelve Years in the Saddle for Law and Order on the Frontiers of Texas*, Sergeant Sullivan devotes an entire chapter[31] to the pursuit that followed:

> I took Jack Harrel, a daring ranger, and we caught the train at once for Wagner [Waggoner's]. . . . Taylor Holt was at the train to meet us, and took us over to the store, where he described the four desperadoes [Hill Loftos (also spelled *Loftis* and *Loftus*), a former Waggoner cowboy wanted for murder, had joined the Waightman trio]. When Holt ex-

pressed the opinion that the men were still in the country, I said that we had better sleep in the store, as I thought the men would attempt to rob the store that night. . . . About ten o'clock someone called at the front door.

Sullivan greeted the party with a six-shooter and Winchester. Alf Bailey, who ran a store and post office a few miles south of Waggoner's, reported that four men had just robbed him of seven hundred dollars worth of merchandise and all the money and stamps in the post office. They had gone toward Red River. While Holt rounded up some horses, Sullivan notified officers "up and down the line" and wired Ranger headquarters. At daylight, he, Holt, Harrel, and Bailey started on the trail.

> The ground was frozen so hard that only one of the four horses made an impression . . . he weighing about twelve hundred pounds. After we had traveled some distance we came to a small house where the four men had spent the balance of the night. There were signs they had fed the horses, and cooked, eaten and slept. We also found a number of fine quirts between the mattresses, some tobacco, and about fifty pounds of coffee in a shed-room, which had been taken from Bailey's store.

They discovered the owner hiding in a shack near by. He denied any knowledge of the quirts, tobacco, and coffee at his house or of the men who had stopped there.

> I thought it best to hold him for a while, so Holt and I took him to the railroad, where we met a local. We hid our horses, boarded the local, went to Iowa Park, and met the passenger train. We then turned our prisoner over to an officer — Eugene Logan — with instructions to jail him at Vernon, and then we quit the train where we had left our horses . . . and returned to Wagner [Waggoner's], where we met the men whom we were with the day before. We also found there Sheriff Moses and Constable Tom Pickett, from Wichita Falls; Bud Hardin, a special ranger from Harrell [Harrold]; Dick Sanders, Sheriff [and] Johnnie Williams, Deputy Sheriff of Wilbarger County; Charley Landers, City Marshal of Vernon; Bob McClure, Billy McCauley and Lee Queen, rangers. . . . I wired Sheriff [S. H.] Tittle, of Mangum, Greer County, fifty-five miles off the railroad, about the robbery.

The posse left at once for Waggoner's headquarters camp on Red River, where Sullivan obtained fresh horses for his men and met Dick Farrell, Tom Waggoner's line camp rider, who lived twenty miles north of the river. Farrell told them there was no one at the line camp when he left. He had seen some objects, but they were so far away that he couldn't tell whether they were horses, cattle, or men.

So we pushed on. About an hour before sundown, a big, blue norther blew up, which we had to face. Just at dusk we came in sight of Dick Farrell's camp, which was a dugout, half rock and half dirt, built in the head of a draw, and there was a light shining out of the mouth of the dugout. . . . Six of my men had fallen behind; so I told the other five that those fellows in the dugout were either the outlaws or some hunters and that we had better wait for the other men. We waited some time, but they failed to come, and I told my men we would try it without the others. We started toward the dugout in a gallop, getting a little faster all the time, and when we got within seventy-five yards of the dugout, the four desperadoes — Joe Beckham, Hill Loftos, Redbuck, and the Kid [Lewis] — ran out and opened fire on us, killing three horses. . . . My horse was rearing and plunging so much to get away from the flare of guns [that] after three trials . . . I succeeded in getting my Winchester out of the scabbard . . . fell off my horse and faced the four men. Three of them were in a trench leading into the dugout, and the fourth, Red-buck, was standing in the door. . . . My first shot struck Redbuck just over the heart, and he fell backward into the dugout. The ball only struck his breast-plate, however, and he fainted, but recovered in a few minutes and again joined the fight. I found out afterward that we hit him again, shattering his collar bone and shoulder blade. I also learned that one of the men in the trench was killed. I heard a gunshot behind me, and I turned and discovered that Johnnie Williams [whose] horse had been killed in the fight. . . had come to my assistance . . . .

We fired several more shots at the three men, but they went into the dugout and fired at us from a window. I suggested to Johnnie that we dismount the men by killing their horses, which we did. . . . There were four animals in the pen, but it was so dark we couldn't see very well, and afterward found that we had killed two of Wagner's [Waggoner's] horses, which they had stolen, and two of his big freight mules, which were used by Farrell. They had stolen two other horses from an old fel-low in the Cheyenne country, but they had turned them out into the pasture. . . .

I suggested to Johnnie that we crawl across the draw and get in the corral behind those dead horses, and kill the men as they came to the door. We started crawling across the draw . . . got out of the gully on high ground, when the three men "sky-lighted" us and opened fire again. Johnnie asked what we had better do, and I replied that it would not hurt to "crawfish" a little . . . and we turned back, when we met the other three men whom we left.

We fought the outlaws until eleven o'clock that night. Every time they saw any of us moving anywhere, they fired at us, and we fired back at them. Finally, we got so cold we couldn't pull a cartridge from our belts [or] work the levers of our Winchesters and we had to quit. We decided to go back that night to Wagner's [Waggoner's] camp . . . walking across the country.

The officers reached the Red River headquarters camp next morning in a blinding storm of sleet and snow. Sullivan made preparations to return to the dugout, but all his men refused to go except Rangers Lee Queen and Billy McCauley. Dick Farrell agreed to guide them but objected to approaching the dugout together because the outlaws would open fire on them as before. He suggested that he go alone, tell them he was the owner of the dugout, and report back to Sullivan as soon as possible.

That evening Farrell returned . . . stated that the desperadoes had left the dugout, but he found Sheriff Tittle, of Greer County, there, with John Byers and Jim Farris, two of his deputies. . . . He instructed Farrell . . . to tell me Joe Beckham had been killed in the fight, that there had been seven horses killed, and for me to come at once. . . .

I immediately got a buckboard and a pair of mules from Tom Wagner [Waggoner], and, with Alf Bailey, Billy McCauley and Lee Queen, went to the dugout, where . . . we recovered nearly all the merchandise that had been stolen from Bailey.

I put Beckham's body in the buckboard, and then loaded in seven saddles, three of which we took off the dead horses, and four which belonged to the outlaws . . . and returned to Wagner's [Waggoner's] station. . . . The next day, Tuesday, we buried Beckham, but the following Thursday I received orders from Adjutant General Mabry to hold an inquest . . . and we had to take the body up and hold an inquest over it that day.

Before burying the outlaw again, Sullivan removed from his finger a valuable ring which he gave to Beckham's sister at Altus.

Loftos was captured some time later, tried on the old murder charge, and acquitted. Kid Lewis was next heard of with Foster Holbrook, former member of the Christian gang in Pottawatomie County, who, after a few escapades of his own, had fled Oklahoma and found employment on Burnett's T Fork Ranch under the name of Crawford.[32]

On February 25, 1896, Crawford and Lewis robbed the City National Bank at Wichita Falls and killed Cashier Frank Dorsey. The Texas Rangers were notified. Captain Bill McDonald and his crack lawmen were at nearby Bellevue. They took the northbound train to Wichita Falls and quickly corraled the robbers without firing a shot, escorted them back to Wichita Falls, and remained on guard the next day and night to keep angry citizens from getting to them in jail. On February 27, McDonald and his men, their duty finished, caught the afternoon train for their headquarters in Amarillo. After nightfall, a mob of three hundred entered the jail with little trouble, took the bandits to the front of the bank, and hanged them from a telephone pole.[33]

Fleeing from the Ranger fight, Red Buck, badly wounded and afoot in the blizzard, made his way back to the Cheyenne country. There are conflicting stories of how and where he met George Miller. One tale has it that Miller, a Texas horse thief, lived with a bachelor named W. W. Glover in a dugout on the latter's claim five miles west of Arapaho. In the summer of 1895, the two men raised a good corn crop, around which they built a taut wire fence. A neighboring rancher, who hated fences and cared considerably less for nesters, offered not even an apology when his cattle tore down the wires in several places and "went tromping about the cornfield." Miller made the necessary repairs, but the next day the cattle were back in the field. This time Miller called on the owner and told him that if his cattle "found their way" through the fence again, they would be shot. The rancher was not to be rebuffed by threats. Hot words were exchanged, and Miller galloped back to the dugout. When he awakened the next morning and saw the cattle for the third time "eatin' their way through his corn," he unlimbered his Winchester, killing a couple of the best cows. The rancher summoned local authorities, and Miller, fearing they would discover that he was wanted in Texas, elicited a promise from Glover to take care of the crops and livestock until things cooled a bit and went into hiding. While on the dodge, he met Red Buck.

If this is true, Miller possibly was the mysterious Charlie Smith who was with Waightman when Gus Holland was slain and his cattle rustled on Cheyenne Creek in September and was the unidentified fourth member of the gang in the Curtis train holdup.

On the other hand, Dolph Picklesimer, then batching in a rock half-dugout house on his Custer County claim five miles north of Canute, says that Miller, whom he had known in Texas, was visiting with him early in January, 1896, when Red Buck, suffering from the bullet wound he received in the shooting affray in Greer County, arrived at his place and sought food and lodging. Miller was "introduced to Red Buck . . . the pair stepped out alone in front of the house, their brief conversation developed into a friendship, and shortly thereafter, they rode off together," Picklesimer fervently hoping that he had seen the last of them.[34]

For the next couple of weeks, while Red Buck's wound healed, the pair sought shelter at the gang's old hideout on the South Canadian near Taloga. On February 14, they appeared at Glover's claim, where Miller induced his old partner to go into Arapaho to buy supplies and ammunition. Glover was not enthused about aiding Red Buck. Once in town, he revealed the presence of the outlaws to lawmen, who promptly formed a posse and rode to the dugout.

Glover was to fire his pistol upon approaching the place as a signal to Red Buck and Miller that all was well. At the same instant, he intended to take shelter and join his seven companions in capturing the desperadoes. The possemen positioned themselves about the dugout. Glover fired. Out came Red Buck and Miller to meet him. A volley rang out, but every shot missed its mark. The posse had "jumped the gun," and before Glover could reach cover, Red Buck, sensing the double-cross, shot and killed Miller's traitor friend. The two desperadoes mounted their horses and fled.[35]

Eluding the posse, Miller and Red Buck

went back to their hiding place on the Canadian, in the edge of D county. Officers of that county, learning of their whereabouts, attacked them but were repulsed by the desperadoes, who then turned south heading for the Wichita mountains with . . . deputies Joe Ventioner, Bill Quillen and Wm. Holcomb, of D county, close on their trail. After reaching the mountains, Miller and Red Buck separated, each starting on the back trail, thinking to elude the officers, but the officers soon discovered the change and turned back, trailing them to the mouth of Elm and from there to Oak Creek. Reaching Oak Creek Tuesday afternoon [March 3], they learned that Miller and Red Buck were at the half-dugout of one Picklesimer, on the head of Oak Creek, and would likely remain there all night. So just before day yesterday morning [March 4], a posse composed of T. L. Shahan, J. T. Duckworth, constables of G county, Louis N. Williams, of Washita county, and deputies Ventioner, Quillen and Holcomb . . . surrounded the dugout and waited for daylight to come, and until the outlaws emerged . . . which was not until the sun was fully two hours high, when George Miller and Picklesimer came out and started to the lot, supposedly to feed their horses. The officers called on them to surrender. Miller went for his revolver, and a ball from one of the officers guns made him drop it. Miller then made for the dugout calling for Red Buck to come to his assistance. Red Buck appeared on the scene, shooting at the officers.[36]

Picklesimer gave this account of the battle:

Holcomb and Joe Ventioner were ambushed along the creek about 83 steps east of the dugout . . . they hit Red Buck and he fell dead at the door. When Miller got to the dugout, he turned Red Buck over and saw he was dead. He got his gun and his watch and started down a draw toward the creek after the two possemen who were directing the firing. Ventioner was on his right, Holcomb on his left.

He traded shots with Ventioner, wounding the latter [the ball struck the deputy in the lower abdomen and passed out just above the left hip, making a serious but not fatal wound]. Another bullet from his gun crashed into the stump which protected Holcomb. But Holcomb took dead aim at the angered desperado. One bullet tore into Miller's right arm above the wrist. Another ripped into his left hand. Miller staggered back into the dugout.[37]

After some time had elapsed, Miller called to the officers

to come to him as he was shot all to pieces. The officers were somewhat slow to venture into the dugout where so desperate a man was, but on being assured by Miller that he was so badly wounded that he could do nothing they went to him and found that three fingers had been shot off his left hand and his right arm broken in two places, which will necessitate amputation.[38]

The posse recovered the watch taken from Red Buck. It was later identified as the property of Charles Noyes. With his right arm and left hand rendered useless, Miller had buried it in the dirt floor with his feet.[39]

Picklesimer applied hot ashes and soot to Miller's wounds as a caustic and wrapped them with cloth. The posse then loaded the desperado, Red Buck's body, and Picklesimer into a wagon and took them to Arapaho, where Picklesimer spent the night in jail convincing officers that he had no option but to offer the two fugitives food and shelter. "Officer Ventioner is at the Hotel Arapaho, resting as easy as could be expected . . . Miller is under guard in the District Court room," both men "receiving all the attention that can be bestowed upon them" by local physicians. Miller "talks quite freely about his partner who has been killed" but "denies that he knows his true name." Mrs. Noyes identified Red Buck by his "coyote eyes," and Deputy Marshal Banks, arriving from his ranch near Cheyenne, "says there is $4,800 in rewards for Waightman." The outlaw's body was roped to an undertaker's board, propped against a wall, and photographed, "apparently to prove that he really was dead."[40]

Miller was never tried for his Oklahoma crimes. After recovering from his injuries, he was

350

escorted to Texas by invitation of the governor of that state and kindly provided with a home in one of her most substantial public buildings as a partial recompense for his artistic and ornamental work in that great commonwealth.[41]

No one claimed Red Buck's body, and it was buried the following day in the Arapaho cemetery at county expense. A common red brick stands at the foot of the unkept grave. Scratched across its surface are two words: Red Buck.[42]

Informed of Waightman's death, Bill Doolin commented that it "showed how much he himself had been maligned . . . the sins of others laid at his door." There was a "wistful look" in his eye, however, as he saw his old gang diminishing.

On May 1, Deputy Marshals Tilghman and Reynolds took Doolin to Stillwater to answer an indictment in the killing of Marshals Hueston, Speed, and Shadley at Ingalls. People packed the courtroom to see the celebrated outlaw. Doolin had agreed to plead guilty on the promise of the U.S. district attorney that he would get only fifty years, the same sentence given Arkansas Tom, but he changed his mind when he was arraigned. He was bound over for trial and ordered returned to the federal jail.[43] On the way back to Guthrie, Tilghman asked: "Bill, why did you go back on your word?" Doolin replied that fifty years seemed a mighty long time and he believed he knew how to beat the charges.[44] A hint of what the bandit chief had in mind came a few weeks later.

While posses were trailing Red Buck, Deputy Marshal Canton received a report that Dynamite Dick Clifton had been slain in the hills between Cleveland and Tulsa but the body had not been identified. Canton, however, already had learned that the fugitive was at his mother's home near Smith Paul's Valley in the Chickasaw Nation. Before he and Deputy Clarence Young could reach that part of the country, Clifton was arrested on a whiskey charge by deputy marshals from Paris, Texas, and sentenced to thirty days in the federal jail under the alias Dan Wiley.

When Canton and Young arrived to identify him, Clifton was wearing a high celluloid collar, a derby hat, and a four-week-old beard. Canton sent for a barber. The outlaw protested. He knew what the marshal was looking for. The shave revealed on his neck a scar the size of a half-dollar; it was the place where the bullet he received in the Ingalls fight had been removed.

Canton and Young went to U.S. Marshal J. Shelby Williams of the Eastern Judicial District of Texas, produced a murder warrant from

Oklahoma, and demanded the prisoner. On June 22, they delivered Dynamite Dick to the Guthrie jail.[45]

Doolin's cell was in front of the main entrance. The moment he saw Clifton, his expression was one of both terror and excitement. He asked to speak to the prisoner; Canton consented. They talked in a whisper, and Canton could not catch their words. As the jailers arrived to put Clifton in a separate cell, Doolin admonished Dynamite: "For God's sake, stand pat!"

The bathhouse at Eureka Springs, Arkansas, where Bill Tilghman captured Bill Doolin.

Red Buck Waightman in death.

Leo E. Bennett, U.S. marshal for the Northern District of Indian Territory at Muskogee.

Marlin rifle, Model 1881, .40 caliber, taken from "Red Buck" Waightman after he was slain March 4, 1896 in a dugout near Arapaho. Photograph courtesy Ralph Foster Museum, School of the Ozarks, Point Lookout, Missouri.

Little Dick West in death.

The Cabinet Saloon in Woodward, operated by Jack Garvey, was the scene of a gun battle involving Temple Houston, Jack Love, and John and Ed Jennings.

Top left: Al Jennings. Right: Jack Love. Bottom left: U.S. Deputy Marshal James F. (Bud) Ledbetter. Right: Temple Houston.

XXIV   The U.S. Jail Looted

GUTHRIE'S FIRST JAIL, an elongated, half-brick affair, stood at the corner of Noble Avenue and North Second Street. Before passage of the 1890 act that created Oklahoma Territory, transgressors of federal laws were taken to Wichita, Kansas, and Fort Smith, Arkansas, for incarceration. After federal courts were organized in Oklahoma, the government continued the practice with its more desperate prisoners, which not only proved risky, inconvenient, and expensive but took away much business the embryo territory desperately needed.

At a meeting in December, 1891, the Commercial Club appointed a committee to estimate the cost and probable benefit that Guthrie would derive from the establishment of a bastille of sufficient capacity and security to accommodate the most hardened desperadoes. It was decided that a second floor could be added to the existing building, and a company of enterprising businessmen proceeded to construct the first real jail in Oklahoma, which they leased to the U.S. Department of Justice. The company was incorporated and the stockholders received good dividends for several years, plus a 50 per cent profit on their investment. In February, 1896, U.S. District Attorney Brooks was authorized to buy the jail for the federal government because he thought prisoners could be taken care of better by Uncle Sam than by private individuals. The jail promptly was given additional improvements, put into first-class sanitary condition, and declared a permanent institution.[1]

The final structure was about forty by one hundred feet in size, two stories high, with native red stone walls eighteen inches thick. Entrance to the main floor was through a heavy steel door on the west (front) of the building, opening into the jail office, or general receiving corridor, ten feet from the ground and enclosed by steel bars and a steel gate at the basement (ground) level. The windows were doubly barred, and the walls of the cells made of sheet iron, with no ventilation except as came through the cell doors. With such security, there had been only one jailbreak of consequence in the history of the institution, and three or four attempted deliveries had been discovered before the schemes materialized.

The office corridor, twelve feet deep and running the width of the building, was divided from the prison area by iron bars extending from floor to ceiling. A big barred door at the far right opened into the bull pen beyond, where the prisoners were allowed freedom in the daytime. Across the back or east side of the bull pen and part way along the north and south walls ran the tier of cells, where inmates customarily were locked up between eight and nine o'clock each night. The most dangerous prisoners were kept in two blocks of cells to the left of the bull-pen entrance. A second door, with a combination lock in a large steel box on each side, opened into a passageway between these cellblocks from the office corridor. The front cells accommodated sixteen prisoners. One jailer and four guards were employed, the jailer and two guards in attendance from 6 A.M. to 6 P.M. and two guards from 6 P.M. until morning.[2]

Bill Doolin was kept in a front cell until the last week of June, 1896, when he "had a number of fits, which were feigned," and "on account of his supposed sickness he was allowed the liberty of the bull pen at day . . . to give him better air and more room to exercise."

At 8:45 P.M. on Sunday, July 5, night guard Joe Miller removed his revolver and placed it in a box near the corridor entrance. With keys in hand, he was then let into the bull pen by night guard J. T. Tull and started toward the cells at the rear.

A bucket of water set to the right of the door on the corridor side so that the prisoners could reach through the bars and get a drink. They were in the habit of filling tin cans to take into their cells at night, so Tull "thought nothing of it" when he saw George Lane, a hulking half-Cherokee, half-Negro desperado charged with selling whiskey in the Osage country, standing in the corner reaching through to the bucket.

As Miller passed into the bull pen, Lane mumbled something about not being able to reach the water and thrust an arm through the door and around to the pail. Miller was halfway to the rear cells. For a moment, Tull's eyes dropped toward the bucket. At the same instant, Lane shoved his head and shoulders through the doorway. With a mighty lunge and quick as a flash, he seized Tull, pinning his arms to his sides in a viselike grip, while three other prisoners—Walter McLain, serving six months for larceny, and Lee

Killian, six months for whiskey peddling, both from Pawnee County, and W. H. Jones of Pottawatomie County, charged with counterfeiting—rushed upon Tull and tore his revolver from the holster under his arm.

Before Miller could run half the length of the bull pen, Bill Doolin leaped through the door, closing and locking it, leaving the guard helpless and unarmed among the prisoners. Doolin grabbed Miller's revolver from the box. "His look of sickness had suddenly disappeared, his eyes shone with the light of hell, his hair fairly bristled all over his head, and with set teeth and a grin of horror he shoved his revolver now in the guard's face, now in his stomach, now in his side, with his fingers clutching the trigger, seeming to need only the beginning of slaughter to complete his demoniacal joy."

He dragged Tull to the middle of the corridor, in front of the combination locks, and ordered him to open them while Killian pointed his revolver at the guard's temple. Bill Dean, a trusty who was sitting at the office desk, ran to Tull's assistance. Doolin knocked him down with his revolver and the others kicked and tossed him down the stairway into the basement. Doolin put his gun against Tull's breast and again ordered him to "open the locks— or die." When the combinations were worked, Doolin opened the passageway door and Dynamite Dick and eight more prisoners joined them from the blocks of cells. The eight were later identified as Charles Montgomery, serving ten months for larceny; James F. Black, awaiting trial for perjury; William Crittenden, serving one year from Pawnee County for larceny; C. E. Lawrence, charged with post-office burglary in Kingfisher County; E. V. Nix, held on bond forfeiture and perjury; Kid Phillips, outlaw and all-around tough, sentenced to one year from Pawnee County for larceny; Henry Irwin, serving a year for post-office robbery in Woods County; and William O. Beck, charged with selling whiskey in the Osage.[3]

Jones and Killian took the big front-door key from Tull, went back to the bull pen, and invited the thirty-five prisoners still there to go with them. When all refused, they locked Miller in the bull pen and Tull in a cell. The gang then took from the wall a half-dozen coats, vests, and hats belonging to the jailer and guards, got a long iron bar and a hatchet from the desk, and ran downstairs into the darkness. Bob Shugart, another prisoner who had come into the corridor but changed his mind, went to a telephone and gave the alarm. A crowd soon gathered at the jail, but it was half an hour before jailer Comley arrived to release Tull and Miller.

Walter McLain, one of the ringleaders, went down Noble Avenue and across into West Guthrie to a house where his wife was boarding. "She had retired for the night but he routed her out, telling her to hurry. . . . In night clothes and barefooted she came, carrying a dress and shoes, and they hurried off on foot. They attempted to stop a man driving toward town, but the horse took fright at the woman in white and dashed past." Later, it was learned "they had succeeded in getting a conveyance further out, and went west."

The other escapees fled north up Second Street to the railroad and followed the tracks out of town. After he had run half a mile, Doolin's rheumatic leg began giving him trouble, and the group sat down and rested. When they started again, they separated, and William Beck turned back to the jail and surrendered. He reported the direction the prisoners had taken, and Deputy Marshals Heck Thomas and Bill Crane set out in pursuit.

At the city limits, they met Alvador Koontz, a clerk in the county treasurer's office, and Winnifred Warner, a young schoolteacher, on the road afoot. Koontz had been taking Miss Warner from her home in the country to a school normal in Guthrie, driving a fine nine-year-old bay mare, a white star on her forehead, hitched to a buggy he had hired the day before from C. E. Scofield on West Noble Avenue. A mile from town, a man leaped from the darkness onto the side of the buggy, poked a revolver in his ribs, and ordered him to get out. Two more men came up on the other side — one with an upraised hatchet — and the young couple complied with alacrity. The three fugitives then climbed into the rig and sped north into the night. Koontz and Miss Warner identified them as Doolin, Dynamite Dick, and Jones, the counterfeiter.

Chief Deputy Kane sent telegrams describing the break to every district marshal. Colcord left Perry with a posse for the Triangle Country southeast of Pawnee; others, from the west, headed for Stillwater and the Ingalls area; and Marshal Nagle "appointed fifteen special deputies with ten-day commissions" to comb Cowboy Flats and the Cimarron east to Perkins. As an additional incentive, jailer Comley offered a one hundred dollar reward for the capture of each of the ringleaders and twenty-five dollars apiece for the others. But Doolin and his confederates had vanished like wraiths.[4]

In the light of Doolin's actions,

> how flat falls all the twaddle he talked about being glad he was caught and having a fair trial and the rot about his giving himself up to Bill Tilghman. Tilghman . . . after risking his life so often and working so hard to capture him . . . loses all the compensation for his arduous

labors, for the rewards were all for arrest and conviction, and he has never been convicted and from present indications never will be.[5]

In the opinion of the *Oklahoma State Capital*,[6]

that fourteen prisoners should walk out of the United States jail in a body and be able to get out of the county without even one being taken does not reflect much credit upon the diligence of the officers whose duty it is to look after the welfare of the law-abiding people of the territory.

Directing its ire at Nagle, the *Guthrie Daily Leader*[7] labeled the delivery

a public crime against law and order and society. It cost the government $50,000 and the lives of many brave men to place Bill Doolin behind bars and will cost the government as much more and most likely the lives of other brave men to recapture him. . . . A terrible condition of official incompetency surrounds the federal jail and calls for prompt and summary action.

It was several days before people realized the enormity of the break and began to present themselves to the public mind in relation to the matter. Individuals and lodges of the Anti–Horse Thief Association complained to Washington that the escape of Doolin and Dynamite Dick again had placed lives and property in jeopardy and demanded a full investigation "to the end that every citizen in the Territory may fully understand whether it was the fault of the officer in charge or the construction of the jail that such was possible."[8]

Nagle's five-page report to the attorney general on August 1 bore no significant variation of the details that appeared in the press. A Justice Department examiner, Plato Mountjoy, was "unable to see wherein Miller was blameworthy" and thought Tull "should not have opened the door under any circumstances till his associate returned." Marshal Nagle reasoned, however, that regardless of whether the two guards were guilty, their efficiency had been impaired greatly, if not destroyed, by the mere fact that the prisoners had escaped, so he discharged both of them.[9] The marshal did not

anticipate any trouble from these escaped prisoners, as all except Doolin and Dynamite Dick are of the class addicted to the petit degree of crime and Doolin for some time past has been in very poor state of health. . . . If they remain in this country after the crops are harvested and the leaves fall, I think they can be re-captured. I do not deem it advisable to incur any extraordinary expense in an effort in that direction while the chances for hiding in the brush and growing crops are as good as they are at present.[10]

Such reasoning to a veteran man hunter like Heck Thomas was asinine. Heck understood Doolin better, perhaps, than any officer in the territory, and he had his own idea how the outlaw might be brought to bay.

On the evening of July 11, Doolin allegedly stopped at a farmhouse fourteen miles east of Oklahoma City and ate supper, returned for breakfast the following morning, and departed after assuring his hosts "he could escape by the aid of his numerous friends from any organized pursuit."[11] Three days later, the *Perry Enterprise-Times* reported "a fight" in eastern Noble County near Morrison between Doolin, Dynamite Dick, and other desperadoes and the deputies who had been pursuing them since their escape. One outlaw was shot but was carried away by the band. The posse was still in pursuit. Hennessey and Wichita newspapers credited Doolin and Dynamite Dick with the July 27 armed robbery of the regular mail and stage in a lonely ravine between Okeene and Lacey in which two bandits took the passengers' money and valuables, then cut the mail sacks and took all their contents, including packages and registered letters.[12]

Heck Thomas put no stock in these "Doolin canards." On August 4, Deputy Marshal John Smith captured one of the escapees, C. E. Lawrence, near Enid, where he had been visiting his father, and returned him to the federal jail.[13] Lawrence told Heck he had not seen Doolin since they separated on the tracks north of Guthrie but that the bandit chief had said then he did not intend to leave the territory without his wife and child.

Heck's interest picked up when the *Enterprise-Times* announced on August 10 that Mrs. J. W. Ellsworth, Doolin's mother-in-law, had driven into Perry from Lawson that morning,

> bringing with her Joe Miller's revolver that Doolin had taken when he broke jail. Mrs. Ellsworth delivered the gun to Granville Morris at the New York hardware, to whom she [also] delivered Doolin's message to Joe Miller: "I thank you, Joe, very much for the use of the gun, and will pay you for the use of it as soon as I strike a job."
>
> It is a very handsome Colt's 45 six-shooter with pearl handles, and Joe is glad to get it back.[14]

The report implied that Doolin was "not far away" and "since he is so generous" might send back Scofield's bay mare and buggy.

Confident that Doolin was hiding near his wife and child, Heck got in touch with Bill Dunn and his brothers and through them engaged the services of Tom and Charlie Noble, two young blacksmiths at Lawson. Charlie was courting the Dunn boys' sister, Rosa, now sixteen. This and the promise of sharing in the rewards for the outlaw "made them approachable for such an enterprise." Doolin, they said, already had visited his wife. On Sunday night, August 2, "he stayed about half an hour and left . . . the next time, Tuesday night, he came back and stayed about an hour . . . and came or went by there the next morning." He had not been seen since, but the Nobles promised to keep an eye on the Ellsworth home, "within rock-tossin' distance" of their blacksmith shop.[15]

Heck Thomas continued to scout the gang's old hideouts along the Cimarron. His eldest son, Albert, who had finished school in Georgia the year before and had come to the territory to ride in his father's posses, accompanied him. On Saturday, August 22, they "stumbled on news" that "Bill Doolin, alias Tom Wilson, alias God" and two others (identified as Dynamite Dick and Little Dick West, who had returned from New Mexico) had been seen south of the river in the Sac and Fox country. Sunday night, August 23, they struck camp on Dry Creek northeast of Chandler, where Deputy Rufe Cannon (who had hotly pursued the Christians after the slaying of Oklahoma City Police Chief Milt Jones) joined them.

The outlaws' appearance apparently was a ruse, for the same night, Doolin again visited his wife at Lawson. It was "rainy . . . and he stayed all night, not getting away very early," and was seen by Tom Noble as he rode down the road west, as he usually did, into the timber on Eagle Creek. Later, the Nobles watched Edith and her father load a wagon with a plow, furniture, and personal possessions. This meant a long journey. A messenger sped to Bill Dunn's ranch. A telephone call to Chandler was relayed to Thomas on Dry Creek, and Heck started immediately for the Dunn ranch with Albert and Cannon.

They "made the drive," twenty-five miles almost due north, by two o'clock in the afternoon, picked up Bill, Dal, George, and John Dunn, and met the Noble boys at sundown "beyond Lawson" with new information. Doolin had returned for his wife and child. They were waiting for darkness to make their departure. The posse moved on the town in the twilight, and Heck "crawled up close enough to watch old man Ellsworth's house with . . . field glasses."[16] Here are the *State Capital*[17] and Guthrie *Leader*[18] versions of what occurred afterward:

[Leader] Bill Doolin, the notorious desperado, is non est . . . his body was brought to the city at 1 o'clock this afternoon [August 25] overland from forty miles east . . . in charge of Heck Thomas and Tom Noble. To Deputy Thomas and posse is due the credit for ridding the country of the last dangerous member of the old Dalton gang. Doolin was quietly shot to death near his home at Lawson, in Payne county. His body, which was cleverly riddled with buckshot is . . . at Rhodes' undertaking rooms on Oklahoma avenue . . . and identification is complete.

When killed the desperado had on the same clothes that he wore in the federal jail and was armed with a six-shooter and a Winchester. During the past six weeks he had greatly decreased in weight and had allowed his auburn beard to grow. When the undertaker washed the body he found twenty buckshot wounds in the chest, four having entered the heart . . . and his left arm bears the scar of one Winchester ball.

After the body had been examined by Dr. Smith . . . it was dressed [and] placed on exhibition in the Gray Brothers building on Oklahoma avenue [where] hundreds of people viewed it . . . and speculated as to what realm the soul of Doolin had lodged in.

Two features of Doolin's make up were his dark, glassy, penetrating eyes, his thin lips and canine teeth. Doolin suffered intensely from rheumatism and his celebrated left leg was rendered almost useless by that ailment. . . .

The State Capital reporter got the true story of the killing of Bill Doolin today [August 26] from an eye witness. He was killed a few hundred feet from the Lawson postoffice, a stone building in which the postmaster, Rev. Ellsworth, runs a grocery store. . . . A wagon had loaded and was ready to take Bill and his wife and baby out of the country. Bill and Mrs. Doolin were . . . away from the house in conversation. Mrs. Doolin went to the house and Bill promised to meet her and the wagon around a certain corner. Heck Thomas, Tom Noble, John Matthews, Charlie Noble, Dell [Dal] Dunn and Bee [Bill] Dunn were hiding on one side of the path where Doolin proposed to go. He came with the rein of his fine riding horse [Scofield's bay mare] on one arm, and the other holding a Winchester. When he was within reach, the marshals cried out to him to throw up his hands. Instead of doing so he wheeled about and lifted his Winchester. At the same moment the marshals on the other side cried, "Stop; throw up your hands!" He turned in the direction of the last voices and fired with his Winchester once, and dropping it, followed up with three shots from his revolver. A volley of Winchesters from the marshals on both sides and the emptying of a double barreled shotgun razed him to the ground. . . .

The killing of Doolin lies between Heck Thomas, John Matthews and Tom Noble. It is insisted by Doolin's friends that Matthews, a part Cherokee who married Mrs. Doolin's sister, is the man who fired the shot, but Matthews has been a long time friend of Doolin's and none here believes he would turn traitor.

[LATER] Young Matthews, Bill's brother-in-law, was not even in the party and had nothing to do with the shooting. Rufus Cannon, a half-blood Cherokee, is the man who killed Doolin. It is understood that Tom Noble gave away the hiding place.

Other sensational stories were circulated but given no credence. The reticence of Heck and his deputies to say who used the shot-gun, plus the absence of bloodstains on the body when it was delivered to the morgue, started a rumor on the streets that Doolin had died a natural death and was set up against a tree and filled with buckshot to "make believe he had been killed." This was spiked by the *Cushing Herald*:[19]

Some well meaning settlers on the grapevine garlanded, ivy-clad creek banks near Lawson, in Payne county, are still quibbling and surmising about the exact way the famous W. H. Doolin came to his death. . . . Some are certain he died a natural death in his father-in-law's cellar, and that some designing persons leaned the dead Bill against a corn shock and shot the corpse so that they could claim the reward. An expert spiritual medium will be asked to state if Doolin died with his boots on, leaning against a corn shock, or if he gave up his ghost like the repented sinner on the cross and started from his reverend father-in-law's cabbage cellar, straight to Paradise.

Later, the scurrilous tale, again altered, was revived by a man named Hicks, who lived in the area and wished to discredit Heck Thomas because Thomas had once jailed him for petit larceny. Hicks swore that Doolin died of "galloping consumption"; that when the officers arrived, they made a deal with his widow for the body, promising her a share of the reward; that Doolin's body was then propped against a tree and filled with buckshot. The story was published widely and was repeated now and again through the years. Government records of the inquest and the records of firms that offered rewards prove Hicks's statement false.

In fact, Doolin bled profusely. Heck's widow, writing to Chris Madsen from Tulsa on January 19, 1939, recalled that her husband "got a wagon and a team of black mules from a farmer and brought the body to Guthrie. The wagon and mules were put on a vacant lot next to our house [at 909 East Springer]," and the mules were unhitched and tied to the rear wheels. "A little Irish woman, Maggie Murphy, who worked for me, came to me and told me to have the men take the wagon out of the lot, as the hay in the bottom was covered with blood and the mules were eating it. The hay was taken out of the wagon and burned and the wagon washed."

Albert Thomas gave this account:

> I knew Doolin while he was in jail at Guthrie. I took him tobacco and magazines on several occasions, and each time I went in the jail he would come up to the bars of the cell and ask me to let him look at my six-shooter—a Colt's .45 my father had given me. Then he would laugh heartily—a joke, of course, even if a weak one. . . .
>
> We arrived in close proximity of the home at which he was staying about 8 o'clock, and after talking over the situation, my father directed Cannon and myself to take our stand down the road about a hundred yards from the spot he and the Dunns and Nobles would guard.
>
> About an hour after we had taken our stand, Rufus and I heard two gun shots in quick succession, then a dull boom of the 8 guage shotgun that B. Dunn and my father had with them. Then everything was quiet, and we rejoined them as quickly as possible.
>
> Mrs. Doolin later told us that while she and Bill were in the house talking, they heard the dogs barking, and Bill said: "That must be those God damned Nobles. I'm going out and run them off." He then picked up his Winchester and got his horse, and went walking down the road toward my father and B. Dunn.
>
> I have never known positively which one fired the shot that killed Doolin. My father did not say, and I never asked him. I did not care to know. I do know my father risked his life many times trying to make arrests without a gun fight, and in this instance Bill Doolin had the first shots, regardless of who used the shotgun.[20]

Here, from a letter to Bill Tilghman dated September 3, 1896, is Heck's account of Doolin's death:

> We waited a long time without seeing anyone, although there was considerable stir about the store and dugout. We learned afterwards that Doolin's wife had told him some of the neighborhood boys had been spying around there too much and that someone was around that night. Finally [Doolin] came out of the stable and to our great surprise, started down the lane coming west, you know how the store is situated on the high prairie. . . . If Bill had wanted to have made his escape he could have had open roads north, south, east, northeast, or . . . northwest through the pasture to those high hills that you have seen many times. Well, he came right down the lane leading his horse by the tip ends of the bridle reins, walking slow in the bright moonlight, Winchester in both hands, well out in front of him, nearly in position to shoot. He was sure on the prowl . . . looking first to one side and then the other . . . for the neighborhood boys who had been spying on him. Then I hollowed to him and had one of the other boys on the other side of the road to hollow to him. . . . He shot at me and the bullet passed between me and B. Dunn. I had let one of the boys have my Winchester and had an old No. 8 shotgun. It was too long in the breech and I couldn't handle

it quick so he got another shot with his Winchester and as he dropped his Winchester from glancing shot, he jerked his pistol and some of the boys thought he shot once and the others twice—and about that time I got the shotgun to work and the fight was over.

Heck listed the members of his posse as "the Nobles, four of the Dunn boys, Rufe Cannon and Albert."[21]

On July 13, 1953, Harry G. Hoke, son of the Lawson farmer who furnished the mules and wagon that hauled Doolin's body to Guthrie, gave me the following eyewitness account of Doolin's death and the circumstances leading to it. It bears out Thomas' report and dispels the allegations of latter-day historians:

The town of Lawson—if you could properly call it a town—consisted of a post office and general store housed in the same building, a two story hotel, and a blacksmith shop. It had a rather odd geographical location. It was at a cross roads which divided Payne and Pawnee counties and four townships, two in Pawnee county, the other two in Payne county, Mound and Eagle. My father [John Hoke] owned the farm which was on the southwest corner of this intersection. The northwest corner was school land occupied or leased by the Ellsworth family.

The family consisted, as I recall, of three daughters Edith, Lottie and Josie and two boys, Frank and Ira. My brother, Charles, and I were about the same age as Frank and Ira, and played together every day. We were about 12 and 13. Edith was married to Bill Doolin and had a fine looking boy about two years old. Lottie was married to Tom Lawson, after whom the town was named. Lawson operated the hotel on the southeast corner of this intersection.

Ellsworth was the postmaster and storekeeper. His supplies had to be trucked in from Perry, then the nearest railroad. My father hauled many a load of freight for him on return trips from taking cotton, corn and hogs to the Perry market. Ellsworth was a respected man and got along well with the farmers of the community, always took part in local religious services, but I don't remember ever hearing him preach as some writers have claimed.

His post office and store was built close to the north side of the road and faced east. The family lived in the back of the store and they had a shed barn with sod walls and hay roof close to the road a short distance west. My father's house was directly across the road south of the Ellsworth barn, but set well back.

We had three bed rooms upstairs. Charles and I slept in the east bed room and the head of the bed was right at the window from which we could see the front yard and beyond that the Ellsworth stable.

Tom Noble was a young man who operated the blacksmith shop on my father's farm southeast of our house. He was a good mechanic and could shoe horses, repair any kind of farm equipment, make coffins, as we called them, or lay a brick or stone walk. He also liked to hunt and was an expert shot with almost any kind of gun. I hung around Tom's shop quite a bit whenever there wasn't much to be done on the farm and really served an apprenticeship to him in the blacksmithing trade, an experience valuable to me later when I took a blacksmithing course in college.

His brother Charlie also was a blacksmith and took care of the shop when Tom had to be away. But Charlie would rather fool around with race horses. He owned a neat little racer called "Little Mose" that could out run nearly everything in that part of the country. He had a courtship with Rose Dunn, a beautiful girl with coal black hair, and later married her.

The Noble boys were not killers. I mean they were not "man" killers, and the only reason they got mixed up in the Doolin affair probably was that they were looking for thrills and notoriety as well as some easy pocket money.

Tom Noble slept at our house and ate most of his meals there. He had a habit of getting up very early and would take his gun and go off down by the creek west of the farm and bring back rabbits or other small game. Tom had been hiding along the road and watching Bill Doolin go out toward his hideout and he told me that a couple of times he drew bead on Bill and would have shot him, but lost his nerve.

He and Charlie were in the posse that killed Doolin. Tom had talked to my father and suggested that he let them get a gun for him and include him in the posse so he could share in the reward, but father told them he wanted no part of it. Father did, however, know what the plans were and the time to listen for the shooting.

The afternoon before Doolin was killed, father, my brother Charles and I had gone to the timber southwest of our place to bring in a load of wood for the winter. We cut deadened trees down, trimmed off the tops and limbs, and hauled the logs home that evening. We had noticed father acting very strangely and wondered what was the matter. On the way home he told us that Doolin would be killed that night, for Doolin would never let the officers take him alive.

As soon as supper was over, father, Charles and I went upstairs and laid across the bed where we could look out across the front yard to the road and shed barn. The sun had gone down and it was beginning to get dusk but still light enough that we could see Bill Doolin and his wife putting the finishing touches to loading the wagon with their entire belongings. They were taking off for parts known only to themselves. Bill's horse was saddled. Bill was to ride out of town, and later Edith and the boy would join with the wagon at a place agreed upon. Edith pleaded with Bill to take another road rather than the one west for she suspected the officers were lying in wait for him, but Bill remarked that it would be only the Noble boys and he'd "scare hell out of them."

I can't describe the feeling we had lying there watching Bill as he started leading his horse off and carrying his Winchester, ready to fire at the least sign or noise, for we knew he wouldn't go far before being challenged by the posse crouched in the edge of my father's cane patch. Soon we heard a clear command: "Halt, Bill!" followed by a shot, then by a volley and very quickly two shots. When Marshal Heck Thomas called to Bill to halt, Bill answered with a shot in the direction from which he thought the sound came. The officers then opened fire with rifles and a shotgun loaded with buckshot. Bill fell and apparently grasped his revolver as he did and fired twice in a death grip.

At the sound of the shooting Edith let out with "Oh, my God, they have killed him" and carried on to a great extent, but neither she nor any of her family ventured to go to the scene.[22]

In a very short time, Tom and Charlie Noble came to our house and insisted that father lend them his wagon and team to haul Doolin to Guthrie to claim the reward. The wagon was still loaded with logs. Tom and Charlie threw off the logs, put the box on the wagon, threw in some straw and a wagon sheet, hitched up the team and were off with father going with them to the scene. There they loaded Bill in the wagon, covered him with the sheet and started for Guthrie. At the shed barn, the Doolin wagon was quickly unloaded by Edith and her brothers, Frank and Ira, and they started just as soon as possible to follow the dead outlaw to Guthrie and claim the body. It was about two weeks later when our wagon and team were returned. Our old dog Shep had gone with the team and he and the team apparently had been well fed. The same night, after the shooting of Doolin, another posse of marshals came to our house and said they were looking for Dynamite Dick, Doolin's partner. They went down to where Doolin was killed and some of them watched the Ellsworth house, but after a while they all came back and father gave them permission to sleep in the hay loft of our barn. . . .

I know that in writing this I am going to stir up dissention for there are persons still living who will say Bill Doolin died of TB or some other cause, and that the officers made a deal with his widow for the body. How such a tale got started is hard to figure. Dead outlaws just do not walk and lead horses down the road and fire rifles and six-shooters.

It was thought the body would have to be taken to Fort Smith for identification, but a telegram from Arkansas authorities advised "it was unnecessary to lug the dead outlaw over the country for the sake of prospective rewards . . . that proof of death would be sufficient."[23] A hearing was held before U.S. Commissioner W. W. Thomas of the First Judicial District on the jail-escape warrant issued in July and returned by Heck Thomas "showing service upon the within named William Doolin . . . killed while resisting arrest on August 24" on the border of Hell's Fringe. Witnesses were examined under oath and identified the corpse. But the Justice Department questioned both the issuance of the warrant and the

369

hearing as "proper or necessary." The matter was still being argued more than a year later, and there is no record that fees were ever paid the witnesses or commissioner.[24]

The escape and killing of Doolin gave many of the companies that had offered arrest-and-conviction rewards an opportunity to "crawl out of their propositions." Heck finally collected $1,425, which he disbursed to posse members as follows:

Charlie Noble		[$]71.00
		25.00
Tom Noble		71.00
		25.00
B. Dunn		71.00
		25.00
		10.00
Dal Dunn		71.00
		25.00
		10.00
Geo. Dunn		71.00
		25.00
		10.00
John Dunn		71.00
		25.00
		10.00
Rufus Cannon	[mileage only]	10.00
Heck Thomas		71.00
		25.00
		10.00

After paying a lawyer for "writing applications for reward," two stenographers for "typing of evidence," and the expense of a half-dozen trips to various points in Kansas, Missouri, and Arkansas, Heck was "out of pocket." On January 7, 1897, he purchased, "for the sum of $30," C. E. Scofield's bay mare, which had been in his custody since the night of Doolin's death. His report does not indicate that the buggy was ever recovered.[25]

Mrs. Doolin reached Guthrie on the night of August 25 and saw her husband's body. She thought it an "outrage" that he had been slain and threatened vengeance "on the Dunn boys [who] have been Bill's friends."[26] She named the Nobles as "her husband's betrayers."[27]

Guthrie photographer W. B. Dougherty made two pictures of Doolin, one with his body propped on the undertaker's board and stripped to the waist, the second after it had been dressed and placed in a casket. Mrs. Doolin and her brothers composed a poem about the outlaw, which they had printed post-card size, and sold it with the pictures to all who would buy them at twenty-five cents each, the "proceeds to be used for burial expenses." That cost, however, was borne by the government:[28]

Sept. 14, 1896
    Attorney General
        Washington, D. C.
    Sir:—
    I have the honor to ask authority to pay enclosed bills incident to the taking off of Bill Doolin, one of the outlaws who broke jail on the night of July 5th, 1896 and was killed by Deputy Heck Thomas and posse August 24th.
    The chief expense of embalming was necessary on account of preserving the body for the purpose of identification.

Very respectfully,
P. S. Nagle
U. S. Marshal

Encl. statement:
W. L. Rhodes, Dr. Furniture, Undertaking, Curtains and Carpets. Embalming a Specialty.

    "Funeral Expence [*sic*] of Bill Doolin"

Coffin	$25.00
Robe	6.00
Embalming	40.00
Hauling to cemetery	1.00
	$72.00

Bill Doolin's funeral was held at eight o'clock Saturday morning, August 29. Marshal Nagle

selected a spot near the heart of Summit View . . . the grave was dug during Thursday night. Mrs. Doolin and [a man named] Sam Trimble were the only mourners, and outside of the cemetery attendants and two attaches of the Marshal's office, there were few lookers-on.[29]

A twisted, rusty buggy axle was thrust into the ground for a marker. The *Stillwater Gazette*[30] commented: "Bill Doolin's left leg will get a rest." Marshal Nagle "reserved another lot near the grave for the reception of . . . Dynamite Dick."[31]

Edith Doolin filed a fifty thousand dollar damage suit against Marshal Nagle for the "unlawful death" of her husband, but it was dismissed the following February. By that time, she had married Colonel Samuel Meek of the original Oklahoma Boomers, who had homesteaded a farm at Clarkson in Payne County.[32] The Reverend Mr. Ellsworth, however, in visiting Stillwater and other area settlements, "expressed himself very emphatically" concerning the fate of his late son-in-law: "Bill didn't die an honest death, but was shot from ambush by the Dunn gang." The bitter feeling, engendered by the brothers' alleged assassination of Newcomb and Pierce, grew.

Canton[33] says the Dunns were still scouting over the Osage and in Pawnee and Payne counties, heavily armed as possemen under the direction of Heck Thomas, and that the citizens of Pawnee County were afraid of them and demanded they be arrested. Still smarting from his failure to share in the rewards for Newcomb, Pierce, and Doolin, Canton had new warrants issued on the Dunns for cattle stealing and sent word to Thomas that he thought it Thomas' duty to deliver these men to him and Sheriff Lake. Thomas, Canton claims, "ignored me absolutely," so he and Lake, with a posse of eight men, moved on Thomas' camp on the Arkansas about sixteen miles east of Pawnee, but Heck and his party had "pulled out through the Osage Hills in the direction of Skiatook in the Cherokee Nation." Canton describes how his posse followed their trail toward Pawhuska, south in the direction of Tulsa, back to the mouth of the Cimarron, and to the head of Shell Creek, where they lost it.

Thomas never concerned himself with Canton's maneuverings. The Dunns, however, blamed their plight more on Canton than on aiding the government in bringing in members of the Wild Bunch. Canton's reactivation of the old charges against them rankled Bill Dunn.

In the first week of November, G. C. Bolton, the Pawnee butcher who was Dunn's partner, was convicted of receiving stolen cattle and was sentenced to five years at Lansing. Judge Bierer fixed his appeal bond at five thousand dollars, which Bolton was "unable to give and is now in jail."[34]

On November 6, the day Bolton was sentenced, Bill Dunn rode into Pawnee. He was standing in a stairway near the butcher shop when Canton came out of a restaurant where he had been serving subpoenas. Several men were lounging on the street. The weather was chilly, and Canton had both hands in his trousers pockets as he started up the plank sidewalk. He was armed with a Colt .45, which he carried on a clip over the waistband of his trousers when he was on town duty. He did not see Dunn until the latter stepped in front of him and said: "Frank Canton, God damn you, I've got it in for you." Dunn's hand was on his revolver, and Canton "saw murder in his eyes." The deputy snatched his .45 from its clip and fired. The bullet struck Dunn in the forehead. Dunn drew his revolver, but it dropped near his body as he fell on the sidewalk, dying and working the trigger finger of his right hand.[35]

Dunn's family arrived in Ingalls with the body on Saturday, November 7. It was kept at Dr. Call's home until Sunday afternoon, then buried in the Ingalls cemetery despite objections by many citizens. The next morning, a pile of fresh hog entrails was found on the grave—an expression of their dissatisfaction.

At Pawnee, Canton's case was

> presented to the grand jury and witnesses examined. The jury was unanimous in deciding that they could not well bring an indictment, since it was plainly justifiable homicide. . . . Canton is a free as well as a brave man, but his life is in danger as he is being shadowed by the brothers of his dead enemy.[36]

Bill Dunn's brothers "threatened to burn the town and ambush Canton."[37]

On the night of November 26, "by the aid of a masked mob," G. C. Bolton escaped from the Pawnee jail.[38] Records do not show that he was ever apprehended. Dal, John, and George Dunn, many warrants on them outstanding, finally left the territory. In the spring of 1897, Canton himself left Oklahoma, joining the gold rush to Alaska.

Heck Thomas might have prevented the Canton-Dunn feud had he not left the Dunn brothers at Shell Creek, gone to Vinita, and boarded a train for Missouri. Thomas had learned from a letter observed by a friendly postmistress that George Lane, whose daring had effected the wholesale jail delivery for Doolin, was stopping with friends near Greenwood, a small town thirty miles east of Kansas City. At Kansas City, Heck contacted Chris Madsen. Being outside his jurisdiction, he asked Madsen to accompany him. On the afternoon of November 19, the two deputy marshals took the train to Greenwood, passing through the settlement so they would not be seen getting off the train, then hired a livery rig and drove to the cabin where Lane was staying a half-mile from town. It had been Lane's boast that he

> would never be taken alive, and the marshals took no chances. About dusk they left their team in the vicinity of the cabin. Thomas went to the rear door and Madsen to the front. As they rapped an old colored woman stepped to the rear door, opened it, while Lane, who had been sitting before the fire whittling, stepped to the front door, the knife

still in his hand. He was covered by the pistols of the two deputies so quickly that he offered no resistance, and his hands went obediently into the air.

Lane was brought to the city last night and this morning the necessary papers for his return to Guthrie were granted.

"I regard him as the real 'bad man' in the territory," said Marshal Thomas to a Times reporter. "His escape proved it . . . Doolin, Dynamite Dick and all of them were afraid to make the break, except Lane."

Lane once served a penitentiary sentence in Texas for horse-stealing . . . but during his youth went to school at Lincoln institute, Jefferson City. He talks well and readily, and expressed no chagrin at his arrest.

"After I broke jail," he said, "they hunted me night and day. Many times I could have reached out and touched them . . . once I swam the Cimarron river with shots whistling around my head. Another time I stepped over the sleeping bodies of the Osage chief of police and two assistants, secured a gun, and walked away. I could have killed them all as they slept.

"I knew the country better than my pursuers . . . but it was a dog's life I led. Green corn was ripe then, thank God, or I would have starved to death. Once I didn't even have that for three days."[39]

Heck reached Guthrie with his prisoner at noon on November 27. Again at noon, on December 19, he arrived in Guthrie with Charles Montgomery in custody. The escapee had been captured at Globe, Arizona.[40] Six weeks later, Heck captured Lee Killian, who jumped guard Tull and grabbed his revolver as Lane held him in the passageway. Killian had been in Colorado until

a short time ago, when he came back to his old home . . . near Joplin, Mo. and at once got into trouble as usual. Thomas found out that Killian was in the neighborhood, and after he had him fully located, quietly walked in on him Saturday [January 30] and brought him back to Guthrie yesterday.[41]

On July 5, the anniversary date of the looting of the U.S. jail, James F. Black was arrested at Ottumwa, Iowa, and returned to Oklahoma by Nagle's deputies.[42] Henry Irwin remained at liberty until May 29, 1899, when he was "taken in Woods county . . . on the farm of a man named Smith with whom he had engaged to work the summer."[43] After eluding officers seven years, Walter McLain was captured on October 29, 1903, by Deputy Marshal Wiley Haines in the Osage Nation.[44] Nix, Jones, Phillips, and Crittenden were never apprehended.

By early summer, 1897, the cause of law and order in Oklahoma again had bogged down in a territorial political hassle.

XXV Populists, Goldbugs, and Pie Hunters

AFTER HIS INAUGURATION, in March, 1893, President Grover Cleveland lost little time in naming a Democratic governor of Oklahoma and making a nearly clean sweep of all lesser Republican appointees. In turn, the political storm of 1896, which swept Republican William McKinley into the White House, resulted in the replacement of Democratic officeholders in Oklahoma by Republican personnel. Democrats and Populists, however, fared not badly.

The economic distress that plagued the nation had put Oklahoma democracy in a hard way and had played into the hands of the People's party. The Populists refused to believe that low farm prices were primarily the result of a huge crop-production increase in the fast-populating Middle West since the Civil War. They were opposed to the federal government's redeeming in gold the bonds and notes that were issued to finance the Union's war machine, and they believed the way to cure a sick commerce was to increase the amount of money in circulation.

As the situation worsened, the Populists' inflationary ideas appealed to more and more people. In fact, the People's party candidate for president in 1892 received more than one-tenth of the total votes cast and drew so heavily from normally Republican states that Cleveland was able to defeat Benjamin Harrison. At the same time, the Populists won control of the state governments of Kansas, Colorado, Idaho, and Nevada, plus ten seats in the U.S. House of Representatives and five in the Senate. With Kansas in Populist hands and fifty thousand votes cast for the party across Red River in Texas, Populism was the political faith of many new settlers who secured lands in Oklahoma during the runs of 1892–93. By 1894, the party had captured a number of county governments in the territory and held the balance of power in the legislature.

The Populists declared that Oklahoma farmers were under a hopeless mortgage and should be given free homes. All land except platted city lots had to be proved up to obtain a patent. This required a registration fee, improvements on the land, and residence six months out of the year for five years (with a two-year credit for Union army veterans) or living on the land fourteen months and paying it off at $1.25 per acre, which amounted to $200 for a quarter-section. Delegate Flynn, however, had been preaching the free-homes issue for a year and had presented such a measure in Congress. The Populists also demanded free and unlimited coinage of silver, protection for school-land lessees, and a graduated service pension.

At the opening of the 1896 campaign, the more conservative Populists and the strong radical faction of Democrats (who already had accepted many of the Populist proposals as elements in their programs and platform) laid plans to fuse the two parties behind a radical candidate for president. The nomination of William Jennings Bryan after his historic cross-of-gold speech at Chicago provided the vehicle. The Populists nominated as territorial delegate to Congress James Y. Callahan, a Methodist minister from Kingfisher County. The fusionists won again in the Democratic territorial convention at El Reno, the Democrats accepting Callahan as their candidate after a spirited fight.[1] Thus their forces were united behind Bryan and free silver.

Callahan sought to take the free-homes issue away from Flynn, arguing that Bryan of Nebraska would be more favorable to the issue than McKinley, the candidate of the hated goldbugs. Even so, the popular Flynn almost eked out a victory, receiving 26,267 votes to 27,435 for Callahan.[2] The fusion forces carried sixteen counties, the Republicans led in seven. This combination also elected a Populist-Democratic majority in the fourth legislative assembly (1897–99).

Callahan's efforts in Congress came to naught. He soon realized that the cards were stacked against anything proposed or sponsored by a Populist. When election time arrived again in 1898, he was back in Oklahoma doing his bit for the Populist cause. But the Populists nominated a man named Hankins, the Democrats chose Judge Keaton as their standard-bearer, and Flynn returned to regain his place for the Republicans. Flynn was the winner by 9,368 votes,[3] and it was the beginning of Populism's ebb tide in the territory. Populists and Democrats fused again in 1900. This time, voters gave Flynn a 3,139-vote plurality,[4] Flynn secured passage of the free-homes legislation sought by the settlers, and the People's party ceased to be a dominant factor in Oklahoma politics.

Republicans split on the presidential issue in 1896. Flynn wanted the territorial delegation pledged to Thomas B. Reed of Maine, who was elected speaker of the House in 1899 and later assisted Flynn with the free-homes bill. But the carpetbag faction of the party decided William McKinley looked like the winner, and Cassius M. Barnes sought to pledge the delegation to him. The six delegates to the Republican National Convention in St. Louis went unpledged but in agreement on a platform plank for free homes and the appointment of only bona fide residents to federal jobs in the territory. Thus Barnes put himself in the position of being the McKinley leader, and soon after his inauguration on March 4, 1897, McKinley did the expected and named Barnes the new Oklahoma governor.[5]

A native of Livingston County, New York, Barnes early in life went with his parents to Michigan, where he was educated in the public schools and Wesleyan Seminary at Albion. He took up telegraphy and made his debut at Leavenworth, Kansas, at age fifteen. He volunteered at the start of the Civil War, serving in various capacities in the Engineering Corps, Quartermaster's Department, and Telegraphic Corps. After the war, he settled at Little Rock, Arkansas, where he served on the city council and was regarded as a man of high executive ability. In 1876, Barnes removed to Fort Smith as chief deputy marshal for the court of Judge Isaac C. Parker, a position he held until 1886. During these years, he enjoyed immediate political contact with the Clayton family and through the influence of Powell Clayton was appointed receiver of the government land office at Guthrie in 1890. This position he held four years, during which time he studied law and was admitted to practice in 1893. He was let out during the Renfrow administration but was elected from the Fourteenth District to the lower house of the legislature, where he became speaker. He was serving a second term as a member of the fourth legislative assembly from the Seventeenth District when he was appointed governor by McKinley.[6]

William M. ("Silent Bill") Jenkins was the "original McKinley man" at the Minneapolis convention that renominated Benjamin Harrison for president in 1892. A native of Alliance, Ohio, in Stark County near Canton, McKinley's home, he was educated in the Alliance public schools and at Mount Union College. While teaching school in Stark County (1876–78), he studied law; in 1880, he moved to Shelby County, Iowa, where he was admitted to the bar, and in 1884, he established residence as a young attorney at Arkansas City, Kansas. He was an ardent Republican and his faith in McKinley was absolute, even when McKinley was in Congress and building a reputation as a strong tariff advocate. With the opening of the Cherokee Outlet, Jenkins staked a claim in Kay County southeast of Newkirk, where he experienced the usual hardships of the homesteader. But he "kept close political touch," and when McKinley moved into the White House, Jenkins asked for an appointment. In June, 1897, he succeeded Thomas J. Lowe as secretary of the territory.[7]

Although the President generally carried out the wishes of Governor Barnes, Flynn, and other Republican leaders in selecting territorial personnel, he made the Department of Justice his own affair. Neither he nor Joseph McKenna, whom he named attorney general to succeed Judson Harmon, received any objections when they decided to retain Caleb R. Brooks as U.S. district attorney for Oklahoma.

On the other hand, both men were "practically inundated" with telegrams and letters from all sections of the territory urging a clean sweep of the judiciary for the broad reason that these offices should be delivered to the party which had come into power regardless of the tenure of the Democratic judges. Although "thoroughly of the idea that, if there is to be any Republican party in the territory in the future, federal patronage must be disposed of on the upbuilding of the party and promoting harmony in its ranks," McKinley held to the rule adopted by his administration to allow federal judges appointed under Cleveland to hold office four years. On July 6, Attorney General McKenna told the *Oklahoma State Capital's* Washington correspondent that such was the intention of his department and that it would be

> carried out rigidly. The only way Republicans will be appointed to these positions prior to the expiration of the terms of the incumbents is in the advent that charges are preferred against them as to their ability to fill the office, or dishonesty in connection therewith. . . . I know of no reason why Judge Dale should not be allowed to serve until the 11th day of September next. The same is true of the associate justices, A. G. C. Bierer, of Perry, January 16, 1898; Justice John L. McAtee, of Kingfisher, February 15, 1898; Justice John C. Tarsney, El Reno, May 15, 1900, and James R. Keaton, Oklahoma City, February 10, 1901. . . .
>
> The candidates who have filed papers at the justice department for the Oklahoma judgeships and who have spent their hard-earned cash visiting Washington to further their claims, had better go home.[8]

The position of U.S. marshal was a different story. Within a week, fourteen Republican stalwarts filed applications with the attorney general's office, and battle lines were drawn.

The most prominent contender was former Deputy Marshal Ransom Payne, who was in Washington at the behest of the John C.

Frémont National Association to act as color-bearer in the McKinley inaugural parade. He was one of the twenty-three deputy marshals, said the *Kansas City Times*,[9] who

> for twelve months constituted the sole executive force which held in check the 100,000 who participated in the memorable rush for homes in Oklahoma in 1889 . . . the first to unfold Old Glory to the breeze on the site of the capital . . . and foremost in the performance of the herculean tasks that the marshal's force was called upon to suppress riots and keep the people from "eating each other up."

The *Times* failed to mention that Payne was dismissed from the marshal's force for supplying unauthorized information about government maneuverings against territorial outlaws to "Eye-Witness," the unidentified author of *The Dalton Brothers* (1892), who bestowed so much false honor upon Payne for running the infamous gang to earth. Payne

> has not figured in Oklahoma blood and thunder since. In July, 1895, he was in trouble at Springfield, Ill., in connection with the strike at the Tudor iron works [where he was] charged with murderously assaulting a deputy marshal.[10]

Nevertheless, Payne "made his bow to the President and modestly told him that it would please him greatly to be named for the lucrative job" of marshal of Oklahoma. He "admitted there were others, but that his endorsements had the only genuine trade mark."[11] Among those other aspirants were George D. Orput, a prominent real estate man and railroad cattle agent from North Enid; former Sheriff C. H. DeFord of Oklahoma County, defeated in the November election; and former U.S. Marshal William C. Grimes.

DeFord bore the endorsement of Powell Clayton of Arkansas, now minister to Mexico, and it was announced on May 21 that he "is dead sure to be marshal . . . the appointment will be made in a few days."[12] Marshal Nagle's resignation was received at the Department of Justice on June 9. Next day, he was notified by letter that it would be accepted upon the qualification of his successor.[13]

On June 14, however, "the situation to the casual observer changes almost hourly. . . . William Grimes is on the scene and making a stiff fight by reason that he formerly held the position and filled it in every way satisfactorily and is chairman of the territorial committee. . . . But the lone star which will hover [over] the successful applicant seems to be slowly gliding midway between DeFord and Ransom Payne. Mark Hanna [the Ohio senator who secured McKinley's nomination in 1896] and Charlie Grosvenor [the statistician of

379

the McKinley campaign] are red-hot for DeFord, and the territorial referee, Governor Barnes, having endorsed him, it looks like his pull is invincible." But DeFord "is overly sanguine." Since arriving in Washington, Ransom Payne "has secured the support and endorsement of a number of prominent western senators and members of the house which he is relying upon to offset the governor's endorsement." Orput "is developing great strength," his candidacy strongly endorsed by Senator W. B. Allison of Iowa and other northern and eastern senators and he "being the one choice of President Cable of the Rock Island railroad, as well as the Santa Fe officials, together with the two express companies, the latter having properly a great interest in the marshalship. . . . Flynn has endorsed Grimes, but is in favor of Orput over DeFord."[14]

On June 19, the contest took on a new phase:

> The marshalship was this morning suspended in the air at the White House and the Gordian knot may not be severed which will let it descend to the senate for some days.[15]

DeFord's nomination "was known to have been settled, on the president's own statement, last Thursday, and its non-appearance among nominations sent into the senate caused no end of comment." A special investigation by the *State Capital* correspondent revealed that "in the last week hundreds of telegrams and letters against DeFord have been received from Oklahoma City at the department of justice. He is charged with nepotism [employing relatives as deputies], malfeasance while in office [refusing to aid deputy marshals in apprehending thieves and train robbers], and other things," all of which DeFord labeled "a lot of malicious lies . . . there is not the slightest foundation for them and the people in the territory know it." The President, "after receiving this information, ordered the nomination destroyed and will call on DeFord this week for an explanation."[16]

More telegrams poured in from Garfield County Sheriff Elzie Thralls, L. B. Sawyer, Lou Messall, Bruce Sanders, and other citizens of South Enid, all urging the President to appoint DeFord. "Coming from within three miles of Orput's home, these telegrams were in the nature of a sensation against Orput, indicating his neighbors don't want him." Orput explained that there still was a bitter war between his town and South Enid and that such could be expected. He further asserted that the "home fight" was the result of a secret agreement in which "Thralls and Sawyer are to be ap-

380

pointed to assistant marshalships, while Sanders is to be appointed clerk to the register of the United States land office at Enid, and Messall is to receive the nomination for treasurer of Garfield county, for their services to DeFord."[17] Orput did not explain his strong backing from the railroad combine.

The chief complaint against Payne "is that too many western senators have taken great interest in his case." Flynn told McKinley in a White House meeting: "We have had one of the finest republican organizations in Oklahoma that has ever been known. . . . You have it within your power to help us perfect that organization and keep it intact, but if territorial appointments are to be controlled by gentlemen living in other states then we will be compelled to do the best we can with the public dissatisfaction, local party success will be retarded and faith in the justice of the administration broken."[18]

Flynn wound up his affairs in Washington on July 2. "Before going home he made a final visit to the White House and buried his Damascus blade deep into the body of DeFord's aspirations." He again urged the appointment of Grimes: "Mr. President, I will be satisfied . . . with Orput . . . but the appointment of Orput would be a recognition of services never rendered and a repudiation of a lifelong republican worker to whom the party is indebted in Oklahoma for a great part of the success it has attained."[19]

On July 13, the *State Capital* correspondent admitted that one could no longer

> predict the outcome . . . lightning may strike the rod which has been elevated by Captain DeFord; it may pass over and descend upon the galvanized steel running up from room 240 of the National hotel occupied by George Orput; it may be drawn westward by the magnetism of the galvanized battery which Payne has constructed. . . . It is becoming generally believed that a dark horse stands the best show.

As the fight continued through the remaining summer months into autumn, the territorial plank in the Republican platform adopted at St. Louis that "all federal officers appointed for the territories should be selected from bona fide residents and self-government accorded as far as practicable" was called forcibly to the President's attention, as was the fact that

> during the Harrison administration four gentlemen were appointed to positions in the territory, residents of the states who were compelled by force of circumstances to resign. . . . Warren S. Lurty was from Virginia . . . his unfamiliarity with the territory and its people operated as

a serious drawback, and accordingly his resignation was tendered after a short career as marshal of less than ninety days.[20]

McKinley wished to "harmonize all factions in some satisfactory way." Since this seemed impracticable, he "dropped all names heretofore prominently connected with the race and decided to appoint a comparatively new man."[21]

Secretary Jenkins was in Washington on another matter in mid-October. McKinley instructed him to return to the territory and select a man whose escutcheon was as free from any taint of wrong-doing as possible. The President jocularly remarked that all men were fallible but that some approached more nearly the standard of infallibility than others. Jenkins proceeded home, returned on October 23, and presented the name of Canada H. Thompson.

Thompson, a native of Henry County, Iowa, had come to Oklahoma at the opening of the Outlet, taking land north of Enid, where he operated a one thousand-acre horse ranch. A lifelong Republican and political whip in the territory, he had canvassed the western counties in Flynn's behalf and had been instrumental in obtaining the appointment of Barnes as governor. His law-enforcement experience consisted of a term as sheriff of Marion County, Kansas, and duty as a special agent for the Rock Island Railroad. He also carried the endorsement of Henry E. Asp, Norman attorney and Republican national committeeman, and of Governor Barnes's newly appointed attorney general for the territory, Harper S. Cunningham.

Here was the "balance" sought by the President, who, weary over the long wrangle, "decided to bring it to an end then and there." He sent for Attorney General McKenna, but "before McKenna had an opportunity to speak his mind, informed him that he had decided on Thompson." McKenna "interposed no objection," and the President informed Asp and Cunningham that "Thompson is appointed Marshal of Oklahoma Territory."[22]

Five months had elapsed since Marshal Nagle tendered his resignation. During that time, his office had to contend with a new bandit gang led by Dynamite Dick Clifton and Little Dick West.

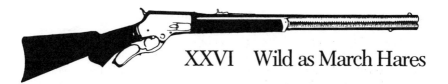

XXVI   Wild as March Hares

FOR SEVERAL WEEKS AFTER THE KILLING of Bill Doolin, Dynamite Dick and Little Dick West hid out on the Deep Fork of the Canadian in the Creek Nation while the hue and cry of the posses that hunted them died along the Cimarron. In mid-October, 1896, they drifted back to the Sac and Fox Reservation. At nine o'clock Saturday night, October 17, they rode into Carney, a small town ten miles northwest of Chandler.

There was a traveling show in town, the Seibert Family, which most of the residents were attending. The outlaws entered the store of B. Fouts and asked for some tobacco. As Fouts turned to hand it to them, he found himself looking into the muzzle of Dynamite Dick's Colt six-shooter. "Hands up!" ordered Clifton. Fouts complied while the outlaw cleaned out the cash drawer. A man named Friend, who had just closed his store and put the day's sales in his pockets, came in and was covered by Little Dick West. Both merchants were "lined up," and Friend was relieved of one hundred fifty dollars. Next, the robbers sacked up four suits of clothes, two pairs of shoes, three blankets, a quantity of canned goods, and other items. "At this moment Pearson, the proprietor of the Carney hotel, Pearson's son and John Miles came in and were each in turn lined up and searched. Then the five men were taken a quarter mile outside of town and turned loose with the injunction not to follow." At midnight, four men on lathered mounts "woke up the liveryman at Mulhall and made him give them a relay of horses. They are supposed to be the same gang who had ridden the twenty miles in three hours . . . the other two were probably on guard outside of Carney with the horses and were not seen."[1]

While officers searched northern Logan and western Payne counties, the gang doubled back into Lincoln County. On the afternoon of October 30, they "held up and looted" the Sac and Fox Agency, a village of about thirty brick, frame, and log structures nestled in the big bend of the Deep Fork five miles south of present-day Stroud. They first rode to the agent's office, presumably to demand the $46,000 in greenbacks to be paid as annuity to the Indians the next week. The agent was absent and the office closed. So the robbers went to the store of Miss Fannie Whistler, covered the inmates and took $486 and valuable papers from the safe . . . then held up J. W. Miffit's place and got $59 and a gold watch. Chief Keokuk's place was robbed of $80 and $3,000 worth of notes. The boldness of the robbers frightened the traders and people so badly they were unable to resist. After robbing Keokuk's place the bandits rushed through the grounds of the government Indian school, firing their weapons. Two of the robbers [Dynamite Dick and West] were recognised as having been in the Carney hold up.[2]

Heck Thomas and posse picked up their trail in the Creek Nation. Twenty miles west of Sapulpa, they

> ran across Dynamite Dick and two others leading their horses in a ravine. They opened fire and a pitched battle ensued. The outlaws having the worst of it took flight, leaving behind a team of mules, a riding horse and their baggage. . . . Darkness coming on, the marshals were unable to pursue them and had to be satisfied with the team, saddle horse and a portion of the loot sacked from Carney and the Indian agency.[3]

In the baggage, Heck found a marriage license issued to Bob Reagin and a girl living near Chandler. Reagin started for Arkansas but decided to return for his bride. Heck and Bill Tilghman were "on deck," however, and arrested him after "a protracted meeting." Reagin implicated "two of the Doolin gang" and John Spurgeon, "a tough character and seemingly proud of his reputation," whom Heck had "suspected of being a member of the notorious Bill Cook gang that robbed the bank at Chandler three years before." Reagin and Spurgeon were "bound over for trial on the agency robbery by Commissioner Galbraith at Shawnee," and Thomas and Tilghman "split a $700 reward for their capture."[4] Dynamite Dick and West remained in hiding in the Creek Nation. When next heard from, in June, 1897, they were accompanied by two pairs of brothers, Morris and Pat O'Malley of Tecumseh and Al and Frank Jennings.

Al and Frank were the younger sons of Judge J. D. F. Jennings, who had gained distinction on many frontiers before coming to Oklahoma. Born in Tazewell County, Virginia, in 1831 and educated at Emory and Henry College, Judge Jennings was for several years a circuit rider for the Methodist Episcopal church. He also studied medicine and was commissioned a surgeon with the Forty-first Virginia infantry during the Civil War. In 1865, he moved his family to Marion, Illinois, where he was a Methodist minister and physician and studied law. In 1872, he was elected to a two-year term as Williamson County attorney. In 1874, he started back to his old Virginia home because of his wife's poor health. She died en route in Adams County, Ohio, and he abandoned the journey. He then located at Manchester, Ohio, where he practiced law until 1880, then practiced at Appleton City in St. Clair County, Missouri, until 1884. In that year he became one of the pioneer settlers of Comanche County, Kansas, where he established himself as a lawyer at Coldwater, served two terms as probate judge, and married Miss Hattie Holt. In 1888, he moved to Baca County, Colorado, practicing law at Trinidad until April, 1889, when he participated in the Oklahoma land rush and secured a claim in Harrison Township seven miles southeast of Kingfisher. Three of his five children by his first marriage—Edward E., John, and Mary Dell—accompanied him. A third son, Frank E., secured the position of deputy clerk in the district court at Denver. The daughter married Austin Eggleson at Kingfisher. Ed and John had learned enough law in their father's office to pass bar examinations and set up practice in El Reno. Alphonso J., who had graduated from the law department of the West Virginia state university and military academy, soon joined Ed and John. In 1892, Al was elected prosecuting attorney of Canadian County.[5]

All the Jenningses were active in Democratic politics. Judge Jennings, a Knight Templar Mason and staunch supporter of Grover Cleveland, was a delegate to territorial and other conventions. With the opening of the Cherokee Outlet, Governor Renfrow appointed him the first probate judge of Woodward County. In the summer of 1894, Ed and John moved their law practice to Woodward, then the "wildest and wooliest cow town on the range."[6]

The shipping point for cattle from the western part of the territory, Woodward was described as "about like Dodge City . . . on a little milder scale," where the first town ordinance, according to one of its founders, admonished its five hundred inhabitants: "If you must shoot, shoot straight upward." The hitchracks along its crooked old main street and its board sidewalks were always lined with the saddle horses of cowboys, buggies, and occasionally a homeseeker's covered wagon. The leading business establishments, in mostly false-fronted frame buildings, consisted of restaurants, dry-goods and general stores, a Chinese laundry, two banks, and twenty-three saloons, complete with mahogany and walnut bars, lewd paintings, and female faro dealers, with the focus on the Cattle King Hotel.

One of Woodward's most prominent figures was Jack Love. Love was born in San Augustine, Texas, on June 6, 1857, and was educated at the Sam Houston Normal in Huntsville. He taught school two terms and saw extended service as a cowboy on the great western ranches of that state before coming to Oklahoma City in 1889 and served as a municipal councilman. "Six feet four inches in height and weighing two hundred and seventy-five pounds with no surplus flesh . . . handsome enough to have served as a model for a Greek sculptor and blessed with a mentality and personality that many more pretentious men might well have envied," Love was Governor Renfrow's choice as sheriff of Woodward County when it was organized. As deputy marshal under Nix, "his firmness and unquestionable courage had a very quieting effect and, more than any other single personal influence, helped to tame northwestern Oklahoma." In 1894, he was an unsuccessful candidate for representative against George Bradfield, the Republican nominee, who defeated him by only two votes. He was unmarried and engaged in the stock business, owning a large number of horses.[7]

Jack Love's intimate friend was Temple Houston, the picturesque and fiery gun-lawyer son of General Sam Houston, first president of the Republic of Texas and idol of the Lone Star State. Educated in philosophy and law at Baylor University, Temple was admitted to the Texas bar in 1878, when he was only nineteen, and was elected Brazoria County attorney before he was twenty-one. His masterful handling of criminal cases attracted such attention that, when the Texas Legislature created the Panhandle (Jumbo) Judicial District of thirty-two counties in 1881, he was appointed its first district attorney. Mobeetie and Old Tascosa were supply centers for the big cattle ranches and meccas for gamblers, cutthroats, and thieves, and Houston often rode in the posses that captured the badmen he later sent to prison. In 1884, he was elected to the Texas State Senate from his district, almost by acclamation. Texas' most powerful politicians thought he should become governor, but Houston belonged to the wide-open spaces of the frontier. The Panhandle was settling up; the opening of the Cherokee Outlet in Oklahoma offered the life he preferred. His second term as senator having ended, he moved his family to Woodward to form a law partnership with Robert Ray, then register of the federal land office, and achieve leadership in political circles of the rapidly developing territory.

At age thirty-four, Houston enjoyed an extensive practice and was one of the most eloquent orators in the Southwest. He stood six feet, was lean hipped and erect, sharp gray eyes snapping beneath jutting brows, with clean-cut jaw and chin and auburn hair flowing to his shoulders. His eccentric dress added glamor to his legend. He wore a beautiful white hat, a Prince Albert coat under which was slung a white-handled Colt, a fancy Spanish-style vest, and satin-striped trousers that flared at the bottom over unusually small Texas riding boots of the finest kid. He spoke French and Spanish fluently, along with seven Indian tongues. He was an avid student of the Bible, Shakespeare, and the Greek scholars, and his words and acts were dramatic in the extreme. Behind his dramatics, however, lay fearlessness and the reasoning of a brilliant mind.

According to Al Jennings in *Beating Back*[8] (co-authored with Will Irwin) and his heavily fictionized autobiography, *Through the Shadows With O. Henry*,[9] brothers Ed and John were the attorneys in "every big case" that came up in the Woodward courts. Defeated in his bid for a second term as county attorney at El Reno, Al visited his father and brothers at Woodward in 1895. Ed and John were representing a cattleman named Frank Garst, who had brought in several hundred head of cattle to pasture on range held under fence by Jack Love. Garst and Love had agreed on a three thousand dollar rental fee, which Garst refused to pay when due, and Love brought suit. The Jenningses won the suit for Garst on grounds that the land still belonged to the government and therefore Love (whom Jennings calls "a gambler and disreputable character" with "a great penchant for . . . appropriating the government's property") had no right to it in the first place and was himself a trespasser. Thus the Jenningses allegedly incurred the displeasure of both Jack Love and the opposing counsel, Temple Houston. Official records are not available, but contemporary sources mention no such lawsuit or a man named Garst. The story appears to have originated with Al Jennings, and later writers have accepted it.[10]

The Jennings-Houston controversy apparently began on October 8, 1895, with a case being tried in Justice of the Peace Williams' court involving some young men charged with stealing a keg of beer from a Santa Fe freight car. Houston, the railroad company's attorney appeared with County Attorney B. B. Smith for the prosecution, and the firm of Jennings & Jennings appeared for the defense. Houston and Ed Jennings "locked horns" over a number of minor points. When Houston asked a witness a question, Ed objected, and an argument followed. Temple accused Jennings of being "grossly ignorant of the law." Jennings' temper flared. Slamming his fist on the table, he shouted, "You're a damned liar!" and lurched at Houston. Temple Houston's life was often tempestuous, but in his monumental dignity, he had never allowed another man to lay a hand on him in anger. "Guns were brought to view . . . but the prompt interference of bystanders prevented their use then and there."[11]

Al Jennings says in his books he was assisting in the case and that it was he, not Ed, who called Houston a liar. "He replied by calling me another liar, then jumped at me . . . Ed came between us and slapped his face." Houston was bursting with rage, but "before he could draw his forty-five, I had mine leveled at him. . . . Somebody dashed the six-shooter from my hand," Houston was "surrounded and disarmed," and the court adjourned in confusion. Feeling ran high. Everybody in Woodward knew about the bad blood between Love and Houston and the Jennings brothers and "expected a shooting before morning." At Ed's office, Judge Jennings reproached his sons for their hot tempers and explained how they had put him "in a ticklish position." Al agreed to apologize to Houston the next morning. Meanwhile, "home was the only place for a Jennings." Ed and John remained to wind up affairs at the office; Al went home with his father and "lay down to wait for them." It was a hot night and he fell asleep. A short time later, he was awakened by someone calling from outside: "Judge! Get up quick! Your boys are killed!" Al states in "The Life Story of Al Jennings":[12]

No one can imagine the sick feeling that came over me. I dressed hastily and ran out of the gate past father, where I met John, who was sorely wounded. He told me to go to Garvey's saloon, that Ed was dead.

I knelt [in the saloon] beside my brother, taking his head in my lap, and found two bullet wounds, one in the back of the head and one over the left ear, both of them ranging forward. I knew then that he had been assassinated, and all of the ambition of life went out of me. The future, which had seemed so bright to me as a young lawyer in a new country, died with my brother. There on my knees on the floor, with his head in my lap, I swore to kill the man who had murdered him.

In his books, Al claims that Ed and John were cornered in the gaming room by Love and Houston, "sneaking, unseen . . . both drunk," and were ambushed. Dispatches from Woodward on October 9 and 10 do not bear him out:[13]

Last night [October 8] about 10 o'clock, this town was aroused by a fusillade of shots in one of the principal saloons here, known as the

388

"Cabinet," and owned by Jack Garvey. Hastening there the spectators beheld Lawyer Ed Jennings weltering in blood, his brain oozing from a bullet hole in the left side of his head, his hand still clinging to a smoking revolver, half concealed by his prostrate form.

Lawyer John Jennings was fleeing up the street with one arm limp and dangling by his side from which the blood poured in streams.

Lawyer Temple Houston and ex-Sheriff Jack Love were on their way to the sheriff's office to surrender their persons to his custody. . . .

Late in the evening, Houston, accompanied by his friend ex-Sheriff Love, went to the Cabinet saloon, a political resort, and as they were taking a drink the Jennings brothers came in and the quarrel was renewed. Very few words passed before all drew their pistols, including Love, who is a game frontiersman and a dead shot. All engaged in a running and dodging fight except Houston. The huge man stood up straight and emptied his revolver without twitching a muscle. At first fire Ed Jennings fell dead on the floor with his brains oozing out. As John Jennings was raising his arm to shoot it was pierced by a bullet and the gun fell to the floor. He was shot again through the body but was able to run out of the saloon and up the street for 200 feet where he fainted from loss of blood. He is now resting easy with every chance for recovering.

Neither Love nor Houston were wounded, although several bullets passed through their clothes and hats.

An inquest by Coroner J. M. Workman was held at once. The jury was composed of the following well known citizens: H. C. Thompson, R. B. Clark, James Hunter, James Haybaugh, Paul McCloud, Joe Hedrick.

The verdict in effect rendered was: Deceased came to his death as a result of a shooting affair engaged in by Temple Houston, J. E. Love and John Jennings.

The trouble is confined to the parties interested. Love and Houston were bound over in the sum of $5,000 each, which they gave and were released. The matter will be settled in the courts and it is thought that no further serious trouble will result.

The case of *The Territory of Oklahoma* v. *Temple Houston and J. E. Love* resulted in a verdict of not guilty on grounds of self-defense, competent witnesses testifying that Ed Jennings had reached for his gun first, and the mitigating circumstance that Ed had been shot through the head from a range at which it would appear that John, who was behind him, must have fired the fatal shot. "Al Jennings grew so bitter . . . that he left the court-room, cursing the courts and threatening vengeance."[14]

In "Life Story,"[15] Al tells us that "through the perfidy of the county attorney the two men were acquitted. Then I telegraphed for my other brother, Frank, who was living at Denver, and when he arrived we arranged to avenge the murder." In *Beating Back*,[16] Al says Frank arrived "the day after we buried Ed" and their father asked if they intended to "pile a new tragedy on him." Daring not to trust themselves in Woodward, where Love and Houston would offer "continual temptation," Al and Frank saddled their horses, took what money they had, and "rode toward Southern Oklahoma . . . to establish some base from which . . . to make our raid and kill those two men. From that time forth . . . we were outlaws in spirit. The rest came as gradually and easily as sliding down hill."

Al was thirty-two, a little more than five feet tall, with a ruddy face that was tanned and sun wrinkled like a baked apple, a shock of bright auburn hair to match his temper, and nervy enough to use his six-shooter without hesitation. Frank was thirty—handsome, stalwart, powerful—and, with either gun or fist, considered an efficient fighter. They rode around for months, "hunting" Houston but never meeting him. They remembered, perhaps, what a quick and accurate shot he was, and Temple Houston made not the least effort to avoid them. The hunting could not have been too zealous, for they never returned to Woodward and generally put in an appearance where Houston wasn't. As Burton Rascoe[17] aptly put it: "No use cluttering up the local graveyard with Jenningses."

Shortly after his traumatic experience at Woodward, Judge Jennings moved to Shawnee, where he continued in the practice of law. In the Populist victory of 1896, because of his wisdom and capability, he was elected probate judge of Pottawatomie County and moved to Tecumseh. By reelection in 1898, he held the office four years, retiring in 1901 and moving to Slater, Missouri, where he died in June, 1903.[18]

John Jennings recovered from his wounds and was probate clerk for his father at Tecumseh. Al and Frank were seen often in the area, "consorting with hard characters," and although their reputations were "bad" among the officers, "there were no warrants for them."[19] They "palled around" with the O'Malley brothers, whom Rascoe calls "a couple of Tecumseh plow-pushers." Actually, Morris O'Malley had served as deputy marshal and Pat as posseman under Nix in 1894 and 1895, when Morris was discharged, on orders from the Justice Department, for padding accounts.[20] Al Jennings characterized them as "two wild Irish boys, who knew nothing but fight and didn't care a damn for anything else."

There are many versions of how and where the quartet joined

Little Dick West, none of which include Dynamite Dick Clifton.[21] In *Beating Back*,[22] Al indicates the idea of the "Jennings Gang" per se was nurtured on the Spike S Ranch of John Harless, near the junction of Snake and Duck creeks in the Creek Nation, where he and Frank found employment after the Woodward affair. "Harless was a cattleman with a habit of rustling other people's livestock," and the Spike S was "a rendezvous for . . . aristocrats in the territorial underworld. . . . Harless had put up a big red barn which was a landmark. Three or four miles south lay a little mountain range, wooded with chestnut and cedar . . . to the east a heavy thicket covered the bottoms of Duck Creek. Once in the mountains, you could laugh at the marshals, and no man who wasn't an outlaw or a friend dared enter the thicket."

It may be that the first exploit of the Jenningses and the O'Malleys as a unit was a wholesale raid in southern Pottawatomie County on Saturday and Sunday nights, June 5 and 6, 1897. They first

> visited Andrew Morrison's general store at Violet Springs, held up the proprietor for several hundred dollars and robbed the store of a large quantity of goods. At Avoca they looted the large store of R. Perkins, Sunday night, securing a large quantity of plunder, and the same evening held up and robbed a party of freighters, securing $225. They next visited the noted Corner saloon, at the junction of Oklahoma, the Chickasaw and Seminole countries, and held up the large crowd there, robbing every man, as well as the till of the saloon, and securing a quantity of whiskey, which they took with them into the thick woods of the Seminole country.[23]

In "Life Story,"[24] Al mentions being in the country at the time, visiting his father at Tecumseh. "He told me I was accused of robbery and was greatly distressed, but I convinced him of my innocence." Judge Jennings insisted that Al face his accusers, but "I had to tell him that it would be impossible for me to prove an alibi. We had some heated words and I rode away again . . . to the Spike S ranch. These men [Dynamite Dick and West?] had long wanted my brother and myself to join them, and now they knew we were with them. We went as wild as March hares."

Of a certainty, by mid-July, veteran U.S. Deputy Marshals James F. (Bud) Ledbetter and Paden Tolbert of Muskogee were on the trail of "Al Jennings and other parties . . . who were going about in the Northern District of the Indian Territory under assumed names." According to later trial testimony by Ledbetter: "We made numerous inquiries, but never did get information of their staying at one place over three or four days at a time, and that was at the mouth of Little Spavinaw."²⁵

Ledbetter and Tolbert were hunting Al and Dynamite Dick for robbery of the post office at Foyil, Cherokee Nation, ten miles northeast of Claremore, which Al described as "only an experimental job." Someone had brought into camp a "set-screw" used for twisting the lock from a safe, and Al wanted to see how it worked. "We took seven hundred dollars just to pay expenses." Al soon would resort to the use of dynamite on safes, which was "cumbersome and dangerous."²⁶

Shortly before midnight on August 16, the southbound Santa Fe passenger train, in charge of conductor Frank Beers of Newton, Kansas, and engineer John Rain of Arkansas City, stopped at Edmond, fourteen miles north of Oklahoma City, for water. As the train left Edmond,

> three masked men climbed over the tender from the blind baggage into the cab . . . "hands up" was complied with . . . and three miles south they commanded the engine man to stop the train. From out of the grass at the side of the track four men arose and ran to the express car. Just then Conductor Beers alighted and started forward to ascertain the cause of the stop, when a couple of shots were fired at him and he was told to get back on the train. He did so. The robbers kept up a continual fire with their Winchesters and yelled to the passengers to keep out of sight. Shots from Winchesters were fired through the express car and Messenger W. H. May and Route Agent Lytle obeyed the order to open the door.
>
> Three of the bandits entered the car and ordering the expressman out, began work on the safe. Two dynamite shots were tried [but] the safe of the Wells-Fargo company resisted all attempts to blow it open, and after some time the robbers . . . bid the train crew good night and disappeared with but little, if any, valuables. It is not known in what direction the outlaws went as they laid in the grass until the train pulled out. The place where the holdup occurred was open prairie and no saddle horses were in sight.²⁷

Conductor Beers ran the train into Oklahoma City and notified the sheriff's office. "Marshal Nagle was telegraphed for at Guthrie," but, disgusted with the political hassle for his position in Washington, he had "gone home to Kingfisher." Heck Thomas received the message, and "posses from both places were soon hot on the trail of the gang."²⁸

Engineer Rain described the bandits who entered his cab as "one man six feet high, black hair and mustache, four to five days' growth [of beard], with black Prince Albert coat; one man heavy set, light hair and mustache, with light suit of clothes, weight 180 to 190 pounds; one man with dark skin and mustache and dark coat and vest with blue overalls [believed to be Frank Jennings, Dynamite Dick, and Little Dick West, respectively]." They did not hide behind the water tank and board the train when it stopped at Edmond, as most writers have indicated; conductor Beers remembered that the three "got on at Ponca City and rode as far as Edmond in the passenger coaches." Messenger May described the trio who entered the express car as "all small in stature, weighing not more than 150 pounds [believed to be Al Jennings and the O'Malleys]. No description of the seventh robber could be obtained."[29]

Heck Thomas and Santa Fe detectives examined the robbery scene at daybreak on August 17. They found the place where

> the horses belonging to the gang had been tied about a quarter of a mile east . . . the trail was easily found and it was learned from those along the route followed that there were four men in the lead followed by the other three at a distance of about five miles apart.
>
> A negro living six miles straight east from the place where the train was stopped saw the advance guard of four about 2 o'clock Tuesday morning. Another party nine miles east saw the other three at 4 o'clock riding very hard . . . toward the Kickapoo line.
>
> The posse is gaining rapidly and it is expected that the robbers will be overtaken before they clear the Kickapoo country. . . . One of the horses rode by the bandits has a deformed hoof on his left hind foot.[30]

It was the horse Dynamite Dick rode when he was trailed by Thomas on the Sac and Fox Reservation after the Guthrie jailbreak. "Tuesday night, the posse lost the trail after crossing into the Kickapoo country and were compelled to give up."[31]

Between their robberies in Lincoln County during the fall of 1896, Little Dick West found sanctuary with a Creek Indian woman on the North Canadian River across from Old Watsonville (present Dustin), and Dynamite Dick hid out around Checotah. Both "caged many free meals" at the farm of Sam Baker east of Bond Switch (now Onapa) and at the home of Willis Brooks, Baker's brother-in-law, in the Dogtown area west of Eufaula. Baker and Brooks, former residents of Cooke County, Texas, and reputed to be gunfighters, had befriended West when he was a spindle-legged waif cleaning up saloons in Decatur and had migrated to Indian Territory about the same time West came to Oklahoma Territory with Halsell. West had kept in touch with them during the years he raided with Bill Doolin. After the Edmond fiasco, the Jennings gang camped near

Baker's farm (Baker, as some authorities believe, may have been the seventh man in the robbery), while Little Dick visited his Creek girl friend on the Canadian. Within two weeks, they had plotted to hold up a train on the Missouri, Kansas & Texas Railroad.[32]

The site they selected was just below Bond Switch, twenty-seven miles southwest of Muskogee. Some ties had been stacked on the right-of-way, and the gang piled the heavy timbers on the rails and set fire to them when they heard the train approaching. The engineer had been piloting locomotives through the Nations long enough to know immediately what was in store for his train. He jerked open the throttle and raced through the obstruction, scattering ties like matchsticks all around the bewildered would-be bandits.

In *Beating Back*[33] and *Through the Shadows With O. Henry*,[34] Al Jennings provides fictionized accounts of this affair in which he garbles details from both the Bond Switch and Edmond holdups and calls it their "first robbery" which "never came off," yet in the same breath he avows the gang obtained "an enchanted treasure chest" of jewelry and six thousand dollars in currency.

The next day, Deputy Marshal Ledbetter came "poking around" the scene. All signs led to the gang's abandoned camp a short distance from Baker's house. Baker admitted having seen the outlaws. Before the marshal left, Baker agreed to notify him if they reappeared in the area.[35] On September 4, Ledbetter struck the gang's trail

> up near Checotah . . . afterwards learned they had been at Barren Fork, a station on the Pittsburg & Gulf, and hunted around there two, three or four days. I next got information they were in the Concharty Mountains. That was about the last of September. I was out there four, five or six days—I don't remember—but I returned to Muskogee on the 2d of October. The evening I got back, I noticed in the papers that they had held up the train at Chickasha.[36]

The gang had struck southwest across the Seminole and Pottawatomie lands into the Chickasaw Nation.

En route, they allegedly decided to burglarize the Santa Fe station at Purcell, a likely place to loot since all express matter was transferred at this point. A night watchman making his rounds spotted some men hiding in the yards. As he approached, they slipped from sight under a platform, but he "had seen their guns and heard the jingle of their spurs" and reported to the agent. The agent notified the city marshal, who rushed to the station with an armed posse, but the men had vanished in the darkness. A few days later, Bill Tilghman supposedly received a report that the gang was planning to rob the bank at Minco and wired President Campbell. Campbell organized a group of citizens to guard the bank day and night. Pat O'Malley was sent in to reconnoiter, saw that a robbery attempt was impractical, and the plan was abandoned. Down to their last penny, their clothing tattered, and eating only such meals as they could obtain from scattered farm houses, "the band became desperate."[37]

During this time, Al Jennings would have us believe,[38] he and Frank—well supplied with loot obtained in train robberies and "$35,000 additional" from a bank holdup in West Texas—boarded a tramp freighter at Galveston and "pulled out without clearance papers for Trujillo, Honduras." There they struck up an acquaintance with William Sydney Porter, self-exiled to beat a bank embezzlement charge at Austin, Texas, and with him embarked on a lengthy spree around the Horn in another boat. They took in most of the South American ports, reached San Francisco, doubled back to Mexico City, and recrossed the Texas border "in August, 1897 . . . practically broke." Al proposed that they rob a bank; Porter declined, said good-by, and went home to face the embezzlement charge. Al and Frank "took the train from San Antonio to Oklahoma," where they "met the old crowd at last," two at the Spike S, the others "at a ranch near Shawnee."

The expedition, according to Al, consumed six months. His movements in 1897 until the last week of September are accounted for. Porter became a fugitive in Honduras in July, 1895, where he remained until January, 1897, when, because of his wife's illness, he took a ship back to New Orleans and wired his father-in-law for twenty-five dollars to pay his rail fare to Austin. His two-thousand-dollar bond had been forfeited; his wife died on Sunday evening, July 25; he was convicted at Austin in February, 1898, and on April 25 became Federal Prisoner No. 30664 at the Columbus, Ohio, penitentiary, where he began the writing that brought him world fame under the pen name O. Henry.[39]

The Jennings gang had camped on the Canadian north of Minco, not to rob the Minco bank, but to "spy out" the twenty-some miles of track along which the southbound Rock Island passenger train would pass shortly after eleven o'clock on the morning of October 1, 1897. Al knew, or had been informed, that a consignment of $90,000 in coin would be expressed through the territory on the railroad that day to Fort Worth banks, and the gang had pulled out of the Muskogee area and the reach of Bud Ledbetter with this as their objective. Al also knew that guards were placed on trains at El Reno and run through to Chickasha at night, "but no guards were carried on day trains as it was not supposed that bandits were nervy enough to rob a train in daylight."[40]

Al decided on a daylight job and selected as the site a "high prairie divide" eight miles south of Minco, "where Pocasset now stands," but "the only human signs then were the track, a section house, and a siding." Here the train could be stopped and the track watched in both directions "against a surprise." On the night of September 30, the gang moved camp to a point southeast of Minco. At 11:15 A.M. on October 1, they "rode to the section house and proceeded to business." Al had cut eye holes in an old bearskin saddle pocket and tied it over his head to conceal his red hair, a glimpse of which "would serve for an identification." The others wore handkerchief masks; "they were not so particular . . . hadn't lived in the region."[41] Some section hands at work on the track saw

> six horsemen approach, coming from the east. They rode up and covered the workmen with Winchesters and ordered them to flag the train, giving them to understand that it meant death to refuse . . . then hid in the brush alongside the track, still keeping the men covered with their rifles. When the train came to a stop one of the robbers stepped into the cab and covered the engineer and fireman, while four of his companions entered the express car, and another took charge of the passenger coaches. . . .
>
> Col. H. E. Havens, of Enid, was a passenger on the ill-fated train en route Chickasha to buy a car load of cattle, and we give his experience as follows: "I was in the chair car and when the train stopped at least fifty shots were fired accompanied by the order, 'Keep your heads inside the car!' I first walked onto the platform, but was ordered to go to my seat or suffer death. I obeyed . . . but thought I would walk through the train and escape from the rear coach which was a Pullman sleeper. When I reached the rear door of the Pullman, a masked robber pointed a Winchester at my bosom commanding me to 'sit down and be quiet or I will put a hole through your anatomy.' I contented myself then by accepting the inevitable results.
>
> "I knew, or surmised, that the robbers were after the money in the express car. . . . They dynamited the safe and the blast shook the whole train and shattered the car. After the first shot the passengers were numb with fear. Twenty minutes later another blast of dynamite exploded. I thought it much stronger than the first shot, but it seems the safe withstood both blasts and the express robbery failed.
>
> "I don't know all that transpired as every time I stuck my head out of the car window I was shot at. . . . I don't believe they meant to kill me, but the bullets whistled too close for me to mistake the desperate intention of the robbers. After blowing up the express safe proved a failure

they entered the mail car and rifled the registered mail. . . . After they got through with the express and mail, they ordered everybody to turn out on the west side of the track alongside a barbed wire fence. . . ." Wayland Wood, of Winfield, Kansas, gives an interesting description of the way the outlaws made the passengers get out of the cars. . . . A man appeared at each end of the car he [Wood] was in and commanded that the people all march out through the front door. While the man near the front door stood up on a seat with a revolver in each hand, the man behind drove them out in the aisle and would rush them along by here and there poking a man in the ribs with his gun. Outside they were all lined up. There were three coaches on the train, and perhaps 115 persons. Twenty of these were women. This made the line quite a long one. . . . While the balance of the outlaws held the crowd covered with their guns, one of them took a leather horse feed bag and made the people dump their valuables into it. Mr. Wood says when his turn came he brought his money out and the outlaw knocked it with his gun into the bag. He had his watch in his vest pocket, with the chain hanging out without being attached to the button hole. He gave it a quick jerk and dropped it inside his pants, his vest being open, and so got it out of sight and saved it.

The outlaws secured about $400, besides several diamond pins and studs. Conductor Dacy was one of the heavy losers. At the alarm the conductor threw his fine gold watch in a coal scuttle. When asked for his time-piece he said he had none. The outlaws knew better and at the point of a revolver, he hurriedly produced the watch. The passengers, women and children excepted, were treated very roughly. . . .

Jim Wright of Minco was the only man wounded. He showed a disposition to refuse to honor the orders of the bandits, and they proved to his satisfaction that his bravery was ill-advised by shooting a part of his ear off.

At one time while the robbery was in progress, the mask fell off the face of the leader. Conductor Dacy saw his features briefly and recognized him as Al Jennings.

The amount they got from the mail car, if any, is not known . . . but it is believed that the brigands received very meagre pay for the desperate chances they took.

It was certainly the boldest holdup in broad daylight ever attempted in history. . . .

The outlaws departed in an easterly direction and had two hours ahead of any pursuit. . . . A large posse from Chickasha is following them closely, while posses from other points that could be reached by telegraph are engaged in an effort to surround the gang.[42]

Marshal Nagle wired Deputy Frank Cochran at Oklahoma City to proceed to Purcell and join Marshal Stowe's posse in belief that the gang would "make a beeline down Walnut Creek and cross the

397

Canadian near Lexington." A special train from Guthrie, carrying a dozen armed men with horses, in charge of Heck Thomas and Tilghman, was transferred at Oklahoma City to the Choctaw line for Shawnee to intercept the gang in the Pottawatomie country. A reward of eight hundred dollars was offered for the arrest and conviction of each robber—five hundred dollars from the Rock Island Railroad and three hundred dollars from the American Express Company. Officers watched all roads and bridges day and night but found no trace of the outlaws.[43]

At Walnut Creek, the gang doubled back, rode west through an uninhabited part of the Wichita Reservation, then circled north, and took refuge at the home of a friendly farmer near El Reno, where they divided the loot and rested. In mid-October, when the pursuit had cooled, they drifted northeast to an old Dalton gang dugout on Cottonwood Creek southwest of Guthrie. Their garments were thin, and the weather turned bitterly cold as, riding at night and lying in secluded camps during the day, they wandered on east below the Cimarron toward the Creek Nation. Shortly after midnight on October 29, they reached the little town of Cushing. About two o'clock in the morning, Lee Nutter was

awakened from his peaceful repose by someone rapping at his bedroom window, which is at the rear of the mercantile establishment of Crozier & Nutter, and calling Lee by name, requested that he get up and wait on them as they wished to purchase funeral apparel for someone who had died somewhere in the country. Mr. Nutter unsuspectingly arose, and on opening the door was startled by the gruff demand of "hands up," and a large revolver thrust into his face. Three robbers then walked into the store and demanded the money. Mr. Nutter, seeing that resistance against such odds was useless, promptly acceded to their request. He opened the safe which contained no money, as he had very fortunately bought checks amounting to $325 that day, and had sent them to Guthrie. The outlaws would not believe Lee and made severe threats against him until they were shown the entry which had been made in the day book. They then rifled the tills, and Mr. Nutter's pockets, getting about $15 in all. Then they went into Mr. Nutter's bedroom, searched his bed thoroughly for money, took a large revolver which was under his pillow, also his gold watch and a Winchester shotgun, which were in the room. Going back into the store they ordered Lee to show them the best hats, gloves, overcoats, etc., which the establishment afforded. They loaded up with these things . . . then took Lee half way to where their horses were hitched at the M. E. church, and left him, with the parting injunction that if he breathed a word of the robbery before they were well out of town they would return and finish him.[44]

Nutter saw only four of the robbers. All were "seemingly very cool, taking their time," and "without further preparation for traveling on a cold night," they rode off with a jug of whiskey, eating some stolen bananas. "It took Lee some time to warm up before the alarm could be given." However, "the identity of the four has been fully established. They are Dynamite Dick, Al and Frank Jennings, and Dick West." A posse of citizens went in pursuit but lost the trail near Kellyville, Creek Nation.[45]

The same day, Heck Thomas wired an old acquaintance, Senator James E. Hazell, of California, Missouri: If you have any friends in the banking business along the borders of Missouri or Arkansas, you can tell them I say to look out. Dynamite Dick's gang . . . is out in your direction and they are going to have money. Hazell immediately forwarded the message to Governor Lawrence V. Stephens at Jefferson City, who in turn released the report to the Missouri and Arkansas press, adding:

> I only give out this information for what it may be worth. Mr. Thomas, who wired Senator Hazell, is a reputable marshal of Oklahoma and has been after this band for several months, but up to this time has missed them. Dynamite Dick, to whom he refers, is supposed to be one of the murders of ex-Auditor Seaborn [killed in the Southwest City bank robbery]. I do not know that there is any danger, as our authorities are able to take care of these outlaws should they make their appearance in our state, but at the same time it is well for our friends in the border counties to be on the lookout until we know they have been caught and penitentiaried or hung.[46]

Heck had just returned from the hunt in Pottawatomie County and did not pursue the outlaws, whom he believed to be fleeing northeast across the Indian Nations. He remained in Guthrie for the reception of Canada H. Thompson, who was taking the reins of federal law enforcement in Oklahoma Territory.

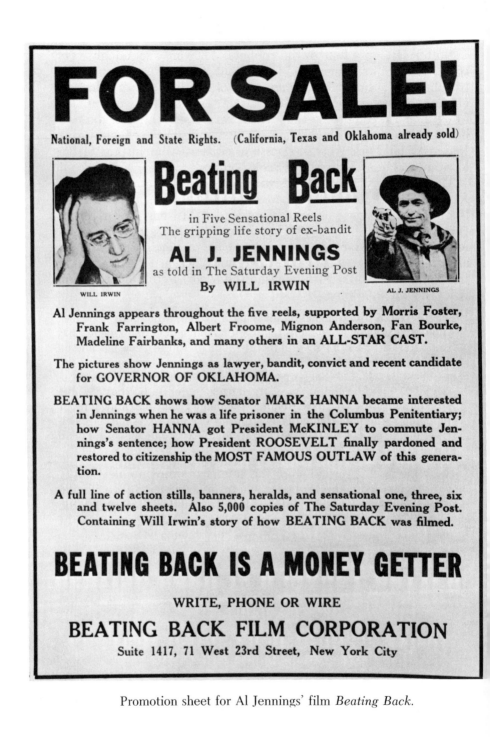

Promotion sheet for Al Jennings' film *Beating Back*.

400

Promotion sheet for Al Jennings' film *Beating Back.*

Advertising placard for *The Passing of the Oklahoma Outlaws.*

Bill Tilghman

35 Years an Official in the West

Presents Oklahoma's Great Historic Photo Drama

"Passing of the Oklahoma Outlaws"

Promotion sheet for *The Passing of the Oklahoma Outlaws.*

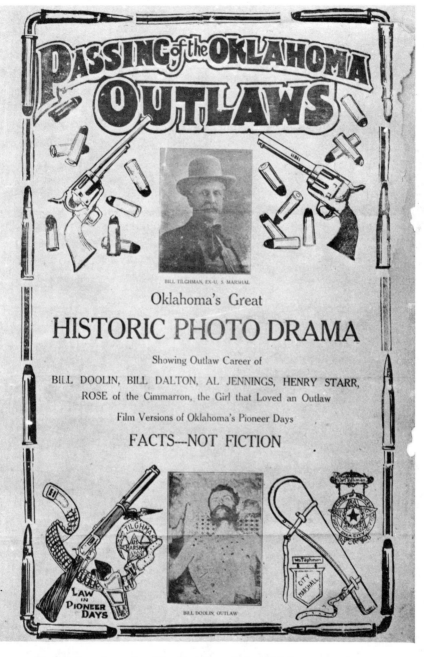

Promotion sheet for *The Passing of the Oklahoma Outlaws.*

Theater advertising display for Bill Tilghman's road show *The Passing of the Oklahoma Outlaws.*

XXVII   The Trail Ends on Cottonwood

CANADA H. THOMPSON, called Harry by his friends, arrived in Guthrie on Friday afternoon, November 5, aboard the passenger train from Enid and at once filed a bond of fifty thousand dollars. On Saturday afternoon, he qualified before Judge Keaton at Oklahoma City, and on Monday morning, he assumed control of U.S. marshal's office. Pat Nagle "stepped down and out, breathing easier now that the responsibility of preserving the peace and fair name of Oklahoma was on another's shoulders, but nevertheless he looked serious and worried."[1] Since tendering his resignation in June, Nagle had been investigated by a Justice Department examiner, who had severely criticized the actions of several field deputies, rejected many of their accounts on grounds of fraud, and reported against allowing other vouchers in the amount of three thousand dollars. But Nagle

is not alone in his troubles. The returns of many of former Marshal E. D. Nix's field deputies have not yet been approved. Even Mr. Grimes, who was marshal prior to Nix, has not been able to obtain an entire settlement of his accounts. And this after a lapse of nearly five years.[2]

In March, 1897, Senator George G. Vest of Missouri introduced in Congress legislation fixing the salary of the U.S. marshal of Oklahoma at five thousand five hundred dollars and that of his chief deputy at one thousand five hundred dollars. He also proposed fixed salaries for clerks of the Territorial Supreme Court and the district courts in an effort to kill the fee system, which was believed to be the root of the problem. The *Oklahoma State Capital* of March 22 attributed the difficulties to

Mr. Plato Mountjoy that federal pie eaters do not know exactly what to make of. Nothing can be found out about his business. He tells neither to warm-hearted federal officials nor the newspapers, but comes here looking into the condition of different departments. It can, however, be seen which way the shoe pinches by the extra politeness and bowings and scrapings, when certain ones who feel that their tenure of office is short, greet him. He is a little man. He is gray and gentle and sweet

405

voiced, but he is as dangerous as Menelik, king of Ethiopia . . . a satrap and autocrat, who can cut off a head by a word and make it fall into the basket.

Thompson was forty-six, above average height, weighed one hundred fifty pounds, was straight as an arrow, his voice soft and musical. His sharp black eyes were piercing but steady and calm; when he laughed, they danced with merriment. He was a man not wanting when called upon to perform duties requiring capacity and cleverness. Nagle offered to acquaint him with the workings of the office, and former Marshal Nix dropped in to pay his respects and put him next.

Marshal Thompson, however, assumed the reins of justice as if he knew just what to do and how to do it. He immediately dispatched five prisoners to the Pawhuska court to stand trial and made arrangements to send others to E Reno that evening. In the afternoon, he issued new commissions to Heck Thomas and Bill Tilghman as field deputies and appointed as chief deputy former Rock Island Detective William D. (Bill) Fossett of Kingfisher. Two days later, he appointed N. E. Sisson of Enid, Thomas J. Taylor, Sr., of Perry, Frank Cochran of Oklahoma City, and Frank E. Smith of Norman district marshal and announced that he would name all of his clerks and deputies by November 15.[3]

Thompson also had made "considerable study" of the Jennings gang's depredations in Oklahoma, but before he could discuss with Thomas and Tilghman his ideas on dealing with these bandits, he received a message from Leo E. Bennett the newly appointed U.S. marshal for the Northern District of Indian Territory at Muskogee, that a man killed by his deputies Sunday night, November 7, had been "fully identified" as Dynamite Dick Clifton.[4]

Disenchanted with the gang's accomplishments after the Cushing robbery, West and Dynamite Dick had separated from the Jenningses and O'Malleys. Agreeing to rejoin them at the Spike S Ranch at a later date, West headed for the North Canadian to visit his Creek girl friend, and Dynamite Dick rode off to his "many hiding places amongst the criminal classes" around Chectoah.[5] Deputy Marshals George Lawson and Hess Bussy

> got the word that the band of outlaws of whom Clifton was the leader had broke up in the neighborhood of Tulsa. . . . Familiar with his regular beat and after laying out several days on top of a hill, ten miles west of Checotah . . . early Sunday morning their man showed up on the trail from the timber to the Sid Williams' place. The officers pulled down on

their man and ordered him to surrender. To Dynamite Dick surrender meant death by the gallows and he obeyed not, but in the twinkling of an eye his Winchester, ever ready, was raised and he fired. A ball from Deputy Lawson's gun broke Clifton's arm, knocking him from his horse . . . he dropped his Winchester and took to the brush. The officers followed and trailed him for some time by the blood from his wound. They lost his trail during the day and . . . it seemed as if their man had escaped. About dark they ran upon a little cabin hid in the woods and circumstances were such as to lead them to believe the wounded desperado was therein. The officers stationed themselves on either side and called for the inmates to come out. After repeated threats of burning the cabin and a few grazing shots to intimidate the occupants, an Indian woman and boy emerged. The officers pulled down on them and ordered them to fire the cabin, threatening instant death unless they complied. The officers could hear someone moving around and trying to knock the clinkers from between the logs so as to get an opening to fire through. Again the officers commanded the woman and boy to burn the house . . . when Dynamite Dick threw open the door, jumped out and commenced firing. With one arm shattered he was badly handicapped and the officers soon brought him down. He was shot several times and lived but a few minutes after the fight was over. The officers immediately loaded their man into a wagon, and after driving all night landed in front of the marshal's office in this city Monday morning. The remains were removed inside the jail stockade until identification was made. . . .

He was a big, heavy set man, well muscled, and . . . the shrewdest scouter and most dangerous criminal that ever infested this section. Writs by the dozen were out for him. He was in the Southwest City bank robbery . . . the Red Rock train robbery and the Ingalls, Ok. fight, where several were killed. He was one of the original Dalton gang . . . also robbed the Foyil postoffice in this territory. He has been in jail at Paris, Texas, Guthrie, Ok. and . . . in conjunction with Bill Doolin, led the famous jail break a year ago. Rewards aggregating three thousand dollars were out for his capture, dead or alive, and the two deputies who trailed him and after two fierce fights brought him down, will be well repaid for their work. . . .

The identification was thorough and complete, and all that was mortal of Dynamite Dick was buried at government expense Tuesday.[6]

The killing of Clifton convinced Deputy Marshal Ledbetter that, Heck Thomas' warning to Arkansas and Missouri authorities notwithstanding, the gang had separated and that the others were still hiding in the Northern District. "Armed with a warrant for the arrest of Al Jennings . . . upon the charge of robbing the post office at Foyil," he reactivated his "wide searching and inquiry."[7]

It is popular belief[8] that Ledbetter enlisted the aid of Sam Baker and Baker met Little Dick West "in a graveyard at Tecumseh" with the tale of a big Indian payment in gold that was to be transported across the country. "Already disgusted" with the Jenningses and O'Malleys, West agreed to "set them up" for the marshal. Since Baker and Willis Brooks were known to these outlaws, it was necessary to bring in a third man, Bob Gentry of Checotah, who stayed close enough to the gang for West to keep him informed of their movements. As the alleged date of the gold shipment drew near and the gang began to assemble on Red Hereford's ranch in the Mounds area south of Tulsa to hide out until the robbery, West again "saddled up one night and unceremoniously parted company with them." Ledbetter got the word and hurried to the ranch. But the gang had become suspicious and "moved out just as the posse was ready to move in."

Ledbetter's testimony[9] shows that he first learned of the gang's whereabouts when four riders stopped at a blacksmith shop in Red Fork on the evening of November 28 to reset a shoe on one of their fagged ponies. They posed as cowboys en route to Red Hereford's ranch. The blacksmith noted their tattered appearance and notified Tulsa District Deputy Marshals Lon Lewis and Joe Thompson.

At dusk, the officers took the road south of Tulsa, accompanied by Gus Thompson, Joe's sixteen-year-old son; John McClanahan; and Jake Elliot. About midnight, the Tulsa contingent was joined by Ledbetter and Tolbert from Muskogee, and the seven-man party lay out on a knoll above the Hereford place until morning. Shortly after daylight, they sent young Gus Thompson to the house to borrow a wood maul and iron wedge, and the boy returned with the information that four riders had taken supper there but had left during the night. The chagrined officers hurried back to the timber and mounted their horses. A wide stretch of prairie lay beyond the ranch buildings, and it was necessary to detour nearly three miles to remain out of view and pick up the trail again. The trail led to the Spike S.

The officers reached the Spike S after dark on November 29. A wind gusted from the north, icy cold; the sweep of sand and dust obscured the stars. The house was a two-story clapboard affair with a bedroom upstairs and three rooms below. This time, Ledbetter sent a man named Kelly, who lived several miles from the ranch, to the house as a spy.[10] Mrs. Harless was alone at the ranch with her young brother, Clarence Enscoe, and her hired girl, Miss Ida Hurst. "John Harless was then in jail on a charge of changing brands," Al Jennings[11] tells us. The outlaws had finished supper. "We talked and laughed and joked; Frank sat down at the organ

408

and we all sang." Someone knocked. "We put our Winchesters within reach, and Mrs. Harless opened the door." Kelly stepped in, covered with dirt, digging his eyes, swollen almost shut; then he saw the rifles and started. He stammered out that he "had got lost." It was so dark he couldn't see his hand before his face until he saw their light. "No, he wouldn't take a cheer. Now he'd found his way, he'd better be going." It sounded fishy to Al, yet Mrs. Harless seemed unsuspecting. Not until the man had mounted his horse did she remark: "He lost! That Kelly! As if he didn't know this country as well as I know my kitchen!" Al sprang to the door with his rifle, but the "sound of hoofs in the distance showed" it was too late to stop him. "It looked terribly suspicious . . . though we joked over it, and Frank drew a laugh by imitating Kelly's manner. We put it out of mind and went on with our music."

On the contrary, after Kelly's departure, Morris O'Malley was posted as a lookout in a wagon between the house and barn, where the outlaws had left their horses. After Kelly reported and departed for home, Ledbetter crawled up to the wagon, thrust his Winchester against O'Malley's body, and told him to climb out and keep quiet. He took the prisoner to the barn, gagged and bound him securely, and left him in a stall.[12] Then the marshal scattered his forces. Joe Thompson and his son were placed 125 yards to the northwest in a point of timber which had served as an escape route for ranch outlaws in the past. Tolbert took his station 80 yards north of the house behind a log cabin with an outside stone chimney. Ledbetter and McClanahan remained in the barn, 200 yards to the northeast, with the horses and prisoner. Lewis and Elliot were posted behind a stone wall south of the barn near the ranch cemetery. Their position commanded the 50 yards of open space between the south side of the house and a peach orchard.

November 30 dawned bright and clear. Clarence Enscoe came out for a bucket of water. Failing to see O'Malley in the wagon, he entered the barn. He, too, was captured, expertly trussed up and gagged, and stretched in the stall.

Within a few minutes, the hired girl came out onto the kitchen porch, called "Breakfast!" then hurried back inside, shivering from a blast of cutting north wind.

A short time later, Mrs. Harless came to the door and called to O'Malley and her brother. Receiving no answer, she threw a shawl about her shoulders and ran to the barn. Ledbetter stepped behind her as she entered. Quietly, the marshal told her who he and those with him were, their official capacity, and that they had a warrant for Al Jennings and knew he was in the house with the other members of the gang. "The place is surrounded and they have no chance to escape," he said. "Go back, tell them those facts and to come out with their hands up. If they refuse to surrender, you and the hired girl must leave the house and go to the cemetery at once."

The frightened woman ran back to the house. Ledbetter joined Tolbert, took a stand behind the stone chimney of the cabin, and waited. He heard voices inside "raised in argument" and there were "demonstrations as if preparations were being made for resistance." Suddenly the door opened and the woman and hired girl, wrapped in heavy blankets, hurried toward the graveyard. They hardly had reached safety when Al Jennings opened fire on Ledbetter from the kitchen window, spattering the cabin chimney with lead. The officers "responded" and "from sixty to one hundred shots flew in both directions, thick and fast."[13]

If one is to believe Al Jennings,[14] it was the battle of the century. His description of the fight, however, is neither convincing nor accurate. Ledbetter and Tolbert, both crack shots and with a good range on the doors and windows, poured such a hail of lead through the clapboard structure that in five minutes the bandits "found the place untenable." Frank Jennings was injured, but a slug from Tolbert's rifle had slashed the muscles of Pat O'Malley's right leg. He was bleeding badly. Al Jennings had a .32-caliber steel-jacketed bullet from Ledbetter's Winchester in his left thigh and slight wounds in both legs above the knees. The trio dashed from the back door for the orchard.

Lewis and Elliot opened fire from behind the stone wall. A charge of buckshot from Lewis' shotgun riddled Frank Jennings' clothing but did no serious damage. Elliot's rifle jammed on the first shot, and before he could extricate the shell, the outlaws gained the concealment of the orchard. They fled from there into the brush thickets of Snake Creek, waded the creek, and vanished into the hills.

It was fully ten minutes before Ledbetter was told the bandits had escaped, and it is said his string of vitrolic curses that filled the air were too warm to be recorded. After searching the hills and creek bottoms for hours without finding a trail, he and Tolbert returned to the ranch, gathered up the outlaws' saddles, and took their horses and Morris O'Malley to Muskogee.

Meanwhile, the fugitives met two Yuchi Indian boys in a wagon. They captured them and their outfit and drove south through Okmulgee that night. After hiding in the brush all next day, Frank Jennings tried to drive them toward Oklahoma but lost his way in the middle of the night and turned back. At daylight, they released the

Indian boys and drove on in the wagon to the home of Willis Brooks.

Al and O'Malley needed medical attention, but with Dynamite Dick dead and Little Dick West out of the picture, Brooks had no interest in the gang. He shuttled them east to Sam Baker's. The latter felt obligated and went into Checotah for a doctor. At the same time, he was thinking of the penalty for aiding and harboring federal fugitives and remembered the promise he had made Bud Ledbetter. While in Checotah, he contacted the marshal and arranged details for delivering the gang to him within twenty-four hours.[15]

On Sunday night, December 5, Ledbetter left Muskogee, accompanied by deputies Isaac Peeples, Paden Tolbert, and John Tolbert, Paden's brother. In the early-morning hours of December 6, they reached a deep cut that led down to the rock crossing on Carr Creek southeast of Baker's home. They felled a big tree across the cut, making it impossible for a wagon to pass. Ledbetter crouched in its branches; the others positioned themselves atop the high banks on each side.[16]

At Baker's house, a wagon was being outfitted with provisions and blankets under a load of straw to take the outlaws to Arkansas. A couple of hours before daybreak, Al and O'Malley, their wounds dressed, crawled beneath the straw and blankets; Frank mounted the driver's seat. Baker gave his final instructions: "Just keep straight along that road until you cross the creek, then turn north, and no one will stop you. Good luck!"

The wagon jolted through the moonlight. Al and O'Malley, relieved that they were leaving Indian Territory at last, dozed. Then the wagon rolled down the cut until the team breasted the barricade. Frank Jennings cursed; Al and O'Malley popped from under the straw. In the same instant they looked into the muzzle of Ledbetter's Winchester and heard his command to surrender; the alternative was to die like rats in a trap. All promptly raised their hands. By nightfall, the trio had joined Morris O'Malley in the Muskogee jail. Marshal Bennett wired Marshal Thompson that the Jennings gang had been taken without firing a shot.[17]

It was believed by the marshal's office at Guthrie that the gang would be taken to Ardmore for trial "as there is $1,000 more reward offered" in the Southern District of Indian Territory, and from Woodward, "word was received today . . . that Colonel Temple Houston, the big-hearted Texan, will defend the Jennings boys if it is a sure thing they have been captured. This is generosity with vengeance," said the *State Capital*.[18] Houston's offer was not accepted.

411

Al, Frank, and the O'Malleys "were arraigned in the federal court at Muskogee Friday [December 24]. . . . They waived preliminary examination and were held in the sum of $5,000 each."[19]

On Monday afternoon, February 21, 1898, a number of business and professional men gathered at Fite & Blakemore Hospital to witness the first use of X rays in Indian Territory. Efforts to locate the bullet in Al Jennings' left thigh had been unsuccessful, and it was giving him much pain.

> Jennings was brought from the jail in charge of Jailer Lubbes and Deputy O'Brian. Drs. [F. B.] Fite, [J. L.] Blakemore, Thompson and Reeves were all present and each more or less in charge of the work, while Mr. Moody had charge of the electrical machinery.
>
> Jennings climbed upon the table and told Jailer Lubbes if "that thing electrocuted him, he [Lubbes] was to be held accountable." Jennings was as much interested in the scientific side of the question as of the purely personal feature of the test.
>
> With drawn curtains the experiment began. The electrical apparatus kept up a terrific rattle, much like the click of a sewing machine, though much louder, and the glass bulb filled up with a greenish, milky light. Jennings' leg was placed near the bulb and then the operator put a funnel-like box [fluoroscope] on the opposite side, put his eye at the spout and looked. The bullet was soon located and everybody in the room given an opportunity to see it for themselves. Later, a sensitized plate was placed where the fluoroscope had been and a good photograph made of the bullet and its location. Owing to the time consumed it was thought best to delay the operation until next day, as the patient had gone through considerable strain.
>
> Tuesday afternoon Jennings was again taken to the hospital, another examination made, and then he was put under the influence of anaesthetic. So perfect had the location been made that Dr. Fite cut straight down through two inches of muscle and touched the bullet at the bottom of the cut. With a pair of forceps . . . the lead tip of a .32 steel ball put there by Deputy Bud Ledbetter . . . and some patches of cloth were quickly removed. The wound was then dressed. . . .
>
> After Jennings was thoroughly free from the chloroform, those present were discussing his good behavior while under its influence, and Jennings . . . finally remarked that he had been a very much misunderstood man.[20]

A federal grand jury disagreed and indicted Al on a charge of assault with intent to kill Deputy Ledbetter in the fight at the Spike S Ranch. He was found guilty in the May, 1898, term of court and on June 4 was sentenced to five years at hard labor in Leavenworth Penitentiary.[21]

Al Jennings was delivered to the U.S. marshal for the Southern

District of Indian Territory and incarcerated at Ardmore until February, 1899, when he was indicted and tried for robbery of the U.S. mails in the train holdup north of Chickasha, found guilty, and, on February 17, sentenced to the Columbus, Ohio, penitentiary for life.[22] Frank Jennings and the O'Malleys received five years each and were taken to Leavenworth.

With word of the capture of the Jennings gang, Little Dick West bid his Creek girl friend good-by and hied back to Oklahoma, where "his acquaintance among old settlers enabled him to find a friendly place to stop whenever he desired." This and the fact that he rarely slept indoors, preferring the open prairie under a blanket, "made it almost impossible to surprise him." On Christmas Day, 1897, he returned to the Cottonwood Creek dugout, where he and the gang had taken refuge after the Rock Island robbery. Within half an hour's ride of the marshals' headquarters, it seemed the least likely place they would search for him. He hired out as a farm hand on the Ed Fitzgerald place near by under an assumed name. Harmon Arnett owned the adjoining farm half a mile away, and Little Dick made frequent visits to his place for extra work until early spring. He even "made himself so bold as to visit Guthrie" on one occasion, then drifted over to Kingfisher. By the first of April, 1898, he was back dividing his time between the Fitzgerald and Arnett farms on Cottonwood Creek.[23]

On Wednesday afternoon, April 6, Mrs. Arnett was in Guthrie and remarked to a friend that Fitzgerald's hired man was trying to get her husband to join him in a robbery. The friend told Mrs. Hart, wife of the district clerk, who told Sheriff Frank Rinehart. Rinehart told Heck Thomas. Heck sparkled when he heard the man's description: undersized, heavy set, dark skinned, always unclean, with a moustache so thick that it drooped over his lower lip, extralong brows that almost ran together at the base of his nose, and furtive eyes set wide in a moonface.

Heck consulted with Chief Deputy Fossett. Thursday night, April 7, they left Guthrie with a posse consisting of Rinehart; Bill Tilghman; Ben Miller, a local policeman; and Heck's son, Albert. The *Oklahoma State Capital*[24] and the *Guthrie Daily Leader*[25] summarized subsequent events:

> The posse arrived at Fitzgerald's farm about 3 o'clock [on the morning of April 8]. A gray horse [matching the description of the round-bellied pony ridden by West in the Rock Island robbery] was found in Fitzgerald's barn. He denied all knowledge of its former owner, saying he had traded for the horse some time ago. . . . Finding no trace of their man, the officers cut across the fields to Arnett's farm. When they had

gone a short distance they saw a man scouting along the timber to the left. Tilghman and Thomas crossed toward him. He changed his course upon seeing the officers. Fossett, Rinehart and the possemen proceeded on to Arnett's. They approached the house from the front and went around toward the barn. Fossett and Rinehart were together, the possemen going to search in another direction. The man [seen along the timber] was standing by a shed connected with the barn. He stepped behind the barn and started running [back] to the timber. The officers called to him to halt. He replied by turning and firing three shots at the officers with a revolver. One shot went dangerously near Rinehart and one by Fossett. The officers then began firing. Sheriff Rinehart fired two shots with a double-barreled shotgun, and Deputy Fossett fired three shots with a Winchester. At the first shots West turned and fired and started to run again, loading his revolver as he ran. The second shot from Fossett's Winchester struck him in the left side and passed through him, coming out [under] his right shoulder. He fell forward and was dead when the officers reached his side.

The body was brought to Guthrie and placed in charge of Undertaker Reder, where it was viewed by hundreds.

Albert Thomas provides a more explicit account of the expedition:

We left Guthrie after dark, using a covered wagon and team and my saddle horse "Limber Jim," which I rode. Miller drove the wagon, the others rode inside. We made dry camp about a mile from the [Fitzgerald] place, and an hour before daybreak moved in and separated—Fossett, Rinehart and Miller taking a stand a hundred yards or so in front of the house, and my father, Tilghman and myself taking a stand about the same distance in the rear. Just before daybreak lamps were lighted in the house and, in accordance with mutual understanding, Fossett and his party advanced to the front door, knocking on it and demanding entrance, which was given them immediately.

They thought that if West was in the house, he would run out the back right into our arms, but there was no evidence that he was around, except a horse in the corral that fully met the description of the one he had been using.

Although we could not get an admission from the farmer or any of his family that they had ever heard of Little Dick, their explanation as to the horse being a stray was not very convincing. Knowing of the other farm house [Arnett's] about a half mile away, and a dugout in the side of a hill about the same distance in a different direction, we again split up, my father and Tilghman heading for the dugout, Fossett and Rinehart going to the other house, and Miller and myself to the horses and wagon with the understanding we would all meet at the second place.

Miller and I had almost reached the wagon when we heard a half-dozen shots in quick succession in the direction of the house where we

414

were to meet—then two more shots at intervals. We made a run for the horses. Miller drove the wagon, and I rode "Limber Jim" on a dead run toward the firing. I can see in my mind's eye now Ben standing up in the wagon, lashing the horses with the ends of the reins, trying to keep up with me, but of course "Limber Jim" and I beat him by at least a hundred yards to the scene, which by this time had switched to a road on the far side of the house.

Little Dick West was dead, lying on his back, right arm stretched above his head, his cocked six-shooter in his hand. This is what happened: As Fossett and Rinehart approached the house, they saw a man step into the breezeway to look close at them. He then stepped from view, but reappeared beside a little building at the rear, walking toward the stable yard. They yelled that they wanted to speak to him, but he jerked his six-shooter, firing and running toward the wire fence enclosing the lot.

Both men fired at him as he dived under the last strand, one shot going under his right shoulder blade and through his body. He ran, I would estimate, about 150 yards beyond the fence, reloading as he ran, and turned in the act of firing again when he died.

Sheriff Rinehart was using my Remington 10 gauge shotgun loaded with buckshot. I had loaded the shells myself. It was claimed that Chief Deputy Fossett, who was using a Winchester, killed West, but my father and Tilghman, after examining the wound in his body, were of the opinion that it was made by a buckshot.[26]

A coroner's jury composed of J. D. Thorpe, Harrison Reed, Hugh McCrary, Ed Laws, M. M. Meek, and Ed Vanderpool returned the following verdict concerning Little Dick West: "He came to his death at the hands of Officer Fossett while resisting arrest."[27]

Although Little Dick was the last checkoff for Doolin's Wild Bunch, one member of the gang would still have to be dealt with: Arkansas Tom, who was in prison.

XXVIII Arkansas Tom's
Last Shot

ON AUGUST 18, 1898, the *El Reno News* noted: "Oklahoma has lived down its reputation of the land of outlaws, by killing them off, and the disreputable news correspondents have scurried for cover." A few scattered robber bands sprang up at the turn of the century, but they belonged to a new era.

Oklahoma was being settled rapidly. Never before had such a heterogenous aggregation of earnest, energetic people assembled themselves so quickly into an organization with a common cause. The Organic Act of 1890 had defined Oklahoma Territory as extending to the South Fork of Red River. Greer County—consisting of the present counties of Harmon, Jackson, Greer, and part of Beckham—had been part of Texas. On March 16, 1896, the U.S. Supreme Court upheld the 1890 act and Texas lost Old Greer.

In May, 1900, Dennis T. Flynn at last realized his dream. His free-homes bill was passed and signed by President William McKinley, thereby saving the settlers an estimated seventeen million dollars. Flynn came home to a series of ovations such as few Oklahomans have ever been accorded. He was unanimously renominated as delegate to Congress and named delegate at large to the Republican National Convention.

The presidential campaign of 1900 was noisy but tame. Whatever the inclination of McKinley's philanthropic gestures of protecting Cuba and the Philippines after the Spanish-American War of 1898 and the 1899 invitation to certain European powers to adopt an open-door policy in Chinese waters, the United States no longer could remain aloof from international issues. The issue of imperialism which William Jennings Bryan tried to raise proved even less successful in stirring voter dissension than free silver had been, and McKinley was returned for a second term in the White House, the vice-presidency going to New York's governor and Rough Rider hero of San Juan Hill, Theodore Roosevelt.

In Oklahoma, Governor Barnes's term expired on April 15, 1901.

Barnes chose to retire, to become president of the Logan County Bank, and to serve two terms as mayor of Guthrie (1903–1905 and 1907–1909). President McKinley elevated William M. Jenkins to the governorship and named former U.S. Marshal William C. Grimes territorial secretary. Horace Speed was returned as U.S. district attorney and Harry Thompson reappointed U.S. marshal with the unqualified endorsement of the territorial organization.

The most important event of Jenkins' brief tenure as governor was the opening of surplus lands belonging to the Kiowa, Comanche, Apache, Wichita, and Caddo Indians on August 6, 1901. In this case, finally, sooners were dealt with effectively. Each applicant for a 160-acre tract had to register and was given a number. The numbers were then thoroughly mixed and drawn from huge boxes. Although only 2,080,000 acres of land were available, more than 160,000 persons registered for claims. The region was divided into three counties, with 320 acres in each reserved as townsites for county seats at Lawton, Hobart, and Anadarko. The towns were surveyed and platted and the lots sold at auction for cash to the highest bidder.

Oklahoma now had twenty-six counties. With this rapid increase of population and property rights came such growth of business in the courts that two additional judges were added to the territorial judiciary, and the new court divided the territory into seven districts.

President McKinley was cut down by an assassin's bullet at Buffalo, New York, on September 6 and died eight days later. Roosevelt succeeded to the presidency, and on November 30 summarily removed Governor Jenkins for official misconduct growing out of charges that Jenkins had financial interests in the Oklahoma Sanitarium Company, which contracted for the care of the territory's insane at Norman. Roosevelt, already whittling out his big stick, based his decision purely on Jenkins' own statements and his oral explanation of them at a hearing in Washington. Jenkins was afforded no further opportunity for defense, and Thompson B. Ferguson, postmaster and publisher of the *Watonga Republican*, who succeeded Jenkins as governor, later thought the President had been too severe with him. Roosevelt retained Horace Speed as U.S. district attorney but soon replaced Marshal Thompson with William D. Fossett.

Ferguson proved to be a capable and wise administrator. An early-day crusader for law and order, he was critical of public officials who took the lesser course of placing personal gain above the demands for honest, sober, economical government. Aside from his

417

sterling service, two outstanding features of his regime were, first, his correction of the situation at the Norman sanitarium by securing legislation transferring the territorial asylum to Fort Supply and, second, the act of Congress on April 21, 1904, by which 231,000 acres of land belonging to the Ponca and Oto-Missouri Indians on the eastern border of the Outlet were allotted, the reservations abolished, a per capita division made of the surplus land to be leased or sold under regulations prescribed by the Interior Department, and the areas attached to the counties in which they were located. By the close of Ferguson's tenure, Oklahoma Territory boasted a population of 700,000, a startling increase from the first census of 60,000 in 1890. Of the 700,000 nearly 74,000 had come with the opening of Indian reservations in the southwest.

The industrial revolution was remaking American Society. Prosperity was felt everywhere when Frank Frantz, a well-known Rough Rider and the seventh and last territorial governor, assumed office on January 5, 1906. Frantz's administration was one of routine and was concerned primarily with unifying the bitter factions that had developed among territorial Republicans so that the party could provide an effective challenge to Democrats in the upcoming elections for the constitutional convention pending statehood.

The Osage Indians and the Kaws, who lived in the northwest corner of the Osage Nation, had resisted all attempts toward allotment of their lands, which totaled some 1,600,000 acres. They were so bitter toward the plan that the Dawes Act of 1887 was not made applicable to these reservations. However, two factions developed in the Osage tribe: the half-bloods wanted allotments; the full bloods, about two-thirds of the population, did not. Discovery of vast quantities of oil, large sums of money owed white traders over a period of years, and the institution of some 400 suits against cattlemen for illegally pasturing their herds on the reservation complicated matters. The country became such a hotbed of corruption that on June 28, 1906, Congress provided for individual division of the lands and funds to the Indians. The mineral and oil rights they retained would make them the richest people per capita in the world.

Finally, the Big Pasture, an area encompassing parts of present-day Cotton, Tillman, and Comanche counties, designated as common grazing grounds for the Indians by the secretary of the interior and reserved from settlement at the Kiowa-Comanche-Apache opening in 1901, together with several small "pastures," the total area exceeding 500,000 acres, was dissolved, sold under sealed bids in December, 1906, and added to the white man's land.

Oklahoma became two almost evenly divided regions: Oklahoma Territory west of Hell's Fringe, including the dissolved Osage, Kaw, Ponca, and Oto-Missouri reservations, and Indian Territory to the east, embracing the lands of the Five Civilized Tribes and their neighbors, the small tribes of the Quapaw Agency.

Oklahoma Territory's tremendous increase in population and the steady drift of whites into Indian Territory, doubling its population to nearly four hundred thousand, were harbingers of doom for the governments of the Five Civilized Tribes. Since 1893, the Dawes Commission had negotiated with these Indians to resign their tribal titles and take allotments. In 1898, they agreed to the plan and were brought under U.S. laws. Existing towns were incorporated, new townsites reserved, and the several Indian nations were divided into recording districts for the filing of deeds, mortgages, and legal papers. In accordance with the agreement, all tribal institutions were to end March 4, 1906. By June, the Dawes Commission found it had practically completed its work of allotting land and could disband, leaving the final details to the Department of the Interior.

New railroads were built into the Nations, connecting the two territories. Trackage in Oklahoma Territory increased from 925 miles in 1901 to 2,611 by 1906. Oil production and mining had begun at the turn of the century, and as early as 1897, Governor Barnes reported that Oklahoma had made a crop record "which astonishes the world." In 1903, Governor Ferguson revealed that for the first time tax receipts had been so large that, in addition to meeting all expenses of government, a payment had been made on the funded deficit that had existed since the territory's birth. Eastern capital was coming in. The free-homes law had wiped out any indebtedness of the homesteader to the government.

Statehood became the leading issue, and without declaring for either single or double blessedness, the territorial legislature adopted a strong memorial to Congress: Oklahoma had an estimated five hundred forty million dollars in wealth "produced in a single decade from the wild prairie and wilderness," three thousand common schools, six "great" institutions of learning, and more churches in proportion to population than elsewhere in the world. "Such people ought not to be longer held in political subjection." Indian Territory was "supplemental" to Oklahoma, with more than three hundred thousand whites and blacks there without political rights, "peasants of the soil to seventy thousand persons of Indian extraction"—"disfranchised" residents who could not levy taxes for roads, schools, colleges, and asylums.

The total thrust was for a single state, notwithstanding the fact that the two territories were exact opposites in natural resources, features, and developments. Even the two populations' natures were different. The Indian leaders of the Five Civilized Tribes met in an attempt to have Indian Territory brought in as a separate state; they drew up a constitution and designated the area Sequoyah. It was an able document. However, both Congress and the President were fully committed to the policy of forming a single state.

Representative Hamilton of Michigan introduced an enabling bill authorizing the admission of the Twin Territories as one. When debate began on January 24, 1906, he told the House:

> These territories are rich in corn, cotton, wheat, coal, gas and oil, and their cities, staked out upon the level plain but a few years ago by a virile population drawn from all parts of the union, have sprung like magic into opulence and power, equipped with every device of energy and luxury. . . . Indian names, once synonyms of savage warfare, have become the musical names of municipalities, of civilized progress.

Representative Charles C. Reid of Arkansas pointed out that Oklahoma Territory alone "possessed more wealth than any state when it was admitted to the union," plus two hundred thousand more people. It had more school children "than many states today have population."

Representative Beall of Texas declared the government had pledged to the Indians that their lands should never be embraced in or annexed to any other territory or state and that without their consent it was proposed to merge them "with other people and another territory." He added, however, that Congress had been driven by necessity to agree to the union because it would be a "greater crime to longer deny a majority of the people of the two territories the right of self-government."

And Bird S. McGuire, Oklahoma Territory's new delegate to Congress, argued: "If we propose to civilize the Indian, if it is the policy of the American government to better his condition, the quickest method, the surest plan to succeed would be immediate statehood for these people."

The Enabling Act was finally passed and signed on June 16, 1906. A constitutional convention in Guthrie provided for a complete court system, the judicial power to be vested in a supreme court, district courts, county and municipal courts, and justices of the peace. The constitution was ratified by a large majority vote of the people, who elected Charles N. Haskell, a Muskogee Democrat, their first governor. At 10:16 A.M. on November 16, 1907, President Roosevelt signed the statehood proclamation.

420

Law enforcement became the responsibility of sheriffs, police departments, and constables. For federal purposes, Oklahoma was divided into the Western District at Guthrie and the Eastern District at Muskogee. Where at one time hundreds of deputy marshals roamed the two areas, each district force was reduced to a half-dozen men, and their work dwindled to federal law violations and routine matters.

The older officers had spent most of their lives in government service. Few had saved anything. Many found employment with the state, counties, or municipalities. Bud Ledbetter rounded out his career as town marshal at Haskell, chief of police of Muskogee, plainclothesman on the police force at Okmulgee, served two terms as sheriff of Muskogee County, and spent his last days in the hills where he had tracked down the Jennings gang.

Heck Thomas became chief of police at Lawton after the Kiowa-Comanche-Apache opening, continuing his service under Marshal Thompson. He was then commissioned by Fossett and by the "wolf-catchin marshal," John L. (Jack) Abernathy, whom Roosevelt appointed in 1906. He carried out many tasks for the government under William S. Cade, marshal for the Western District of Oklahoma, appointed by William Howard Taft in 1911, before his death at Lawton on August 15, 1912.

When Jo Shelby died at Kansas City in February, 1897, Chris Madsen resigned and returned to Oklahoma. In 1898, he was off to Cuba as quartermaster sergeant with the Rough Riders. After the Spanish-American War, he accepted a deputy's commission under U.S. Marshal John S. Hammer of the Southern District of Indian Territory at Ardmore until statehood, then served as chief deputy under Abernathy until the latter resigned in 1910 and was chief deputy under Cade until 1913. He became auditor for the Tulsa Police Department during World War I and later was clerk of the police court. From Tulsa, he was special investigator for Governor J. B. A. Robertson until July 1, 1922, then bailiff in the federal court at Oklahoma City, retiring in 1933. He died at Guthrie on January 6, 1944, at the age of 93.

Bill Tilghman served two terms as sheriff of Lincoln County, a brief term in the legislature as senator from the Lincoln-Pottawatomie district, and was police chief at Oklahoma City from 1911 to 1913. In 1914, he was back in state politics, actively campaigning for his friend J. B. A. Robertson, Chandler attorney and presiding judge of the Supreme Court Commission, who was making his first bid for the governorship.

The Democratic primary was one of the hottest ever waged in

Oklahoma from the standpoint of mudslinging and vituperation. The other leading contenders among the six candidates were Charles West, state attorney general; Oklahoma Supreme Court Chief Justice Robert L. Williams, a crusty, pugnacious bachelor who had achieved strong party support with his prominent role in the 1906 constitutional convention; and Al Jennings, who had become a national figure through the serialization of his co-authored biography in the *Saturday Evening Post.*

Jennings' conviction for assault on Bud Ledbetter had gone to the U.S. Court of Appeals for Indian Territory, and the judgment of Muskogee District Court was affirmed on October 26, 1899, while he was in the penitentiary at Columbus.[1] On June 23, 1900, through the persistent efforts of his brother John and Judge Amos Ewing, a friend of the family at Kingfisher, President McKinley commuted Al's life sentence, received at Ardmore, "to imprisonment for five years, with all allowances for good conduct." Thus Jennings' term would have expired June 20, 1902, but a few days before that date, on an order signed by the U.S. district attorney for the Northern District of Indian Territory, he was taken from the Ohio prison and transported to the penitentiary at Leavenworth, Kansas. On petition for a writ of habeas corpus by his Kansas City attorneys, S. C. Price and Frank P. Sebree, to the Circuit Court for the Eastern District of Missouri, it was held that the marshal of the Northern District of Indian Territory had acted without authority of law in surrendering Jennings to the custody of the Southern District marshal after a judgment and sentence had been pronounced committing him to Leavenworth for assault with intent to kill, "thereby postponing execution of the first sentence indefinitely." Because of these circumstances, the prisoner had been "undergoing imprisonment since June 4, 1898 — a part of the time in jail at Ardmore, a part of the time in the penitentiary at Columbus, and a small part of the time in the penitentiary at Leavenworth." Deducting the allowance in his favor for good behavior at the rate of two months per year, as prescribed by federal statute, his term would have expired before he filed his application for a writ of habeas corpus. Jennings was ordered discharged.[2]

Jennings returned to Oklahoma in mid-November, 1902. He spent a few days at El Reno, "paying short visits to old friends . . . looked in at the doings in the district court," and considered the merits of reestablishing his law practice in the city.[3] He finally located at Lawton, forming a law partnership with his brother John, who was then with Leslie P. Ross (who lost the governor's race to Lee Cruce of Ardmore in 1910). Al lived on a five-acre tract at the southwest edge of town and married Miss Maude Deaton, talented musician and singer and graduate of Drake University in Iowa, to whose influence Al credited his success in winning back a respectable place in society, where, by nature, he felt he belonged.[4] On February 2, 1907, President Roosevelt granted him a full-citizenship pardon.

Jennings moved to Oklahoma City, opening a suite of law offices in the State National Bank Building, and in 1912 again plunged into politics by announcing his candidacy for Oklahoma County attorney. His campaign appeal was at least unique: "When I was a train robber and outlaw I was a good train robber and outlaw. If you choose me as prosecuting attorney I will be a good prosecuting attorney."[5] Although his opponents publicly questioned his sincerity—"if Jennings is in earnest about reforming, his place would be beneath the redeeming blood and cross of Christ"—enough voters took him at his word to give him the Democratic nomination.[6] He lost, however, to Republican D. K. Pope in the general election.

Jennings wasn't disappointed. Charles J. Hite of Thanhouser Film Company put up the money to make a motion picture of Al's life (starring Al) based on the story he had co-authored in *Saturday Evening Post*. Jennings closed his law office and departed for New York. *Beating Back* was completed in the Thanhouser studios at New Rochelle and on a rented farm near Ogdensburg, New Jersey, in April, 1913, but was not released for several months because of litigation. Jennings had assigned his story rights to two men, for which he was to receive 297 shares of stock at a par value of $100 each. He took them to court in Oklahoma City, contending that his name had been forged on the stock certificates and the certificates sold and that some of the shares were now held by his partners in the Beating Back Film Corporation.

Al's Democratic primary victory, together with the wide publicity from the lawsuit and his filmed biography, encouraged him to seek the governor's chair in 1914.

While Williams promised to bring harmony to the Democratic party and establish confidence in government and the influential *Daily Oklahoman* labeled Robertson a stooge to incumbent Governor Lee Cruce, whose administration was "attempting to steal the election," Attorney General West accused Williams of serving on "a rich man's court" which "always ruled against cripples who sued corporations" and of financing his campaign with a ten-thousand-dollar mortgage on six hundred acres of land that had been "grafted from ignorant Indians." Williams' enemies tagged him Corporation Bob, and Robertson, because of his several initials, became Old Alphabet. West's attack was so vicious that he found himself steadily losing ground; in desperation, he challenged Williams to a public debate. This proved to be a tactical blunder. Williams, who had resigned his office before announcing his candidacy, promptly stated that he would not debate a man still on the payroll and seeking office at the expense of the taxpayer.[7]

Jennings' platform called for honesty in government. "But it takes a real man to make that word HONEST mean something," he declared. "Not a man who has managed all his life to avoid open conflict with the law . . . but a man who has run the gamut of human experience . . . who understands the psychology of crooks he will have to deal with. You have a rough job in Oklahoma. I have the nerve, the ability, the determination, and the comprehension of human nature necessary . . . to do it."[8]

He toured the state via passenger train, spoke on busy street corners, and generally drew large crowds. He made no effort to gloss over his sins. In fact, he greatly exaggerated them and asserted that when leaving the home of some poor farm woman who had prepared him a meal he would often toss five or fifty dollars. At Konawa early in July, he lashed out at Robertson and Williams, declaring they were guilty of more looting and disregard for the rights of others than he ever knew as an outlaw. A few days later in an unscheduled speech at a picnic in Wapanucka, he called attention to how the large state newspapers either ignored or made a joke of his campaign and charged that Williams had used his mortgage money to buy the support of the *Daily Oklahoman*. Whereupon Williams unexpectedly emerged from the audience and declared: "The man who says I bought the support of the press . . . is a liar." Turning to Jennings and looking him squarely in the face, he said: "You are a liar! I was never an outlaw and am not a coward. I do not need the office of governor to reform me. If I am defeated I shall continue to be a good citizen."[9] There was an uproar from the crowd. Jennings flushed. He started to say something, then left the platform quietly, perhaps remembering the consequences of a lie that had passed between his brother Ed and another man several years earlier.

Al wound up his campaign with an address at First and Robinson in downtown Oklahoma City. He pledged himself to law enforcement and noted his "special qualifications" for dealing with prison reform. "I will parole every prisoner who shows himself worthy. . . . However, I do not intend that the prisons remain empty," he assured a crowd of nearly 10,000. "I would replace the men who are there now with Oklahoma's crooked politicians."[10]

Williams won the nomination by a narrow margin, receiving

424

35,605 of the votes cast; Robertson received 33,504 and Jennings 21,732. In the general election, Robertson gave his support to Williams. Jennings turned his back on the Democrats and supported the Republican nominee, John Fields, whom Williams narrowly defeated, 100,597 votes to 95,904.[11]

The results hardly had been tabulated when Jennings again departed for New York. *Beating Back* was scheduled for release, and Al toured the country, proudly displaying his citizenship pardon from Roosevelt in the theaters where the five-reeler was showing. Eventually, he landed in California, where he spent the next three decades in the "picture business,"[12] but his dark influence in Oklahoma continued for many years. *Beating Back* depicted Al's bandit life about as accurately as it did the life of a butterfly. His followers were gallant heroes, "forced" by one reason or another to live outside the law, and their deeds were made to appear both glamorous and profitable. Deputy marshals were alternately contemptible, bloodthirsty assassins or sniveling cowards who didn't stand a chance against brave criminals.

In the battle at the Spike S Ranch, for example, the Jennings gang, a handful of men, held off more than one hundred officers. And in a chase scene, Bud Ledbetter was portrayed streaking over a rise on a long, gangling horse, lying low over the saddle horn and firing promiscuously as he rode, his coattails and exaggerated moustache streaming in horizontal lines. Behind him raced the posse, long guns waving, six-shooters blazing, their horses shying left and right at every shot.

Emmett Dalton, who had been out of prison since 1907 and was traveling the lecture circuit with a film about his own career, wrote Ledbetter from Wheeling, West Virginia:

> I have just witnessed the exhibition of "Beating Back" by Al Jennings, and I hasten to inquire, what's the chance to borrow the long-tailed Prince Albert coat, boots, star, and heavy fierce black mustache you wear in the picture. . . . I had one hell of a good laugh when I saw a party impersonating you dressed up as above mentioned, and knowing you as I do, I could not help think while looking at it, how I would like to hear you express yourself.[13]

Even lawyers who had helped Jennings reestablish himself after his release from prison were indignant and told Bill Tilghman: "Somebody ought to make a picture showing the truth."

E. D. Nix had left Guthrie in 1898 and reentered the wholesale mercantile business in Joplin, Missouri. He was now living in St. Louis, dealing in bonds, stocks, and investments. Tilghman contacted him; Nix liked the idea and agreed to finance the venture. He, Tilghman, and Chris Madsen formed the Eagle Film Company, with Nix as president, Tilghman vice-president and treasurer, and Madsen secretary. J. B. (Bennie) Kent, an expert cameraman and longtime friend of Tilghman, was the photographer. Captain Lute P. Stover of Iola, Kansas, a successful magazine writer and scenarist with considerable experience in directing, was hired to write the script. The company, with a corps of actors, arrived at Chandler on Monday, January 18, 1915, secured offices in the Raedeker Building, and made plans to film *The Passing of the Oklahoma Outlaws*.[14] Nix outlined their purpose to the *Chandler News-Publicist* on January 22:

> We are undertaking the production of a moving picture story of the decline and end of the practice of outlawry in Oklahoma territory. . . . The robbing of different banks and railroad trains, and the pursuit, capture and punishment of the outlaws engaged will be shown, as will also the different battles in which the outlaws engaged against the deputies. The reproduction of all the important events connected with the breaking up of such notorious gangs as the Doolin and Dalton organizations will be given. The famous cave in the Creek Nation, where the outlaws were accustomed to meet and divide their loot will be an important portion of our setting; for the pictures are to be taken . . . as near the exact spots where the actual events occurred as our data and memories will enable us to place them. Interwoven with the accounts of the outlaws are many unusual romances. . . . We will show the capture of two noted women outlaws who were taken, armed and ready for fighting, while masquerading in men's clothing. . . .
>
> While we are of course concerned with making our undertaking a great success financially, and our motives are therefore not wholly philanthropic, we hope to impress upon the young people of the country . . . that never did the outlaw succeed in his defiance of the law; that the only life worthy of living is the upright and law-abiding life and any other life must inevitably result in ruin.

In 1908, 520 territorial convicts were transferred from Lansing, Kansas, to the old federal stockade at McAlester, which Oklahoma had rented for a state prison. Among them was Arkansas Tom.

The Reverend Sam Daugherty, pastor of a Methodist church at Greenville, Texas, Tom's brother, had worked long and diligently for his pardon, "obtaining scores of signatures and testimonials as to his uprightness" before Tom joined Bill Doolin in Oklahoma.[15] At a hearing in Guthrie on April 16, 1908, Governor Haskell denied executive clemency in the face of "vigorous protest of Payne county citizens in general . . . strong individual remonstrances drawn up by officials involved in his capture and trial, and relatives of deputy marshals who fell in the battle with the Doolin gang."[16] This did not stop the Reverend Mr. Daugherty, who finally visited Nix in St. Louis. Time had mellowed the former marshal's feelings in the matter, and, impressed with Tom's record as a model prisoner during his fourteen years of incarceration, he used his influence with other federal officers who had participated in the arrest and prosecution.[17]

During the last months of his administration, Governor Haskell granted pardons or paroles to "no less than twenty life termers and to nearly sixty persons serving sentences for homicides of various degrees." The list was "smothered and not discovered" until after Haskell left office, "when it was brought out to be indexed and filed as required by state statute and the constitution with the upcoming legislature." Among the "most famous names" was "Roy Daugherty, alias Tom Jones." He was paroled on November 29, 1910, with orders to report to Bill Tilghman at Oklahoma City.[18]

Tilghman found work for Tom in the store of an old friend, and for a time he operated a restaurant in Drumright. He later visited Nix in St. Louis, where the former marshal "got him a position as an accountant" and found him to be "very accurate and reliable."[19] When the Eagle Film Company was organized, Tom was brought back to Oklahoma to play himself in *The Passing of the Oklahoma Outlaws.*

Nix, Madsen, former Chief Deputy Hale, and former U.S. District Attorney Brooks also appeared in the film. Impersonating other well-known characters were Ed Lindsay and his wife, both excellent riders; Lem Rogers, Montana Williams, and Bill McNamee, former members of the 101 Ranch and Pawnee Bill Wild West shows; and F. A. Gleason, "a soldier of fortune and adventurer . . . with Captain Lawton's troop at the surrender of Geronimo." Mrs. J. B. Kent and Miss Faye Kent played leading feminine roles, and other Chandler residents were outlaws and possemen. Excepting Tilghman's capture of Cattle Annie and Little Breeches, his "Cave of Death" episode, and the mythical Rose of Cimarron (who allegedly leaped from the hotel window and carried guns and ammunition to her sweetheart, Bitter Creek, as he lay helplessly wounded in the street at the height of the Ingalls fight), the motion picture was reasonably accurate. These bits of fiction, which have confounded historians for half a century, originated with Captain Stover, who, in addition to directing, prepared *Oklahoma Outlaws* under a pen name, Richard Graves, "to give a short history of each of the reproductions given in the film . . . these books to be sold at the theaters in which the picture is shown."[20]

The train robbery scenes were shot early in February, "utilizing the beautiful and picturesque scenery" of Lincoln County. Then the company moved to Guthrie to stage the federal jailbreak, traveled to Eureka Springs for the capture of Doolin, and spent several days with Bud Ledbetter filming the battle at the Spike S Ranch and the capture of the Jennings gang.

They were back at Tilghman's ranch for the concluding scenes on March 27 when word came that Henry Starr, noted Indian Territory desperado, and his gang had just galloped into nearby Stroud and robbed both banks. As the gang was marching down the street with the terrorized bankers and clerks as hostages to make their escape, a seventeen-year-old boy named Paul Curry shattered Henry's leg bone below the left hip with a "hog rifle." His second bullet struck another robber in the neck, breaking his left shoulder and injuring a lung. Both men were captured.[21]

Tilghman and his cameraman hurried to Stroud to film the bandits under guard and being bandaged in the doctor's office and obtained additional footage as they were being brought to the Chandler jail. The fiasco was added to *The Passing of the Oklahoma Outlaws*, and a brief account of Starr's career was included in Stover's red paperbound book.

Photographer Kent now had "four sets of reels, about 9,000 feet to the set; a total of approximately 36,000 feet, or seven miles of film" and "outside the cost of the raw material and finishing work, the estimated total expense of $10,000 had been spent in Chandler for salaries, labor, props and rent." The film was premiered at Chandler on May 25, and people from throughout the area "crowded the Odeon theater until after midnight."[22]

In keeping with the tradition of the time, Tilghman went on the road with the picture, lecturing his audience from the theater stage and introducing Arkansas Tom as the lone survivor of the Doolin gang. He did good business and soon bought out his partners. However, he finally grew tired of the schedule. During a slack period in 1924, he accepted a job policing the oil boom town of Cromwell in Seminole County and was slain by a drunken prohibition officer he had trusted.

Long before that, however, Arkansas Tom had quit the show and returned to St. Louis. Traveling with the film had made him restless, and he was frequently seen hanging around with the tough element. In December, 1916, he became involved in a bank burglary at Neosho, was found guilty in the February term of Newton County Circuit Court, and was sentenced to eight years in the state penitentiary at Jefferson City. His Oklahoma parole was revoked, but somehow the revocation was canceled. He was discharged from the Missouri prison on November 11, 1921, again a free man.[23]

For the next two years, Tom worked in and around the tri-state areas of Kansas, Oklahoma, and Missouri, living most of time with a cousin at Galena, Kansas. It seemed that he had turned over a new leaf, as promised. Then, about 2:30 on the afternoon of November 26, 1923, four men held up the bank in the small farming town of Asbury, Missouri. By the summer of 1924, two members of the gang had been captured and were serving fifty-year sentences in the penitentiary, a third member was in jail charged with first-degree robbery, and Joplin police were searching for Tom. They finally located him on August 16, hiding at the home of a friend on West Ninth Street:

> W. F. Gibson, chief of detectives, narrowly escaped death when Daugherty opened fire on him as he stepped on a rear porch of the house to cut off escape, one bullet clipping the officer's hat. Gibson returned the fire, three of his four shots taking effect. Daugherty then ran into another room to meet Detective Len Van Deventer, who had entered the house through a front door while the bandit had been engaged by Gibson at the rear.
>
> Van Deventer fired first, the fatal bullet striking immediately above the heart and the bandit pitched on a bed, his pistol clutched in his upraised hand.[24]

At the Hurlbut Undertaking Company, more than five thousand persons viewed the remains of the last of Bill Doolin's Wild Bunch. The death of Arkansas Tom Daugherty brought to an end the story of the great horseback gangs west of Hell's Fringe.

Notes, Comments and Variants

CHAPTER I

1. Dr. Delos Walker, *Daily Oklahoman*, Apr. 22, 1909.
2. Cassius M. ("Cash") Cade to *Kingfisher Free Press*, Golden Anniversary Edition, Apr. 17, 1939.
3. James Marshall, *Santa Fe: The Railroad That Built an Empire* (New York, Random House, 1945), 233.
4. As the train passed Oklahoma City and slowed opposite a fine piece of land near Edmond, Miss Daisey jumped off the cowcatcher, struck an attitude of defiance, and flung her shawl to the wind, shouting: "This claim is mine against all the world, take it who dare."
5. Marion Tuttle Rock, *Illustrated History of Oklahoma* (Topeka, C. B. Hamilton & Son, 1890), 23–24.
6. Walker, *loc. cit.*
7. Rock, *op. cit.*, 22, 24.
8. Bunky (Irving Geffs), *The First Eight Months of Oklahoma City* (Oklahoma City, McMaster Printing Co., 1890), 7.
9. J. A. Newsom, *The Life and Practice of the Wild and Modern Indian* (Oklahoma City, Harlow Publishing Co., 1923), 100–101.
10. *Vinita Indian Chieftain*, Apr. 23, 1889.

CHAPTER II

1. Hamilton S. Wicks, "The Opening of Oklahoma," *Oklahoma Daily Capital*, Apr. 27, 1890.
2. Angelo C. Scott, *The Story of Oklahoma City* (Oklahoma City, Times-Journal Publishing Co., 1939), 15.
3. A. Z. Clark, "One Oklahoma Pioneer," *Oklahoma State Capital*, Apr. 23, 1904.
4. *Topeka State Journal*, Apr. 23, 1889.
5. Victor E. Harlow, *Oklahoma: Its Origins and Developments* (Oklahoma City, Harlow Publishing Co., 1934), 252.
6. Dan W. Peery, "The First Two Years," *Chronicles of Oklahoma*, Vol. VII, No. 3 (September, 1929), 284–86.
7. Chris Madsen to *Guthrie Daily Leader*, Apr. 16, 1939.
8. *Ibid.*; Peery, *loc. cit.*

9. Marshall, *op. cit.*, 232–33.

10. Luther B. Hill, *A History of the State of Oklahoma* (Chicago and New York, Lewis Publishing Co., 1909), I, 218.

11. *Ibid.*, 215.

12. *Ibid.*, 209–210.

13. Evan G. Barnard, *A Rider of the Cherokee Strip* (Boston and New York, Houghton Mifflin Co., 1936), 142–43.

14. April 24 dispatch from Fort Reno, *Oklahoma City Times*, Apr. 29, 1889.

15. Madsen, *loc. cit.*

16. *Oklahoma City Times*, Apr. 29, 1889; *Vinita Indian Chieftain*, May 2, 1889.

17. *Ibid.*

18. *Ibid.*

19. *Ibid.*

20. Dennis T. Flynn, *Daily Oklahoman*, Apr. 23, 1939. Flynn, a lawyer and journalist who lived through Guthrie's first three turbulent years as its postmaster, served for eight years as the territory's delegate to Congress.

21. John Alley, *City Beginnings in Oklahoma Territory* (Norman, University of Oklahoma Press, 1939), 9–10.

22. *U.S. Statutes at Large*, XXII, 383–90.

23. *Ibid.*, XXV, chap. 333, sec. I.

24. Hill, *op. cit.*, 230.

25. *Vinita Indian Chieftain*, May 2, 1889.

26. The *New York Herald*, Apr. 24, 1889, and the *Chicago Tribune*, Apr. 26, 1889, also noted this condition in Guthrie.

27. Each of these subdivisions organized provisional governments under charters adopted at public meetings. The provisional governments assumed and exercised all the powers, functions, and authority of legally constituted municipal corporations and continued to do so until August, 1890, when they were consolidated and organized as a village corporation under and pursuant to the laws of Nebraska as adopted and extended over the territory by the Organic Act of May 2, 1890.

28. O. H. Richards, "Memories of an '89er," *Chronicles of Oklahoma*, Vol. XXVI, No. 1 (Spring, 1948), 3–4.

29. Rock, *op. cit.*, 27–28.

30. Editor Frank H. Greer, *Oklahoma Daily State Capital*.

31. Evett Dumas Nix, *Oklahombres* (St. Louis and Chicago, Eden Publishing House, 1929), 21.

32. *Guthrie Daily News*, Aug. 1, 1889.

33. Greer, *loc. cit.*; Hill, *op. cit.*, 230.

34. *Oklahoma City Times*, Apr. 29, 1889.

35. Cade, *loc. cit.*

36. Berlin B. Chapman, "The Founding of El Reno," *Chronicles of Oklahoma*, Vol. XXXIV, No. 1 (Spring, 1956), 79–108; Alley, *op. cit.*, 59–72.

37. *Daily Oklahoman*, Apr. 23, 1939; *Norman Transcript*, Sept. 13, 1964; Alley, *op. cit.*, 73.

38. *Oklahoma State Capital*, Oct. 4, 1894; Gaston Litton, *History of Oklahoma at the Golden Anniversary of Statehood* (New York, Lewis Historical Publishing Co., 1957), I, 431.

39. *Daily Oklahoman*, Apr. 23, 1939. The story of Stillwater's beginnings and growth has been told admirably by Berlin B. Chapman, *The Founding of Stillwater* (Oklahoma City, Times-Journal Publishing Co., 1948), and Robert E. Cunningham, *Stillwater: Where Oklahoma Began* (Arts and Humanities Council of Stillwater, Oklahoma, Inc., 1969).

40. Hill, *op. cit.*, 222.

41. Robe Carl White, "Experiences at the Opening of Oklahoma 1889," *Chronicles of Oklahoma*, Vol. XXVII, No. 1 (Spring, 1949), 60–62.

42. Scott, *op. cit.*, 37.

43. White, *loc. cit.*

44. *Oklahoma Pioneer* (Oklahoma City), May 11, 1889.

45. Roy Gittinger, *The Formation of the State of Oklahoma, 1803–1906* (Berkeley, University of California Press, 1917), 189; Hill, *op. cit.*, 228.

46. *Oklahoma City Times*, Sept. 19–27, 1889; Scott, *op. cit.*, 43–45, 65–67; Peery, *loc. cit.*, 297–315; Berlin B. Chapman, *Oklahoma City: From Public Land to Private Property* (1960), reprinted from *Chronicles of Oklahoma*, Vol. XXXVII, Nos. 2, 3, 4, 1–96.

47. Albert McRill, *And Satan Came Also* (Oklahoma City, Britton Publishing Co., 1955), 22.

48. *Ibid.*, 23.

49. *Ibid.*, 5, 73.

50. "Oklahoma City Was Born in One Day," *Daily Oklahoman*, Jan. 3, 1943.

51. Colonel D. F. MacMartin, *Thirty Years in Hell* (Topeka, Capper Printing Co., 1921), 21.

52. Joseph B. Thoburn and Muriel H. Wright, *Oklahoma: A History of the State and Its People* (New York, Lewis Historical Publishing Co., 1929), II, app. LVI–2, "Agitation for Territorial Government," 925–26.

53. The counties were Logan, Oklahoma, Cleveland, Canadian, Kingfisher, and Payne; the seat towns, Guthrie, Oklahoma City, Norman, El Reno, Kingfisher, and Stillwater, respectively.

54. Quapaw, Peoria, Ottawa, Shawnee, Modoc, Wyandotte, and Seneca.

55. The portion of the Outlet occupied by the Ponca, Tonkawa, Oto-Missouri, and Pawnee tribes was included.

56. Cattlemen and homesteaders occupied No Man's Land shortly after the Civil War. In 1887, they sought to create the Territory of Cimarron but gained no encouragement from Congress. To meet their needs, Congress now added the Panhandle to Oklahoma Territory as Beaver County, with the seat at Beaver.

57. Grant Foreman, "Horace Speed," *Chronicles of Oklahoma*, Vol. XXV, No. 1 (Spring, 1947), 5–6.

58. W. W. Jenkins, *Political Death by Assassin's Bullet: The Story of William M. Jenkins and His Family* (Denver, Dingerson Press, 1970), 76–77.

59. Homer Croy, *Trigger Marshal: The Story of Chris Madsen* (New York, Duell, Sloan & Pearce, 1958), "Sources," chap. 3, p. 247.

60. Ex parte Hally, I Oklahoma Reports 12; William Dysart et al. v. Warren S. Lurty et al., III Oklahoma Reports 601.

61. *Oklahoma State Capital,* Jan. 16, 1906; Joseph B. Thoburn, *A Standard History of Oklahoma* (Chicago and New York, American Historical Society, 1916), II, 653.

62. "Agitation for Territorial Government," in Thoburn and Wright, *op. cit.,* 925–26.

63. Report of the Governor of Oklahoma for 1891, *House Executive Documents,* 52nd Cong. 1st sess., XVI (2935), 449–50.

64. Oklahoma prisoners worked in the Kansas coal mines to pay the cost of their maintenance. This arrangement was continued until after statehood.

CHAPTER III

1. Fred E. Sutton, *Hands Up! Stories of the Six-Gun Fighters of the Old Wild West* (Indianapolis, Bobbs-Merrill Co., 1927), 186–87; Nix, *op. cit.,* 14–16; Newsom, *op. cit.,* 102–103; Croy, *op. cit.,* 36; Paul I. Wellman, *A Dynasty of Western Outlaws* (Garden City, N.Y., Doubleday & Co., 1961), 14; Richard S. Graves, *Oklahoma Outlaws* (Oklahoma City, State Printing and Publishing Co., 1915), 28–29.

2. Graves, *op. cit.,* 61–62; Newsom, *op. cit.,* 103; Zoe A. Tilghman, *Outlaw Days* (Oklahoma City, Harlow Publishing Co., 1926), 23.

3. Stanley Vestal, *Short Grass Country* (New York, Duell, Sloan & Pearce, 1941), 251.

4. Nix, *op. cit.,* 33.

5. Wellman, *op. cit.,* 14.

6. Often misspelled *Louis.*

7. In the *Kansas City Star,* May 10, 1931, Emmett Dalton is quoted: "Poor mother; we gave her plenty of trouble. She was a sister to Henry Younger—father of Cole, Bob and Jim, the outlaws. They were my cousins." See also Emmett Dalton, *When the Daltons Rode* (New York, Doubleday, Doran & Co., 1931), 19. Fred Harvey Harrington, *The Hanging Judge* (Caldwell, Idaho, Caxton Printers, 1951), 81, says Henry Washington Younger was her half-brother. Wellman, *op. cit.,* 159, accepts. Harold Preece, *The Dalton Gang* (New York, Hastings House, 1963), 13, states that no records have turned up to prove such a relationship.

Actually, Adeline was the daughter of Charles F. Younger, brother of Colonel Henry Washington Younger, father of Cole, Bob, Jim, and John. The Younger boys and the Daltons were *second* cousins.

8. David Stewart Elliott, *Last Raid of the Daltons* (Coffeyville Daily Journal, Oct. 22, 1892), 54; S. W. Harman, *Hell on the Border: He*

Hanged Eighty-eight Men (Fort Smith, Ark., Phoenix Publishing Co., 1898), 633.

9. Dalton, *op. cit.,* 25.

10. Harman, *op. cit.,* 634.

11. Glenn Shirley, *Heck Thomas, Frontier Marshal* (Philadelphia and New York, Chilton Co., 1962), 66–67, 78–81; Dalton, *op. cit.,* 202–208.

12. D. S. Elliott and Ed Bartholomew, *The Dalton Gang and the Coffeyville Raid* (Fort Davis, Tex., Frontier Book Co., 1968), 58.

13. Elliott, *op. cit.,* 55; Harman, *op. cit.,* 635.

14. T. A. McNeal, *When Kansas Was Young* (New York, MacMillan Co., 1922), 271; Elliott, *op. cit.,* 55; Elliott and Bartholomew, *op. cit.,* 57.

15. Shirley, *Heck Thomas,* 122–123.

16. Dalton, *op. cit.,* 35.

17. *Ibid.,* 36.

18. McNeal, *op. cit.,* 272.

19. Croy, *op. cit.,* 176.

20. *Oklahoma City Times-Journal,* Aug. 26, 1891; Nix, *op. cit.,* 37; Sam P. Ridings, *The Chisholm Trail* (Guthrie, Okla., Co-operative Publishing Co., 1936), 468–69.

21. Dalton, *op. cit.,* 91.

22. McNeal, *op. cit.,* 271.

23. Shirley, *Heck Thomas,* 124–25.

24. *Vinita Indian Chieftain,* Feb. 30, 1890.

25. *Ibid.,* Apr. 17, 1890.

26. *Laws Governing U. S. Marshal and His Deputies, Western District of Arkansas* (Fort Smith, J. H. Mayers & Co. 1892).

27. Emmett Dalton, "Beyond the Law" [I], *Wide World Magazine,* Vol. XLI, No. 241 (May, 1918), 3.

28. These forays of horse thievery also are narrated, with additional detail, in the *Vinita Indian Chieftain* of September 11, 1890. Harry Sinclair Drago, *Outlaws on Horseback* (New York, Dodd, Mead & Co., 1964), 203–204, is mistaken in saying they occurred in Old Oklahoma and the Cherokee Strip, that the Cherokee Strip Livestock Association hired stock detectives to identify the Daltons, and that no one has produced evidence to support Grat's involvement and release.

Records of the U.S. commissioner's court at Fort Smith show that warrants were issued for Grat, Bob, and Emmett on September 6, 1890, for horse stealing. Grat was arrested at Claremore and delivered to the U.S. commissioner's court by Deputy Marshals L. P. Isbell and Barney Connelly. No evidence was presented connecting him with the thefts, although the evidence against Bob and Emmett was conclusive. Grat was released and departed for California in October.

29. "An Eye Witness," *The Dalton Brothers and Their Astounding Career of Crime* (Chicago, Laird & Lee, 1892), 66–72; C. B. Glasscock, *Bandits and the Southern Pacific* (New York, Frederick A. Stokes Co., 1929), 37–44; Stewart H. Holbrook, *The Story of American Railroads*

(New York, Crown Publishers, 1947), 379–80; Eugene B. Block, *Great Train Robberies of the West* (New York, Coward-McCann, 1959), 93–95; Preece, *op. cit.*, 87–97; Richard Dillon, *Wells, Fargo Detective: The Biography of James B. Hume* (New York, Coward-McCann, 1969), 248–49.

30. Nix (pp. 37–38) and Wellman (pp. 165–66) are incorrect in putting the Starmer killing after the Wharton train robbery. Starmer was killed May 2, 1891, and the train robbery occurred a week later. Drago (pp. 210–11) accepts the error and places the Twin Mounds fight on Skeleton Creek, nearly twenty miles west. Preece (pp. 210–11) gives a fictionalized account in which the incident occurs on "a pair of strategically placed Ozark [?] hillocks . . . a mile or two from the banks of Beaver Creek."

31. "An Eye Witness," *op. cit.*, 76–78.

32. Pp. 87–89.

33. Emmett Dalton, "Beyond the Law" [II], *Wide World Magazine*, Vol. XLI, No. 242 (June, 1918), 94.

CHAPTER IV

1. Dalton, *op. cit.*, 91–93.

2. *Ibid.*; Emmett Dalton, "Beyond the Law" [III], *Wide World Magazine*, Vol. XLI, No. 243 (July, 1918), 199.

3. *Op. cit.*, 106.

4. Frank C. Cooper, "Santa Fe Passenger Train Holdups in Oklahoma During the '90's," *Santa Fe Magazine* (April, 1955).

5. Colonel Bailey C. Hanes, *Bill Doolin, Outlaw O. T.* (Norman, University of Oklahoma Press, 1968), 31.

6. "Beyond the Law" [II], *loc. cit.*, 95.

7. *Ibid.* Drago (p. 210) says there were seven in the gang; Hanes (p. 31) accepts and names the additional three as Bill Doolin, Dick Broadwell, and Bill Powers. Hanes also dates the holdup incorrectly as Friday, May 8.

8. Drago (p. 209) says northbound.

9. *Op. cit.*, 95.

10. *Op. cit.*, 104.

11. *Op. cit.*, 95–96.

12. *Op. cit.*, 209.

13. *Op. cit.*, 104.

14. *Op. cit.*, 95.

15. *Op. cit.*, 98–100.

16. *Op. cit.*, 165.

17. "Beyond the Law" [II], *loc. cit.*, 96.

18. May 15, 1891.

19. Dalton (p. 96) claims Miss Moore had learned this "through her access to official circles," and Preece (p. 106) accepts.

20. Hanes (p. 32) credits Bill Doolin with discovering this five hundred· dollars.

21. Dalton, *op. cit.*, 97.

22. *Op. cit.*, 274.

23. *Op. cit.*, 40.

24. *Op. cit.*, 210.

25. *Op. cit.*, 108–109.

26. *Fort Smith Elevator*, May 15, 1891.

27. *Ibid.*

28. "Beyond the Law" [II], *loc. cit.*, 97.

29. *Fort Smith Elevator*, May 15, 1891.

30. Carolyn Lake (ed.), *Under Cover for Wells Fargo: The Unvarnished Recollections of Fred Dodge* (Boston, Houghton Mifflin Co., 1969), 124 (cited hereafter as *Dodge Recollections*).

31. Dalton, *op. cit.*, 97.

32. *Fort Smith Elevator*, May 15, 1891.

33. *Dodge Recollections*, 123–24.

34. May 15, 1891.

35. "Beyond the Law" [III], *loc. cit.*, 193.

36. "An Eye Witness," *op. cit.*, 105.

37. *Dodge Recollections*, 126.

38. *Ibid.*

39. *Op. cit.*, 105.

40. *Op. cit.*, 87.

41. *Op. cit.*, 88–89.

42. *Op. cit.*, 89–90.

43. *Sheriff's Report of U. S. Prisoners in County Jail, Sedgwick County, Kansas (1886–1894).*

44. *Op. cit.*, 69–71.

45. *Op. cit.*, 214.

46. *Op. cit.*, 121.

47. "Ed Short's Career," *Oklahoma City Times-Journal*, Aug. 26, 1891; "Ed Short, Fearless Gunman," *Daily Oklahoman*, Feb. 29, 1920; George Rainey, *No Man's Land: The Historic Story of a Landed Orphan* (Guthrie, Okla., Co-Operative Publishing Co., 1937), 201–209; Ridings, *op. cit.*, 464.

48. There was no sister Daisy or brother, Jim Bryant, living near Mulhall. This fiction originated with "An Eye Witness" (pp. 106–111).

49. The "Eye Witness" and Emmett Dalton's two versions of Bryant's capture and his gun battle with Ed Short are replete with manufactured dialogue and sentimental inaccuracies.

Graves (pp. 40–41), Zoe A. Tilghman, *Outlaw Days* (pp. 35–37), Sutton (pp. 273–77), Nix (pp. 40–43), Barnard (pp. 193–95), Ridings (pp. 463–69), and Wellman (pp. 167–70) all incorrectly place the event *after* the Red Rock robbery of June, 1892, and claim Bryant was wanted for the murder of the Wharton station agent. Sutton even claims to have been present when Black-Faced Charley was rolled down the car steps onto the Waukomis station platform and that the outlaw, still alive, asked him, "Please pull my boots off, and don't tell the folks back home."

The most accurate accounts appear in the *Oklahoma State Capital,*

Aug. 24, 1891; *Oklahoma City Times-Journal,* Aug. 26, 1891; *Vinita Indian Chieftain,* Aug. 27, 1891; and George Rainey, *The Cherokee Strip* (Guthrie, Okla., Co-Operative Publishing Co., 1933), 255–61.

CHAPTER V

1. *Op. cit.,* 113–15.
2. *Op. cit.,* 38.
3. "Beyond the Law" [III], *loc. cit.,* 198–99.
4. *Ibid.*
5. *Vinita Indian Chieftain,* Sept. 17, 1891.
6. Dalton, *op. cit.,* 133; "Beyond the Law" [III], *loc. cit.,* 199; Preece, *op. cit.,* 138–39; Hanes, *op. cit.,* 40.
7. Sept. 17, 1891.
8. "Beyond the Law" [III], *loc. cit.,* 199.
9. *Op. cit.,* 135.
10. *Vinita Indian Chieftain,* Sept. 17, 1891; *Fort Smith Elevator,* Sept. 18, 1891.
11. Dalton, *op. cit.,* 135.
12. Sept. 17, 1891.
13. Oct. 8, 1891.
14. Sept. 18, 1891.
15. Sept. 17, 1891.
16. E. Bee Guthrey, "Early Days in Payne County," *Chronicles of Oklahoma,* Vol. III, No. 1 (April, 1925), 77–78 (Guthrey thought the robbery had occurred at Clarksville, Arkansas).
17. Sept. 4, 1891.
18. Glasscock, *op. cit.,* 55–56.
19. *Op. cit.,* 112–19, and "Beyond the Law" [IV], *Wide World Magazine,* Vol. XLI, No. 244 (August, 1918), 313.
20. *Op. cit.,* 72–74.
21. *Op. cit.,* 163–64.
22. *Op. cit.,* 206–208.
23. (New York, Frederick Fell), 24–25.
24. "Beyond the Law" [IV], *loc. cit.,* 312–13.
25. Dalton, *op. cit.,* 122.
26. "Beyond the Law" [III], *loc. cit.,* 197–98.
27. Dalton, *op. cit.,* 117–19, 141.
28. "Beyond the Law" [IV], *loc. cit.,* 314.
29. Misspelled *Mock* by Hanes (p. 44).
30. Misspelled *Whitteny* by Hanes (p. 45).
31. *Fort Smith Elevator,* June 10, 1892; Rainey, *The Cherokee Strip,* pp. 233–234.
32. *Ibid.* Nix (pp. 39–40) has Bob, Emmett, and Powers robbing the coaches and herding frightened passengers on and off the station platform. Wellman (pp. 166–67) follows the Nix version, robbing passengers of watches and jewelry, tumbling the safe from the express car, and opening it on the ground outside. Drago (p. 216) accepts. Preece (pp.

164–69) follows the facts fairly accurately but fictionizes heavily. Emmett Dalton (p. 149) incorrectly states that the robbery was done quickly, without resistance. Not a shot was fired, and, except for the station agent, Red Rock "hadn't even turned over in its sleep."

33. [IV], *loc. cit.*, 315.

34. P. 149.

35. *Op. cit.*, 119.

36. Rainey, *The Cherokee Strip*, 235.

37. Especially Dalton, *op. cit.*, 149–52.

38. *Dodge Recollections*, 156.

CHAPTER VI

1. *Dodge Recollections*, 157.

2. *Daily Oklahoman*, Aug. 17, 1952.

3. Interview with Ben Beckley [n.d.], Vol. 51, p. 106, *Indian-Pioneer History, Foreman Collection*, Oklahoma Historical Society.

4. Interview with Fred Dunlap, December 14, 1937, Vol. 23, p. 110, *Indian-Pioneer History, Foreman Collection*, Oklahoma Historical Society.

5. Interview with Cam Hornbeck [n.d.], Vol. 29, p. 447, *Indian-Pioneer History, Foreman Collection*, Oklahoma Historical Society.

6. *Op. cit.*, 216.

7. *Op. cit.*, 48.

8. *Op. cit.*, 123–24.

9. *Op. cit.*, 165.

10. July 21, 1892.

11. Dalton, *op. cit.*, 167; Preece, *op. cit.*, 191–92.

12. *Vinita Indian Chieftain*, July 21, 1892.

13. July 21, 1892.

14. July 15, 1892.

15. [IV], *loc. cit.*, 315–17.

16. *Op. cit.*, 130.

17. *Op. cit.*, 193.

18. *Op. cit.*, 48–52.

19. *Op. cit.*, 219.

20. *Op. cit.*, 181.

21. [IV], *loc. cit.*, 317.

22. Preece, *op. cit.*, 214.

23. *Vinita Indian Chieftain*, July 28, 1892.

24. *Op. cit.*, 181–82, and "Beyond the Law" [V], *Wide World Magazine*, Vol. XLI, No. 245 (September, 1918), 380.

25. Dalton, *op. cit.*, 183–84, 301–303.

26. "An Eye Witness," *op. cit.*, 138–39.

27. *Ibid.*; Emerson Hough, *The Story of the Outlaw* (New York, Outing Publishing Co., 1907), 380.

28. *Oklahoma State Capital*, Oct. 24, 1894.

29. *Dodge Recollections,* 159–71.

30. Emmett Dalton (pp. 210–11) mentions the incident but says it occurred while they were crossing the Arkansas in escaping from the Adair robbery.

31. Nix, *op. cit.,* 44.

32. [V], *loc. cit.,* 379–80.

33. Pp. 222–25.

34. Pp. 152–53.

35. Pp. 53–55.

36. *Op. cit.,* 161–62.

37. Pp. 47–49.

38. *Op. cit.,* 188–90.

39. *Op. cit.,* 51–53.

40. *Op. cit.,* 175–76, 186–87.

41. *Op. cit.,* 222–23.

42. (Albuquerque, University of New Mexico Press, 1955), 58–59.

43. P. 143.

44. Pp. xii–xiii.

45. P. 162.

46. *Coffeyville Journal,* Oct. 7, 1892.

CHAPTER VII

1. *Op. cit.,* 24.

2. (Tulsa, Okla., George Henry Printing Co., n.d.), 4.

3. Hanes, *op. cit.,* 25.

4. Interview with Jim Williams, August 20, 1937, Vol. 49, p. 519, *Indian-Pioneer History, Foreman Collection,* Oklahoma Historical Society.

5. Graves, *op. cit.,* 57–58; Newsom, *op. cit.,* 163; Nix, *op. cit.,* 56–57.

6. Hanes (p. 59) places them at Dave Fitzgerald's horse ranch eleven miles northeast of Guthrie on Cowboy Flats. Fitzgerald homesteaded there in the Oklahoma opening, near a creek that bore his name, and was a close friend of Halsell's employees.

7. Oct. 26, 1892.

8. *Coffeyville Journal,* Oct. 14, 1892; *Stillwater Gazette,* Oct. 21, 1892.

9. *Ibid.*

10. *Op. cit.,* 209.

11. *Op. cit.,* 66–68.

12. *Coffeyville Journal,* Oct. 14, 1892.

13. Preece, *op. cit.,* 111–17.

14. *Dodge City Globe,* Nov. 2, 1892; *Vinita Indian Chieftain,* Nov. 3, 1892.

Nix (p. 61) includes Bill Dalton, making the number *four,* adding that "other members of the gang were too busy arranging their affairs to join the outfit permanently" and did not participate. Wellman (p. 192) and Drago (p. 232) accept, and Hanes (p. 69) gives the time as "about 2 P.M.," contemporary reports to the contrary.

15. Hanes (p. 69) claims that Doolin went to the cashier's desk and began negotiations for a personal loan (not likely, since he was wearing a mask) while Newcomb stepped to the opening at the counter, suddenly drew his six-shooter, and told Baird to throw up his hands "damn quick" and that Baird dropped behind his desk to seize a gun kept there for just such an emergency but the pair pounced on him before he could use the weapon.

16. Hanes (p. 69) says they overlooked quite a sum of gold and silver hidden under some loose papers on Baird's desk; Nix (p. 61) sets the amount taken at "several thousand dollars"; Wellman (p. 193) and Drago (p. 232) claim a fantastic $18,000!

17. *Dodge City Globe*, Nov. 2, 1892; *Vinita Indian Chieftain*, Nov. 3, 1892.

18. This story first appeared in Graves's *Oklahoma Outlaws* (pp. 41–42); was repeated by Newsom (p. 155), who includes Heck Thomas in the posse; and was repeated in *Outlaw Days* by Zoe A. Tilghman (pp. 37–39), who still believed it (p. 207) in *Marshal of the Last Frontier* (Glendale, Calif., Arthur H. Clark Co., 1949) and added that Madsen, who was at Fort Supply and was warned by telegraph, almost caught the Spearville robbers with a squad of soldiers as they fled through western Oklahoma and that in the running fight Doolin was wounded in the foot. This didn't happen until months later.

Nix (pp. 61–62) enlarges on the tale. Yantis, discovering Beeson trailing him, became frantic and, in his haste to put as much distance between himself and pursuer as possible, rode his horse to exhaustion. Yantis then encountered a farmer riding a very good horse, and when the latter refused to exchange mounts with him, Yantis shot and killed him instantly, than raced on to his sister's home fifteen miles away. The murder of the farmer aroused the entire community. Meanwhile, Sheriff Beeson came upon the outlaw's exhausted horse and followed the trail to the home of Yantis' sister.

Wellman (pp. 192–93) and Drago (pp. 232–33) accept Nix, and I believed the story in *Six-Gun* (pp. 67–68) and *Heck Thomas* (p. 152) until I was unable to locate such a report in official records or the territorial press.

19. *Stillwater Gazette*, Dec. 2, 1892; *Dodge City Globe*, Dec. 2, 1892.

20. *Ibid.*

21. Yantis v. Hueston et al., Case No. 211, District Court, Payne County, O. T.; U.S. Attorney C. R. Brooks to Attorney General Richard Olney, June 22–July 21, 1894, *passim*, Records of District Attorney for Oklahoma Territory, Guthrie, 1894.

CHAPTER VIII

1. *Coffeyville Journal*, Dec. 23, 1892.

2. *Ibid.*

3. Vest to Miller, December 25, 1892, Department of Justice, File 12014.

4. Walker to Attorney General, December 26, 1892, Department of Justice, File 12014.

5. Needles to Attorney General, December 26, 1892, Department of Justice, File 12014.

6. Dickerson to Attorney General, December 29, 1892, Department of Justice, File 12014.

7. Yoes to Attorney General, December 29, 1892, Department of Justice, File 12014.

8. Grimes to Attorney General, December 29, 1892, Department of Justice, File 12014.

9. *Coffeyville Journal*, Nov. 4, 1892.

10. Emmett Dalton served a little less than fifteen years. In November, 1907, his sentence was commuted by Kansas Governor Edward M. Hoch. A year later, he married Julia Johnson of Bartlesville, Oklahoma, his childhood sweetheart, who, with his mother, had worked so hard for his freedom. Emmett justified the belief of the parole board that he would become an upright citizen. He did some theatrical work and became known to thousands in a new generation by writing of his experiences for the movies, books, and western magazines. In the early 1920's, he moved to California to be close to his Hollywood friends and joined church. Until ill health prevented his activities, he engaged in the real estate business and was a building contractor. He died peacefully in Los Angeles on July 13, 1937, at sixty-six. On July 14, his shot-scarred corpse was removed to a crematory. His ashes were taken to Coffeyville and buried beside his older brother, Bob, whom he loved so much and with whom he had come near losing his life while attempting the latter's rescue in Death Alley.

11. Nix, *op. cit.*, 57–58.

12. *U.S. Statutes at Large*, XXVI, 749, 794, 1016, 1025; XXVII, 989–93.

13. Report of the Secretary of the Interior for 1891, *House Executive Documents*, 52nd Cong. 1st sess., XIV, 2933; Thoburn and Wright, *op. cit.*, 555; Gittinger, *op. cit.*, 197–98; Dora Ann Stewart, *The Government and Development of Oklahoma Territory* (Oklahoma City, Harlow Publishing Co., 1933), 61–62.

14. *U.S. Statutes at Large*, XXVII, 1018–21; Thoburn and Wright, *op. cit.*, 555–56; Stewart, *op. cit.*, 68.

15. Report of the Governor of Oklahoma, 1892.

16. Nix, *op. cit.*, 30–31, 64–65.

17. Organic Act, secs. 9 and 10; in re Terrill, 144 Federal Reporter 616.

18. Dan W. Peery, "George W. Steele, First Governor of the Territory of Oklahoma," *Chronicles of Oklahoma*, Vol. XII, No. 4 (December, 1934), 383–92; John Bartlett Meserve, "The Governors of Oklahoma Territory," *Chronicles of Oklahoma*, Vol. XX, No. 3 (September, 1942), 218–19.

19. "Oklahoma Governors," *Oklahoma State Capital*, Jan. 16, 1906.

20. "Oklahoma Governors," *loc. cit.*; "Autobiographical Sketch of Ex-Governor A. J. Seay's Public Life," *Oklahoma State Capital*, Apr. 11, 1909; Meserve, *loc. cit.*, 219–21.

21. "Oklahoma Governors," *loc. cit.*; Meserve, *loc. cit.*, 221–22.

22. Nix, *op. cit.*, 1–8, 29–31, and biographical data in *Oklahoma State Capital*, May 29, 1893; *Guthrie Daily Leader*, Oct. 7, 1894.

23. Nix, *op. cit.*, 66–67.

24. Original petition, To His Excellency, Grover Cleveland, President of the United States, Cloud Chief, O. T., February 17, 1893 (photo copy in author's collection).

25. Parker to Cleveland, Fort Smith, Arkansas, February 21, 1893 (photocopy in author's collection).

26. *Oklahoma State Capital*, May 29, 1893.

27. *Ibid.*

28. June 7, 1893.

29. June 17, 1893.

30. *The Autobiography of Charles Francis Colcord, 1859–1934* (Privately printed, 1970).

31. *Oklahombres*, 81–82.

32. *Ibid.*, 71.

33. *Ibid.*; *Oklahoma State Capital*, July 6, 1893.

34. Nix, *op. cit.*, 83–85.

35. Shirley, *Heck Thomas*, 120–21.

36. June 11 dispatch from Cimarron, Kan., *Oklahoma State Capital*, June 12, 1893.

Graves (p. 65), Newsom (p. 166), Zoe A. Tilghman, *Outlaw Days* (p. 61) and *Marshal of the Last Frontier* (p. 208), Croy (p. 166), and Wellman (p. 197) give the date incorrectly as May 28. Drago (p. 234) uses May 26. Nix (p. 87) mentions no date and calls the holdup a bank robbery. Hanes (p. 80), generally accurate on various aspects of the affair (except that Arkansas Tom did not participate), gives June 10.

37. *Op. cit.*, 198.

38. *Op. cit.*, 234.

39. June 11 dispatch from Cimarron, Kan., *Oklahoma State Capital*, June 12, 1893.

40. *Op. cit.*, 166–67.

41. Wellman (p. 198), Drago (pp. 234–35), and Hanes (pp. 82–83) accept this story.

42. *Guthrie Daily News*, June 16, 1893; *Oklahoma State Capital*, June 16–17, 1893.

43. Dictated to Harold L. Mueller, serialized in the *Daily Oklahoman*, Nov. 17, 1935–Mar. 15, 1936, and reprinted in *Farmer-Stockman*, May 1, 1941–Feb. 15, 1942.

44. *Dodge Recollections*, 182–83.

45. Reminiscences of Billy McGinty (332 pages), dictated to Glenn Shirley at Ripley, Oklahoma, 1957–1958 (in author's collection).

The *Stillwater Gazette* of June 4, 1904, states in its sketch of Daugherty's early life: "Giving up the idea of preaching, Jones—but that's not his correct name, for he gives an alias after getting into trouble . . . wandered into western Texas and finally became a cowboy in the Panhandle district, afterward in Western Oklahoma, along the Woods and Woodward county line. Early in 1893 he was attracted by the successful career being made as outlaws by the Dalton and Doolin gangs, and rode overland to Ingalls, where he joined the gang which was then making its headquarters [there]."

46. *Guthrie Daily Leader*, Aug. 11–Sept. 1, 1893; *Oklahoma State Capital*, Aug. 26–30, 1893; Thoburn and Wright, *op. cit.*, 556–57; Gittinger, *op. cit.*, 201–205.

47. *Op. cit.*, 88–89; "Letter of Suggestions," Governor William C. Renfrow, U.S. Attorney Horace Speed and U.S. Marshal E. D. Nix to President Cleveland, Guthrie, O. T., July 15, 1893 (photocopy in author's collection).

48. "Four Score Years A Fighter," *loc. cit.*

49. Zoe A. Tilghman, *Marshal of the Last Frontier*, 15–185, *passim*; W. B. (Bat) Masterson, "Famous Gunfighters of the Western Frontier," *Human Life* (July, 1907).

CHAPTER IX

1. Mrs. Frank Garrett, "Jesse Denton Ramsey," *Chronicles of Comanche County*, Vol. II, No. 1 (Spring, 1956), 10.

2. Named by settlers from Falls City, Nebraska.

3. George H. Shirk, "First Post Offices Within the Boundaries of Oklahoma," *Chronicles of Oklahoma*, Vol. XXVI, No. 2 (Summer, 1948), 240, and Vol. XXX, No. 1 (Spring, 1952), 70.

Hanes (p. 27) misspells the name *McCurty*; Leslie McRill, in "Old Ingalls: The Story of a Town That Will Not Die," *Chronicles of Oklahoma*, Vol. XXVI, No. 4 (Winter, 1958–59), 429, misspells it *McCurtry*.

4. Records of Payne County Clerk's Office, Stillwater, Oklahoma.

5. Nix (pp. 103, 105) calls it the Trilby; Wellman (p. 199) and Drago (p. 237) accept. James D. Horan, *Desperate Women* (New York, G. P. Putnam's Sons, 1952), in his fictionized chapter on the mythical "Rose of the Cimarron" (p. 245), claims the buildings were two saloons: Trilby's, "a gambling place," and Ransom's saloon, "a drinking place." The name *Trilby* does not appear in contemporary reports or official records.

6. Drago (p. 237) calls Mary Pierce a widow. She was the wife of Henry Pierce, and they had four children. In 1901, Pierce moved to Stillwater, where he dealt in livestock and managed the Globe Hotel. In February, 1905, he was murdered and robbed while on a mule-buying trip at Perry.

7. Hanes (p. 78) spells Wagner as *Wagoner*, Comley as *Conley*, and Sadie's maiden name as *McCloskey*. He thinks she was a waitress at an Ingalls restaurant.

8. Nix (pp. 103–104) attributes this operation to Mary Pierce.

9. *Op. cit.*, 103.

10. Newsom (p. 179) claims they were married in the spring of 1894, Wellman (p. 221) in 1894, and Drago (p. 259) in the summer of 1894.

11. *Op. cit.*, 74–75.

12. *Op. cit.*, 178.

13. *Outlaw Days*, 68–70.

14. *Op. cit.*, 436.

15. *Op. cit.*, 84–85.

16. *Stillwater Gazette*, Sept. 1, 1893; *Guthrie Daily Leader*, Sept. 5, 1893; *Perkins Journal*, Sept. 7, 1893.

17. *Dodge Recollections*, 182–83.

18. *Oklahoma State Capital*, July 10, 1893; *Stillwater Gazette*, July 14, 1893.

19. July 10, 1893.

20. P. 22.

21. *Tulsa Daily World*, Dec. 20, 1936.

22. Interview with Orrington Lucas, December 29, 1937, Vol. 61, pp. 470–76, *Indian-Pioneer History, Foreman Collection*, Oklahoma Historical Society.

23. *Oklahoma State Capital*, Sept. 2, 1893; *Guthrie Daily Leader*, Sept. 2 and 5, 1893; *Stillwater Gazette*, Apr. 10, 1908.

24. H. A. Thompson (Reminiscences of the Ingalls Battle) to Glenn Shirley, June 3, 1940 (in author's collection).

Thompson was born in Jasper County, Indiana, in 1870. He came to Oklahoma in 1889, living at Stillwater until 1897, where he was under-sheriff of Payne County and U.S. deputy marshal. In 1897, he moved to Tulsa, serving as deputy marshal until 1904, at which time he was employed by the St. Louis & San Francisco Railway Company to protect its trains out of St. Louis during the World's Fair. In 1909, he was appointed chief of police at Tulsa and in 1911 became a special agent for the Department of Justice, working on the Mexican border with headquarters at San Antonio, Texas. In 1919, he returned to the St. Louis & San Francisco as district special agent and in 1929 became superintendent of the Bureau of Identification, Oklahoma City Police Department, where he was employed until his death on March 2, 1945.

25. Sutton (p. 193) claims "Bill Tilghman was in charge but his team ran away, his leg was broken and he was not in the battle." Nix (p. 104) says "Tilghman had planned to lead the group of officers, but he had broken an ankle and was confined to his home in Guthrie" (apparently his ghost writer was relying on Sutton, for Nix had sent Tilghman to Perry). Zoe A. Tilghman, *Marshal of the Last Frontier* (p. 209) has Bill "laid up at this time . . . he and his horse having plunged off a broken bridge into a swollen creek . . . in the rain." Wellman (p. 199) and Drago (p. 242) accept Nix and Sutton. Drago is mistaken in including Frank Canton and Charles Colcord in the posse.

26. Thompson to Shirley, *loc. cit.*

27. Stansbery, "'Cops and Robbers' in Territorial Days," *op. cit.*; Elmer T. Peterson, "A Ghost Comes to Life," *Daily Oklahoman*, Sept. 11, 1938.

28. O. W. Sollers to Glenn Shirley, July–August, 1937 (in author's collection). Sollers had replaced Thomas J. Hueston as city marshal in the

spring of 1893. In his last years, Mr. Sollers and I discussed the Ingalls fight often.

29. *Oklahoma State Capital*, Sept. 2, 1893.

30. E. D. Nix to Attorney General Olney, July 30, 1895, Records of United States Marshal for Oklahoma Territory, Guthrie, 1893–1895; *Perkins Journal*, Sept. 7, 1893.

Dan Nelson, "The Ingalls Raid," *Daily O'Collegian*, May 2, 1926, says "the bullet struck the magazine . . . and split . . . half of it entered his body near the right groin, clipping off the end of his spinal column, then curved back to make its exit near the left groin." With such a wound, Newcomb hardly could have ridden out of Ingalls. Hanes (pp. 106–107) relies on this fiction and adds: "Bitter Creek shifted his Winchester to his left hand . . . drew his Colt with his right hand" and finished off Speed with "a .45 slug."

31. Territory of Oklahoma v. Tom Jones, Case No. 323, District Court of Payne County, November 30, 1893; *Oklahoma State Capital*, Sept. 2, 1893; *Perkins Journal*, Sept. 7, 1893; *Stillwater Gazette*, Apr. 10, 1908.

32. McRill, *op. cit.*, 433.

33. *Stillwater Gazette*, Sept. 1, 1893; *Guthrie Daily Leader*, Sept. 5, 1893; *Perkins Journal*, Sept. 7, 1893.

34. Nix to Attorney General, *loc. cit.*

35. *Guthrie Daily Leader*, Sept. 5, 1893; *Stillwater Gazette*, July 30, 1906.

36. Nix to Attorney General, *loc. cit.*

37. Territory of Oklahoma v. Tom Jones, *loc. cit.*; *Stillwater Gazette*, June 9, 1904, and Apr. 10, 1908.

38. Thompson to Shirley, *loc. cit.*; *Stillwater Gazette*, July 20, 1906.

39. *Stillwater Gazette*, Apr. 10, 1908.

40. "How Shadley Fell," *Oklahoma State Capital*, Sept. 13, 1893.

41. *Op. cit.*, 435.

42. *Op. cit.*, 114–15.

43. *Op. cit.*, 115.

44. Nelson, *loc. cit.*

45. *Stillwater Gazette*, July 20, 1906.

46. Wellman (pp. 210–211) claims that Doolin (not Dynamite Dick) received this ball "at the base of [his] skull," and it "remained there the rest of his life," causing severe headaches and occasional seizures "similar to short epileptic fits."

47. *Oklahoma State Capital*, Sept. 2, 1893; *Stillwater Gazette*, July 20, 1906.

48. *Oklahoma State Capital*, Sept. 4, 1893; *Perkins Journal*, Sept. 7, 1893; *Stillwater Gazette*, July 20, 1906.

49. *Ibid.*

50. *Oklahoma State Capital*, Sept. 2, 1893.

51. Sollers to Shirley, *loc. cit.*

52. P. 195.

53. Pp. 109–111.

54. P. 255.
55. P. 207.
56. Sollers to Shirley, *loc. cit.*
57. *Guthrie Daily Leader*, Sept. 2, 1893.
58. *Oklahoma State Capital*, Sept. 7, 1893; *Oklahoma City Press-Gazette*, Sept. 8, 1893.
59. Sept. 8, 1893.
60. Sept. 4, 1893.
61. *Perkins Journal*, Sept. 7 1893.
62. *Ibid.*, Sept. 21, 1893.
63. *Stillwater Gazette*, Sept. 8, 1893.
64. *Oklahoma State Capital*, Sept. 4, 1893.
65. *Oklahoma State Capital*, Sept. 11, 1893; *Guthrie Daily Leader*, Sept. 13, 1893.
66. *Oklahoma State Capital*, Sept. 16, 1893; *Guthrie Daily Leader*, Sept. 16, 1893.
67. *Ibid.*
68. *Ibid.*

CHAPTER X

1. *Guthrie Daily Leader*, Sept. 19, 1893.
2. *Ibid.*; *Oklahoma State Capital*, Sept. 20, 1893.
3. Oct. 3, 1893.
4. *Oklahoma State Capital*, Sept. 23, 1893.
5. *Ibid.*, Oct. 3, 1893.
6. *Ibid.*, Sept. 30, 1893.
7. *Guthrie Daily Leader*, Nov. 10, 1893.
8. *Oklahoma State Capital*, Nov. 18, 1893.
9. *Ibid.*, Sept. 30, 1893.
10. *Ibid.*
11. *Ibid.*, Sept. 20, 25, and 30, 1893.
12. Nix, *op. cit.*, 98.
13. The exploits of Thomas and Tilghman during these few months are described in Shirley, *Heck Thomas*, 176–87.
14. *U.S. Statutes at Large*, XXVIII, 20.
15. *Oklahoma State Capital*, Jan. 9, 1894; *Oklahoma Daily Press-Gazette*, Jan. 9, 1894.
16. *Oklahoma State Capital*, Feb. 3, 1894; Thomas H. Doyle, "The Supreme Court of the Territory of Oklahoma," *Chronicles of Oklahoma*, Vol. XIII, No. 2 (June, 1935).
17. *Oklahoma State Capital*, Mar. 21, 1894; *Oklahoma Daily Press-Gazette*, Mar. 22, 1894.
18. *Oklahoma State Capital*, Nov. 13, 1893.
19. *Ibid.*, Nov. 20, 1893.
20. *Ibid.*, Nov. 22, 1893.

21. Nov. 24, 1893.
22. Dec. 1, 1893.
23. *Oklahoma State Capital,* Dec. 7, 1893.
24. *Stillwater Eagle-Gazette,* Jan. 5, 1894.
25. Department of Justice, File 12014, No. 687.
26. *Oklahoma State Capital,* Jan. 24, 1894; *Pawnee Times,* Jan. 26, 1894; *Pawnee Scout,* Jan. 26, 1894; *Stillwater Eagle-Gazette,* Jan. 26, 1894.
27. Jan. 26, 1894.
28. Mar. 7, 1894.
29. Department of Justice, File 12014.
30. *Ibid.,* No. 1951.
31. *Ibid.,* No. 2225.
32. *Oklahoma Daily Press-Gazette,* Mar. 14, 1894.
33. *Ibid.; Oklahoma State Capital,* Mar. 13 and 14, 1894; *Guthrie Daily Leader,* Mar. 14, 1894.
34. *Oklahoma Daily Press-Gazette,* Mar. 14, 1894; *Guthrie Daily Leader,* Mar. 15, 1894.
35. *Guthrie Daily Leader,* Mar. 15, 1894.
36. *Oklahoma State Capital,* Mar. 14, 1894.
Graves (pp. 81–82), Zoe A. Tilghman, *Outlaw Days* (p. 76) and *Marshal of the Last Frontier* (p. 210), and Newsom (pp. 183–84) attribute the robbery to Newcomb and Raidler, claim the express packages contained "$6,500 consigned to a local cattleman," and say the pair spent their "suddenly accumulated" wealth in "riotous living" at the Columbian Exposition in Chicago (the exposition closed October 30, 1893, nearly five months before the Woodward affair).
Nix (pp. 185–88) includes Charley Pierce as a third robber and provides a fictionized account. Wellman (pp. 220–21) and Drago (p. 263) accept Nix.

CHAPTER XI

1. *Guthrie Daily Leader,* Mar. 29, 1894.
2. *Daily Oklahoman,* Mar. 31, 1894.
3. *Op. cit.,* 187–88.
4. *Oklahoma State Capital,* Apr. 5, 1894; *Guthrie Daily Leader,* Apr. 5, 1894.
5. Graves (p. 80), Zoe A. Tilghman, *Outlaw Days* (p. 74), and Newsom (p. 182) say the gang rendezvoused at Hot Springs, Arkansas. Hanes (p. 133) says they met at Fairland, in present Ottawa County, and includes Dalton and Newcomb in the Southwest City raid. Graves, Zoe A. Tilghman, Newsom, and Horan (p. 258) give the date as May 20.
6. *Afton Herald,* May 11, 1894; *Oklahoma State Capital,* May 12, 1894; *Oklahoma Daily Press-Gazette,* May 12, 1894; *Cherokee Advocate,* May 23, 1894.

447

Wellman (p. 214) and Drago (p. 259), apparently relying on Nix (p. 99), set the amount of loot at $15,000 and allege that it was on the return trip to Oklahoma Territory that the gang "cleaned out the bank at Pawnee, getting $10,000."

7. Territory v. Jones, *loc. cit.*; *Oklahoma State Capital*, Nov. 27, 1893, and May 15, 1894; *Stillwater Eagle-Gazette*, Dec. 1, 1893, and May 17, 1894.

8. Dale to Attorney General Olney, May 21, 1894, Department of Justice, File 12014, No. 5955; *Oklahoma State Capital*, May 19, 1894.

9. *Oklahoma State Capital*, May 22, 1894; *Oklahoma Daily Press-Gazette*, May 23, 1894; *Stillwater Eagle-Gazette*, May 24, 1894.

10. *Ibid.*; Territory v. Jones, *loc. cit.*

11. *Oklahoma State Capital*, June 8, 1894.

12. Tom Jones v. The Territory of Oklahoma, 4 Oklahoma Reports 45.

13. June 14, 1894.

14. Nix, *op. cit.*, 113.

CHAPTER XII

1. May 23 dispatch from Longview, *Daily Oklahoman*, May 24, 1894; *Oklahoma Daily Press-Gazette*, May 25, 1894.

2. Dispatch to Marshal Nix from Paris, Tex., *Oklahoma State Capital*, June 1, 1894.

3. J. S. Williams, U.S. Marshal, Eastern District of Texas, to Attorney General, July 19, 1894, Department of Justice, File 12014, No. 8638; *Oklahoma State Capital*, June 11, 1894.

4. Interview with Mike Gorman, March 15, 1937, Vol. 4, p. 114, *Indian-Pioneer History, Foreman Collection*, Oklahoma Historical Society.

5. *Daily Oklahoman*, June 9-10, 1894; *Oklahoma Daily Press-Gazette*, June 11, 1894; *Oklahoma State Capital*, June 11, 1894.

6. Nix (p. 215), Wellman (p. 226), and Drago (p. 268) give the date incorrectly as September 25.

7. *Daily Oklahoman*, June 9-10, 1894; *Oklahoma State Capital*, June 9, 1894; *Guthrie Daily Leader*, June 10, 1894.

8. Emmett Dalton, in *When the Daltons Rode* (pp. 309-310), provides a tear-jerking version of the killing of his brother and claims that the officers involved "came in for considerable public censure" and "one by one were discharged" or "drifted to other parts." Of course Emmett, still in prison, admits this information was "conveyed" by letter from his mother.

9. *Daily Oklahoman*, June 9, 1894; *Guthrie Daily Leader*, June 10, 1894; *Oklahoma Daily Press-Gazette*, June 11, 1894; *Oklahoma State Capital*, June 12, 1894.

10. *Daily Oklahoman*, June 9, 1894; *Oklahoma State Capital*, June 9, 1894.

11. *Oklahoma Daily Press-Gazette*, June 11, 1894; *Daily Oklahoman*, June 12, 1894; *Oklahoma State Capital*, June 12, 1894.

12. *Daily Oklahoman,* June 10, 1894.
13. *Ibid.*
14. *Ibid.,* June 12, 1894.
15. *Oklahoma State Capital,* June 16, 1894.
16. *Daily Oklahoman,* June 13–14, 1894.
17. *Ibid.,* June 12, 1894.
18. Ed Bartholomew, *The Biographical Album of Western Gunfighters* (Houston, Frontier Press of Texas, 1958), 56.
19. *Guthrie Daily Leader,* June 10, 1894; *Oklahoma Daily Press-Gazette,* June 11, 1894.
20. *Op. cit.,* 216.
21. June 13, 1894.
22. June 12, 1894.

CHAPTER XIII

1. Nix, *op. cit.,* 189.
2. *Enid Daily Wave,* Mar. 30, 1894; *Oklahoma State Capital,* Mar. 30, 1894.
3. *El Reno Democrat,* Apr. 5, 1894; *Oklahoma State Capital,* May 24, 1894; *Oklahoma Daily Press-Gazette,* May 25–26, 1894.
4. *Oklahoma State Capital,* Oct. 23 and Nov. 15, 1894; *Oklahoma Times-Journal,* Nov. 15, 1894.
5. *Ibid.*
6. Henry M. Shoemaker v. The Territory of Oklahoma, 4 Oklahoma Reports 118.
7. *Guthrie Daily News,* June 16, 1893.
8. Rainey, *The Cherokee Strip,* 248–49.
9. *Oklahoma State Capital,* Aug. 9, 1894; *Enid Daily Wave,* Aug. 8, 1895; Rainey, *The Cherokee Strip,* 244–48.
10. *Ibid.*
11. Marquis James, *The Cherokee Strip: A Tale of An Oklahoma Boyhood* (New York, Viking Press, 1945), 27.
12. *El Reno News,* Jan. 28, 1898; Marquis James, *They Had Their Hour* (Indianapolis, Bobbs-Merrill Co., 1934), 288.
An allegedly "true" statement by Bill Tilghman in the Western History Collections, University of Oklahoma Library, printed in the *Guthrie Daily Leader,* Apr. 18, 1965, refers to Black's wife as "Buck-skin Mabel" and Freeman as "a man named Winters." Details of Wyatt's early career also are incorrect.
Nix (p. 203) calls Freeman *Winters,* Black's wife *Pearl,* and includes S. T. Watson as a member of the gang. Sutton (p. 280) adds two fictitious characters, Rattlesnake Charlie and Indian Bob, a half-blood.
13. *Oklahoma State Capital,* June 7, 1895.
14. *Ibid.,* Apr. 12, 1894; *North Enid Tribune,* Apr. 12, 1894; *El Reno Democrat,* May 17, 1894.

15. *Enid Daily Wave*, Apr. 10, 1894; *Wichita Daily Eagle*, Apr. 10–11, 1894; *North Enid Tribune*, Apr. 12, 1894.

16. *Enid Daily Wave*, Apr. 13, 1894.

17. *Ibid.*

18. *Ibid.*, Apr. 10, 1894.

19. *Ibid.*

20. *North Enid Tribune*, Apr. 12, 1894.

21. *Oklahoma State Capital*, Apr. 12, 1894.

22. *Ibid.*

23. *Daily Oklahoman*, May 26, 1894.

24. *El Reno Democrat*, May 17, 1894; *Canadian County Republican*, May 18, 1894.

25. *Ibid.*

Nix (pp. 189–90) claims that Madsen located Henry "Silva" and Felix Young in an El Reno gambling house. "Silva surrendered without a fight, but Young tried to make his getaway through the back door of the joint," running to his horse "hitched two blocks down the street." The deputy commandeered a horse hitched near by, and there ensued an exciting chase in which the bandit found his .45's ineffective against the deputy's Winchester. Madsen killed the bandit's horse and, as the animal tumbled into the dust, "jumped to the ground beside the fallen man and disarmed him."

In "Four Score Years A Fighter" (*Daily Oklahoman*, Jan. 19, 1936), Madsen says W. D. Fossett, a Rock Island detective, learned that "Ned Silva" and Young were in El Reno, hurried there with warrants, and called on him to help make the arrests. After a stroll around town, they located "Silva" and arrested him without trouble. Young saw Madsen and dodged around the block to his horse hitched west of the Kerfoot Hotel, and Madsen dropped his horse with the first shot from his *revolver*. Young injured his leg in the fall but kept running and got tangled up in a wire fence. Madsen got tangled in another wire fence in trying to catch him, and Young fired at him before he could free himself. Fossett came to his aid. "Young might have given us quite a chase, but he did not see a Negro woman's clothesline . . . it caught him under the nose and threw him to the ground," which gave the officers time to get close enough to make him realize that he must either surrender or "a bullet would stop him."

Croy (p. 78), with characteristic humor, accepts Madsen's version.

26. *Daily Oklahoman*, May 19, 1894; *Guthrie Daily Leader*, May 29, 1894; *Oklahoma Daily Press-Gazette*, June 8, 1894.

Nix (p. 190) says Sylva and Young were taken to the Enid jail. Croy (p. 79) claims that Young escaped at Enid, but was recaptured and taken to Guthrie, where he was "sent to prison and passed out of public interest"; Sylva was "thrust in the El Reno jail," which "he didn't like and left, going to Texas."

27. *Op. cit.*, 189–90.

28. *Daily Oklahoman*, Jan. 19, 1936.

29. *Daily Oklahoman*, May 22, 1894; *El Reno Democrat*, May 24, 1894;

Canadian County Republican, May 25, 1894; *El Reno Globe,* May 25, 1894.

Nix (pp. 123–24) provides a completely erroneous version.

30. *Daily Oklahoman,* May 22, 1894; *El Reno Democrat,* May 24, 1894; *Canadian County Republican,* May 25, 1894; *El Reno Globe,* May 25, 1894.

31. *Canadian County Republican,* May 25, 1894.

32. *Daily Oklahoman,* May 25 and 27, 1894; Nix, *op. cit.,* 123.

33. *El Reno Globe,* May 25, 1894; *Oklahoma State Capital,* May 25, 1894; *Daily Oklahoman,* May 27, 1894.

CHAPTER XIV

1. *Railway Review,* June 1, July 12, and Oct. 4, 1889, and Jan. 17, 1892; *Railroad Gazette,* Sept. 16, 1893.

2. William Edward Hayes, *Iron Road to Empire: The History of 100 Years of the Progress and Achievements of the Rock Island Lines* (New York, Simmons-Boardman Publishing Corp., 1953), 135–36.

3. *Ibid.,* Rainey, *The Cherokee Strip,* 371–72.

4. *Op. cit.,* 546–47.

5. Rainey, *The Cherokee Strip,* 366–69.

6. Hayes, *op. cit.,* 137–38.

7. *Op. cit.,* 548.

8. G. E. Lemon, "Reminiscences of Pioneer Days in the Cherokee Strip," *Chronicles of Oklahoma,* Vol. XXII, No. 4 (Winter, 1944–45), 452.

9. Rainey, *The Cherokee Strip,* 373.

10. James, *The Cherokee Strip,* 13.

11. Lemon, *loc. cit.,* 453.

12. Rainey, *The Cherokee Strip,* 373–74.

13. Lemon, *op. cit.,* 454; Rainey, *The Cherokee Strip,* 375.

14. *Ibid.*

15. *Oklahoma State Capital,* June 7, 1894; *Guthrie Daily Leader,* June 7, 1894; *Oklahoma Daily Press-Gazette,* June 7, 1894.

16. May 14, 1894.

17. *Oklahoma State Capital,* Apr. 28, 1894.

18. *Oklahoma Daily Press-Gazette,* May 28, 1894.

19. Nix, *op. cit.,* 159–63.

20. *Oklahoma Daily Press-Gazette,* June 8, 1894.

21. Rainey, *The Cherokee Strip,* 378.

22. *Op. cit.,* 139–40.

23. *Op. cit.,* 454–55.

24. Department of Justice, File 6968.

25. *Ibid.*

26. Rainey, *The Cherokee Strip,* 378–79.

27. *Ibid.*

28. *Enid Daily Wave,* June 7, 1894.

29. Debate on the subject fills sixty-five pages of the *Congressional Record* from September, 1893, through July, 1894 (photo copies in author's collection).

30. *Enid Daily Wave,* June 19, 1894.

31. *Ibid.,* June 23, 1894.

32. *Ibid.,* July 11, 1894.

33. *Ibid.,* July 13, 1894.

34. *Ibid.*

35. *Oklahoma State Capital,* July 13, 1894.

36. Nix to Attorney General, July 13, 1894, Department of Justice, File 16-1-59A.

37. Attorney General to Brooks, July 13, 1894, *ibid.*

38. *Oklahoma Times-Journal,* July 16, 1894.

39. *Enid Daily Wave,* July 16, 1894.

40. *Oklahoma State Capital,* July 18, 1894.

41. *Ibid.; El Reno Democrat,* July 19, 1894.

42. Madsen to Brooks, July 17, 1894, Department of Justice, File 6968.

43. Brooks to Olney, July 17, 1894, *ibid.*

44. *El Reno Democrat,* July 19, 1894.

45. Brooks to Attorney General, July 18, 1894, Department of Justice, File 7181; Smith to Attorney General, July 19, 1894, *ibid.*

46. *Oklahoma State Capital,* July 17, 1894; *El Reno Democrat,* July 19, 1894.

47. Cable to Olney, July 18, 1894, Department of Justice, File 6968.

48. Brooks to Olney, July 18, 1894, *ibid.*

49. Olney to Dale, July 18, 1894, Department of Justice, File 7181; Frank Dale to Richard Olney, July 19, 1894, *ibid.*

50. Brooks to Attorney General, July 17, 1894, *ibid.*

51. Nix to Attorney General, July 19, 1894, *ibid.*

52. Nix to Olney, July 23, 1894, Department of Justice, File 6968.

53. Brooks to Olney, July 23, 1894, *ibid.*

54. Nix to Attorney General, July 24, 1894, *ibid.*

55. *Ibid.*

56. Brooks to Attorney General, July 24, 1894, *ibid.*

57. July 25 dispatch from Kingfisher, O. T., *Wichita Daily Eagle,* July 26, 1894.

58. Brooks to Attorney General, July 26, 1894, Department of Justice, File 6968.

59. Brooks to Attorney General, July 27, 1894, *ibid.*

60. Judge John L. McAtee to Olney, July 28, 1894, *ibid.*

61. *Enid Daily Wave,* July 25, 1894.

62. *Ibid.,* July 26, 1894.

63. July 28 dispatch from Kingfisher, O. T., *Wichita Daily Eagle,* July 29, 1894.

CHAPTER XV

1. *Oklahoma State Capital,* Feb. 6, 1894.

2. *Guthrie Daily Leader,* Apr. 5, 1894; *Oklahoma Daily Press-Gazette,* Apr. 5, 1894.

3. *Oklahoma State Capital*, May 11, 1894; *Oklahoma Daily Press-Gazette*, May 12, 1894.

4. *Oklahoma State Capital*, June 6, 1894.

5. *Enid Daily Wave*, June 20, 1894.

6. *Oklahoma State Capital*, Aug. 1, 1894.

7. *Ibid.*, Aug. 15, 1894.

8. *Ibid.*, Nov. 13, 1894.

9. *Guthrie Daily Leader*, Nov. 25, 1894.

10. *Oklahoma State Capital*, Nov. 26, 1894.

11. *Stillwater Eagle-Gazette*, Dec. 6, 1894.

12. *Oklahoma State Capital*, Dec. 1, 1894.

13. *Ibid.*, Apr. 21, 1894.

14. Apr. 21, 1894.

15. *Oklahoma State Capital*, May 17, 1894.

16. *Oklahoma Daily Press-Gazette*, May 24, 1894; *El Reno Democrat*, May 31, 1894.

17. *Guthie Daily Leader*, July 16, 1893.

18. Dec. 10, 1893.

19. *Oklahoma State Capital*, Aug. 18, 1893; *Wichita Daily Eagle*, Dec. 10, 1893.

20. July 23, 1893.

21. *Oklahoma State Capital*, Aug. 18, 1893.

Croy (pp. 159–60) calls the victim "a Kansas man" whom he "fascinated with her charms" until she could get word to officers that he was Bob Dalton, knowing that they would "come on the run" and believing they would kill him when he "resisted arrest" and pay her the reward on Dalton's head.

Preece (pp. 182–86) embellishes the tale and gives the date as June, 1892, following the Red Rock train robbery. Flora is "Florence" and "Flo," and Mundis is "Munday" and "Mundy."

22. *Vinita Indian Chieftain*, Apr. 20, 1893; *Stillwater Gazette*, May 5, 1893.

23. *Oklahoma State Capital*, June 7, 1893.

24. *Guthrie Daily News*, June 30, 1893.

25. *Ibid.*

26. Letter from Chris Madsen to Mrs. Matie Thomas, Tulsa, Oklahoma, June 9, 1937 (photo copy in author's collection).

From the *Oklahoma State Capital*, Nov. 19, 1907; "Bartlesville, Okla., Nov. 18—United States Deputy Marshal George Williams and Earnest Lewis, an alleged 'bootlegger,' were killed in a pistol duel here tonight when Williams and Fred Keller, another United States deputy marshal, attempted to arrest Lewis. Lewis owned a livery stable and was well to do. He was suspected by the authorities of having sold liquor during the last few days. He has been in a number of shooting scrapes and had the reputation of being a 'bad man.' When Williams and Keller entered his place to arrest him, Lewis, before either of the officers could draw a pistol, sent a bulet into Williams' heart, killing him. Before Lewis could fire again

Keller had killed him. Williams was 26 years of age. He was unmarried. His parents live at Collinsville."

27. *Guthrie Daily Leader*, July 16, 1893.
28. *Oklahoma State Capital*, Aug. 11, 1893; *Guthrie Daily Leader*, Aug. 12, 1893.
29. *Oklahoma Sate Capital*, Dec. 9, 1893; *Wichita Daily Eagle*, Dec. 9, 1893.
30. *Wichita Daily Eagle*, Dec. 10, 1893.
31. *Guthrie Daily Leader*, Dec. 17, 1894.
32. *Ibid.*
33. *Oklahoma Daily Press-Gazette*, Mar. 8, 1894.
34. *Stillwater Eagle-Gazette*, May 4, 1894.
35. *Oklahoma State Capital*, Aug. 7, 1894; *Oklahoma Daily Times-Journal*, Aug. 8, 1894.
36. Aug. 16, 1894.
37. Preece, *op. cit.*, 275.
38. *Oklahoma Daily Times-Journal*, Apr. 2, 1896.
39. Shirley, *Heck Thomas*, 163.
40. Annual Report of William P. Hazen, Chief of U.S. Secret Service, Washington, 1894; Nix, *op. cit.*, 144.
41. *Oklahoma State Capital*, July 17, 1894.
42. *Ibid.*, July 20, 1894.
43. *Ibid.*, Aug. 10, 1894.
44. *Ibid.*
45. *Ibid.*, Nov. 22, 1894.
46. *Ibid.*, Dec. 17, 1894.
47. *Op. cit.*, 149–53.
48. *Ibid.*, 144.

CHAPTER XVI

1. Brooks to McAtee, Aug. 8, 1894, Records of District Attorney for Oklahoma Territory, Guthrie, 1894, p. 101.
2. Brooks To Wrightsman, Aug. 8, 1894, *ibid.*, pp. 99–100.
3. Brooks to Beale, Aug. 10, 1894, *ibid.*, p. 106.
4. Brooks to Morgan, Aug. 11, 1894, *ibid.*, pp. 114–15.
5. Brooks to O'Bryan, Dec. 20, 1894, *ibid.*, p. 383.
6. Brooks to Capt. Woodson, Jan. 2, 1895, *ibid.*, p. 408.
7. *Oklahoma State Capital*, Nov. 30, 1894.
8. *Ibid.*, Dec. 12, 1894.
9. Sept. 28, 1895.
10. *Oklahoma State Capital*, Feb. 11, 1895.
11. Sept. 21, 1895.
12. *Oklahoma State Capital*, Sept. 20, 1895; *Oklahoma Daily Times-Journal,* Oct. 4, 1895.
13. *Oklahoma State Capital*, Jan. 12, 1895; *Oklahoma Daily Times-Journal*, Jan. 14, 1895.

14. Brooks to Olney, Dec. 17, 1894, Records of District Attorney for Oklahoma Territory, Guthrie, 1894, pp. 97–98.

15. Brooks to Olney, March 14, 1895, *ibid.*, pp. 697–98.

CHAPTER XVII

1. Brooks to McMechan, Nov. 7, 1894, Records of District Attorney for Oklahoma Territory, Guthrie, 1894, p. 289.

2. Jan. 7, 1895.

3. *Oklahoma State Capital*, Jan. 7, 1895.

4. Brooks to Olney, Nov. 13, 1894, Records of District Attorney for Oklahoma Territory, Guthrie, 1894, pp. 79–84.

5. *Ibid.*

6. *Oklahoma State Capital*, Jan. 2, 1895.

7. Apr. 26, 1895.

8. *Oklahoma State Capital*, Apr. 23, 1895.

9. *Ibid.*, Sept. 19, 1894; *Stillwater Eagle-Gazette*, Sept. 27, 1894.

10. Graves, *op. cit.*, 82–83; Newsom, *op. cit.*, 178; Zoe A. Tilghman, *Outlaw Days*, 76–78, and *Marshal of the Last Frontier*, 210.

11. *Guthrie Daily Leader*, Nov. 29, 1894.

12. Dec. 4, 1894.

13. *Guthrie Daily Leader*, Feb. 18, 1895.

14. *El Reno Globe*, Nov. 8, 1895; Sergeant W. J. L. Sullivan, *Twelve Years in the Saddle for Law and Order on the Frontiers of Texas* (Austin, Von Boeckmann-Jones Co., 1909), 84–85.

15. *Oklahoma State Capital*, Dec. 26, 1894.

16. *Ibid.*, Dec. 24, 1894.

17. *Ibid.*, Jan. 21, 1895; *Stillwater Eagle-Gazette*, Jan. 31, 1895.

18. March 14, 1895.

19. (Boston and New York, Houghton Mifflin Company, 1930), 113.

20. *Op. cit.*, 78.

21. *Op. cit.*, 174–75.

22. P. 72.

23. Graves, *op. cit.*, 87.

24. Pp. 87–92.

25. Newsom (pp. 180–82) closely follows Graves's account, Zoe A. Tilghman reproduced it in *Outlaw Days* (pp. 82–86), Sutton (pp. 200–204) accepted, and Nix's ghost writer in *Oklahombres* (pp. 165–69) embellished it, identifying the dugout occupant as Will Dun (the uncle) and one of the outlaws hiding in the bunks as Bill Dalton, who had been dead seven months.

In *Marshal of the Last Frontier* (pp. 210–11), Zoe A. Tilghman claims the gang had just returned from the Canadian, Texas, robbery and the dugout occupant was a cousin of the man Tilghman sought. Croy (pp. 167, 189) describes the Rock Fort as a dugout on the Dunn ranch near Ingalls, built in the upper end of a ravine and fortified with rock walls, but places the Tilghman incident at a dugout in a hillside near Yale. Wellman (p.

214) locates the hideout "at the Will Dunn ranch . . . near the Cimarron";
Drago (p. 260) says it "belonged to Will Dunn"; Hanes (p. 139) thinks it
was "in the area south of Ingalls."

26. *El Reno Democrat*, Apr. 26, 1894.

27. Madsen to Mrs. Thomas, Jan. 27, 1937 (photo copy in author's
collection).

28. Zoe A. Tilghman, *Marshal of the Last Frontier*, 214.

29. *Perry Daily Times*, Mar. 3 and 5, 1895; *Eufaula Indian Journal*,
Mar. 8, 1895.

30. *Op. cit.*, 110.

31. Canton, *op. cit.*, 111–13.

CHAPTER XVIII

1. Details of the Dover robbery appear in the *Kingfisher Free Press*,
Apr. 4, 1895; *Enid Daily Wave*, Apr. 4, 1895; *Hennessey Clipper*, Apr. 4,
1895; *Oklahoma State Capital*, Apr. 4, 1895; *El Reno Globe*, Apr. 5, 1895;
and *Guthrie Daily Leader*, Apr. 6, 1895.

Graves (p. 93), Newsom (p. 183), Zoe A. Tilghman, *Outlaw Days* (p.
89), and Nix (p. 181) give the date incorrectly as May, 1895. Wellman (p.
218) says May 4, 1895. Drago (p. 261) accepts and sets the time at noon.
All claim the amount of the collection to be "several thousand dollars."
Hanes (p. 141) reports a startling *thirty-five thousand*!

2. Barnard, *op. cit.*, 209.

3. Nix (p. 180), Wellman (p. 219), and Drago (p. 262) put the time at
"just before sundown."

4. *Hennessey Clipper*, Apr. 4, 1895.

5. *El Reno Globe*, Apr. 5, 1895; *Oklahoma Daily Times-Journal*, Apr. 8,
1895; *Oklahoma Daily Star*, Apr. 9, 1895.

6. *Hennessey Clipper*, Apr. 4, 1895.

7. *Oklahoma Daily Times-Journal*, Apr. 8, 1895; *Oklahoma Daily Star*,
Apr. 9, 1895; *Guthrie Daily Leader*, Apr. 10, 1895.

8. Apr. 8, 1895.

9. *Oklahoma State Capital*, Apr. 9, 1895.

10. *Guthrie Daily Leader*, May 8, 1896.

11. *El Reno Globe*, Apr. 5, 1895; *Oklahoma State Capital*, Apr. 6, 1895.

Contemporary reports and Justice Department records do not reveal
which member of the gang killed Godfrey. Barnard (pp. 210–11) states
that Bitter Creek ordered Pierce to "get the horses." The old man picked
up a shotgun, and "instantly Bitter Creek shot him."

Graves (p. 95), Zoe A. Tilghman, *Outlaw Days* (p. 89), and Sutton (pp.
214–15) credit Red Buck. Nix (pp. 181–85) has Doolin present and claims
that the cold-blooded murder of the old man made such an impression on
the bandit leader that he ordered Bitter Creek to bring up the saddlebags
in which the Dover loot was carried, handed Red Buck his share, and told
him: "Drag your lousy, cowardly carcass out of my sight! If I ever see you
again I'll kill you! You could have taken that outfit without harming a hair

on the old man's head. You are too damn low to associate with a high class gang of train robbers. Git!" And the gang rode off, leaving Red Buck disarmed, "mouth agape" and "staring after them in his surprsie."

This Red Buck-Doolin exchange is retold variously by Croy (pp. 182–83), Wellman (pp. 219–20), and Drago (p. 262). Drago judiciously admits that "it can not be documented."

It didn't happen. Doolin did not participate in the Dover robbery and was never charged with the crime. "There were *five* bandits in the hold-up and Raidler is the only one left of the five, the other four [Tulsa Jack, Pierce, Newcomb, and Waightman] having since been killed. "Brooks to Attorney General Judson Harmon, April 11, 1896, Records of the District Attorney for Oklahoma Territory, Guthrie, 1896, p. 331. See also In the Matter of the Application of William J. Raidler for a Writ of Habeas Corpus, 4 Oklahoma Reports 417.

12. *Oklahoma State Capital*, Apr. 11, 1895.

13. James, *The Cherokee Strip*, 27.

14. *El Reno Globe*, Apr. 5, 1895.

15. Canton, *op. cit.*, 114–15.

16. *Ibid.*, 116.

17. *Ibid.*, 119.

18. May 3, 1895.

19. *Guthrie Daily Leader*, May 3, 1895; *Oklahoma Daily Times-Journal*, May 3, 1895.

20. Canton, *op. cit.*, 119–20.

21. *Pawnee Times-Democrat*, May 10, 1895.

22. Nix (pp. 196–97) does not mention the name but credits the killing to Tilghman and Heck Thomas. Graves (pp. 95–96), Newsom (p. 193), and Zoe A. Tilghman, *Outlaw Days* (pp. 89–91) say Tilghman and Thomas arranged the trap but had gone "some distance from the house" when they heard shooting; they "hurried there," were met by two of the Dunn brothers with shotguns, and saw the bandits lying dead near the yard gate. These writers give the date as "in July." Croy (pp. 184–87) fictionizes the four accounts and in Sources, Chapter 20, gives the date as July 20. Wellman (pp. 221–23) and Drago (pp. 264–65) accept Nix. Barnard (p. 212) claims the Dunns wanted the rewards and during the night, when all were in bed, went to the room where the outlaws were quietly sleeping and killed them. Hanes (p. 152), following Barnard's version (the popular one among old-timers), places the sleeping pair in an upstairs bedroom and identifies the killers as Bill Dunn, using Dr. W. R. Call's old eight-gauge shotgun, and John, using a Winchester rifle. Colcord states in his autobiography (p. 171) that he investigated the affair and "found that [the outlaws] were shot lying flat on their backs . . . while asleep . . . in Bee Dunn's yard."

23. Nix to Attorney General, May 3, 1895, and May 14, 1895, Department of Justice, File 7114.

24. *Guthrie Daily Leader*, May 5, 1895.

25. James Newcomb to *Oklahoma State Capital*, May 8, 1895.

26. *Oklahoma State Capital*, May 16, 1895.
27. *Pawnee Times-Democrat*, May 10, 1895.

CHAPTER XIX

1. Berlin B. Chapman (ed., "The Cherokee Commission at Kickapoo Village," *Chronicles of Oklahoma*, Vol. XVIII, No. 1 (March, 1939), 69–73.
2. *Oklahoma Daily Times-Journal*, Mar. 26 and May 20, 1895.
3. *Oklahoma State Capital*, May 20, 1895; *Oklahoma Daily Times-Journal*, May 21, 1895.
4. *Oklahoma State Capital*, May 23, 1895.
5. *Oklahoma Daily Times-Journal*, May 24, 1895.
6. *Ibid.*, May 23, 1895.
7. *Oklahoma State Capital*, May 23, 1895.
8. *Oklahoma Daily Times-Journal*, May 27, 1895.
9. *Oklahoma State Capital*, May 31, 1895.
10. *Ibid.*, June 21, 1895.
11. *Oklahoma Daily Times-Journal*, May 24, 1895.
12. Jeff Burton, *Black Jack Christian: Outlaw* (Santa Fe, N.M., Press of the Territorian, 1967), 2. Burton thinks they took part in the 1891 run, but there is no evidence that the family filed a claim.
13. Bill Deister (as told to Jane Pattie), "Outlaws I Have Known," *Old West*, Vol. 9, No. 3 (Spring, 1973).
Newsom (pp. 203–204) locates the Christians at Violet Springs in 1895 and claims he and the boys "were comrades in the wild days of the Southwest." He is wrong in stating that "they began their outlaw life in the year 1900."
14. July 13, 1895.
15. Deister, *loc. cit.*
16. *Oklahoma State Capital*, Apr. 30, 1895.
Newsom (pp. 204, 207–208) alleges that, at The Corner saloon, Bob and Bill Christian encountered a man named Yoakum, who accused them before their drinking and gambling friends of stealing his horses. The brothers drew their six-shooters, and Yoakum was swearing a lie to the "inspiration of bullets spraying about his feet" when "one Turner, a federal officer and [Yoakum's] brother-in-law," intervened. "He demanded the two boys to surrender . . . for he had a warrant and was going to serve it." The warrant, "issued at Oklahoma City," was "for the arrest of Bob Christian, charged with bootlegging whiskey in Indian Territory" from a Violet Springs saloon owned by Deputy Marshal Carr. "Bob resisted the officer by saying, 'You may go to a hotter climate and eat your warrant also.' Turner shot Bob just over the left eye" and Bill, "being a gunsman true to type . . . took the life of the officer who fell headlong from his horse."
17. *Oklahoma State Capital*, May 24, 1895.

18. *Ibid.*, May 31 and July 1, 1895; J. H. Garver v. The Territory of Oklahoma, 10 Oklahoma Reports 197.

Burton (p. 3) says Bill Christian was sentenced to *five* years and gives May 24 as date of the brothers' transfer to the Oklahoma County jail.

19. Newsom (pp. 209–210) identifies Bob Christian's sweetheart as Emma Johnston, who had followed him from Texas and was cooking for a crew of men running a gristmill at Sasakwa, Seminole Nation. He also is incorrect in stating "she secured a couple of U.S. army forty-five Colts revolvers . . . used at the time by soldiers at Fort Sill" and took them, "with belts, scabbards and ammunition," into the jail "concealed underneath her garments."

20. *Oklahoma Daily Times-Journal*, July 1, 1895.

Newsom (pp. 210–11), Nix (pp. 129–30), McRill (pp. 65–67), and Burton (p. 4) give varied versions of the bloody affray. Newsom, Nix, and Burton reverse the roles played by Bob and Bill Christian. Newsom incorrectly identifies the third escapee as Buttermilk John Mackey.

21. July 1, 1895.

22. July 1, 1895.

23. *Oklahoma State Capital*, July 6, 1895.

24. *Loc. cit.*

25. *Oklahoma Daily Times-Journal*, July 11, 1895; *Oklahoma State-Capital*, July 12 and 13, 1895.

26. *Ibid.*

27. *Oklahoma State Capital*, July 13 and 17, 1895; *Oklahoma Daily Times-Journal*, July 17, 1895.

28. Garver v. The Territory of Oklahoma, *loc. cit.*; Reeves v. The Territory of Oklahoma, *loc. cit.*

29. *Oklahoma State Capital*, July 17, 1895; *Oklahoma Daily Times-Journal*, July 30, 1895.

30. *Oklahoma State Capital*, July 22, 1895.

31. *Oklahoma Daily Times-Journal*, July 23, 1895.

32. *Ibid.*, July 24, 1895.

33. July 29, 1895.

34. July 30, 1895.

35. July 29 dispatch from South McAlester, I.T., *Oklahoma Daily Times-Journal*, July 30, 1895.

36. July 29 dispatch from Eufaula, I.T., *Oklahoma Daily Times-Journal*, July 30, 1895; *Oklahoma State Capital*, July 31, 1895.

Burton (p. 5) dates the robbery July 26.

37. Aug. 6 dispatch from South McAlester, I.T., *Oklahoma Daily Times-Journal*, Aug. 6, 1895.

38. Aug. 10 dispatch from South McAlester, I.T., *Guthrie Daily Leader*, Aug. 11, 1895.

39. Aug. 23 dispatch from Hartshorne, I.T., *Oklahoma State Capital*, Aug. 23, 1895.

40. *Oklahoma Daily Times-Journal*, Aug. 22, 1895.

41. *Ibid.*, Aug. 24, 1895; *Oklahoma State Capital*, Aug. 26, 1895; *Arapahoe Argus*, Aug. 29, 1895; *Daily Oklahoman*, Sept. 15, 1895.

Burton (pp. 5–6) claims Hocker was shot by one of two gang members, "Claude Nuckells" or "Ted Edwards." These names do not appear in official records.

42. *Oklahoma State Capital*, Aug. 28, 1895.

43. *Oklahoma Daily Times-Journal*, Sept. 4, 1895; *Oklahoma State Capital*, Sept. 4, 1895.

44. *Daily Oklahoman*, Nov. 7, 1895; *Oklahoma Daily Times-Journal*, Nov. 15, 1895.

45. *Oklahoma State Capital*, Dec. 10, 1896; Reeves v. The Territory of Oklahoma, *loc. cit.*

At Lansing, Reeves became the prison butcher and a trusty. After serving eleven years, he was pardoned by Oklahoma's last territorial governor, Frank Frantz.

46. *Oklahoma State Capital*, Sept. 10, 1896.

47. *Oklahoma Daily Times-Journal*, Nov. 25–29, 1895.

48. Garver v. The Territory of Oklahoma, *loc. cit.*

49. *Oklahoma State Capital*, Apr. 14, 1898.

50. *Ibid.*, June 14, 1900.

51. Newsom (p. 204) says that "after several years of bandit life . . . the boys passed out of the knowledge of anyone . . . and it cannot be truthfully said by one who knew them, whether or not they are dead or alive. Their desperate lives greatly affected their parents and hurried them to their grave, for they did not live long after . . . their bodies sleep somewhere today on the lone prairies near [Sacred Heart or Violet Springs]."

Nix (p. 130) writes: "The last they were heard of . . . they had joined the Cuban Army, remaining there until after the Spanish-American War. From there it was stated they located somewhere in Mexico."

A dispatch from Fort Smith on October 7, 1895, reported that six men held up a northbound Frisco passenger train at Caston Switch, Indian Territory, about thirty miles east of Wilburton; "they cut the express car loose and ran it up the track, but failed to open the through safe and only got eighty-five cents from the local safe . . . the passengers were not molested. . . . It is thought to have been the work of the Christians."

Burton (pp. 6–7) thinks "Bob and Will Christian and three other men" committed this holdup and credits them with the robbery on December 7, 1895, of a mining company's store at Coalgate, Choctaw Nation, in which the haul was "about $220 in cash, and goods to the value of some $200."

52. *Oklahoma State Capital*, Sept. 13, 1895.

53. *Loc. cit.*

54. (Phoenix, H. H. McNeil Co., 1915), 50–53.

55. Burton, *op. cit.*, 8–10.

56. These exploits are detailed in the Wilson opus (pp. 56–59) and more particularly by Burton (pp. 11–32).

CHAPTER XX

1. Graves, *op. cit.*, 83–84; Newsom, *op. cit.*, 179; Zoe A. Tilghman, *Outlaw Days*, 78.
2. *Op. cit.*, 134.
3. Golden Anniversary Edition, Apr. 16, 1939.
4. This article was reprinted over the years under various headings in special issues of the *Leader* from 1958 to 1966.
5. *Beaver Herald*, Sept. 12, 1895; *Oklahoma State Capital*, Oct. 3, 1895.
6. *Oklahoma State Capital*, July 6, 1895; *Oklahoma Daily Times-Journal*, July 8, 1895.
7. "Midkiff's Manifesto," *Pawnee Times-Democrat*, Sept. 13, 1895.
8. *Oklahoma State Capital*, July 6, 1895.
9. *Ibid.*; *Guthrie Daily Leader*, July 7, 1895.
10. Nix, *op. cit.*, 132.
11. *Oklahoma State Capital*, Aug. 20, 1895.
12. *Blackwell Times-Record*, Aug. 29, 1895; *Payne County Populist*, Sept. 5, 1895.

Graves (pp. 84–86) states: "Marshal Tilghman and Burke heard . . . they were stopping at one of their old hold outs and went there to capture them. . . . Upon learning of the approach of the officers, the girls tried to make a get away. Burke ran around the house and remained outside, and Tilghman went in, expecting a warm reception, for the girls were armed and it was known that they would shoot. Cattle Annie leaped from a window. She was caught by Burke and attempted to draw her revolver as she fell, but the marshal got her too quickly. Little Breeches escaped and gave the officers a long chase. She fired over her shoulder at them as she fled, but her aim was not good. . . . Marshal Tilghman finally shot the horse the girl was riding and horse and rider came to the ground with a crash. Little Breeches fought wildly, but was soon captured."

Newsom (p. 185) and Zoe A. Tilghman, *Outlaw Days* (p. 80) repeat this road-show tale, and Nix's ghost writer (pp. 132–34) embellishes it. Edwin L. Sabin (pp. 317–18) in *Wild Men of the Wild West* (New York, Thomas Y. Crowell Co., 1929), Horan (p. 265), and Wellman (pp. 212–13) accept.

13. *Beaver Herald*, Sept. 12, 1895; *Oklahoma State Capital*, Sept. 16 and Oct. 3, 1895; *Payne County Populist*, Sept. 26, 1895; *Oklahoma Daily Times-Journal*, Nov. 13, 1895.
14. *Ibid.*
15. *Oklahoma State Capital*, Oct. 19, 1896; *Blackwell Times-Record*, Nov. 12, 1896.

Graves (p. 86) says "nothing was ever heard of [the girls] again" and "it is not likely they ever returned to the Southwest." Nix (p. 135) thinks both were discharged and took up settlement work in New York and he "often wondered . . . what they were able to make of their lives." Zoe A. Tilghman, *Outlaw Days* (p. 81), Horan (p. 266), and Wellman (p. 213) claim that Little Breeches died in the East and Cattle Annie returned to Oklahoma.

16. *Tulsa Sunday World*, May 24, 1964.

CHAPTER XXI

1. Interview with William D. Fossett (Second Interview), Aug. 18, 1937, Vol. 63, pp. 18–19, *Indian-Pioneer History, Foreman Collection*, Oklahoma Historical Society.

2. *Oklahoma State Capital*, June 6, 1895.

3. *Ibid.*, June 7, 1895; *Kingfisher Free Press*, June 27, 1895.

Nix (pp. 204–205) locates the hideout "in a clump of hills on a farm near Galena" and credits the encounter and capture to a posse led by Deputy Marshal Halsell. As the officers neared the camp, they heard a wagon rumble over the stony trail, so they spread themselves and waited. A man named Watson was driving, with the women in the back. Black sat in the rear of the wagon, his legs dangling, and Wyatt brought up the procession on a stolen horse. Halsell fired at Black. Black cried out, grabbing one foot, then jumped from the wagon and vanished between two sand hills. Both horses hitched to the wagon were wounded by posse fire, but Watson whipped them into a run. Halsell and two possemen took after Black; the other pursued Wyatt and the wagon. It was late afternoon, and a heavy storm had gathered. With rain pouring down in torrents and in the darkness, it was impossible to follow the fugitives. The posse caught their trail the next morning. Watson, Zip, and the women had succeeded in crossing the Cimarron during the night, and Black had rejoined the party. The posse searched all day, finally discovering them in a deep canyon on Gypsum Creek, and in a second gun battle, Zip, Black, and Watson again escaped, but the women were captured.

Watson is not mentioned in official or contemporary records. Nix (pp. 209–210) states he was arrested "some time later" after a running fight with Deputy Sam Bartell "on the Washita River about twenty-five miles from Anadarko" and "was the only male member [of the gang] who lived to serve a prison term."

James, *They Had Their Hour* (p. 287), includes "Bill Doolin and Buck Wateman [*sic*]" in the "long-range fight . . . on the edge of Steer Canon."

4. *Oklahoma State Capital*, June 7, 1895.

5. *Kingfisher Free Press*, Aug. 8, 1895.

6. *Oklahoma State Capital*, July 24, 1895.

7. *Kingfisher Free Press*, Aug. 8, 1895; James, *They Had Their Hour*, 288.

8. *Oklahoma State Capital*, July 30, 1895; *Hennessey Clipper*, Aug. 1, 1895.

9. Aug. 1, 1895.

10. *Oklahoma State Capital*, Aug. 2, 1895; *Oklahoma Daily Times-Journal*, Aug. 3, 1895.

11. *Kingfisher Free Press*, Aug. 1, 1895.

12. Accounts of the pair's flight from the Glass Mountains and the killing

of Black appear in the *Oklahoma Daily Times-Journal*, Aug. 3 and 8, 1895; *Oklahoma State Capital*, Aug. 5 and 8, 1895; and *Kingfisher Free Press*, Aug. 8, 1895.

Nix (p. 208) claims Black "died with a chew of tobacco in his mouth big enough to choke a horse . . . his body literally tattered with bullet holes"; that one bullet "hit a scrub oak tree which smashed it flat and it glanced, striking Yeager on the breast bone . . . deflected, turned around under the man's arm and lodged almost in the middle of his back without entering the vital cavity."

James, *They Had Their Hour* (p. 290) says the outlaws were ambushed by a posse of fifteen men who "lay on their bellies" in the field and "fired without warning"; that Wyatt was "terribly wounded in the bowels" but "whipped out his pistol and retreated behind its fire" into the corn; and that "so greatly did the posse respect this demonstration," they did not follow him.

13. Accounts of Wyatt's final pursuit and capture appear in the *Oklahoma Daily Times-Journal*, Aug. 3 and 5, 1895; *Enid Daily Wave*, Aug. 5, 1895; *Oklahoma State Capital*, Aug. 5, 6, and 12, 1895; *Kingfisher Free Press*, Aug. 8, 1895; *Enid Eagle*, Aug. 12, 1895. See also Rainey, *The Cherokee Strip*, 249–53.

Varied and somewhat fictional versions appear in Sutton (pp. 281–82), Nix (pp. 208–209), James, *They Had Their Hour* (pp. 291–93), and Croy (pp. 86–87).

14. Aug. 6, 1895.

15. *Enid Daily Wave*, Sept. 7, 1895.

16. *Ibid.*, Sept. 10, 1895.

17. *Oklahoma State Capital*, Nov. 7, 1895.

Sutton (p. 280) makes no disposition of the Freeman woman but calls Belle Black "Pearl" and erroneously reports her "last robbery" as the "Rock Island train near Dover" and her "last fight" as occurring when "a posse overtook the gang at Cottonwood crossing on the Cimarron and Indian Bob [?] and Rattlesnake Charlie [?] were killed." He says that "when the gang regained its share of the money and the best horse in the remuda and disappeared." Sutton further alleges that Bill Tilghman found her years later, "a respected wife and mother, in a little town in western Oklahoma" but "came away without even disclosing his identity" because "the law could not have been vindicated or justice done by exposing her husband and children to shame."

Nix (p. 209) claims: "The two women were given short terms in the federal jail at Guthrie by Chief Justice Dale."

18. *Daily Oklahoman*, Sept. 11, 1895; *Vinita Leader*, Sept. 12, 1895; *Fort Smith Elevator*, Sept. 13, 1895.

Sutton (pp. 220–21) says Tilghman trailed Little Bill into the "Sac and Fox Indian country" for "a crime done in Woodward" and found him asleep on the open prairie!

Graves (p. 96), Zoe A. Tilghman, *Outlaw Days* (p. 91), and Wellman

(p. 224) give the date as Sept. 7. Nix (p. 213) gives Sept. 1. Hanes (p. 154) calls the outlaw Little *Dick* Raidler.

19. *Fort Smith Elevator*, Sept. 13, 1895.
20. *Ibid.*

Wellman (p. 224) and Drago (p. 266), perhaps relying on the Sutton account of the alleged prairie duel in the Sac and Fox country, claim Raidler wounded Tilghman in the shoulder and Tilghman shot Raidler in the lung with a Winchester.

21. *Guthrie Daily Leader*, Sept. 11, 1895; *Daily Oklahoman*, Sept. 11, 1895.
22. *Kingfisher Free Press*, Apr. 9, 1896; *Oklahoma State Capital*, Apr. 10, 1896.

Graves (p. 98), Newsom (p. 190), and Zoe A. Tilghman, *Outlaw Days* (p. 93) and *Marshal of the Last Frontier* (p. 216) state: "He was tried for train robbery." Wellman (p. 225) and Drago (p. 267) say he was "for multiple robberies and sentenced to twenty-one years." Hanes (p. 165) gives the trial date as April 11.

23. In the Matter of the Application of William F. Raidler for a Writ of Habeas Corpus, 4 Oklahoma Reports 417; *Kingfisher Free Press*, June 25, 1896.
24. *Guthrie Daily Leader*, May 8, 1896.

CHAPTER XXII

1. *Daily Oklahoma Times-Journal*, May 8, 1895.
2. *Beaver Herald*, Jan. 2, 1896; *The South and West*, Jan. 2, 1896; *Kingfisher Free Press*, Jan. 2, 1896; *Oklahoma Daily Times-Journal*, Jan. 4, 1896.
3. Jan. 3, 1896.
4. Dec. 31, 1895.
5. *Guthrie Daily Leader*, Jan. 16, 1896.
6. (Boston, Houghton Mifflin Co., 1938), 28.
7. Zoe A. Tilghman, aware of the Rhodes biography in *Marshal of the Last Frontier* (p. 229), admits Doolin "stayed at the ranch several weeks . . . making plans to bring his wife and baby there and start a new life."

W. H. Hutchinson, *A Bar Cross Man* (Norman, University of Oklahoma Press, 1956), discusses Doolin's presence with some disagreement about when he was there (pp. 49–50, 242–43, 295–96).

Hanes (pp. 145–49) enlarges on the visit with details from *The Trusty Knaves*.

8. *Oklahoma State Capital*, July 16 and 20, 1895; *Yukon Weekly*, July 18, 1895; *Payne County Populist*, July 25, 1895.
9. *Stillwater Eagle-Gazette*, Mar. 2, 1894.
10. *Guthrie Daily Leader*, Jan. 16 and 17, 1896.

Graves (pp. 100–101), Newsom (p. 185), and Zoe A. Tilghman, *Outlaw Days* (p. 96) claim Tilghman intercepted a letter written to Mary Pierce at the O. K. Hotel, where Edith had left a ring Doolin gave her while they were sweethearts. She asked Mrs. Pierce to send it to her, and Tilghman learned the address of Mrs. Will Barry, to whom the package was shipped.

Nix (pp. 216–18) says: "We decided to try to locate the Doolins through Mrs. Pierce. . . . Tilghman went to call on Mrs. Pierce and she expressed deep appreciation for our treatment of her . . . realized we could have placed a charge against her for harboring bandits at the time of the Ingalls fight. . . . She had received a letter from Doolin's wife, requesting that she mail a wedding ring that had been left in the hotel on her last visit. The package was to be addressed to Mrs. Will Barry at Burden. . . . I loaned Tilghman a Prince Albert coat and a black derby hat and he procured the other necessary accessories to complete his costume. He was to go to Burden as a preacher."

Zoe A. Tilghman, *Marshal of the Last Frontier* (p. 218), gives still another version and maintains Tilghman donned the preacher garb for his trip to Arkansas later.

Wellman (pp. 221, 228–29) accepts Nix.

Drago (pp. 263, 270–71) labels the ring business "hocus pocus," surmises that Tilghman "got the address from Bee [Bill] Dunn," and that Doolin "bought a small farm near Burden," where he lived for "six months, unsuspected, law-abiding and church-going."

Hanes (pp. 149–50) thinks Edith and her son joined Doolin "in mid-May, 1895" upon selecting Burden as a place to "settle down," yet Doolin sent for them *after* drifting back from New Mexico.

11. *Guthrie Daily Leader*, Jan. 16 and 17, 1896.

12. *Ibid.*

13. *Ibid.*

14. *Guthrie Daily Leader*, Jan. 17, 1896; *Oklahoma State Capital*, Jan. 17, 1896; *Daily Oklahoman*, Jan. 17, 1896; *Vinita Indian Chieftain*, Jan. 23, 1896; *Oklahoma Daily Times-Journal*, Jan. 24, 1896.

15. *Guthrie Daily Leader*, Jan. 17, 1896.

16. *Oklahoma State Capital*, Jan. 17, 1896.

17. *Guthrie Daily Leader*, Jan. 17, 1896.

18. *Ibid.*

19. *Ibid.*; *Oklahoma State Capital*, Jan. 17, 1896.

CHAPTER XXIII

1. *Oklahoma Daily Times-Journal*, Sept. 25, 1895.

2. *Ibid.*, Nov. 25, 1895.

3. *Ibid.*, Dec. 16, 1895.

4. *Ibid.*

5. *Oklahoma State Capital*, Dec. 19, 1895.

6. Jan. 20, 1896.

7. Jan. 27, 1896.

8. *Oklahoma Daily Times-Journal*, Jan. 24, 1896.

9. *Oklahoma State Capital*, Jan. 21, 1896.

10. *Oklahoma Daily Times-Journal*, Jan. 24, 1896.

11. *Ibid.*

12. Jan. 25, 1896.

13. Brooks to Harmon, Jan. 27, 1896, Records of District Attorney for Oklahoma Territory, Guthrie, 1896 (no page number).

14. Jan. 25, 1896.

15. Jan. 30, 1896.

16. *Oklahoma Daily Times-Journal*, Jan. 27, 1896; *Stillwater Gazette*, Jan. 30, 1896.

17. *Oklahoma Daily Times-Journal*, Jan. 31, 1896.

18. *Oklahoma State Capital*, Feb. 1, 1896.

19. *Oklahoma Daily Times-Journal*, Feb. 15 and 19, 1896.

20. *Guthrie Daily Leader*, Feb. 28, 1896; *Oklahoma State Capital*, Feb. 29, 1896; *Oklahoma Daily Times-Journal*, Mar. 7, 1896.

21. Feb. 4, 19, and 28, 1896.

22. Feb. 24, 1896.

23. Feb. 20 and 26, 1896.

24. *Oklahoma Daily Times-Journal*, Mar. 28, 1896.

25. *Ibid.*

26. Albert Bigelow Paine, *Captain Bill McDonald, Texas Ranger* (New York, J. J. Little & Ives Co., 1909), 166–69, 176.

27. Sept. 12 special from Woodward, O. T., *Oklahoma Daily Times-Journal*, Sept. 13, 1895; *Oklahoma State Capital*, Sept. 13, 1895.

28. *Oklahoma State Capital*, Sept. 13, 1895.

29. *Ibid.*, Mar. 21, 1896; *Oklahoma Daily Times-Journal*, Apr. 4, 1896.

30. Dec. 6 special from Woodward, O. T., *Oklahoma State Capital*, Dec. 6, 1896.

31. *Op. cit.*, XXXIV, 145–54.

32. *Oklahoma Daily Times-Journal*, Mar. 14, 1896.

33. Paine, *op. cit.*, 199–213; Jonnie R. Morgan, *The History of Wichita Falls* (Wichita Falls, Texas, Nortex Offset Publications, 1971), 87–90.

34. "Posse's Guns End Red Buck's Crime Career," *History of Custer and Washita Counties* (Clinton Daily News, 1937).

35. *Ibid.*

36. *Arapaho Argus*, Mar. 5, 1896.

37. "Posse's Guns End Red Buck's Crime Career," *loc. cit.*

38. *Arapaho Argus*, Mar. 5, 1896.

39. Graves (p. 98), Newsom (p. 184), and Zoe A. Tilghman, *Outlaw Days* (p. 94) date Red Buck's death as Mar. 15, 1896.

Nix (p. 216) gives Oct. 2, 1896, and credits the killing to "Chris Madsen and a posse of citizens."

Croy (p. 193) states: "Chris and his posse cornered Red Buck in a dugout near Cheyenne, Oklahoma, March 5, 1896."

Wellman (p. 226–28) accepts the Nix date and provides a fictional account of how Madsen "deputized" a party of Rangers who had "traced the two outlaws from Texas" after killing Joe Beckham "in a running fight."

Drago (pp. 268–69) combines the Nix and Wellman versions and gives the year as *1894*, "when [Bill] Dalton was killed."

40. *Arapaho Argus*, Mar. 5, 1896; *Oklahoma State Capital*, Mar. 10 and 21, 1896; *Oklahoma Daily Times-Journal*, Mar. 10, Apr. 4, 1896; "Posse's Guns End Red Buck's Crime Career," *loc. cit.*

41. *Oklahoma State Capital*, Feb. 6, 1900.

42. "Posse's Guns End Red Buck's Crime Career," *loc. cit.*

Nix (p. 216) writes: "Red Buck's body was brought to Guthrie and, to our great surprise . . . claimed by as dear an old lady as I ever had known. . . . Mrs. Lucy Waightman was such a motherly character that I was greatly puzzled as to how such a demon could come from such a lovable mother."

43. *Oklahoma Daily Times-Journal*, May 2, 1896; *Guthrie Daily Leader*, May 3, 1896; *Stillwater Gazette*, May 7, 1896.

44. Zoe A. Tilghman, *Marshal of the Last Frontier*, 227.

45. *Guthrie Daily Leader*, June 22, 1896; *El Reno News*, July 3, 1896; Canton, *op. cit.*, 132–34.

CHAPTER XXIV

1. *Oklahoma Daily Times-Journal*, Jan. 1, 1892; *Oklahoma State Capital*, Feb. 15, 1896. See also *The Autobiography of Charles Francis Colcord*, 168.

2. Nagle to Attorney General, Aug. 1, 1896, Department of Justice, File 12014, No. 12637.

3. *Ibid.*

4. Details of the escape appear in Nagle to Attorney General, Aug. 1, *loc. cit.*; *Oklahoma State Capital*, July 6, 1896; *Daily Oklahoman*, July 7, 1896; *Guthrie Daily Leader*, July 7 and 8, 1896.

Nix (p. 225) says the break occurred "on a cold night in the early part of January, 1896," and gives an erroneous account of how it was engineered.

Zoe A. Tilghman, *Marshal of the Last Frontier* (p. 228), claims "both guards were quickly marched into cells, bound and gagged . . . thirty-seven prisoners slipped out and off into the darkness."

Wellman (p. 232) and Drago (p. 273) accept Nix and claim every man in the jail was liberated.

5. *Guthrie Daily Leader*, July 7, 1896.

6. *Guthrie Daily Leader*, July 8, 1896.

7. *Guthrie Daily Leader*, July 11 and 12, 1896.

8. Citizens' Letters, July 10–31, 1896, Department of Justice, File 12014, Nos. 11309 and 12680.

9. Mountjoy to Attorney General, Dec. 17, 1896, Department of Justice, File 12014, No. 19536.

10. Nagle to Attorney General, Aug. 1, *loc. cit.*

11. *Daily Oklahoman*, July 16, 1896; *Oklahoma Daily Times-Journal*, July 16, 1896.

12. *Oklahoma State Capital*, July 29, 1896.

13. *Ibid.*, Aug. 6, 1896.

14. *Ibid.*, Aug. 10, 1896.

15. Heck Thomas Clippings, Correspondence and Marshals Records (in author's collection; cited hereafter as Heck Thomas Papers).

16. *Ibid.*

17. Aug. 25 and 26, 1896.

18. Aug. 26 and 27, 1896.

19. June 25, 1897.

20. Albert M. Thomas to Glenn Shirley, October 7, 1957.

Sutton (p. 208) says that when Doolin escaped, he promised to take his wife to some far-off place and begin life anew as soon as he "pulled just one more bank robbery"; that he "called his gang together," robbed a Missouri bank of "several thousand dollars," and returned to his wife and baby "in a little cabin near Quay [the new name for Lawson after February, 1903]," but "the marshals arrived at that very same midnight."

Nix (p. 229) writes: "Three or four months after Doolin escaped we learned his wife took the boy to the home of her father near Lawton [Lawson] and we assigned a scout to watch the little woods cabin." Nix had been out of office since February.

Croy (p. 200) dates the killing August 28; Hanes (p. 176) gives August 25. The Hanes date appears on the monument erected over the outlaw's grave in 1961.

Wellman (p. 233) accepts Nix and Sutton, killing Doolin at *Lawton* on Aug. 25 after the outlaw had "helped his wife and baby into the wagon and turned to mount his saddle horse tied to a front wheel."

Drago (p. 274) claims the Ellsworth home was watched "for months" and the outlaw was slain on the night of August 25 as he walked down the road behind the wagon driven by his wife, his saddle horse "tethered to the endgate."

21. Hanes (pp. 177–78) includes Hy Cotts, "brother of Mrs. Bee Dunn," and says Bee killed Doolin with his stepfather's eight-gauge shotgun, "the same gun he had used to kill Pierce."

22. Graves (p. 107) says that when Mrs. Doolin "heard the shots, so close together they sounded like only one," she "snatched up her baby" and ran toward the posse gathered about the dead outlaw. "They tried mercifully to shield . . . her dead husband from her sight, but she pushed them aside and kneeling beside the body wailed in the agony of a broken heart."

Newsom (p. 194) and Zoe A. Tilghman, *Outlaw Days* (p. 103), repeat Graves. Sutton (p. 209), Nix (p. 230), Wellman (p. 234), and Drago (p. 275) accept. Hanes (p. 179) writes: "Heck Thomas restrained her and would not let her near the body . . . sent her back to the house."

Sutton says he later acquired the Winchester Doolin was carrying, describes many notches filed and cut in its barrel and stock, and states: "With that rifle Doolin killed thirty men."

23. *Oklahoma State Capital*, Aug. 28, 1896.

24. Brooks to Attorney General Harmon, October 14, 1896, Records of District Attorney, Guthrie, O. T., October, 1896, pp. 425–27; U.S. Attorney to Joseph McKenna, Attorney General, December 3, 1897, *ibid.*, December, 1897, pp. 587–88.

25. Heck Thomas Papers.

26. *Oklahoma State Capital*, Aug. 26, 1896.

27. *Ibid.*, Aug. 27, 1896.

28. Department of Justice, File 12014, No. 14620.

29. *Guthrie Daily Leader*, Aug. 30, 1896.

Graves (p. 107), Nix (p. 230), Wellman (p. 234), and Drago (p. 275) claim hundreds of people, including most of the deputy marshals who had hunted the outlaw for years, witnessed the last scene.

30. Aug. 27, 1896.

31. *Stillwater Gazette*, Sept. 4, 1896.

32. *Oklahoma State Capital*, Mar. 2, 1897; *Edmond Sun-Democrat*, Mar. 5, 1897.

33. *Op. cit.*, 138.

34. *Guthrie Daily Leader*, Nov. 10, 1896.

35. *Oklahoma State Capital*, Nov. 7, 1896; *Stillwater Gazette*, Nov. 12, 1896; *El Reno News*, Nov. 20, 1896; Canton, *op. cit.*, 136–37.

36. *Guthrie Daily Leader*, Nov. 12, 1896.

37. *El Reno News*, Nov. 20, 1896.

38. *Perkins Journal*, Nov. 27, 1896.

39. *Oklahoma State Capital*, Nov. 20, 1896.

40. *Oklahoma State Capital*, Dec. 19, 1896.

41. *Ibid.*, Feb. 6, 1897.

42. *Ibid.*, July 9, 1897.

43. *Ibid.*, June 3, 1899.

44. *Ibid.*, Nov. 1, 1903.

CHAPTER XXV

1. *Oklahoma State Capital*, Aug. 5 and Sept. 11, 1896.

2. W. B. Richards (comp.), *The Oklahoma Red Book* (Oklahoma City, 1912), II, 305.

3. *Ibid.*

4. *Ibid.*, 306.

5. *Oklahoma State Capital*, Apr. 1–2, 1897.

6. Meserve, *loc. cit.*, 222–23; *The Oklahoma Red Book*, II, 160–61.

7. *Oklahoma State Capital*, June 7, 1897; Meserve, *loc. cit.*, 224; Jenkins, *op. cit.*, 1–4, 28.

8. *Oklahoma State Capital*, June 6, 1897.

9. Feb. 28, 1897.

10. *Oklahoma State Capital*, Aug. 2, 1895; *Oklahoma Daily Times-Journal*, Aug. 2, 1895.

11. *Oklahoma State Capital*, Apr. 1, 1897.

12. *Ibid.*, May 21, 1897.

13. *Ibid.*, June 10, 1897.
14. *Ibid.*, June 14–18, 1897.
15. *Ibid.*, June 19, 1897.
16. *Ibid.*, June 16, 23, and 28, 1897.
17. *Ibid.*, June 22, 1897.
18. *Ibid.*, June 17, 1897.
19. *Ibid.*, July 2 and 8, 1897.
20. *Ibid.*, Sept. 28, 1897.
21. *Ibid.*, Oct. 13, 1897.
22. *Ibid.*, Oct. 25–26, 1897.

CHAPTER XXVI

1. *Oklahoma State Capital*, Oct. 19, 1896; Heck Thomas Papers.
2. *Oklahoma State Capital*, Oct. 31, 1896.
3. *Ibid.*; *El Reno News*, Nov. 6, 1896; Heck Thomas Papers.
4. Heck Thomas Papers.
5. Morris Swett, "Al J. Jennings," *Chronicles of Comanche County*, Vol. VI, No. 2 (Autumn, 1960), 82–83.
Burton Rascoe, *Belle Starr: The Bandit Queen* (New York, Random House, 1941), Appendix "The Jennings Gang: Comic Relief," is mistaken in stating (p. 268) that "Ed hung out his shingle in Enid . . . Frank dealt cards in a gambling house for a living; Al just loafed."
6. Swett, *loc. cit.*, 82; *Oklahoma State Capital*, Jan. 8, 1894, and Nov. 16, 1902; *Kingfisher Free Press*, Golden Anniversary Edition, Apr. 17, 1939.
7. *Arapaho Bee*, Oct. 18, 1895; Thoburn and Wright, *op. cit.*, II, Appendix XLVIII-1, "Jack Love," 915–16.
Wellman (p. 277) and Drago (p. 277) claim Love was still sheriff and also was collecting fees as corporation commissioner, an appointment obtained through the influence of Temple Houston. Houston died at Woodward on Aug. 15, 1905, and Love did not become a member of the Oklahoma Corporation Commission until 1907, a race he was importuned to make rather than run for governor. He was the commission's first chairman, a position he held until his death on June 1, 1918.
8. Serialized in *Saturday Evening Post* in 1913 and published as a book by D. Appleton and Co., in 1914: see pp. 40–41.
9. (New York, H. K. Fly Co., 1921), 27–28.
10. Nix, *op. cit.*, 245; Rascoe, *Belle Starr*, 269; Wellman, *op. cit.*, 277; Drago, *op. cit.*, 277.
11. *Oklahoma State Capital*, Oct. 10, 1895; *Oklahoma Daily Times-Journal*, Oct. 10, 1895; *Daily Oklahoman*, Oct. 11, 1895.
12. "The Life Story of Al Jennings" (as related himself), *Daily Oklahoman*, Aug. 15, 1912 (cited hereafter as "Life Story").
13. *Oklahoma State Capital*, Oct. 10, 1895; *Oklahoma Daily Times-Journal*, Oct. 10, 1895; *Daily Oklahoman*, Oct. 11, 1895; *Vinita Leader*,

Oct. 17, 1895; *Chickasaw Enterprise*, Oct. 17, 1895; *Arapaho Bee*, Oct. 18, 1895.

14. Nix, *op. cit.*, 246.

15. *Loc. cit.*

16. P. 43.

17. *Op. cit.*, 270.

18. Swett, *loc. cit.*, 83.

19. Graves, *op. cit.*, 107; Newsom, *op. cit.*, 188; Zoe A. Tilghman, *Marshal of the Last Frontier*, 240.

20. Brooks to A. Jones [field deputy], Tecumseh, O. T., February 21, 1895, Records of District Attorney for Oklahoma Territory, Guthrie, 1895, p. 553; *Oklahoma State Capital*, July 17, 1894, and Feb. 4, 1895.

21. Rascoe, *Belle Starr*, 270–72; Eugene B. Block, *Great Train Robberies of the West* (New York, Coward-McCann, 1959), 143–44; Swett, *loc. cit.*, 84; Wellman, *op. cit.*, 276, 278; Drago, *op. cit.*, 279–81.

22. Pp. 45–56.

23. *Oklahoma State Capital*, June 12, 1897.

24. *Loc. cit.*

25. Jennings v. United States, II Indian Territory Reports 670. See also 53 Southwestern Reporter 456.

26. Jennings, *Beating Back*, 155–56.

27. Aug. 17 dispatch from Edmond, O. T., *Oklahoma State Capital*, Aug. 17, 1897; *Daily Oklahoman*, Aug. 17, 1897.

Graves (p. 108), Newsom (p. 188–89), Zoe A. Tilghman, *Outlaw Days* (pp. 104–105) and *Marshal of the Last Frontier* (p. 241), and Rascoe (p. 272) give the date incorrectly as August 18 (Nix says the early part of 1896). They claim the train was halted "about a mile" south of Edmond, where "an extra man held the bandits' horses," and that the robbers, frightened when the conductor came toward them with his lantern, leaped to their mounts and fled "like jack rabbits" with "only a few hundred dollars," obtained, according to Wellman (p. 278) and Drago (p. 281), from a "cashbox" or "strongbox" broken open inside the express car.

28. *Guthrie Daily Leader*, Aug. 17, 1897.

29. *Oklahoma State Capital*, Aug. 17, 1897; *Daily Oklahoman*, Aug. 17, 1897.

30. *Guthrie Daily Leader*, Aug. 18, 1897.

31. *Oklahoma State Capital*, Aug. 19, 1897; Heck Thomas Papers.

Zoe A. Tilghman, *Marshal of the Last Frontier* (p. 241), claims that "within twenty-four hours Bill [Tilghman] had a sworn statement from the man who held their horses," and "warrants were issued for" Al and Frank Jennings, the O'Malleys, and Dick West.

Nix (pp. 249–50) relates that "all the gang except Al fled to a camp on Laury Whipple's place near the Pottawatomie county line. . . . Al spurred his horse in the direction of his father's home at Tecumseh," where he remained the rest of the night to establish an alibi, rejoined the gang at the Whipple place next morning, and "together they headed for the south-

471

eastern part of the Territory near the Texas line"; that en route they met
Deputy Sam Bartell, who knew Al Jennings quite well but "knew nothing
about the Edmond robbery" and invited the gang to "the little farm house
where he and his wife were making their temporary home"; that Bartell's
wife "prepared a good meal for them," for which Al "handed Mrs. Bartell
twenty dollars," then bade the couple good-by, and "he and his men rode
on their way."

32. Helen Starr and O. E. Hill, *Footprints in the Indian Nation* (Muskogee, Okla., Hoffman Printing Co., 1974), 83–84.

33. Pp. 50–55.

34. Pp. 45–51.

35. Starr and Hill, *op. cit.*

36. Jennings v. United States, *loc. cit.*

37. Graves (pp. 108–110), Newsom (pp. 195–96), Zoe A. Tilghman,
Outlaw Days (pp. 105–106), and Nix (pp. 250–51).

These events are not mentioned in available contemporary reports or
official records.

Nix (p. 251) continues: "About this time Al Jennings secured a grub-
stake . . . and left the country. I was never able to learn just what particular depredation supplied the money. . . . He was in Honduras for some
months, finally making his way back through Mexico and into the United
States. He had not been in this country long when he gravitated toward
his old gang and brought them together once more."

Again, Nix had not been in the marshal's office for more than a year.
His ghost writer obviously relied on Jennings' books, in print years before
Oklahombres appeared in 1929.

38. *Beating Back*, 88–99; *Through the Shadows With O. Henry*, 61–96.

39. Richard O'Connor, *O. Henry: The Legendary Life of William S.
Porter* (Garden City, N.Y., Doubleday & Co., 1970), 54–65.

40. *Guthrie Daily Leader*, Oct. 3, 1897.

41. *Beating Back*, 108.

42. *Oklahoma State Capital*, Oct. 2 and 4, 1897; *Daily Oklahoman*,
Oct. 2, 1897; *Guthrie Daily Leader*, Oct. 3 and 5, 1897; *Enid Daily Wave*,
Oct. 4, 1897.

Latter-day writers claim only *five* bandits participated.

43. *Daily Oklahoman*, Oct. 2, 1897; Heck Thomas Papers.

44. *Cushing Herald*, Nov. 5, 1897.

45. *Ibid.*; *Oklahoma State Capital*, Nov. 3, 1897.

46. *Oklahoma State Capital*, Oct. 29, 1897; Heck Thomas Papers.

CHAPTER XXVII

1. *Oklahoma State Capital*, Nov. 6 and 8, 1897.

2. *Ibid.*, Nov. 1, 1897.

3. *Ibid.*, Nov. 8, 1897.

4. *Guthrie Daily Leader*, Nov. 12, 1897; *Oklahoma State Capital*, Nov.

16, 1897; Bennett to Thompson, Nov. 14, 1897, in Heck Thomas Papers.

5. Graves (pp. 112–13) does not mention the Cushing robbery but states that the Jennings gang obtained "a jug of whiskey and bunch of bananas from the wrecked express car . . . making a dinner off the bananas" as they fled westward after the Rock Island holdup.

Nix (p. 254) says that as the outlaws started toward Indian Territory after resting in the dugout on the Cottonwood, "Little Dick West could not help but compare this band of battered wanderers with his former companions of the dashing Doolin-Dalton gang [and] on one chilly evening when the others were saddling their horses for a night's ride . . . Little Dick bade them good-bye and rode off to the south without an excuse or a word of comment." Drago (p. 284) accepts.

Zoe A. Tilghman, *Marshal of the Last Frontier* (p. 242), thinks "Dick West left them . . . on Cottonwood river."

Wellman (p. 281) claims West's pride was so "utterly scarified" by a gallon of whiskey and a bunch of bananas as loot for a train robbery that he left his "tattered and chapfallen" comrades then and there, and they never saw him again.

The whiskey-banana story first appeared in Al Jennings' *Beating Back* (pp. 117–18), serialized two years and printed as a book one year before Graves produced *Oklahoma Outlaws*.

6. *Muskogee Phoenix*, Nov. 10, 1897.

Graves, Newsom, and Zoe A. Tilghman, strangely, make no disposition of Dynamite Dick Clifton.

Croy (p. 205) says he was killed "the first week in December" after the Guthrie jailbreak in July "on a ranch sixteen miles west of Newkirk, Oklahoma."

Nix (pp. 198–99) says he was badly wounded in the right arm, hip, and lungs in a gun battle with Deputies Will Nix, W. O. Jones, and Steve Burke "at a country store about twenty miles from Perry . . . on an afternoon following" the slaying of Bitter Creek and Pierce in Payne County in 1895 and that he was brought to the federal jail at Guthrie, his wounds were dressed, but "in a few days contracted pneumonia . . . and died. His body was claimed by his father, who lived south of Ardmore, near the Texas line."

Wellman (p. 223) and Drago (p. 265) accept this piece of Nix fiction.

7. Jennings v. United States, *loc. cit.*

8. Graves, *op. cit.*, 114; Zoe A. Tilghman, *Outlaw Days*, 110; Nix, *op. cit.*, 255; Starr and Hill, *op. cit.*, 84.

9. Jennings v. United States, *loc. cit.*

10. *Ibid.*

11. *Beating Back*, 134–35.

12. Jennings v. United States, *loc. cit.*

13. *Ibid.*

14. *Beating Back*, 137–44.

15. Starr and Hill, *op. cit.*, 84; "Life Story," *loc. cit.*

16. December 6 and 7 dispatches from Muskogee, I. T., *Wichita Daily*

Eagle, Dec. 7, 1897; *Guthrie Daily Leader*, Dec. 7 and 8, 1897; *Oklahoma State Capital*, Dec. 8, 1897.

17. *Ibid.*

18. Dec. 8, 1897.

19. *Oklahoma State Capital*, Dec. 27, 1897.

20. *Muskogee Phoenix*, Feb. 24, 1898; *Oklahoma State Capital*, Feb. 28, 1898.

21. Jennings v. United States, *loc. cit.*

22. In re Jennings, 118 Federal Reporter 479.

23. *Oklahoma State Capital*, Apr. 8, 1898; *Guthrie Daily Leader*, Apr. 9, 1898.

24. Apr. 8, 1898.

25. Apr. 9, 1898.

26. Albert M. Thomas to Glenn Shirley, Oct. 7, 1957.

Graves (p. 127) and Zoe A. Tilghman, *Outlaw Days* (pp. 122–23), claim that "as Marshals Tilghman and Thomas, Sheriff Rhinehart [*sic*] and Bill Fossett . . . approached the orchard they saw Little Dick currying a horse back of the barn. He saw the officers at the same time. . . . They called to him to surrender, but he replied with a six-shooter in each hand. The officers fired several shots . . . and one bullet hit him as he was stooping, going in at the hip and coming out at the shoulder. He straightened up, jumped high in the air and fell dead."

This horse-currying, twin-six-shooter act is repeated by Nix (p. 261) and accepted by Wellman (p. 286) and Drago (p. 288), who also credit Little Dick's death to Thomas and Tilghman.

27. *Guthrie Daily Leader*, Apr. 9, 1898.

CHAPTER XXVIII

1. Jennings v. United States, *loc. cit.*

2. In re Jennings, *loc. cit.*

3. *Oklahoma State Capital*, Nov. 16 and Dec. 11, 1902.

4. *Ibid.*, Nov. 25, 1903, and Aug. 21, 1910; "Life Story," *loc. cit.*; Swett, *op. cit.*, 87–88; Duane Gage, "Al Jennings: The People's Choice," *Chronicles of Oklahoma*, Vol. XLVI, No. 3 (Autumn, 1968), 244.

5. *Daily Oklahoman*, Aug. 3, 1912; "Life Story," *loc. cit.*; "From Prosecuted to Prosecutor," *Literary Digest*, Vol. XLV, No. 12 (Sept. 21, 1912), 487.

6. Gage, *loc. cit.*, 244.

7. *Daily Oklahoman*, July 13–26, 1914; Edward Everett Dale and James D. Morrison, *Pioneer Judge: The Life of Robert Lee Williams* (Cedar Rapids, Iowa, Torch Press, 1958), 216–17, 222–23.

8. Gage, *loc. cit.*, 244.

9. *Durant Weekly News*, July 10, 1914; *Daily Oklahoman*, July 24, 1914.

10. *Daily Oklahoman*, Aug. 3, 1914.

11. Dale and Morrison, *op. cit.*, 224.

12. Al Jennings died with his boots off in his tree-shaded white frame home at Tarzana on Dec. 26, 1961.

13. *Muskogee Phoenix*, Jan. 1, 1915.

14. *Chandler News-Publicist*, Jan. 22, 1915; Zoe A. Tilghman, *Marshal of the Last Frontier*, 316.

15. *Oklahoma State Capital*, July 12, 1906.

16. *Ibid.*, Mar. 26, 1908; Stillwater Gazette, Mar. 27, Apr. 10–24, 1908.

17. Nix, *op. cit.*, 114–15.

18. *Oklahoma State Capital*, Nov. 29 and Dec. 11, 1910; Mar. 4, 1911.

19. Nix, *op. cit.*, 115.

20. *Chandler News-Publicist*, Jan. 22 and 29 and Feb. 12, 1915.

21. For details of this robbery, see Glenn Shirley, *Henry Starr, Last of the Real Badmen* (New York, David McKay Co., 1965), 167–72.

22. *Chandler News-Publicist*, May 28, 1915.

23. J. T. Lamar, Record Clerk, Missouri State Penitentiary, Jefferson City, to Glenn Shirley, Oct. 30, 1951; C. W. Wilson, Record Clerk, Kansas State Penitentiary, Lansing, to Glenn Shirley, Nov. 1, 1951.

24. *Joplin Globe*, Aug. 17 and 18, 1924; *Stillwater Gazette*, Aug. 29, 1924.

Index

476

477

478